THE NEW TESTAMENT CODE

COMPANION EDITION

ROBERT EISENMAN

The New Testament Code

Companion Edition

The Way Publishing

3rd Edition
ISBN-13: 9781796396546

ENDNOTES

Chapter 1

1 See my *James the Brother of Jesus* and *The Dead Sea Scrolls and the First Christians*

2 Josephus, *War* 2.120–58, *Ant.* 18.18–22, and Philo, *Quod Omnis Probus Liber*, 75–91; see, for instance, Epiphanius, *Haeres.* 29.1 and 29.4

3 132–6 CE. For Eusebius, *EH* 4.6.2–6, for instance, there do not appear to have been 'Christians' as such in Jerusalem until after Hadrian renamed it after himself and Justin Martyr (c. 100–65 BCE), *Dial.* doesn't even seem to know the Gospels as separate entities.

4 See both 'fearing God' and 'God-Fearers' in CDxx.20.19–20.

5 See for example, Ian Wilson, *The Blood and the Shroud*, New York, 1998, pp. 143–54

6 *Ant.* 20.20

7 Acts 9:2–17

8 Cf. Eusebius in *EH* 1.13.2

9 Acts 9:11

10 *Ant.* 20.34–43

11 Koran 27.20–47

12 *EH* 1.13.4–5

13 *Ibid.*, 2.23.7

14 See *James*, pp. 930–9

15 Acts 6:5–6

16 Acts 6:1–8:2

17 Cf. the names of two of Plato's most famous Dialogues, *The Timaeus* and *The Parmenides*; note too, Nicanor was the name of the fabulous bronze Gate at the entrance to the Court of the Women in the Temple given by a Rich Alexandrian Jew by that name.

18 *Ant.* 16.299, 333–55, etc., cited by Josephus *inter alia* as a source in *Apion* 2.84

19 See 'the Nilvim' in CDiv.3 and 'the Nobles of the People' in CDvi.4–8, discussing at length in Chapters 21–2 below.

20 *War* 2.228/*Ant.* 20.113

21 For the Sanhedrin and James, see *Ant.* 20.200.

22 For the attack on James by the 'Enemy' Paul in the *Recognitions*, see 1.70

23 *Vita* 430; also see *Ant.* 1.8, *Apion* 1.1, 2.1, and 2.296.

24 For a later 'Clement,' evidently related to these, see 'Clement of Alexandria'—a.k.a. 'Titus Flavius Clement.'

25 Suetonius 8.14.4–17.3 and Dio Cassius, *Roman History*, 67.4.1–5. There is some debate about the year of Josephus' death and some think he lived till 104 CE, but he definitely seems to leave the scene in 96 right before Domitian's assassination.

26 *EH* 3.18.4,

27 Ps. *Rec* 1.170; also see parallel reference in Ps. *Hom.* 11.35 of Jesus disputing with the Devil in the wilderness and Peter following James' directives.

28 This was first revealed by a *London Times* correspondent, Philip Graves, in a series of articles in *The New York Times*, August 6–8th, 1921. Also see W. Eisner and Umberto Ecco, *The Plot: The Secret Story of the Protocols of the Elders of Zion*, New York, 2005

29 Cf. Matthew 4:5/Luke 4:9.

30 See Ps. *Rec.* 1.70 above; note the actual use of this word *'headlong'/'prenes'* in 1:18, but with the additional telltale note of his head *'breaking open'* and *'his bowels gushed out'*!

31 See *EH* 2.23.3, 2.23.16–8, 1 *Apoc. Jas.* 25.9–20 and 2 *Apoc. Jas.* 61.21–63–31.

32 See *EH* 2.23.12, 13, 17, etc.

33 *EH* 2.23.13.

34 *EH* 2.23.16.

35 1QpHabxi.12–5.

36 The mistake Acts 7:16 has *'Stephen'* make here is twofold: it thinks it is Abraham who is having this intercourse with *'the sons of Hamor'* and Abraham's and not Joseph's burial site is in Shechem though here, too, there may be a trace of Samaritan tradition of some kind. That the author is pillaging Joshua at this point is unmistakable.

37 *EH* 2.1.1.

38 See *James*, pp. 240–2 and 304.

39 *Ant.* 20.113 and 118–36; also see *War* 2.229 and Tacitus, *Annals* 12.54.

40 See *M. San.* 9:6, Numbers 25:6–13 on Phineas, and S. G. F. Brandon, *Jesus and the Zealots*, pp. 41–5.

41 Jude 1:1.

42 *EH* 2.13.2–3 quoting Justin Martyr's *Apology* 1.26. Also see Ps. *Rec.* 2.7 and *Hom.* 6.7. Another confusion here is the *'Salamis'* in Acts 13:5, which does not seem to have been on Cyprus, but this may be just another mix-up with *'Samaria.'*

43 *Ant.* 20.142

44 *Rec.* 1.72, 2.7–8, and *Hom.* 1.22 and Epiphanius, *Haeres* 21.2.3–5.1.

45 *War* 1.63, *Ant.* 9.288–90, 11.19–20, 11.85–8, etc.; cf. also *James*, pp. 495–6 and 533–5. Note that the 9th/10th century Karaite heresiologist and teacher Al-Kirkisani, in his *History of Jewish Sects*, tr. by L. Nemoy, *Karaite Anthology*, New Haven, 1952, p. 49, knows that *'the Samaritans were known among the Jewish People as the Cuthaeans'* and explains this by 2 Kings 17:24, asserting that *'the King of Assyria settled men from Babylon and Cutha'* in Samaria—a point echoing with just the slightest more specificity Epiphanius in Haeres. 8.8.10–1 below.

46 See Genesis 10:4, Numbers 24:24, Isaiah 23:1–12, Jeremiah 2:10, etc.

47 See *James*, pp. 130–1 and 605. One assumes *'Timothy'* is the name in Greek; *'Titus'* in Latin—this despite the fact both are mentioned in 2 Corinthians and 2 Timothy.

48 See genealogy page on *'The Herodians'*—*'Mariamme'* in Greek Josephus comes from *'Miriam'* in the Old Testament and becomes *'Mary'* in the New Testament.

⁴⁹ *Ant.* 19.299 and 317–25, but in *War* 2.520 and 3.11–9 a second or later, possibly his descendant and a '*Babylonian*', deserts from Agrippa II's army and becomes a principal Rebel Commander. With '*John the Essene*', he is killed at Ascalon while '*Niger*' escapes.

⁵⁰ Cf. CDvi.21, xx.19, and 33 but also see James' title '*Oblias*'/'Strength of the People' in *EH* 2.23.7.

⁵¹ Cf. for example Acts 15:1 and 5 or Galatians 2:12 on the '*some from James*.'

⁵² This word actually means '*Assembly*' of '*Church*' and parallels "*Ezah*' at Qumran.

⁵³ 4QpPs 37iv.9–10.

⁵⁴ *Ant.* 14.121–2 and *War 1.181.*

⁵⁵ *War* 4.359–63. It would be hard for anyone reading this to escape the resemblance.

⁵⁶ For these overlaps, see *James*, pp. 166–7, 177–9, 412–3, 913–5, etc.

⁵⁷ Here Paul is '*Saulos*.' Nine lines later (13:9), in the context of evoking the '*Enemy*' terminology and '*Sergius Paulos*,' he is '*Paulos*.' Is there an adoption going on here?

⁵⁸ Ps. *Hom.* Epistle of Peter to James 1–5; Epistle of Clement to James 1 and 7.

⁵⁹ See *War* 7.437–54; *Vita* 424.

⁶⁰ *EH* 1.13.1–20 and J. B. Segal, *Edessa 'The Blessed City,'* Oxford, 1970, pp. 62–80.

⁶¹ *EH* 3.11.2 and 4.22.4 quoting Hegesippus.

⁶² See fragments in *ANCL* and *EH* 3.39.

⁶³ See my discussion in *James*, pp. 839–50.

⁶⁴ Recently an ossuary inscribed with the name of '*Cepha*' was found, though this has been interpreted in terms of a third homophone '*Caiaphas*'; see Zvi Greenhut, Burial Cave of the Caiaphas Family' in *BAR*, Sept/Oct, 1992, pp. 29–36.

⁶⁵ See the whole issue of '*going out into the Land of Damascus*' in CDiv.3, vi.3–vii.9, and xix.21–xx.22.

⁶⁶ See the parallel to this in Jerome's citation from the Gospel of the Hebrews, *Vir. ill. 2.*

⁶⁷ *Ibid.* See discussions in *James*, pp. 198–9, etc.

⁶⁸ What Jerome has done to come up with 'cousins' is simply identify the '*Mary the sister of his mother*,' '*the wife of Clopas*' in John 19:26 with '*Mary the mother of James the Less and Joses and Salome*' in the Synoptics.

⁶⁹ Cf. *James*, pp. xviii, 95–7, 141–2, etc.

⁷⁰ In Acts 3:1–9 the James character is missing and in 1:20 the '*election*' to the '*Episcopate*' is to replace '*Judas*'—a curious replacement.

⁷¹ Mani (216–77 CE) was born in Mesene, an Elchasaite center to this day.

⁷² Edessa is in Northern Syria. Adiabene, bordering it, is in Northern Iraq.

⁷³ For the numerous '*Antioch*'s at this time, see Pliny, *Natural History* and Strabo, *Geography.*

⁷⁴ For Abraham's central role there, see Koran 2.124–140, 3.67–68, 4.125, 14.35–52, etc.

⁷⁵ For Josephus' superior description, see. *Ant.* 18.116–19.

ENDNOTES

[76] See also the reference in Romans 16:7 to another putative Herodian, *'Junius my kinsman'*—most likely Julius Archelaus, probably the nephew who helps rescue Paul from *'oath-taking'* Sicarii in Act 23:16–20

[77] *Ant.* 18.137.

[78] Cf. Ps. *Rec.* 1.70 with *EH* 2.23.16–8.

[79] See *War* 2.554–6; also see Paul in Philippians 4:22.

[80] *Ant.* 18.109–25.

[81] *Ant.* 18.116–19.

[82] Note the Simon who wishes to bar Herodians like Agrippa I from the Temple as foreigners in *Ant.* 19.332–4; also see *M. Sota* 7:8, *M. Bik* 3.4 and *Siphre* Deut 17:15.

[83] See Moses of Chorene, 2.29–35.

[84] Herod's father had been given citizenship for services rendered to Rome; *War* 1.194.

[85] See *Ps. Hom.* 10.1, 26, 11.1, 28–30, and 12.6.

[86] *Ibid.*, 2.19 (here, comparing Gentiles to *'dogs'* in the meat they consume), 7.3, 8.19, and 11.351.

[87] In Acts 13:1, the reason for John Mark's departure had been unclear; cf. 1QSviii.16–26 and CDxx.1–17 and 22–27.

[88] See, for instance, the allusion to *'raising up David's seed and establishing the Throne of his Kingdom'* in 4QFlor 10.

[89] Ps. *Rec.* 1.45–54 and 62–64.

[90] *War* 1.95 and *Ant.* 13.379 and 18.20.

[91] Ps. Rec. 1.71; cf. Mark 8:9–20 and *pars.*

[92] Tiberius Alexander did not come to Palestine until 46–48; cf. *War* 2.20/*Ant.* 20.100–3.

[93] Cf. CDvii.10/xix.22–3.

[94] Cf. Ps. *Rec.* 1.72, 2.7 and Ps. *Hom.* 2.22–4.

[95] Cf. its use in CDii.11, iv.4–5, xx.21 and 34.

[96] See 1QpHabxii.1–10.

[97] Cf. James 4:4 with Galatians 1:1 and 10–1.

[98] See 4QpNahii.7–8.

[99] Matthew 25:33 and pars.

[100] 1QpHabxi.13.

[101] CDi.12–6 and viii.22/xix.34

[102] See CDi.16 and viii.14–18/xix.27–31.

[103] 1QpHabii.4 and CDvii.21–23/xix.33–35.

[104] See *Surahs* 2.87–91, 3:21, 4:155, etc.

[105] Cf. *War* 2.143 with 1QSviii.16–26, CDxx.1–17, and CDxx.22–27.

[106] Note his constant reiteration of *'not Lying'* in Galatians 1:20, 1 Corinthians 11:31, etc.

[107] Cf. Ps. *Rec.* 1.71 with 1 Corinthians 15:6, 18, and 51.

[108] Cf. *EH* 2.23.13 and Matthew 24:30 and 26:64/Mark 13:26 and 14:6 *pars*.

[109] See Ps. *Hom.* 7:3–4, 7.19, and 11:35.

[110] See my article: '*Joining*'/'*Joiners*' in *DSSFC*, pp. 313–31 and CDiv.3, 4QpNah, iv.4, etc..

[111] 1QpHabvii.11, viii.1, and xii.4–5.

[112] *Ant.* 19.366.

[113] See *Ant.* 19.329–31.

[114] See *M. Sota* 7:8, *M. Bik.* 3.4, and *Siphre* Deut 157 on 17:15 above.

[115] See *EJ* article '*Sikarikon*' and Origen, *Contra Celsus* 2.13.

[116] See Hegesippus' characterization of James as '*not respecting persons*' in *EH* 2.23.11.

[117] Cf. CDxx.19–20 above.

[118] CDi.1 and ii.2.

[119] But also earlier in CDii.11 and iv.4.

[120] *Ibid.*, xx.18–20.

[121] CDxx.33–4.

Chapter 2

[1] Ps. *Rec.* 1.70 above—only known in Latin and Syriac; Ps. *Hom.* —which actually came down in the Greek and more detailed—begins with the Introductory Letters of Peter to James and Clement to James, then moving on to discourses by Clement, omitting all really early historical material.

[2] See my notes about '*delivering up*' in CD, the anti-Acts history, in *James* and *DSSFC*.

[3] Cf. '*the Disciples of God*,' '*the Men of Perfect Holiness*,' '*the House of the Torah*,' or '*the Penitents from Sin in Jacob*' in CDxx.4–17.

[4] For '*Camps*,' see 1QMi.3, vii.1–7, CDxii.22–xv.8, 4QD266, and *MMT*ii.34–5 and 66–8.

[5] See '*Perfect of the Way*'/'*Walkers in Way*'/'*Way in the Wilderness*' in 1QSviii–ix and CDxx.

[6] Ps. *Rec.* 1.70.

[7] Cf. '*causing to stumble*'/'*casting down* 'in 1QpHabxi.8, Jerome, *Vir. ill.* 2, etc.

[8] 1QpHabxi.4–7—here are all the allusions, including '*swallowing*,' '*pursuing*,' etc.

[9] See 1QpHabvii.17–viii.3 and xii.4–5.

[10] *MMT* ii.8–9.

[11] Hippolytus, *Phil.*, 9.21 and *War* 2.152–3.

[12] The use of the term '*the Poor*'/'*Ebionim*' permeates the literature at Qumran: 1QpHabxii.3, 4QpPs 37.ii.10, iii.10, and iv.11 calling the Scroll Community '*the Assembly of the Poor*'; also see 1QHv.23, '*Ebionei-Hesed*.'

[13] Cf. my comments about this language in *DSSFC*, pp. 362–5; also see 4QD171, even before the First Column of CD, applying '*linzor*'/'*keep away from*' to '*the Sons of Light*.'

[14] See *EH* 3.27 and 6.17, Epiphanius, *Haeres.* 30.1.1–34.6l, and Irenaeaus, *Ad Haer* 1.26.2.

15 Ps. *Rec.* 1.70–3 and *Vir. ill.* 2.

16 See Letters of Peter and Clement to James and *Hom.* 11.35.

17 *Rec.* 1.71.

18 See 'Bones of Contention,' *Time Magazine*, Aug 6, 2001, p. 55; AP Report by Steve Weizman, 'Archaeologists Uncover Ancient Graves near Site where Dead Sea Scrolls were Found,' 7/26/01; also H. Eshel and M. Broshi, 'Excavations at Qumran, Summer of 2001,' *IEJ* 53, 2003, pp. 61–73.

19 'Digging for the Baptist,' *Time Magazine*, 8/12/02; also see M. Broshi and H. Eshel, 'Whose Bones? New Qumran Excavation, New Debates,' *BAR* (2003), pp. 26–33 and 71.

20 Al-Biruni, *The Chronology of Ancient Nations*, tr. E. Sachau, London, 1879, 8.38–39, 18.10, and 20.25–26; but see also *The Fihrist* 9.1. For al-Biruni, there are two groups of Sabaeans, the original ones, whom he calls pagan idolaters and Jewish ones who emigrated there presumably at the time of the Assyrian exile. It was the descendants of latter who prayed towards the North while the former, the South. In 20.28, he says the same thing about the Manichaeans, namely that *'they prayed towards the North because it was the middle of the Dome of Heaven.'*

21 See P. Bar-Adon, 'Another Settlement of the Judean Desert Sect at 'Ein el-Ghuweir on the Shores of the Dead Sea,' *BASOR*, 1977, p. 12; also see, K. D. Politis, 'Rescue Excavations in the Nabataean Cemetery at Khirbat Qazone,' *AJDA*, 1998, pp. 14–16 and Bar-Adon's 'Excavations in the Judean Desert,' *Atiqot* 9, 1989, pp. 3–14 and 18–29.

22 See J. Zias, 'The Cemeteries at Qumran,' *Dead Sea Discoveries*, 2000, pp. 220–53.

23 Compare Ps. *Rec.* 1.72–4 with Acts 8:9–25. This *'Taheb'* was a Messianic Samaritan Redeemer figure, ruthlessly suppressed by Pontius Pilate. Further to this, it may be that some Gospel accounts are keyed on stories connected with him; cf. Acts 9:36–41's *'Dorcas'/'Tabitha'* story succeeding this.

24 Ps. *Rec.* 1.73.

25 Cf. 1QpHab xi.4–8 above alluding to *'pursued.'*

26 Cf. John 19:31–3 with *War* 4.317 describing the care the Jews showed in taking down those crucified before sunset and how *'God condemned (Jerusalem) to destruction'* as *'polluted'* because of the treatment of Ananus' and his friend Jesus ben Gamala's corpses.

27 See Eshel, Broshi, Freund, *et. al.*, 'New Data on the Cemetery East of Khirbat Qumran,' *DSS* 9/2, 2002, pp. 135–65.

28 See AP report of 7/26/01 and *Time Magazine* of 8/6/01 above.

29 *Ibid.*, but also see J. Zias, 'Tombes bedoine: histoire d'une erreur,' *Le Monde de la Bible*, June, 2003, pp. 48–9 and Broshi and Eshel's reply, 'Zias' Qumran Cemetery,' *Revue de Qumran* 21/3, 2004, pp. 487–89.

30 And further to this, see J. Zias, 'Qumran Archaeology: More Grave Errors,' *Bible and Interpretation*, February, 2004.

31 See Broshi and Eshel in 'Whose Bones?' in *BAR*, 2003, pp. 26–33 above.

32 'Digging for the Baptist,' 8/12/02 above.

³³ Cf. *MZCQ*, pp. 28–35 and 78–94; *James*, pp. 80–90 and variously.

³⁴ For *'earlier vs. later'* and *'relative dating'* generally, see *MZCQ*, pp. 81–9. Our point was that, if the *'relative dating'* was wrong, that was sufficient to question the whole structure—not to look for *'absolute dates.'*

³⁵ May 15th, 1989. See Baigent and Leigh, *The Dead Sea Scrolls Deception*, London, 1991, pp. 80–2 and 242. Also see 'They Used the Wrong Dating Curve: Wishful Thinking and Overstating in Qumran Radiocarbon Dating Analysis,' *The Qumran Chronicle*, September, 2003, pp. 21–4.

³⁶ My previous appearances having been *'scrapped'* because of protests, apparently, by other participants, they had not realized I had all the photographs of the unpublished Scrolls.

³⁷ Though *'officially'* it was announced that the archive was open to all scholars; in view of legal threats, the Library, in fact, took a *'wait-and-see'* attitude until things clarified.

³⁸ Cf. the names of who was assigned to translate and comment on documents first appearing in *DSSU*, 1991 in M. Wise, M. Abegg, and E. Cook, *The Dead Sea Scrolls: A New Translation*, San Francisco, 1996.

³⁹ H. Shanks, 'C14 Tests Substantiate Scroll Dates,' *BAR*, Nov/Dec, 1991, p.72.

⁴⁰ See G. Doudna, 'Dating the Scrolls on the Basis of Radiocarbon Analysis' in *The Dead Sea Scrolls after Fifty Years* (eds. P. Flint and J. Vander Kam), Leiden, 1998, pp. 430–71.

⁴¹ See *ibid.*, p. 430 and J. Atwill and S. Braunheim, 'Redating the Radiocarbon Dating of the Dead Sea Scrolls' in *DSD* (11/2), Leiden, 2004, pp. 144 and 149.

⁴² G. Bonani, M. Broshi, i. Carmi, S. Ivy, J. Strugnell, and W. Wolfi, 'Radiocarbon Dating of the Dead Sea Scrolls,' *Atiqot* 20, 1991, pp. 127–32 and 'Radiocarbon Dating of Fourteen Dead Sea Scrolls,' *Radiocarbon* 34, 1992, pp. 643–49.

⁴³ The Chicago detour was arranged through M. Wise and N. Golb—my colleagues; cf. acknowledgements on p. 430, *op. cit.* above.

⁴⁴ See 'Queries and Comments': 'Why not more C-14 Tests on the Scrolls?', *BAR*, May/June, 1992. Also note Editor Shanks' response (*'send us a check'*) as well as his 'Did a Letter to *BAR* End a Cornell Student's Career?', *BAR*, July/August, 1995 following Doudna's initial note to ANE, the U of Chicago online digest, November 7, 1994 about how his *'PhD program was destroyed in 1991 because of mailing a letter to BAR (urging C-14 testing on the DSSU).'*

⁴⁵ See *BAR*, September/October, 1991: 'BAS Publishes Dead Sea Scrolls: *A Preliminary Edition of the Unpublished Dead Sea Scrolls—The Hebrew and Aramaic Texts from Cave Four*, edited and reconstructed by Ben Zion Wacholder and Martin Abegg (Sept, 1991).'

⁴⁶ This communicated to me by someone who worked in *BAR's* office at the time, though no actual acknowledgement or note of thanks was ever received by me.

⁴⁷ See the thoroughgoing criticism of all three labs but, in particular, this Arizona lab—whether real or sensationalized—in H. Kersten and E. R. Gruber, *The Turin Shroud and the Truth about the Resurrection*, U.K., 1992, pp. 74–100 and 314–33. *Par contra*, see Doudna's own championing of it the next day on the ANE/U of Chicago list on November 8, 1994: *'I am of course partial to the NSF–Arizona AMS Facility which is doing the current Dead Sea Scrolls testing. They are an excellent lab with a wide range of experience...'*

⁴⁸ See T. Jull, D. J. Donahue, M. Broshi, and E. Tov, 'Radiocarbon Dating of Scrolls and Linen Fragments from the Judean Desert,' *Radiocarbon* 37, 1995, pp. 11–9 and *BAR*'s own report: May/June, 1995, 'New Carbon-14 Results Leave Room for Debate.'

⁴⁹ See the points made by Braunheim in the first version of their article in *The Qumran Chronicle*: 'Wishful Thinking and Overstating in Qumran Radiocarbon Dating Analysis' and comments like those of M. Broshi about me, one of those conducting the tests, they publish there, pp. 23–4.

⁵⁰ Cf. *James*, pp. 82–5 and Atwill/Braunheim, 'Overstating,' pp. 24–8 and 31–4.

⁵¹ P. Wearne and J. Kelly, *Tainting the Evidence*, New York, 1998, pp. 9–36; also see general press coverage at the time, such as Online Newshour: *'FBI: Feeling the Heat,'* 4/15/97 or CNN: *'Report Finds Flaws in FBI Crime Lab,'* 4/15/97 and earlier ones before these.

⁵² See G. Rodley and B. Thiering, 'Use of Radiocarbon Dating in Assessing Christian Connections to the Dead Sea Scrolls,' *Radiocarbon* 41, 1999, pp. 169–82. For first recalibration, see M. Stuiver and P.J. Reimer, 'Extended 14 C Data Base and Revised CALIB 3.0 14 C Age Calibration Program,' *Radiocarbon* 35, 1993, pp. 215–30; but also see discussion in 'Redating,' pp. 145–50.

⁵³ For a comparison of these, see the chart in Rodley and Thiering, p.170; for the newest 1998 calibration, see Stuiver, Reimer, Bard, *et. al.*, INTCAL.98 Radiocarbon Age Calibration, 24,000–0 cal BP,' *Radiocarbon* 40, 1998, pp. 1041–83 and Doudna, pp. 433–6.

⁵⁴ See both N. Caldararo, 'Storage Conditions and Physical Treatments Relating to the Dating of the Dead Sea Scrolls,' *Radiocarbon* 37, 1995, pp. 21–32 and R. E. M. Hedges, Radiocarbon Dating by Accelerator Mass Spectometry: Some Recent Results and Applications,' *Philosophical Transactions of the Royal Society of London*, v. 323/1569, 1987, pp. 57–72 and cf. T. Jull, *et.al.*, pp. 11–12.

⁵⁵ See Atwill/Braunheim, 'Redating,' pp. 145–50.

⁵⁶ For overlaps between the Habakkuk and Psalm 37 *Peshers*, see Chapters 23 and 27.

⁵⁷ One should look at the 'first sigma' dates of this *Pesher*, 29–81 CE, 1998 Calibration. The 'second sigma' extend it to 111 CE. The 'second sigma' Habakkuk, peculiarly, remained about the same as the first.

⁵⁸ I first made this point at the New York Academy of Sciences Conference in 1992; for a description, see Neil Asher Silberman, *The Hidden Scrolls*, New York, pp. 14–27 and my paper there 'The Theory of Judeo-Christian Origins: The Last Column of the Damascus Document,' *Methods of Investigation of the Dead Sea Scrolls, Annals of the New York Academy of Sciences*, 1994, pp. 355–70. The repartee at the end of this article with Prof. Schiffman and others, pp. 367–70, is particularly refreshing and revealing.

⁵⁹ See Rodley and Thiering, pp. 170–2; Atwill and Braunheim, 'Redating,' pp. 144–7.

[60] See Braunheim and Atwill in *Qumran Chronicle* and *DSD* above.

[61] *Ibid.*, pp. 153–7 and 32–5.

[62] See their discussion and Calibration Data charts, pp. 149–54/28–32. Actually, the chart-illustrator here made a mistake on the two-sigma range of the Habakkuk *Pesher* which, to some extent, illustrates the point. So anomalous were its 'two-sigma' results in 1994—which uniquely in this case were identical with the one-sigma (a curious happenstance!)—that the illustrator erred.

[63] This in a letter of 11/29/1992 to T. Jull, *et. al.*, quoted in a footnote to the *Atiqot* version of their article, 28, 1996, pp. 85–91 and also referred to in Rodley/Thiering, p. 175. The reader should note that this letter was sent *before the tests were actually carried out*, thereby alerting those conducting them what to look for—which, to some degree, explains the special treatment this document received (an improper methodology or way of proceeding to say the least)!

[64] G. Vermes, *The Dead Sea Scrolls in English*, 4th Ed, 1995, p. xxx and *The Complete Dead Sea Scrolls in English*, 1997, 1998, 2004, etc., p. 21 and n. 58. Actually in the whole of DSSU there is not a single reference to Paul as *'the Wicked Priest.'* On the contrary.

[65] *MZCQ*, p. xv, *JJHP*, pp. 49–72, *James*, pp. 128–31, 145–8, 508–20, and variously.

[66] See J. L. Teicher, in *The Journal of Jewish Studies*, vols. ii, iii, and iv, from 1950–3.

[67] 'Overstating,' p. 34 and 'Redating,' p. 156.

[68] This issue of 'absolute' dates has always been on the mind of all commentators and still is; cf. S. A. Birnbaum, *The Hebrew Scripts*, Leiden, 1971, pp. 130–61 and F.M. Cross, 'The Development of Jewish Scripts' in *The Bible and the Ancient Near East*, 1961, p. 135.

[69] See, for instance, M. Wise, *The First Messiah*, San Francisco, 1996 and A. Ellgard, *Jesus One Hundred Years Before Christ*, New York, 1999.

[70] *Op. cit.*, pp. 433–6, 462–64, and 469–71.

[71] Except for Doudna, there have been few if any retractions and little rethinking.

[72] It was with this expression I started my work in *James*, pp. xxx–xxxi. The quote is from one of Pirandello's most famous plays.

[73] *Op. cit.*, pp. 21–6; also see Hedges, pp. 58–64 and 68–70; for the number of 'samples'/'runs' they took, see Jull, *et.al.*, pp. 11–6.

[74] See the routine reference to palaeographic date as if almost sacrosanct in most Qumran documentary analysis.

[75] H. Eshel, '4Q348, 4Q343, and 4Q345: Three Economic Documents from Qumran Cave 4?,' *Journal of Jewish Studies* (52/1), Spring, 2001, pp. 132–5.

[76] The point is that all these documents refer to the same *dramatis personae*, events, pseudonyms, and '*Messianic*' passages. Consequently all must have been written at more or less the same time. The reader, therefore must choose: do they reflect events and issues of the 2nd c. BC or 1st c. CE?

77 Even H. Shanks in *BAR*, May/June, 1995, p.61, called the 1994 tests *'too gross and too iffy to settle any arguments'*; but see Bonani, Wolfi, Strugnell, *et. al.* in 1991–2, pp. 847–8 and Jull, Donahue, *et.al.* in 1994, pp 13–7 (including the self-serving note on p.14) and the heavy nod in both to palaeography.

78 1QSviii.12–6 and ix.16–24; also see *'the Penitents of the Wilderness'* in 4QpHabiii.1 and *'the Golah of the Wilderness'* in 1QMi.2

79 Jeremiah 31:31, CDvi.19–vii.9, viii.21/xix.33 and cf. Jesus/Paul in 1 Corinthians 11:25, 2 Corinthians 3:6, Luke 22:20 and *pars.* and Hebrews 8:8–9:13 and 12:24.

80 1QpHabvii.17–viii.3 and cf. Romans 1:17, Galatians 3:12, Hebrews 10:28, etc.

81 Cf. Matthew 22:37–9 and *pars.*, James 2:5–26, and Justin Martyr, *Dial.* 23, 47, and 93.

82 For John's teaching, see *Ant.* 18.117; for 'the Essenes', see *War* 2.122 and 139.

83 For *'zeal'* at Qumran, see 1QSii.15, iii.10, and ix.23 (*'for the Law and the Day of Vengeance'*); Paul, Galatians 1:14 and 3:17–8 (sarcastically and attacking his enemies); also see Matthew 2:23 on Jesus, alluding to *'Nazoraean'*, but obviously basing it on *'Nazirite'* scriptural allusion, and the *'keeping away from'* language associated with James' directives to overseas communities—as well as *'N-Z-R'* language generally at Qumran above.

84 See Eusebius and 4QpPs 37ii.10, etc. above.

85 1QpHabxii.2–3; note too the use here (as in 4QpPs 37iv.9) of the key *'gamul'*/*'pay.'*

86 F. M. Cross, *The Ancient Library at Qumran*, New York, 1958, pp. 152–60 is typical; but see also Vermes, *Les Manuscript du Desert du Juda*, Tournai, 1953, pp. 92–100. Both Vermes in his translations and A. Dupont-Sommer in *The Essene Writings from Qumran*, Oxford, 1961 actually formulate the usage here as *'walking in the ways of drunkenness'*—the cause of much of the misunderstanding. As opposed to this, see J. T. Milik, *Ten Years of Discovery in the Wilderness of Judea*, 1959, pp. 64–70 and, of course, myself.

87 See 1QpHabxi.9–xii.6 and 4QpPs 37iv.9f.

88 See my Appendix on *'The Three Nets of Belial'* and *'balla^c'*/*'Bela^c'* in *JJHP*, pp. 87–94 and *DSSFC*, pp. 208–17.

89 *Ibid.* and see genealogy of *'The Herodians'* on pp. 1010–11 below.

90 Also see this same kind of grouping in CDiv.15–v.15 and vi.14–vii.9.

91 See Cross, pp. 122–7, M. Burrows, *The Dead Sea Scrolls*, NY, 1955, pp. 128–42, and G. R. Driver, *The Judaean Scrolls*, Oxford, 1965, pp. 197–225.

92 4QpNahii.3.

93 1QpHabix.3–7.

94 For Pompey's restraint, see *War* 1.152–4/*Ant* 14.71–4; for Herod's, *War* 351–7/*Ant* 483–6.

95 See Louis H.Feldman, 'Financing the Colosseum,' *BAR*, 27/4, July/August, 2001.

96 1QpHabvi.3–8.

97 For the arguments for Roman military practice, see Driver, pp. 168 (where he attributes to observation to then Major General Yigal Yadin) and 178–96. In fact the deifications began

in 42 BC when the Senate voted Julius Caesar—whose image was the first *'man'* to appear on a Roman coin—*'Pater Patriae'* and *'Divus Iulius'* and Augustus, therefore, *'Divi filius'* (*'Son of God'*—thus!); but these deifications continued throughout the 1st century and included Augustus' wife Livia, Augustus himself by Tiberius in 14 CE, Caligula, and even Claudius by Nero.

[98] 1QpHabvi.6–11 and cf. *War* 3.532–41.

[99] 2:1–3, *Ant* 1.1–3/*War* 2.117–8

[100] See A. N. Sherwin-White, *The Roman Citizenship*, Oxford, 1939, pp. 270–5.

[101] See 1QpHabxi.4–8.

[102] See, for instance, b. *RH* 31a–b, *San* 41a, *AZ* 8b, etc. and my 'Interpreting *Abeit Galuto in the Habakkuk Pesher*,' DSSFC, pp. 247–71.

[103] CDvii.13–viii.1 and see Chapters 21–2 below.

[104] See *EH* 2.23.13 above. For 'Jesus,' see Matthew 24:30 and 26:64 and *pars.*

[105] 1QMxi.17–xii.11 and xix.1–2.

[106] *War* 6.312–4. This must also be seen as including Isaiah 10:33–11:5 subjected to exegesis at Qumran in the Isaiah *Pesher* as well.

[107] Andre Lemaire, 'Burial Box of James the Brother of Jesus,' *BAR*, 28/6, November/December, 2002—and endlessly since, e. g., 'Brother of Jesus Ossuary, 29/4, July/August, 2003, 'Cracks in James' Bone Box Repaired,' January/February, 2003, etc. See too, my first comments in R. Lorenzi, Discovery Channel News 10/21/02 'First Proof of Jesus Found?'

[108] See AP Report, 6/18/03: 'Israel Says James Ossuary is a Fake' or Ha'aretz English Edition, 6/19/03: 'Antiquities Team Declares Ossuary a Forgery,' and further to this, AP Article of 7/22/03, 'Antiquities Dealer Arrested on Suspicion of Forging Artifacts.'

[109] See, for instance, the excellent article in *Ha'aretz English Edition*, 11/9/2002 by Sara Leibovich-Dor, 'Bones of Contention,' in *The Jerusalem Post* by Calev Ben David, 6/20/03, 'Jesus for Suckers,' or my short piece in *Folia Orientalia*, 2002, 'The James Ossuary—Is it Authentic?', pp. 233–6.

[110] See my response to 5/2/04 to David Samuel's *New Yorker* article of 4/12/04, 'Written in Stone.'

[111] See my comments in 'A Discovery That's Just Too Perfect,' *Los Angeles Times Op-Ed*, 10/29/02 and in Ha'aretz, 11/9/02 and *Discovery Channel News*, 10/21/02 above, as well as L. Peat O'Neil's *National Geographic News* article, 4/18/03, 'Bible-Era Artifacts Highlight Archaeology Controversy,' or Carol Eisenberg's *Newsday* article, 4/16/03, 'An Archaeological Detective Story.'

[112] At first the enthusiasm of many palaeographers (Lemaire, F. M. Cross, J. Fitzmyer, and others— one even judging it to be in the 'perfect handwriting' of the Fist Century CE) was palpable; but afterwards, chastened by increasing questions about patina, etc., Cross became more circumspect (though not Lemaire); see the correspondence published by Shanks on B.A.S.: '*Update—Finds or Fake*,' June 27, 2003.

[113] To be fair, Kyle McCarter did remark this in his original 2002 Toronto presentation and Carol Eisenberg's 4/16/03 *Newsday* article, but the best presentation was in Rochelle Altman, 'Official Report on James Ossuary,' article, 10/29/2002, *Bible and Interpretation*—reprinted 'Ossuary was Genuine, Inscription was Faked' in *Israel Insider*, 2/10/2003; see Paul Flesher, 'The Experts and the Ossuary: A Report on the Toronto Sessions' in *Bible and Interpretation*.

[114] See *Ant.* 20.200.

[115] The last in a note by reviewer A. Auswaks, Jerusalem Post on April 22nd, 1997. It has since become known that Oded Golan was connected for good or for ill with Shlomo Moussaieff, the billionaire Israeli antiquities collector (dealer?) in London. The latter was introduced to and knew my work intimately since the late 80's because of a long personal relationship with Michael Baigent (cf. *The Jesus Papers*, pp. 269–72); for Golan and Moussaieff, see 'Trial Sheds Light on Shadowy Antiquities World,' *Boston Globe*, 5/16/06.

[116] See Introduction to *James*, xxiii.

[117] *EH* 2.23.17–19 and Jerome, *Vir. ill.* 2.

[118] See L.Y. Rahmani, *A Catalogue of Jewish Ossuaries in the Collections of the State of Israel*, Israel Antiquities Authority, 1994.

[119] The first reference to him would appear to be in Tacitus (c. 116 CE), *Annals* 15.44, regarding the fire in Rome, who calls him '*Christus*'—which to some extent, echoes the allusion to '*Chrestus*' in Suetonius 5.25.4 which appears a more general rather than specific one. The reference in Josephus, *Ant.* 18.63–4 is considered interpolated.

[120] In the Scrolls, there are references to '*seeing Yeshuᶜa*'/'*Salvation*' and '*the Messiah of Aaron and Israel*'/'*Heaven and Earth*'/'*Righteousness*'—but not specifically to '*Jesus*.'

[121] See *EH* 3.11.2 and 3.32.1–3 above

[122] *Ibid.* 2.23.7

[123] *B. Sukkah* 52a.

[124] *EH* 2.23.3 quoting Clement and 18 quoting Hegesippus.

[125] For the relationship to Santiago de Compostela, see *James*, pp. 621–2 and 861.

[126] See Paul Flesher's description of John Painter's remarks at 'The Toronto Sessions,' *Bible and Interpretation* above.

[127] See R. Altman's 'Official Report' and Flesher's description K. McCarter's remarks in *Bible and Interpretation* above.

[128] See John 19:38–20:14 and *pars*.

[129] See Copper Scroll, items 52 and 53, and J. M. Allegro, *The Treasure of the Copper Scroll*, New York, 1960, pp. 104–12.

[130] See N. Avigad in *Jerusalem Revealed*, ed. Y. Yadin, Jerusalem, 1975, p. 18. Recently a plaque was identified on the Absalom Pillar by J. Zias and E. Puech attributing it, too, to '*Zachariah*' (John the Baptist's father?).

[131] See 1 Chronicles 24:15 identifying this line as the '*Seventeenth* Priestly Course.'

[132] For Mariamme daughter of Boethus, see War *Ant.* 15.320–2; for this '*Joseph and Mary*' story, see *Ant.* 15.65–72, 81–87, etc.

[133] See John 19:38 and *pars.* above.

[134] 'This has now proceeded to trial—cf. 'Trial Sheds Light,' *Boston Globe*, 5/16/06 above.

[135] See L.Y. Rahmani *Catalogue* above.

[136] *Los Angeles Times* Op-Ed, 10/29/02.

[137] See N. Silberman and Y. Goren, Faking Biblical History: How Wishful Thinking and Technology Fools Some Scholars—and Makes Fools of Others,' *Archaeology*, September/October, 2003, pp. 20–29 and David Samuels, 'Written in Stone,' *The New Yorker*, 4/12/04.

[138] See Y. Goren, 'An Alternative Interpretation of the Stone Tablet with Inscription Attributed to Jehoash King of Judah,' *Bible and Interpretation*, 2002 and F. M. Cross, 'Notes on the Forged Plaque Recording Repairs to the Temple,' *IEJ*, 2002, pp. 119–22.

[139] See Summary of Official IAA Report in *BAR*, September/October, 2003.

Chapter 3

[1] See *EH* 2.23.5, Jerome, *Vir. ill.* 2 and *Comm. on Gal.* 396 (1:10), and *Haeres.* 78.7.7.

[2] See Paul's competitive claim in Galatians 1:15 and 2 Corinthians 7:1.

[3] See *Haeres.* 30.2.3 and 78.13.2 and 78.14.3.

[4] For 'Banus', see *Vita* 11 and cf. *War* 2.120.

[5] See *Protevang* 8.2–12.3.

[6] See *Ant.* 15.72–87 and 2.168 above.

[7] See '*brothers*' in Matthew 12:46–9, John 2:12, 7:3–5, etc.; for '*sisters*,' see Matthew 13:56/Mark 6:3. etc.

[8] Jerome in *Vir. ill.* 2 calls James '*the son of Mary sister of the Lord*' in John 19:25 (sic!).

[9] See *Protevang* 25.1.

[10] See *b. B.B.* 60b, *Naz.* 19a, *Ned.* 10a and 77b, and *Ta'an* 11a; *James*, pp. 309, 764, and 898.

[11] In Paul, 1 Corinthians 12:12–27, Ephesians 2:18–22, etc. Gospels—John 2:21/Matthew 26:61 and *pars.*

[12] Cf. Matthew 9:11, 11:19, Mark 2:16, Luke 5:30, 7:34, 15:2, etc. and the allusions to '*eating and drinking*' in Matthew's '*Little Apocalypse*' 24:38 and 49 (including an allusion to '*drinking with drunkards*'—'*gluttons*' obviously being implied too) and Luke 10:7.

[13] We have already seen the use of this '*Cup*' imagery in 1QpHab xi.8–xii.6; but see also Revelation 14:8–11 and 1:1–21.

[14] For the allegorization of '*Damascus*,' see Chapters 26–8 below.

[15] See *b. B.B.* 60b, *Naz.* 19a, *Ned.* 10a, 77b, and *Ta'an* 11a above.

[16] See *James*, pp. 309, 764, 898, and 1028 and Benjamin of Tudela, *Travels*: Year 1165, where he describes these '*Mourners for Zion*' as '*eating no meat and abstaining from wine and dressing only in black and living in caves*'!

[17] See A. Paul, *Ecrits de Qumran et Sectes Juives aux Premiers Siecles de L' islam: Recherches sur l'origine du Qaraisme*, Paris, 1969.

[18] *Ibid.*, pp. 115–140.

[19] Benjamin, for instance, also in Year 1165, describes the Uprising of David Alroy (c. 1155). But there were earlier ones like Abu ʿIsa al-Isfahani and his disciple Yughdan (preceding Anan ben David and patterned on similar Shiʿite Islamic ones from the Seventh Century and Karaism onwards), both of whom—like other *'Mourners for Zion'* and James—*'prohibted all meat and wine'*; see al-Kikisani in L. Nemoy's *Karaite Anthology*, New Haven, 1952, pp. 51 and 334. Al-Biruni, too (the 10th–11th Century Muslim geographer and encyclopaedist), in *The Chronology of Ancient Nations* 3.20, also knows about the teachings of both Abu ʿIsa al-Isfahani and Yughdan.

[20] See M. Baigent, R. Leigh, and H. Lincoln, *Holy Blood, Holy Grail*, London, 1982, pp. 85–109. Though this inner circle or *'kabal'* is probably imaginary, still the choice of this designation is curiously interesting.

[21] 1QHxvii.30–5.

[22] Matthew 11:18–9/Luke 7:33–4, accompanied by a distinctly antinomian polemic and cf. *EH* 2.23.5 and *Haeres.* 78.13.3.

[23] See for instance *Zohar* 1.59b on *'Noah'* and Proverbs 10:25.

[24] See CDiv.17–8, vi.15–vii.3, *MMT*ii.3–24 and cf. *Haeres.* 30.16.7.

[25] See *War* 2.129 and Hippolytus 9.16, , Ps. *Hom.* 7.8, 10.1, 11.1, 24–8, and *Haeres.* 17, 19.5.7, 30.2.4–6, etc.

[26] Cf. Luke 5:36–9 and *pars.* with 1QSvi.4–5 where *'new wine'* is specifically mentioned.

[27] Cf. 1QSv.13, vi.2–5, 20–21, vii.19–20, etc. with *War* 2.130–3—but see too War 2.143–4

[28] 28. Cf. *EH* 2.23.5, *Haeres.* 78.13.3, and Luke 1:15 and 7:33/Matthew 11:18.

[29] See in Hippolytus 9.21 how he uses the same expression to explain why the *'Zealot'/'Sicarii Essenes'* enduring any torture and preferred death rather than *'blaspheme the Law or eat things sacrificed to idols.'*

[30] *EH* 4.22.4, *Haeres.* 19.1.1–6, 19.5.7, 20.3.1–4, 29.1.1–4, 29.5.1–29.7.7 30.1.1, and 53.1.1–4. Also see Apost. Const 6.6, which calls *'Masbuthaeans', 'Basmuthaeans',* and Pliny, *N.H.* 5.81, who knows a group in Northern Syria called the *'Nazirines.'*

[31] See S. Goranson, 'Essenes: Etymology from ʿAsah,' *Revue de Qumran*, 1984, pp. 483–98.

[32] This is also the case with a name like *'Abgarus'* which becomes *'Agbarus', 'Acbarus', 'Augurus', 'Alburus',* etc. in many translations.

[33] See *Haeres.* 53.2.2.

[34] See, for instance, *Haeres.* 30.17.1–18.1; but also 53.1.1–4 and Hippolytus 9.9 and 10.25.

[35] *Ant.* 18.112–9.

[36] See Eshel, Broshi, Freund, *et.al.*, 'New Data on the Cemetery East of Khirbat Qumran,' *DSD* 9/2, 2002, pp. 135–65 and P. Bar-Adon, 'Another Settlement of the Judean Desert Sect at

'Ein el-Ghuweir on the Shores of the Dead Sea,' *BASOR*, 1977, p. 12 above. But also see, K. D. Politis, 'Rescue Excavations in the Nabataean Cemetery at Khirbat Qazone,' *AJDA*, 1998, pp. 14–6, J. Zias above, 'Qumran Archaeology: More Grave Errors,' *Bible and Interpretation*, February, 2004, and Eshel and Broshi, 'Zias' Qumran Cemetery,' *Revue de Qumran* 21/3, 2004, pp. 487–89.

37 See Al-Biruni, *The Chronology of Ancient Nations* 8.23 and *The Fihrist* 9.1 above. Note that for al-Biruni, who seems to know a lot about Mani (just as *The Fihrist* in the previous generation does)—like the Prophet Mani, called himself '*the Messenger of God to Babylonia*' and referred to himself as '*the Seal of the Prophets*'—8.6–11.

38 Cf. A. N. Sherwin-White, *The Roman Citizenship*, Oxford, 1939, pp. 270–5 with CDvii.10/xix.23 on '*the Kings of the Peoples*'—which it considers identical with '*the Greek-speaking Kings*.'

39 In CDiv.17–v.15 and viii.4–10/xix.18–22, these '*Princes*' are called '*diseased without a cure*.'

40 The point is that it was only in this Period that the Roman Emperor was the Head of an underling body of Greek-speaking Kings in the Eastern part of the Empire like the Herodians.

41 Cf. *War* 3.522–42 with 1QpHabvi.10–1 on the '*Kittim*' and the general picture in the Gospels of activities in and around the Sea of Galilee or '*Gennesareth*', as Josephus calls it.

42 See for instance Tacitus in *Annals* 6.44 and 12.12 in his references to '*Acbar King of the Arabs*' or Edessenes generally. Strabo in *Geography* 16.1.28 considers almost all Mesopotamians '*Arabs*' as he does '*Osrhoeans*'; for Pliny, *H.N.* 6.31.136–9, so are the inhabitants of Charax Spasini on the Persian Gulf where Izates originally lived; for Juvenal, *Satire* 1.127, even the famous Roman Governor, Tiberius Alexander, is an '*Arabarch*.'

43 In Dio Cassius, *Roman History* 68.21, it can be either '*Augurus*'/'*Albarus*'/or '*Agbarus*'; the same for Hippolytus in *Codex Baroccian* 26.

44 Cf. *EH* 1.13.2;.

45 These are the cities which are the heart of the present political situation concerning Kurdistan; see our maps.

46 These are also the names of eponymous heroes in Syriac sources, the First Apocalypse of James, and in the Koran — as well as of the aboriginal '*Yazidis*.'

47 Cf. Moses of Chorene, *History of Armenia*, 2.35, with *Ant.* 20.18, who sees Helen as the first and principal of Abgar's wives. This is also the position somewhat of The Teaching of Addai.

48 See *Ant.* 20.17–53 and 75–92.

49 See *James the Brother of Jesus*, pp. 856–66 and 923–36. '*Thaddaeus*', of course, certainly bears some linguistic relationship to '*Addai*' as he does in Gospel Apostle lists to '*Judas of James*' (cf. Luke 6:16). '*Theudas*', of course, bears a linguistic relationship to '*Thoma*' ('*Twin*' in Aramaic)/'*Yehudah*'—as he does in the Second Apocalypse of James to '*Theuda the brother of the Just One*.'

50 See Moses of Chorene 2.35 above.

51 For the history of this monarch, see Eusebius, Moses of Chorene, *loc. cit.*, and J. B. Segal, *Edessa 'The Blessed City*,' pp. 62–82 above.

52 One of these several *Judas*'es, all of whom overlap, would be a reasonable guess but it is *Judas Thomas* and *Addai*/*Thaddaeus* who appear in Eusebius'/Syriac Conversion of King Agbar stories.

53 In Josephus, this occurs in *Ant.* 20.34–48.

54 Strabo 17.1.54–2.4 calls her *the Ruler of the Ethiopians in (his) time*, but he clearly means Meroe in Nubia on the Nile (c. 50–25 BC), a point Pliny consolidates in *N.H.* 6.35.

55 See *Ant.* 20.38–46, which is supported and even more fully fleshed out in Gen. *R.* 46:10–47:11.

56 One should note that Josephus makes it clear that *Queen Helen sent her representatives* (plural) *to Alexandria to buy grain* to relieve the Famine—a point he repeats in discussing Theudas' reverse exodus to the Jordan; *Ant.* 20.51 and 97–102.

57 This disparity between Acts 12:1–24 and Galatians can be explained by considering that Paul and Barnabas were among those who went either to Alexandria or Cyprus on these grain and fig-buying missions.

58 Cf. *Ant.* 20.35–47 above.

59 See J. B. Segal, *op. cit.*, pp. 15 and 66ff., who makes it clear *Ezad* is *Izates* and, at one point in *War* 4.567, Josephus seemingly even calls him *Izas*.

60 Cf. *Haeres.* 19.2.1–4.2, 30.1.3–3.7, and 53.1.1ff. with Hippolytus 9.8.

61 See A.F.J. Klijn and G. J. Reinink, *Patristic Evidence for Jewish Christian Sects*, Leiden, 1973, pp. 54–67—in particular, the quotation they provide from Bar-Khonai who thinks the name *Sampsaeans* derives from *Churches* (*Ecclesiae*, i.e., *Elchasaites*); also see L. Cirillo, *Elchasai e gli Elchasaiti: Un contributo alla storia delle communita guideo-cristiane*, Cosenza, 1984.

62 For the use of the term *ʿEdah* at Qumran, see CDvii.20, xx.3, 1QpPs 37ii.10, iii.10, etc.

63 *EH* 3.32.1–8.

64 For Simeon bar Yohai and the *Zohar*, see *James*, p.821 and *MZCQ*, pp. 54 and 71.

65 *Haeres.* 19.1.1–5.7, 30.1.1–3.7, and 53.1.3.

66 See *EH* 1.13.1–20, 2.12.1–3, and *Ant.* 20.1–117 and Chapters 3 and 28 below.

67 Cf. *Ant.* 20.21 with John 1:14–8 and 3:16–8.

68 *Ant.* 20.22–3 and 34–5.

69 Acts 9:10–8 and in Chapter 1 above and variously below.

70 See CDvi.19–vii.9 and below Chapters 21 and 22.

71 CDiv.2–3 and vi.2–11.

72 See CDv.6–9, vi.30–vii.4, and xx.27–32.

73 The *Fihrist* 9.1; cf. as well al-Biruni, 8.44ff.

74 See E. S. Drower, *The Mandaeans of Iraq and Iran*, Oxford, pp. 1–10 and 100–24 and *The Secret Adam*, Oxford, 1960, pp. 88–106; also see *The Haran Gawaita and the Baptism of Hibil-Ziwa*, tr. E. S. Drower, Biblioteca Apostolica Vaticano, Citta del Vaticano, 1953, pp. viii–xi and 2–17. According to Mandaean tradition, the followers of John the Baptist fled eastward in 37 CE—the approximate year Josephus actually gives for his execution.

[75] See "2004 Refugees International" (Update, Jan, 2006) and articles there referred to.

[76] See *James*, pp. 324–31.

[77] See the descriptions of this in Hippolytus 9.8–9 and 10.25 and *Haeres.* 19.4.1, 30.3.1–6, and 5.1.8–9. For Simon *Magus*, see Ps. Rec. 1.72 and 2.7–8 and Ps. *Hom.* 2.22–4, Epiphanius 21.2.3–4, and *Haeres.* 10.8.

[78] See, for instance, Matthew 12:46, Luke, 24:36, John 20:14, 20:19, 20:26, 21:4, and Acts 1:10, 7:55–6 (Stephen's James-like 'Great Power'/'Primal Adam' proclamation and cf. Matthew 26;64 and Mark 14:62 and even the *'two Angels'* in Luke 24:4).

[79] In the Koran, see 2.124–133, 3.33, 3.95–7, 21.51–75, 26.69–103, etc.

[80] For Paul, see Galatians 3:6–18 and Romans 4:1–16; for Muhammad, see Koran 2.135–40 and 3.95 and 113–5, etc.

[81] In CD, paralleling the Koran, one finds this in iii.2–20, ending in evocation of *'the Primal Adam'* ideology. But even more impressively *MMT*ii.30–3 ends with evocation of Genesis 15:6's *'reckoned to you as Righteousness'*, applying it to its Kingly recipient and his *'People'*—Koranic and 'Jamesian' works Righteousness with a vengeance. One should also see the point about Abraham's circumcision from CDxvi.4–6 based on Genesis 17:10–4 and the basis of the conversion episode of Izates and Monobazus in both the *Talmud* and Josephus above. For these controversies in Scroll Studies, one can see M. Baigent and R. Leigh above, *The Dead Sea Scrolls Deception*, New York and London, 1991; N. A. Silberman, *The Hidden Scrolls*, New York, 1994; and my own Introduction *DSSU*, 1992, pp. 1–16.

[82] This, as opposed to James, the Koran, and of course CD and *MMT* above.

[83] For the *'Friend'* terminology, see CDiii.2–4 above and for *'Perfection'/'Perfection of the Way,'* see 1QSviii.1–10, 18–25 (in exegesis of Isaiah 40:3: *'making a straight Way in the Wilderness*) and CDii.15–6, vii.4–6, xx.2–7, etc.

[84] See, too, the Scrolls' condemnation of the *'Emptiness'* of the Lying Spouter's teaching in 1QpHabx.9–12 and our analysis of this in Chapters 26 and 27 below.

[85] Koran 37.101–14—though all Muslims seem to think these lines unequivocally refer to Ishmael, he is nowhere mentioned as such by name—whereas Isaac explicitly is.

[86] Koran 7.59–79, 9.70, 11.25–68, 14.9, 22.42, 26.106–59, 29.14–40, 51.41–6, 69.5–8, etc.

[87] See both *Ant.* 20.25–6 and Hippolytus 9.8 and 10.26.

[88] See Koran 4.126.

[89] *'Lying'* in James usually comes in connection with the *'Tongue'*—as in 1:26 or 3:5–15; *'Lying'* in Paul usually comes in connection with the protestation, *'I lie not'* or *'I do not lie'*—as in Galatians 1:20, Romans 3:7/9:1, and 2 Corinthians 11:31; in the Scrolls, of course, the antagonist of the Righteous Teacher is *'the Man'/'Spouter of Lying'* and the allusion is omnipresent.

[90] See CDiii.2–20 and MMTii.30–3 above, which evoke imagery having to do with Abraham to make the ideological point of *'holding fast to the Covenant.'*

[91] The *'King'/'Kings'* would appear to be referred to in ii.21–9 (where an earlier letter is alluded to) introducing this evocation of Abraham's *'works'* being *'reckoned as justifying him'* and this *'King'*'s *'People'* in ii.30 above.

[92] For detailed arguments regarding the identity of these two, see *James*, pp. 862–939

[93] See the references to '*the Land of Noah*,' particularly in conjunction with the ark in 11.25–49—which certainly did not come down in Arabia as such—introducing ᶜAd and Hud. The same is true of 26.105–49 where latter's typically Northern-Syrian-style, cattle-grazing land is described; this is also the conjunction of 29.14–38, etc.

[94] See *James*, pp. 853–958 above.

[95] Few in either Koranic or Early Christian Studies have ever even imagined that '*Hud*' is just a contraction of the Hebrew '*Yehudah*' and simply relates to '*Addai*'/'*Thaddaeus*,' '*Judas Thomas*,' '*Judas Barsabas*,' and '*Judas of James*.' See my article 'Who Were the Koranic Prophets ᶜAd, Thamud, Hud, and Salih?' in *The Journal of Higher Criticism*, 11/2, Fall 2005, pp. 86–107—first given at a session of the American Academy of Religion in 1997,

[96] See the article on '*Yezidis*' by Christine Allison in *Iranica* of 2/20/05. They are an extreme Shiᶜite sect in Kurdistan who venerate the grave near Mosul (*in Adiabene* of course) of their founder and Holy Man, '*Shaykh ᶜAdi*' (the son of someone called '*Musa*'/'*Moses*'). Considered heretics and '*Devil-Worshippers*' by Orthodox Muslims; in reality, they are Kurds representing an out-growth of Mithraism with elements of Judaism, Christianity, and paganism (they pray three times a day, keep the Sabbath, and pray towards the sun!), and call themselves '*Ezdis*' or '*Ezidis*,' from which '*Yezidis*'—i.e., once more '*Ezad*'/'*Izates*'?

[97] See *E.H.* 2.23.4 and 12–8 where Eusebius drawing first on Clement of Alexandria and then on Hegesippus, uses James' cognomen, '*the Just*' or '*Righteous One*' in place of his very name itself. So does Origen in his famous testimony about Josephus having attributed the fall of Jerusalem to the death of James—not Jesus—in *Contra Celsus* 1.47, 2.13, and *Comm. on Matt.* 2.17.

[98] *Ant.* 20.24–6.

[99] One should note that in 20.26, Josephus specifically observes that it was in this Kingdom, given to Izates by his father, that the ark—'*whose remains are shown to everyone to this day*'—came to rest. Over a thousand years later, Benjamin of Tudela makes the same claim in the year 1163–4 of his *Travels* when he describes the way from Haran via Nisibis to Mosul.

[100] For '*Justification*' theology and '*the Sons of Zadok*,' see CDiv.7 (*par contra*, see CDi.19); for the several evocations of '*the Love Commandment*,' see 1QSix.19, CDvi.20–22, 20.17–18, etc. (*par contra*, see viii.6/xix.18 directed against '*the Herodian Establishment*').

[101] In the Koran, Abraham, Ishmael and Isaac, Jacob, the Tribes, etc. are all designated original '*Muslims*' in 2.126–41. This parallels the way in CDiii.2–4 above, Abraham, Isaac, and Jacob are described as '*Friends*' or '*Beloved of God and Heirs to the Covenant forever*.'

[102] See vii.14–xx.12 and Chapters 21–2 below.

[103] See my article '*MMT* as a Jamesian Letter to "the Great King of the Peoples beyond the Euphrates,"' *Journal of Higher Criticism*, 11/1, Spring, 2005 (first given to the Society of Biblical Literature in 1997), pp. 55–68.

[104] See G. Williams, *Eastern Turkey: A Guide and History*, 1972, London, 1972, pp. 166–7—this was supposed to have been in a cave under the Great Mosque. Even the spring at Callirhoe is

attributed to Abraham. Par contra, see C. H. Gordon, 'Abraham and the Merchants of Urfa,' *JNES* 17, 1958, pp. 28–31 and A. R. Millard, 'Where was Abraham's Ur?,' BAR, May/June, 2001.

105 See W. Dalrymple, *From the Holy Mountain: A Journey among Christians of the Middle East*, London, 1997, p.74, the Official Turkish Government site '*Sanliurfa*,' and cf. Luke 1:24 and *Protevang*. Jas. 22.3

106 In *Ant.* 20.18 and 20.26, Josephus also calls him '*Monobazus*'—which, like '*Abgarus*' in neighboring Syriac Tradition. seems to be a name coursing through multiple generations of this family. In 20.24, Josephus calls this Kingdom, '*Carron*'/'*Carrae*,' a designation that has never been made sensible.

107 See Turkish Government '*Sanliurfa*' above and *Wikipedia* articles: '*Edessa, Mesopotamia*' and '*Sanliurfa*.'

108 Cf. Gen R. 46:10–1 and *Ant.* 20.38–45 with Acts 8:26–40. The key connection here, apart from the fantastic elements in Acts, is the fact of a '*Queen*''s Treasury Agent and the question asked by the teacher, Philip in Acts—'Eleazar from Galilee' in Josephus—'*Do you understand what you are reading?*' See *James*, pp. 883–922.

109 Cf. Acts 8:38–9 with *Ant.* 20.46.

110 Cf. 'Jesus" '*not one jot or tittle*' speech in Matthew 5:18/Luke 16:17; for the Scrolls' emphasis on '*the exact letter of Torah*,' see CDiv.8, vi.14, vi.20, xx.6, 1QSi.15–17, viii.17, etc.

112 In Dio Cassius 68.4, Nerva reapplied the traditional body of Legislation against castration, known as the *Lex Cornelia de Sicarius et Veneficis*; while Hadrian—obviously in the wake of the Bar Kochba War—outlawed 'circumcision' completely with his '*Ius Sicaricon*'; cf. *The Augustan History* 13.10ff. and Chapter 28 below.

113 *Ant.* 20.35–43 and 46–8.

114 Paul continues these attacks in 4:7–6:15 and refers to this '*Party*' sarcastically in Philippians 3:2 as '*the Concision*' or '*Cutters*' and cf. Chapters 20 and 28 below.

115 *E.g.*, Matthew 19:12 (concerning '*eunuchs*'), Mark 14:4 (concerning '*the Poor*'), Luke 19:39 (concerning '*Pharisees*'), John 6:64 (concerning '*belief*'), 9:16 ('*the Pharisees*' again), 9:40 (concerning Matthew's '*Blind Pharisees*'), etc.

116 CDxvi.6–8.

117 The usage '*Satan*' does not occur as such at Qumran. Rather this '*Angel of Mastema*.' Therefore, all references to '*Satan*' one sees in some translations are almost always to '*Belial*' in the original.

118 CDxvi.4–6.

119 See 1QSv.2–3 and v.9.

120 Cf. Hebrews 11:17 with *Ant.* 20.20 above.

Chapter 4

[1] Hippolytus 9.8–12.

[2] Hippolytus 9.9; cf. *Haeres.* 19.5.1.

[3] *Zohar* 63a and 67b on 'Noah.'

[4] Cf. Koran 7.59–79, 11.29–68, 26.106–58, etc.

[5] Hippolytus 9.8.

[6] See *James*, pp. 328–36 and E. S. Drower, *op. cit.*, pp. 1–19, 100–24, and 258–62. Also E. S. Drower, *The Secret Adam*, Oxford, 1960, pp. ix–xvii and 88–106.

[7] Koran 2.62, 5.69, 22.17, etc.

[8] The 'Sabaeans' of Southern Arabia (a Kingdom functioning rather in the 10th to 7th Centuries B.C. and known in the Hebrew Bible as 'Sheba') is spelled somewhat differently than those considered here as 'Peoples of the Book.' The consonant here is a 'sadi' as opposed to a 'sin' (cf. *Surah* 27.22–44, where it is immediately followed by reference to 'Thamud' and 'Salih' in 27.45ff.; also see 34.15–20). Those relating to 'bathing' in Syriac and Aramaic are also spelled with a different 's,' but also with an 'ayin' as they are in Arabic and would be in Hebrew too.

[9] See Al-Biruni, *The Chronology of Ancient Nations*, 8.23ff., 18.26ff., and 20.26ff. and *The Fihrist* 9.1.

[10] For 'Protected Persons' or 'Dhimmis' in the Koran, see 2.62, 5.69, and 22.17; for the concept of 'Peoples of the Book'/'Ahl al-Kitab' upon which it is based, see 2.105–141, 3.64–79 but especially 100–15, 4.123–26, 153–77, 5.68–69 (again including 'Sabaeans'), etc.

[11] See, for instance, the material on Abraham in 2.124–36, 3.65–7, 4.125, etc.

[12] In giving these testimony, Muhammad makes it clear in 3.113 that all '*Peoples of the Book are not the same*,' some '*standing*' or being '*more staunch*' than others; cf. James 2:17–24. To paraphrase James, this reads: '*O Empty*' or '*Foolish Man, do you not know that Abraham was saved by sacrificing Isaac* (this being a 'work') *and that is how we are justified. Not by Faith alone, but rather by Faith and works working together*'—the final point, as should be clear, basically paralleling Muhammad's '*believe and do good works*' repeated throughout the Koran.

[13] In CD, see i.1–2, 10, 12, ii.1, 20–21, iii.6, xx.2, 6, 21, etc.; in James, see 1:4, 22–25, 2:8, 13, 17–25, etc.; but in Paul *par contra*, see Romans 2:13–15, 25, 3:27f., 11:6, Galatians 2:16, 3:10, etc.

[14] Cf. 1QSvi.6–7 and *War* 2.128–36.

[15] Koran 3.113–114.

[16] Cf. *EH* 1.13.4–10 and see the two variant manuscripts of *Apost. Const.* 8.25 on '*Lebbaeus surnamed Thaddaeus*,' a.k.a. '*Judas the Zealot*' and '*Judas of James*'; for these overlaps, also see *James*, pp. 930–8 above.

[17] See Haeres. 29.1.1 and 29.4.1–5.1 where he claims this was the name applied by Philo either to those he denotes as '*Theraputae*' or '*Essenes*.' For Epiphanius, anyhow, that this was just an earlier name for '*Christians*.'

[18] James 1:22, 1:23, and 1:25

[19] 1QpHabvii.10–1 on Habakkuk 2:3 and *'the Delay of the Parousia,'* viii.1–3 on Habakkuk 2:4, and xii.4–5 on *'the Ebionim'* or *'the Poor.'*

[20] See *Haeres.* 20.3.4 and 29.1.1–7.1.

[21] Cf. *EH* 4.22.6 with *Haeres.* 1.3.1 and 19.5.7, but also Justin Martyr, *Dial.* 80.

[22] The only group both Eusebius'/Hegesippus' and Justin Martyr's *'Galileans'* can be are those Epiphanius variously refers to as either *'Nazoraeans'* or *'Nasarenes'* whom he hardly distinguishes from either *'Ossaeans'* or *'Ebionites'*—or, for that matter, *'Sampsaeans.'*

[23] *Haeres.* 19.2.10 and 20.3.2–4. Here, too, he basically contends that all have been absorbed into *'the Ebionites.'*

[24] *Haeres.* 29.1.1–4, 29.5.4–7.4, and 30.2.3–3.7; for a polemical view of Ebionite doctrine, see *EH* 3.27.1–6.

[25] For Hegesippus, *EH* 2.23.5–6 and *Haeres.* 78.14.2, James *'did not enter the* (public) *baths'* and, like the Essenes, *'did not anoint himself with oil'*; but he did *'enter the Temple alone.'* For Epiphanius in *Haeres.* 29.4.1–5, supported by Jerome, this was *'the Holy of Holies'* where, as High Priest, he proceeded to make a typical *'Yom Kippur Atonement'* on *'behalf of the whole People.'* But certainly anyone doing such things and entering the Temple in such manner (especially *'Priests'*) was obliged to take a ritual bath; see *M. Middah* 1:4, 5:3, *M. Par.*3:7, *b. Tam* 26b, *j. Yoma* 40b, *b. Yoma* 30a–31a, *Ant.* 12.1456, *War* 4.205, etc. The solution to this conundrum would seem to be found in Josephus' statement that *'the Essenes preferred dry skin'*, not that they did not bathe—meaning they did not anoint themselves with any oils and probably did not take Greco-Roman-style hot baths; but they certainly took cold ones as did James' counterpart *'Banus'* below. So probably and almost assuredly did James. See also, *James*, pp. 344–5 above.

[26] See *Haeres.* 30.21.1 and Ps. *Hom.* 8.2, 10.1, 10.26, 11.1, etc.

[27] See the description he gives of *'Banus'* in *Vita* 11 and, of course, his lengthy description of *'Essenes'* in *War* 2.12–61.

[28] See, for instance, Ps. *Rec.* 4.35 and Ps. *Hom.* 7.3, 7.8, 8.14, 8.19, 11.35, 12.6 (showing Peter as a vegetarian), etc.

[29] E. S. Drower, *op. cit*, pp. 102 and 155.

[30] Cf. Matthew 19:13–5 and *pars.* and Acts 6:6, 8:17–9, 13:3, and 28:8.

[31] *Haeres.* 30.18.1–21.1. In fact, just as Josephus' *'Essenes'*—according to the Ps. *Hom.* 12.6, Peter also *'wears only threadbare clothes'*. At Qumran, see 1QpHabxii.3, 4QpPs 37ii.16, iii.10, iv.11, and 1QHv.23 (*'the ʿEbionei-Hesed'*/*'the Poor Ones of Piety'*).

[32] *Haeres.* 30.18.1.

[33] *Ibid.* 30.21.1

[34] *Ibid.* 30.21.2.

[35] *EH* 3.27.2; cf. *Ad. Haeres.* 1.26.2, 3.21.1, 4.33.4, 5.1.3, and *Contra Celsus* 5.65 and *Hom. in Jer.* 18.12.

36 The point is that it was their name that meant *'the Poor'* not that their Christology was *'poverty-stricken.'*

37 Ps. *Rec.* 1.39–47, 5.10, and 8.59; Ps. *Hom.* 2.6–12; in the Gospels see Matthew 21:11, Luke 1:76, and John 6:14 and 7:40–1. This is based on Deuteronomy 18:15–9, cited in 4QTest 4–8 but also see 1QSix.11 where it is coupled with *'the coming of the Messiah of Aaron and Israel.'* For the Manichaeans, Mani too is the Seal of the Prophets and, in the Koran, see for instance, 3.84, 7.157, 33.1–59, etc.

38 *Haeres.* 30.2.4–5, 16.1.1, and 21.1–43.

39 See Acts 2:23, 2:36, 3:15, 4:10, etc.

40 See, for instance Peter, in Ps. *Rec.* 1.13–43 and throughout the *Homilies.*

41 We say *'Historical'* because the picture in the Gospels and the Book of Acts is rather more polemically retrospective and even sometimes inverted.

42 Hippolytus 9.21.

43 Cf. Hippolytus 9.21 with *War* 2.159–63.

44 See *War* 1.3–6.

45 Al-Biruni, *op. cit.,* 8.23

46 Benjamin of Tudela, *Travels:* Year 1164.

47 *Haeres.* 20.3.4, but also see 19.4.1, 30.3.1–6, and 30.17.5.

48 Al-Biruni, *The Chronology of Ancient Nations,* 8.38–9 and 20.26–9 above; see also *The Fihrist* 9.1 as well.

49 See P. Bar-Adon, 'Another Settlement of the Judean Desert Sect at ʿEin el-Ghuweir on the Shores of the Dead Sea,' *BASOR,* 1977, p.12; 'Excavations in the Judean Desert,' *Atiqot* 9, 1989, pp. 3–14 and 18–29; K. D. Politis, 'Rescue Excavations in the Nabataean Cemetery at Khirbat Qazone,' *AJDA,* 1998, pp. 14–6; and J. Zias, 'The Cemeteries at Qumran,' *DSD,* 2000, pp. 220–53 above. Also see, R. de Vaux, *Archaeology and the Dead Sea Scrolls,* Oxford, pp. 52 and 88. G. R. Driver, *The Judaean Scrolls,* Oxford, 1965, pp. 45–8, also observes that Karaite Jews observe this custom.

50 See H. Eshel and M. Broshi, 'Excavations at Qumran, Summer of 2001,' *IEJ* 53, 2003, pp. 61–73; Eshel, Broshi, Freund, *et. al.,* 'New Data on the Cemetery East of Khirbat Qumran,' *DSD* 9/2, 2002, pp. 135–65; J. Zias, 'Qumran Archaeology: More Grave Errors,' *Bible and Interpretation,* February, 2004; and finally H. Eshel and M. Broshi, 'Zias' Qumran Cemetery,' *Revue de Qumran* 21/3, 2004, pp. 487–89 above.

51 *Chronology* 8.23, 18.10, and 20.29. For Methusaleh's other son, called *'Sabi',* see al-Biruni, *Chronology of Ancient Nations* 8.41–2. The reference to *'Yusufus'* leading here into a consideration of Samaritan matters is erroneous and a proofing error, but the fact of John's Samaritan connections and their knowledge of this remains. The point that was being made here was that John was also referred to *'as-Sabiʿ'* in the Arabic version of Josephus, The *'Yusufus.'*

52 Cf. *The Fihrist* 9.1 with CDv.7–10, vii.1 and 11QTlvi.19–lvii.19 and lxvi.14–5. The point that was supposed to be indicated here was two centuries after the Prophet. The author of

The Fihrist, Ibn al-Nadim, as everyone knows, was a younger contemporary of or lived in the previous generation before al-Biruni—the 10th Century.

[53] Koran 2.172, 5.3, 6.146, and 16.115.

[54] Ps. *Hom.* 7.9; cf. Acts 15:20, 15:29 and 21:25.

[55] Cf. Acts 10:14 and 10:28, Hippolytus, 9.21, and CDv.7 and vi.17–8. Also see 1QSv.14–20.

[56] Ps. *Hom.* 7.19.

[57] For this same *'Perfection'* ideology at Qumran, see CDvii.3–5 above and 1QSviii.21–ix.6.

[58] See Koran, *loc. cit.* above.

[59] The transmission has to be seen as quite straightforward: from James' directives into the Pseudoclementines and, via the Elchasaites and Manichaeans, into Islam.

[60] *The Fihrist* 9.1. Even Mani's ban on wine and his vegetarianism is described here; cf. al-Biruni 8.43ff.

[61] E. S. Drower, *The Mandaeans of Iraq and Iran*, pp. 3–5 and *The Secret Adam*, p. ix.

[62] See 1QSv.2 and v.9 and, for instance, Psalm 25:8–10 and Psalm 119:1–5 where *'Notzrei ha-Brit'* is used synonymously with *'Shomrei ha-Brit'* and 4QTesti.17's Messianic citation of Levi's admonition to his children in Deuteronomy 33:9: *'Britcha yinzor'/'they will keep Your Covenant.'*

[63] Of course, this *'Keepers of the Secret'* vocabulary is known to the Pseudoclementine *Homilies'* Epistle of Peter to James 3–4 as, to some extent, it is at Qumran, *e.g.,* 1QSix.21–2.

[64] See *The Secret Adam*, pp. 21–34 and see, for instance, the *Zohar* 55b–56a on Genesis 1:27's reference to *'Adam.'*

[65] See, for instance, Ibn al-ʿArabi, *The Bezels of Wisdom.*, tr. R. W. J. Austin, New York, 1980, pp. 51–6, 84–8, 149, 253, and 281, speaking about *'The Perfect Man'* and basically echoing *Kabbalah*.

[66] See Hippolytus 9.9, 10.25, *The Fihrist* 9.1, and *The Secret Adam*, xi–xiv. The Mandaean *Haran Gawaita*, the title of which even refers to this flight, puts it around 37–8 CE. Today there are even *'Christians'* in South India, who call themselves *'Knanaya Zealots'*, that is, *'Canaanite'/ 'Cananaean Christians'*, who claim to be descendants of emigrants who left Edessa in 345 CE, follow *'Thomas'* but shun more normative *'Christian'* followers of *'Thomas'* as backsliders, will marry no one outside their own blood group, and claim descent from Palestinian Jews; cf. *www. knanayadiocese.org*. For CD, see iv.2–3, vi.3–vii.5, and further below.

[67] See *EH* 1.13.4 and 10–20, *The Acts of Thomas* 1–11, and the Syriac *Doctrine of Addai* and *The Teaching of the Apostles* 27.

[68] *B. Suk.* 52a–b; see also *b. San.* 97a; Genesis R. 75.6, 95, and 99.2; and Song of Songs R. 2.13.4 in *b. San.* 43a and 67a. There is also the character known as *'Ben Stada'* (probably a variation on *'the Standing One'* and identical to *'the Messiah ben Joseph'*), who, according to *b. Shab.* 104b, was said to have brought sorcery from Egypt. He too was crucified at Lydda. *B.B.* 10b and *Pes.* 50a also pointedly speak of *'the martyrs at Lydda.'* One should note that Justin Martyr in *Apology* 2.14–5 actually refers to *'Sotadists'* when speaking about Simon *Magus*.

⁶⁹ See the allusion both to '*leading Ephraim astray with a Lying teaching and a Tongue full of Lies*' in 4QpNahii.8 and that to '*the Simple of Ephraim joining*' or '*rejoining the Many*' or '*Majority of Israel*' in 4QpNahiii.5, itself using the language of '*ger-nilveh*'/'*resident alien*' or '*Nilvim*'/'*Joiners*', i.e., '*Gentile Converts.*' For '*Ephraim*' as '*Samaria*', see Isaiah 7:9, 11:13, Ezekiel 37:16–19, Hosea 4:17, 5:3, and throughout.

⁷⁰ See my article 'A Discovery That's Just Too Perfect' in *Los Angeles Times Op-Ed* of 10/29/02 and above.

⁷¹ *B. Suk.* 52a–b above. Even Josephus, *War* 2.234–46, records many difficulties between Jews and Samaritans in this border area, which resulted in numerous executions.

⁷² *Ant.* 18.85–9. Here Pilate is removed and sent to Rome because of the outrages he committed against this Samaritan 'Messiah' and his followers, but not before Tiberius had already died in 37 CE.

⁷³ See *EH* 2.13.3, quoting Justin Martyr (who came from Samaria), *Apology* 1.26 and 1.56, and Ps. *Rec.* 2.7 and Ps. *Hom.* 2.22; also see Irenaeus, *Ad. Haeres.* 1.23, Hippolytus 6.2, Epiphanius 21.1, *etc.*

⁷⁴ *Ant.* 20.142. The Latin version of this work and several variant Greek ones identify this character as '*Simon.*' There is also, of course, the overlap with Paul's confrontation on Cyprus with the character Acts 13:8 is calling '*Elymus Magus*' (i.e., '*Sorcerer Magician*'). Of course, in Ps. *Rec.* 2.7/ *Hom.* 2.23, Irenaeus, *Ad.Haeres.* 1.23, and elsewhere, it is clear that Simon's principal doctrine was '*the Primal Adam*' or '*Standing One.*' The confusion here with '*Atomus*' should be patent. Where '*Cyprus*' goes (often '*Kitta*'/ '*Kittaeans*' in classical Hebrew), we have already discussed the confusion of this term in *James*, pp. 494–5 with '*Cuthaeans*', the term by which '*Samaritans*' were often known in Jewish Literature. Cf. Josephus, *Ant.* 9.288–90, 11.19–20, *War* 1.63, etc. This is the same in Rabbinic literature and even in Benjamin of Tudela above.

⁷⁵ For statements of this doctrine relative to Simon, see Ps. *Rec.* 2.7 and *Hom.* 2.23 above; relative to the Na'assenes, see Hippolytus 5.3; the Elchasaites, Hippolytus 10.25; the Sampsaeans, Epiphanius, *Haeres.* 53.1.8–9; Christ himself, Tertullian, *The Flesh of Christ*, 1.16–7.

⁷⁶ See Ps. Rec. 1.72 and 2.7; for '*laying on hands*,' see the Epistle of Clement to James 2, 19, Ps. *Hom.* 9.23, and E. S. Drower, *The Mandaeans of Iraq and Iran*, pp. 102 and 155.

⁷⁷ Justin Martyr, *Apology* 1.26, *EH* 2.13.3, Ps. *Rec.* 2.7/Ps. *Hom.* 2.22, Irenaeus, *Ad. Haeres.* 1.23, Hippolytus, 6.2, Epiphanius 21.1, etc.

⁷⁸ Ps. *Rec.* 1.72–4.

⁷⁹ See Acts 8:17–8, E. S. Drower, *op. cit.*, p. 155, and Ps. *Rec.* 2.7/Ps. *Hom.* 2.22 above.

⁸⁰ The most well-known example of this, of course, is the story of '*the Good Samaritan*', illustrating the two '*Love Commandments*' in Luke 10:25–37, just before 'Jesus" encounter with Luke's version of Martha's '*complaint*' at '*having to do all the serving*' in 10:38–42. But there is also the encounter with the Samaritan leper in 17:11–19 (one of ten), whom Jesus cures and which also includes allusion to '*standing*' in 17:12, as well as the episode in John 8:48, where Jesus is both accused of '*being a Samaritan and having a demon*'—in reply to which he only denies the

second. This episode too (like Luke 17:18) is full of the language of '*Glory*'/'*glorying*' and the idea that the portrait of '*Jesus*' owes much to Samaritan tradition is something we have already treated above and will treat further below.

[81] Cf. al-Biruni, *Chronology of Ancient Nations*, 8.23, 18.10, and 20.29; *The Fihrist* 9.1; and E. S. Drower, *Mandaeans*, pp. 7 and 258–62.

[82] See Ps. *Rec.* 2.7–11 and Ps. *Hom.* 2.22–4.

[83] See Origen, *Contra Celsus* 6.11, Eusebius, *E.H.* 4.22.5, and Epiphanius, *Haeres.* A13, 8.9.1, 10.1.1, 13.1.1–4, and 20.3.4.

[84] See *Ant.* 20.129–33. Loeb notes '*Dortus*' and '*Doitus*' as variant readings for its '*Doetus*.'

[85] All of this is very circular, but perhaps the main point is the association of Lydda with the crucifixion of '*the Messiah ben Joseph*' in the various Rabbinic contexts—cf. n. 68 above.

[86] See *Ant.* 18.85–7, M. Gaster, *The Samaritans*, Oxford, 1925, pp. 90–91, who directly connects this episode to the Samaritan '*Taheb*' or '*Restorer*' ideology. The Fourth-Century *Memar* of Marqah also makes it clear that the idea has something to do with the '*True Prophet*' Prophecy of Deuteronomy 18:18–9—an ideology, as we have seen, basic to both Pseudoclementines and the Messianic compendium of Qumran proof-texts known as 4Q*Test*. Not only can this '*Restorer*' idea in a general sense have to do with being a '*Penitent*'—itself widespread as well at Qumran—but the reference to '*Mount Gerizim*' and a wonder-worker doing a '*sign*' there also makes it clear that it is something of a '*Joshua*'/'*Jesus*' *redivivus* episode—'*Joshua*,' of course, transliterated in the Greek into '*Jesus*.'

[87] *Ant.* 18.88–90. Here it is the Samaritans who sent a delegation to Rome to complain. Cf. too similarly Philo's *Mission to Gaius* 299–305 very soon afterwards.

[88] Cf. *Ant.* 18.116–9 with *Ant.* 18.85 and note the sequentiality here. For Joseph, the denouement concerning John comes after the demise of the Samaritan '*Impostor*' and, for that matter, after the recall of Pontius Pilate from Palestine.

[89] *Ant.* 18.85–6.

[90] Cf. *Ant.* 18.88 with Matthew 27:11–26 and *pars.*

[91] Cf. Acts 21:38 with *War* 2.261–3 and *Ant.* 169–72. Josephus says this individual claimed to be '*a Prophet*'—n.b., '*the True Prophet*' ideology again. Acts only says he wanted to '*lead four thousand Sicarii out into the wilderness*'; cf. too *War* 4.323 and 5.19 and *Ant.* 20.168.

[92] *War* 6.300–9 and Chapter 18 and variously below.

[93] *Ant.* 18.89. N.b. the matter of Pontius Pilate's recall is noticeably missing from Josephus' *War*. He rather skips right from the episode, where Pilate sneaks the standards with the bust of the Emperor upon them into Jerusalem by night and then bludgeons those who came to Caesarea to plead against this (2.169–70), to Caligula's order to Petronius—then Governor of Syria— to kill himself (fortunately for us, he did not, for this apparently is the same Petronius who authored *The Satyricon*) during the episode Josephus describes about Caligula's attempt to have a giant statue of himself erected in the Jerusalem Temple (2.2.184–204).

[94] Acts 8:26–39. This, of course, occurs right after the confrontations in Acts with Simon in Samaria. Here Philip adds, in response to the eunuch's interpretation, 'I believe the Son of God to be Jesus Christ': 'If you believe from the whole heart, it (meaning immersion in water or baptism—that is, in place of 'circumcision') is lawful' (8.36–7). One should compare this, as we have, with the story of Izates' conversion in *Ant.* 20.43–5 and Gen. R. 46.10, which even claims to know the passage Izates and his brother Monobazus were reading, Genesis 17:11.

[95] Cf. *Didache* 1.1

[96] See, for example, 1QSi.9–10, ii.7–16, iii.3–25, iv.8–26, etc., and throughout the War Scroll.

[97] See 1QSiv.9–14; CD, i.14–ii.1, iv.19, viii.12–13;1QpHabv.11–12, x.9–13, etc.

[98] This 'Judas' is probably not to be distinguished from 'Judas of James' and 'Judas the brother of James' in Luke and the Letter under his name—nor, for that matter, 'Judas Iscariot'/'the Iscariot' or 'Thaddaeus'/'Addai' in other Apostle lists and the First Apocalypse of James. 'Saba' in 'Barsabas' is hardly to be distinguished from 'Saba' as in 'Sabaean'/'Sobiai'/'Masbuthaean'; see *James*, pp. 853–963.

[99] *The Haran Gawaita and the Baptism of Hibil-Ziwa*, tr. E. S. Drower, Biblioteca Apostolica Vaticano, Citta del Vaticano, 1953, pp. vii–xi and 3–8 and cf. her *Mandaeans of Iraq and Iran*, p.6.

[100] For 'Peoples' in the New Testament, see mainly the way Paul uses the term in Galatians 2:2–8, 1 Corinthians 10:20–32 and 12:2–13, Romans 2:14–3:29, 9:24–30, 11:1–25, and 15:9–27, etc.; but also see Matthew 4:15, 10:5–18, 12:18–21, etc. and *pars*. At Qumran, see CDvi.4–10, viii.8–10, viii.16, 1QpHabii.5–iv.14, vi.7–9, ix.4–x.9, etc.

[101] See E. S. Drower, *The Haran Gawaita and the Baptism of Hibil-Ziwa*, p.4 and cf. *The Mandaeans or Iraq and Iran*, pp. 3–6 and *Right Ginza* 3–15.

[102] See, for instance, the reference in Ps. Rec. 1.70 to the 'Enemy,' who leads the attack on James in the Temple and then gets letter from the High Priest to pursue the Community to Damascus, as 'Simon, a Magician.'

[103] See *James*, pp. 807–958.

[104] See *EH* 2.23.7 and *Haeres.* 78.7.7.

[105] Cf. Matthew 10:4/Mark 3:18 with Luke 6:15/Acts 1:13.

[106] See *EH* 1.13.4 and 1.13.10 and cf. such documents as The Acts of Thomas which begins with Thomas in India. We have already noted above the two communities ascribed to Thomas in India, one normative Christian and the other calling itself 'Knanaya Zealots'—obviously based on 'Cananaean'/'Kanna\`im' above, the connection with whom needs further investigation.

[107] Cf. for instance *EH* 1.9.5 with *EH* 1.12.2–4 where Eusebius is unclear concerning whether 'Cephas' is an 'Apostle' or 'Disciple' or whether there are one or two of them. The same for 'Thaddaeus.'

[108] For Matthew 10:4 and Mark 3:18 above, the Apostle is 'Thaddaeus' or 'Lebbaeus who was surnamed Thaddaeus' (whatever this means); for Luke 6:15 and Acts 1:13, he is 'Judas (the brother) of James.'

[109] For *'the Mebakker,'* see CDix.18–9, xiii.7–19, xiv.8–14, etc. and Chapters 18 and 22 below.

[110] See *The Haran Gawaita and the Baptism of Hibil-Ziwa*, p. 4 and *The Mandaeans of Iraq and Iran*, pp. 4–6 above and E. S. Drower,'s 'Mandaean Polemic' in *BSOAS*, no. 25, 1962, pp. 438–48.

[111] Note that in the *Ant.* 18.116–9 John's death is presented as occurring after Pontius Pilate's removal from Palestine and after the Samaritan *'Taheb'* affair.

[112] See Josephus in *War* 2.128 and 2.139 and cf. CDvi.21, James 2:5–8, and *Dial.* 23, 46–47, 52, and 93.

[113] *War* 2.118–9—*n.b.*, the *'head'* part of this scenario would seem to come from the previous episode in *War* 2.116 when Josephus describes the angry Tiberius as commanding his Governor in Syria Vitellius *'to send him his (Aretas') head'* when he caught him (which of course he did not).

[114] Cf. *Ant.* 18.116–8 with Luke 3:6 where John attacks *'the multitudes that went out to be baptized by him,'* referring to them as *'off-spring of vipers'*; for Matthew 3:7, these are *'the Pharisees and Sadducees'*—in either event, the portrait is clearly tendentious.

[115] Matthew 14:6 and *pars.* Again, we have the Roman interest in birthday parties—mot evinced by Jews in Palestine. Titus shows a similar interest at the end of the *Jewish War*. Moreover, the portrait of John's head upon a platter, even though it does not occur in Josephus as we just said, nor in John, has been a fixture of Western painting from Renaissance Times to Pre-Modern.

[116] See *Ant.* 18.106–29.

[117] *Ant.* 18.108–15; the information that Salome was Philip's wife and it was he that died childless is given by Josephus in *Ant.* 18.136–7 and that Herodias was originally married to a half-brother of Herod Antipas, himself named *'Herod'* and not *'Philip',* is given by Josephus in *Ant.* 18.109 and 18.136. Nor is there any way out of these New Testament contradictions whatever facile apologetic stratagem is chosen.

[118] Hippolytus 9.8 and *EH* 6.38. One should note that it is in the library of Caesarea that Origen saw the copy of Josephus' *War* testifying to the fact that Jerusalem fell because of the death of James (not 'Jesus'). The date Hippolytus gives here for this preaching is the 3rd Year of Trajan, which would be about 101 CE and would make him a contemporary in Palestine, both of James' successor Simeon bar Cleophas and the famous Simeon bar Yohai of *Zohar* tradition. The reference to *'Alcibiades'* here, which has puzzled so many, is obviously just a Greek approximation of *'Elchasai'*!

[119] For the Mani Codex, see L. Koenen and C. Romer, *Der Kolner Mani-Kodex*, Bonn, 1985 and *Codex Manichaicus Coloniensis*, ed. L. Cirillo, Cosenza, 1990—in particular, the article by L. Koenen, pp. 1–34. Also see L. Cirillo, *Elchasai e gli Elchasaiti*, Cosenza, 1984 and the actual quotations from Mani's *'Book called the Shaburkan'* (after the Persian Ruler, for whom he composed it) which al-Biruni claims to give in his *Chronology of Ancient Nations*, pp. 8.1–8. He also claims in 3.11–16 that *'the Manichaeans have a Gospel of their own',* which they call *'The Gospel of the Seventy,'* the contents of which *'really are what the Messiah thought and taught, that every other Gospel is false and its followers are Liars against the Messiah'*—ideas that in one form or another also went into the Koran.

120 See L.T. Stuckenbruck, *The Book of the Giants from Qumran*, Tubingen, 1997, pp. vii–ix and pp. 1–4.

121 For an Islamic view of the Manichaeans, see *The Fihrist* 9.1 and al Biruni 8.41ff., for whom Mani—whose followers were called Siddiks (i.e., *Zaddiks*) and who taught poverty, 'separation from the world,' sexual continence, abstinence, vegetarianism, and '*the Right Path*'—came from an Elchasaite family in Messene (i.e, Charax Spasini/Basrah again). The only '*Essene*'/'*Ebionite*'/'Jamesian' thing he did not teach was bathing—which is the same for Islam. For *The Fihrist*, Mani was taught by an Angel called '*the Tawm*' (i.e., '*Thomas*' again), which he even knows means '*Companion*'/'*Twin*', and his principal doctrine yet again is '*the Primal Adam*.' Now that we have found his '*book*,' it is hard to see just how this would differ from '*Elchasai*''s '*book*.'

122 See E. S. Drower, *The Mandaeans of Iraq and Iran*, pp. 3–7 and 'Mandaean Polemic' in *BSOAS*, no.25, 1962, pp. 438–48.

123 See, for instance, the reference to the Simon *Magus*-type '*Magician*' called '*Elymus the Magus*' on '*Cyprus*' in Acts 13:8 and the Samaritans as '*Cuthaeans*' in *Ant.* 9.288–90, 11.19–20, *War* 1.63, etc. above—'*Cuthaeans*' obviously doubling for for '*Kittim*'/Cypriots, Cretans, or Greeks elsewhere. One should note that, according to *The Scholia* of Theodore bar Konai, a Nestorian Syriac scholar of the 8th–9th Century, the group he calls '*the Cantaeans*' (obviously meaning '*the Cuthaeans*' or '*Samaritans*') preceded the Mandaeans in their doctrines—again, obviously true. But also see, Epiphanius' claim in *Haeres.* 8.6–11 above (echoing 2 Kings 17:24 and repeated by al-Kirkisani as well) how the Babylonians settled the Assyrian '*Cutha*' in Samaria!

124 See 1QSi.12–8, viii.12–8, and ix.4–20.

125 Acts 21:16.

126 *Ant.* 18.109–17 above.

127 As I argued earlier, if Paul was an Herodian, then it was probably he—not the so-called '*Manaen*'—who was '*a foster brother of Herod the Tetrarch*' and the '*Herod*' responsible for the death of John the Baptist.

128 *Surahs* 2.62, 5.69, and 22,17.

129 To see how the Koran spells '*Sheba*' or the '*Saba*" of Southern Arabia, see *Surahs* 27.21–45 and 34.12–5. This '*Saba*', at least from the 10th Century BC forward, extended across the Straits of Hormuz into what we now call Ethiopia which accounts for some of the confusion in the traditions regarding the two. The two peoples are, in any event, genetically-related even today.

130 *Geography* 17.1.48–2.3. Note that it is clear here that what Strabo is calling '*Ethiopia*' and '*Ethiopians*' is what we would call '*Nubia*,' a little further up the Nile from Egypt, and the capital he is talking about is clearly Meroe, whose ruins still exist today (cf. Pliny, *H.N.* 6.35.29–30). This is clearly Acts 8:27–39's source. Nor is there any castration ever noted in any of these locales. The idea of this '*Queen*''s Treasury Agent being a '*eunuch*' clearly reflects the Roman *Lex Cornelia de Sicarius et Veneficis*, which we shall discuss further in Chapter 28 below.

131 For a good description of the stories surrounding this '*Saba*' (i.e., today's '*Yemen*') and its capital Ma'rib, see R. A. Nicholson, *A Literary History of the Arabs*, Cambridge, 1907/1969, pp. 1–30.

[132] See Koran 27:20–53—'Thamud,' of course (like the 'Angel Taum' among the Manichaeans), reflecting 'Judas Thomas'; and 'Salih,' 'the Just One' James.

[133] On Helen's three successive 'Nazirite' oaths, see *b. Naz.* 19a–20a; for her gifts to the Temple, see *b. Yoma* 37a, *b. Git.* 60a, and *Tosefta Pe'ah* 4:18.

[134] See *The Travels of Rabbi Benjamin* Year 1164. This is to say nothing about all the various Karaites and 'Mourners for Zion' he is encountering.

[135] *Ant.* 20.97.

[136] This is an extremely telling bit of dissimulation, since why Judas' position should have been so important and why the Leadership of the early Church was never regulated according to Acts are probably questions impossible to answer; see *James*, pp. 164–209. For James as 'Bishop' or 'Bishop of Bishops,' see Ps. Rec. 1.66 and 1.68, the Epistles of Peter to James 1.1 and Clement to James 1.1 and see *EH*, quoting Clement of Alexandria, 2.1.3 and *Haeres.* 29.3.8, 66.19.7, and 78.7.7.

[137] See, for instance, *EH* 2.1.4 and 2.23.10–6.

[138] *EH* 2.1.2, 2.23.1, and *Haeres.* 78.14.2.

[139] For 'Judas the Zealot,' see the variant mss. of *Apost. Const.* noted in *ANCL*, asserting that 'Thaddaeus, also called Lebbaeus' in Matthew, '*was surnamed Judas the Zealot, who preached the Truth to the Edessenes and the People of Mesopotamia when Abgarus ruled over Edessa, and was buried in Berytus (Beirut) of Phoenicia.*' For 'Theudas the brother of the Just One,' see 2 Apoc. Jas. 44.18 above.

[140] See 'Nusairi' article by Louis Massignon in *Encyclopaedia of Islam*, 1st ed.

[141] See L. Massignon, 'Nusairi' in *E.I.* above and H. Field and J. B. Glubb, 'The Yezidis, Sulubba, and other Tribes of Iraq and Adjacent Regions,' *General Series in Anthropology* 10, Menasha, Wisconsin, 1943, pp. 5–16.

[142] *Ad. Haeres.* 5.1.3 and *Haeres.* 30.3.1–7 and 17.4, 53.1.8–10.

[143] Cf. 1QSiv.19–24 on '*the Two Spirits*' and '*Holy Spirit*' baptism, CDiii.18–20 introducing the definition of '*the Sons of Zadok*,' 1QHiv.29–34 referring both to '*Enosh*' (John's name among the Mandaeans) and '*the Son of Man*' (Adam), and 1QM x.11 interpreting '*the Star Prophecy*' of Numbers 24:17 in terms of Isaiah 31:8's '*the sword of no mere Adam.*'

[144] See 4QTest 4–8, 1QSix.11 (where it is coupled with '*the coming of the Messiah of Aaron and Israel*') and, for instance, Ps. Rec. 1.39–47, 5.10, 8.59, and Ps. Hom. 2.6–12 above.

[145] *N.b.,* all the references to Jesus '*standing*' in Luke 24:36, John 1:26, 20:14, 20:19, 20:26, and 21:4, Acts 4:10, 7:55–6, etc. and see *Haeres.* 30.3.2–6, describing the 'Sampsaeans, Ossaeans, and Elchasaites.'

[146] CD.vi.10–1, viii.24, xii.23–xiii.1, xiv.19, and xx.1 and cf. 4QFlor 11 and 13. Certainly in Ezekiel 37:10 the reference is to Resurrection. This is true, too, in Daniel !2:13, which uses '*the Last Days*' exactly as in CDvi.10 above and is almost an exact parallel to this reference. But it is also true in Lam. R. 2.3.6 and Zohar i.62b in exposition of Daniel 12:13. Zohar iii.22a on 'Phineas,' expanding Ezekiel 37, also uses '*stand*' in precisely this manner.

[147] For the Apostles as *'standing,'* see John 18:5–25, 19:26, and Acts 1:11; for the two Angels, see Luke 24:4; for Mary Magdalene, see John 20:11, etc.

[148] Cf. Ps. *Rec.* 2.8–11 and Ps. *Hom.* 2.24.

[149] See the variant manuscripts of the *Apostolic Constitutions*, noted in *ANCL* above, and the reference in the fragments of Hippolytus 'On the Twelve Apostles' to the effect that *'Judas who is also (called) Lebbaeus (thereby combining Luke with Matthew) preached to the People of Edessa and to all Mesopotamia, and fell asleep at Berytus and was buried there.'*

[150] John 6:71, 13:2, and 13:26.

[151] Luke 6:15 and Acts 1:13 but see also Hippolytus 'On the Twelve Apostles' in *ANCL*, who also identifies this 'Simon' as *'the son of Clopas (i.e., 'Simeon bar Cleophas') who is also (called) Judas'* (meaning he is placing the name in the context of the *'Judas of Simon Iscariot'* complex) and *'became Bishop of Jerusalem after James the Just and fell asleep and was buried there at the age of one hundred and twenty years'*—that is, not only is he basically identifying *'Simon the Zealot'* with *'Simeon bar Cleophas,'* but he is also incorporating the story of the death of the latter in Trajan's time; see *James*, pp. 817–50.

[152] 2 Apoc. Jas. 44.11–25.

[153] 1 Apoc. Jas. 36.4–24, here even including reference to the *'secret'* or *'hidden'* ideology.

[154] *Ant.* 20.97 above.

[155] Matthew 14:13–21 and 15:33–8 and *pars.*

[156] Cf. CDiv.2–3, vi.19–21, and vii.16–7.

[157] CDv.6–16 and vi.19–vii.6.

[158] See *War* 2.259 and 264–5 and *Ant.* 20.160 and 167–8.

[159] For use of terms *'Innovation(s)'/'Innovator(s)'* in Josephus, see *War* 2.5, 2.224, 2.407–10, and 2.513; *Ant.* 18.93 and 20.129 (followed by one of the crucifixions at Lydda); and even *Vita* 17 and 28.

[160] See John 4:45–54 and 6:3–14 (ending in reference to *'the True Prophet'* ideology) and Matthew 14:14–21, 15:29–38, and 16:5–12 (moving on to *'the leaven of the Pharisees and Sadducees'*) and *pars.*

[161] One should note how defensive Josephus is in *Vita* 17–20 following his journey to Rome at the age of 26 to help some *'Priests'* who had gone there to plead their case before Caesar, his defensiveness against Justus of Tiberius in *Vita* 335–93 who was evidently accusing him of sedition, and his final defense of himself in *Vita* 407–30.

[162] For Helen, see *Ant.* 20.17–96 which is immediately followed in 20.100–1 with the *'Theudas'* affair and the mention of Queen Helen's *'famine relief'* activities following this in 20.102 by the note about the crucifixion of Judas the Galilean's two sons, James and Simon—whom I take to be the type of *'the two sons of Thunder,'* James and John (Mark 3:17) who would have to *'drink the Cup'* 'Jesus' drank in Matthew 20:22–3/Mark 10:38–9—and the note there about *'the Census of Quirinius'* which causes the anachronism about Judas the Galilean coming chronologically after Theudas in Acts 5:37.

163 See Chapter 1 above and *James*, pp. 111–9. Since Josephus is zealous of recording most such executions, the conclusion probably is that *'James the brother of John'* in Acts probably substitutes for *'Judas'* or *'Theudas the brother of James'* in Josephus and elsewhere.

164 This, of course, is the introduction of James in Acts. Nor can it be avoided that this is the *'house'* of *'Mary the mother of James'* (*'and the brothers'*), not of John Mark, only the author of Acts is chary of telling us this.

165 See *James*, pp. 51, 111–9, 192, etc.

166 Cf. Acts 5:34–40 with Ps. *Rec.* 1.65–71.

167 See *Ant.* 20.102 above and cf. Acts 5:36–7.

168 *Haeres.* 27.1.2 and 31.1.1–2.1. For the Valentinians, see Hippolytus 10.9 and throughout *Haeres.* For Valentinus as a *'hearer of Theudas'* and he or Theudas as Paul's pupil, see Clement of Alexandria's *Stromata* 7.17; for Clement's full name—*'Titus Flavius Clemens'*—which would, doubtlessly, make him a descendant of the famous Flavius Clemens, see *EH* 6.13.2. One should note that, if *'Theudas'* is to be identified with *'Thaddaeus'*/*'Addai'*/*'Judas the brother of James,'* then Paul gives every indication of knowing *'the brothers of the Lord'* in 1 Corinthians 9:5—a designation which would include this *'Judas'*/*'Theudas.'*

169 *EH* 3.4.10. For Flavius Clemens' execution in 95–6 CE by Domitian for his Christian sympathies, see *EH* 3.18.5, Dio Cassius 67.14.1–2, and Suetonius 8.15.1. For the *'Clement'* in the Pseudoclementines as a Roman nobleman of the family of Caesar, see Ps. *Rec.* 1.1, 7.8–10, and 10.72 and Ps. *Hom.* 4.7, 12.8–10, and 14.8–10. Curiously for *b. Git.* 56b and *A.Z.* 10b, the conversions of both Flavius Clemens and Domitilla are to Judaism.

170 See Suet. 8.14.4, Dio Cassius 67.14.4–5, and Josephus' dedication to Epaphroditus in *Vita* 430 and *Ant. Preface* 8–9. Though many do not think that Josephus died until early in Trajan's reign, there is no real evidence of his surviving any of these events. Furthermore, if Epaphroditus is the Epaphroditus in Suet. 6.49.4 and 8.14.4, it is doubtful Josephus could have survived the death of his patron. *N.b.*, that in Philippians 4:18–22, Paul actually sends Epaphroditus to Nero's household.

171 *EH* 3.18.5 has Flavia Domitilla exiled and calls her Flavius Clemens' niece. Dio Cassius 67.14.1–2, while agreeing that she was exiled, calls her his wife. Interesting, too, it has been observed that the Domitilla Chapel in this Catacomb is arranged in the Jewish manner.

172 Suet. 8.18.1–3 and Dio Cassius 67.17.1–18.2

173 See Commentary on John 6.6 and *Contra Celsus* 6.11.

174 See *b. B.B.* 60b. Cf. how the Rabbis in *Ned.* 77b and *Naz.* 77b discourage not only this kind of Naziritism, but Naziritism in general going so far in *b. Taᶜan.* 11a and *Ned.* 10a to term such Nazirites *'Sinners.'* But we have already seen that Benjamin of Tudela, *Travels*, 1165 CE—a thousand years later—reports encountering precisely such cave-dwelling, Jewish *'Rechabites'* who *'sustain the Poor and the ascetics called "Mourners for Zion" or "Mourners for Jerusalem"'* who *'eat no meat, abstain from wine, and dress only in black.'*

[175] To make this *'freedom'* plain, one should note the *'allegory'* he himself quotes later in the same Letter (Galatians 4:22–31) of *'the free woman*—by whom he means *'Sarah'*, though he does not actually name her—and *'the slave woman'* Hagar, who *'is Mount Sinai in Arabia'*, whom he does name and compares to *'the present Jerusalem in slavery with her Children.'* His conclusion famously is—quoting Genesis 21:10—therefore *'cast out the slave woman'*, and his meaning, which he reiterates often, could not be plainer. For him *'slavery'* is *'slavery to the Law'*; and *'freedom,' 'freedom from the Law'*, and not *'from Rome'*, as we should have expected. For comparison purposes, note our Illustration picturing the Jewish coin from Year 2 of the Revolt with the logo *'Freedom of Zion'* on the reverse. This certainly expresses the *'Palestinian'* view of this period; but also see Romans 8:2–9:9, using the same basic allegory and actually naming *'Sarah'*. For Paul's view of political freedom, see Romans 13:1–8.

[176] *EH* 3.20.1–8. Though Eusebius is tentative about the second point, obviously there was a round-up of *'Messianic'* Agitators in Trajan's time coinciding with very serious outbreaks of unrest in Egypt ending with the elimination of almost the entire Jewish Community there; cf. EH 3.32.1–7, quoting Hegesippus, who mentions the same round-up — this time ending with the crucifixion of Simeon bar Cleophas.

[177] For this point, see the variant manuscripts of the *Apostolic Constitutions* noted in *ANCL* above, which mention *'Judas the Zealot'*, identifying him with *'Lebbaeus surnamed Thaddaeus'*; but also the fragments of Hippolytus *'On the Twelve Apostles'*, who only speaks about *'Judas also called Lebbaeus.'* Nevertheless, both contend that *'Judas of James'* was buried in Berytus.

[178] For these manuscripts *'Simon the Zealot'* (a.k.a. probably *'Simon Iscariot'*) *'became Bishop of Jerusalem after James the Just and fell asleep and was buried there (meaning, in Jerusalem) at the age of 120'*, by whom they obviously mean *'Simeon bar Cleophas.'* N.b., Hippolytus *'On the Twelve Apostles'* says as much as we saw, denoting *'Simon the Zealot, the son of Clopas'*—thus!

Chapter 5

[1] *EH* 2.23.4–8, *Haeres.* 29.4.1–4, 30.2.6, and 78.7.7–8, and *Vir. ill.* 2. Note that, whereas the allusion from Hegesippus quoted by Eusebius is rather vague, speaking of *'entering the Temple alone'* (itself a patent impossibility!); both Epiphanius and Jerome make it clear that they regard this as *'the Holy of Holies'* and that what James was clearly involved in effecting was a *Yom Kippur* atonement of some kind *'seeking forgiveness for the People,'* as Eusebius/Hegesippus would have it; see my *James*, pp. 310–410.

[2] The first scholar to grasp this idea was R. Eisler in his ground-breaking tour de force, *The Messiah Jesus and John the Baptist*, London and New York, 1931, pp. 540–6 and 584, which he wrote without benefit of the Dead Sea Scrolls, though he did have the Cairo Damascus Document. Unfortunately his productive life was cut short by time in Hitler's concentration camps, even though he did live to see the appearance of the Scrolls in 1947. His work was echoed and developed by S.G.F. Brandon in *The Fall of Jerusalem and the Christian Church*, London, 1951 and *Jesus and the Zealots*, London, 1957.

[3] This is also supported by the Greek Orthodox writer, Andrew of Crete, who was born in Jerusalem in 660 CE (d., c. 740) and was a monk at Mar Saba, who also quotes Hegesippus—*Vita et Martyrium S. Jacobi Apost. Frat. Dom.* 1.10.21 (also cited by Robert Eisler, p. 541 above).

[4] For Epiphanius, citing *'Clement, Eusebius, and others,'* James actually wore the miter or breastplate of the High Priest with the inscription upon it *'Holy to God'*; *Haeres.* 29.4.3–4 78.14.1.

[5] *EH* 2.23.7. This means that James' cognomens—cognomens which included *'the Zaddik,' 'Oblias,'* and *'Protection of the People'*—were to be found in Scripture. The same can be said for *'Jesus'*, who was said to *'be called a Nazoraean'* (obviously meaning *'a Nazirite,'* because *'Nazoraean'* is nowhere to be found *'in the Prophets'*—Matthew 2:23), and for *'the Righteous Teacher'* at Qumran.

[6] Cf. *Vita* 11–12 above. For James and the Essenes wearing only *'linen,'* see *EH* 2.23.6, *Haeres.* 78.13.3, *Vir. ill.* 2, *War* 2.128, and Hippolytus 9.16 (both of whom also speak of Essene *'ablutions in cold water'*). For Priests and Levites inside the Temple, see Ezekiel 44:17 and 2 Chronicles 5:12.

[7] *Vita* 11 above. *'Banus'* is the perfect *'Rechabite.' 'Linen,'* of course, like *'things growing on trees,'* is vegetable not *'animal'* matter—the whole point.

[8] *Haeres.* 78.14.2.

[9] For the archetypical moment in all such *'Holy Places,'* see Moses in Exodus 3:5.

[10] Cf. *EH* 2.23.5 with *War* 2.123. There is probably no more important point connecting James with the Essenes than this.

[11] Cf. *EH* 2.23.5 with *Haeres.* 78.13.2.

[12] As Josephus makes clear in *War* 2.128 and Hippolytus in 9.16 above, *'Essenes'* regularly made *'cold water ablutions'* just as *Banus* regularly took *'cold water baths'*; so none of these obviously preferred having *'dry skin.'*

[13] Clearly James would have had to immerse himself if he went on the Temple Mount in the manner described in early Church sources; cf. *M. Mid.* 1:4, 5:3, *M. Par.* 3:7, *b. Tam.* 26b, and *j. Yoma* 40b; also see *Ant.* 12.145 and *War* 4.205. If James did perform one such *Yom Kippur* atonement (even as a Rechabite *'Opposition High Priest,'* as already described), then he did most certainly. See *b. Yoma* 30a–31a—recently, in fact just such an underground bathing facility has been found leading onto the Temple Mount.

[14] Even Peter, as we have seen, is portrayed as a *'Daily-bathing Essene'*-type in the Pseudoclementines (where he is portrayed as following James' directives to the letter) and in Epiphanius' picture of *'Ebion''s Travels of Peter* in *Haeres.* 30.15.3 and 30.21.1 for the same reasons as *Banus* in *Vita* 11 but also, as should be clear from the reference of *'bathing before partaking of bread'* in the latter, *'the Essenes'* as well.

[15] Cf. *CDiii.21–iv.4,* following allusion to *'the Primal Adam'* ideology.

[16] *CDiv.4.* Since this is an eschatological exposition turning on the allusion to *'standing,'* we are once more in the realm of *'the Standing One'* ideology—to say nothing of the Hebrew understanding of the word *'standing'/'ʿomdim'* to mean *'to be resurrected'* as well.

[17] Here Paul's use of the phraseology *'to fall asleep'* is the same as that used in 15:18 to in the aftermath of his allusion to a post-resurrection appearance to James and Jerome's description of just such an appearance in the Gospel of the Hebrews—*Vir. ill.* 2.

[18] That is, both are eschatological; cf. the definitions of *'Standing One'* in Epiphanius' description of *'Ebion"s/'Elchasai"s* idea of *'Christ'* in *Haeres.* 30, 17.6 or under the *'Ossaeans,'* 19.4.1.

[19] CDiv.7 and cf. the eschatological interpretation of Habakkuk 2:4 in 1QpHabviii.1–3 and the references in xii.14 and xiii.2–3 to *'the Day of Judgement,'* there being no doubt that we are speaking (as in Islam and the Koran) of *'the Last Judgement'* here.

[20] CDi.19. The allusion here is to *'the Seekers after Smooth Things'* who *'transgressed the Covenant... and banded together against the soul of the Righteous One and all the Walkers in Perfection.'* The reversal here is not unlike the reversal one encounters in 2 Corinthians 11:13–5 where *'the Pseudo-Apostles... transform themselves into Apostles of Christ'*—Satan's *'Servants whose end shall be according to their works'* (a play on James' *'Righteousness of works'* doctrine).

[21] One should note all the passages in the Gospels where *'Jesus'* either *'justifies'* or prefers *'Sinner(s),'* *e.g.,* Matthew 9:10–13, 11:19, Luke 5:30–32, 7:37–39, 15:7–10, and *pars.*

[22] See Paul in Galatians 2:15–7 and 5:1–7 following upon his *'freedom vs. slavery'* allegory in 4:22–31—also his remarks in 1 Corinthians 6:12 and 10:23 concerning *'all things being lawful for'* him and in 8:12 on *'sinning against Christ'* and *'wounding the brothers' weak consciences'* because of the issue of *'eating things sacrificed to idols'*—the very essence of James' directives to Overseas Communities and Hippolytus 9.21's *'Zealot'* or *'Sicarii Essenes'* martyrdom ethic.

[23] Cf. the references to basically the same *'table of demons'* in Ps. *Hom.* 7.3, 7.4, 8.23, etc., also in the context of alluding to *'things sacrificed to idols',* but from the opposing ideological perspective.

[24] 1QSv.2–5 and v.9–13.

[25] Cf. *EH* 2.23.5 and *Haeres.* 78.13.3 above about James with *War* 2.123–9 and Hippolytus 9.16 about "Essenes".

[26] Even better ones, related to Peter's teaching, are to be found in Ps. *Hom.* 7.8 and 8.19, both of which actually include the category of *'that which is strangled';* but also see Koran 2.173, 5.3, 6.146, and 16.115 above.

[27] *Haeres.* 78.14.1–3

[28] *Ant.* 20.51 and 101–2.

[29] *Haeres.* 78.14.1.

[30] Note that in *'the Little Apocalypses,'* *'Jesus'* compares events occurring in the present time in their eschatological significance to *'the Days of Noah'* and, *'Magician'*-style, does all sorts of miraculous things—though not, significantly, *'rain-making'* except, as we shall see, in an esoteric *'Judgement coming upon the clouds'* eschatological sense; cf. Matthew 24:30, 24:37, 26:64, and *pars.* It is at this point that Epiphanius (*Haeres.* 78.14.2), just as Eusebius/Hegesippus (in *EH* 2.23.7ff., but without the *'rain-making'*), avers that *'the Just One'* (in Hebrew *'Zaddik'/'Zadok'*) was used in the place of James' very name itself.

[31] Note here that, in this first Biblical torrential rain flood episode, Noah is the first *‘Zaddik* and see, for instance, Hebrew *Ben Sira* 44:17; for the *‘Perfection’* ideology at Qumran, see CDi.20–1, ii.15–6, xx.2–7, 1QSi.13, iv.22 (followed by allusion to *‘the Primal Adam’* ideology in iv.23), viii.18–ix.6, etc.; for *‘Jesus,’* of course, see the paradigmatic conclusion in Matthew 5:48: *‘So be Perfect as your Father in Heaven is Perfect.’*

[32] *EH* 2.313 and cf. Daniel 7:13 and Matthew 24:30 and 26:64/Mark 13:26–7 and 14:62 above. At Qumran, see CDiv.3–9, 1QpHabv.4, and Chapter 15 below.

[33] In addition to 1QpHabv.4, just cited above, see 1QMxii.1–10 and xix.1–2.

[34] CDiv.4–7 and note here the expression *‘called by Name,’* anticipated in CDii.11, paralleling such New Testament expressions as *‘called by this Name’* or *‘called by the Name of’* in Acts 2:21, 15:17, 22:16, etc., and *‘name’* and *‘naming’* symbolism generally in the New Testament and even Jewish *Kabbalah.*

[35] 1QMxii.4–9 and xix.1 and see my article *‘Eschatological “Rain” Imagery in the War Scroll from Qumran and in the Letter of James,’ JNES,* v. 49, no. 2, April, 1990, pp. 173–84—reprinted in *DSSFC,* pp. 272–87.

[36] Matthew 24:30 and 26:64/Mark 13:26–7 and 14:62 above.

[37] Not only is this *‘Power’* language is widespread in the Gospels—see, for instance, Matthew 9:6, 28:18, Luke 4:14, 5:24, 9:1, and *pars.*; but one also even sees it at Qumran—see 1QMi.4 and cf. *Haeres.* 19.4.1 on the *‘Ossaeans’* and 21.2.3 on the *‘Simonian’* followers of Simon *Magus* and similarly in the Pseudoclementines.

[38] This idea of *‘Stephen’* as a stand-in for James was first proposed by H. J. Schoeps in *Theologie und Geschichte des Judenchristentums,* Tubingen, 1949, pp. 441ff.; see also *James,* pp. 166–87 and 444–53. Cf. too, the *‘wilderness Temptation’* scenarios in the Synoptics, Matthew 4:5 and *pars.,* where the idea of James standing on *‘the Pinnacle of the Temple’* is retrospectively absorbed into the story of *‘Jesus’*—but this time negatively as *‘Temptation by the Devil’* (*‘Belial’*)!

[39] Cf. 1QHix.26–35.

[40] Cf. 1QMxii.9–10.

[41] *ARN* 4.4.

[42] *War* 2.6–7 and n.b., Hebrews 7:11–8:2 and 9:9–15.

[43] *ARN* 6.3 and *b. Ta͑an.* 19b–20a.

[44] See 1 Kings 17:1, 18:2 and 45, and 19:11 and Chapters 5-6 below.

[45] See the list of such persons in *ARN* 2.5—*‘Tam’/‘Perfect’* meant for the redactors of such traditions, *‘being born circumcised.’*

[46] See Hebrew *Ben Sira* 44:17 above—which starts its enumeration of *‘Pious Men’* (*Anshei-Hesed*) with *‘Noah the Righteous,’* anticipating succeeding such individuals in the *‘Hesed’/‘Zedek’* tradition.

[47] The point here, of course, is that this more or less parallels the note in Eusebius/Hegesippus following the death of James (*EH* 2.23.18) that *‘immediately Vespasian besieged them’*; but one should also see the note in Rabbinic literature (*ARN* 4.5), when R. Joshua following R.

Yohanan leaving Jerusalem, looks back and, seeing the city, cries out 'Woe'—just as 'Jesus' here in the Gospels.

[48] Cf. *Zohar* i.63a and 67b on '*Noah*.' For John as Elijah, see Matthew 11:14, 9:8–13, and *pars*. *Par contra*, cf. John 1:21–5.

[49] Note the inversion here of '*the Friend of God*' language, applied to Abraham in James 2:23–4 and CDiii.2–3, to say nothing of in the Koran.

[50] Note the passages that follow this in Galatians 4:17–8, attacking those who '*are zealous*' (*zeloute*) as well as the '*Essene*'/Qumran practice of '*excluding*' (i.e., '*excommunication*'); also see James 5:19 on '*straying from the Truth*' and note this notion of '*Truth*' is a widespread one at Qumran. In these passages, Paul also refers in 1:20 and, by implication, to the notion of '*Lying*' so widespread at Qumran and in James 3:5–14 ('*Do not lie against the Truth*' and on '*the Mouth*' or '*Tongue*' out of which comes both '*blessing and cursing*').

[51] See James 2:12 and 5:7–9 and Jude 14–5. That '*Jude*' (actually '*Judas*') is the same as '*Judas of James*' and other '*Judas*'es and '*Thaddaeus*'es is hardly to be doubted.

[52] *B. Taʿan.* 6a. Interestingly the word *Taʿanith* uses to express this is '*yorah*,' meaning '*former*' or '*spring rain*' (that is, '*not torrential*'). But this is exactly the allusion—long puzzling to scholars—CDvi.10–1 and xx.13–22 use to refer to '*the Teacher*'/'*Moreh*.' For *b. Taʿan.* 7b, evoking Isaiah 45:8 on '*the Heavens sending down Victory like rain*' and '*the clouds pouring down Righteousness*' and '*Salvation*' ('*Yeshaʿ*'—cf. CDxx.37 above) in continuation of this theme of rain-making, '*the day on which rain falls is as great as the day on which Heaven and Earth were created*'—n.b., the relation of this to the appointment *Logion* in Gos. Th. 12: '*go to James the Just, for whose sake Heaven and Earth came into existence*' and the relation of this last, in turn, to the interpretation of *Zohar*, i.59b on '*Noah*' or Proverbs 10:25: '*the Zaddik is the Pillar of the World*'—or '*the Torah was given... No rain falls unless the sins of Israel have been forgiven*.' Yet again, note the relation of this to James' atonement activities in the Holy of Holies in the Temple. Jerome—to continue this theme of James, '*clouds*,' '*rain*,' '*Salvation*,' and '*Righteousness*'/'*Judgement*'—reads Isaiah 45:8 as '*Let the clouds rain down the Just One*.'

[53] Cf. too 1 Maccabees 2:58, but also 2:54 on Phineas and *Ben Sira* 48:1–2.

[54] Luke 4:25–6 also has Jesus refer to this '*three and a half years*' with regard to drought and, by implication, rain-making and the time frame will also have relevance to Daniel 12:7's '*a time, two times and a half*,' as it will to the period between James' death and the outbreak of the War against Rome.

[55] For this '*whirlwind*' and '*quaking mountains*,' reminiscent of the most vivid Koranic imagery, see 4QpNahi.1–11; for Ezekiel, see 13:12–4 following his allusions to '*Lying prophets*' with their '*empty visions*' and '*the plasterers on the wall*' in 13:9–11 (cf. CDiv.18–20 and viii.12–3) .

[56] See Hippolytus 9.20–1 and cf. Josephus, *War* 2.143 and 2.152–3.

[57] Also see Romans 10:2–6 and 11:14 and note that the former is precisely the passage Jerome used against Origen to rebuke him for having become a '*Sicarius*' or for castrating himself—Letter 84 to Pammachius and Oceanus—i.e., he did this out of '*zeal for God, but not according to Knowledge*.'

58 That the issue here is, not only their *'zeal for God,'* but also *'for circumcision'* is clear from Paul's further comments (continuing the *'Hagar'*/*'freedom'* allegory in Galatians 4:21–31) in 5:1–14, culminating in 5:12 with his ribald defamation of *circumcision* and ending with what is obviously a play on James'*'Royal Law according to the Scripture'* in 5:14. Cf. the same *'Commandment'* used to justify *'paying taxes'* to Rome in Romans 13:7–8. But also see the *'Essene'* use of this in *War* 2.138–9, ending in 140 in almost a complete parallel to Paul in Romans 13:1.

59 *EH* 2.1.4 and 23.10–3, *Vir. ill.* 2, *Haeres.* 78.14.5–7, etc.

60 Also see Daniel 9:27 and 11:31 and cf. *Ant.* 12.253, Matthew 24:15, and Mark 13:14. One of the first to make this suggestion was Louis Ginzberg in an article in the *Jewish Encyclopedia*, but Antiochus Epiphanes seems to have been particularly attached to this Deity; see Livy's *History of Rome* 41.20.1–4 and the *Periochae* (175 BC—5 CE).

61 See *War* 2.407–420. If one compares this with the coming of the mournful prophet, Jesus ben Ananias, in *War* 6.300–9 in Tabernacles, 62 CE, seemingly in the aftermath of or just following the death of James, then the *'three and a half years'* is complete.

62 If one connects the two, particularly the appearance of the mysterious *'Prophet,'* Jesus ben Ananias on *Succot*, 62 CE, James' death as reported in *Ant.* 20.200 and James' known antagonism to *'pollution of the idols'* (Acts 15:20); then this is something of the conclusion that can be reached. Note this is also something of the way Josephus presents things with his evocation of *'the World Ruler Prophecy'* in *War* 6.312–4 as the moving force behind the War against Rome.

63 *EH* 2.23.17–25 and note the progression of events here in Eusebius—James' death, followed by the appearance of the Roman Armies, followed by the fall of Jerusalem.

64 *Contra Celsus* 1.47, 2.13, and *Comm. on Matt.* 10.17. Since this testimony seems to have appeared in the *War*, the only place it probably could have been was in the discussion of the death of Ananus in *War* 4.296–332.

65 For *'yizzil'*/*'save,'* see 1QpHabviii.1–3 (in exegesis of Habakkuk 2:4: *'The Righteous shall live by his Faith'*) and xii.14 (including reference to *'the Day of Judgement'*); for *'Yesha*ʿ*'*/*'Yeshu*ʿ*a,'* see CDxx.18–20 (following reference to *'the Yoreh,' 'the Penitents from Sin in Jacob,'* and *'a Book of Remembrance for God-Fearers,'* i.e., *'Gentiles'*) and 4QD416–8.

66 Cf. *B. Ta*ʿ*an.* 6a–7b with James 5:4–8, specifically mentioning *'early'* and *'late rain'* in the context of *'the coming of the Lord.'*

67 Cf. *Ta*ʿ*an.* 7b above.

68 Cf. CDvi.8–11 and xx.13–8 above. In the former, *'the Yoreh ha-Zedek'* can mean *'the One who Pours down Righteousness at the End of Days'*; but in the latter, the so-called *'Yoreh'* has already *'been gathered in'*—whatever this means.

69 Of course, this is James' cognomen in all works associated with his name; cf. *EH* 2.23.7 and *Haeres.* 78.7.7 above. For *'the Moreh ha-Zedek,'* one should note that in all exegeses leading into his person the underlying text is almost always a *'Zaddik'* one; cf. Habakkuk 1:4, 1:13, 2:4, Psalm 37:12, 21, 25, etc.

70 1QMxii.12 and xix.3.

[71] Matthew 24:35/Mark 13:31/Luke 21:33.

[72] See, for instance, Acts 23:12 how the telltale *some* again *of the Jews make a plot* (the *plotting* language too again), *putting themselves under an oath* (clearly now, 'a temporary Nazirite' one), *not to eat or drink until they have killed Paul* (repeated in Acts 23:21); also see *B.B.* 60b, *Ned.* 10a and 77b, *Naz.* 77b, and *Ta'an.* 11 for the Rabbinical view discouraging such oaths; *par contra*, see Benjamin of Tudela in *Travels* 1175 above, whose *'Mourners for Zion...eat no meat and drink no wine.'* For Paul's position on *'eating and drinking,'* see, for instance, 1 Corinthians 8:8, 10:25, and 11:29; for the Gospels' portrait of how *'the Son of Man came eating and drinking,'* while John—a typical *'Rechabite'/'Nazirite'*—did not and *'Jesus'* as *'a glutton and a wine-bibber,'* see Matthew 11:18–9 and Luke 7:33–4.

[73] On the seven Noahide Laws incumbent upon all mankind or *'Sons of Noah,'* which include *'fostering Righteousness and prohibiting idolatry, fornication, blasphemy, manslaughter, carrion or eating parts of living animals including its blood, and theft,'* see *San.* 56a–59b (n.b., here *'Adam,'* since he came before Noah's sacrifice permitting him to eat the flesh of animals but not the blood, is portrayed like James as a vegetarian), *A.Z.* 2b, 5b-6b, 64b, *Yoma* 28b, *B.K.* 38a, 92a, etc.

[74] See *EH* 2.23.7 and 3.7.9 and *Haeres.* 78.7.7, the implication of all these testimonies being that, once James' presence was removed, the City could no longer survive. Of course, in Eusebius, this *'Bulwark'* testimony is immediately followed by the description of Jesus ben Ananias' prophecy in 3.8.7–11.

[75] It should be noted that this is a part of all James' prohibitions as pictured in Acts 15:20, 15:29, and 21:25. Furthermore, in the Rabbinic testimony above, this concern over eating any part of *'living'* animals (itself an aspect of the *'carrion'* ban) is particularly insistent.

[76] For Hippolytus, see 9.21 above; for the Koran, see 2.173, 5.3, 6.146, and 16.115; for Peter's seeming abstention like James from, see Ps. *Hom.* 7.3–4, 7.8, etc.

[77] For *MMT*, see ii.7–9 and below Chapter 13.

[78] Cf. above *'John came neither eating or drinking'*—Matthew 11:18/Luke 7:33—and Peter in Ps. *Hom.* 8.15 and 11.35. For Adam as a primordial vegetarian, see *b. San.* 59b above.

[79] It is difficult to know what Paul means by *'the cup of demons'* here, but he seems to be speaking about *'the Israel according to the flesh... eating the sacrifices'* or *'those sharing (communing) with the altar'* of 10:18 as, in the same breath, he goes on to talk about *'eating at the table of demons'* and *'things sacrificed to demons'*—now, not *'idols'*—while averring a second time that *'all things are for me lawful.'* The rhetorical dissimulation here is quite astounding—but not so Ps. *Hom.* 7.3–4, 7.8, and 8.8–19 above on the same subject of *'demons'* and *'the table of demons.'*

[80] See the perfect definition of *'carrion'* in Ezekiel 44:31.

[81] See *Zohar* i. 59b on *'Noah'* above. It also explains both *Logion* 12 of the Gospel of Thomas and *'why Heaven and Earth should have come into existence for his sake'* as well as the *'Bulwark'* allusion in *EH* 3.7.9 above.

[82] One can also probably say that this '*Covenant*' is the same as both the '*Zadokite*' and the '*Zealot*' one; see my '*Eschatological Rain Imagery*,' *MZCQ*, pp. 4–16/*DSSU*, pp. 23–80 and *JNES*, pp. 175–6 above.

[83] See 1 Maccabees 2:1. For Phineas', Zadok's, and Yehozedek's genealogy, see 1 Chronicles 5:30–41. For the course of Joiraib, see 1 Chronicles 24:1–7.

[84] For Phineas as the paradigm, see Numbers 25:6–15 and its evocation in 1 Maccabees 2:26–7, 2:50, 2:54, and 2:58 (here, even for Elijah). Also see *Ben Sira* 45:23–29, referring to Phineas as '*Third in Glory*' and Hebrew *Ben Sira* 51:12, coupling '*the Sons of Zadok*' with such a '*Zealot*' appeal in the case of '*Simeon the Zaddik*.' Note, that for Num *R.* 21.3–4, Phineas is also a '*Zaddik*.'

[85] Cf. Ezekiel 44:15 with CDiii.21–iv.4

[86] One should note how this '*Covenant of Peace*' is associated with Phineas' name in Numbers 25:10–2 just as it is with '*Noah's* ('*Noah the Righteous*' in Hebrew *Ben Sira*) in *Zohar*, i, 66b and 68b—a '*Covenant*' that is clearly being described in Genesis 9:9–17.

[87] 1QMxi.4–xii.9.

[88] Cf. *Chronicles of Jerahmeel* 59.17, *Pseudo Philo* 48.1, and *Sifre* Numbers 131.

[89] CDiv.2–3 and vi.4–7.

[90] The point was that Enoch was described in Genesis 5:21–4 as being '*taken up*' and '*walking with God*'—for the Qumran Literature in his name, see J. T. Milik, *Book of Enoch*, Oxford, 1976; for Literature in general, see R. H. Charles, *Book of Enoch*, London, 1917 and *The Old Testament Pseudepigrapha*, ed. J. H. Charlesworth, New York, 1983, i, pp. 5–315.

[91] The important thing here is the allusion in both sets of data to '*fourteen years*'. This to say nothing of James' alleged mystical experience, nor the issue of Paul's typical reticence where '*Leadership*' issues were concerned.

[92] See, for instance, the *Zohar*, i, 26a–b, on Genesis 2:8 and *b. Hag.* 14b on '*the four who entered Paradise*' ('*Pardess*,' meaning literally—as it does in Islam—'*Orchard*' or '*Gardens*'; cf. Koran 2.25 and 111, 7.40, 15.45, 56.12, 80.12, etc.).

[93] One should note that at Qumran, '*the Mebakker*' ('*the Overseer*' or '*Bishop*') '*is the master of every secret of men and of all Tongues*' (CDxiv.9–10), to say nothing of the link of this with its caricature in the '*speaking in Tongues*' in 1 Corinthians 13:1–14:39 and Acts 2:3–11; cf. also James 1:26 and 3:5–6's concern for '*Tongue*' issues generally.

[94] Haeres. 30.16.7. Part of this lost work is supposed to have been included in the Pseudoclementines and ostensibly seems to have dealt with James' lectures on the Temple steps portrayed there—therefore its name. But it also cannot be unrelated to '*Hechalot*' Literature in Jewish *Kabbalah*, i.e., '*The Literature of Heavenly Ascents*'.

[95] See Solomon Schechter's *Fragments of a Zadokite Work*, Cambridge, 1910.

[96] See Y. Yadin, *Masada: Herod's Fortress and the Zealots' Last Stand*, London, 1966, pp. 174–7.

[97] See Ezekiel 40:46, 43:19, 44:15, and 48:11.

[98] See Ezekiel 44:7–19 and 48:11. This is the name originally given the document by S. Schechter

above—but also echoed in R. H. Charles' publication of it in *Apocrypha and Pseudepigrapha of the Old Testament*, ii, Oxford, 1913, pp. 785–834.

[99] See, for instance, *War* 2.402–10 where '*the Innovators*' even bar Agrippa II and his sister Bernice—later the mistress of Titus— from all of Jerusalem; but also see the '*Simon*' the '*Head of an Assembly*' or '*Church of his own*' (*Ecclesia*) in Jerusalem in *Ant.* 19.332–4 who wants to bar all Herodians from the Temple '*as foreigners*'—but cf. Paul in Ephesians 2:19, denying there are any '*foreigners or resident aliens (i.e., 'Nilvim')*, *but (all) fellow-citizens of the Saints* (note the language of Roman '*Citizenship*' here as well) *and of the Household of God...*'

[100] See *War* 2.411–5, in continuation of this episode, but also raising the charge of '*Impiety*' against such '*Innovators*' and noting that this '*even put Caesar outside the pale.*'

Chapter 6

[1] *Ant.* 14.22–5.

[2] Cf. *War* 2.147–8 and Hippolytus 9.20.

[3] *Ant.* 14.22. For Honi as a '*Rain-maker*' in the *Talmud*, see *j. Ta˓an.* 66b and *b. Ta˓an.* 23a, the '*Jerusalem*' being the traditions as they were retained in Palestine and the '*Babylonian*' (which is far longer and exhaustive), those retained in Mesopotamia. Note here that the passage *b. Ta˓an.* 23a quotes to describe the circles Honi draws—comparing them to the Prophet Habakkuk's— is Habakkuk 2:1: '*I will stand upon my Watchtower and take my stand upon my Fortress,*' which 1QpHabi.2–vii.14 basically expounds in the name of '*the Righteous Teacher, to whom God revealed all the Mysteries of the words of His Servants the Prophets*' (i.e., '*the Righteous Teacher*' is God's earthly Exegete *par excellence*; cf. below, Chapter 27), in terms of the '*Last Era*' or '*Final Age being prolonged,*' '*beyond anything the Prophets have foretold,*' i.e., '*the Delay of the Parousia.*'

[4] For this '*Famine,*' which Josephus, echoed by Acts 5:36–7 (even with its anachronism) and 11:28–30, connects both the coming of '*Theudas*' and Queen Helen's grain-buying activities in Egypt and Cyprus, see *Ant.* 20.48–53 and 97–102.

[5] *B. Ta˓an.* 23a/*j. Ta˓an.* 66b and cf. James 5:17–9 and 1 Kings 18:1–45.

[6] Cf. 1 Kings 17:1 and Matthew 11:14 above and *pars*.

[7] CDiii.2–3 and cf. too James 2:10 and 2:21–4 above. James also knows '*Keepers*,' '*Friend*,' etc.

[8] Koran 2.130–41.

[9] In this '*allegory,*' Paul parallels similar things he is saying in Romans 8:12–9:8, starting with '*loving God*' (as James in 2:5) in 8:28, once again affirming he '*does not lie*' in 9:1, and ending with '*the Children of the Promise are to be reckoned for the seed*' (and, in fact that all should '*be called the Sons of the Living God*'—9:26/Cf. Hosea 1:10).

[10] John 19:26, 20:2, 21:7, and 21:20.

[11] *EH* 2.23.10.

[12] The issue of '*Letters of Recommendation*' or '*Authorization*' is an important one and is regulated in the Pseudoclementines in *Rec.* 4.35 and *Hom.* 11.30. Plus, one should note that these narratives themselves are formed in the manner of the yearly or seven-yearly reports demanded of Peter (and in continuation of whom Clement) by James in *Rec.* 1.71.

[13] CD iv.17–v.11 and vii.1–2 and *MMT* ii.47–55 and 83–9.

[14] Although some of the episodes in Talmudic literature are overtly ridiculous—for instance, Hanan being called *'the Hidden because he used to lock himself in the outhouse'* in *Ta'an.* 23a or the pseudonymous 'Bar Daroma' (evidently an opponent of some kind) dropping his bowels in the outhouse when he encountered a poisonous snake and immediately dying in *Git.* 57a or the picture of R. Zadok, who observed fasts for forty years so Jerusalem would not be destroyed, sucking the pulp of a fig in *Git.* 56a or Vespasian inspecting the straw in the excrement of the defenders of Jerusalem to find out if they were starving and thereafter chastising his troops in terms of *'eating and drinking'* in *ARN* 6, 21a; in Acts, one rather has the picture of *'the Jews'* doing one negative thing after another to alleged Early Christians.

[15] CD iv.19–20 and viii.18–9/xix.31–2.

[16] That this is very relevant to *'the Pharisees'* and the rest of *'the Establishment Alliance,'* who seek accommodation with Foreign Power and, particularly the Authorities in Rome, is very clear from Josephus' own description of *'the Peace Alliance'* in *War* 2.411–22 consisting of *'the Men of Power'* (obviously *'the Herodians'*), *'the High Priests,'* and *'the Principal Men of the Pharisees.'*

[17] *Ant.* 14.24.

[18] See *Ant.* 20.200 and cf. *EH* 2.23.2–23.

[19] *M. Ta'an* 3.8 and *b. Ta'an* 23a.

[20] *Ant.* 14.19–22; *n.b.*, how Josephus refers here to how Honi *'had hidden himself.'*

[21] Though originally Josephus did not identify which Party was which, later in *Ant.* 14.24 he makes it clear that those supporting Aristobulus II were *'Priests'* and in *War* 1.131–51, that those supporting Pompey, Antipater, and Hyrcanus II were *'Pharisees.'*

[22] We say *'Messianic Sadducees'*—a rather unique appellation—because it is clear that those responsible for the literature at Qumran regarded themselves both as *'Sons of Zadok'* (i.e., they are a species of *'Sadducees'*) and are intensely and apocalyptically *'Messianic'*; see *MZCQ*, pp. 19–26 and *DSSFC*, pp. 49–80. This is a term, to be sure, one never hears in Dead Sea Scrolls Research.

[23] At one point in 1QS ix.13, the term would appear to be *'Sons of the Zaddik,'* considered by some to be a scribal error, but it probably is not. This is also true of 1QS iii.20 where the term is *'the Sons of Zedek'* / *'the Sons of Righteousness.'* It should also be appreciated that Hebrew *'waw'* and Hebrew *'yod'* are almost indistinguishable and basically interchangeable in Qumran epigraphy. In any event, it is clear that *'the Sons of Zadok'* double as *'Zaddikim'* as does, in fact, their most prominent representative, *'the Teacher of Righteousness'* himself.

[24] See *War* 1.327–64, 1.431–43, 1.562–99/*Ant.* 14.13–5.9, 15.164–238, 15.320, etc.

[25] One sees that his opponents are Pharisees in the note Josephus gives in *War* 1.113. For *'Purist Sadducees,'* see *MZCQ*, pp. 12–6.

[26] For John Hyrcanus as a *'Sadducee',* see *War* 1.54–67 but, in particular, *Ant.* 13.230–300.

[27] *War* 1.107–12/*Ant.* 13.399–406.

[28] See *War* 1.120–55 and *Ant.* 13.408–14.78, etc. *N.b.*, for instance, *War* 1.143: Hyrcanus' supporters are always in favor of *'opening the gates to Pompey.'*

29 *Vita* 2–7.

30 *War* 1.131–2. This is a tragic happenstance and sealed Aristobulus II's doom and, probably, as the inevitability of history progressed that of the Jewish People's in Palestine thereafter and all occasioned by the rivalry and enmity of two brothers as usual in Jewish Biblical History! The description is slightly different in *Ant.* 14.41–7.

31 *Ant.* 18.17.

32 *Ant.* 14.22–4.

33 *B. Ta'an.* 23a/j. *Ta'an.* 66b. As in James' case, the reason that emerges in this conversation between R. Simeon b. Shetach and Honi is Honi's presumed 'blasphemy' or taking the Divine name in vain.

34 *Ant.* 14.14–21/*War* 1.123–32.

35 *Ant.* 14.21 and 14.25–6.

36 *Ant.* 14.27–28.

37 *Ant.* 14.27.

38 *War* 1.148. Interestingly, *Ant.* 14.65–68 credits Strabo, Nicolaus of Damascus, and Livy of attesting to similar points.

39 *War* 1.150/*Ant.* 14.69. The reference to 'Herod's father Antigonus' is also obviously erroneous and a proofing error. It should read 'Herod's father Antipater' and will be corrected in subsequent editions, as will 'as-Sabi' ibn Yusufus' earlier, which should have read: 'as-Sabi' in the Yusufus.'

40 One should note how the Pharisaic approach of 'seeking accommodation with foreigners' is reflected in the recommendation by Hyrcanus' supporters in *War* 1.143 above to 'open the gates to Pompey.' That this is characteristic can be seen in the defense of Herod by Sameas the Pharisee (probably Shammai though possibly Shemaiah) in *Ant.* 14.172–6 and with Pollio (probably Hillel) in *Ant.* 15.3–4 to the defenders of Jerusalem in 37 BC to, once again, 'open the gates to Herod,' the citizens of which directly demur demonstrating the Pharisees, whatever their and later pretenses, were not the popular party in Jerusalem at this time. The 'Zealots' or 'nationalists' were, as nationalist parties predictably are. The same thing occurs in 66 CE, when in *War* 2.411–8, 'the Pharisees' send to Roman troops outside the city to Florus to come in and crush the Revolt that had by that time broken out.

41 *Ant.* 14.28.

42 Cf. *Ta'an.* 7b above. N.b., the allusion to 'Saba'im' with an 'alif not an 'ayin' in Isaiah 45:13, designating 'Sabaeans' of Southern Arabia and Ethiopia (the root of the parallel Islamic usage) even here in the 6th–5th Century and not the 'Sabaean' Bathers of Southern Iraq and Northern Syria.

43 Cf. 1QM, xii.9–10 and xix.2 above with Matthew 5:45.

44 In *Ant.* 20.201–2, Josephus specifically notes that 'the most fair-minded and those most concerned with observance of the Law objected to what had been done.'

45 *B. Berakhot* 48a. She would also appear to be mentioned in the Dead Sea Scrolls under her Hebrew name 'Shlomzion'—4Q322 (Calendrical Document C).

⁴⁶ *B. Ta^can.* 23a/*j. Ta^can.* 66b.

⁴⁷ Cf. *M. Ta^can.* 3.8 with *EH* 2.23.14–23 and *Ant.* 20.200–2.

⁴⁸ Cf. *EH* 2.23.7 and *Haeres.* 78.7.7. For Jerome in *Comm. on Galatians* 1:19, so 'Holy' was James that the People of Jerusalem used to crowd around him and try to 'touch his garments as he walked by.'

⁴⁹ Cf. *M. Ta^can.* 3:8 and *b. Ta^can.* 23b. Cf. *Ant.* 14.21 above.

⁵⁰ For Simeon as one of the original Pharisee 'Pairs,' see *Abboth* 1.9 and *ARN* 10.1 (22a). One should note, not only the parallel charge against James, but also that of 'blasphemy' or 'Profanation of the Name' against 'Jesus' in Matthew 26:65 and *pars.*

⁵¹ *EH* 2.23.6, *Haeres.* 78.14.1, *Vir. ill.* 2, etc.

⁵² *Ant.* 14.22.

⁵³ *B. Ta^can.* 23a–b.

⁵⁴ See R. Eisler, *The Messiah Jesus and John the Baptist*, p. 244.

⁵⁵ See, for instance, the note in the *Yalkut on Jeremiah* 35:12 that 'Rechabites' (such as these ancestors of John like Honi) married the daughters of Priests and their descendants ministered as Priests in the Temple.

⁵⁶ Cf. Koran 3.33–49 and note how Muhammad calls John both 'a Prophet to the Righteous' and 'celibate' (3.39); but also note the use of the word 'hidden' in Koran 3:44. Unfortunately in this *Surah*, Muhammad (or his redactor) mixes up Moses' family with Jesus' both generationally and genealogically. This is because of confusion over the name 'Maryam', which in Hebrew and Arabic can be both 'Miriam' (Moses' sister) and 'Mary,' Jesus' mother. This leads him to consider Moses' father 'Imran' ('Amram' in Exodus and the reason for the name of this *Surah*, 'The Family of Imran,' by which it intends 'Jesus'' family but rather focuses on Moses'), supposedly Miriam's father (Exodus 6:20), Mary's father as well (Koran 3:35–6); and *Surah* 19.1–35: 'Mary' where, once again, Muhammad knows the name of John's father ('Zachariah') though not his mother (Elizabeth), and also that 'he had Wisdom when just a child' and 'he was of the Consecrated' (19:12–5—this material is certainly from Mandaean sources which he, no doubt, encountered in the caravan trade in visits to Southern Iraq). Furthermore, he makes it clear, once again, that he is mixing up Moses' family with Jesus' by calling Mary the 'sister of Aaron' in 19:28. Moreover, he also knows 'the Primal Adam' ideology and something of the narrative of the Protevangelium of James (19.17–25).

⁵⁷ This is, of course, both 'the Insan al-Kamil' of Mandaean doctrine and 'the Adam Kadmon' of Jewish *Kabbalah.* It is also 'the Primal Adam' of both the Pseudoclementines and the Ebionites.

⁵⁸ These different forms of Shi^cism, as well as offshoots such as 'the ^cAlawwis' or 'Nusayris,' are named after the number of imams that are reckoned before their going into 'occultation' or 'becoming Hidden.'

⁵⁹ This connection with the 'Buddha' doctrine is not so far-fetched—note how Hippolytus 9.8 notes that an individual named 'Alcibiades,' by whom he clearly means 'Elchasai' in Greek, came to Rome from Apamea right in the center of the Edessene Kingdom and the Land of

the Osrhoeans ('*the Assyrians*'), bringing a book attributed to '*a certain Righteous One named Elchasai*,' which he, in turn had received further East in the Kingdom of the Persians, describing '*the Standing One*' (i.e., '*the Buddha*'), '*96 miles high and 16 miles wide*,' and which had been preaching to one '*Sobiai*' there, i.e., a '*Sabaean Baptist*.' Of course, we know that Buddhist teachers were coming into these areas probably ever since the time of Alexander the Great and that early converts to Islam some centuries later such as Ibn al Muqaffa^c, the translator of *The Fables of Bidpai* into Arabic, and Abu Muslim, the Leader of the Uprising that led to the establishment of the ^cAbbasid Caliphate, were probably originally of Buddhist origins.

[60] Cf. John 21:20–3 with 1QpHab, vii.9–15.

[61] Cf. *Ant*. 18.117 with Koran 3.59, 19.17, etc.

[62] Note that in 15:45, Paul actually refers to '*the First Man Adam*' (i.e., '*the Primal Adam*') which '*became a living soul*,' but '*the Second*' or '*Last Adam, a life-giving Spirit*'—i.e., again his '*spiritualization*' of things; and see the Mandaean *Book of John*, the *Right Ginza* 49ff. and 199ff., and R. Eisler, pp. 231–2 and 240–4 In these passages, Jesus is '*Barnasha*' (i.e., '*Bar-Enosh*'/'*Son of Man*').

[63] Also see Ezekiel 1:27–8 and the '*no mere Man*'/'*no mere Adam*' citation of Isaiah 31:8 in 1QMxi.11–2 above.

[64] Cf. 1QHi.6, ii.32–35, iii.21–25 (and note here the '*standing*' imagery), iii.35–36, iv.4.24, etc. 1QHiii.37 speaks of God as a '*Wall of Strength*'—words used to characterize James in early Church literature

[65] 1QHiv.21–25 (again note the language of '*standing*' here).

[66] 1QHiv.30–33—*n.b.* how G. Vermes translates '*all His works*' in iv.32 here as the less eschatologically-charged '*all His deeds*.'

[67] Cf. 1QHvi.24–29 and ix.28–35 (and *n.b.*, the '*Rock*' and '*Fortress*' language here) with Matthew 5:9 and John 1:12.

[68] Cf. 1QHvii.6–10 (including the '*Tried Wall*' and '*Fortress*' symbolism again) and ix.28–30 with *EH* 2.23.7, 3.7.9, and *Haeres.* 78.7.7 above.

[69] See, for instance, CDvi.14–15 and vi.17–vii.3, including the '*Nazirite*' language of '*separation*' as well and the definition of '*the New Covenant in the Land of Damascus*' as '*setting up the Holy Things according to their precise specifications*'—directly followed by James' '*Royal Law according to the Scripture*': '*to love each man his brother as himself*.' Also see viii.8-9 condemning '*not keeping apart from*' or '*away from* (the language of James in Acts 15:19–26) *the way of the People(s)*.'

[70] Cf. '*The Rishonim*' or '*the First*' in CDi.16 and viii.17–18/xix.19–21, following allusion to '*turning aside from the way of the People(s)*' again and cf. '*Jesus*' in the New Testament speaking—clearly tendentiously—about '*the First shall be Last and the Last shall be First*'; Matthew 20:16 and pars.

[71] See the '*Belial*' allusion in CDiv.15 and that of '*swallowing*' (*ba-la-^ca*) in 1QpHabxi.5, 7, and 15, '*Beliar*' in 2 Corinthians 6:15, that of '*casting down nets*' generally in New Testament allusion and my appendix to *JJHP* and my article '*The Final Proof that James and the Righteous Teacher are the Same*' in *DSSFC*, pp. 208–17 and 332–51.

72 Cf., for instance, the bizarre 'Rip van Winkle' story in *b. Ta'an.* 23a about Honi falling asleep under a carob tree for 'seventy years' and then, when waking up in his grandson's time, being so disconsolate that 'he prayed (for his own death) and died'—Talmudic humor at its finest!

73 Nor are they without relationship to Buddha under the Bhodi Tree. Not only does John 1:49 portray Nathanael as being the first to recognize Jesus as both 'the Son of God' and 'the King of Israel,' but 1:51 presents a prelude of James' (and Stephen's) vision at the time of his/their stoning.

74 See the *Chronicles of Jerahmeel* 59.17 and *Pseudo Philo* 48.1 above. For Phineas as a 'Zaddik,' see Num. *R.* 21.3–4; and for the twelve miracles associated with his name, *Sifre* Numbers 131.

75 Numbers 25:6–15.

76 For this original 'Covenant,' see Genesis 9:9–17, but also see *Ben Sira* 45:23–29 referring to Phineas above and the *Zohar*, i, 66b and 68b on 'Noah' above too.

77 *B. Ta'an.* 23a–b.

78 See *EH* 1.7.15, meaning the family of 'the Lord' according to the flesh from the Greek 'Despot'/ 'Lordship.'

79 *B. Pes.* 57a and *Tos. Men.* 13.21.

80 See *Ant.* 20.160 beginning with Felix's putting to death many of the 'Impostors and Brigands' (*Lestai*—the same word used in the Gospels to express the two so-called 'thieves' between whom 'Jesus' was crucified—Matthew 27:38 and *pars.*) and the assassination of the High Priest Jonathan and continuing on through the judicial murder of James by Jonathan's brother (there has to be some causality here) to what he considers to have been Agrippa II's completion of the Temple and Albinus' clearing of the jails and filling the land with the same 'Lestai' he says also doubled as 'Sicarii'—*Ant.* 20.215/*War* 2.254ff.

81 *Ant.* 20.181 and 20.206–7.

82 This rioting either before or after the death of James, involving one 'Saulos,' is very similar to the events portrayed in both Acts and the Pseudoclementine *Recognitions* before the death of someone allegedly called 'Stephen'—see below Chapters 17-20 too.

83 For Jesus ben Ananias, see *War* 6.300–9. He is not the only one to be involved in such 'Woes.' See, for instance, R. Joshua in *ARN* 4 (20a), when following R. Yohanan out of Jerusalem he looks back and sees the ruins of the Temple; or when R. Yohanan meets his nephew, 'Ben Battiah,' the Head of the *Sicarii* in Jerusalem in Lam. *R.* 1.5.31 (in *Gittin*, therefore, 'Abba Sikra') and, frightened of him, tells him he cried out 'Wah' when he really cried out 'Woe'! For the 'Pella Flight,' see *EH* 4.3.5, Epiphanius, *De pond. et mens.* 15, and below Chapter 18 too.

84 *War* 6.308–9.

85 1 Chronicles 5:27–34. Note that he and Ezra were supposed have the same father, 'Seraiah', and of course, both go back to David's High Priest of the First Temple, 'Zadok.'

86 We treat this artificiality in *DSSFC*, pp. 24–26/*MZCQ*, pp 8 and 46; but note that Josephus in *Ant.* 20.224–31 lists some eighteen High Priests from Solomon's time until Nebuchadnezzar 'took Josadek the High Priest captive'; while in 10.152–3, he lists only six names for the same Period—*pace* both genealogical and chronological knowledge in Josephus' time.

[87] Cf. Nehemiah 8:4 with 12:7 and 21—but see too Ezra 7:1 and Nehemiah 11:11.

[88] Acts 12:17 introduces James in an off-hand manner—after disposing of the other James in 12:2—as if we should already know who he is. Aside from the missing election of James—probably overwritten by the meaningless and somewhat dissimulating election to succeed Judas *Iscariot* in 1:21–6—Matthew 27:9 quotes *'Jeremiah the Prophet'* to describe the circumstances of Judas *Iscariot*'s death again and *'the Price'*/*'Field of Blood'* associated with him/it when the quote is, in fact, from Zechariah. It is in this complex of materials that we feel the missing Introduction of James in the New Testament's sources is to be found and which, no doubt, really did include these curious passages from Jeremiah 35:3–19 on the descendants of *'Jonadab son of Rechab.'*

[89] Cf. 2 Kings 22:4–20/2 Chronicles 34:14–35:18—n.b., *'Hilkiah'* is definitely designated as *'the Priest'*/*'the High Priest'* here.

[90] There does appear to be some confusion here since, in Jeremiah 29:3, there are two individuals who deliver this letter from Jeremiah to the captives in Babylon—one *'the son of Shaphan'* and the other *'Gemariah the son of Hilkiah'*; but later, in 36:10–2, it is *'Gemariah'* who is denoted as *'the son of Shaphan.'* The writer is unable to reconcile these discrepancies.

[91] For Shaphan's role in this (called *'the Scribe'*), see 2 Kings 22:3–14 and 2 Chronicles 34:8–20. Note that it is one of his descendants who is condemned as *'an idolater'* in Ezekiel 8:11.

[92] This is clearly a paradigmatic episode connecting the father of the Rechabites with Kingly/High-Priestly *'zeal'*—but also see how Acts 8:27–39's transforms another *'Zealot'* episode and *'circumcision'* (the sign of the Covenant) in the way it pictures *'Philip'* as *'joining'* himself to the chariot of the Ethiopian Queen's eunuch.

[93] Again, the ideal of *'keeping the Commandments'* and its combination with antagonism to *'ba-la-ᶜa'*-type idolatry are strong.

[94] 2 Apoc. Jas. 5.4. This *'Pillar'* is probably *'the Stone of Lost Property'* mentioned in Talmudic Honi stories below—cf. Chapter 7.

[95] The important points of contact here are the one in Jeremiah 35:10–18 *'to keep the Commandments of (their) ancestor'* and, of course, to *'drink no wine'*—35:8–14; cf. Numbers 6:1–21 and *James*, pp. 302–10.

[96] See *EH* 3.11.2, 3.32.1–6, and 4.22.2–4 (the last two quoting Hegesippus). For his probable appearance with James in the encounter with Jesus on the Emmaus Road, see Luke 24:13–35; and on the relationship to *'Simon the Zealot'* and Jesus' brothers generally, *James*, pp. 817–52.

[97] *EH* 2.23.17 and note how Epiphanius in *Haeres.* 78.14.6 now calls this person *'Simeon bar Cleophas.'* But note, too, how Epiphanius in Haeres. 78.8.1 preceding this calls 'Jesus'' second brother *'Simeon'* not *'Simon.'* From our perspective, it should be clear that to call someone *'a Priest of the Sons of Rechab'* is the same as calling him an *'Essene'* or *'Ebionite'* Priest—even a *'Son of Zadok'* as the term is used at Qumran.

[98] Note how in Acts 6:8–8:3's recreation of these events, the witness to the stoning of Stephen and the fomenter of the rioting thereafter is *'Saul'* or *'Paul.'* Here, of course, it should be observed that in Jewish stoning procedures, it is not *'the witnesses'* who *'lay their clothes at the feet of'* anyone

(Acts 7:58—also note the very words, *'cried out with a loud voice'* repeated twice, as in Hegesippus' account in *EH* 2.23.12–3 and 17 of the stoning of James), but rather the condemned who must undress prior being stoned!

99 Cf. *Haeres.* 78.14.1 with *b. Taᶜan.* 23a–b.

100 *B. Taᶜan.* 23b.

101 See Jerome, *Comm. on Galatians* 1:19 above.

102 Cf. how in the Ps. *Hom.*'s Prelude in the Letter of Peter to James, the assembled *'Elders'* are *'in an agony of terror'* on having heard James' words on *'keeping this Covenant'* and, therefore, *'joining the Heavenly Holy Ones'* and swearing, in addition to all these things, *'not to lie'* on pain of *'being accursed living and dying and punished with an Everlasting Punishment'* (cf. Paul in Galatians 1:19, 2 Corinthians 11:31, etc. on similarly swearing *'not to lie'* but in a totally different context!).

103 Cf. Matthew 8:2–15, 9:20–31, 14:35–36, 20:30–34/Mark 3:10–12, 6:55–56, 8:22–26/Luke 5:12–15, 6:19, 7:1–17, and *pars.*

104 Cf. James 5:7–8 (followed in 5:9 by the allusion to the *'not grumbling'* of 1QSvii.17–8) with John 21:22–3 and 1QpHabvii.5–14 above.

105 See *A.Z.* 16b–17a and *j. Shab.* 14:4(14d). For his famous snakebite cure in the name of *'Jesus b.. Panthera'* (a favorite Talmudic way of referring to 'Jesus'), see *A.Z.* 27a–b, j. *A.Z.* 12:2 (40d), *Tos. Hul* 2:22–3, and Eccles. *R.* 1.8.4.

106 Cf. *EH* 2.23.10–13 with Ps. *Rec.* 1.44.

107 See *A.Z.* 16b, Eccles. *R.* 1.8.3, and *Tos. Hul.* 2:24. N.b., this name *'Jesus ha-Notzri'* is conserved in one Talmudic ms. redaction too.

108 Along with Eliezer, R. Joshua ben Hananiah ('Jesus'?) was one of the five *'Disciples'* making up R. Yohanan b. Zacchai's inner circle and (probably following the School of Hillel) more liberal than though perhaps not as luminous as R. Eliezer, e.g., he was much more liberal on the subject of proselytes and conversion generally than R. Eliezer; cf. Gen. *R.* 70.5, Eccles. *R.* 1.8.4 (possibly having to do with Queen Helen of Adiabene), and *Tos. San.* 13.2. Noteworthy too, for our purposes perhaps, he rejected the extremism of *'mourning for Zion'/'mourning for the Temple'* of *'eating no meat and drinking no wine'* (b. *B.B.* 60b) and, after the Bar Kochba War, apparently tried to pacify the People when Hadrian rescinded his promise to rebuild the Temple (Gen. *R.* 64.10). Furthermore, as opposed by R. Eliezer, he seems to have assisted the convert Aquila (Acts 18:26?—the writer is aware of chronological difficulties here and elsewhere, but simply pointing out the parallels whatever they're worth) in translating the Pentateuch.

109 Though married to Rabban Gamaliel's sister, *'Imma Shalom,'* their disputes were legendary and Eliezer was ultimately excommunicated by the latter (the Patriarch Gamaliel II); see b. *B.M.* 59b and *Nid.* 7b–8a. Though he disputed with R. Joshua (a character very much like 'Jesus'), the two were friends and both took R. Yohanan's coffin out of Jerusalem and went back to get R. Zadok's—see *Git.* 56a, *Yeb.* 48b, *Abbot* 2.8, *Lam. R.* 1/5/31 and *ARN* 14 (24a). After his death, R. Joshua annulled Rabban Gamaliel's ban of excommunication on R. Eliezer; cf. b. *San.* 68a, *Git.* 83a, j. *Shab.* 2.6 (5b), and *ARN* 25.8f. Not only was he probably the most interesting of the Rabbis, but the most colorful. R. Yohanan was his teacher and R. Akiba his student.

[110] Cf. 'Jesus' portrayed (we employ single quotes here, as already noted, because we are not sure such episodes or portraiture are historical) as *eating and drinking*—our *'eating and drinking'* theme again—*with publicans and Sinners'* ('publicans' surely including Herodian *'tax-collectors'* and 'Sinners,' *'prostitutes'* in Matthew 9:10–11, 11:19, Mark 2:15–16, Luke 5:29–30. But particularly absurd in this regard is 'Jesus" contention in Matthew 21:31–2 that *'the publicans and prostitutes go into the Kingdom of Heaven before'* even the Apostles or, for instance, that *'the publicans justified God'* (Luke 7:29—for the Pauline view of this, see Romans 13:6–8)! The reason that the coupling of these two has to represent *'Herodians'* is because 'Herodian' women of this period (Herodias, involved in the death of John the Baptist, Bernice involved in the destruction of the Temple and accused of incest with her brother Agrippa II, Mariamme, her sister, and Drusilla who married Felix, one of the most brutal of all Roman Governors) were looked upon as no better than *'prostitutes'*—it is not that Judea was crawling with 'prostitutes' in this period! But the reason given by 'Jesus' ('Asclepius'?) here is the most absurd of all and reveals the patent dissimulation involved in such portraits: *'For John came to you in the Way of Righteousness* (so far so good) and *you did not believe him, but the tax-collectors and the prostitutes believed him.'* Nothing could be more preposterous than this and, of course, it is totally contradicted by Josephus in *Ant.* 18.116–9 above.

[111] See, for instance, *War* 2.406–16 above.

[112] For recent research on the Akeldama, see L. and K. Ritmeyer, 'Akeldama—Potter's Field or High Priest's Tombs?' and G. Avni and Z. Greenhut, 'Akeldama—Resting Place of the Rich and Famous,' *BAR*, 20/6, November/December 1994, pp. 36–46 and, by the same authors, 'The Akeldama Tombs: Three Burial Caves in the Kidron Valley', Jerusalem, *IAA Report*, no. 1, 1996, Jerusalem, pp. 57–72.

[113] For the replacement of this election by the all but meaningless *'election'* to replace *'Judas Iscariot'* as *'Twelfth Apostle,'* see *James,* pp. 165–208; but the key here, as we shall see below, is the Greek translation of the reference to *'Office'* in Psalm 109:8 as *'Bishopric'* or *'Episcopate'*—that is, this was the *'election'* actually held at this time which would have been normal to determine the *'Successor'* to 'Jesus' not 'Judas.' Nor is this to say anything about the name of the defeated candidate in Acts 1:23: *'Joseph Barsabas Justus'*—nothing could be more indicative of the *real* nature of the underlying material in Acts' original source than this!

[114] See n. 88 above and variously.

[115] Cf. John 12:4–6 where, in 'Judas ("the son" or "brother") of Simon Iscariot"s mouth, this become 'three hundred'; for 'Mary'/'Martha,' see Chapter 8 and Chapter 11 below.

[116] Cf. the promises made to *'those that love Him'* in CDvii.3–6/xix.1–4 and xx, 17–22.

[117] See James 1:26 and 3:5–11; for 'the Liar' and 'Tongue' imagery in the Scrolls, see CDi.14–16, iv.19–20, v.11–15, viii.13, etc.; 1QpHabv.11, x.9–13; 1QSiv.9–11, etc.

[118] See 1QHii.32–34, iii.25, v.13–23; CDvi.16–21 on *'the New Covenant,'* 1QpHabxx.5–10; 4QpPs 37ii.10, iii.10, etc.

119 The usage is based on the all-important allusion in Isaiah 53:11: '*My Servant the Righteous One will justify Many*' (*Rabim*), the basis for Qumran exegetical organization; for Qumran Community generally, see 1QSvi.8–21, vii.3–25, viii.19–ix.2, etc.; and for its use, for instance vis-à-vis '*the Liar*' or '*the Lying Tongue*,' see CDi.14ff., 1QpHabx.9ff., and 4QpNahiii.8.

120 In it we have the tell-tale allusions to '*the Many*,' '*the Poor*,' '*standing*,' '*saving*,' and the '*soul*'; cf. 4QpPs 37ii.8–9, iii.10, iv.11, iv.20–21, etc., and 1QS, 1QH, 1QpHab, and CD above.

121 If one inspects the texts subjected to exegesis at Qumran one will find, as we saw, that basically these are the usages that determine the exegetical framework and the choice—e.g., Psalm 37, Habakkuk 1–2, Nahum 1–3, Isaiah 10:20–11:5, 5:6–30, 8:7–11:5, 29:10–31:1, and 54:11 (one wonders what else might have been connected to this fragment), Hosea 2:8–8:14, etc.

122 This usage '*Pekudah*' will be of premier importance in the Damascus Document below, where it will in various contexts relate to a Divine Visitation, Judgement, and even a reference such as '*the High Priest Commanding the Many*'; cf. CDi.7, v.15–6, vii.9, vii.21/xix.11, viii.2/xix.14, etc., and 4QD266.8

123 As can be seen from Zechariah 11:11–13, none of these words in the manner Matthew 27:9–10 reproduces them, not '*the Sons of Israel setting a price*' nor '*a Potter's Field*,' nor anything else for that matter appear—not even in The Septuagint. Nor is the sense remotely similar. Not only has Matthew got the name of the 'Prophet' wrong, but he has deformed the content beyond anything that could be considered properly recognizable—this in the interests of a patently anti-Semitic and tendentious exegesis. But the end of the passage, as it appears from Zechariah 12:4–13:2, is actually quite hopeful with '*all the Nations on Earth that gather together*' and '*come up to destroy Jerusalem*' being '*struck dumb*' and '*blind*' and '*all the inhabitants of Jerusalem made Mighty in their God*' and '*the Chiefs of the Thousands of Judah*' and '*the House of David*' raised on high—and a '*a well being opened*' for them that we shall again encounter in CDvi and xix in Chapters 21-22!

124 Cf. the tendentious presentation of Acts 1:15–26 and the results; whereas the election as direct successor to 'Jesus' at this time—'*immediately after the ascension of our Saviour*'—is clearly alluded to in *EH* 2.1.3–4, citing and quoting the Sixth Book of Clement of Alexandria's *Institutions*. 'Khalifa' in Arabic means 'to succeed' or 'Successor' and this is clearly the most important problem in the formation of Islam after the death of the Prophet as well (an excellent *obiter dictum*) and has continued to be till the present day.

125 I have discussed this term '*Sicarios*' in *James*, pp. 171–84, 489–96, and 952–8, but the point is that what seems to have happened is that the first '*sigma*' and '*iota*' have just been reversed and a '*tau*' substituted for the second '*sigma*' in the suffix. Cf. as well Origen, *Contra Celsus* 2.13, who speaks about the '*Sicarius*' in his day and, of course, Josephus on the whole subject of '*the Sicarii*.'

126 For '*the Mebakker*' or '*Overseer*' at Qumran, see 1QSvi.20, CDix.18–19, xiii.6–7, xiv.13, 4QD266.16, etc. F. M. Cross, to his credit in *The Ancient Library at Qumran*, New York, 1961, p. 232, properly recognizes the synonymousness of the two terms.

[127] Cf. Acts 1:26 and note the name of the purported defeated candidate in Acts 1:23, '*Joseph called Barsabas who was surnamed Justus*'—'*Justus*' a Latin characterization, now transliterated into Greek, and, of course, James' cognomen in all early Church texts. Note, too, that '*Barsabas*' reappears in Acts 15:22 and 32 as one of the couriers for James' letter to Northern Syria and is also never heard from again at least in Scripture but he bears the name of James' perhaps most famous brother and is probably synonymous with '*Thomas*' and/or '*Thaddaeus*'—as well as numerous other '*Judas*'es per se.

[128] The '*not drinking of wine*' is, of course, characteristic of James (*EH* 2.23.5), '*Mourners for Zion*' generally, Manichaeans (*The Fihrist* 9.1), and on into Islam—but also one of the basic tenants of Naziritism and Nazirite oaths—see Numbers 6:1–5 and Tractate *Nazir* of the *Talmud* generally. It would also seem to be characteristic of '*the Siddiks*' among al-Biruni's '*Manichaeans*' (8.27ff.), who resemble nothing so much as Jewish '*Rechabite*' or Judeo-Christian '*Ebionites*' (and, for that matter perhaps, '*Buddhist*' itinerants).

[129] Cf. Jeremiah 35:7 with *War* 2.150 and Hippolytus 9.21.

[130] This '*Keeper*' terminology is, of course, strong throughout the Dead Sea Scrolls as is the idea of '*doing*' what one was '*commanded to do*'—see 1QSi.2–15, v.1–11, v.20–22, CDii.17–iii.20, vi.18–vii.9, xx.2, 21, 27–34, etc.

[131] See Koran 2.219 and 5.90.

[132] Jeremiah 35:5–8.

[133] CDvi.20, vii.16, and xx.12. But paralleling this is the use of the same allusion concerning '*raising up the fallen Tabernacle of David*' in 4QFlori.12–3, but also and perhaps even more germane, '*raising up (his) seed*' and '*establishing the Throne of his Kingdom*' from 2 Samuel 7:12–4 in 4QFlori.10f.

[134] CDvii.16 and xx.12, the latter actually picking up the same promises in CDvii.4–9/xix.1–2 preceding it.

[135] See 1 Corinthians 11:24–9 and Luke 22:19–20 and *pars.*, placed right between the reference to '*not drinking the fruit of the vine until the Kingdom of Heaven has come*' and the pointing out Judas *Iscariot* as the one '*who would be delivering me up at the table*'; and Chapters 27-28 at the end of this book.

[136] For this body of traditional Roman legislation, named after the Second Century BC Consul, Publius Cornelius Scipio responsible for the defeat of Carthage, see *James*, pp 184 and 922 and Dio Cassius 68.3–4 for its application in Nerva's time—and see also Chapter 28 again at the end of this book.

[137] For '*doing*' and '*works*,' which is such an important usage throughout the Qumran corpus (and which some translators—like Vermes—reduce to triviality by rendering it as '*acts*' or '*deeds*'), see CDi.20, ii.1–15, iii.6–12, xx.2–3 (perhaps the most perfect exposition of it), 1QSi.2–7 (as is this), v.20–4 (and this), vi.18, viii.13–18 (in exposition of Isaiah 40:3's '*going into the Wilderness to prepare the Way of the Lord*'), ix.20–23 (again in exposition of '*the Way in the wilderness*' in ix.19), and 1QpHabvii.10–viii.3 (here James 1:22–25's '*be a Doer*') in interpretation of '*the*

Delay of the Parousia' and Habakkuk 2:3–4. For more references to *'doing'/'works'* in the Letter of James, see 1:4, 2:12–13, 2:14–26, 4:11, 4:17, etc.

138 Mark 5:25–34 and *pars.*

139 See, for instance, Matthew 9:10–11, 11:19, 21:31–32. Mark 2:15–16, Luke 5:29–30, and 7:29 above.

140 For these issues of *'niece marriage'* and *'sleeping with women during their periods'* as the chronological determinant for the Damascus Document at Qumran, see my appendix to *JJHP*, pp. 87–94/ *DSSU*, pp. 208–17 and note the Herodian genealogy in the Appendix of this volume which vividly illustrates the Herodian family policy of marrying close family cousins and nieces— to say nothing of divorce and Herod's own polygamy. There is no similar indication among Maccabeans, not even Alexander Jannaeus.

141 See my Appendix to *JJHP*, just cited above, and CDiv.14–v.18 and note here the evocation of Deuteronomy 17:17: *'He shall not multiply wives unto himself'* in v.2 (as Herod certainly did) and the famous *'Offspring of Vipers'*-type language of Matthew 3:7 and *pars.* in v.14–5. Note, too, how the charge of *'sleeping with women during their periods'* combines both the *'fornication'* and *'pollution of the Temple'* charges of *'The Three Nets of Belial'* preceding it.

142 CDv.14–5. The point, of course, here is that Priests during the Herodian Period were accepting their appointment from Herodian Kings or Roman Governors or both—thereby acquiring their pollution.

143 The charge of *'not observing proper separation (in the Temple as prescribed) by Torah'* is to be found in CDv.7, exactly in between the accusations of *'polluting the Temple'* and *'sleeping with women during their periods'* and *'niece marriage'/'close family cousins'* charges. The import of all these points should be clear to all but the most insentient reader.

144 See *War* 2.409–23 above.

Chapter 7

1 John 1:46–51. It is important to note that al-Biruni, who knows about figures like Buddha and Zarathustra and their religions, in *Chronology* 8 says that *'the Sabaeans'* in Northern Iraq—of which he knows two groups, one indigenous and the other descending from the Jewish Exiles there—knows of a teacher called *'Budhasaf* (obviously based on *'the Buddha'*), whom he says *'came from India'* and *'introduced the Religion of the Sabaeans'* there.

2 B. *Taᶜan.* 23b. Note that in the same tractate *'Hanan the Hidden'* is introduced as the son of Honi's daughter and the story told about him that the Rabbis—because they were afraid of him—used to send school children to him to take hold of his garment to ask him to pray for rain. It is here the ribald aside is added that he was called *'ha-Nehba'/'the Hidden because he used to lock himself in the privy'*!

3 J. *Taᶜan.* 66b. Here the same story is told about going into *'a mountain cave'* and falling asleep for seventy years, but this time it is connected to both the destruction and rebuilding of the Temple. It is unclear if this is just another variation of the original *'Honi'* story or another *'Honi.'*

[4] *Ibid.*

[5] See, for instance, 1QMi.1–ii.14 and the *'Visitation'*s referred to in CDi.7, v.15–6, and vii.9–21/xix.1–13.

[6] Where James is concerned, we have already seen this occurring in the detail that *'he was a Nazirite from his mother's womb'*—cf. Matthew 2:23; 'Jesus' being taken to *'the Pinnacle of the Temple'* and being *'tempted by the Devil'* (*'Diabolos'/'Belial'*) *'to cast himself down'*—Matthew 4:6–7 and *pars.*; James' proclamation *'on the Pinnacle of the Temple'* of *'the Son of Man sitting on the right hand of the Great Power and about to come on the clouds of Heaven'*—EH 2.23.12–4 and Matthew 24:30/Mark 13:26 and 26:64/14:62; and having been *'cast down'* and being stoned, kneeling and saying, *'Forgive them father, for they know not what they do'*—cf. 'Jesus' in Luke 23:34, but not in the other Gospels.

[7] Take, for example, in the *'Stephen'* episode (which we consider—like H.-J. Schoeps—an overwrite and conflation of the attack on and stoning of James), in Acts 7:55–60 after making the *'blood libel'* accusation again and referring to the *'uncircumcised heart'* of Ezekiel and 1QpHab, ending with the *'bowing down on his knees'* (always an important detail where James is concerned) and the variation on the *'forgive them Father, they know not what they do'*—now *'Lord, do not lay this sin on them'*—'Stephen,' *'looking into Heaven,'* rather sees *'the Glory of God* (not *'the Son of Man coming in Glory'*) and Jesus standing (not *'sitting'*) at the right hand of God', i.e., the *'Standing One'* allusion again.

[8] Forget 'Jesus'" really questionable greeting in John 1:47 (hardly written by an *'Israelite'*)—for 'Nathanael' (Hebrew: *'Given by God'*) for John 1:51 it is now Jesus' prediction to him that he *'will see the Heavens opening and the Angels of God going up and coming down on the Son of Man'*—whatever this is supposed to mean. *N.b.*, the *'ekbalontes'* here, not only parallels what Essenes do to their *'Backsliders'* in Josephus' *War* 2.143 (*ekballousai*), but also how James is *'cast down'* the Temple steps by the *'Enemy'* Paul in the Pseudoclementine *Recognitions* and from *'the Pinnacle of the Temple'* in the reports of his stoning in Hegesippus/Clement/Eusebius.

[9] Cf. Matthew 11:18–9/Luke 7:33–4.

[10] John 2:19–21 and cf. with Matthew 26:61/Mark 14:58, introducing *'the Son of Man coming on the clouds of Heaven'* in 26:61/14:62 (it is at this point the High Priest cries out *'Blasphemy'*) and 27:40/Mark 15:29.

[11] See b. *San.* 86a and Shab. 33b–34a.

[12] See 1 Maccabees 2:24–7, 2:54, and the whole approach of CDi.3–4, i.14–18, iii.5–12, vii.21–viii.19, xx.2–4, 1QS, ii.4–18, iv.9–14, v.5–7, ix.23–25, 1QpHabix.4–6, etc.

[13] Cf. 1QSv.2–14 and CDiv.3–9.

[14] For such *'Servant'* language coupled with *'Righteousness'* at Qumran, see CDxx.20–22, 1QSiv.9 (here the usage actually is *'Service of Righteousness'*), ix.22–24, etc. For *'the End'/'Last End'* and *'works,'* see CDiv.7–9, 1QpHabvii.1–viii.3, x.9–12, and xii.12–14.

[15] 1QpHabvii.15–16. The text is fractured here, but it actually continues in viii.2 in terms of *'the House of Judgement.'* For this *'House of Judgement'* as *'the Last Judgement,'* see x.3–5 and for the actual *'Day of Judgement,'* see xii.14 and xiii.2–4.

[16] Cf. the *'Temptation'* episode *'in the wilderness'* for *'forty days and forty nights'* by *'the Devil'* in Matthew 4:1–12 and *pars.* above.

[17] Ps. *Hom.* 11.35.

[18] See *War* 2.259 and *Ant.* 20.160–1 and 20.168. For Josephus, these individuals were *'Innovators,'* *'claiming Divine inspiration,'* and the word he uses for *'Bandits'/'Brigands'* at least in The *Antiquities* is *'Lestai,'* the actual term the Gospels use for the *'two thieves,'* as we saw, between whom 'Jesus' allegedly was crucified (Matthew 27:38 and *pars.*). In the *War*, this is preceded by the introduction of *'the Sicarii'* and followed by *'the Egyptian pseudo-prophet'* and *'Deceiver'* (also referred to in Acts 21:38—note the actual allusion to *'Sicarii'* here). This is also true for The *Antiquities* where, in the second citation, it is preceded by Josephus' *'mea culpa'* too (which has itself probably drifted into Matthew 27:25) and his charge of *'Impiety'* and *'pollution of the Temple,'* from which he contends even *'God turned away in loathing,' 'bringing on the Romans'* to *'purify the City by fire'* and *'inflict slavery upon us'* (sic)!

[19] The key here is the allusion to *'signs,'* the *'signs'* of course which 'Jesus' does across *'the Sea of Tiberius'* (*'Gennesareth'*) when he goes out with the 'four' to 'five thousand' and multiplies the loves and fishes in Matthew 14:13–23 and 15:29–16.12/Mark 6:31–45 and 8:1–21 and *pars.* For John 2:11 below, it is: *'These are the signs Jesus did in Cana of Galilee'*—but also see John 6:1–15. Of course, for these same wilderness *'signs,'* see Matthew 4:1–17 above and *pars.*

[20] This is the theory behind the opening *Surah* 86: *'The Clot,'* followed by allusion in *Surah* 87 to *'the Night of Power,'* in which *'the Angels and the Spirit'* (in this case, a direct allusion to *'the Holy Spirit'*—in Islam *'Gabriel'* and *'the Holy Spirit'* being considered synonymous) are said to have *'descended'* and *'peace until the rising of the dawn.'*

[21] Cf. 1 Kings 19:4–14 (including allusion to *'in the wilderness,' 'sitting'* and then *'sleeping under a tree,'* and *'forty days and forty nights'*) with Koran 3.113–15, 73.1–6, 74.1–6, 84.16–21, etc.

[22] 1 Kings 19:7–8.

[23] See Koran 78.17–20, 81.1–12, 82.1–5, 84.1–4 (ending in 19 with an image from *Hechalot* Mysticism and in 25 with the typical 'Jamesian' admonition to *'believe and do good works'*—n.b., again, the key emphasis on *'doing'*), etc., but also see the same imagery in 1QHiii.31–32 and xvii.11–12.

[24] CDxx.20.

[25] See j. *Ta'an.* 3:3 (iv.a).

[26] Cf. 1QSviii.7–8, 1QHvi.24–26, vii.7–9, etc.; in the Gospels of course, Peter is *'the Stone'* and Jesus, *'the Precious Cornerstone'*; cf. Matthew 16:18, 21:42, Acts 4:11, Ephesians 2:20, and *pars.* Also see 1 Corinthians 3:9–11 for Paul's view of *'God's Building'* which he, *'as a wise architect, has laid upon the Foundation of Jesus Christ'* (thus!).

[27] 2 *Apoc. Jas.* 61.21–25.

[28] *M. San.* 6:4—this is the same section in which it is averred that the body of the hanged one *'is not to remain all night upon a tree'* (Deuteronomy 21:23).

[29] B. *Ta'an.* 19b–20a.

30 See, for instance, how in 1 Corinthians 8:1–3, in discussing the all-important *things sacrificed to idols* of James' Directives to Overseas Communities, Paul plays off the *'puffed up'* allusion, one finds in the Habakkuk *Pesher* (vii.14–6 leading into *'the Righteous shall live by his Faith'*), where it is used to condemn the *'non-Torah-Doers'.* Paul rather uses it to condemn the Leadership (i.e., James the Just and others), playing off their supposed *'Knowledge'* (*Gnosis*). He also plays off the *'building'* language and *'knowing'* language (cf. CDi.1, addressed to *'all who know Righteousness'*—*Zedek*). He does the same in 1 Corinthians 3:8–14 above, where he plays of the language of *'building,' 'reward,'* and *'works(s)'*—as he does in Galatians 4:21–31, where he plays off the *'freedom* vs. *'slavery'* issue and the Essene *'casting out'* language, as we saw. Even this is preceded in 4:16–8 by plays off the *'Enemy,' 'Truth,'* and *'zeal'* vocabulary. In 5:12–15, in the context of quoting the *'All Righteousness'* Commandment, as we have also seen, he plays off the *'cutting off'* language, that one finds, for instance, in CDiii.7, xx.25–6, and 1QS, ii.16, as well as that of *'eating'* and *'swallowing.'* This should do for a start.

31 The actual description of this event comes in *M. Taʿan.* 3.8–9, but in b. *Taʿan.* 23a, the passage from Habakkuk 2:1–2 that one will also find in the Habakkuk *Pesher* is actually connected to Honi's rain-making.

32 Habakkuk 2:4 is the exegetical basis of Paul's understanding of *'Christian'* Faith in both Romans 1:17 and Galatians 3:11, as it is in James 2:14–26—no matter how much the conceptualities of these two might diverge. The same can be said for Habakkuk *Pesher* vii.17–viii.3 and Hebrews.

33 B. *Taʿan.* 23a.

34 1QpHabvi.12–vii.14.

35 1QpHabvii.15–6: *'and they will not be pleased when they are judged.'*

36 Cf. CDiv.10–12 with 1QpHabvi.12–13. Here the relevant word from Habakkuk 2:1 is *'metzuri'* in place of CDiv.12's *'metzudo'*—almost indistinguishable in any case.

37 1QpHabvii.4–14 and note here the use of *'God making known to the Teacher of Righteousness'* (would one say he was *'puffed up'*?) as opposed to Paul's *'being known by Him'* in 1 Corinthians 8:3 above.

38 Cf. *'being saved from the House of Judgement because of their works and Faith in the Righteous Teacher'* in 1QpHabii.2–3, the allusions to *'not being pleased with their Judgement'* in vii.16, *'the End'* and *'the Last Era'* in vii.5–14, *'the House of Judgement'* as God's *'Judgement ('with fire and brimstone')* in the midst of many Peoples'* in x.2–5, , and *'the Day of Judgement'* when *'God will destroy all the Servants of idols and Evil Ones off the Earth'* in xii.14–xiii.4.

39 See *M. Git.* 5:6 (44a) and its explanation in b. *Git.* 55b. This is continued, particularly where business transactions regarding such property were concerned in 58a–b and *B.B.* 47b. The *'Sicaricon'* was something like *'The Administration of Confiscated Enemy Property Bureau'* instituted against the *Sicarii* after the Bar Kochba War, who were obviously still functioning during that War. Simeon bar Yohai and his son may have been seen as in some manner connected to this, as his teacher R. Akiba was. His area of operations would again seem to have been Galilee.

[40] See L. Nemoy's translation of 'Al-Qirqisani's Account of the Jewish Sects' in *HUCA*, v. 7, 1930, pp 326–7 and 363–5 which is more complete than the abridged one he includes in his later *Karaite Anthology*, New Haven, 1952, pp. 50–1 above. For the ban on 'niece marriage' at Qumran, see CDv.6–11 (here for the same reason as given in al-Kirkisani for 'Zadok''s 'Sadducees'—the extension of the ban on paternal and maternal aunts—by analogy) and 11QTlxvi.14–6.

[41] *Loc. cit.*, pp. 364–5 and 50–1.

[42] Note that for Hippolytus, 5.1–3 and 10.5, 'the Naassenes' (whoever they were supposed to be) come before 'the Essenes' (9.14–23), i.e., the group we would consider to be 'the Sons of Zadok' or 'Zadokites' at Qumran—but also see Epiphanius in *Haeres*. 8.9.1, 10.2, 11.1–3, 12.1. and 20.3.4 where 'Sebuaeans' (whom he considers contemporaries of 'the Essenes') are concerned.

[43] Cf. 15:1–10 and note how he begins this with allusion to the word 'stand' in 15:1 and the same allusions to 'being saved,' 'holding fast,' and 'in vain' in 15:2, we shall repeatedly encounter in both the Damascus Document and the Habakkuk *Pesher* below. Note, too, that the first part of this formula on post-resurrection appearances: 'first to Cephas (there is no recorded first appearance to 'Cephas'—even if 'Peter' and 'Cephas' are the same individual—but rather, in the Gospels, the first appearance is either to Mary Magdalene or 'the two' on the Road to Emmaus), *then to the Twelve*' (in any event, there were allegedly only 'eleven' Apostles at the time—'Judas Iscariot' supposedly already having disappeared), and it is impossible to say anything about the one to 'over five hundred brothers at the same time' that comes next in 15:5. But one can say something about 15:7–9: 'He appeared to James, then to all the Apostles (unnumbered), *and Last of all, as if to an abortion, he appeared to me.*' This at least contains no contradictions and Jerome in *Vir. ill.* 2, as we have already seen, does preserve the record of just such a first appearance to James in what he calls 'The Gospel according to the Hebrews' (at least this 'Gospel' has the picture of 'the grave clothes being given to the Servant of the High Priest'—unlike the picture in Acts' portrayal of the witnesses to the stoning of Stephen 'laying their clothes at the feet of a young man named Saul' in Acts 7:58—correct), which very much parallels the appearance to 'Cleopas' in Luke 24:13–35 (allegedly Jesus' 'uncle,' but in this case probably 'Simeon bar Cleophas, his first cousin or even possibly his second brother—note the actual allusion here to 'the Eleven' in Luke 24:33).

[44] 1QpHabx.5–15 and Chapter 27 below.

[45] See Koran 2:31–38 on 'Adam' being above the Angels and the Angels (including 'Iblis,' i.e., 'Belial') being subject to his command—'Jesus' being the incarnated 'Adam'—and their equation in 3:59 above.

[46] *Haeres*. 30.3.2–6.

[47] *Ad. Haer*. 5.1.3.

[48] Cf. 'Belial' for the name of 'the Devil' in CDiv.14–7 or, for instance, in 1QSii.4–19 or 4QBer (286–7): 'The Community Council curses Belial'—the 'r' in Paul's 'Beliar' is obviously defective but, nevertheless, illustrative.

[49] 1QMxii.11–2 and xix.2 above.

[50] Cf. 1QMxii.4–7 and xix.1–5 above. For '*works*' in the sense of '*doing the Torah*' at Qumran (both based on the same root in Hebrew), as opposed to '*work*' meaning '*labor*,' '*mission*,' or '*service*,' see 1QpHabx.9–12 (describing '*the Liar's vain*' and '*worthless service*') or numerous allusions in 1QS, such as i.2–7, vs. iv.9–11 or ix.19–24.

[51] 1QMxii.11–2 and xix.2 above.

[52] See 4Q203–12 for what must be considered the earliest fragments of any '*Enochic*' literature ever found.

[53] Actually '*Balaam*' is one of the four commoners whom Rabbinic Literature designates as having '*no share in the world to come*'; cf. b. *San.* 104b–110b and *JJHP*, pp. 90–94/*DSSFC*, pp. 213–17.

[54] Cf. CDiv.14–16, 1QHiv.10, and Revelation 2:14, which all use the language of '*nets*' when evoking either '*Belial*' or '*Balaam*.' For their parts, Peter 2:15 and Jude 11, who also evoke '*Balaam*' (the latter together with Cain or Korah), only speak of '*the error*' or '*reward of Unrighteousness*.' For b. *San.* 105a, echoing the '*swallowing*' language at Qumran, the import of '*Balaam*' is '*he who swallows the People*' which the '*Herodians*' (in our view, the real '*Sons of Bela*ᶜ'/'*Belial*' and the key to this particular '*nom a clef*') did as a matter of course.

[55] Cf. James 1:26 (amid the language of being '*a Doer of the work*' and '*bridling one's Tongue*'), 4:11 (following allusion to '*the Diabolo*' and together with being '*a Doer of the Law*'), and 5:9 (following allusion to '*early and late rain*' and '*the coming of the Lord*') with vi.26 and vii.17; and see CDiii.5–12 on the Sons of Jacob '*murmuring in their tents*' in the wilderness. For the imagery of '*light vs darkness*' see, for instance, 1QSi.9–11, iii.2–3, iii.18–26, iv.9–11, etc. It is interesting to note that the allusion to '*guffawing*' in 1QSvii.14–5 overlaps the same kind of allusions and penances in CDxiv.20ff. and 4QD266 (Frag. 10.ii.11–5), showing the two to be not really completely separate documents.

[56] See, for instance, Romans 1:7, 5:1, 5:11, etc. and 1 Corinthians 1:3–8, 5:4, 15:3, but especially 15:57 where he speaks of '*giving thanks to God for the Victory He gives us through our Lord Jesus Christ*'—a '*Victory*,' of course, not over '*the Kittim*' as in the War Scroll but a '*Victory*,' as we shall see, in the Greco-Roman style '*over death*'—something almost totally alien to the Judeo-Palestinian mindset.

[57] 1QMxi.4–xii.17. This too grows very triumphant as the reader may see for him or herself. This Prophecy is also subject to exposition in CDvii.18–viii.1 and 4Q*Test.* 8–13; see Plate 49 and Chapters 21-22 below.

[58] Cf. 1QMxi.11–3 (which includes the allusion to Isaiah 31:8's '*the sword of no mere Adam*') with 1 Corinthians 15:45–7.

[59] See Sermon 191 and cf. Koran 3.45, 4.157, and 19.19–23.

[60] Koran 2.111–39 (including the stark language of '*works Righteousness*' and the point that Abraham and Ishmael founded the Kaᶜabah and they, along with Isaac and Jacob, are all '*Muslims*'/'*those who have surrendered*') and 3.65–97 (note here in his '*Lying*' accusations he is following the '*Jewish Christian*'/'*Ebionite*' false pericopes in Scripture ideology, not to mention that a good deal of his construct in these passages comes from Mani and the Mandaeans preceding him— the former also making the claim of '*the Seal of the Prophets*')

[61] See Romans 2:25–4:25 (beginning with all our categories: *'being a Doer of the Law,' 'keeping the Law,' 'breaking the Law,' 'in my Lie, the Truth of God overflowing to His Glory,' 'works of the Law,'* and ending with *'a Righteousness of Faith'*), 9:1–11 (including yet another reiteration that he *'does not lie'* and attacking *'works'* Righteousness) and the classic Galatians 3:2–4:31 (which we have already considered somewhat above, but including Habakkuk 2:4: *'the Righteous shall live by Faith,'* an outright attack on *'works of the Law',* and ending by asserting that *'the Children of the Promise'* or *'the Spirit'* are the real Children of Sarah while the Jews in their stubborn attachment to the Law are really *'the Children of Agar'* (*'who is Mount Sinai in Arabia'*—thus)!

[62] This is the clear import of CDi.10–6 (beginning with *'And God considered their works,'* i.e., *'works Righteousness'*!) and using the language of *'the First'* for the Ancestors—Abraham, Isaac, Jacob, and Moses. This imagery is reprised in the *'The High Priest Commanding the Many''s 'Blessing'* in the newly-discovered Last Column of 4QD266 and 4QD270, 8–13.

[63] Cf. *War* 2.143 above.

[64] The key to all these things is Paul's attitude towards *'the Law',* as he expresses it in Romans 2:12–4:25 above; but see also how, starting with the *'Piety'* Commandment of *'loving God,'* he uses the words *'separation,' 'cursing,'* and ends with the conclusion that *'the Children of the flesh are not the ones who are the Children of God but the Children of the Promise are counted as the seed'* in Romans 8:28–9:8 that follows.

[65] The key equivalence, as we just saw above, is the totally tendentious identification of *'Agar'* in Galatians 4:25 as *'Mount Sinai in Arabia'* which, in the Philo-like *'allegory'* Paul constructs here, *'corresponds to the present Jerusalem'*—a real stretch, to say the least—which *'is in slavery with her Children.'* One would normally infer here, given the meaning of words and the historical situation, *'slavery to Rome'*; but this is not Paul's Pharisee-like and toadying point. What he means, as we have now amply explained, is *'slavery to the Law'*—forget about Rome!

[66] For *'fishermen* (or *'Apostles') casting their nets'* (an obvious parallel to the *'Belial'/'Balaam'* material we noted above), see Matthew 4:18, 13:47, Mark 1:16, John 21:6, etc.; for *'casting pearls before swine,'* and *'bread to dogs,'* see Matthew 7:6, 15:26, and Mark 7:27; for *'casting out devils'* or *'demons,'* see Matthew 8:16, 9:16, 9:33, 10:1, 12:24–28, Mark 1:34, 3:15–23, 6:13, 7:26, Luke 11:18–20, 13:32, etc.; for *'casting into a furnace of fire,'* see Matthew 3:10, 13:42–50, 18:8–9, Mark 9:18–47, Luke 3:9, John 15:6, etc.; and see my article 'The Final Proof that James and the Righteous Teacher are the Same' (first given at the Society of Biblical Literature in Chicago, 1994), in *DSSFC*, pp. 332–51.

[67] Cf. *EH* 2.23.14–6, *Ps. Rec.* 1.71, *2 Apoc. Jas.* 5.3.61, Jerome, *Vir. Ill.* 2; or, for instance for *'Stephen,'* Acts 7:58; for *'the Essenes,' War* 2.143 above.

[68] CDiv.13–7 and 1QHiv.7–9.

[69] For *'Beelzebub,'* see Matthew 10:25 and 12:24–7, Mark 3:22, and Luke 11:15–8; for *'Babylon,'* see Revelation 14:8, 16:19, 17:5, 18:2, and 18:21 (together with *'casting'* imagery repeated twice in the same line).

[70] 1QpHab xi.5–xii.6—this language of *'ba-la-ᶜa'/'swallowing'* repeated three times in this section. Note too that the allusion to *'the Wicked Priest destroying the Poor'* (*Ebionim*) is purposefully introduced in exposition of Habakkuk 2:17 here and the only parallel allusion does not occur in Habakkuk until 3:14 where the term in question is *ᶜAni'/'the Meek'* or *'Downtrodden'* not *'Ebion'* ('the Poor'). For a discussion of *'the Ebionim,'* however tendentious, see *EH* 3.27.1–7.

[71] Philo is well-known as a Neoplationist of the Alexandrian School from the Richest Jewish family in Egypt known as that of *'the Alabarch of Alexandria,'* which some consider meant *'Arabarch'* (i.e., *'Head of the Arabs'*; see Juvenal, *Satires* 1.127). His nephew, Tiberius Alexander, was the type of the ideal Roman Civil Servant and a backslider from Judaism (*Ant.* 20.100—also mentioned in Acts 4:6), later Governor of Egypt, and finally Titus' Commanding General, who stood in for Vesparian when he went to Rome to become Emperor, at the siege of Jerusalem (*War* 6.237). His family too intermarried with *'Herodians'* (*Ant.* 20.147). Known for his allegorical method, his most famous work, *Mission to Gaius* (see *Ant.* 18.257–61 and *EH* 2.5.1–7)—the second part of which did not survive—contains an indictment of Pontius Pilate. Eusebius in *EH* 2.17.1–18.8 exhaustively lists his works and says he met Peter in Rome (this is probably apocryphal but, if Paul was an *'Herodian',* he probably met *him* and Paul does show, as we have been demonstrating, more than a passing familiarity with his *'allegorical'* method).

[72] Cf. Ps. *Rec.* 1.71 and *EH* 3.27.4. Also see Irenaeus, *Ad Haer.* 1.26.2, and Origen, *Contra Celsus* 5.65 and *Hom. in Jer.* 18.12.

Chapter 8

[1] B. *Taᶜan* 19b–20a and cf. *ARN* 6.3(21a).

[2] Gen R. 42.1. This, by the way, in the context of an exposition by Rabbi Eliezer b. Hyrcanus (*'Liezer'*—thus!) of Psalm 37:14—an exposition extent at Qumran.

[3] See *War* 5.24–6 for how the Famine began in the purposeful burning of all the stores by John of Gischala and Simon, the Temple Captain and son of the High Priest Ananias, and 5.420–41 and 5.512–8 for the effects of this.

[4] Cf. b. *Taᶜan* 19b–20a and *ARN* 6.3 with b. *Taᶜan* 23a and 1 Kings 17:1–8 and 18:41–19:14.

[5] *ARN* 21a.

[6] Cf. *ARN* 9 (22b) on Numbers 12:9–15.

[7] *War* 2.148–9. For the Prophet Habakkuk, too, as a *'Circle-Drawer'* like Honi in exposition of a passage extent at Qumran (Habakkuk 2:1: *'I will take my stand upon my Watchtower'*), see *Taᶜan* 23a. For the exposition of this, which has to do with *'the Delay of the Parousia'* and *'the Last Era,'* see Chapter 27 below.

[8] These fabulous *'Rich Men'* permeate the historical portions of the *Talmud* and its associated literature. See, for instance, b. *Git* 56a, *Ket.* 66b–67a, *Taᶜan* 19b–20a, *ARN* 6.3 (20b–21a), etc. For the New Testament, see in particular Luke 1:53, 6:24, 12:16–21, 16:1–22, 21:1, Matthew 19:23–24, 27:57, Mark 12:41 and pars.; but also see James 1:10–2:6 and 5:1ff.

[9] See b. *Ta'an* 19b–20a and *ARN* 6.3 (20b–21a) above. The play of '*Sabu'a*' here is on the Aramaic '*sabbi'a*'/'*satiated*'. Not only is this a usage, as will become apparent, widespread in all our traditions; but in the Syriac and, following that, the Arabic, it is related to '*Immersion*' as, for instance, '*Sabaeans*' or '*the Subba' of the Marshes*' above.

[10] See Chapters 8, 9, 10, 11, ec. below and *n.b.*, that the pun here in the Greek '*kunes*'/'*kunaria*'/'*kunariois*' is on the Hebrew word for '*Zealots*'—'*Kanna'im*' and see Chapter 13..

[11] See Chapter 3-4, etc. above.

[12] In b. *Git* 56a, this is also '*twenty-one years*'—in *ARN* 21a, this is '*twenty-two*'; in Lam. R. 1.5.31, the number give is rather '*ten*' and there are rather '*four councillors*': '*Ben Zizzit, Ben Gurion, Ben Nakdimon, and Ben Kalba Shabua*' (thus!).

[13] *ARN* 6.3 (21a) and cf. Josephus in *War* 5.24–6 and 5.420–518 above.

[14] For this plaque, see *Git* 60a and *Yoma* 37a; for Helen's three successive Nazirite oath penances imposed on her by the Rabbis, see *Naz* 19a–20b—but also see the Fifth-Century Armenian historian, Moses of Chorene 2.35. The imposition of these '*oaths*', as we shall see below, certainly seems to have had something to do with an aspect of the charge of '*fornication*'.

[15] See *War* 5.147, *Ant.* 20.95, and *E.H.* 2.12.3. In these matters folklore is often an interesting guide. It should be appreciated that this tomb—now known, not incuriously as '*the Tombs of the Kings*'—were in times past known by the Jews of Jerusalem as '*the Cave of Kalba Sabu'a*,' a not unimportant testimony to their true identity—see article '*Izates*,' *Encyclopaedia Judaica*, Jerusalem, 1971.

[16] See the pictures we provide of its entrance and interior in Plates 85 and 88.

[17] See Chapters 8-12 and variously below and *Ket* 62b–63a and *Ned* 50a. Cf. too *ARN* 20b.

[18] This is how he is referred to in *Git* 56a and Gen R. 42.1; in *ARN* 20b, it is '*Siset Hakkeset*' which implies it has something to do with the '*silver*' (*kesef*) of his wealth—in this case the '*silver couch*', upon which he reclined '*at the head of the Great Ones of Israel*.' For the former, the name rather is presented as having to do with '*his zizzit (fringes) which used to trail on cushions*' (*kesset*), though '*couch*' and '*cushions*' are hardly very distinguishable.

[19] *Ibid.* Either way the name is mysterious and has to do with wealth and luxury—just as in Luke 16:19 above. In the one derivation, he is presented as sitting at the Head of the Jewish Nobility; in the other, the Roman—all very peculiar, but obviously a *nom a clef* for a very wealthy and famous personage—probably an '*Herodian*' (Agrippa I?—II?) or one of Philo's relatives.

[20] *Ket* 66b–67a, 104a, *Git* 56a, and Lam R. 1.16.47–9 and see variously below.

[21] See *War* 1.242, 432–8, *Ant.* 15.81–5, 202–46, etc. and *War* 1.562 and *Ant.* 18.136. For Josephus, these are sometimes transliterated as '*Mariamme*,' the translation we have used, for '*Mariamne*.' There are about four more Herodians by the same name in Josephus. Recently a tomb, which gripped the imagination of the public for which reason it was dubbed '*The Jesus Tomb*,' had two such ossuaries inscribed with the names '*Maria*' and '*Mariamne*'—the latter of the two being taken by enthusiasts for Mary Magdalene's remains. But as one can see, '*Mariamne*' for '*Mary*' is the widespread usage in Greek works of the Period and, therefore, no particular connection

with *'Mary Magdalene'* on this basis can be either assumed or deduced. For mix-ups in the New Testament between the *'Mary's* and *'Martha's*, see Luke 10:38–42 and John 11:1–12:3.

[22] See b. *Ta'an* 19b–20a and *ARN* 6.3 (21a) above for Nakdimon's *'rain-making'* and *'cistern-filling'*. For his and the other *'Rich men'*'s grain storage, see *Git* 56a, *ARN* 21a, and *Lam R.* 1.5.31 above as well. These *'miracles'*, of course, parallel (as we shall see below) many of *'Jesus''* reported *'water'* or *'oil-filling'* and *'feeding'* episodes. See, for instance, Matthew 14:15–21/Mark 6:36–44, Matthew 15:32–8/Mark 8:1–20, Luke 9:12–17 on the *'feeding of the four–five thousand'* and the *'multiplication of the loaves,'* 16:1–12 ('Jesus'' parable about the *'baths of oil'* and *'kors of wheat'*, which introduces his versions of the *'serving two masters'*/6:13 and the *'not one jot or tittle'*/6:17 aphorisms and precedes the *'Rich man'* feeding the *'Poor man Lazarus under the table'* in 16:19–31), and John 2:1–11 and 6:42 and see Chapters 10, 12, and variously below.

[23] B. Ta'*an* 19b–20a and *ARN* 6.3 (21a). It is interesting that the Jerusalem *Talmud Ta'anith* 3.9–10 doesn't record this episode but only Honi's similar miracles and, curiously enough, that of his *'grandson'*—also called *'Honi.'* One should also note in this context all the Gospel allusions to *'fill'*/*'full'*/or *'being filled'*—see, for example, Matthew 4:20/Mark 6.42, Matthew 15.37/Mark 7:27(*'let the children first be filled'*—the *'Canaanite little dogs'* episode)/8:8/Luke 9:17, 16:20–1 (the equivalent *'Poor Lazarus'* and *'the dogs under the table'* episode, *'desiring to be filled'* and *'full of sores'*), and John 2.7, 6.12–3/6:26 (*'the Disciples'* and *'the baskets being filled'*—cf. Luke 6:21 and Mark 7:27 above), and 21:11 (Peter pulling *'the net full of large fishes'* to land), and 1QpHabxi.14 variously below.

[24] B. Ta'*an* 20a and *ARN* 21a but, where this *'filled to overflowing'* or *'overflow'* referred to in both these Rabbinic contexts is concerned, also see *'the twelve baskets full of overflow'* or *'leftover'* in Matthew 14:20/Mark 6:43/Luke 9:17, *'the seven baskets full of the overflow of broken fragments'* in Matthew 15:37/Mark 8:8 (and again in Matthew 16:9–10/Mark 8:19–20), and also discussed Chapter 10 below.

[25] See *M. Naz* 3:6 and b. *Naz* 19b–20a. According to Rabbinic tradition, she had sworn that if her son (presumably Izates) *'returned safely from war,'* she would *'be a Nazirite for seven years,'* vividly confirming a passage in Josephus' *War* 2.313 that *'it was the custom for someone in difficulty or danger to undertake a Nazirite vow.'* Notwithstanding, at the end of that time, when she came up to *'the Land of Israel,'* she was told by those of *'the Beit Hillel'* (*'the School of Hillel'*) that vows of that kind observed outside of Palestine where not valid because of the *'uncleanness'* there. Therefore, she would have to do an additional seven years. At the end of this period too, for some reason (it is this which is obscure, but all seem to relate to something sexual), she once again contracted *'uncleanness'* and was instructed to do a third, which she did—but the whole smacks of artificiality and there seems to have been something else at work here and person or persons wishing to keep her in the Holy Land. It was during this time, too, that she was said *inter alia* to have erected a large *sukkah* at Lydda for the Feast of Tabernacles which all frequented (*Tos. Suk* 1:1 and b. *Suk.* 2b–3a—here it is argued that her *Sukkah* was too high, *i.e.*, *'over twenty cubits'*—probably by *'the Beit Hillel'* again—a perfect example of Rabbinic *pipul*). N.b., that above, Lydda would also seem to have been the locale of the crucifixion of the

Messiah b. Joseph.' It would also appear to be the place where both Rabbis Eliezer b. Hyrcanus and his student Akiba completed their studies. One should note its importance, too, in the 'Peter' cycle of stories in Acts both above variously and below.

26 *M. Yoma* 3.10, b. *Yoma* 37a–b, *Tos. Pe'ah* 4.18, and *ARN* 41.12 (34b), but see *War* 7.148–50 and Plate 113. Josephus' sycophantic description of Vespasian/Titus/Domitian's Triumphal Parade here is chilling in the extreme and marks him forever as the turncoat of turncoats. The portrait of Simon bar Giora's torture and execution as leader of the Jews anticipates that of 'Jesus" in the Gospels and makes it plain that Helen's golden candelabra was deposited in *'the Temple of Peace'*, Vespasian immediately had built like Augustus before him in Rome, though the Temple veils and Torah Scrolls he seems to have taken directly into his palace—*ARN* agrees with most of this.

27 In this context, it is certainly not incurious to remark that Simon *Magus* himself at a chronologically contemporaneous time had a consort or *'Queen'* called *'Helen'*, whom Early Church Fathers considered no better than a *'prostitute'* and say he picked up *'in a brothel in Tyre'* (typical theological or linguistic hyperbole)—see *EH* 2.13.4, Irenaeus, *Ad. Haer.* 1.23.2, Justin Martyr, *First Apology* 1.26, Hippolytus 6.15, and Epiphanius, *Haeres.* 21.2.1–3.6. In Ps. *Rec.* 2.8–12, she is called *'Luna.'* It would seem, however, that the first reference—aside from the *'Simon'* in Josephus—is in Justin (c. 140 CE) and for him, Helen has only committed *'fornication'* or some sexual indiscretion of some kind. It is to Irenaeus (c. 180 CE) we seem to owe *'the brothel in Tyre of Phoenicia'* magnification, as we do much else. But these writers even seem to see her as an incarnation of *'Helen of Troy'*—her archetype—and, therefore seemingly all the other *'Helen'*s and the Greek epitome of the originator of all female evil. For *'Tyre in Phoenicia'*, of course, one should have regard to the story of *'Jesus'* and the *'Canaanite'/'Syrophoenecian woman'* and *'the dogs under the table'* of Matthew 15:21–8/Mark 7:24–31 referred to variously below.

28 For this Golden Plaque, see b. *Yoma* 37a, *Git* 60a, and *Tos. Pe'ah* 4:18—in *Gittin*, the Rabbis even find reason to complain about this. It is interesting that, in referring to the imposition of another *'seven year'* Nazirite penance-period on Helen, *Ket.* 7a refers to a decision R. Yohanan supposedly gave at Sidon (i.e., *'Zaidan'* or also possibly *'Beitsaida'*) forbidding *'performing the first intercourse on Shabat.'* Whatever one makes of all this, it is probable that the issue necessitating this (at least her so-called *'third'* Nazirite penance) had to do with perceived sexual impurity or impropriety of some kind which, in turn, would relate to Helen's demonstrated interest in *'the suspected adulteress'* accusation in Numbers preceding the one defining the kind of Naziritism she seemed to become involved in.

29 See *James*, pp. 896–922 and *Ant.* 20.49–53 and 92–104. Also see Moses of Chorene 2.35. It is interesting the amount of space Josephus devotes to the Helen/Izates/Monobazus story. In the first place, it would appear that Helen is on pilgrimage to give thanks for her blessings concerning Izates (thus Josephus) when all these issues pertaining to the Famine and her second Nazirite oath occur around 43–47 CE. In the second, one should note the miraculous story centering about Izates' birth in Josephus, *Ant.* 20.18–9, for which reason he seems to have been

named *'Izates,'* which in Persian apparently meant *'Godly Being'* or *'God';* and, finally, the number *'twenty-four'* Josephus associates with his offspring in *Ant.* 20.92, which carries with it just the slightest echo of the R. Akiba story—not unrelated as I have pointed out to this *'Adiabene'* family—and his *'Twenty-Four Thousand Disciples'!*

[30] For the *'Famine,'* see Josephus, *Ant.* 20.51 and 101 above. Queen Helen seems certainly to have been in the country at the time. For the stopping of sacrifice on behalf of foreigners and the rejection of their gifts, see *War* 2.409–10. The time, therefore, is *'twenty-one years.'* Of course, Helen was dead by this time, having died around the time of her son in 55 CE; but her offspring were not and, as we have seen, were participants in the War against Rome—see *War* 2.520, 4.567, and 6.356.

[31] B. *Taʿan* 9b–20a. Here is our number *'twenty-four'* again, just encountered in the formulary presentation for the number of Izates' offspring—both male and female—in Josephus' *Ant* 20.92 above, should one choose to regard it. Once again, it may simply be accidental, but the number in these various contexts is certainly insistent.

[32] See Ps. *Rec.* 1.72, 2.7–11, etc. These are, of course, Roman *'miles,'* but Epiphanius in his chapter about *'Ossaeans'* gives the equivalent in Greek *'shoeni,'* that is, *'twenty-four'* again—19.4.1. For him, too, it is the width of this *'Standing One,'* who is *'the Primal Adam'* or *'the Hidden Power'* who is *'the Christ'*—n.b. here, too, the derivation of the name *'Elchasai.'* It is difficult to understand what all these overlaps or numerical coincidences might mean, unless it again has something to do with the Revolutionary or *'Messianic'* ideology of all these Eastern *'bathing'* groups.

[33] See Koran 73.1, 74.1, etc.

[34] B. *Taʿan 20a.*

[35] See *M. Taʿan* 3.8 and b. *Taʿan 19a* and *23a/j. Taʿan 3.9–10.*

[36] This is the position of *M. Taʿan* 3.8, which is further fleshed out in *Taʿan 23a.* These texts, the latter of which compares Honi (or *'Onias'* as the case may be) to both *'the prophet Habakkuk'* (Habakkuk 2:1: *'I will stand upon my watchtower and take my stand upon my fortress,'* a passage extant at Qumran introducing 1QpHabvii's eschatological portions—see below, Chapter 27) and Elijah, refer to either Honi or others alluding to Honi's *'being a son'* of God's *'household'* and basically initiate the issue of being *'a son of God'* in the Hebrew/Judaic framework. In the Babylonian *Talmud,* this is connected to the derivative story about Nakdimon making rain (20a) which is itself further fleshed out, as we have seen, in *ARN* 6.3 (21a), which now adds the words *'the Glory of my fathers's house'* to those just alluded to in *M. Taʿan* 3.8 above. It is not incurious that just following *'Jesus''* reported allusion in John 2:16–7 to his *'Father's house'* and *'his Disciples''* application of the passage from Psalm 69:10, *'zeal for Your house consumes me',* to his *'cleansing'* of the Temple and an allusion to *'the sign(s)'* or *'miracle(s)'* Jesus' was doing—most notably, *'destroying this Temple and raising it up again in three days'* (John 2:18–23); John 3:1, probably not unintentionally or unwittingly first introduces the character it calls *'Nicodemus'* (our *'Nakdimon'?),* *'a man of the Pharisees, a Ruler of the Jews'* (thus!) —a character missing from the other Gospels and with whom John then pictures Jesus as carrying on quite a sophisticated discussion about *'Christology',* *'being born again',* and *'Light'* theology, which twice employs the

phraseology *'only begotten,'* present in the Synoptic account of 'Jesus'' baptism but, of course, missing from John's (3:1–22). This then is followed by an account—certainly not accidental—of a discussion between 'Jesus'' *'Disciples'* and John *'beyond the Jordan'* (because 'Jesus' and 'his Disciples' had by that time *'come into the Land of Judea'* (cf. CDiv.3 and vi.5 below on *'going out from the Land of Judah'*) on the subject of exactly who was *'the Christ'* (3:26–36), which includes quite a clear allusion to *'the Primal Adam'* ideology, completely reminiscent of Paul in 1 Corinthians 15:45–50. But more astonishing than any of this and, in our view, definitive in showing the dependence of New Testament versions of *'sonship'* on materials of this kind, the words of the prayer Nakdimon is pictured as making in *ARN* (and, to a lesser extent, both he and Honi are pictured as using in *Ta'anith*) to *'fill'* the cisterns and bring the rain are as follows: *'Master of the Universe, it is revealed and known to You that not for my own Glory did I do this, nor for the Glory of my father's house* (does he mean the *'Glory'* of his own family or the *'Glory of God's House'*—for John's Gospel, as for the story of Honi, it is clearly the latter) *did I do this, but only for Your Glory I performed it, so that there might be water for the pilgrims.'* The use of the word *'Glory'* here will have many ramification in the Documents we will consider below. The reader might wish to catalogue these.

[37] See Matthew 26:59–67/Mark 14.55–65 and *pars.*, a passage which takes up where John 2:28 leaves off above. Cf. too John 10:29–39, itself beginning with evocation of *'My Father.'*

[38] Cf. *Ant.* 14.26–8.

[39] B. Ta'an 20a.

[40] B. Ta'an 23a–b. and cf., for instance, the description of James in *Haers* 78.14.1.

[41] *Ta'an* 23b and note how this *'Hanin'* (*'John'?*) is described as *'the son of Honi the Circle-Drawer's daughter'*—and note, too, how this tradition again involves *'little children'* or *'school children'* who, like *'the people of Jerusalem'* in Jerome's tradition about James in *Commentary on Galatians* 1:19 (who, because he was so *'Holy,'* used *'to crowd around him and try to touch his garments'*), *'take hold of the hem of his garment'* or *'his fringes.'*

[42] See above fns. 27–9 for Helen's three successive *'Nazirite'* oaths for some infraction, probably having to do with *'purity',* and her interest in the *'suspected adulteress'* passage of Numbers 5:11–31.

[43] See Ps. *Rec* 1.72 and 2.7 and 12 above, etc.

[44] *Haeres.* 19.4.1, which also may be—as we progress—one of the reasons for the constant references to the *'feet'* of the Messiah (all that would have been visible, of course, according to this measurement scheme, to a mere mortal) —to say nothing about the constant allusion to *'Standing'* in all sources.

[45] B. *Ned* 50a and *Ket* 62b. For Monobaz's connection to R. Akiba, see b. *Shab* 68b.

[46] *ARN* 6.2 (20b). Later Akiba seems to take a Roman matron as his wife. Had Rachel died? This is all very curious. For relations with R. Eliezer b. Hyrcanus, see, for instance, *B.M.* 59b, *Hag* 14b, j. *Hag* 2.17 (7b), *Tos. Hag* 2.2, b. *Meg* 3a, etc.

47 For the New Testament, see Matthew 2:1–12's '*Star in the East*' replete with allusions to '*King of the Jews*,' '*the Christ*' '*a Leader shall come forth*' (cf. the Messianic Leader Prophecy at Qumran), and '*the Star standing over*' (i.e., '*the Standing One*' ideology again). In the Scrolls, see CDvii.14–21 (which includes Amos 5:26–7 and 9:11 and Numbers 24:17: '*The Star Prophecy*'), 1QMxi.5–15 (which again includes '*The Star Prophecy*' and Isaiah 31:8: '*Ashur falling by the sword of No Mere Man*'—'*The Primal Adam*' ideology), 4QFlori.6–13, which includes 2 Samuel 7:11–4 and Amos 9:11, and 4QTest 5–13 (which includes Deuteronomy 18:18–9, '*The True Prophet*' Prophecy and Numbers 24:15–17 ('*The Star Prophecy*' yet a third time), discussed variously in Chapters 21–28 below. For Josephus, see *War* 6.288–314 on '*the signs and portents*' accompanying the fall of Jerusalem and the destruction of the Temple, which include both the portent of '*a star resembling a sword, together with a comet, which stood over the city for a whole year*' and the portrait of '*one Jesus the son of Ananias*'—with which we began this work—who, directly following the death of James (*Succot*, 62 CE) for seven long years, went around the City crying, '*Woe, woe to Jerusalem*,' until he was struck by a projectile and killed just before its fall. Josephus' portrait ends with the important historical note that '*the thing that most moved the Jews to revolt from Rome was an ambiguous Prophecy* (i.e., Isaiah 10:33–4 and Numbers 24:14–7—'*ambiguous*' because it was capable of manifold interpretation and he didn't know whether it applied to Vespasian, who destroyed the City, or '*a Messianic Leader*' of their own) among their writings that '*a World Ruler would come out of* Palestine.

48 Lam. *R.* 2.2.4 and j. *Ta'an* 4.5(68a). For the vivid portrayal of this Uprising and the unimaginable casualties sustained, one should read the whole of this section of Lamentations *Rabbah*.

49 B. *Ned* 50a and *Ket* 62b above.

50 B. Ta'*an* 23b above.

51 This is rather Gen R. 42.1, which is the same section in which '*Nakdimon*' is called '*Nakodimon*'; but see also Lam R. 1.5.31, following evocation of '*The World Ruler Prophecy*' of Isaiah 10:34 ('*Lebanon shall fall by a Mighty One*') and the story of the various '*woe*'s and '*wah*'s when R. Eliezer and R. Joshua carry R. Yohanan's body out of Jerusalem, just preceding the story of R. Yohanan sending them back in to bring out R. Zadok—as well as Eccles *R.* 1.8.3–7, where R. Eliezer tells R. Akiba the story he heard from '*Jacob of Kfar Sechaniah*' about '*Jesus the Nazoraean*' and the picture of R. Eliezer's stricter approach to the *Torah*, where a Gentile sinning woman wanted to convert, than that of the '*Jesus*' prototype R. Joshua. Importantly, this story concerns a female proselyte of the type '*Jesus*' encounters in Matthew 15:23 and Mark 7:24 in Tyre and Sidon, which we will analyse in greater detail as we proceed.

52 Again, the spelling of this in Josephus is rather '*Eleazar*' (*Ant.* 20.43) not '*Eliezer*,' as we have it spelled here. Still his approach echoes that of Eliezer ben Hyranus in the above story in Eccles. *R.* 1.8.4. But these disputes between R. Eliezer and R. Joshua—Yohanan ben Zacchai's—favorite two pupils, are famous in Rabbinic literature. But, in particular, where '*circumcision*' as a *sine qua non* for conversion is concerned, see b. *Yeb* 46a, where R. Eliezer specifically takes the position of Josephus' '*Eleazar*' here. This is varied somewhat in j. *Kid* 3.14, where R. Joshua is portrayed as also requiring '*baptism*'—an interesting addition.

53 *Ant.* 20.18. It is interesting that here Josephus calls him '*Monobazus surnamed Bazeus*,' two names which would appear to be the same. However, elsewhere in 20.24–6 he is satisfied simply to call him '*Monobazus*.' Depending on whether we are looking at a Greek or Latin version of the name '*Abgar*', we encounter '*Agbarus*' or '*Abgarus*' and sometimes even '*Acbarus*,' '*Augurus*,' or '*Albarus*,' e.g., see Tacitus, *Annals.* 6.44 and 12.12 or in *ANCL*: Hippolytus on the Twelve Apostles and Codex Baroccian 206. These confusions in transliterating Semitic names to Greek or Latin ones are widespread and even remarked by authors of the time, who comment that the Greeks had a hard time with Arabic or Syriac-based names. It is difficult to know whether Abgar and Monobazus are parallel or identical clusters of names. Moses of Chorene 2.29–35, for instance, thinks Helen's husband is '*Abgarus*'—so apparently to some extent does Eusebius in *EH* 1.13.1–2.12.1 where, according to some chapter headings, she is '*Queen of the Osrhoeans*,' i.e.,'*the Assyrians*.'

54 *War* 2.520.

55 For the connection of this '*Kenedaeus*' with Luke's name for this mysterious '*Kandakes*'— Queen Helen's parallel or double, see *James*, pp. 883–88 and 906–22—but also see Strabo, *Geography* 17.1.54 and Pliny, *H.N.* 6.35 and *Ps.* Philo 25.9–28.10 celebrating '*Kenaz*' as a quasi-Messiah!

56 *Loc. cit.* (*War* 2.520 above). The parallel with Leonidas should not be lightly taken. Even 1 Macc. 11:21 considers '*the Jews and the Spartans to be brothers*'—a probable confusion having to do with the Mycenaean heritage of the Philistines along the Coast.

57 These allusions to '*filled*' or '*full*' permeate the Gospels and one should probably catalogue each one of them, as we have above—but for a particularly relevant example, see Luke 16:22's '*Poor Man Lazarus longing to be filled from the crumbs that fell from the Rich Man's table*' below or the constant '*filling of baskets*' (paralleling Nakdimon's '*filling of wells*') in Matthew 14–6/Mark 6–8 above. In John 12:3, see how '*the house was filled with the odor of the ointment*' with which '*Mary anointed Jesus*' feet and wiped his feet with her hair' (sic)! The most important reference of this kind in the Scrolls occurs in 1QpHabxi.13–14 in interpretation of Hab 2:14–15 about how '*the Wicked Priest walked in the way of satiety*' or '*in the way of drinking his fill*'—not in the way of '*drunkenness*' as most '*Consensus Scholars*' mistakenly think, but in '*drinking the Cup of the Wrath of God*,' which '*would swallow him*'—that is, '*the Cup of Divine Vengeance*'; cf. Rev.14:10 and 16:19 ('*the Cup of the Wine of the Fury of His Wrath*').

58 B. Git 56a, but see *ARN* 6.3 (21a) above: '*Whoever entered his house hungry as a dog came away filled*.' In these passages, one has to understand that '*Sabu͑a*' is based on the Aramaic '*sabbi͑a*'/ '*satiated*'—in both Arabic and Syriac this usage, as we have seen, is related to '*immersion*,' that is, '*immersion in water*' or '*baptism*.'

59 Cf. *War* 2.143 and *Ps. Rec.* 1.70, which even includes the '*headlong*' language of Acts 1:18's picture of the James-like '*fall*' Judas *Iscariot* takes and, for Luke 4:29, what the citizens of Nazareth wish to do to '*Jesus*' when he compares himself to Elijah in the matter of '*rain-making*,' and going to '*Zarepta the widow of Sidon*'—another allusion to Queen Helen or Luke's parallel to Matthew 15:22/Mark 7:26's '*Canaanite*'/'*Greek Syrophoenician woman*' (also from Tyre and

Sidon)?—and Elisha only having *'cleansed'* the single leper *'Naaman the Syrian,'* i.e., his support in his own alleged home of the Pauline *'Gentile Mission'*!

[60] See 1QpHabxi.4–15 and the discussions in *James*, pp. 252–54, 444–50, 504–13, etc., which are extensive and cannot be repeated here in full. The gist of these are also summarized in *DSSFC*: *'The Final Proof that James and the Righteous Teacher are the Same,'* pp. 332–51; also see Appendix, pp. 87–94 in *JJHP*: *'The "Three Nets of Belial" in the Damascus Document and "Ballaᶜ"/"Belaᶜ" in the Temple Scroll'*—pp. 208–17 in *DSSFC*.

[61] 1QpHabviii.14–ix.5. Here the reference is to how *'the Last Priests of Jerusalem gathered Riches and profiteered from the spoils of the Peoples,'* which is easily interpreted in terms of the predation activities of *'the Herodians'* and *'the Men of Violence'* in this Period—vividly described in Josephus' *Ant.* 20.181–214 in the run-up to James' death and the War against Rome. But, in addition, what *'the Yeter ha-ᶜAmim'* or *'the Army of the Kittim'* do here is, in turn, plunder *'the High Priests'/'Last Priests'* and take their *'spoils'* or *'Riches'* to Rome.

[62] B. *San* 105a–106b, Once one realizes that this *'Belaᶜ'/'ballaᶜ'/'Balaam'* terminology is a blind for Herodians, then a good deal of chronological misinformation and disinformation at Qumran is clarified.

[63] See my Appendix, pp. 87–94 in *JJHP*: *'The "Three Nets of Belial" in the Damascus Document and "Ballaᶜ"/"Belaᶜ" in the Temple Scroll'* and pp. 208–17 in *DSSFC* above. For Revelation, the references are 2:14ff. and 14.8–13 above; but also see 2 Peter 2:15 and Jude 1:11. At Qumran, see CDiv.14–5 and 1QHiv.10 and 11QTxlvi.10.

[64] Cf. Ps. *Rec* 2.4, 3.1, etc. and Ps. *Hom* 2.19–22. The presentation in the *Homilies* is by far the more detailed and itself very curious. It is this presentation that names the Canaanite/Syrophoenician woman as *'Justa,'* identifying her as *'a Gentile though living like the Sons of Israel,'* by which it seemingly means she kept Jewish Dietary Laws. Besides her daughter, whom she married to one of the *'Poor'* (in 3.23 she is identified as *'Bernice'*), she is described as having two sons, one of whom seemingly the famous *'Aquila.'* These sons she had educated by Simon *Magus*, who is identified as *'the son of Antonius and Rachel'* and *'a Samaritan.'* It is in this discussion that Aquila identifies *'Helen'* as a *'Queen'* and, like Simon and Dositheus, originally one of John's *'thirty'* Disciples. It was in this manner that she supposedly fell in with Simon and not—as later Fathers suggest—in a brothel in Tyre which seems rather to reflect this story about the Canaanite/Syrophoenician woman—thus far the *Homilies*!

[65] Ps. *Rec* 1.72–2.1. Here *'Zacchaeus'* as one of the founding members of the Caesarea Community but so too are *'Aquila'* and his brother, though the story of their mother's conversion is missing. Still Aquila does then tell the story of Simon *Magus'* origins, which roughly agrees with the one he is pictured as telling in the *Homilies* above. *'Zacchaeus'* also plays a significant role in this part of the *Homilies* 2.1–2.21 where his role as *'a publican'* as in the Luke 19:2 is signaled too. One wonders whether this character has anything to do with the *'Zacchaeus,'* signaled as the father of R. Yohanan b. Zacchai, or whether this resemblance is purely coincidental. The matter of *'strangled things'* as *'carrion'* appears in Ps. *Hom* 7.4, 7.8 and 8.19, but *n.b.*, 11.35 too, where *'Peter'* is pictured as a complete *'Jamesian.'*

66 1QpHabxii.3–10; but also see 4QpPs 37ii.10, iii.10, and iv.11 on *'the Church'* or *'Congregation of the Poor'* and 1QHv.23 on *'the Poor Ones of Piety.'*

67 4QpPs 37iv.10.

68 1QpHabxii.2–3, echoed in 4QpPs 37iv.9–10.

69 *ARN* 6.27 (21a). In *Git* 56a it is *'Ben-Zizzit ha-Keset'* because, as we saw, *'his fringes (zizzit) used to trail on cushions'* (keset) or *'his seat (kise) was among the Great Ones of Rome'*—but in both there may be a play on the word *'kesef,'* having to do with all the *'silver'* he amassed. Whatever the case, he was clearly an Establishment Personality in league with the Romans.

70 See *ARN* 6.15–7 (20b), b. *Ned* 50a–b, and *Ket* 62b–63a. This *'crown'* seems to have related to a youthful prediction about what he would give his wife Rachel that *'She would wear a crown like the City of Jerusalem'*—itself relating to his future wealth and fame, For more on this *'crown'* or *'Golden Jerusalem,'* which Rabbi Akiba is said to have given his wife Rachel, see *Shab* 59b. According to *ARN* 20b, *'before he departed from the world, he owned tables of silver and gold and mounted his couch on ladders of gold'*—again, typical Talmudic hyperbole. But there is a conundrum here that has not failed to go unremarked among rabbis and scholars, one of the earliest of whom seems to have been R. Luria of Safed in the Sixteenth Century, and that is that, since his wife Rachel—the obvious source of his early wealth—seems to have disappeared from the Traditions, to be replaced by the curious story in *Ned* 50b and *A.Z.* 20a of the conversion of a *'Rich'* and irresistibly beautiful Roman matron—the alleged wife of the Roman Prefect Tinius Rufus (cf. *Git* 90a), whom some traditions even hold responsible for his death—how is this to be squared with his fame as a Jewish Messianist and Patriot? In fact, some traditions even claim to know her name, *'Rufina,'* which seems itself suspect in the extreme. In these traditions about R. Akiba, one should also note the mention of one *'Aquila'* or *'Onkelos,'* whom it calls *'the son of Kalonymus'*/*'Kolonikos'*—whom many take to be Flavius Clemens or *'Clement'* of Pseudoclementine fame, just as in these materials about Peter, Simon *Magus,* and *'the Church'* at Caesarea, itself the largest neighboring town to Samaria—see *A.Z.* 11a, *Git* 56b, *B.B.* 99a, etc. For his interest in the Samaritans (*'Cuthaeans'*), whom he considered legitimate converts and which would link him further to some of the materials above, see *Kid* 75b.

71 *Ket* 66b and cf. Lam *R.* 1.16.48. For Boethus' daughter with her proper name, *'Martha,'* see *Git* 56a and *Ket* 104a. For Boethus' daughter as *'Miriam,'* see Lam *R.* 1.16.47 (the *'Mary'* and *'Martha'* names again).

72 This *'levirite marriage'* theme is important in the extreme, particularly as regards Boethus' daughter Martha's marriage to her second (or third) husband, Josephus' friend Jesus ben Gamala. For the patently tendentious issue of *'levirite marriage,'* raised according to Synoptics portraiture by John the Baptist vis-à-vis Herodias' marriage to *'Philip,'* see Matthew 14:3–4/Mark 6:17–8/and Luke 3:19. But, as we have several times pointed out, Herodias did not marry *'Philip'* but rather, according to Josephus' testimony, another son of Herod himself also called *'Herod.'* Philip was married to Herodias' daughter Salome and it was he, whom Josephus specifically informs us, *'died childless'*; so here the issue of *'levirite marriage'* would have been appropriate. Rather, the issue here seems to have been what Qumran calls *'fornication'* and *'divorce'* and *'marrying close family cousins.'*

[73] The point here is that it is Paul in Galatians 2:15 who makes it clear that 'Gentiles' were to be identified with 'Sinners', thereby unraveling this bit of cryptography which could have been deduced anyhow from his doctrine of 'Original Sin'. But the main doctrine at Qumran is 'Righteousness'—'a Righteousness of the Law' which fairly permeates all documents there—to say nothing of its principal sage, 'the Teacher of Righteousness'.

[74] *Ket.* 62b–63a.

[75] 1 Apoc. Jas. 31.2–32.10. Of course now, with the recent discovery of the Gospel of Judas, it has be re-appropriated to 'Judas'—but, however this may be, one or another of these 'brother's was clearly seen as the Successor at least as far as 'teaching' or 'Gnosis' was concerned.

[76] See *ARN* 4 (20a) and *Git* 56a–b.

[77] Cf. my comments on CDiii.2–4 and James 2:20–4 and 4:4 above.

[78] *ARN* 6.3 (20b)

[79] For the 'Maschil' or 'Guide' at Qumran, a title of course that develops out of the Biblical Psalms, see in particular 1QSi.1, iii.13, viii.11, etc.; but, in particular, see CDi.7–11 about how God 'visited them and caused a Root of Planting to grow' and how 'they knew that they were Sinners,' i.e., John's doctrine of 'repentance from sin'. 'And they were like blind men groping for the Way for twenty years (more imagery of 'the Way in the wilderness') and God considered their works (Jamesian 'works') and, because they sought him with a whole heart, He raised up for them a Teacher of Righteousness to guide them in the Way of His heart.' Here the language of 'the Guide' and, of course, that of 'being like Blind Men'. For more on this subject, see my Chapter 10: 'Every Plant which My Heavenly Father has not Planted will be Uprooted' below. One of the reasons we decipher both the euphemisms 'Pharisees' and 'Blind Guides,' as we shall see below, as 'the Party of the Circumcision of James' is because Acts 15:1–5—the prelude to 'the Jerusalem Council'— makes it very clear (as does Paul in Galatians 1–2) that the 'some' who are 'coming down from Judea ('Jerusalem') and saying that 'unless you are circumcised according to the custom of Moses' and generally 'troubling' communities, such as Paul's, were of 'the Heresy of the Pharisees' (clearly these so-called 'Pharisees' were not 'Normative Pharisees', but a 'Heresy'). As we have been showing too above, this also represents a fundamental debate in Rabbinic Judaism of this Period.

[80] For 'hear and understand' at Qumran, see for instance these very same passages in CDi.1: 'Hear all you Knowers of Righteousness (the 'Righteousness' doctrine again) and comprehend the works of God' (the 'works' doctrine above) and ii.2, including even the idea of 'unstopping your ears' (cf. Mark 7:32–5 and pars., where Jesus cures a deaf and dumb man by 'sticking his fingers in his ears' and 'spitting on his tongue'—sic! In Mark, this directly follows his explanation of the 'Toilet Bowl' Parable below and the 'Greek Syrophoenician woman' and 'the dogs under the table' episode and several allusions to 'he who has ears, let him hear'. In 8:23, after explaining the meaning of his having 'filled' the baskets, 'Jesus' then even 'spits into the eyes of a blind man'—again thus)!

[81] Matthew 15.20 adds for good measure, 'eating with unwashed hands does not defile the man'—for him the original issue of the 'Parable'; while Mark 7:19 makes it clear the point of the whole exercise (reflecting Pauline doctrine in 1 Cor 8–11) was 'to declare all foods clean'—a point

which 'Peter' was presumably unaware of in the *Heavenly Tablecloth* episode of Acts 10:14–5, to say nothing of Gal 2.

[82] John 11:39: *'he already stinks for it is four days'* (since he has been in the tomb). Here *'Martha'* is described as *'the sister of him who had died.'* Of course, in Luke 16:20's version of Matthew and Mark's *'dogs under the table'* episode, Lazarus (who is portrayed as *'a certain Poor Man...full of sores, desiring to be filled'*) was not yet dead—nor did he have a sister named *'Martha'*; likewise in Luke 10:38–42's version of the *'Martha'* events —only this time she does not have a brother called *'Lazarus'*, only a *'house'* and a sister called *'Mary'* (*'Miriam'*)! Of course, Martha's complaint in John 11:21–2: *'whatever you ask of God, I know He will give it to you,'* reflects almost word-for-word what the Jewish crowd requests of Honi in both *Taʿanith* and Josephus as well as, by implication, what Simeon ben Shetah consider's God's opinion of Honi to be.

[83] One admits the dizzying quality of all this, but this is what the New Testament writers depended on to mystify and overwhelm the untutored innocent. It is important to keep one's eyes on the different usage of *'cask'* and *'flask'* as well as those to *'very precious ointment,' 'spikenard ointment of great value,'* and *'alabaster'* when following the path of dependency and variation. Mostly in these episodes, it is *'Judas Iscariot'* (literally *'Judas of Simon Iscariot'*) or *'the Disciples'/'they'* doing the *'complaining'* as in John 12:4–7 or Matthew 26:6–13/Mark 14:3–9. Of course, the switches from *'Simon Iscariot'* to *'Simon the Pharisee'* to *'Simon the Leper'* and the constant shell game going on about the location *'Bethany'* and whose *'house'* it really was—bearing in mind what I have already said above—are a good joke. In John 12:3, of course, it is *'a litra of pure spikenard ointment of great value'*—*'litra'* to appear later in John's picture of Jesus' burial scenario. For its part, to bring all these usages full circle, Luke 7:37 just keeps the allusion to an *'alabaster flask of ointment.'*

[84] All these allusions to *'reclining'* are very important and imply in the Greco-Roman/Etruscan style *'dining'* or *'eating.'* This, for instance, is how Josephus depicts Agrippa II as *'reclining'*—presumably with his dinner guests on the balcony of his Palace overlooking the Temple Courtyard and the sacrifices in the all-important episode involving *'the Temple Wall'*, preceding the death of James and its pobable immediate cause—that is, *'he was reclining and eating while he* (and his guests—some of whom presumably *'uncircumcised'*) *gazed on everything being done in the Temple'*; *Ant.* 20.189–96.

[85] Even I am becoming confused here. One should have said *'Miriam the daughter of Nakdimon ben Gurion'*—*ARN* 6.3 (20b); but it is the theme here of 'levirite marriage' regarding both characters which causes the confusion. As noted above, Boethus' daughter Martha was also actually waiting for permission to marry Josephus' friend Jesus b. Gamala. For another version of this tradition regarding Nakdimon's daughter, see Lam *R.* 1.16.48 and *Ket* 66b above (repeated in 65a as if it is rather his, that is, *'Nakdimon's daughter-in-law'*). It is in Lam *R.* 1.16.47, preceding this, that Boethus' daughter like Nakdimon's is called *'Miriam'* and here the statement is made that *'the Rabbis granted her two seʾah of wine daily,'* that is, while she was awaiting the decision of *'the levir'*. For traditions incorporating *'Martha'*'s proper name, see *Git* 56a and *Ket.* 104a above. Still, the mix-ups here between the two are widespread and

not just because, so often, both are called *'Miriam'* or *'Mary.'* In fact, it is the subject of being a *'widow'* and awaiting the decision of the *'levir'* that seems to make it clear we are often speaking about *'Martha'*—unless both were *'widows.'* Plus, it is not clear which of these two daughters survived the fall of the Temple. At one point *'Martha'* seems to die in the Famine in Jerusalem during the Roman siege, but other traditions seem to imply that she was alive and met a tragic fate afterwards. Nakdimon's daughter *'Miriam'* does seem to have died under terrible stress after the fall of Jerusalem. What is incontestable is that both are clearly well-known enough to have become proverbial—so well-known, in fact, as to have provided a template for Gospel writers—particularly John.

[86] See, for instance, 1QpHabx.9 and CDiv.19–20 and viii.13, where *'the Man of Lying'* actually is called *'the Mattif* (from the verb *'hittif')* or *'Pourer out of Lying'*—otherwise known as *'the Spouter of Lying.'* This is another instance where more precise translations can help precisify possible connections, reformulations, and/or refurbishments.

[87] CDi.14–15. The verb here is *'hittif,'* the root of *'Mattif,'* making it clear precisely what *'the Man of Lying'* or *'Jesting'* was actually doing—*'removing the boundary markers which the First'* or *'Forefathers had set out as their inheritance,'* i.e., the Mosaic *Torah.* The allusion to *'choosing the fair neck'*—which so parallels Jesus' statement in Luke 10:42 that *'Mary has chosen the good part'*—occurs in i.19 and means, in this context, *'choosing the easiest way.'*

[88] This is how it is stated in Mark 14:24 also. In Luke 22:20, this is *'poured out for you'*; but cf. CDi.14–15 above on the rise of *'the Scoffer'* or *'Comedian who poured over Israel the waters of Lying'*!

Chapter 9

[1] At Qumran, one should note, *'mumuring'* of this kind is an important infraction. In the first place in CDiii.7–14, *'murmuring in their tents'* (i.e., *'in the wilderness'*) against *'the Voice of their Maker and the Commandments of their Teachers'* (i.e., Mosaic Law) is a severe offence and is to be contrasted with *'holding fast to the Commandments of God.'* It *'kindles the Wrath of God against their Assembly'* (in Greek, *'Church'/'Ecclesia'*) and *'because of it, their Kings were cut off,'* *'their Mighty Ones perished,'* *'their Land became desolate,'* and *'they were delivered up to the sword.'* In 1QSvi-vii, where there is much attention paid to *'speaking rudely or impatiently'* (vi.25–26), *'slandering the brother'* and, worse, *'slandering the Many'* (vii.15–16), *'murmuring against the Foundation'* or *'Leadership of the Community'* (the meaning is unclear here, but it can be intuited) is punishable by expulsion without possibility of return (Paul?); *'murmuring against one's fellow without justification'* is only punishable by *'six months penance.'*

[2] We have already examined the historicity of *'Stephen'* above and in *James the Brother of Jesus*, pp. 606–14. In our view, *'Stephen'* is a deliberate fictionalization based on the attack on the Roman Emperor's *'Servant Stephen'* in this Period (note the idea of *'Servant'* here) in Josephus and covering up the attack by Paul on James in the Pseudoclementine *Recognitions* (H.-J. Schoeps was the first to suggest this). One should note that *'the stoning of Stephen'*, c. 44–45 CE in Acts, is an actual transposition of *'the stoning of James'* in 62 CE in Josephus.

³ See, for instance, Paul in 2 Corinthians 10:12–12:11, who is very upset about the Jerusalem *'Super Apostles'* who are undoing his work in the *Diaspora*—particularly as regards the unnecessariness of attachment to the Mosaic Law and *'circumcision'*—even includes allusion to the fact that he *'does not Lie'*: *'Hebrews are they? So am I. Israelites are they? So am I. The seed of Abraham are they? So am I...but I have worked harder,'* etc., etc. (thus)!

⁴ See *Ket* 62b–63a (n.b., here is one of the episodes where *'Rachel falls upon her face and kisses his feet'*), *Ned* 50a, *ARN* 4.5 and 6.1(20a–b), etc.

⁵ CDxx.17–22. One should pay particular attention to the fact that this is addressed to *'the Penitents from Sin in'* or *'of Jacob'* (James?), *who kept the Covenant of God,'* that is they were *'Shomrei ha-Brit'* or *'Keepers of the Mosaic Covenant'*—the definition of *'the Sons of Zadok'* in the Community Rule. Here, too, each is instructed *'to speak to his neighbor, strengthening his brother to support their steps in the Way of God'*—a variation on James 2:8's *'Royal Law of Scripture'* (the *First Love Commandment*); plus *n.b.*, the variation here on *'the Way in the wilderness'* terminology. This ends with the promise from Exodus 20:6 that *'He does Mercy to the thousands of them that love him* (the second of the two *Love Commandments*—cf. James 2:5 on *'the Kingdom promised to those that Love Him'*) *and his Keepers for a thousand generations'* (again the language of *'the Shomrei ha-Brit'*)! This is from Ms. B. The same promise is made in vii.4–6 of Ms. A.

⁶ *Ket.* 66b–67a.

⁷ *Haeres.* 78.14.1

⁸ *Commentary on Galatians* 1:19 above. This tradition is more or less repeated in b. *Ta'an* 23b in regard to Honi's grandson, *'Hanin,'* a contemporary of either John the Baptist or James, or both, and now it is the *'school children'* who are substituted for *'the People of Jerusalem'* or the *'little children,'* who as here in Jerome's tradition, *'take hold of the hem of his garment'* or *'his fringes.'*

⁹ Aside from the general thrust of the Gospels to give the impression that Jerusalem fell because of the death of Jesus (counter-indicated in Origen, Eusebius, Jerome, *et. al.*), the several pictures of the proclamation of the *'coming of the Heavenly Host upon the clouds of Heaven,'* and the alleged charge against James of *'blasphemy'* (there was no *'blasphemy'* where 'Jesus' was concerned, even in the portrait of the Gospels—which involved pronouncing the forbidden Name of God— unless it be the Honi-like infraction: *'speaking to God as a son'*); there was the unique portrait in the Synoptics of *'the Devil taking'* Jesus and *'placing him upon the wing'* or *'Pinnacle of the Temple'* and *'tempting him'* to *'cast himself down'* (katabale)—here the *'casting'* language of all of the James' death scenarios, we have encountered—not to mention the attack by Paul on James in the Pseudoclementine *Recognitions.* 'Jesus'' response is, of course, the typically wise-guy *'You shall not tempt the Lord your God'* (Matthew 4:5–7 and *pars.*—the reader should not worry about my approach here. *None of these things ever happened!* This is what I have tried to explain is what is meant by *'Literature',* not *'History'*).

¹⁰ See, for instance, Matthew 8:2–15, 9:20–31, 14:35–36, and 20:30–34, Mark 3:10–12, 6:55–56, and 8:22–26, Luke 5:12–15, 6:19, 7:1–17, etc., and *pars.*).

[11] 1QpHab xi.4–8. This is, of course, one of the most famous and most labored-over passages in the Dead Sea Scrolls. Not only does it contain the *'swallowing'* language and imagery, it also contains both that of *'casting down'* (*'causing to stumble'*) and *'his House of Exile'*, which we shall explain in great detail in Chapters 25 and 26 towards the end of this book. It should also be appreciated that, if the *'blasphemy'* trial of James—as reported by Josephus in *Ant.* 20.200–202—had to do with his entering the Holy of Holies and pronouncing the forbidden Name of God, then this too occurred on *Yom Kippur* (*Yom ha-Kippurim—the Day of the Atonements* in the Habakkuk *Pesher*) and its aftermath.

[12] Lam *R.* 1.16.47. Though she is called here *'Miriam the daughter of Boethus'*, this must be *'Martha the daughter of Boethus'*, as we have seen, since the matter again clearly involves awaiting the decision of *'the levir'* in order to marry Josephus' close friend Jesus ben Gamala (later killed by 'the Zealots' and 'Idumaeans'). Here the mix-ups in Rabbinic literature between *'Miriam'* and *'Martha'* become patent.

[13] In this same section, for instance, Lam *R.* 1.16.50 quotes Zechariah 14:4 about how God Himself, whose *'Feet will stand on that Day upon the Mount of Olives'*, will take the field against all the Nations (this exactly parallels the War Scroll at Qumran) after already having recounted how R. Eleazar b. Zadok applied the passage from Deuteronomy 28:56–7 concerning *'the tender and delicate woman… who would not set the sole of her feet upon the ground'* (Lam *R.* 1.16.47). In the second tradition attributed to R. Eleazar b. Zadok (also quoted in *Ket.* 67a below), where he rather quotes Song of Songs 1.8 and sees her *'picking barley corns at Acco'*—there *'the feet'* are *'horses' hoofs'* or *'feet'*! For *Git* 56a, in a particularly graphic episode which we shall also have occasion to note further below, *'Martha the daughter of Boethus'*—this time the designation is correct—dies during the siege of Jerusalem because she wanted *'some fine flour'* and, when her servant could find none, she *'took off her shoes'* and went out on the street herself whereupon *'some dung ('dung'* will be an ongoing theme) *stuck to her foot and she died'* (*sic*)! Here the passage from Deuteronomy 28:56–7 is rather applied by R. Yohanan. For *Ket.* 66b–67a, as we have and shall see, it is Nakdimon b. Gurion, *'for whose feet woolen clothes were spread, when he walked from his home to the House of Study which the Poor, who followed behind him, then rolled up.'* This will not be to mention all these *'hair-wiping'* and *'foot-kissing'* episodes in both Gospels and Talmudic Literature, already alluded to above and which we shall have occasion to analyse further below. Of course, for Luke 16:21's *'Poor Lazarus under the table'*, the proverbial *'dogs'* don't *'come and lick his'* feet, but only rather *'his sores'* (sic)!

[14] *Ket.* 67a above. This theme of *'the Poor'* will appear over and over again.

[15] Matthew 19:24/Mark 10:25. Of course, the words *'Glory'* and *'Glorified'* appear throughout the Gospels, but the main *'glorying'* and *'glorifying'* appear in Paul—1 Corinthians 1:31, 5:6, 6:20, 9:15, 10:17; 2 Corinthians 3:7–11, 4:4, 7:4, 9:13, 12:11; Romans 1:17, 8:21, Galatians 1:24, etc. By the same token, see 1QpHab x.10–2 on *'the worthless city built upon blood and the Assembly'* or *'Church erected by the Spouter of Lying upon Lying, tiring out (the) Many with a worthless service for the sake of his Glory.'* One should also note that in *Ta'an* 20a, when Nakdimon allegedly enters the Temple, wraps himself in his cloak, and makes rain; he does so *'not for his own Glory, nor the Glory of his father's house—but for (God's) Glory'*!

16 As an example of this kind of thing, one should see the way the 'Man-God' or 'God Dionysus' is treated or demands to be treated in Euripides' *Bacchae*—but this is only one example among many.

17 See *War* 2.122–23, but also see CDxiii.11–13 on the duties of 'the Mebakker' or 'Overseer' on the matter of property.

18 There are so many 'Ananias'es in Josephus that it is difficult to count them all. Of particular interest is the '*Jesus son of Ananias*,' we cited at the beginning of this book. Also interesting is the '*Ananias*'—instrumental in the conversion of Queen Helen's household and her favorite son Izates—who in Eusebius is the courier between Jesus and the King in Northern Syria. Where '*Sapphira*' is concerned, there are two characters that come to mind—the first is '*Jesus son of Sapphias*,' the Leader of the Galilean boatmen and the Party of the Poor on the Sea of Galilee. They poured out their blood until the whole sea ran red.' The second is '*Judas Sepphoraeus*,' who seems to have been the prototype for '*Judas the Galilean*' and started the disturbances in Galilee at the end of Herod's life. The reason I call attention to these parallels is because, obviously, none of these things really actually ever happened, anymore than did the '*foot-cleaning*'/'*hair-wiping*' or '*sore-licking*' episodes, I have already cited above and will cite further below—to say nothing of '*spitting*' in someone's eyes or ears or recommending '*eating with unwashed hands*' or '*declaring all foods clean*'—all the product of Hellenistic '*Mystery Cult*' Religion and popular literature of the time or superstition.

19 *Epistle of Peter to James* 5.1.

20 *Ibid.*, 4.1. For '*the Fountain of Living Waters*' at Qumran and, in particular, related to '*the New Covenant in the Land of Damascus*,' see CDiii.16–17 and viii.22–23 and Chapters 21–22 below. For '*baptism*' or '*immersion*,' see 1QSiii.4–9 and iv.20–23, etc.

21 *Ibid.*, 4.2.

22 For this kind of language at Qumran, see 1QSix.3–6, CDvii.4–6, xv.19–20, 1QMvii.5–7, xii.1–10, etc. Of course, the language of '*keeping the Covenant*' at Qumran is intrinsic and occurs throughout but, in particular, it is the definition of '*the Sons of Zadok*' in 1QSv.2–5 and 8–14 and CDiii.2–20, viii.1–2 (on '*breaking the Covenant*'), xx.17–18, etc.

23 In particular, see Paul in Galatians 1:20, 2 Corinthians 11:31, and. if one wishes from the Pastorals, 1 Timothy 2:7, 4:2, etc.

24 *Epistle of Peter to James* 4.5

25 Matthew 26:21–25/Mark 14:18–21.

26 The '*delivering up*' in Hebrew, as we have over and over again emphasized in our works, is an important usage and concept at Qumran, but there it generally means '*being delivered up to the sword*' or '*Divine Vengeance*' as a result of Communal or Historical infractions based on '*backsliding from*' and/or not observing '*the Law*' ('*the Mosaic Law*') in as clear-cut and '*Faithful*' manner as necessary, not '*delivering up*' or '*betraying*' (as the case may be) the Messiah 'Jesus'—cf. CDi.4–6, i.17–18, vii.13, etc.

[27] Perhaps the best discussion of this kind of censorship is to be found in Robert Eisler's *The Messiah Jesus and John the Baptist*, pp. 49–112, London/New York, 1931 with numerous examples and illustrations with particular reference to *'the Testimonium Flavianum.'*

[28] CDv.6–18. This is a key passage for it explains how the Establishment *'pollutes the Temple,'* i.e., because *'they do not separate according to the Torah'* (i.e., between *'clean'* and *'unclean,' 'Holy and profane'*) and *'they lie with a woman during the blood of her period and each man takes (to wife) the daughter of his brother and the daughter of his sister.'* Of course, this can be no other Establishment than *'the Herodian'* as I have explained in the Appendix to *JJHP*, pp. 85–94. Other evidences of this concern over *'blood'* (as in James' directives to Overseas Communities in Acts 15:21–9 in CDiii.6–6: *'they ate blood and their males were cut off in the wilderness,'* ascribing the length of the *'wilderness sojourn'* after the Exodus to this, and 1QpHabx.5–12, attacking *'the Spouter of Lying for leading Many astray'* (Paul?) and *'building a Worthless City upon Blood and erecting an Assembly ('Church') upon Lying for the sake of his Glory, tiring out Many with a Worthless Service and instructing them in works of Lying so that their* [c]*Amal (really 'Activity', 'Effort', or 'Suffering Service'*—not *'Works') would count for nothing.'*

[29] See Matthew 14:13–21, 15:28–16:12, Mark 6.32–44, 8:14–21, etc. and Chapters 10, 11, and 14 below.

[30] As should be clear, as in the Biblical Naomi and Ruth episode, *'the Levir'* must give his permission for the new marriage—an idea which seems to have percolated into the John the Baptist episodes in the Synoptics (though it is nowhere stated in so many words however this seems to be the popular view—only that John *'objected'* on the basis that she had been his *'brother's wife')* where John is presented in the Synoptics as raising the issue in the remarriage of Herodias to a second of her uncles (i.e., both the *'divorce'* and *'forbidden marriage with a niece'* issues outlined in the Damascus Document above) even though levirite marriage would appear to have nothing to do with the situation (Matthew 14:3–5/Mark 6:17–18/Luke 3:18)—see, for instance, *Ket* 65a which specifically says that *'the Rabbis granted the daughter-in-law of Nakdimon ben Gurion a weekly allowance of two se'ahs of wine for her spice puddings'* because *'she was a woman awaiting the decision of the levir.'* In ARN 6.3 (21a), now it is *'the daughter of Nakdimon ben Gurion'* and *'she needs a Tyrian Gold Dinar every Sabbath (i.e., 'weekly') just for her spice puddings'* (thus)! Moreover the comment is added: *'she was then a childless widow awaiting the decision of her brother-in-law* (the *levir*). But in Lam. *R.* 1.16.47–8 above, this is *'Miriam the daughter of Boethus'* (sic), as we have seen and now the allowance is rather *'two se'ahs of wine daily'* (not *'weekly'*), because her husband Josephus' friend Jesus b. Gamala had died! This moves right into the story about *'Miriam the daughter of Nakdimon'* and her *'allowance of five hundred golden dinars daily just for her perfume basket'* (retold in *Ket* 66b above). That it is clearly *'Martha'* that is so intended in terms of the permission of *'the Levir'*—if not the widow's allowance—is made clear in *Yeb* 61a and *Yom* 18a, where the story of how she bribed the Rabbis to allow how to marry Jesus b. Gamala is told.

[31] *ARN* 6.3 (21a).

[32] *Ket* 66b and Lam. *R.* 1.16.48 above. In *Ketuboth* it is *'four hundred gold dinars daily',* while in Lamentations *Rabbah,* it is *'five hundred.'*

³³ *Git.* 56a,

³⁴ The plaque in this tomb is nicely described in N. Avigad's article in *Jerusalem Revealed*, ed. Y. Yadin, Jerusalem, 1975, p 18. There, the names on it make it clear that this is the family of 'the Boethusians' from Egypt who, in fact, were making '*Bnei Hezir*' Priestly claims (cf. Nehemiah 10:20)—therefore the name accorded this Tomb. Herod imported this clan, which was therefore absolutely beholden to him and the Establishment he created, from Egypt at the end of the previous Century after executing his Maccabean wife, the first '*Mariamme*'/ '*Miriam*'/or '*Mary*' (See *Ant.* 15.320–2), and marrying the second—the '*Boethus' daughter*' of an earlier generation—again named '*Mariamme*' or '*Mary*'. Perhaps it is from this that the mix-up between the two names '*Miriam*' and '*Martha*' starts—not to become too obsessed with it, though John's Gospel clearly is and Luke, to some extent, as well. The other two Gospels, clearly, don't even seem to know these two persons even exist. The traditions regarding the '*casting down*' of James or the '*fall*', he is pictured as having taken took from '*the Pinnacle of the Temple*' or '*the Temple steps*' *can* be found, as we have seen, in Eusebius' *E.H.* 2.1.4, 2.23.18, Jerome's *Vir. ill.* 2, Epiphanius' *Haeres.* 78.14.5–6, and Ps. *Rec.* 1.70.

³⁵ See *James*, p.p. 455–6.

³⁶ See earlier in Chapter 1 and n. 30 above. The relevant Synoptic passages are: Matthew 14:3–5/Mark 6:17–18. One should also remark that this is the first '*Joseph and Mary*' story. For Herod's execution of his sister's husband '*Joseph*'—seemingly for adultery with his Maccabean wife '*Mariamme*' (the real first '*Mary*')— and the tragic story ultimately of his execution of her as well, see *War* 1.441–3 and *Ant.* 15.64–95 and 202–39 (which for some reason tells the story somewhat less harshly).

³⁷ *Ant.* 18.136–7. This fact alone undermines the main points of this particular New Testament scenario as, not only secondary, but inaccurate as well—despite the attempts by manifold apologists to rescue it by claiming Herod had *two sons* named '*Philip*' (sic!) and the '*Herod*' who was Herodias' original husband was, in fact, also named '*Philip*'. Notwithstanding, the attempts, to which such persons are willing to go to impart Historicity to such clearly-damaged narratives, strain credulity.

³⁸ Of course, it is patently absurd to think that anyone connected to this '*Herod*' could have been a members of Paul's incipient '*Antioch Community*'—or is it? See earlier above Chapter 1 and *James*, pp. 98–99, 560–63, and 874 for '*Manaen*''s probable mix-up with Paul's associate '*Ananias*.'

³⁹ For these matters, see CDiv.20–v.11, but also the proscriptions in the Temple Scroll, lvii.15–20 on the '*King*' having one and only one wife, not divorcing her, and not taking a wife from among the Gentiles, and lxvi.15–7 for the general ban on '*niece marriage*' which the Herodians practised so promiscuously—but, even more germane than any of this, the very words attributed to John the Baptist in Matthew and Mark: '*It is forbidden to take to wife the wife of one's brother and uncover the nakedness of one's brother, the son of his father or the son of his mother. It is unclean.*'

⁴⁰ This is to be found in *ARN* 6.3 (21a) —but also see *Lam R.* 1.16.47–8 above.

[41] The '*Tyre and Sidon*' references are, of course, to be found in Matthew 15:21/Mark 7:24 and 31—in the latter both introducing and following the curing of the Canaanite/Greek Syrophoenecian woman's daughter episode. This, too, is not so surprising as in all contexts—Gospel, Rabbinic, Early Church—the subject is a woman of one kind or another, usually extravagant, but also suffering from '*uncleanness*' or an '*unclean spirit*.' In Luke 6:17, it is displaced and comes just following the call of the Apostles and just before the first highly-circumscribed version of Matthew's '*Sermon on the Mount*' but, interestingly enough, still in the context of '*healing those with unclean spirits*' (thus!). The other '*Tyre and Sidon*' references are those in Matthew 11:21–2 and *pars.*, condemning Israel and claiming that if '*mighty works*' of this kind had been done there, their inhabitants would long ago have believed'! But, of course, an obvious truism, since these were not the kinds of '*mighty works*' the inhabitants of Judea and Jews in the surrounding Areas were expecting. The '*mighty works*' they were expecting are better described in the War Scroll from Qumran!

[42] For the '*Tyre*' reference in the Simon *Magus* stories, see above and especially n. 28, the first of which would appear to be Irenaeus, *Ad. Haer.* 1.23.2—but also a host of others, including Hippolytus 6.15.

[43] This in the Judas *Iscariot* '*betrayal*' or '*delivering up*' scene in Matthew 27:3–9.

[44] This is *Ket* 65a but in *Lam R.* 1.16.47, where '*carpets were laid from the door of her house to the entrance of the Temple so her feet should not be exposed*' so she could '*see her husband Jesus b. Gamala reading on the Day of Atonement*'; it should be recalled that this was '*Miriam (Martha) the daughter of Boethus*.'

[45] This is a position we have reiterated in all our works from *MZCQ* to *JJHP* to *James the Brother of Jesus*. For the clear allusion to '*taking Vengeance*' for what had been done to '*the Priest*' (meaning '*the High Priest*')/'*the Righteous Teacher*,' see 1QpPs 37ii.20 and iv.9–10. The '*paying him his reward*' language repeats in 1QpHabxii.2–3—to say nothing of the picture of James' death in Early Church Literature and the quotation there of Isaiah 3:10–21. But here it is for the destruction with which '*he rewarded the Poor*'—the name of course of James' Congregation and '*the Congregation*'/'*Church*'—to which almost the whole of the *Pesher* on Psalm 37 is directed. For further analysis, see Chapters 24 and 25 below. For the horrifying circumstances of the deaths of Jesus b. Gamala and Ananus at the hands of '*the Violent Ones of the Gentiles*,' i.e., Josephus' '*Idumaeans*,' see *War* 4.315–25.

[46] *Ket.* 65a and *Lam R.* 1.16.48 above. The point is that in the former case, the Rabbis are talking about her '*two se'ahs of wine daily*' and '*her sweetmeats*' or '*spice puddings*'; in the latter, her '*five hundred gold dinars daily to be spent on her perfume box*.'

[47] *Lam R.* 1.16.47.

[48] *Git* 56a. The picture of R. Zadok here is excruciating. *Git* 56b explains how he was restored. No Asclepius-type miraculous cures or the like here—the opposite.

[49] *Lam R.* 1.16.48. These '*barley corns*' or '*grain*' themes will also reappear in both *ARN* 6.3 (20b–21a) and *Git* 56a's '*Rich Men feeding Jerusalem*' traditions. Of course, we also have similar references in the '*Jesus*' feeding '*the Multitudes*' materials in Matthew 14–6 and Mark 6–8.

⁵⁰ *Ket* 67a and cf. *Lam R.* 1.16.48 above.

⁵¹ *Ket* 66b.

⁵² *ARN* 6.3 (21a). Here again, one should note both the *'grain'* and *'dung'* motifs so typical of these Rabbinic accounts. Of course, where the motif of *'loaves'* in the Gospels is concerned, one has only to note the *'feeding'* episodes in Matthew 14–6/Mark 6–8—as well as Luke 9:13–6 and John 6:9–26.

⁵³ *Ibid*. For the burning of the stores episode in Josephus, see *War* 5.24–6 and cf. Tacitus, *Histories* 5.12. For the Talmudic description of such *'Mourners for Zion. who vow not to eat or drink until they have seen the Temple rebuilt,'* see *B.B.* 60b. Also see Benjamin of Tudela, *Travels* Year 1165 where, somewhere in the North Yemen area of Arabia, he claims to have seen thousands of Jewish *'Rechabites'* (as he calls them), *'living in caves and continually fasting'*—being *'Mourners for Zion'* and *'Jerusalem'*. But even earlier in these notices in *ARN* 4.5 (20a) about R. Yohanan and Vespasian, Yohanan seems to start the tradition of *'Mourning for Zion'*—viz., *'When R. Yohanan ben Zacchai heard that Jerusalem was destroyed and the Temple in flames, he tore his clothing and his Disciples tore their clothes* (note again, R. Yohanan has *'Disciples'* just like *'Jesus'* has) *and they wept, crying aloud and mourning'*. For Talmudic discouragement of such behavior—which was seen as a form of *'Naziritism'* (i.e., *'Rechabitism'*)—see *Ta'an* 11a, *Naz* 19a, and *Ned* 10a and 77b. Further to this tradition about the bravery of Jerusalem's defenders and the extremity of their hunger, *ARN* 6.3 (21a) also provides a tradition about how those stationed on the walls would promise—if given five dates—to behead five of Vespasian's men. When given them, they would go down and capture five heads of the men from Vespasian's army.

⁵⁴ *Ket* 66b–67a. It is important to note these references to *'the Poor,'* which will not only resonate with both the Dead Sea Scrolls and the members of James 'Community—called *'the Poor'*—but also the complaint of *'Judas of Simon Iscariot'* (i.e., *'Simon the Zealot'*—cf. the Apostle lists in Luke 6:15 and Acts 1:13) —as we shall enumerate it below—in John 12:3–6 when he sees Martha's sister Mary *'taking a litra of pure spikenard ointment of great value'* and *'anointing Jesus' feet and wiping his feet with her hair'* (thus!).

⁵⁵ *Ket* 104a

⁵⁶ See n. 45 above and *War* 4.315–25.

⁵⁷ See the Picture Plates nos. 102–3 and *War* 4.1–83. For Judas' *'Gaulonite'* origins, despite his *'Galilean'* cognomen—and specifically Gamala on the Gaulon—see *Ant.* 18.4.

⁵⁸ *ARN* 6.1(20b). It should not go unremarked that this is followed by reference to the same *'little children'*, we shall so often encounter with regard to *'Jesus'* person and activities, viz.: *'and if they plead, "Because of our little children," it should be replied, "Did not R. Akiba have many sons and daughters...?"'* Interesting, too, this is followed by the statement that *'he* (R. Akiba) *was forty years old when he began to study Torah and, by the end of thirteen years, he taught Torah in public'*. The time frame in this second clause is not unlike Luke 2:46's picture of *'Jesus'* teaching the elders in the Temple at the age of *'twelve'* (we all know that in *Vita* 9, Josephus claims that he was only *'fourteen'* when those learned in the Law came to consult him about points of *Torah*—

thus!). Furthermore, preceding this in *ARN*, R. Akiba's training at the feet of R. Eliezer b. Hyrcanus and R. Joshua (probably at Lydda—a tradition attributed to R. Simeon b. Eleazar) is compared to *'a stone mason's uprooting a mountain in order to cast it into the Jordan by chipping away at it to bring it down to size.'* This is followed by how, because of this, R. Akiba was able *'to bring the hidden things to light'*—all usages with particular import when it comes to looking at parallels regarding 'Jesus' in Mark 6–8, Matthew 14–6, etc. to R. Akiba, et. al.

[59] It is perhaps germane to point out that, where such *'plots'* or *'plotting'* is concerned, it is perhaps Paul's biography more than any other that reflects this (cf. Acts 23:12ff. on how *'the Jews made a plot, putting themselves under a curse, saying that they would neither eat or drink until they had killed Paul'*—here, of course, not only the language of *'plotting,'* but also the 'Nazirite' language of *'putting themselves under an oath'* and the all-important allusion to *'not eating or drinking'* regarding such 'Terrorist' Nazirite behavior)—not to mention the *'plotting'* that had to have occurred between Agrippa II and the High Priest Ananus to destroy James. Where this latter is concerned, one should note the language, we shall explore further below, of *'zamam'/'zammu'* in 1QpHabxii.6 relating to the *'judicial conspiracy'* or *'plot to destroy'* the Righteous Teacher and his followers among 'the Poor' (also known as 'the Simple of Judah doing Torah') and its reflection in 1QHiv.7ff. referring to 'the Sons of Belial' (probably 'the Herodians') and their *'nets.'*

[60] We have emphasized this *'do'* or *'doing,'* meaning 'works of the Torah,' at both Qumran and in the Letter of James in all our work—see, for instance, in *James*, pp. 277–8, 302–8, 854–6, etc. and Chapters 26-27 later in the book below. One should not ignore the fact that the allusion to *'why are you troubling this woman'/'leave her alone. Why are you troubling her'* in Matthew 26:13 and Mark 14:6 is a direct reflection—nay, even a borrowing—from Paul's position on *'circumcision'* in Galatians 5:6–14 (ending with the facetious evocation of James' *'Love Commandment'* no less!): *'You were running well* (cf. the material on *'running'* too in the Habakkuk *Pesher*)... but *(ominously) he who is troubling you shall bear the Judgement'* (though slightly different vocabulary—cf. too Galatians 1:7, 5:12, and 6:17) —notwithstanding that in Matthew and Mark we are simply dealing with something so trifling as anointing his head *'with an alabaster cask'* or *'flask of very precious spikenard ointment'* and not *'circumcision or uncircumcision'* as in Paul. But this is the way of the Gospel artificers!

[61] This *'Memorial'* or *'Remembrance'* is, of course, directly referred to at the end of the Damascus Document (xx.18–20), where *'God-fearing'* or *'God-Fearers'* are twice specifically evoked but now, not in the context of antagonism to the Law, but in that of direct tutelage to observe it—see too Chapters 22 and 28 at the end of this book below. In this context, too, one should not forget to remark the allusion in Ps. Rec. 1.71 in the context of the miraculous *'whitening'* of the tombs of two of the brothers, demonstrating *'that our brethren were held in Remembrance before God.'*

[62] CDi.1 and ii.1.

[63] Here the *'touching,'* Elchasaite *'Great Power,'* and Asclepius-like *'healing'* language is, as usual, remarkable; but, also, should one choose to regard it—though once again expressed in slightly different vocabulary in the Greek—the *'troubling'* language of Paul in Galatians 1:7, 5.10, 5:12,

and 6:17 above. Of course, if this does have any relevance, then it truly comes in an extremely comical yet telling context, i.e., that of the *'healing of unclean spirits'* once again. Here, it is the *'clean'* vs. the *'unclean'* aspect of the language which is determinant.

[64] Where this imagery of *'house'* is concerned, one should note—again, should one choose to regard it—the *'House'* imagery in the Damascus Document (iii.19–20: *'and He built a House of Faith for them in Israel which has never stood from ancient times until now'* and the all-important xx.10–3: *'the House of the Torah'*—repeated two times—as opposed to *'the House of Peleg'/'the House of Separation'*, xx.22) —not to mention Paul's equally important *'house'* imagery in 1 Corinthians 3:9–17.

[65] Matthew 15:22/Mark 7:26. When considering this *'Greek Syrophoenician'/'Canaanite woman'* on the *'Borders'/'Coasts of Tyre and Sidon,'* one should not forget the whole tradition of Simon Magus taking his *'mistress'/'Queen'* out of a brothel there; and, where *'the dogs'* or *'little dogs'* are concerned, the connections with Queen Helen's *'Zealotism'* (that is, *'kuon'/'kunarion'* with *'Cananean'/'Kanna^cim'*). Any who would claim the Gospels are unaware of Queen Helen of Adiabene should have regard for Luke 7:11–6's account of *'Jesus'* with a *'touch'* resurrecting (note the usual *'coming,' 'standing,'* and *'touching'* language here) the *'only-begotten son of the widow of Nain'* (of course, not only is Izates called Helen's *'only-begotten'* in Josephus, but the non-existent *'Nain'* is easily recognized as but a contraction of *'Adiabene'*)! This episode also, not only ends with the crowd as usual *'glorifying God',* but crying out *'God has visited His People'*! This is the same *'Visitation'* language that permeates the Damascus Document below.

[66] See *Ant.* 18.4–10, 18.23–25, and *War* 2.18. For the rise of *'the Sicarii'* derivative from them and their mass suicide at Masada, see *War* 2.254–57, 7.253–62, and *Ant.* 20.186.

[67] We consider the so-called *'Zealot'/'Sicarii'* (*'Christian'?*) and *'Messianic'* Movements to be identical or synonymous because of the notice at the end of Josephus' *Jewish War* explaining the fall of the Temple in terms of various signs and prophecies, in which he admits that *'the thing which most inspired the Jews to go to war* (with Rome) was an ambigiuous prophecy from among their sacred writings (he calls it *'ambiguous'* because *'some applied it to one of their own'* but others, like himself and R. Yohanan b. Zacchai, obsequiously applied it to the rise of Vespasian!) *that one from their own Country would arise to rule the whole habitable Earth'* (*War* 6.312–3 above)—see *James*, pp. 171–2, 251–4, 417–9, 678–84, and variously below.

[68] See, in particular, the many scenes of this kind in Euripides' *Bacchae,'* p. 252 and n. 73 below and the kind of respect the Man-God Dionysus is demanding, even in disguise, from the people of Thebes and the vengeance his followers enact when he does not receive it. For another good example of this kind, see the scene on the huge relief from the Temple of Hathor at Dendera in Egypt, where the famous Cleopatra and her son by Caesarion by Caesar are depicted, showing just this kind of awe and respect before personalized depictions of the Gods Isis and Horis (and possibly even a miniature of Osiris). There are many depictions of this kind in Egyptian Tomb paintings and wall reliefs as there are in many of the seats of Hellenistic Mystery Religions generally.

[69] *War* 2.427.

[70] For additional *'House'* imagery in the Scrolls this time *'the House of the Torah'*—see above, n. 64 and CDxx.10–3.

[71] This is how Origen—who himself seems to have mutilated himself as a *'Sicarius'* (see Jerome, Letter 84 to Pammachius and Oceanus below, mocking Origen's attempt to make himself *'a eunuch for the Kingdom of Heaven'*)—uses the term in *Contra Celsus* 2.13.

[72] According to Dio Cassius 68.3–4, the ban on circumcision seems to have come into effect under Nerva (96–8 CE). This would make sense as it occurs directly after the troubles with this continuing Revolutionary *'Sicarii'* agitation. Origen (*Contra Celsus* 2.13 above) says that the judges in his own time were particularly harsh in applying it and few *Sicarii* in his own time escaped the death penalty. This *'Law,'* which was attributed to Publius Cornelius Scipio (therefore its name and perhaps, in a kind of satirical reflection, that of the Roman Centurion *'Cornelius,'* the *'Pious'* and *'God-Fearing Soldier'* in Acts 10:1–11:18 who learns to call *'no man profane and no food unclean'* and, about whom, *'Peter'* has to argue with *'those of the Circumcision'*), was a traditional body of Legislation forbidding deliberate mutilation of the flesh—particularly *'castration,'* of which *'circumcision'* was considered an especially onerous example especially after the War against Rome in 66–73 CE and the Second War in 136–38 CE. For our view of it, see *James*, pp. 183–84 and 814–16 and the last sections of Chapter 28 below.

[73] Not only does the Man-God Dionysus hold the citizens of Thebes in some contempt for the way he is treated in *The Bacchae*, but he also requires and receives a degree of punishment by his *'Bacchae'* (therefore its name) of its ruler Pentheus. In Apuleius' *Golden Ass*, one will also encounter similar if more satirical presentations of man-gods or gods and goddesses—the most impressive of which occurs at the beginning of the last chapter (Chapter Nineteen) when he *'falls at the feet of'* the *'Many-Named Goddess'* (in this case, *'Isis'*). Not only does he *'bathe them with (his) tears,'* but he *'prays to her with a voice choked with emotion,'* Earlier there are scenes with Osiris and almost every known god or goddess of the ancient world, one of the most striking of which is to be found in Chapter Eight when Psyche *'falls on her knees'* before a representation of Juno—*'the great Jupiter's sister and wife'*—and, *'wiping away her tears, embraces her, pleading to her.'* Even Josephus in *Ant.* 18.65–80, directly following the disputed testimony about *'Jesus'* being *'the Christ'* (see *James*, pp. 65–7) adds an odd scene about one *'Paulina'*—a devotee of the Goddess Isis—who is willing to totally submit to a man impersonating the Egyptian God Anubis to the extent of being willing to share his bed. Though many dispute this section—since even Tacitus in *Annals* 2.85 implies an earlier date 19 CE for these things— the reference in the account of *'Ida'* (a variation on *'Ioudas'*?) as the one responsible and the razing of the Temple of Isis (*'Isidos'*—thus!) and the *'casting'* (*balein*) of her statue into the river—not to mention the expulsion of the Jews (*Ioudaious*) from Rome which follows—are nothing if not noteworthy.

[74] See *Ket* 66b and 104a above. This theme of *'self-Glorification'* is not far removed from the picture in Matthew 26:11/Mark 14:7/John 12:8 of *'Jesus'* allowing the woman from *'Bethany'* (*'Mary, Lazarus' sister'* in John—*'at Simon the Leper's house'* in the two Synoptics) to anoint his head and wipe his feet. Where Luke is concerned, not only does this seemingly purposefully obscure parable in the run-up to its thematically-parallel *'crumbs falling from the Rich Man's table'* episode

include—when characterizing the illusory nature of '*the Riches the Unrighteous*'—the same genre of personage again referred to in 16:5–8 by the '*Master*'/'*Lord*' denotations ('*Kurios*'/'*Kurion*'). Not only this, but from the outset in 16:1, it raises the same tell-tale concern over '*wastefulness*' of the Rabbinic '*Nakdimon*'/'*Miriam*' traditions and these complaints by Jesus '*Disciples*' or '*Judas of Simon Iscariot*' in the other three Gospels. Furthermore, Luke 16:8 even incorporates the important Qumranism, '*the Sons of Light*' to say nothing of '*digging*' in 16:3 and '*scoffing*' in 16:14, we shall see to be so pivotal to crucial contexts of the Qumran Documents in Chapter 10 and variously below.

[75] Mark 10:25/Luke18.25. Aside from these traditions in *Ketuboth*, it should perhaps be observed in passing that *ARN* 8.8 (21b) conserves a curious tradition that quotes Genesis 24:31 on how '*Laban made room for*' or '*fed (Abraham's) camels*'—the former being interpreted in the first in terms of clearing out his house of idols!—to show that '*the Righteous of old were Pious, but so were their beasts.*' Even this tradition, in addition to '*abjuring idolatry,*' contains the usual motifs of '*the Piety of the Righteous,*' '*their beasts,*' '*not eating and drinking,*' and '*straw, barley, and water.*' Moreover, if one consults the original passage, one finds—for whatever it's worth—that the next line, Genesis 24:32, contains an allusion to '*washing their feet*'!

[76] For instance, '*two by two they went into the ark*' in Matthew 19:4/Mark 10:6 is the basis of the ban on polygamy in CDv.1ff. and '*not putting away one's wife and marrying another*' in Matthew 19:9/Mark 10:11 is basically reiterated in 11QTxlvii.17–20. On the other hand, in both Qumran contexts, the bans are part of '*the Royal*' or '*King Law.*'

[77] The '*Perfection*' doctrine is, of course, widespread at Qumran—'*the Perfect of the Way*' being , seemingly, another name for the Community and '*Perfecting the Way*' being perhaps its principal objective (that is, to seek '*Perfect Holiness*'—cf. Paul in 2 Corinthians 7:1)—see 1QSviii.9–11 introducing the exposition of Isaiah 40:3's '*Prepare in the wilderness the Way of the Lord,*' viii.18–20, viii.25, and ix.8–9 following it; CDi.20–21 and xx.1–8, etc.

[78] Note too how Paul also quotes this Commandment in Galatians 5:19 against his opponents who are '*troubling*' his Communities with '*circumcision*' and cf. CDvi.14–21: '*to do according to the precise letter of the Torah..., to separate from the Sons of the Pit, to keep away (lehinnazer, i.e., to be a 'Nazirite') from polluted Evil Riches..., to separate between polluted and pure, and to distinguish between Holy and profane...according to the Commandment of those entering the New Covenant in the Land of Damascus—to set up the Holy Things according to their precise specifications* (this, as opposed to what '*Peter*' is pictured as learning, however dissimulatingly, in Acts 10:15 above), '*to love each man his brother as himself*'—so once again here it is, James 2:8's '*Royal Law according to the Scripture*'!

[79] See *War* 2.118 and *Ant.* 18.4–10 above and note that for Judas, '*to pay a tax to the Romans and to submit to mortal men, as if to their Lords*' (i.e., '*not to call any man Lord*'), was anathema and the basis of the Revolt.

[80] *War* 2.139–40. As Josephus expresses this: '*Before touching the pure food, one is obliged to swear tremendous oaths that he will practice Piety towards God* (the first '*Love Commandment*') *and exercise Righteousness towards his fellow man*' (the second).

81 To understand this and bring it full circle, one should consult *Ant.* 18.117–18's description of John the Baptist as *'commanding the Jews to exercise virtue both as regards Righteousness towards one another and Piety toward God,'* i.e., the *'Righteousness/Piety Dichotomy.'* I have also discussed this in *James*, pp. 236–8, 853–5, and variously.

82 Matthew 5:48 and see above n. 77.

83 *ARN* 2.5 (18b). The rationale given here for Noah is Genesis 6:9: *'And Noah was a man, Righteous and Perfect in his Generation'*—for Adam, as in *'male and female He created them'* above, Genesis 1:28: *'And God created man in His own image.'*

84 For James, see Eusebius, *EH* 2.23.5, Jerome, *Vir. ill.* 2, and Epiphanius, *Haeres.* 78.7.7 above. For this passage in Hymns, see vii.17–9: *'You created the Zaddik and from the womb prepared him to stand according to Your will, to keep Your Commandments, and walk in all (Your Pathways)'* and xvii.30–6: *'You have known me since (the time of) my father and chosen me from the womb... My father did not know me and my mother abandoned me to You. You are a father to all the Sons of Your Truth'!*

85 For the *'Judgements'* made by the *Mebakker* at Qumran, see CDxiii.5–19, xiv.8–19, xv.8–17.

86 See Origen, *Contra Celsus* 2.13 above. As 'Jesus' is presented as putting this in Matthew 19:12: *'There are eunuchs from the mother's womb* (it is this which parallels the *ARN*'s list of Patriarchs who *'were born circumcised'*),*...eunuchs who were made eunuchs by men* (this is something like the parody of Queen Helen's Treasury Agents in Acts 8:27 above), *and eunuchs who have made themselves eunuchs for the sake of the Kingdom of Heaven.'* It is this last, which is not paralleled in the other Gospels, that seems to have played a part in Origen's reported castration. But the material prefacing this on *'divorce'* in 19:3–9, which does have a parallel in Mark 10:2–12, to wit, *'Moses allowed you to put away your wives because of the hardness of your hearts'* and *'whosoever shall put away his wife and marries another, commits adultery against her',* has a negative parallel of sorts from the life of R. Akiba, above too, in seemingly explaining why R. Akiba took a second wife (if he did) and particularly the wife of Tinius Rufus, if he did (nuch of this has the sound legend as we already suggested). *M. Git.* 9.10 (90a) pretends to quote R. Akiba on 'divorce' (after 'Beit-Shammai,' which almost exactly replicates 'Jesus' here, and 'Beit-Hillel') to the effect that 'a man may divorce his wife even *if he finds another more attractiver than she.'* Though having the sound of authenticity, the provenance and context of this saying must be seriously questioned because even at Qumran, as we have explained above, 'divorce' was frowned upon—especially where 'the Ruler' was concerned.

87 Letter 84 to Pammachius and Oceanus aabove. Paul's attack here in Romans on those Jews who *'have zeal for God'* is very detailed and also reflects his more emotional one on the same group—the one which is disturbing his Communities with *'circumcision'* in Galatians 4:16–8—clearly *'the Party of the Circumcision'* or the *'some from James'* earlier, i.e., *'those who are zealous to exclude'* and, one might add, *'cut off.'* Not only does he make it clear too that, as at Qumran, the issue is *'Righteousness'* but, criticizing Moses' *'Righteousness of the Law'* (Romans 10:5) and speaking about those who *'set up their own Righteousness' 'being ignorant of God's Righteousness,'* he quotes similar passages as those in CDvii–viii and xx from Deuteronomy

7:9 about *'living for a thousand years'* and from Leviticus 18:5 *'that the man who practiced these things shall live by them.'*

88 Hippolytus 9.21.

89 See Dio Cassius 68.3–4 and n. 72 above. Here, not only does the *'eunuch'* parody the Roman view of *'circumcision'* and the fact that Helen's two sons insisted on *'circumcising themselves'*, despite her opposition; but also *'the Ethiopian Queen'* (who did not exist at this time and certainly did not send her *'Treasury Agent'* to Jerusalem) plays off *'the Queen of Adiabene'*, who did exist at the time and did send her *'Treasury Agents'* to Jerusalem. As a matter of fact, she sent them further afield to Egypt (therefore the picture in Acts 8:26–40 of Philip's encounter with the *'eunuch'* on the road to Gaza, when Philip was supposed actually to be on his way to Caesarea—sic!) and Cyprus to buy grain to relieve the Famine.

Chapter 10

1 *Ket.* 66b–67a. and cf. *EH* 4.22.6. In *EH* 4.22.1, he implies that this whole testimony is from Hegesippus' *Memoirs*. Since, according to this testimony, these sects boiled down to *'Essenes, Galileans, Daily Baptists, Masbuthaeans* (the same, seemingly, as *'Daily Baptists'*), *Samaritans, Sadducees, and Pharisees'*; it stands to reason, that the *'Galileans'* here—obviously named after *'Judas the Galilean'*—must be the same as what in other contexts would be called *'Zealots'* or *'Sicarii.'*

2 See, for instance, *War* 2.259, 2.264–5, and *Ant.* 20.168. For the *'Temple Wall Affair,'* which they seem also to have provoked, see 20.189–96. For their barring King Agrippa II and his sister— Titus' future mistress, the profligate Bernice—and his seeming consort (both appear in Acts too); see *War* 2.407.

3 In regard to this last, it should be observed that neither James nor the Essenes used *'oil'* or, as Josephus so delightfully puts it in *War* 2.123–4: *'oil they considered a defilement and...made a point of keeping the skin dry'* (i.e., not anointing the skin with oil); for James, see *EH* 2.23.5 and pars.: *'he did not anoint himself with oil and he did not use the bath',* i.e., obviously meaning Roman hot baths—for he certainty took Essene-style cold baths or immersed himself as otherwise he could not have gone up to the Temple Mount in the manner described. The issue of *'drinking no wine'* is self-evident and we have already covered it in *James* as we have many of these matters.

4 For Jesus' *'mother and his brothers'* in the Synoptics, see Matthew 12:47/Mark 33:1–4/Luke 8:19–21, but these derogatorily or belittlingly. The issue of *'Glory,'* we have already covered to some extent both in Rabbinic literature and at Qumran above and will do so further and in greater detail below; but for the matter of both Nakdimon's and Honi's *'Glory,'* see *ARN* 6.3 (21a) and *Taᶜan* 19b–20a and 23a above.

5 See *ARN* 6.3 (21a) and *Taᶜan* 19b–20a above. This *'doing'* ideology is so widespread at Qumran that it would be hard to catalogue all the instances of it, but see *MZCQ*, pp. 41–3. It is also strong in James 1:22–25, 2:8, 2:13, 4:17, etc., as we have seen.

[6] *ARN* 6.3 (21a). One should also note that in these matters relative to the Gospel of John, Nathanael (in our view, the stand-in for James) will be said to come from '*Cana of Galilee*' (21:2). Where the numerous repetitions of the verb '*fill*'/'*filling*', etc. are concerned, it should be appreciated that Nakdimon '*fills twelve wells*', whereas Jesus '*fills twelve baskets*' (John 6:13, Matthew 14:20, Mark 6:7–8:19).

[7] *James*, pp. 842–922.

[8] We have already treated these matters in *James*, pp. 770–83 but see the Papias Fragment 10 in *ANCL*, which states in no uncertain terms that '*Mary*', who was '*the wife of Cleophas or Alphaeus*', '*was the mother of James the Bishop and Apostle, Simon, Thaddaeus, and one Joseph*'!

[9] This, of course, agrees with Papias above, but now Simon and Judas—'*Thaddaeus*' in both the 'Apostle lists' of Mark and Matthew—are left out.

[10] There is constant slippage here where the names of 'Jesus'' mother and brothers go. To add to the confusion, in Matthew 27:56 she is also called '*the mother of the sons of Zebedee*'—unless this is yet another woman or another '*Mary*'. It is difficult to say.

[11] The interest centering about Mary Magdalene has grown exponentially over the last two decades. This began with the discovery at Nag Hammadi of the Gospel attributed to her but also with various cryptic references in other documents like the Apocalypses of James to characters seemingly spun off from her. This was fostered by the Feminist Movement, also gathering steam at that time and several gender-specific authors who seem to have made Mary their chief interest, and a vast popular literature, stemming from the Baigent-Leigh-Lincoln thriller, *Holy Blood, Holy Grail* and ending in *The Da Vinci Code*. It was followed up, more recently, by a parallel such intellectual gospel, The Gospel of Judas. As such, it has reached fantastic proportions and this based upon perhaps three references in the received Gospels.

[12] See b. *Git* 56a, where the amount is the *pro forma* '*twenty-one years*'; in *ARN*, 6.3 (21a), this amount changes to '*twenty-two*' and it is *Kalba Sabuᶜa*'s own stores alone that '*can supply enough food for every citizen of Jerusalem for twenty-two years*'; in Lam R. 1.5.31, this is '*ten*'—i.e., each of '*the four Councillors*' or '*Rich Men*' ('*Ben Zizzit, Ben Gorion, Ben Nakdimon, and Ben Kalba Shabua*'—thus!). For Josephus in *Ant.* 20 above, it is rather Queen Helen who is able to do this and in Rabbinic literature the '*twenty-one*', as we saw, is the time of her three successive Nazirite oath periods which the Rabbis imposed—seemingly as a penance—upon her for some reason.

[13] '*The Sons of Light*' language is a well-known designation in the Scrolls—particularly in 1QSi.9, ii.16, iii.24–25, xi.15, 1QMi.3, 7, 9, 11, CDxii.4–5, etc. The allusion to '*digging*'/'*Diggers*' ('*of the Well*') comes in CDvi.3–9. The '*scoffing*' language at Qumran is to be found in 1QHii.31 and iv.9–10: '*the Scoffers of Lying*' (*Malitzei-Chazav*), CDi.13–5: '*the Scoffer who pours over Israel the waters of Lying, causing them to wander astray in a trackless waste without a Way, bringing low the Everlasting Heights, ..removing the boundary markers*' (the Mosaic Law). Not uninterestingly, the '*nets*'/'*malitzim*' language is tied to the '*Lazon*'/'*Scoffing*' in that both are based on the same Hebrew root. Therefore, '*the Scoffer*' even '*sets up nets*'. This ties in with our Paul as '*Herodian*'

theorizing because it is these '*nets*' which '*ba-la-ᶜa*'/'*devour Israel.*' Interestingly, too, this is given as a plural (*Anshei ha-Chazav*) in CDxx.34, who '*spoke negatively about the Laws of Righteousness and rejected the New Covenant and the Compact which they set up in the Land of Damascus.*' These '*have put idols on their hearts and walked in stubbornness of their heart*' (cf. Paul in 1 Corinthians 8:4–7) and '*shall have no share in the House of the Torah.*' The Damascus Document could not be more explicit than this.

[14] Matthew 15:22/Mark 7:23.

[15] The '*Righteousness*' and '*Light*' language at Qumran is so widespread that we need not delineate it here. As for the language of '*Servant(s)*' or its correlatives, it is strong throughout Hymns. In 1QSi.3, '*the Prophets*' are called '*all His Servants*', as they are in 1QpHabii.8–9 and vii.5 (in interpretation of Habakkuk 2:2–4); and in CDxx.21, we actually have the language of '*Servants of God.*' But perhaps the best examples of these come in the climax of the Habakkuk *Pesher* in Columns xii.10–xiii.4, in which '*the Servants of idols*' and '*those who but serve stone and wood*' ('*the idols of the Nations*')—basically the contrapositive to Paul here—are being condemned: '*These will not save them on the Day of Judgement.*' One should also note the use of this '*Servant*' simile in 1QSix.22 in interpretation of Isaiah 40:3 and in anticipation of '*being a Man zealous for the Law whose Time is the Day of Vengeance.*'

[16] The '*cutting off*' is an important usage, too, at Qumran as we have seen. Perhaps the most relevant use of it is to be found in CDii.17–iii.1 where '*the Sons of Noah*' are '*cut off,*' because '*they walked in the stubbornness of their heart*' and '*did not keep the Commandments of God.*' In particular, the Sons of Israel '*were cut off in the wilderness,*' because '*they ate blood*'—important where James' rulings are concerned—and '*murmured in their tents*' (CDiii.6–9). Again, in the climax in CDxx.25–6, it is specifically averred that '*with the appearance of the Glory of God to Israel, all among the members of the Covenant who transgressed the boundary of the Torah shall be cut off from the midst of the camp.*' Again, one cannot get much more specific than this. Where Paul goes, he is basically using the allusion against his opponents within the Movement—doubtlessly the Jamesian '*Party of the Circumcision*'—whom he bitingly wishes '*would themselves cut off.*' His sarcasm and intense parody here should again be obvious—as should the double entendre involved.

[17] We have seen the references to '*not anointing themselves with oil*' in n. 3 above. For Peter as a '*Daily Bather,*' see Epiphanius, *Haeres.* 30.21.1, which is probably based on the numerous testimonies in this regard in the Pseudoclementine *Homilies*, we have already alluded to above as well.

[18] An amalgam of CDi.10–1 and ii.7–8—but for '*heart,*' also see ii.17–8, iii.5–12 ('*following the stubbornness of their own hearts*'), viii.19, xx.33 ('*the hearts*' of those '*listening to the voice of the Righteous Teacher,*' who '*did not desert the Laws of Righteousness…will be strengthened*' and '*they will be victorious over all the Sons of the Earth*'), 1QSii.12 (the '*idols upon the heart of*' the backslider), iii.3 ('*no Justification by that which one's stubborn heart permits*'—Paul again?), 1QpHabii.8, xi.13 ('*he did not circumcise the foreskin of his heart*'), etc.

[19] For this linkage, see CDiv.17–v.11 ('*two by two they went into the ark*').

[20] Cf. *Ned.* 50a. with John 11:2, 12:3, and Luke 7:38–44.

[21] See *ARN* 6.3 (21a) above, Lam R. 1.5.31, and Josephus, *War* 5.24–6 and cf. Tacitus, *Histories* 5.12.

[22] See variously below and *Ket.* 66b–67a, Lam R. 1.16.46–8, and *Git.* 56a. In *Kethuboth*, R. Yohanan is leaving Jerusalem with his Disciples when he sees Nakdimon's daughter Miriam *'picking barley grains from the dung of Arab cattle'*; but R. Eleazar b. Zadok, as we saw, rather sees *'her picking barley grains from among the feet of horses in Acco.'* In *Gittin*, 'Martha the daughter of Boethus' goes out in Jerusalem to *'find something to eat'* and *'some dung stuck to her foot, so she died.'* In Lamentations *Rabbah*, this is rather *'the Romans binding her hair to the tails of Arab horses and making her run from Jerusalem to Lydda'* and, as we have seen, she is rather *'Miriam the daughter of Boethus,'* etc. All of this, both in *Talmud* and Gospels, resembles nothing so much as the code one finds in Arab *Sufi* poetry some 10–12 centuries later where words like *'hair,'* *'feet,'* *'face,'* and the like have their own specific mystic meaning and are varied according to the wishes of the poet/narrator (if one looks hard enough, one can also find the same thing in Charles Baudelaire's poetry eight centuries later, obviously influenced by the importation of Arab/Persian Sufi poetry from North African milieux newly connected to France).

[23] *Ned.* 50a. In James 5:9, the exact quote is *'The Judge is standing before the Door'* (more *'Standing One'* imagery). In *EH* 2.23.8 and *pars.*, the question the crowd supposedly *'cries out'* to him on Passover in the Temple is, *'What is the Door to Jesus?'* There is also the constant reiteration of the words *'cry'*/*'crying out,'* should one choose to regard it, which is also replicated in the picture of *'Stephen'* in Acts 7:56–60 undergoing the same tribulation (*'casting out'*/*'casting down'*) and stoning as James two decades later, upon which picture it is obviously based as we have already remarked.

[24] See further, Chapter 11 below.

[25] Cf. *ARN* 6.1 (20b) with Matthew 26:11/ Mark 13:7/John 12/8. It is more than a little interesting that the *'accusation'* (the *'accusation'* language is also noteworthy here) in the latter is made by *'Judas ('the son' or 'brother of Simon') Iscariot.'* It is interesting too, as already remarked above, that this is followed in *ARN* by reference to the same *'little children,'* we shall further consider below—now not those who *'Jesus suffers to come unto him',* but those of the Rabbis who plead *'we were too Poor''* and, for example, R. Akiba himself. It is also followed by the note that R. Akiba *'started studying Torah and, by the end of thirteen years, he taught Torah in public,'* we have already compared above to Luke 2:46's picture of Jesus teaching in the Temple at a not unsimilar age—more parallels.

[26] See *Vita* 338–67, in which Josephus makes it clear that Agrippa II is now in retirement (along with him) in Rome and quotes two letters he claims to have received from him.

[27] See Chapter 11 below and, for example, CDi.10–12, xii.20–21, xiii.22, 1QSiii.13, ix.12, ix.21, etc.

[28] CDi.7–8. This is followed by the note about *'remission of sins'* (i.e., knowing they *'were Sinful Men'*) *'being like Blind Men,'* *'seeking Him with a whole heart,'* and God *'raising up for them a*

Teacher of Righteousness to guide them in the Way of His heart,' i.e., 'the Guide.' There is also the first note here about God 'visiting them'— we shall discuss this further in Chapter 21 below.

29 *Ket.*66b and 104a.·

30 Matthew 18:2–4, 19:13–15, Mark 9:42, 10:14–15, Luke 17:2, 18:16–17, and John 13:33.

31 See Chapter Nine, n. 76 above and CDiv.20–v.11.

32 Galatians 5:15. The sarcasm and antipathy of his language here should be clear and it is paralleled throughout the Habakkuk *Pesher* and elsewhere at Qumran in the *'eating'/'consuming'/'swallowing'* language one finds there—cf. 1QpHabvi.5–11, xi.5–15, xii.4–6, even including the language of *'dumb beasts'/'consuming,'* etc. For *'the freedom'* he *'enjoys in Christ Jesus,'* see Galatians 2:5. The butt here is those who wish *'to enslave'*—but *'enslave'* to Mosaic Law, not to Rome. He continues this simile in Galatians 4:21–31—after referring now to his *'little children'* (4:19)!

33 The defect here—which was first recognized by A. Von Harnack in *'Die Verklarungsgeschichte Jesu, der Gericht des Paulus (1 Cor. 15.3ff.) under die Beiden Chistusvisionen des Petrus,' Sitzungsberichte der Preussischen Akademia,* 1922, pp. 62–80—has to do with two versions of the sighting order in 1 Corinthians 15:6–7: *'first to the Twelve'* (there were only supposed to be *'Eleven'* at the time) and *'then to James, then all the Apostles'* (a redundancy)—the latter obviously being the authentic tradition.

34 For *'the First'* at Qumran, which usually represents *'the Forefathers who received the Torah,'* see CDi.16. *'The Last'* or *'Last Generation'/'Last Times'* is already making its appearance in i.11–12 here, but also see i.4, iii.10, iv.6–9, vi.2, viii.16–17, 1QpHabii.7, vii.2–12, ix.4–5, etc.

35 Paul also makes this very clear in Galatians 4:24–5 where, in relation to the bondservant Hagar *'being Mount Sinai in Arabia'* or *'the Covenant from Mount Sinai which brings slavery,'* he affirms: *'Such things are allegorized'*—plainly harking to Philo of Alexandria's allegorical method of interpretation. Did Paul know Philo personally? Possibly. If he was an *'Herodian,'* as we have already argued, then he did most certainly, since one of Agrippa I's daughters was married to Philo's nephew. However, whereas Philo is mainly applying this to what we would call *'The Old Testament',* as Paul is to some extent here; the difference is that *'The New Testament'* is already applying the method to presentday events.

36 It is interesting that Luke 18:15 changes the *'little children'* language to *'babes,'* but resumes the *'little children'/'child'* language again in 18:16–17. John 13:31–34, though completely befuddled, struggles manfully to reproduce the meaning, combining it with the *'glorified'/'Glorification'* language and James' Royal Law according to the Scripture: *'Love one another'*—*'The Love Commandment.'*

37 For this kind of *'Power'* language in the Gospels, see Matthew 9:6–8, 10:1, 24:30, Mark 6:7, Luke 4:6–5:24, 10;19, John 1:12, 10:18, and *pars.* We have also already discussed the *'Power'* language in Chapters 1 and 4-6 above.

38 Jerome, *Commentary on Galatians* 1:19

39 See *Ket.* 63a.

[40] This *plotting* language is clear in the Scrolls. See, for instance, 1QpHabxii.2–4 relating to *'the Wicked Priest'*'s judicial conspiracy to destroy *'the Righteous Teacher,' 'the Poor,'* and *'the Simple of Judah doing Torah'* or 1QHiv.7ff. relating to *'the Sons of Belial'* (in our view, *'Herodians'*), their *'nets,'* and all *'the Lying Scoffers'* (*Malitzei-Chazav* above), who lead the people astray *'with Smooth Things,' 'give vinegar to the thirsty'* (another favorite Gospel image), and whose *'works are boasting.'*

[41] This is so strange because in John 12:10–11 it is *'Lazarus'* whom *'the Chief Priests plotted to put to death'* because *'many of the Jews were believing on Jesus because of him'*; whereas in the similar passages earlier from 10:45–57, it is Jesus whom *'they (particularly Caiaphas) wanted to put to death'* after the miracle of *'Lazarus'* being raised from the dead. The only word for all this is *'bizarre'*!

[42] See 1QpHabxi.4–xii.10 above.

[43] 1 QpHabxi.14–5.

[44] As this reads in Revelation 14:8 and 14:10, *'he shall drink of the Wine of the Wrath of God'* which would *'be poured out full strength into the Cup of his Anger.'* The parallel is so precise that there can almost be no doubt of the literary dependency. One can add to this 14:8: *'she has given to all nations to drink of the wine of the Fury of her Fornication'* or 16:19: *'And Babylon the Great was remembered before God to give her the Cup of the Wine of the Fury of His Wrath.'* Again, setting aside their playfulness, these correspondences are almost precise

[45] For *'the Poor'* at Qumran, see 1QpHabxii2–10 above, 4QpPs 37ii.10, iii.10, and iv11 (all actually mentioning *'the Congregation'* or *'Church of the Poor,'* 1QHv.24 (here *'the Ebionei-Hesed'*/*'the Poor Ones of Piety'* in a Document which also speaks of *'the soul of the Poor One'* in ii.32, iii.25, and v.18), and 1QMxi.9–13, xiii.13–14, CDvi.21, xiii.13, etc. Also see 'The Hymns of the Poor'—4Q434–6. For James' Community as *'the Poor,'* see Paul in Galatians 2:10, James 2:5, and Eusebius in *EH* 3.27.1 and *pars.*

[46] See Mark 6:38–41/Matthew 14:17–9/John 6:13 and Luke 9:16 and further below.

[47] One should also note the Jewish Revolutionary in Libya or Cyrene, known both to Eusebius in *EH* 4.2 and Dio Cassius 68.32 during the uprising in Trajan and Hadrian's time in 115–18 CE, which definitely ended up in the virtual elimination of the Jews of Egypt. Eusebius call him *'Lucuas'* (*'Luke'*/*'Lucius of Cyrene'*—Acts 13:1 and cf. Paul in Romans 16:21), but Dio Cassius makes it clear he was also known as *'Andreas'* or *'Andrew'* (*'Man'*?). Both make it clear that he was considered to be a Jewish *'King'* (i.e., a Messiah) and both call him by the well-known New Testament expression *'King of the Jews.'* For interesting references to both terms in the same context at Qumran, see 1QHxii.30–32, referring to both *'Righteousness'* or *'Justification'* and *'Perfection of the Way.'*

[48] See *Antiquities* 20.153, 20.195, and *Vita* 16 and Tacitus, *Annals.* 14.64.2 and Dio Cassius 62.13.1–4—in this account, it is Nero laughing at one Plautus' head that is mentioned.

[49] *Ant.* 20.97–8 and cf. the anachronism in Acts 5:36–7 which is based on a too hasty (or perhaps even a sloppy or inaccurate) reading of these passages in Josephus since, in discussing Queen

Helen's famine-relief activities and the crucifixion of Judas the Galilean's two sons, James and Simon, which follow in 20.101–3; Josephus then goes on to mention how this same Judas '*had aroused the people to revolt against the Romans at the time of the Census of Quirinius*.'

50 *Ant.* 20.50–1, repeated in 20.101. Eusebius makes reference to this famine relief directly following, of course, his account if the '*Impostor Theudas*' and Talmudic sources too are much enamored of this theme.

51 If Paul really was involved in '*famine relief*' activities, as I have argued elsewhere and as Acts 11:28–30 and 12:25 proclaim, then it was as part of these famine-relief activities of Queen Helen and her son Izates. The point is that the '*Antioch*' in question had to have been '*Antioch Orrhoe*' or '*Antioch-by-Callirhoe*,' the capital of '*the Great King of the Peoples beyond the Euphrates*' (either Izates or his putative father '*Abgarus*'/'*Agbarus*') and not '*Antioch-on-the-Orontes*,' as Acts implies but never specifically says. But I have argued this earlierin Chapter 1 and in *James*, pp. 154–9, etc.

52 The parallel here is fairly strong: cf. CDiv.3 and vi.5. In those two instances it is '*going out from the Land of Judah to dwell in the Land of Damascus*.' But the language parallels are clear, since Paul has just gone out to '*those of the Way*' in '*the Synagogues of Damascus*' in Acts 8:2—whatever Acts may mean by this.

53 For '*Thaddaeus*' ('*Judas the brother of James*' in Lukan variations) and '*Theudas*,' see *James*, pp. 930–5 and earlier in Chapter 4 above.

54 The sequencing here is pretty clear and is followed by Eusebius in *EH* 2.9–11—not to mention Acts 5–12 in its own tendentious way. Since Josephus is very keen on documenting most of the gruesome executions in this period, there can be little doubt that these two '*brothers*' in these two contexts have to be seen as interchangeable—the one bowdlerizing the other. It is interesting that the '*sign*,' Josephus portrays '*Theudas*' as claiming to be able to perform, is a Joshua-style parting the Jordan River in reverse (i.e., he is a '*Jesus redivivus*'—as we have elsewhere argued) and leading a reverse Exodus (into '*the Land of Damascus*,' as it were). Elsewhere in *War* 2.259 and *Ant.* 20.167–8, Josephus characterizes these '*signs*,' which '*the Deceivers*' (like '*Jesus*'), '*Impostors*,' and '*Pseudo-Prophets*' were performing, were to '*lead the people out into the wilderness*'—there to '*show them the signs of their impending Redemption*' or '*Freedom*'—a '*Freedom*' (i.e., from Rome) which Paul totally reverses, allegorizing it into a '*Freedom from the Law*' as we have seen.

55 See, for instance, this kind of language in CDii.14–6 and iii.5–12 (here the language is '*walking in the stubbornness of their heart*,' but the effect is the same).

56 For the story of this plaque, see *Naz* 19b–20a, *Yoma* 37a and *Git* 60a.

57 In the first place, there were no '*Ethiopian Queens*' at this time called '*Candakes*,' the last documented one, according to Strabo, *Geography* 17.1.54 and Pliny, *H.N.* 6.35, having ruled in '*Nubia*'—the undoubted sources of Acts' malevolent parody here—was killed in approximately 22 BC; and certainly none who sent her '*treasury agents*' up to Jerusalem at this time, as Queen Helen had done. In the second place, we have already shown that this episode plays off Josephus' story of the conversion of Queen Helen's two sons who, when reading about the '*circumcision*' by

Abraham of his whole household, immediately go out and do likewise (thus!), *Ant.* 20.43–6. Gen R. 46.10 actually knows the passage Queen Helen's two sons were reading at the time—Genesis 17:14. Finally, aside from the possible play on 'Cananaean', I have already described the possible one on Helen's other descendant—the freedom fighter 'Kenedaeus' who lost his life in the first engagement of the War against Rome at the Pass at Beit Horon—*James*, pp. 915–22.

[58] See, for instance, the *Epistle of Peter to James* 5.1 introducing the *Homilies.*

[59] This 'holding fast' is perhaps one of the key usages in CD. See, for instance, CDiii.20, vii.13–4, viii.2, xix.14, xx.27, etc. The usages of 'keeping' and 'breaking' are so numerous as to be almost inexhaustible; but in 1QSv.1–2 (including an allusion to 'holding fast') and v.9, 'keeping'/'Keepers' is the definition of 'the Sons of Zadok'—but for 'keeping'/'breaking' generally, see also CDii.18–21, v.3–4, v.21, vii.6–9 on Deut 7:9 and again in xx.22 (of Ms. B) on Exodus 20:6, xviii.22, xix.1, xx.25, 1QpHabii.3–6, viii.10, etc.

[60] In James, for instance, see 1:26, 2:20, 3:5–8, 3:14, 4:5, 4:8, etc. and in CD, see i.11, ii.18, iii.5, v.12, vi.12 (they 'shall not kindle its altar in vain'), etc. The same imagery abounds in the Habakkuk *Pesher*, Hymns, and more newly-published works such as 4Q434–6 ('*The Hymns of the Poor*') or 4Q416 ('*Sapiential Works.*')

[61] See *The Republic*, Books II–III (377a–408d) and Book X (595a–609d).

[62] Cf. how Paul does this allegorically in Galatians 4:21–31 or in 1 Corinthians 6:12 (also about 'food' and 'the belly')-10:29: '*All things are for me lawful*'; and my conclusion in Chapter 28 at the end of this book.

[63] The '*walking upright*' or '*in Perfection of the Way*'/'*Perfect Holiness*' is absolutely fundamental at Qumran; e.g., 1QSi.15 (here '*walking neither to the right or the left*'—cf. Acts 21:24: '*walking orderly keeping the Law*'), ii.2, iii.10 ('*not straying to the right or the left*' again), viii.10, viii.18–25, ix.9, etc.

[64] In our view, this is particularly clear in 1QpHabviii.11–13 in its description of how '*the Wicked Priest*' profiteered from '*the Riches of the Men of Violence*'/'*the Peoples* (both referring to 'Violent Herodians'), *heaping upon himself iniquitous sinfulness*' (meaning, he took their polluted gifts and sacrifices into the Temple), and CDvii.10–1 on '*the Kings of the Peoples*' (a term used in Roman jurisprudence for ethnic Rulers like the Herodians in the East) *and "their wine" is their ways*'—see Chapters 24 and 28 below.

[65] For '*separating oneself*'/'*themselves*' and '*walking in Perfection of the Way*' or '*Perfect Holiness*' in the context of exegesis of Isaiah 40:3, see 1QSviii.13–21 above; for the language of '*Naziritism*' or '*lehinazzer*'/'*keeping away from*' in the Damascus Document, see CDvi.14–7 ('*separate from the Sons of the Pit*' and '*polluted Evil Riches*'), vii.1 ('*and fornication*'), and viii.8 (and '*the People*'/'*Peoples*'). In these regards, one should not forget the description of James' Directives to Overseas Communities in Acts 15 and 21—always commencing with the words '*keep away from.*'

[66] Cf. CDxx.18–21.

[67] See Chapter 10 above, where the Masoretic only reads: '*they have taught the Commandments of men*'—not '*teaching as doctrines the Commandments of men.*'

[68] It should be appreciated, however, that in Matthew 15:24 the notation *'House'* does reappear, but now it becomes *'not being sent except to the lost sheep of the House of Israel.'* One should also note that in Matthew 15:13–4 the language of *'falling into a pit'* also occurs—as does *'uprooting plants'*—both of which will also recur, as we shall see, in CDi.7 and xi.13.

[69] This is recapitulated in CDii.14–5 but now the exhortation includes *'uncovering your eyes that you may see and understand the works of God...in order that you may walk in Perfection in all His ways and not follow after the thoughts of a Sinful imagination or fornicating eyes.'*

[70] In Mark 7:31, it is said that *'he came to the Sea of Galilee,' 'having left the borders of Tyre and Sidon',* but passing *'through the Borders of the Decapolis'*—a fairly roundabout way to go. In other words, he passed through modern Lebanon, Syria, and the Golan to get to the Decapolis—but how he did this (if he did) is left unexplained.. The same goes for Philip in Acts 8:26–40.

[71] The language of *'seeking'* is widespread in the Damascus Document, which actually starts out in CDi.10–11 stating—following the allusions to *'knowing they were Sinners'* and *'being like blind men groping for the Way'*—that *'God considered their works, because they sought Him with a whole heart and raised up for them a Teacher of Righteousness to guide them in the Way of His heart.'* But even more important is the material about *'the Doresh ha-Torah'/'the Seeker after the Torah'* in CDvii.17–20 in exposition of *'the Star Prophecy'* of Numbers 24:17. Here, too, there is some esoteric language that could possibly be interpreted in terms of *'sign'/'signs'* or *'images'* in CDvii.14–7—see Chapter 21 below.

[72] In these allusions in Acts, it becomes clear that *'Mark's desertion'* of the team (as Paul would have it) to report what was transpiring back to Jerusalem was not an amicable one, but clearly involved a good deal of ill-will—and this in the usually more accurate *'We document.'* Here, since Mark 7:1 had already used the verb *'come'* to describe the usual *'coming down from Jerusalem',* while Matthew 15:1 had rather expressed this as: *'then come to Jesus from Jerusalem, Pharisees and Scribes'* (forgetting both the *'some'* and the *'down'*)—to avoid redundancy, Mark must now use the basically meaningless phraseology *'there gathered unto him the Pharisees and some of the Scribes'*—n.b., how Mark has added here the usual *'some'* to complete the implication of the *'some from James coming'* down from Jerusalem of Paul in Galatians 2:12 and elsewhere in the Gospels, e.g., earlier in Mark 14:4 or Luke 19:39 or John 9:40.

[73] Even the allusion in Mark 7:21–3 (in this instance, the most prolix Gospel), to the heart's *'Evil thoughts, murder, adulteries, fornications, thefts, false witness, railings'* as *'defiling the man,'* recalls the Community Rule's depiction of *'the Spirit of Unrighteousness'* or *'of Evil'* as: *'greediness of soul, stumbling hands in the service of Righteousness* (cf. Paul in 2 Corinthians 11:15), *Wickedness and Lying, pride and proudness of heart, duplicitouness and deceitfulness, cruelty, ill-temper, impatience, much folly, and zeal for lustfulness, works of Abomination in a Spirit of Fornication, and Ways of Uncleanness in the Service of Pollution, a Tongue full of blasphemies, blindness of eye and dullness of ear, stiffness of neck and hardness of heart in order to walk in all the Ways of Darkness and Evil inclination'* (1QSiv.9–11 and cf. Matthew 15:19).

[74] That the issue is *'table fellowship with Gentiles'* is just strengthened by all these allusions to *'blindness'* (as in John 9:13–41 above), *'Blind Guides,'* and *'hypocrites'/'hypocrisy.'* At Qumran, as

reiterated variously in the Damascus Document, the position is *doing according to the precise letter of the Torah* and *setting up the Holy Things according to their precise specifications* (iv.8, vi.20, xx.6, etc.); whereas in Paul and the New Testament following him, it is *not to separate Holy from profane* (Acts 10:14–5) and *all things are for me lawful...Eat everything sold in the butcher shop in no way inquiring because of conscience* (Paul's favorite euphemism for *the Law*—1 Corinthians 10:23–25).

[75] The reference is to 1QSiv.4 on *the Two Spirits.* The parallel kind of expressions in Hymns are to be found in ii.15, v.24, ix.3 and 23, xiv.13–14, etc.

[76] See James 3:4–8.

[77] This is the second part of *the Two Spirits* in the Community Rule above—*the Spirit of Righteousness* or *Cleanliness*—1QSiv.9–11.

[78] Cf. CDi.11–2, xii.20–1, xiii.22–3, 1QHiii.13, ix.12–26, 1QHxii.11, etc.

[79] See James as *Oblias* or *ʿOz-le-ʿAm,* as well as *a strong Bulwark* in E.H. 2.23.7 and 3.7.9 and *pars.* For the same *Fortification*/*Tried-Wall*/and *Strengthening* language applied to the Righteous Teacher and Community Council at Qumran, see CDvi.21, xx.33, 1QSviii.7, 1QHv.38, vii.7–9, ix.8, etc.

[80] 1QSix.12–4.

[81] For *the Elect* see, for instance, CDiv.3–9 which basically identifies *the Sons of Zadok* as *the Elect of Israel...who would stand up in the Last Days* (i.e., *be resurrected* or *go on functioning*) and *justify the Righteous and condemn the Wicked* (i.e., for all intents and purposes—participating in *the Last Judgement*) or 1QpHabv.4–5 to the same effect. For *the Way,* see for instance 1QSviii-ix's exegesis of Isaiah 40:3 on *the Way in the wilderness*—which includes such expressions as *walking in Perfection of the Way* (viii.18, 21, and ix.9), *Perfecting the Way* (viii.25), *washing their Way* (ix.9), and *the rules of the Way* (ix.21).

[82] 1QSix.15–9. This last, of course, means *loving your neighbor as yourself*—as this is put explicitly in the definition of *the New Covenant in the Land of Damascus* in CDvi.19–21 and the definition of *the Community of Truth* in 1QSii.24–5 and, by implication, in 1QSviii.2 and CDxx.17–18 above—*the Royal Law according to the Scripture* of James 2:8 and the second of the two *All Righteousness Commandments* of the *Hesed*/*Zedek* dichotomy as we have seen.

[83] CDxx.17–20 and meaning, as we have shown in *DSSFC,* pp. 313–31, *Gentiles.*

[84] For *Loving God* at Qumran, the first of the two *All Righteousness Commandments* (together with *Righteousness towards one's fellow man* above), see, for example, CDxx.21 and 1QSii.24.

[85] 1QSix.21–2. This kind of hatred is palpable in the *blessing and cursing* sections earlier in 1QSii.4–17 and iv.11–9 in discussing *the Visitation* or *Judgement upon all who walk* in this manner. One should also note the *cursing* in a document like *The Community Council Curses Belial* (4QBer 286–7). Actually this doctrine of *returning Good for Evil* seems to go back to Josephus' description of Agrippa I, whom he describes in *Ant.* 19.329–31 as *scrupulous in keeping the Laws of his Country,* *gentle,* *benevolent to foreigners,* and *compassionate to his own Countrymen.* In explaining how such behavior would *heap coals upon his (detractor's) head,* Josephus even applies the Greek term *chrestos* to him—in this instance meaning *gentle.*

86 One can see this 'amal' in 1QpHabviii.2–3's interpretation of Habakkuk 2:4: 'the Righteous shall live by his Faith.'

87 Translators such as Vermes as we have seen, often translate terms of this kind as 'Precept' or 'Ordinance'; but to do so in this context diminishes the significance of what is being alluded to here. 'Hok'/'Hukkim', just as later in CDvi.9, have to be translated as 'Law'/'Laws.'

88 One finds similar vocabulary among extreme Fundamentalist Islamic groups like al-Qaida today but, once again, without the echo of non-violence.

89 1QSix.23—here one has the 'doing' (which is the basis of the 'works'/'Righteousness' ideology) associated with 'the hands' but now, of course, not in the context of 'washing' before eating but rather in the context of the Attributes of God.

90 1QSix.24. If one want to see this 'Rechabite' vocabulary of 'commanding,' one should see Jeremiah 35:6–18 on 'the commands the sons of Rechab were commanded to do' (here even including the 'doing' vocabulary). We have already shown that, according to Eusebius' version of Hegesippus' picture of James death (E.H. 2.23.17), the individual who attempts to interfere in his stoning is identified as 'one of the Priests of the Sons of Rechab, a son of the Sons of Rechab'—which we take to be a euphemism for 'Essene' Priests or 'Nazirite' or 'Nazorean Priests' and an individual whom Epiphanius in Haeres. 78.14 identifies as James' so-called first 'cousin' or, in our view, his putative second brother, Simeon bar Cleophas—but, in any event, his Successor to Leadership in the Movement he led in Palestine

91 In the incredible Hymn attached to the end of the Community Rule in 1QSx-xi, the Council is even pictured as 'joined to the Sons of Heaven' and described as 'a Building of Holiness' and 'an Eternal Planting' or 'Plantation' (xi.8–9—but see also viii.4–9: 'With the existence of these in Israel, the Council of the Community will be established upon Truth like an Eternal Plantation, a House of Holiness for Israel…,a Tested Rampart, a Precious Cornerstone, the Foundations of which will not shake or sway in their place…,a House of Perfection and Truth in Israel'). In so many of these contexts in the Community Rule, the Damascus Document, and Hymns, one encounters the 'laying the Foundations' imagery that Paul uses in 1 Corinthians 3:9–14, as well as the 'Building' imagery with which the Habakkuk Pesher attacks the Man of Lying 'who built a Worthless City upon Blood'—as we shall see, as we proceed, in our view Paul's understanding of 'Communion with the Blood of Christ.' This is not to mention 'God causing a Root of Planting to grow' itself of the Damascus Document which will also be directly parodied not only in Paul, but here in the Synoptics as well. Nor is this to say anything about the idea of 'God's Building' or 'House' which will be, of course—as already alluded to above—the very imagery CDiii.19 ('He built for them a House of Faith in Israel') and which CDxx.10 and 13 ('a House of the Torah') also uses to describe its view of the Community.

92 CDi.5–8.

93 See, for instance, 1QSviii.4–9 and xi.7–9 above and 1QHvi.24–6 and vii.8–9 on 'the Foundation which will be set upon Rock,' 'the Doors of Protection which will not sway' and 'the Tried-Wall,' 'Fortified Tower,' and 'Ramparts' which are 'an Eternal Foundation,' 'Building,' or 'Rock', which also 'will never sway.'

[94] 1 Corinthians 2:6–7.

[95] See 1QSix.18 and xi.3–19 above, but also see iii.23, iv.6 and 18, v.25–26, CDiii.18, 1QMxiv.9–10, xvii.9, etc.

[96] 1 QpHabx.9–13.

[97] For these correspondences, see Chapters 28-29 at the end the book.

[98] CDiii.18–20. As this continues, it reads: *'And for them that hold fast to it, there will be Victorious Life and all the Glory of Adam will be theirs'* (cf. Paul in 1 Corinthians 14:22–15:58 and note both the *'Glory'* and Ebionite *'Primal Adam'* vocabulary there. For this *'Faith'* or *'Compact'* as *'a House of the Torah,'* see CDxx.10–13 above).

[99] CDvii.4–6, xx.10–13 and xx.21–22.

[100] This *'Pit'* language is very important and, as we shall see, is duplicated in Matthew 15:14 however tendentiously. Probably the best example of it is to be found in CDvi.12–14, including the *'Nazirite'* language of *'keeping away from'* and *'separation'*—as well as Acts 21:30's *'barring the door',* introducing the definition of *'the New Covenant in the Land of Damascus'* in vi.16–8; but also see xiii.14 and xiv.2 and 1QSix.16–21 above. In my view, the use of it in CDvi is equivalent to *'the Daubers on the Wall'* attack on *'the Seekers after Smooth Things,' 'Zaw-Zaw,'* and *'the Windbag'/'Man of Confused Spirit'* in iv.19–20 and viii.12–13/xix.24–26.

[101] CDxi.13–4.

[102] See our discussion of *'internal'* vs. *'external evidence'* in Chapter 2 above.

[103] There is some evidence that *'Jesus'* (whoever he may have been) came in 19–21 CE. This comes in Eusebius' citation from what he considers to be the fraudulent *'Acti Pilati'* which places the crucifixion in that year (*E.H.* 1.9.3–4). But Tacitus, too (*Annals.* 2.85), places the expulsion of the Jews from Rome under Tiberius in most peculiar and suspicious circumstances in this Period as well—not later as in Josephus' version of similar events—see *James,* pp. 66 and 863. In this manner, the mysterious *'twenty years'* at the beginning of CDi.10 evaporates. Furthermore, this would explain why Paul, who is supposed to be functioning, c. 37 CE onwards, knows so little about the *'Christ Jesus'*—his eye-witness testimony about whom is almost nil—he is talking about. If there is an *'Historical Jesus'*—aside from the Samaritan one—this is probably the best way of understanding him.

[104] See, for instance, 4QFlori.11–3 and CDvii.16–20 and Chapters 21-22 below. Cf. too 4QTxl.5–13.

[105] CDii.9–11.

[106] See, for instance, the document, Prof. Wise and myself discovered (4Q285—we called it *'The Messianic Leader'*), which identifies *'the Root of Jesse'* with *'the Branch of David'* and, in turn, *'the Nasi ha-ᶜEdah'/'the Leader of the Assembly'* or *'Church.'* This *Messianic Leader*, of course, then reappears in documents like 4QFlori.11–3 and CDvii.16–20 above, not to mention the interpretation of *'the Shiloh Prophecy'* of Genesis 49:10 in 4Q252 or the so-called *'Genesis Pesher'*—see *DSSU,* pp. 24–9 and 77–89 and variously below. It should be appreciated that the reason we released 4Q285 when we did was because, in attempts to dissimulate and send

the public away in other directions, responsible persons were letting it be known that *'there was nothing interesting in the unpublished Scrolls fragments.'* We disagreed. Therefore the release— to show that there was. This was the important thing. It was not to grab headlines as some contended. The opposite. The preliminary translation (such as it was) was Michael Wise and his University of Chicago team's. We all relied on this. They had their interpretation. I had mine. Mine appears on pp. 24–7 of *DSSU*. In my personal view, there never was a *'Suffering Messiah'* at Qumran though—who knows—there might have been.

Chapter 11

[1] Cf. CDi.7–9 above for *'God causing a Root of Planting to grow'*; for the widespread use of *'Pit'* imagery in CD, see vi.15 (in conjunction with the *'Nazirite'* language of *'lehinnazer'/'keeping away from'*), xiii.14–5, 1QSix.16, 21–22, etc.

[2] Despite the repetitions, contradictions of locale, and the more elegant manner of expression; the point being made in both Matthew and Mark here (in conjunction with this 'Parable') is the same as what 'Peter' is pictured as having learned *for the first time* in Acts 10:9–16 and Paul in 1 Corinthians 10:25. The conclusion that 'to eat with unwashed hands does not defile the man' and that 'declaring all foods clean' are to be found in Matthew 15:20 and Mark 7:19 in the text above.

[3] See *ARN* 6.2 (20b). The 'Parable' here (about 'a Stone-Cutter'/"Peter'?) is told by one R. Simeon ben Eleazar but, however this may be, the thrust has to do with what R. Akiba did with the teachings of R. Eliezer ben Hyrcanus and his colleague R. Joshua ('Jesus'?); and what the 'Stone-Cutter' did was *'chip away'* the *'tiny pebbles'* of a great *'mountain'* in order *'to uproot it'* and *'cast it into the Jordan.'* It is this which is compared to what R. Akiba did to the teachings of R. Eliezer and R. Joshua. Here, too, the *'little children'* are R. Akiba's *'sons and daughters,'* as we have seen, and R. Akiba (who is supposed to have been *'forty years old'* before he began to study) studies *'thirteen years'* before *'he taught Torah to the multitudes'* (cf. Luke 2:42–9 above, which to some extent echoing Josephus as well, has 'Jesus' as *'twelve years old'* when he was sitting for *'three days'* among the teachers in the Temple and answering their questions).

[4] For another one of these *'little ones'* episodes, this one quite humorous and combined with the 'Rich Man' motif, see Luke 19:1–10 about one 'Zacchaeus' who was *'a chief tax-collector and a Rich Man'* but *'too short'* to see Jesus *'in the crowd'* (that is, so many people apparently wanted to see him!); so he *'climbed up a sycamore tree'* (thus—what detail!). It's nice to know there were *'sycamore trees'* in Jericho at this time; but, however this may be, the fact that Jesus ends up *'staying at his house'* despite the fact *'he was a Sinner,'* identifies it with the probably more-historical 'Zacchaeus' episode in the Pseudoclementine *Recognitions* 1.73–74, at whose house 'Peter' stayed when he was sent to Caesarea by James on his first *'missionary'* journey. Also, note the connection with R. Yohanan b. Zacchai's name here should it prove of any relevance.

[5] These sorts of *'falling down'* at or *'kissing'* someone's *'feet'* and *'feet'* stories generally are to be found relevant to Rabbis such as R. Akiba, R. Eliezer b. Hyrcanus, and the like in *Ket* 63a, *ARN* 6.3

(21a), *Git* 56a, etc. above. It is not incurious that the parallel in Luke to the Rabbinic story of Nakdimon *'filling the lord'* or *'master's cisterns'* comes in 16:1–8, ending with a telltale allusion to the Qumran-like *'Children of Light.'* This story, too, begins with reference to another *'Rich Man,'* *'a master'* or *'patron'* and, as usual, ends by condemning *'the Pharisees'* as *'lovers of money'* (thus!). Furthermore, it also introduces the famous Lukan version of Matthew's *'Sermon on the Mount'* including *'not serving two masters,'* the *'not one jot or tittle disappearing from the Law'* material, and finally his version of *'the dogs'* episode.

[6] It is very strange, but in view of what he says in 1 Corinthians 10:18 introducing this about *'Israel according to the flesh participating with'* or *'sharing the sacrifices at the altar'*—meaning, *'in the Temple';* it is hard to avoid the conclusion that it is this he then goes on to refer to as *'the Cup of Demons'* or *'the Table of Demons.'*

[7] His usage of the word *'conscience'* is always important. One can find it fully explained in the crucial Corinthians 8:7–12 preceding this. Here, it is used in their context of *'being weak,'* *'causing to stumble,'* and *'things sacrificed to idols'*—all important usages where Qumran, *Sicarii* Essenes, and the Letter of James are concerned. But one can also find it in Romans 2:14–5 (in connection with *'works of the Law,'* *'Doers of the Law being justified,'* *'Gentiles,'* things *'being written on their hearts'*—favorite imageries of his) and 9:1 (in conjunction with *'telling the Truth'* again *'and not Lying,'* *'the Children of the Promise counting as the Seed,'* and *'Standing'*).

[8] So here now, we have the *'going out'* from Mark's *'toilet bowl'* excursus or *'Parable'*—itself relating, of course, to *'clean'* and *'unclean'* things and *'purity,'* as opposed to Matthew 15:17's *'casting out into'* (ekballetai) now used to describe the rectification of *'Mary'*'s *'unclean'* state. But in the parallel or similar description of Mary in Mark 16:9 depicting a *'first appearance'* to Mary the morning after the crucifixion, this is now reformulated in the manner of Matthew above as *'out of whom he had cast seven demons'* (ekbeblekei) and so our various conundrums and textual interchanges continue—this one more puzzling than ever.

[9] 2 Maccabees 7:1–42. Of course, in this episode (again, probably not completely historical and embroidered but still meant to be moving and to encourage martyrdom for the Laws), each brother is in turn encouraged by the mother to sacrifice himself *'for the sake of His Laws'* and the promise being held out is *'Resurrection of the dead'* or, as this is put here, *'to live again'*—an excellent context in which to consider the mass suicide at Masada. Josephus, too, recounts a similar episode in *War* 1.312–13/*Ant.* 14.420–30—probably the basis of all the traditions— when Herod is on the way down to take Jerusalem in 37 BC and he encounters *'the cave-dwellers'* (whom he calls *'Bandits'* or *'Robbers'*) near Arbela in Galilee and an old man on these cliffs who, despite Herod's efforts to dissuade him (thus!), slays his wife and their seven children and then jumps into the ravine after them!

[10] *Par contra,* one should note how in Mark 12:13–18/Matthew 22:15–26 (here the issue is, not surprisingly, whether it is right *'to pay tribute to Rome'*) and Mark 3:6 (here, again not surprisingly, the Herodians *'plotted with the Pharisees how to destroy him'*), *'the Herodians'* are listed with the Pharisees (in this, quite realistically) as being among those opposed to *'Jesus'*' teachings—the only question is, which teachings of *'Jesus,'* the real ones or the mythological/

literary ones? On the other hand, it should be noted, that it is Paul in Acts 24:10–26:32 who enjoys easy relations with '*Herodians*' and, as we have suggested earlier, may himself have even been an '*Herodian*'—cf. Romans 16:7–11.

[11] Mark 15:47 also thinks it knows a '*Mary the mother of Joses*.'

[12] Cf. *James the Brother of Jesus*, pp. 74f., 142–5, 770–83, 842–50, 924–39, etc.

[13] For more of these '*coming*' episodes, see the incident about the raising or curing of Jairus' daughter in Mark 5:21–43/Matthew 9:18–26/Luke 8:40–56, Chapter 11 below (once again, contrary to normative expectation, Mark is the most prolix of the three; for Matthew 9:18 the '*little daughter*' is already dead, so it is a Raising; while for Mark 5:23 and Luke 8:42, she is only at the point of death, so it is a curing), which leads into the '*certain woman who had been sick with a flow*' or '*fountain of blood for twelve years*' who '*comes*' up to Jesus and '*touches the fringe of his clothing*.' As we shall see below as well, this appears to either play off or pun on Jewish scrupulousness about 'blood' generally and/or CDvii.22/xix.34's '*Fountain of Living Waters*.' Moreover, in all three Gospels, these two episodes follow another peculiar one about '*coming*' into '*the country of Gedara*' in the area of the Decapolis above the Sea of Galilee, where 'Jesus' encounters '*a certain man of the city possessed*' either '*by demons*' (which later turn out to be '*Legion*'—Mark 5:15) or the usual '*unclean spirit*' (Mark 5:2), whom he finds out was named '*Legion*'—an odd episode indeed.

[14] CDi.18–20 below. Note how this is directed against '*the Seekers after Smooth things*' and '*those who chose illusions*,' who are then described as '*justifying the Sinners (Paul's activities?) and condemning the Righteous*,' and leads into the attack on '*the life of the Zaddik and all those walking in Perfection*' by '*those transgressing the Covenant and breaking the Law*.' For another such allusion to '*leaving*' someone to do something, see 1QS.ix.19–22, which also speaks about '*walking in Perfection each with his neighbor*' (i.e., '*the All Righteousness Commandment*'/'*the Royal Law according to the Scripture*'), '*making a Way in the wilderness*,' '*the Guide*,' '*everlasting hatred for the Sons of the Pit*,' and '*leaving them to their Riches and the work of their hands, like a servant to his master or the meek one to the one dictating to him*.')

[15] CDiv.7–10.

[16] In all such materials, one should note the overlap with the character Josephus calls '*Eleazar ben Jair*'—a descendant of Judas the Galilean and kinsman of that '*Menachem*' tortured and probably stoned to death by his opponents on the Temple Mount when he put on the Royal Purple—*War* 2.433–49 and 7.253–399.

[17] This '*go your way*' allusion is a curious one and is discussed in Chapter 11 and variously below.

[18] For James' directives in Acts, see 15:20.15:29, and 21:25; for Qumran, see CDii.7–9 and iii.5–7.

[19] CDv.7—again the word '*blood*' is specifically included.

[20] CDvii.21–4/xix.33–xx.1, but also see CDvi.14–vii.9 where this '*Covenant*' is specifically defined.

[21] See Chapters 27-28, the last sections of this book below.

[22] One can see that this is true from the same kind of statement Jesus makes to characterize the *'Canaanite woman'* in Matthew 15:28 above. There it is: *'O woman, great is your Faith.'* One should also note that in that episode, just as the woman *'having come, did homage'* or *'bowed down to him'* (here again, just as with the Hellenistic or Greco-Roman *'Man-God'* stories as, for example, Dionysus in Euripedes' *Bacchae*) in Matthew 15:25 (in Mark 7:26 she rather *'falls down at his feet'* as we saw); so too in Mark 5:6 *'the man with the unclean spirit'* called *'Legion'* also *'ran up to him and did homage'* or *'bowed down to him'*—again as if to a Greco-Hellenistic *'God Man'* (one should also note, as in Acts' picture of *'Stephen'* before the Jewish crowd and James in the Temple in early Church literature, this demoniac also *'cried out in a loud voice'*).

[23] See our discussion in Chapter 4 above.

[24] See *'the Taheb'*'s place of activity *'Tirathaba'* and variously above.

[25] In Hebrew, there is also the feminine of *'lamb'* as in *'dorcas'/'doe'* for *'Tabitha'* above.

[26] *Ned.* 50a. One should note, too, how in this episode in *Nedarim*, R. Akiba is portrayed (as *'Jesus'* is in the Gospels) as repulsing *'his Disciples'* when they try to prevent his family (in this case, his long-suffering wife *'Ben Kalba Sabuʿa's daughter'*) from approaching him—in the Synoptics, it will be recalled, it was the family that cannot get close to him because of the crowds!

[27] *Ibid.* Cf. Luke 2:4–21. Here it is *'the Angel of the Lord,' 'the shepherds,'* and *'the multitude of the Heavenly Host'* who take the place of *'Elijah the Prophet'*; but note here how the last-named preach *'Glory to God in the Highest and Peace on earth, good will towards men'* (2:14)—however kind-spirited, another reversal to what one might expect to find in the War Scroll from Qumran where *'the Heavenly Host'* is concerned. As for Elijah, he will then reappear in the descriptions of John the Baptist, either pro or con.

[28] The issue of *'the son of Joseph'* has particular relevance vis-a-vis the supposed *'Ossuary'* which recently surfaced, we discussed above earlier, in the name of *'Jacob'/'James the son of Joseph brother of Jesus'*. As we pointed out earlier, there would have been numerous ossuaries with the formula *'son of Joseph'* on them and this was most likely the only authentic part of the inscription. Moreover, where *'James'* name was concerned (for the Ossuary *'Jacob'*), in most classical Early Church texts, the name of his father was usually rather *'Cleophas'/'Clopas'*—probably corrupted into *'Alphaeus'* or *vice versa*. Moreover, it also has relevance vis-a-vis the Samaritan Messiah or *Taheb* above, who really would have ben a *'Jesus son of Joseph'*—therefore the patronym vis-a-vis R. Akiba is all the more convincing or impressive.

[29] *Ket.* 63a.

[30] *Ibid.*

[31] *Ibid.*

[32] See Ps. *Rec.* 172–4 above.

[33] See Y. Yadin, 'The Excavation of Masada,' *Israel Exploration Journal* 15, 1965, pp. 81–2 and 105–8, and *Masada*, London, 1966, pp. 173–90.

[34] See, for instance, 4Q521, 'The Messiah of Heaven and Earth,' Fragment 1, Column i.12—but there are others.

[35] The criticism of him in Lam. R. 2.2.4 and j. *Ta'an* 4.5 (68d) for applying the Messianic '*Star*' Prophecy (the probable origin of Bar Kochba's name) to Bar Kochba by the other Rabbis gives some proof of this, as do the tremendous numbers of '*his Disciples*' described above in *Ket.* 62a–63b and *Ned.* 50 (seemingly some 24,000!) and the description of his imprisonment and horrific death at the hands of the Romans in *Ber.* 61b. In the latter, a '*Bat Chol*' or '*Heavenly Voice*' cries out, much in the manner of the Synoptics: '*This is my only begotten son, etc., etc.*'— only in Akiba's case, it is: '*You are destined for the life of the world to come.*'

[36] For John's teaching '*Righteousness towards one's fellow man*,' see *Ant.* 18.117; for Josephus' '*Essenes*,' see *War* 2.139. For James, of course, see 2:8.

[37] Hippolytus 9.21.

[38] See 2.2.4 and *Ber.* 61b above and cf. 1QMxi.6–xii.17 and Matthew 24:30/Mark 13:26 and 26:64/14:62 and *pars.*

[39] *Ber.* 61b–62a

[40] CDxx.20–21 and James 2:5 on '*loving God.*' Also see, Josephus' '*Essenes*' in *War* 2.128–33.

[41] *Ket.* 62a–63b.

[42] See 1QpHabxi.4–8 which even includes a reference to '*casting them down*' (in normative translations, a little misleadingly, '*causing them to stumble*'). For James' *Yom Kippur* Atonement in the Temple, see Chapters 2, 4, and variously above.

[43] Lam *R.* 1.16.47. Though here she is '*Miriam*'/'*Mary*,' in *Git* 56a (where her death is described quite differently) and *Ket.* 104a, she is quite properly '*Martha the daughter of Boethus*', as we have seen. In *Yoma* 18a, she bribes Agrippa (obviously Agrippa II—called '*King Yannai*' in *Yeb.* 61a) with '*three measures of gold coins.*'

[44] Lam *R.* 1.16.47. Cf. *Git* 56a above.

[45] Lam *R.* 1.16.47–8. In *Ket* 67a, as we have seen, he rather '*sees her picking barley grains among the horses' hoofs in Acco.*' This '*Zadok*' is an extremely important name/character in both the Dead Sea Scrolls and Talmudic Tradition. For Josephus in *War* 2.451 and 628, he would appear perhaps to be the father of one '*Ananias b. Zadok*,' who is part of a delegation that takes the surrender of the Roman garrison in the Citadel at the beginning of the Uprising and, later in Galilee, is part of another delegation that relieves Josephus of his alleged '*Command*' there. In *Git.*56a he is someone who '*fasts for forty years so that Jerusalem might not be destroyed.*' In 56b, he is someone on whose behalf R. Yohanan convinces Vespasian (*sic*) to allow him to send back into the city to rescue. In Lam R. 1.16.46, it seems to be his children who are taken captive to Rome and die in each other's arms (see our dedication page). Having said this, later in *ARN* 16.1 (24b)—which confirms the fact that, though a Rabbi, he is of '*the High Priestly Line*' and calls him '*the greatest man of his generation*'—he himself is taken captive to Rome and, like Joseph in the Bible, supposedly resists the advances of a highborn Roman matron there.

[46] *ARN* 6.3 (21a). In *Git* 56a, as we have also seen, he is rather denoted as '*Ben Zizzit ha-Kesef*'/'*Silver*' *and* this is supposedly because '*his fringes (zizzit) used to trail on cushions (Keset) and here, 'his seat (kise) was*' rather '*among those of the Roman Nobility*'! The folkloric character of these

appellations and traditions should be clear as should their '*nom-a-clef*' character; but whoever he was, he was clearly an Establishment character of some kind and, therefore probably an 'Herodian' or one of their hangers-on.

[47] *ARN* 4.5 (20a—here the passage cited is Isaiah 10:34, which is also extant at Qumran). See also *Git* 56a–b, which cites Isaiah 10:34 too but clearly with quite a different interpretation; but the episode is so fundamental to Rabbinic tradition that it is also alluded to in Lam. *R* 1.5.31 and again the citation is Isaiah 10:34. One should also see *Yoma* 21a and 39b.

[48] See CDvii.18–9, xix.10–1, and 4Q*Testi*.12 and cf. Chapters 21, 22, and 28 below.

[49] This is about the most pro-Roman episode in any of the Gospels or Acts. Here the Centurion is seen as being so respectful of 'Jesus,' as well he might, that he does not even permit the 'Man/God' to enter his house. When one hears that Matthew is the most '*pro-Jewish*' of all the Gospels, one must range against such judgements passages such as these. Certainly this episode is meant to conciliate ex-Roman Centurions and Army members and, that the promises '*of the Kingdom*' are now being given over to them—the destroyers of Jerusalem, the Temple, and the Jewish People in Palestine—can hardly be more opportunistic and cynical. Actually the language here matches Paul in Galatians 4:19–31, where somehow he manages to present the Jews as we saw ('*such things being allegory*'—sic!) as '*Hagar*' because of their attachment to the Law—she, '*being Mount Sinai in Arabia*.' This is the kind of '*Slavery*' Paul is talking about. Therefore he concludes in 4:30, in another tendentious use of Scripture: '*Cast out the slave woman*', and the verb he uses, '*ekbale*', is the same verb Matthew 8:12 is applying to '*the Children of the Kingdom*,' i.e., '*the Jews*' and the same one Acts 7:56–7 is applying to what '*the Jews*' do to '*Stephen*.' It is for this reason one calls this episode and its conclusion a pure '*Gentile Mission*' one and one of the first reversals. It is also the same verb (in perhaps its original embodiment), as we have seen, that Josephus uses to describe what '*Essenes*' do to backsliders, '*cast them out*' (*War* 2.143)!

[50] The use of '*standing*' or '*stand up*' in the Damascus Document and elsewhere at Qumran is extremely important. Not only does it relate to '*the Standing One*' doctrine of the Pseudoclementines, Ebionites, Simon *Magus*, and others, as we have seen; it also relates to '*being resurrected*' and '*the Resurrection*' and was, probably based on Ezekiel 37:10–4—the Hebrew way of expressing this. For CD, see iv.3–4, vii.12, vii.19, xiii.23, xiv.19, xx.1, etc. and cf., for example, 4Q*Flori*.10 and 13 below.

[51] See *Ant.* 20.21—already mentioned above too. It is worth cataloguing all the usages of this particular adjective, but one particularly interesting one comes in Paul's speech at '*Antioch of Pisidia*' in Acts 13:33. This speech is, not only addressed to '*God-Fearers*' in 33:16 and 26 (Cf. CDxx.18–23), speaks of '*raising up David*' and '*his seed*' (Acts 33:22–3—cf. 4Q*Flori*.10–3), alludes to '*the Shiloh Prophecy*' of Genesis 49:10 and 4Q252v.1–4 (Acts 33:28—note the basic allusion to the Messiah's '*feet*' all round); but finally quotes Psalm 2:7 which it translates into Greek as the '*begotten*' or '*only-begotten son*.' This is the same passage quoted in Hebrew 1:5 and 5:5 and, according to Jerome, the Hebrew Gospel of the Ebionites, i.e., the adoptionist '*This is my only-begotten son; on this day I have begotten him*'—in place of the Synoptic: '*This is my beloved son; in him I am well pleased*' of Matthew 3:17 and *pars.*,

[52] This '*offspring of vipers*' epithet was originally used by Matthew 3:7 and 12:34—the first in John the Baptist's attack supposedly on '*the Sadducees and Pharisees*' (Luke 3:7 rather uses it to portray John as attacking the entire '*crowd that came out to be baptized by him*'—thus!); the second, and here in Matthew 23:33 (in the context of many other allusions) to portray '*Jesus*' attacking only '*the Pharisees*' (in our view, as already indicated, in such contexts, a *nom-a-clef* for James''*Jerusalem Church*' Leadership); but one can find a parallel to it in two places in CDv.13–7 amid other patently John the Baptist-like allusions and viii.9–12 to attack '*the Daubers on the Wall*' and '*the Kings of the Peoples*'—in our view, the first being individuals like Paul who claimed to be '*a Pharisee of the Pharisees*,' and the second, '*the Herodians*' (see Chapters 22, 24, and 28 below). We have already noted above the Qumran parallel to Matthew 15:14 and 23:16–24's '*Blind Guides*' in CDi.9–11.

[53] Cf. *ARN* 6.2 (20a), *Ned* 50a, and *Ket.* 62b–63a above.

[54] Though in Matthew 24 discards the '*widow's mites*' material, not surprisingly it keeps Mark 13's '*going forth out of the Temple*' material which Luke 21 neglects. In these series of encounters and allusions from Mark 12–3, Matthew 23–4, and Luke 21, it would be hard to be more anti-Jewish or Judaism than these showing that such an attitude was well-established by this time. For Titus' destruction of the entire City, see *War* 7.1–2.

[55] Cf. Mark 12:19, 12:32, 13:1, etc.

[56] This '*leading astray*' language is, of course, basic to Qumran and, in particular, the presentation of the position of '*the Man of*'/'*Spouter of Lying*' who '*leads Many astray*'; cf. CDi.13–6, 1QSiii.22, 1QpHabx.9–13, etc.

[57] One should note that the whole issue of '*the Poor*' vs.'*the Rich*' is not only paramount at Qumran but was, along with the '*tax*' issue and gifts from non-Jewish foreigners in the Temple related to it, the driving issues behind the War against Rome. One can see this in the picture of Agrippa II's last speech to the crowd bent on Revolution, where he and his sister (Bernice—later Titus' mistress) are portrayed as '*bursting into tears*' and making it clear that they '*have not paid their tribute to Caesar*.' It is in continuance of this that Josephus, the Chief Priests, the most prominent Pharisees, and the Principal Citizens (i.e., '*the Herodians*') call stopping sacrifice and refusing gifts on the part of foreigners in the Temple '*a peculiar innovation into their Religion*' and an '*Impiety*' (thus!), setting the stage for and meaning it would ultimately inevitably lead to the destruction of the Temple. Cf. too *War* 2.426–9, where '*the brigands*,' '*Sicarii*,' and '*Innovators*' burn the palaces of Ananias the High Priest and Agrippa and Bernice and burn the debt records too, '*turning the Poor against the Rich*,' and 2.402–17. All of these matters are certainly being alluded to and, to some extent, played on or parodied in these pregnant passages in the Synoptics!

[58] Of course, as we have already repeatedly seen, '*the Poor*' (*Ebionim*, i.e., '*the Ebionites*') is a fundamental conceptuality at Qumran—cf. 1QpHabxii.2–7. In fact, 4QpPs 37iii.10 and iv.11 makes reference to '*the Congregation*' or '*Church of the Poor*' on at least two separate occasions even in the extant text.

[59] This passage in 1QpHabvi.7 is of the utmost importance because it makes it clear that the interpretation of *'sacrificing to their standards and worshipping their weapons of war,'* that is, *'parceling out their yoke and their taxes (i.e., 'tax farming'), consuming/eating all the Peoples year by year, giving many Countries over to the sword,'* relates to the Romans—and, in particular, the Imperial Romans—and no one else.

[60] *War* 6.301–9 and Chapter 18 below.

[61] Cf. CDi.9–11, xii.20–1, xiii.22, 1QSiii.13, ix.12, ix.21, etc.

[62] For R. Yohanan's *'woes'* upon leaving Jerusalem with his *'Disciple'* R. Joshua ('Jesus'?) and Vespasian's behavior, see *ARN* 4.5 (20a)—note here that Isaiah 10:34 (the *Pesher* concerning which is extant at Qumran) is applied to this fall, as it is by implication at Qumran as well. (Reader note: line editor improperly interrupted footnote sequence here and nn. 63–64 have been overstepped).

[65] Cf. CDvi.3–10, vi.19–vii.6, and viii.21–23/xix.31–xx.7 and below in Chapters 21 and 28.

[66] For Queen Helen, see Josephus, *Ant.* 20.17–96 and above Chapter 8. One should also note the relevance of this individual to a Qumran document like *MMT*; see below, Chapters 19 and 28.

[67] See *Ant.* 20.94–6 and *War* 5.55, 119, and 147 and Plates 85–8 of the second picture section.

[68] Cf. CDi.7–9.

[69] CDi.17, vii.9–13, vii.21–viii.3/xix.5–16, etc.

[70] This *'glorying'* permeates both the Gospels and Paul's letters; cf. Luke 4:15, 5:26, 7:16, 13:13, 17:15, 23:47, John 7:39, 12:16–28, 13:31–32, 14:13, 15:8, 17:4, and *pars.*; but also see the description of *'the Spouter of Lying'* in 1QpHabx.9–13 as we have seen.

[71] See CDiii.19, iv.4, vii.18–20, xii.23, xiv.19, etc. and 4QFlori.10–13 and 4QTesti.12–13; for *'the True Prophet,'* see 1QSix.12 and in 4QTesti.5–6.

[72] For *'the True Prophet'* ideology, see Ps. Rec. 1.16, 1.40–1, 1.44 and variously/Ps. Hom. 1.21, 2.4–12, and variously; for Muhammad and the Koran, a good example is 33.1 and 33.30–59; for Mani, see al-Biruni 8.206–9.

[73] 1QSix.12 above.

[74] See CDxix.2–3 and Chapter 21 and variously below.

[75] CDiv.14–21 in interpretation of Isaiah 24:17 and viii.12–3/xix.24–6 (while Ms. A has *'one of confused spirit,'* Ms. B has *'walking in the Spirit'!*).

[76] 1QSviii.10–6, in describing the *'Naziritism'* and *'Study of the Torah'* of *'the Perfect of the Way'* and ix.18–24, the necessity of *'separating from any man who has not turned his Way away from all Unrighteousness,'* *'eternal hatred for the Men of the Pit,'* and *'zeal for the Law'* and *'the Day of Vengeance.'*

[77] For the *'woollen clothes'* that were spread beneath Nakdimon's feet while *'the Poor gathered them up,'* see *Ket.* 66b and the *'carpets'* that were laid from the door of Martha's *'house to the entrance of the Temple so her feet would not be exposed,'* see Lam R. 1.16.47 and Chapter 9 above.

78 For *'the ᶜAm ha-Aretz'* in the *Talmud*, see for example, *M. Toh* 7.5–8.5 (and note, in passing, the allusion to *'dog'* where *'clean'* and *'unclean'* foodstuffs are concerned in 8.6), *B.B.* 57b–58a, *Shab* 13a, 15b, 23a, *Pes.* 42b, 49a–49b, and variously; at Qumran, we must have regard for the expressions *'ᶜamim'* and *'yeter ha-ᶜamim'* in 1QpHabviii.5–ix.5 and CDvii.5–12/xix.17–25 and xx.24, and Chapters 18 and and 23 below.

79 Of course, the incidences of the allusion to *'Standing'* and its variations, both at Qumran and in the New Testament, must be catalogued as we have done to a certain extant here and above, and in *James*, pp. 269, 327, 370–8, 449, 700–90, etc.; for *'the Standing One'* in the Pseudoclementines and in Elchasaite ideology, see variously above as well.

80 CDvi.11–7. Importantly, this allusion to *'barring the door'* and *'not kindling the Temple altar in vain'* from Malachi 1:10, not only is paralleled in the picture in Acts 21:30 of Paul being unceremoniously ejected from the Temple and the doors being *'barred behind him'*; but in CD, it also forms the introduction of the description of *'the New Covenant in the Land of Damascus'* which involves *'setting up the Holy Things according to their precise specification,' 'distinguishing Holy from profane,' 'loving each man his brother as himself* (James 2:8's *'Royal Law according to the Scripture'*, as we saw), and *'separating from all pollutions according to their Statute.'*

81 Lam R. 1.16.48; for the word *'geviot'* for *'corpse'*—in this case, the *'corpse'* of *'the Wicked Priest'*—see 1QpHabix.2; for the transformation of *'looking upon their privy parts'* (*meᶜoreihem'*) in received Habakkuk 2:15 into *'their Festivals'* (*'meᶜodeihem'*), see 1QpHabxi.2–3 and its exploitation— also concerning *'the Wicked Priest'*—in xi.4–15 (including both allusion to *'Festivals'/'the Day of Atonements'* and *'circumcising the foreskin',* i.e., *'the Wicked Priest'*'s) and Chapters 24-25 below.

82 See Lam R. 1.16.47 above and *pars*.

83 *Ket.*66b. This kind of confusion and/or overlaps between the *'Miriam's/'Mary's* and *'Martha',* as we have seen, is not surprising. Even in Gospels, *'Mary'* says the same thing as *'Martha'* (cf. John 11:21 with 11:32 while Luke 10:38–42 below, while keeping some of the elements envisions a wholly other scenario).

84 Not only should one correlate all these *'Glorification'/'self-glorying'* themes, as we have done; but the allusions to these *'camel'* aphorisms in Rabbinic literature occur in *Ket.* 66b–67a and 104a. For parallels in Lam R., including material about her husband Josephus' friend Jesus b. Gamala (to which the *'camel'* aphorism relates as well), see Lam R. 1.16.47-48 above and *Yoma* 9a and 18a and above (for more on this *'Jesus,'* see *Yoma* 37a, *Yeb.* 61a, and *B.B.* 21a).

85 Since *Ket.* 66b thinks this is *'Miriam the daughter of Nakdimon ben Gurion,'* the amounts are quite high and R. Yohanan is pictured as commenting on this; but he sees her just outside Jerusalem as he *'left'* the City, as we saw, *'picking barley grains in the dung of Arab cattle'* (thus!)— the reduction in her previous state which these Talmudic traditions seem to revel in presumably because of her former imperiousness—and it is at this point that R. Eleazar b. Zadok is also pictured as applying *'the consolation of Zion'* aphorism to her, though he seems to see her *'picking barley grains among the horses' hoofs at Acco'* (about one hundred miles further North along the Coast). For Lam R. 1.16.47. he too applies *'the consolation of Zion'* aphorism to *'Miriam*

the daughter of Boethus' (read *'Martha'*), whom he sees, as already remarked, *'the Romans bind her hair to the tails of Arab horses* (n.b., the *'Arab'* parallel here) *and make run from Jerusalem to Lydda.'* In the very next line, he also applies the Song of Songs 1:8 passage to *'Miriam the daughter of Nakdimon'* as in *Kethuboth*; but no matter—the lack of sympathy is the same. *Ket.* 104a, in applying the *'camel'* aphorism to her, makes it clear in the end that this is *'Martha the daughter of Boethus.'*

[86] *Ket.* 104a above.

[87] See *War* 4.236–325. Here Josephus presents his friend (who had warned him of a plot on the part of Simon ben Gamaliel—the son of Paul's presumable teacher and a Pharisee Patriarch in Palestine—to remove him in Galilee; see *Vita* 204) as making a long speech to *'the Idumaeans'* to try to dissuade them from joining causes with those Josephus has now taken to calling *'Zealots.'* These last—presumably music to Roman ears—he now accuses of all form of *'Impiety,' 'pollution,'* and *'gathering spoils.'* But in the end, *'the Zealots'* do finally let these *'Idumaeans'* inro the city by stealth and together they end up butchering *'Jesus ben Gamala,' 'Ananus ben Ananus,'* and as many of the other High Priests as they can find. There is an error in the text here: *'James' judicial murderer'* should read *'Ananus ben Ananus,'* not *'Jesus ben Ananias'*— *'the Prophet'* who bemoans James' death, not his murderer.

[88] *Git* 56a, One should note that in the death scenario for *'Martha the daughter of Boethus'* here, though the *'dung'* motif remains; now the scenario is that *'by this time she had taken off her shoes,'* but *'some dung stuck to her foot and she died'*—again, too, the *'foot'/'feet'* element, as we have seen above.

[89] *Git* 56a, but in *ARN* 6.3 (20b–21a), where these three are also named, the period is *'twenty-two years'* while in Lam R. 1.5.31, where there are *'four councilors'* (*'ben Gurion'* being separated from *'ben Nakdimon'*), the figure is *'ten'*—each is *'capable of supplying the city with food for ten years.'*

[90] See Robert Eisler, *The Messiah Jesus and John the Baptist*, Dial Press, 1931, pp. 252–5.

[91] In this regard, one should take seriously Acts (normally rather tendentious before the introduction of *'the We document'* in 16:10, but in this case pretty accurately incisive) 11:26's contention that it was at *'Antioch'* and among the members of Paul's *'Gentile Christian Church'* that *'the Disciples were first called Christians.'* Of course, that means that in Palestine earlier than approximately the mid-Fifties CE, they were called something else. What was that *'something else'*—*'Nazirites,' 'Essenes,' 'Sicarii',* or *'Zealot 'Sicarii Essenes'*? The only problem, as we have tried to call attention to in our first chapters, is which *'Antioch'* are we talking about here?

[92] The New Testament knows this category of persons, *'the Herodians'* (Mark 3:6 and 12:13/Matthew 2:16), which we find exceedingly useful as a designation. We take it to mean all those who owe their position to or have an interest in the continuation of *'the Herodian Establishment.'* Of course, this *'Peace Party'* do invite the Roman Army into the City, as they did the Seleucids way back in Judas Maccabee's and Alexander Jannaeus' time and as they did to Herod when he was supported by Roman troops in 37 BCE; thus bearing out Josephus' again rather tendentious assertion in the Introduction to *The Jewish War* that it was *'the Jews own Leaders who invited*

the Romans into the Country'—but this was hardly the popular position or that of the mass (in other words, a very self-serving statement to say the least—oft-repeated!).

93 *War* 5.24–6; cf. Tacitus, *Histories* 5.12. For these '*Biryonim*,' one should see the parallel narratives in *Git* 56a and Lam R. 1.5.31 above. The Head of these '*Biryonim*' of Jerusalem in *Gittin* is '*Abba Sikra*'—clearly the Leader of the *Sicarii* there—and he is designated as R. Yohanan's nephew ('*the son of R. Yohanan's mother's sister*'); but in Lamentations *Rabbah*, he is actually named as '*Ben Battiah*' and portrayed as leading R. Yohanan's coffin (carried by his two '*Disciples*,' R. Eliezer and R. Joshua) out of the city—a very curious scene indeed!

94 *Git* 56a. For a parallel proper ascription, see *Ket.* 104a above applying the '*camel*' aphorism to her because of her deceased husband Jesus ben Gamala.

95 *Git* 56a–b.

96 *Git* 56a.

97 *Git* 58a and Lam R. 1.16.48.

98 See *Ant.* 20.179–82. He is a curious figure because, though he was appointed High Priest by Agrippa II, he also seems to have been connected to '*the Temple Wall Affair*'—in the context of which, he was sent to Rome to plead the case with ten others before Nero and his wife Poppea (who, for some reason, kept him back); cf. *Ant.* 20.189–96 and *War* 2.270. It was directly thereafter that James was stoned under the direction of Agrippa II and a new High Priest he had appointed, Ananus ben Ananus ('Ananus the Younger'). For the *Talmud*, *Yoma* 9a, Ishmael was High Priest for ten years which, in this context, seems rather implausible but there was also an earlier such '*Ishmael*' in *Ant.* 18.34. In any event, his clan '*the Boethusians*' are named in '*the Zealot woes*' in *Pes.* 57a (as is he) as '*beating the people with sticks*.' Nevertheless, he is a contradictory character and at times seems to have had quasi-'Zealot'-like sympathies as '*the Temple Wall Affair*' might illustrate and here where he is also called (perhaps erroneously) '*Phineas' Disciple*.' In such a context in *War* 6.114, he is possibly the one beheaded in Cyrene for unspecified (but obviously seditious) offences, though in the same breath his sons are portrayed as fleeing to the Romans for security.

99 So important do I consider this story to be as illustrative of the times, that I have used it as one of the Dedication Pieces to this book and explained many of these points in my Preface.

100 Cf. Matthew 3:17/Mark 1:11/Luke 3:22 where the cry '*This is My beloved son; in him I am well pleased*' is actually attributed to '*a Voice out of the Heavens*' or '*out of Heaven*,' i.e., '*a Bat-Chol*,' and Acts 10:13–16—Peter's '*Heavenly Tablecloth*' vision. Also see Jerome's *Gospel to the Hebrews*.

101 In Git 57b, the unnamed woman who encourages her children to Martyrdom in the face of the Roman Emperor also '*went up onto a roof and threw herself down and was killed*.' In this story, too, there is a '*Voice from Heaven*' which cries out in the words of Psalm 113:9: '*A joyful mother of children*'! Moreover, the connection with this one in Lamentations *Rabbah* and the one in 2 Maccabees 7 is obvious. These, in turn, are certainly connected with Josephus' story of how Herod pleads with the father of the seven children in the caves outside Arbela on his way with the Roman General Sossius down to take Jerusalem in 37 BC—*War* 1.309–14 and, in

the author's view (stated several times), parodied by the nonsense story told of the Sadducees in M. 22:23–34 and *pars*. In the author's view, these stories about *'Bat-Chol's* really do give the ethos of this Period and not the more idealized Greco-Roman ones, one finds in the Gospels and the Book of Acts.

[102] Lam R. 1.16.50–51.

[103] *Yoma* 38b.

[104] 1QMxi.13–14; for *'the Star Prophecy,'* see 1QMxi.6–7 and CDvii.16–21. Also see 4QTesti.12–13.

Chapter 12

[1] *Git* 56a. This *'casting into the streets,'* of course, recalls Matthew 27:3–7's picture of Judas *'casting the thirty pieces of silver into the Temple'*—whatever is meant by this—of course, whatever is meant, the reversal of the tragic sense of the Rabbinic is always obvious. This is supposed to fulfill a passage from *'the Prophet Jeremiah'* when, in fact, the passage being quoted is a broadly-doctored version of *'the Prophet Zechariah'* (11:12–3), which does not really have the connotation Matthew is trying to give it (see my *'Gospel Fiction and the Redemonization of Judas'* in *The Huffington Post*, 12/19/07). Where Ezekiel goes, at Qumran—to be sure—there is *'the Zadokite Statement'* of Ezekiel 44:15 in CDiii.21–iv.10; but there is also the repeated reference to *'the Builders of the wall'* and *'the Daubers with plaster'* of Ezekiel 13:2–23 (the context of which is *'foolish prophets following their own spirit,' 'empty visions'*—this is repeated in 1QpHabx.9–13 in the accusations against *'the Spouter of Lying'* of *'leading Many astray'*—and *'crying "Peace" when there is no Peace')* in the several descriptions of *'the Liar'* / *'the Spouter'* / or *'the Windbag,' 'walking in the Spirit'* or *'being of confused spirit'* in CDiv.20–21, viii.12–13 (Ms. B: xix.24–26), etc. Nor is this to say anything of Ms. Bxix.1–4, quoting Ezekiel 9:4's *'putting a mark on the forehead of those who weep and cry,'* following Zechariah 13:7 and paralleling Ms. A's quotation of Amos 5:26–7 and 9:11 about *'escaping to the Land of the North'* and *'exiling the Tabernacle of your King'* (interpreted in terms of *'re-establishing the fallen Tent of David'*), all relating to *'escaping the Era of the Visitation...with the coming of the Messiah of Aaron and Israel'* (see futher below Chapter 21).

[2] *Ant.* 20.145–7 and *Vita* 119. The former also deals with her reputed incest with her brother Agrippa II. For her relationship with Titus Caesar, see Suetonius, Titus 7; Tacitus, *Hist.* 2.2, and Dio Cassius 66.15 and 18; for a seeming satiric reference to her incest, see Juvenal 6.156–60.

[3] See *Yeb.* 61a and *Yoma* 18a. In both, the *'King'* is called *'King Yannai,'* but this is typical of either Talmudic imprecision or disinformation. The *'King'* involved is clearly Agrippa II and Josephus confirms this in *Ant.* 20.213. One should also see Lam R. 1.16.47 where she is called *'Miriam daughter of Boethus'* (sic!).

[4] Cf. *Yoma* 9a and 18a above. The former statement is literally reproduced in marginal notes of a Sixteenth Century Edition called *Bayit Hadash* with glosses by R. Joel b. Samuel Sirkes.

[5] See *Ket.* 104a and cf. too *Ket.* 66b, where a seemingly similar situation regarding extremely high

dowries and the like is being told about Nakdimon's daughter Miriam, whom R. Yohanan (*'riding on an ass followed by his Disciples'*—thus!) sees on his way out of Jerusalem *'picking barley grains out of the dung of Arab cattle.* It should also be recalled that in Lam R. 1.16.47, it is pointed out that, after she married Joshua b. Gamala, *'the King (Agrippa II) appointed him High Priest.'* Here too, the question of her maintenance after his death (*'two se'ahs of wine daily'*) is discussed in the context of the extravagant nature of the widow's allowance, they accorded her, and the point about her *'once going to see (her husband) reading on the Day of Atonement in the Temple'*; wherefore *'they laid carpets for her from the door of her house to the entrance of the Temple so that her feet might not be exposed. Nevertheless, they were exposed.'* This is a marvelous tradition.

6 For these materials about *'Martha the daughter of Boethus'* (*sic*—really *'Miriam'*, as we have seen), called *'one of the Richest women in Jerusalem'* and the story of her death, when she is supposed to have gone out and took off her shoes, *'some dung stuck to her foot and she died'*; see Git. 56a (already so noted several times above). It is at this point that R. Yohanan is supposed to have applied the verse from Deuteronomy 28:57: *'The tender and delicate woman among you who would not adventure to set the sole of her foot upon the ground.'* For the parallel material in CD, see xix.9–13 and Chapter 21 below.

7 For the true picture of the relationship of Salome to Philip and John the Baptist generally, see *Ant.* 18.116–19 and 137 and, for a real picture of *'levirite marriage'* issues as they related to the remarriage of Martha the daughter of Boethus and Josephus' friend Jesus ben Gamala, see *Yeb.* 61a, *Yoma* 18a, *Ket.* 104a, and Lam *R.* 1.16.47 above.

8 For the ban on *'niece marriage,' 'close family cousins,'* and *'divorce'*, see CDiv.17–v.10, viii.6–7, 11QTlxvi.12–16, etc.; for the *'Simon'* in Josephus, see *Ant.* 18.332–4 and for Herodian marital practices generally, see *Ant.* 18.130–42 and the Herodian Genealogical Chart we have provided below.

9 For *'the Sicarii,'* see *War* 2.254–57, 425–29, and 4.400–5, *Ant.* 20.186, etc. It is interesting that, as first really observed by Morton Smith, Josephus only begins using the term *'Zealots'* in *War* 2.651, long after most of these references. The second such references come in *War* 4.162–365 when, beginning with his discussion of *'the Peace Party'* of Ananus ben Ananus, Jesus ben Gamala, Rabban Simeon ben Gamaliel (Paul's alleged teacher's son), and even one *'Gurion'*— probably a descendant of the family of *'Nakdimon ben Gurion'* above—and ending with their alliance with *'the Idumaeans'* and other *'Brigands',* they destroy such persons as this Ananus, Josephus' friend Jesus ben Gamala and finally the *'Rich'* Traitor, Josephus calls, *'Zachariah ben Baris'* (cf. Matthew 23:35), whom they slew in the Temple and whose body they *'cast down'* into the ravine below. It is odd that these so-called *'Zealots'* first really appear in Josephus during the course of this seeming *'Vengeance'* being taken for the death of persons such as James, the greater part of whose partisans according to Acts 21:21 were made up of *'Zealots'!*

10 *War* 7.262-68.

11 It is very important to chronicle these so called *'Idumaeans'* in Josephus and I have done so to

some extent in *MZCQ*, pp. 62–63, 95; *JJHP*, pp. 26–27, 43, 49–50, 64, 71, *James*, pp. 406–8, 522–27, 814–15, and Chapters 23-24 below; in Josephus, these are chronicled in key passages of the *War* in 4.224–353, 4.566–72, and later in 5.248–49, 358, 6.378–81, and 7.262–74. Aside from Niger of Perea, whose death we have already noted as being perhaps the palimpsest for that of the 'Jesus' of Scripture; they had two brave leaders, Josephus constantly cites, named *'John'* and *'James the son of Sosas,'* who seem to have been brothers and who bear an uncanny parallel to the names of the two *'Disciples'* of Jesus in Scripture, known as *'John and James the sons of Boarneges'.* For these two, see Josephus, *War* 4.235, 290 (John's death by an *'Arab'*s arrow), 521–28, 5.249, and 6.92, 6.148, and 6.360, where he is ultimately arrested by Simon bar Gioras and probably executed. There is also one *'Simon son of Cathlas'* and, where *'the Zealots'* are concerned, *'Simon and Jude the sons of Ari'* (obviously *'Jairus'*—6.92 and 6.148). Note, too, the plethora of Maccabean and later 'Christian' names throughout these notices.

[12] See *War* 4.224–325 above. He repeats this charge of butchering all the High Priests in *War* 7.267–68.

[13] For *'Ben Zizzit',* see *Git.* 56a, *Gen R.* 42.1, *Lam R.* 1.5.31, and *ARN* 6.3 (20b–21a). For the famous Talmudic episode where the Rabbis cry out to Agrippa I, when he comes to read the Deuteronomic King Law on *Succot,* that *'You are our brother, you are our brother, you are our brother'* on account of his Piety; see *M. Sota* 7:8 and *pars.* (*Bik.* 3:4 and *Siphre* Deut. 157 on 17:15).

[14] See *Git.* 56a, which here calls *'the Zealots', 'Biryonim',* and cf. *ARN* 6.3 (21a), *War* 5.24–26, and Tacitus, *Hist.* 5.12

[15] *Git.* 56a. It is here R. Yohanan is pictured as applying the verse from Deuteronomy 28:57 to her pathetic state: *'The tender and delicate woman among you who would not venture to set the sole of her foot upon the ground'*; but in *Ket.* 66b, it is rather *'Nakdimon ben Gurion's daughter'* Miriam whom R. Yohanan sees *'picking barley grains from the dung of Arab cattle',* as we saw (again the mix-up between *'Martha'* and *'Mary'* even in these Talmudic/Rabbinic traditions). Nonetheless, directly following this, in *Ket.* 67a and repeated verbatim in *Lam R.* 1.16.47–8 (where she is actually correctly named *'Miriam the daughter of Nakdimon'*), it is rather R. Eleazar b. Zadok who is the bearer of the tradition and, as we have also repeatedly seen, what she is doing when he sees her is *'picking barley grains from among the horses' hoofs in Acco'.* Furthermore, it is concerning her fate that the latter allegedly applied the passage from Song of Songs 1:8 (not the one from Deuteronomy 28:57 in the previous tradition): *'O fairest among women, go thy way forth among the footsteps of the flock and feed your bodies'* (*geviotayik* and not *'kids'/'gediyotayik'* as in the original—at Qumran, one sometimes gets the same sort of tampering with Biblical quotes to develop a preferred exegesis—as one does often in the Gospels and in Acts). In the conversation with R. Yohanan in *Ket.* 66b (not with Eleazar ben Zadok, as we just saw, as in *Ket.* 67a and *Lam R.* 1.16.48) and as we shall see below, not only does Nakdimon's daughter address him as *'Master'* (cf. see how in conversation with *'her sister Mary'* in John 11:28, *'Martha'* refers to *'Jesus'* as *'Master'*); but the only thing she really requests of him (R. Yohanan)—after *'wrapping herself in her hair'* and *'standing up'*—is *'feed me'* (our *'dog'/'dogs under the table longing*

to be fed' or *Ben Kalba Sabu^c a's* 'Poor'/'the Poor man Lazarus' at the 'Rich Man's door' language in Luke 16 again); however we are clearly dealing with the same episode. It is here that R. Yohanan enters into his discourse on *'the Riches'* of both her father and father-in-law's houses, noting in an aside to *'his Disciples'* how the marriage contract he signed in her regard reckoned her surety at *'one million dinars'* and comparing it, by implication, to her present fallen state. Here the exchange between R. Yohanan and Nakdimon's daughter—who, to repeat, instead of Lamentations *Rabbah's* and 67a's description of her in the name of R. Eleazar b. Zadok, as *'picking grain among the horses' hoofs in Acco,'* is now rather *'picking barley grains out of the dung of Arab cattle'*—is more detailed and focuses more on the utter reversal of her fortune and the complete obliteration of the *'Riches'* of both her father and her father-in-law's house (whoever these may have been—is there a mix-up here too with *'Boethus' daughter Martha'*?). This kind of confusion and/or overlap between the *'Miriam's'/'Mary's/* and *'Martha'* is not surprising. Even in Gospels, *'Mary'* says the same thing as *'Martha'* in John 11:21 and 11:32. Moreover, the kind of rebuke *'Jesus'* is pictured as giving to all these various complainers, as we have already several times remarked, is the same as in Luke 7:37–4 where it is yet another unnamed woman—simply identified as *'a Sinner'*—'washing' Jesus' feet again (though now *'with her tears'*) *'and wiping them with her hair.'* In parallel materials about R. Yohanan in *Kethuboth* 66b, he is once again pictured, like 'Jesus' in reverse, *'leaving Jerusalem riding upon a donkey while his Disciples follow him'* (66b). In this picture, too, of the miserable state to which *'Nakdimon ben Gurion's daughter Miriam'* had fallen, the motif of *'her hair'* is added as well. To repeat, now *'standing up'* to answer the *'Master'*'s questions, she wrapped (not *'wiped his feet'* as in John 11:2, 12:3, Luke 7:37–38, etc.) *herself with her hair and stood before him'*—here also, two incidences of these *'Standing'/'stood'* allusions). Nor in *Kethuboth* is she explicitly going out *'barefoot'* as *Gittin* relates rather of *'Boethus' daughter Martha'* above who, as we just saw too in the picture of her fate, is depicted—Rabbinic hyperbole aside—as dying *'when some dung stuck to her foot'*! To this heart-rending end, R. Yohanan was also pictured, as we just saw as well, as applying the verse from Deuteronomy 28:56 above about *'the tender and delicate woman who would not set the sole of her foot upon the ground'* and which we have already observed *'R. Eleazar b. Zadok'* apply in Lam R. 1.16.47 to *'Boethus' daughter Miriam', 'picking grain among the horses' hoofs in Acco'*—but, Rabbinic hyperbole again aside, whose *'hair'* the Romans are now pictured as *'binding to the tails of Arab horses and make run from Jerusalem to Lydda'* (sic)!

[16] *ARN* 6.3 (21a) above.

[17] In CD (Ms. B) xix.9–13, the passage being quoted is Ezekiel 9:4 about *'putting a mark on the foreheads of those who weep and cry'* (we have already called such persons *'Mourners for Zion'*), which is clearly meant to parallel the more detailed quotes from Isaiah 7:17, Amos 5:26–27 and 9:11, and Numbers 24:17 (*'the Star Prophecy'*) in CDvii.7–21 in Ms. A. Both are, in some sense, dealing with the *'coming of the Messiah of Aaron and Israel'* (singular), the destruction which would be visited upon *'the Backsliders'* and *'Evil Ones, when God visits the Earth,'* and *'the Little Ones'* and *'the Meek of the Flock'* (Zechariah 13:7) who would escape to *'the Land of the North.'* See Chapter 21 again below and note the parallel with Matthew 27:3–10 about *'Judas*

Iscariot' (sic) supposedly *casting the pieces of silver into the Temple* which thinks it is quoting *the Prophet Jeremiah* when, in fact, it is quoting a very loose version of *the Prophet Zechariah* as we saw (11:12–13). Still, the ambiance of all these passages have in some sense to do with the fall of Jerusalem and the destruction of the Temple, the coming of some kind of *'Messiah,'* and the *'escape'* of some group or other (*'the Meek'* or *'the Poor'*) *'who weep and cry.'*

[17a]Matthew 27:3–10 above and *ARN* 6.3 (21a). *Git.* 56a, as we have seen, gives a slightly different derivation of his name, i.e., *'Ben Zizzit Hakeseth'*—that *'his fringes used to trail on cushions'* and *'his seat was among the Nobility of Rome,'* not *'of Israel.'* Who could he be? One of the *'Herodians'* perhaps? For the *'cistern'* stories about Nakdimon as a kind of *'Honi'/'Elijah redivivus'* and his *'daughter's bedspread,'* see *Ta'an* 19b and *ARN* 21a above as well.

[18] *Git.* 56a–b.

[19] Ephesians 2:19–22, too, continues this metaphor of *'Jesus'* or the body of the Community (which in 1 Corinthians is *'Christ Jesus'*) as Temple and it does so by emphasizing there *'are no longer (any) strangers and foreigners'* in *'the Household of God.'* Moreover, it also emphasizes *'Circumcision'* and *'Uncircumcision'* (2:11), *'Separation'* in a purely allegorical or spiritualized manner (2:12), *'the Blood of Christ'* (2:13), *'Peace'* (i.e., the Roman *'Pax Romana'*—2:14), and a general plethora of *'Foundation,' 'Cornerstone'* (cf. 1QSviii.7–8 below where the context is also spiritualized *'Temple'* imagery, i.e., *'a Dwelling of the Holy of Holies for Aaron'*), and *'Building'* imagery—all spiritualized.

[20] Lam R. 1.5.31 and Eccles. R. 7.12.1.

[21] For our comments on these *'Abba'* names, as well as more material on *'Jacob of Kfar Sechania'* or *'Sihnin,'* see Chapter 4 above. One should note, as well, that Lam R. 1.17.52 also knows a Rabbi known as *'R. Joshua of Sihnin'* as we saw.

[22] Eccles. R. 7.12. Here, the passage is about *'Ben Battiah'* or *'Abba Sikkra,'* R. Yohanan b. Zacchai's nephew, *'the Head of the Sicarii in Jerusalem'* who, in this capacity, *'burned all the stores'* as we have already seen as well. But what should have been written here is the Aramaic *'Sikrin'* while instead we find the designation *'Kisrin.'* We have also already remarked mix-ups like this in the *'Judas Iscariot'* designation in the Gospels and the Book of Acts above. Of course the story about *'Jacob'* (possibly *'James'*) is to be found in Eccles. R. 1.8.3, A.Z. 17a, and *Tos. Hul.* 2:24 above. One should also see j. *Shab.* 14.4 (14d). For more on this *'Jacob,'* also see A.Z. 27b. While some authorities consider this *'Kisrin'* to be *'Katzrin'* on the Golan Heights, reconquered from the Syrians in modern times in 1967 and where an archaeological dig has been in progress for some time; others simply identify it as a Hebrew/Aramaic approximation of the coastal town of *'Caesarea.'* Still *'Kfar Sechania'* or *'Sihnin'* is doubtlessly a Galilean town—and just such a town exists among the Arabs in Galilee today, not far from the Sea by that name. For *'Sihnin,'* see Josephus, *Vita* 188 and 265 and *War* 2.573 and Chapter 6 above. Also in addition to the Talmudic references there, see j. *Meg* 4:5, 7b.

[23] *Git.* 56a–b and cf. Lam R. 1.5.31 and *ARN* 4.5 (20a).

[24] *Ber.* 62a. This is an amazing passage because, not only does it show the earthiness of the *Talmud*

and its concerns for the mundane bodily things—such as which way to sit in the privy, how one should behave when one 'consults nature,' or how to indulge in sexual relations (to each such schoolboyish indiscretion concerning which, the narrator replies: *'It is a matter of Torah and I am required to learn'*); but it comes right after the gruesomely detailed description of R. Akiba's public death and martyrdom—itself following upon and in exposition of the citation of how one *'should love the Lord your God with all your soul and with all your might'*—the 'Piety' Commandment of all our Opposition/Resistance groups above.

[25] *Git.* 56a and Lam R. 1.5.31. In these presentations, of course, we have what is perhaps the original prototype for *'the Pierced Messiah'* material. This is a question that has vexed Qumran Studies ever since Prof. Wise and myself informed the world of the existence of just such a text in the unpublished Qumran manuscripts in 1991 (4Q285)—after we published it, dubbed by popularizers like Hershel Shanks (the Editor of *The Biblical Archaeology Review*) *'The Pierced Messiah',* but which we called *'The Messianic Leader (Nasi)'*; cf. *DSSU,* pp. 27–29. For my original interpretation of this text, see the introduction of it in *DSSU,* pp. 24–27 (which I wrote—Prof. Wise and his Team at the University of Chicago doing redactions and translations, while I wrote most of the commentaries). It is interesting that in the presentation in *ARN* 4.5 (20a), the *'pierced'* material is omitted as is any reference to R. Yohanan's nephew, *Abba Sikkra*/Ben Battiah, the context in which one finds it in the *Gittin* and Lamentations *Rabbah* presentations above. Nonetheless, the episode does move on to R. Yohanan's anachronistic interview before Vespasian, in which the former does apply it to the latter (as Josephus does with slightly more reliability in the *War* 3.399–405), one part of what I have been referring to as *'the Messianic Prophecy'*—Isaiah 10:34: *'Lebanon shall fall by a Mighty One.'* That passage is introduced by the material about *'a Shoot arising from the Root of Jesse',* both extant at Qumran—the first in 4QpIsaᵃ (161–3) below and the second in 4Q285 above. A second prophecy contributing to this *'Messianic'* couplet is *'The Star Prophecy'* of Numbers 24:17 which we have referred to above, but see Chapters 12, 14-15, and 21 below. Again, to reiterate, Prof. Wise and myself were the first to call attention to this incredibly pivotal fragment buried in the hitherto unpublished materials. To Prof. Wise's Team goes the credit of discovering it and first translating it, though others—also recognizing its importance—have since capitalized on and exploited it for their own purposes (the first, and most notable, perhaps, being—hardly months after we first publicly revealed its existence—Prof. G. Vermes of Oxford in *'The Oxford Forum for Qumran Research: Seminar on the Rule of War 4Q285, JJS,* 1992, pp. 85–90. In that somewhat opportunistic and not very charitable publication, he criticized the translation of Prof. Wise and his team (unaware at the time, perhaps, that I was not among those doing this aspect of the work), as others—like Prof. Wacholder of H.U.C.—had already done before him (perhaps justifiably); while at the same time giving the impression that he and his colleagues were the ones really bringing this key fragment to the attention of the public. Perhaps as a reward for this, he and his student/associate, P. Alexander, were the ones ultimately given responsibility for *'the Editio Princeps'*—as he terms it—of this text in *DJD* XXIII by the Qumran *'Editorial Team.'* Others who exploited the existence of this pivotal fragment included institutions like the Israel

Antiquities Authority which, while initially condemning our part in calling attention to and making this fragment public, have made it a featured part of almost every exhibition of the Dead Sea Scrolls they have sponsored ever since at Museums around the world—while all the time, like some others, usually neglecting to acknowledge our part in discovering it and bringing this fragment to the attention of the world—not to mention the published catalogues that usually accompanied these exhibits. In their anxiety to usurp and condemn the fact that we originally found this fragment, they almost always misunderstand the purpose of Prof. Wise and myself in revealing the existence of this fundamental fragment (overlooked by 'the *Official Team*' previously responsible for the publication of the Scrolls for some 35 years) was not to give a definitive final translation; but rather to counter the endless palliatives one was hearing at the time, attempting to discourage the public from inquiring further into the matter of the previously-unpublished Scrolls—namely, that '*there was nothing important in the unpublished materials*.' We disagreed and this was the reason we went public to the press—where they had been handing out these tendentious reports to counter-indicate this mantra, citing the existence of this pivotal fragment identifying '*the Branch of David*,' the '*Shoot from the Root of Jesse*,' with '*the Nasi ha^cEdah*.' This '*Nasi*,' as we have seen, is also mentioned in Column vii of the Damascus Document in connection with the crucial exegesis of '*the Star Prophecy*' of Numbers 24:17—just mentioned above—as '*the Scepter who would arise out of Israel*.' We considered it highly important even if the translation provided by Michael Wise and his associates was only a rough preliminary at the time. The point of this exercise was to show the world just how important some of the materials to be found in the unpublished corpus actually were—not to provide a final accurate and precise translation. We left this to those obliged to us for having found it.

[26] Once again, this has to be seen as Isaiah 10:34–11:5, a *Pesher* concerning which is completely extant at Qumran (4QpIsa^a—also reflected, however fragmentedly, in 4Q285 above), augmented by Numbers 24:17, as we just saw, which is found in at least three places in the extant Qumran corpus: the Damascus Document, the War Scroll, and *Testimonia*. In the first place, it has to be said that in all these contexts at Qumran, '*the Nasi ha-^cEdah*'/'*the Prince of the Congregation*' is mentioned (in the Isaiah *Pesher*, for instance, however fragmentary, it is in Column ii.15); and '*the Branch of David*' in at least two of these, as well as in the Genesis *Pesher* in the exposition there of the '*Shiloh*' Prophecy of Genesis 49:10. Furthermore in all the Isaiah *Pesher*s, '*the Remnant*'—an expression also to be encountered in Columns vii and xix in the Damascus Document below, and '*the Last Days*,' pervasive in the Literature—are mentioned repeatedly. Paralleling the Damascus Document too, '*the Time of the Visitation*' is evoked. The Enemy are clearly '*the Kittim*' and, not insignificantly, '*Lebanon*' (because of the '*whitening*' imagery) is definitively identified as '*the Temple*.' Here, however, the resemblance between these positions and the Rabbinic ends because the interpretation attributed to R. Yohanan—not to mention Josephus—appears to reverse that at Qumran, This should not be surprising as one finds the same kind of reversal going on in 'Christian' Literature almost without pause. Of course, '*the Star Prophecy*' appears as well in Rabbinic Literature but, once again, there it is more

to belittle it or belittle R. Akiba—otherwise perhaps the most heroic Rabbi in the *Talmud*—because of his perceived application of it to Bar Kochba from which report, it would appear certain, the latter took his name. This is because in most other contexts—such as 2.2.4 and b. *Ta'an*. 68d, which tell the whole story of R. Akiba and '*Bar Koziba*' (as well as the latter's death) and the Bar Kochba Letters found at Wadi Murabba'at—he is called '*Bar Kosiba*'. Of course, in Rabbinic Literature, not unlike the opponent of the Righteous Teacher in the Scrolls, '*Bar Koziba*' is re-interpreted to refer to '*the Liar*'—an interesting parallel with the operative manner of the Documents at Qumran.

[27] The point here is that we have actual Rabbinic confirmation that all these allusions—*ARN* 4.5 (20a), Lam R. 1.5.31, and *Git.* 56a–b—refer to the fall of the Temple in 70 CE and not any earlier one. In fact, as *ARN* progresses, a number of other prophecies, referring to this event and using this kind of '*Lebanon*' language to refer to the Temple, are listed. One also finds the same sorts of '*Lebanon*' passages in *Yoma* 39b, some also including '*cedars*' language which almost always refers to '*the Temple*'. Another favorite, where this kind of imagery is concerned, is Zechariah 11:1: '*Open your doors O Lebanon that the fire may devour your Cedars*'!

[28(26)] This does begin to undermine the believability of the account in Matthew right from the start, which is largely contradicted in Acts 1:18–20 anyhow (see my '*Gospel Fiction and the Redemonization of Judas*' in *The Huffington Post*, 12/19/07 above). But curiously, the account too in Acts 1:20 appears to apply two tendentious prophecies from what it terms '*the Holy Spirit by the mouth of David concerning Judas*' Psalms 69:29 and 109:8 to these events concerning Judas' demise and the immediate alleged election to replace him, where the defeated candidate's '*surname*' was '*Justus*.' We have treated this subject at length in *James*, pp. 154–257, 406–60, etc. and the point is that the word Greek Acts uses to express Psalm 109:8 ('*let someone else take his Office*', to say nothing of the uncharitability the passage from Psalm 69:25: '*let his camp be reduced to ruin; let there be no one to live in it*'—what does this mean?) is '*Episkopon*,' which all will recognize as precisely the position accorded James (where the epithet '*Justus*' is used in sometimes in place of his very name itself) in Early Church Literature and not either '*Judas*' or his substitutes. Equally curious, not only is there no description of the missing election of James as '*Bishop*' of the early Church—found in almost all early Church sources—which should have occurred at approximately this time; there is no introduction of who, in fact, this '*James*' actually was; though Acts 12:17, following upon the beheading of the other James and Peter's alleged miraculous escape from prison, seems to think we either know or should know who he is. Finally, if we see James as a kind of '*Essene*' or '*Rechabite*', then at this point the material from Jeremiah 35:1–19 probably would have been an appropriate text to cite at this point, were one interested in citing proof texts. So here actually '*the Prophet Jeremiah*' would have been appropriate, whereas in the parallel account in Matthew 27:3–10 above, it would not have been—rather Zechariah 11:12–3 as we have seen. Of course Zechariah 12:10 cited in John 19:36 (which omits any mention of '*Judas*' in its discussion of the death of '*Jesus*', as do Mark and Luke), the first '*pierced*' text in the Gospels, really does find a parallel in the materials about R. Yohanan's escape from Jerusalem in Rabbinic Literature as we have seen above.

[29(27)] To show that Paul is aware of this method, see his statement in Galatians 4:27 where, in tendentiously applying Abraham's marital situation in Genesis to that of his congregants *'wish to be subject to the Law'*, which plays upon the *'freeborn wife'* Sarah, as opposed to *'the daughter of the slave woman'* Hagar (who is supposed to stand for *'Mount Sinai in Arabia, whose children are in slavery'*, i.e., a thinly-disguised aspersion for being subject to *'the Law of Moses'*), whereas the real *'Children of the Promise'* (meaning his Communities) are *'free'*; he therefore quotes, again rather tendentiously but full of ill-will and bad temper and itself playing on the *'Essene'* practice of *'casting out'* backsliders as reported in Josephus: *'Therefore cast out the slave woman'*—this in place of what might have been considered real *'Freedom'* and *'Slavery'* by his opponents, i.e., those fighting against Rome or in the so-called *'Zealot,'* *'Messianic,'* or *'Sicarii'* Movement and a point actually expressed on their coinage from 66–69 CE and even later in the Bar Kochba Uprising (another of these *'Star's*): *'the Freedom of Israel.'* But where Paul is concerned, as he puts this following the precedent of Philo (whom, if he was an *'Herodian,'* as we shall argue again presently and have done previously —*'Herodians'* having married into Philo's family, he probably even knew): *'Such things are allegory.'*

30 See n. 27 above.

31 Lam R. 1.5.31 and 2.2.4 and *ARN* 4.5 (20a) above, but also see Eccles. *R.* 7.12.1 and *Git* 56b as well.

32 See, for instance, 4Q163 (Isaiah *Pesher*), Fragment 21.7–9, where the passage being cited is Zechariah 11:11 just after these quotes from Talmudic Literature above, and Fragments 8–10, where the passage being quoted is Zechariah 3:9.

33 See, for instance, 1QpHabv.12–vi.11, where the passage being expounded is Habakkuk 1:14–16 and the exposition has to do with *'the Kittim'* (in our view, the Romans), who *'eat'* or *'consume all the Peoples year by year giving many Countries over to the sword'* (hardly the Seleucids). *'They destroy many by the sword...and have no pity even on the fruit of the womb.'* This pericope is very compelling, particularly for dating purposes. For this kind of *'destruction'* applied to *'the Righteous Teacher,'* *'the Poor,'* and, in turn, via *'God's Judgement,'* *'the Wicked Priest'* and *'all the Servants of Idols'* taken as one; see 1QpHabxi.4–xii.4 below.

34 1QpHabxi.16–xii.5. Note here that this reference to *'Lebanon'* as *'the Council of the Community'* comes amid evocation of *'the dumb beasts'* as *'the Simple Ones of Judah doing Torah'* and *'the Ebionim'*—and presumably their *'Blood'* (*'the Blood of Man'*/*'Adam'* in Habakkuk 2:17)—as consisting of these and *'the Council of the Community.'* For *'the Essenes'* wearing only *'white linen'* (like *'Priests'* in the Temple), see Josephus, *War* 2.122. It should be noted too that, in the interpretation of Zechariah 11:1 in *ARN* 4.5 (20a): *'Open your doors, O Lebanon, that fire may devour your cedars,'* *'Lebanon'* would appear to stand for *'the High Priests'* and here the exposition involves hurling the keys to the Temple up to Heaven.

35 For this list of the virtues and characteristics of *'the Community Council,'* see 1QSvii.1–12 (immediately preceded by a rehearsal of *'Essene'* expulsion practices and directly followed by evocation of Isaiah 40:3's *'Prepare in the wilderness the Way of the Lord'* as descriptive of the Community's own *'separation from the midst of the Habitation of the Men of Unrighteousness to go into the wilderness'*). Note, too, that in this perhaps fundamental description these also include

'*paying the Wicked their Reward*' of 1QpHabxii.2–3 above and '*those bent in the dust*' in the War Scroll, the '*steadfastness*' of Columns vii–viii and xix–xx of the Damascus Document, the '*Precious Cornerstone*' imagery of 'Jesus' in the New Testament, and the '*spiritualized*' Community as Temple imagery of Paul in 1 Corinthians.

[36] *ARN* 4.5 (20a). For being '*made white*,' see *Yoma* 39a and 39b below.

[37] *Yoma* 39b. Note that in 39a, preceding this, there is even an allusion (as in Isaiah 1:18) to '*whitening*' of the scarlet strap that was tied between the horns of a bullock in the Temple for sacrifice. For the exposition of this passage in Nahum at Qumran, see 4QpNahi.4–9 which, once again though fragmentary, clearly centers on what '*the Kittim*' are doing to the Land including the Temple.

[38] Lam R. 1.5.31. In this narrative, which rather takes place in the presence of his nephew '*Ben Battiah*' (in *Gittin*, '*the Head of the Biryonim in Jerusalem*'), it is the difference—as we have already seen—between a '*woe*' and a '*wah*' that make all the difference.

[39] *Ibid.*

[40] Cf. Lam R. 1.5.31 with *ARN* 4.5 (20a) and *Git* 56b above.

[41] *War* 6.312–3. In another curious parallel, it is interesting to note that, even in the story of 'Jesus ben Ananias' that precedes this in *War* 6.300–9, 'Jesus'' cry of '*Woe, woe to Jerusalem*,' repeated some four times, is also anticipating the fall of Jerusalem and the destruction of the Temple.

[42] Cf. *War* 2.151–3 with *Ant.* 18.23 and note that, while Josephus is calling the latter 'the Fourth Philosophy' followers of 'Judas the Galilean' without specifically naming it either 'Zealot' or 'Sicarii,' but obviously rather 'Galileans'; the description of the courage they show under torture and the threat of imminent death is the same. In fact, it is this indifference to torture and death that Hippolytus 9.21 is rather describing as characteristic of those he is calling either 'Zealot' or 'Sicarii Essenes.'

[43] See Josephus, *War* 4.585–663 and cf. Tacitus, *Hist.* 2.78–5.13, Suetonius 8.5.1–8.85, etc.

[44] See Josephus, *War* 3.399–405 above.

[45] We first began to call these '*Movements*' '*Messianic*' and insist on a *singular* Davidic Messiah at Qumran in *MZCQ*, Leiden, 1983, pp. 20–27, 36–38, and 96–97. The finding, of course, of '*The Messiah of Heaven and Earth*' text (4Q521) in *DSSU*, 1991, pp. 19–21 did not hurt this hypothesis at all. See also my comments introducing this section, pp. 17–19 but, also, my more general ones in pp. 10–12.

[46] See 4QFlori.7–11 on 2 Samuel 7:11–14 and Amos 9:11 and Chapters 21-22 and variously below. One should note that in all such contexts—4Q285, the Messianic *Florilegium* on the Promises to David, Columns vii and xix of the Damascus Document, and in the Genesis *Pesher*—the adjectival, verbal, and pronominal usages surrounding all these allusions are invariably *singular*.

[47] 4Q285 above, *DSSU*, pp. 24–30.

[48] See my comments in n. 25 above. Though this was widely trumpeted as a text which I found, it

was not I who either found this text or translated it. As already stated, my purpose in releasing it in 1990 was to show how significant some of the materials in the unpublished corpus actually were, as opposed to what some members of the Qumran Editorial Team were publicly insisting. See my comments as well in *DSSU*, pp. 24–7, in 1990–1. This introduction, written solely by myself, was also my sole contribution to the decipherment of this text. The idea of 'a Suffering Messiah' at Qumran always seemed to me to run counter to the militancy and Apocalyptic aggressiveness of the general thrust of the texts there. Though possible, it was to say the least highly improbable despite the equivocal and ambiguous nature of the allusion in question.

49 CDvii.18–21, xii.23, xiv.20, and xix.10–11 and see my comments in *DSSU*, pp. 10–12 and 17–19 above.

50 See 4Q252v.1–6, DSSU, p. 89 and my comments there on pp. 83–85. Of course, the allusion here to the Messianic *'feet'* are all-important to the numerous accounts in the Gospels—which we have covered *ad nauseum* above—of anointing Jesus' feet with expensive *'spikenard ointment'* or *'wiping'* them with one's hair or *'bathing'* them with one's tears. But also one should see the numerous allusions to *'making Your enemies Your footstool'* of Psalm 110:1 (another aggressively *'Messianic'* Psalm which also speaks of *'sitting on the Right Hand'* of God, the *'Scepter in Zion,'* *'a Priest after the Order of Melchizedek forever,'* *'shattering kings,'* *'smashing skulls,'* and *'holding His Head high in Victory'*) in Matthew 22:44, Mark 12:36, Luke 20:43, Acts 2:35, and Hebrews 1:13 and 10:13 and cf. 1QMxii.11–12 and xix.3–4.

51 See Lam R. 1.16.51 which has many of the quotations found here at Qumran, not to mention in Paul—cf. *'the Comforter'* or *'Deliverer'* of Isaiah 27:9 in Romans 11:26, as well as in John 15:26 and 16:7.

52 See CDvii.18–21 where *'the Scepter arising out of Israel'* is said to be *'the Nasi chol ha-ʿEdah',* at whose *'rising'* or *'standing up'* (Resurrection?), *'shall utterly destroy all the Sons of Seth'*—this again in line with the aggressive quality of Psalm 110:5–7 despite later 'Christian' attempts to transmute it.

53 See *ARN* 4.5 (20a) above.

54 *Git.* 56b above.

55 See our comments about *'the Mourners for Zion'* in *James*, pp. 309, 709, 764, and 898.

56 CDvii..18–20, 1QMxi.5–9, and 4QTesti.9–13.

57 *Loc. cit, War* 3.399–405.

58 Lam R. 1.13.41 and Song of Songs R. 8.9.3. It should be noted that Numbers 24:17 is also quoted in the latter 2.3.5.

59 1QpHabix.6–7 (note that the context here is the fall of Jerusalem and, in particular, the destruction of *'the Last Priests of Jerusalem'*). The *'Oracle to leave Jerusalem'* is known as *'the Pella Flight Oracle'* and, for a description of it, see *E.H.* 3.5.3 and Epiphanius, *De pond. et mens. 15*. For our treatment of it, see Chapter 17 below. It is interesting that, directly following this reference in *E.H.* 3.8.1–11, Eusebius gives all of Josephus' *'signs'* from the *War* for the destruction of Jerusalem and the Temple, including the whole story of *'Jesus ben Ananias'* oracle,

which we discuss below and compare both to '*the Pella Flight Oracle*' and '*Agabus*'' reverse oracle in Acts 21:10–14 '*not to go up to Jerusalem*,' One should also note that it is in this same section, *E.H.* 3.8.10–11, that Eusebius remarks Josephus' application of '*the World Ruler Prophecy*' to Vespasian (and here, quite clearly, he is using the language of Numbers 24:17 not Isaiah 10:34), arguing that this was incorrect and should rather have been applied to '*Jesus*,' '*since Vespasian did not rule the whole world, but only that part of it which was subject to the Romans*' (sic)! For Paul's receipt of another reverse revelation—this time to '*go up to Jerusalem*,' see Galatians 2:1–2.

[60] *Ket.* 66b.

[61] Cf. *Ket.* 66b–67a with Lam R. 1.16.48 and n. 15 above.

[62] Cf. *Ket.* 66b and 67a with *Git* 56a and Lam R. 1.16.47 and, again, see n. 15 above. We have already paid sufficient attention to all these '*hair*' motif allusions, but for the various ministrations of women '*anointing*' Jesus' '*feet*' with their '*tears*' or '*wiping*' them with their '*hair*' in the New Testament, see Matthew 26:7–12, Mark 14:3–4, Luke 7:38–44, and John 11:2 and 12:3, etc. In the latter two cases, as we have seen, it is again another '*Mary*'—this time identified as '*Martha's sister*' (sic!).

[63] *ARN* 6.3 (20b)

[64] For the '*sweet fragrance*' of the '*Righteousness, et. al.*' of Community Council at Qumran, see 1QSviii.9–10. It should be noted, as we shall again below, that this is the same Epaphroditus that Paul addresses earlier in Philippians 2:25 as his '*brother*,' '*fellow-worker and fellow-soldier*,' '*Minister*' and '*Apostle*' seemingly to those he later calls '*the Saints*' in '*the Household of Caesar*' in Philippians 4:22 (speak about Rabbinic hyperbole). It is hardly to be doubted that this is the same '*Epaphroditus*' (also '*in the Household of Caesar*'—in this case, both '*Nero Caesar*,' whom he seems to have helped commit suicide, and, after that, the Flavians— to whom Josephus dedicated most of his works. In 2 Corinthians 2:14–7, Paul really surpasses himself with this '*sweet fragrance*' imagery, using it in every way imaginable.

[65] For '*the Sons of the Pit*' in the Scrolls, see 1QSix.15 in exposition of Isaiah's '*Way in the Wilderness*' citation, CDvi.14–6 with the same sense of '*separation*' from them and in the context of allusion to the '*Nazirite*' language of '*keeping away from*' (Hebrew: *lehinnazer*—the same sense of Matthew 15:14's '*leave them alone*'), i.e., '*the Pharisees*' and their '*Blind Guides*,' etc.

[66] 4QMMTii.56–66 (4Q396–7). It is interesting that these passages on '*pure*' and '*impure liquids*' and '*the vessels*' that hold them are sandwiched in between references to '*the blind who cannot see*' (so as to keep apart from uncleanness and impurity) and '*the deaf who cannot hear the Law and the Ordinance and the Precepts of Israel on cleanliness and purity*'—followed by allusion to '*barring the dogs from the wilderness camps*.'

[67] *ARN* 25.3 (27a), somewhat palely reflected in *San.* 68a. It is interesting that in this discussion R. Eliezer, not only seems to cantankerously reverse many of the purity regulations his Disciples had previously recognized and, dying with the words '*clean*' on his lips—thereby prompting either R. Eleazar b. Azariah or R. Joshua to cry out, '*the ban is annulled*' (meaning '*the ban of excommunication*' Rabban Gamaliel had placed upon him—see below *B.M.* 59b), '*because his

soul departed with the word "clean" upon his lips, he is clean for the world to come' (thus!) —but also, in discussing the miracles attributed to R. Eliezer, one uses the very language of *'planting'* and *'uprooting,'* we have just described, and attributed in Matthew 15:13 to 'Jesus" teaching on the subject of *'the Blind Guides'* and *'the Pharisees'* that *'every Plant which My Heavenly Father has not planted shall be uprooted'.* As this is put in typical Rabbinic hyperbole, *'an entire field of cucumbers'* which *'with a word'* he both *'planted and uprooted'* and *'taught'* others how to do so.

67 2.2.4 and j. *Taʿan* 68d.

68 *ARN* 25.3 (27a) and *San.* 68a above. It is here he is said to prophesy the manner and harshness of R. Akiba's death and others of his generation, *'because they did not come to study under (him)',* *'taking no more than the paint brush takes from the palette.'*

69 See *A.Z.* 16b–17a, j. *Shab.* 14d, *Eccles. R.* 1.8.3, and *Tos. Hul.* 2.24 above. In this encounter, the *sitz-im-leben* would appear to have been the charge of *'heresy'* leveled in some quarters against R. Eliezer. To explore these, the traditions have R. Akiba—clearly R. Eliezer's favorite student— ask him sympathetically, *'Perhaps you heard an heretical opinion and it appealed to you?'* It is in response to this query by an adoring Disciple that R. Eliezer tells the story of his encounter with Jacob of Kfar Sechania, who told him the story in the name of *'Jesus the Nazorean'* or *'Jesus ben Pandira.'* Whatever one's view of the authenticity of this story (the writer considers it perhaps the only really authentic tradition regarding this mysterious teacher we have), it is clear that R. Eliezer sympathizes with this story and the position it represents and considers it quite funny which, of course, would be even more the case of *'Jacob of Kfar Sechania'* ('James'?) were more hard-line and the opposite of what Received Scripture has attempted to transform him and his colleagues into, i.e., at the very least, more sympathetic to Rome in the manner of R. Yohanan, R. Joshua, and Gamaliel II beelow, rather than the more extreme approach represented by the Dead Sea Scrolls (clearly documents of *'the Minim'* or *'Sectarians'*—the very thing R. Eliezer is being accused of here).

70 See, in particular, their dispute over the *'cleanness'* or *'uncleanness of the oven of Akhnai'* in *B.M.* 59b above which led to R. Eliezer's excommunication. In this dispute, after first causing a *'carob tree to be uprooted a hundred cubits out of its place'* (Cf. 'Jesus" *'miracle',* on *'coming back into Jerusalem'* in Matthew 21:19–22, of making *'the fig tree'* wither and even the possibility of *'moving a mountain into the sea'* by *'Faith'*—a matter also referred to in *ARN* above in relation to R. Eliezer), R. Eliezer appeals to *'a Bat Kol'* which promptly cried out from Heaven in favor of his opinion (cf. Peter and his vision of the Heavenly Tablecloth in Acts 10:11–20, when a Heavenly *'Voice'* accompanies it, instructing him three times *'to kill and eat'*). It is at this point that R. Joshua quotes Deuteronomy 30:12: *'It is not in Heaven,'* insisting one should, *'pay no attention to a Bat Kol,'* but rather quoting Exodus 23:2, *'follow the majority',* proceeding then to cast the deciding vote vis-à-vis R. Eliezer's excommunication. Other notable disputes between them occur when a woman who had committed incest in *Eccles R.* 1.8.4 and *Tos. San* 13.2 came to both and R. Eliezer in the manner of the more hard-line School of Shammai drove her away, but R. Joshua accepted her (cf. Gospel portraits of 'Jesus' keeping *'table fellowship'*—and I use the term *'portrait'* advisedly—with *'prostitutes'* and *'sinners'*); or *Ned* 74a on widow's *'waiting period'*

important for the situation of Jesus b. Gamala above. In general portrayed as sympathetic to 'Gentiles,' he is quoted in *Tos. San.* 13.2 as saying; '*Pious Gentiles have a share in the world to come*' and lamented in Tos. Sot. 15.3 with the words: '*Since R. Joshua dies, good counsel has departed from Israel.*' Not only was R. Joshua with Rabban Gamaliel and others a prominent member of the '*Peace Party*' and participated in several voyages to Rome in this regard (cf. *Bek.* 8b, *Hul* 59b–60a, *Nid.* 69b–70a, and Gen R. 64.10), his approach contrasted markedly with that of R. Eliezer who, for instance, in *M. Shab.* 6.4 supported the wearing of weapons on the Sabbath and in *A.Z.* 23a supported '*banning sacrifices from Gentiles in the Temple*'—one of the issues that began the First War against Rome (R. Joshua almost always being the more lenient and R. Eliezer in the spirit of the more rigorous School of Shammai—cf. *Nid.* 7b and *Shab.* 130b— being the more stringent as opposed to that of Hillel). He was even reputed in *Bek.* 8b above to have conversed with the Emperor Hadrian in Athens! But besides these various resemblances to the picture of 'Jesus' in Scripture, perhaps the most interesting episode concerning R. Joshua is his argument with '*the Mourners for Zion*' in *B.B.* 60b who, because of the destruction of the Temple, refuse any longer '*to eat meat or drink wine.*' Here, he is pictured as quoting Malachi 3:9: '*You are cursed with a curse, yet you rob me—nay, even the whole Nation.*' To be sure, anyone familiar with the New Testament Book of Acts will immediately recognize the resemblance of this to Acts 23:14: '*with a curse we have cursed ourselves not to eat or drink until we have killed Paul*' (which is to say nothing of the Synoptics' various insistences that '*the Son of Man came eating and drinking*')! Nonetheless, in the end, R. Joshua is pictured as being among the first to proclaim the abolition of the ban against R. Eliezer and his Halachot (legal rulings— '*the ban is annulled, the ban is annulled*') in the account of *San.* 68a above and, in arguments concerning widowhood and intervening marriage (in this case, we have a subject being treated by Muhammad in the *Koran* 2.230 taking basically the same position and a '*divorce*' law in Islam to the present day!). In *Git* 83a–b; he was forced to admit, basically restoring all of R. Eliezer's opinions, '*You should not refute the Lion after he is dead.*'

[71] For more arguments with R. Yohanan and his 'School' (including R. Joshua and Gamaliel II), which basically continue those, as just noted, between Hillel and Shammai, see *Ned.* 19a on '*unclean fluids*' again, *M. Neg.* 9.3 on the proper application of *Halachic* Tradition, *Ta°an* 25b in another episode regarding a '*Bat Kol*' which supposedly criticized R. Eliezer's lack of '*forbearance*' *in* the matters of the stopping or making of rain again, and *B.B.* 10b, *M. Shab.* 6.4, *Nid.* 7b, *A.Z.* 23a, and *Git.* 83a–b above. By the same token and as opposed to many of these examples, *Pirkeh Abbot* 2.8 reports that R. Yohanan '*used to say: "If all this sage of Israel were on one scale and Eliezer b. Hyrcanus on the other, he would outweigh them all"*'!

[72] See *B.M.* 59b above. Because of this excommunication, Rabban Gamaliel was said to have been swept over by a great wave at sea. For his sister, '*Imma Shalom,*' see *Shab.* 116a–b, *°Er* 63a, and *Ned.* 20a–b.

[73] *ARN* 6.3 (20b) above and Gen R. 42.1; cf. too Pirke de Rabbi Eliezer 7 and Ps. Philo 12.1.

[74] For the *Zohar* 1.31b–132a too, the actual explanation of this mystical designation has to do

with *'the light on Moses' face'*; cf. *James*, pp. 133–4. In Islamic Sufi tradition, a similar tradition holds sway.

[75] For the use of this allusion, *'House of Judah,'* at Qumran, see CDiv.11, 1QpHabviii.1, 4QPs 37ii14, etc.

[76] *ARN* 25.3 (27a).

[77] *ARN* 25.1 (27a).

[78] *ARN* 6.3 (20b) and Gen R. 42.1.

[79] *Ibid.* Actually in this account the allusion to *'a silver couch'* makes some commentators feel this name should actually be *'Ben Sisit'* or *'Ben Zizzit Hakksef'* (*'Silver'*), that is, not either *'Keset'* or *'Keseth'* / *'Couch'* or *'Cushions'*

[80] Eccles R. 7.12.1. Actually here there are again only three *'Councillors,'* *'Ben Gurion'* and *'Ben Nakdimon'*—probably correctly—being combined into one. It is in Lam R. 1.5.31 that the four *'Councillors'* are named. Still, in both accounts, it is *'Ben Battiah,'* Yohanan b. Zacchai's nephew (not Abba Sikkra—if there is any difference between the two terminologies), who is *'Head of the Zealots in Jerusalem'* and who *'burned the storehouses.'* It is at this point, too, that R. Yohanan rather applies the Prophecy *'Lebanon shall fall by the hand of a Mighty One'* from Isaiah 10:34 above to his *'Prophecy'* about Vespasian—not *'the Star Prophecy'*—in any event, as we have seen, both are extant at Qumran.

[81] *Git.* 56a but also, one should note, here two derivations of his name are given: 1) *'because his seat (kise) was among the Great Ones of Rome'* above and 2) *'because his fringes (zizzit) used to trail on cushions'* (*keseth*). However, as we have already suggested, whoever he was, he was clearly an Establishment person and I would imagine a member of the Herodian Family or that of the Alabarch of Alexandria—see n. 69 in Chapter 8 above and n. 46, Chapter 11 above.

[82] For the story of this woman—supposedly named *'Rufina'* (also rumored as being responsible for his death) and supposed to be the wife of the Roman Prefect Tinius Rufus—and this marriage, see *Ned.* 50b, *A.Z.* 20a and n. 70, Chapter Eight above. It should be noted that this same 'Saintly' R. Akiba did makes some peculiar rulings—for instance, in *Git.* 90a, that it was permissible to divorce one's wife if one wished to marry a more beautiful woman and in *Shab.* 64b, allowing women to use beauty aids during menstruation. For *'Tinius Rufus,'* one should also see *Git.* 90a.

[83] 1QpHabxi.8, This allusion, which is normally translated *'cause to stumble'* and describes what the Wicked Priest did to the Righteous Teacher and his followers (*'the Poor'* / *'the Ebionim'*) actually translates out as *'cast them down'*—a usage pregnant with meaning for this Period.

[84] 4 QpPs 37ii.13–20.

[85] Cf. 4QpPs 37ii with Gen R. 42.1.

[86] See 4QpPs 37ii.14–6, iii.1, iii.5–7, and iii.11, and below, Chapters 23 and 27. It should be noted that this term, *'Doers of the Torah',* which circumscribes the application of Habakkuk 2:3–4 on *'the Delay of the Parousia'* and *'the Righteous shall live by his Faith'* in the Habakkuk *Pesher* where it is a fundamental usage, is also fundamental to the Letter of James 1:22–2:26[81]

Git. 56a but also, one should note, here two derivations of his name are given: 1) '*because his seat (kise)* thereby via internal parameters focusing them into the same Era.

[87] 4QpPs 37ii.18–20.

[88] See *MZCQ*, pp. 29, 32–3, and 92–6. The use of the term '*Nasi*'/'*Nasi Chol ha-ᶜEdah* '(a term also found in the exegesis of Numbers 24:17 in the Damascus Document as we have seen) in iii.14 and v.1 in the War Scroll from Qumran—a term we know was in use on Bar Kochba coinage—further solidifies this possibility.

[89] Cf. 4QpNahiii.8 and iv.4–5 and also the use of the term '*Nilvim*' in CDiv.2–3 and 4Q448('*Paean for King Jonathan*)ii.4 (*DSSU*, pp. 273–80), which is based on the word '*joining*'/'*Joiners*' and which I have identified as '*Gentiles attaching themselves to the Community*' as in Esther and Isaiah below.

[90] CDiv.3 in exposition of the term '*ha-leviyyim*' and Chapters 14, 18, 19, 21, 23, 27, and 28 below.

[91] See Luke 10:33, 17:16, John 4:39–40, 8:48, and Acts 8:25; but *par contra*, see Matthew 10:5. Nor is this to take into account the point that I have paralleled the portrait of the fate of the Samaritan *Taheb* in Josephus (another '*Joshua ben Joseph*') with that of '*Jesus*' in the Gospels and, furthermore one should note that in the Pseudoclementines some of the followers of John the Baptist, such as '*Dositheus*,' were very definitely considered to be '*Samaritans*.'

[92] Note that this concept of '*Salvation*' is very important. The Gospels themselves are aware that 'Jesus" name actual means or alludes to '*Saviour*'/'*Salvation*.' This concept, expressed as '*Yeshaᶜ*'/ '*Yeshuᶜa*' is fundamental to Documents like the Damascus Document (especially in the final promises in Columns xix–xx of the B Document). As I have expressed this—particularly in my *Preface*, but also in the piece I have referred to in *The Huffington Post*, '*Gospel Fiction and the Redemonization of Judas*' (12/19/07)—this is a new concept for the Hellenistic Greco-Roman World which had personified with '*gods*' or '*man-gods*' for almost every kind of abstract intellectual 'Power'/'Force'/or 'Concept,' but never the relatively new 'Hebrew' concept of '*Salvation*.'

[93] 4QpPs 37ii.9–10 and iii.10 and cf. 1QpHabii.6–11, v.5–12, vii.4–16, ix.9–10, and xi.2–10 and Paul in Galatians 2:10 and James in James 2:5.

[94] 4QpPs 37ii.18–20. For Josephus; vivid picture of this alliance and these events, see *War* 4.300–325 and how the havoc wrought by '*the Zealots*' or '*Sicarii*' in Jerusalem continues into 5.26.

[95] 1QpHabxi.10–xii.3. This language of '*being paid the reward of*' or '*paying the reward*' is crucial and is, not only to be found in 1QSviii.6–7 referring to the Community Council, but also in the Isaiah 3:10–11 proof text, applied to the circumstances of James' death at the hands of '*the Wicked Priest*'; *E.H.* 2.23.15–6. It is this which is being reflected in the language of the Habakkuk *Pesher* above.

[96] CDiv.2–3 but cf. too CDvi.3–5 about '*the Diggers*' from Numbers 21:18, which parallels this, in xix.17—also called '*the Penitents from Sin in Jacob*' who '*kept the Covenant of God*,' i.e., they were '*Keepers*,' that is, they were '*Sons of Zadok*' according to the precise definition in the Community

Rule v.2 and 9.

97 4QpPs 37ii.9–10 and iii.10 above and note that this is really the same as James 2:5 above as well on 'the Kingdom reserved for those who love Him'—'loving God' being the first part of the 'All Righteousness' dichotomy of 'loving God' or 'Piety' and 'loving your fellow man'—the 'Righteousness Commandment'— also found in at least two places in the Damascus Document as we have seen and, to some extent, here in the Habakkuk *Pesher*.

98 CDvii.5–9 following the 'Nazirite' language of 'keeping away from' (lehazzir/lehinnazer—familiar too in Acts 15 and 21's picture of the outcome of 'the Jerusalem Council'), 'fornication,' 'separation,' and, of course, the 'Righteousness' Commandment: 'loving each man his brother as himself' from CDvi.17 to CDvii.3, we have been following throughout.

99 CDiii.19–20: 'And He built for them a House of Faith in Israel the likes of which has never stood from ancient times until now and, for them that hold fast to it, there will be Victorious Life and all the Glory of Adam will be theirs'!

100 Cf 4QpPs 37iii.1–2 with CDi.7–8. The allusion in the latter to 'inherit His Land and prosper on the good things of the Earth' is exactly parallel, once again bearing out my contention that most of these so-called 'Sectarian' documents at Qumran were written at more-or-less the same time regardless of relying on the tendentious results of either palaeographic reasoning or carbon test dating. Note here, too, the allusion to 'knowing they were Sinners', one finds there, corresponds to the allusions 'the Penitents from Sin in Jacob', one finds later in the Document, as we have seen, and the whole idea of allusions like 'John taught Repentance from Sin' in the wilderness'. one finds peppered throughout the New Testament. For this 'Covenant and the Compact, which they raised in the Land of Damascus—and this is the New Covenant' and the fact that God 'does mercy to (the thousands) of them that love Him and to His Keepers for a thousand generations' (Exodus 20:6), see CDxx.11–23 which also includes reference to 'the Penitents from Sin in Jacob', just mentioned above, 'Yesha*ᶜ*'/'Salvation', and 'God-Fearers' or 'fearing God's Name,' a fairly common way of alluding to right-guided 'Gentiles' in this Period.

101 Gen R. 42.1.

102 See Chapters 13, 21-22, and 28 below.

103 Cf. CDi.7–8 above and in 1QSxi.7–9 on 'the Building of the Holy Ones' and 'joining one's Assembly to that of the Sons of Heaven.'

104 See CDxx.21 above but also in relation to 'the Penitents of Israel' in CDvii.16–18 again, a kind of 'Grace,' in that God 'so loved the First who testified on His behalf, that He loved those coming after them.'

105 4QpPs 37iii.4–6.

106 CDvi.3–11. One should also note the allusion preceding this in CDiii.16 and following those to 'the Testimonies of His Righteousness and the Ways of His Truth, which a man must do in order to live through them' (note the Jamesian emphasis again on 'doing' here), to 'digging a well rich in waters' and the material following this up about 'the New Covenant in the Land of Damascus,' also alluded to as 'the Well of Living Waters' in viii.21–23. In CDvii.18–19, Numbers 24:17's

'Star,' of course, is identified with *the Interpreter of the Torah*—just as 'the Staff' of Numbers 21:18 and Isaiah 54:16 is here in Column vi.

Chapter 13

[1] *DSSU*, pp. 182–200. In fact, if one will note the way I arranged these texts—the Introductions and commentaries to which I wrote—I divided this reconstructed document, which was made up of some seven plates, 4Q393–99, into two Documents because of an allusion in ii.29–32 about writing its respondent(s) earlier *some works of the Torah which we reckoned for your own Good and for that of your People* (implying, as I have argued elsewhere and will proceed to argue here, that this is the King of a foreign *'People'* or converts to Judaism who require such tuition and because, introducing this in ii.28–9 with the example of David, a former *'King'*), *for we see that you possess discernment and knowledge of the Torah.'*

[2] This passage is to be found, as we have previously noted, in *MMT*i.62–70, which is preceded by allusion to the Blind and the Deaf *'trespassing on the Purity of the Temple'* and the whole issue of the cleanness of *'poured liquids'* and the effect of this on the *'purity'* of their containers—which was something of the issue, it will be recalled, between R. Eliezer and Rabban Gamaliel and his supporters among the rest of . the School of R. Yohanan in *B.M.* 59b above.

[3] For the 'Official' publication of this document, which came out about a two years after that of Prof. Wise and myself , see E. Qimron and J. Strugnell, *DJD X: Qumran Cave 4*, Oxford, 1994 (though I don't recall ever having received an acnowledgement footnote from these two authors). Again, the present writer was the first to point out that this term implied the charged expression *'works'* and not either *'words'* or *'acts'*, which has since—backed up by Prof. F. Garcia Martinez in his translation of *The Dead Sea Scrolls*, Leiden, 1998, ii. pp. 790–804, who was the first to realize that I was right in this insight, followed up by M. Abegg, '4QMMT, Paul, and "Works of the Law,"' in *The Bible at Qumran: Text, Shape, and Interpretation*, Grand Rapids, 2001, pp. 203–14, who picked up the idea of the whole relationship with the Letter of James, first enunciated by myself in Poland in the Summer of 1990 (one might add: first, one has to know what is in the Letter of James—something not too widespread in Dead Sea Scrolls Studies—then one might be able to see some relationship). For my original presentation of these ideas, which was written even before the entire 'Composite Document' became widely available in 'samizdat' copy, see my 'A Response to Schiffman on *MMT*' in Z. J. Kapera's publication, *The Qumran Chronicle*: 'Qumran Cave IV and MMT Special Report,' Krakow, 1990/91, nos 2/3, pp. 95–104, which still reads as fresh today as the day it was given. I also presented a more developed version of these ideas to the Society of Biblical Literature in 1994: '*MMT* as a Jamesian Letter to "*the Great King of the Peoples beyond the Euphrates*" or Izates,' which was later published in *The Journal of Higher Criticism*, vol. 11, no. 1 in Spring, 2005, pp. 55–68. For the references to this usage, see *MMT*ii.26–33, which actually ends in an allusion to *'doing them'*—meaning of course these *'Works of the Torah.'* Of course, too, important portions of 1QpHabvii.11–viii.3 and xii.2–6 invoke this usage *'Oseh ha-Torah'* as a qualifier, as we have seen. For Paul's famous allusions to Genesis 15:6—together with Habakkuk 2:4, one of the basic building blocks of

'Gentile Christianity'—see Romans 2:13 (which also even includes a reference to 'Doers of the Law'), 4:2–5:9, and Galatians 2:16–17, 3:11–24, and 5:4; for James', see 2:21–25. Moreover, once again, we are encountering verification that all of these Documents were written at more or less the same time, despite the widely disparate parameters being applied to them. It is worth remarking that some have even thought the term 'Essene' in Greek—the derivation of which is unsure—actually comes from the term ᶜOseh ha-Torah' and not the Aramaic for 'Piety', i.e., ᶜOsim'/'Essenes'/'Doers.' I would not be opposed to this derivation.

4(2) See my several analyses in 'A Response to Schiffman on *MMT*' in *The Qumran Chronicle*: 'Qumran Cave IV and MMT Special Report,' Krakow, 1990/91, nos 2/3, pp. 95–104. In my view, the addressee of this 'Letter'—the only 'Letter' in the Qumran corpus—and found in multiple copies too, showing just how important it was, was either 'Agbarus'/'Agabus'/'Abgarus'/ or 'Izates'—the favorite son of Queen Helen of Adiabene as we shall see below—if in fact the they can be differentiated at all; see *James*, pp. xxxiii, 194, 296, 484, 881, and 991 and 'MMT as a Jamesian Letter to "the Great King of the Peoples beyond the Euphrates" or Izates,' *The Journal of Higher Criticism*, vol. 11, no. 1, Spring, 2005, pp. 55–68, etc.

5(3) The expression I am referring to occurs in *MMTii.29–30* above and begins the portion I will now proceed to translate. But it also harks back to the somewhat reconstructed phrase in *MMTii.1–2* where the word '*maᶜasim*' definitely occurs, though the sense is somewhat obscure because of the poor state of the redaction preservation at this point. Nevertheless, it is clear that this term '*works*' (in the plural) is being used to describe what the '*some of (these) words*' referred to. The reconstructed phrase '*miksat-divareinu*' does appear in i.1; but, if this were what the abbreviation '*MMT*' stood for, then it should have read '*MDTE*' (based on the reconstruction '*Miksat Divareinu ba-Torah-El*') and not '*Miksat Maᶜasei* (based on the root '*to do*'/'*doing*' and, therefore very definitely, meaning '*works*' and not some other formulation such as that employed by G. Vermes in his translations, '*Observances*'—more often, he uses the word '*Acts*' or '*Deeds*' to translate such an Hebraicism which, of course, misses the point entirely and the charged usage involved—anything to avoid the formulation '*works*' which in his case has to be seen as intentional)! By the same token, it is true that the allusion to '*words*' reappears at the end of the Second Letter, together with allusion to '*the Last Times*' and '*it will be reckoned to you as Righteousness*' (presumably meaning, '*your having done what was Upright and Good before Him*'— obviously implying these same '*works of the Torah*' just spoken of), i.e., '*you will rejoice at the End of Time when you find some of our words to be True.*' Once again, were anyone doubting it, verifying the contemporaneity of it and documents like 1QpHab and CD above, regardless of the imprecise and tendentious palaeographic arguments or carbon test analyses being applied to them. This is an issue, as I said in my original Preface, the public will have to decide for itself as both judge and jury. It is the crucial one. Without agreement on it, there is no proceeding forward—that is: will internal data take precedence over tendentious external date, or *vice versa*?

6 See the key exegesis of '*the Last Age*' or '*Final Era*' in 1QpHabvii.2–14, based on Habakkuk 2:3 (preceding Habakkuk 2:4): '*For there shall yet be a vision of the Appointed Time and it will speak of the End and will not Lie,*' which includes allusions to '*the Doers of Torah*' and '*the Men of*

Truth' and leads into allusion to the Last *'Judgement'*, and ix.3–7, which pictures the fall of the Herodian High Priestly clans (plural) and more, of course, on *'the Last Judgement'* in x.3 and xii.14–xiii.4. *Inter alia*, in CDiii.21–iv.12, see the key exegesis of *'the Sons of Zadok as the Elect of Israel who will stand up at the End of Days'* (an allusion to *'the Resurrection of the Righteous'* as we have seen) and who would *'justify the Righteous and condemn the Wicked'*—again, obviously eschatological.

7 *MMTii.29–32.*

8 The key phraseology, of course, is *'reckoned to you as Righteousness'* (*nachshveha lecha le-Zedakah*), which actually echoes the language of Genesis 15:6 and not that found elsewhere in the Scrolls, such as in the definition of *'the Sons of Zadok'* in CDiv.7 above: *'yazdiku Zaddik'* (the Scrolls, it would seem, can use a plural verb when they mean a plural verb!); but for a parallel usage in 4Q266 (the Last Column of the Damascus Document), see *DSSU*, pp. 218–19, Lines 6–7: *'yachshevah'*—*'he will not be reckoned among all the Sons of His Truth, for his soul has rejected the Foundations of Righteousness'* (i.e., Mosaic Law—which Paul refers to in Galatians 4:24–5 as *'Agar'*, which *'is Mount Sinai in Arabia'* and *'brings forth Slavery'*). One should also see the reference in 4QMMTii.29–30 about *'some works of the Torah which we reckoned for own Good and for that of your People,'* though here the verb is simply the active *'hashsavnu.'* To some extent, the same can be said for Psalm 106:31 related, interesting enough, to Phineas—the patronymic father of the *'Zealot Movement'*—*'and it was reckoned to him as Righteousness until all Generations forever.'* The importance of this allusion in this context in terms of all the positions we have been evaluating in this book cannot be underestimated.

9 CDvi.19–21, the actual definition of *'the New Covenant in the Land of Damascus.'* The second citation is from vi.18–19 introducing this. Bbut also see v.7 on *'pollution of the Temple'* and *'not separating (clean from unclean as) per Torah'* in the matter of *'fornication,'* i.e., *'lying with a woman during the blood of her period'* (as, for instance, someone like Drusilla—*'a Jewess'* according to the dissimulation in Acts—marrying Felix) and *'each man taking the daughter of his brother and the daughter of his sister (to wife).'*

9(2) The reference is to be found in 4QMMTii.29–30 above: *'And finally, we (earlier) wrote you concerning some of the works of the Torah which would be reckoned for your own Good and that of your People.'* As just indicated, this very definitely harks back to 4QMMTii.1–2, implying there certainly was an earlier *'letter'* or *'letters'*—much like in the New Testament 1 and 2 Corinthians or 1 and 2 Thessalonians.

10 For *'King Ezad,'* see *James*, pp. 906–10 and J. B. Segal, *Edessa, the Beloved City*, p. 15 above. Also see Chapter 28 below. Where the identification with *'Izates'* is concerned, it is not without relevance that at one time Josephus in *War* 4.567 also denotes Queen Helen's son as *'Izas.'* This person would also seem to be known as *'Abgar VII.'*

11 See Hippolytus 9.21 which also includes, surprisingly enough, references to *'good conscience'* in the sense of *'despising death'* and going the final mile—in particular, in the matter of not *'blaspheming the Law or eating things sacrificed to idols.'* But see, in particular, *'for (one of these 'Sicarii' or 'Zealot Essenes') submits to death and endures any torture rather than violate his 'conscience.'* For Paul's use

of the word *'conscience,'* see Romans 2:11–7 (including reference to *'the Doers of the Law being reckoned as Righteous,'* *'work of the Law,'* and *'not being a respecter of persons'*—an allusion known from Early Church descriptions of James), 1 Corinthians 8:7–12 specifically relating to *'eating things sacrificed to idols,'* and 10:15–25 including reference to *'all things being for me lawful'* and *'Communion with the blood of Christ.'* For Josephus' *'Essenes,'* the allusion is the less specific *'nor blaspheme their Law-Giver or eat forbidden things'*; cf. *War* 2.152–3 above.

[12] See above CDvi.19–vii.4 and xx.17–20 (here again including reference to the term *'reckoning,'* *'revealing Salvation'*/*'Yesha^c,'* and *'Justification to those fearing His Name'*/*'God-Fearers'*—often an allusion to *'Gentiles'*).

[13(12)]Cf. *James*, pp. 661–64 and 832–35 and Romans 2:11–17, 1 Corinthians 8:7–12 specifically relating to *'eating things sacrificed to idols,'* and 10:15–25 including reference to *'Communion with the blood of Christ'* as in n. 11 above.

[14] For the antagonism to *'blood'* in CD, see ii.8, iii.6–8, v.7, etc.

[15] See, for instance, the use of this verb in exactly this sense in CDvi.14–5 about *'keeping away'* from *'the Sons of the Pit'* and *'the polluted Evil Riches of the Temple,'* vii.1–2 on *'keeping away from fornication'* and sexual relations with *'near kin'*, including nieces and close cousins, and viii.8 on *'keeping away'* from the Traitorous Establishment, *'wallowing in the ways of fornication,'* *'approaching near relatives for fornication,'* *'Evil Riches,'* and *'profiteering.'*

[16] This linkage is specifically to be found in CDv.6–11, where the *'pollution of the Temple'*— the *'*Third Net of Belial*'*—is specifically tied to the *'ban on fornication'* one, i.e., *'marrying nieces'* and *'sleeping with women during their periods.'* See in particular my Appendix in *JJHP*, pp. 87–94 on *'The "Three Nets of Belial" in the Damascus Document and 'Balla^c'/"Bela^c" in the Temple Scroll.'*

[17] These definitions are to be found, as we have seen, in CDiv.20–v.11—but they also may be found reflected in 11QTlvii.15–21 and lxvi.12–7 and 4QMMTii.47–57 and 83–9.

[18] Josephus speaks of just this kind of rejection of, for instance, Gentile sacrifice in the Temple, the stopping of which he designates as the immediate cause of the War against Rome in *War* 2.408–420.19.

[19] See n. 17 above. But also all the additional references to *'fornication'* in CDii.16, viii.5–7, and Documents like 1QSi.6–7, iv.10, 1QpHabv.7, viii.7, and 1QHxiv.7.

[20]4QMMTii.84. In this sense it is perhaps helpful to look upon Qumran and *'Essenes'* generally as a Community of *'Holy Ones'*/*'Kedoshim'* or, as we shall presently attempt to call attention to, *'Nazirites'* —probably, life-long *'Nazirites'*—*'dedicated to'* or *'Holy to God.'* For these kind of allusions expressing the *'Holiness'* of Israel,' see, for instance, Leviticus 19:2–21:22 and Deuteronomy 7:6, 14:2–21, 23:14, 26:19, 28:9, etc.

[21] 4QMMTii.84–8.

[22] Cf. for instance Exodus 28:36 and 39:30

[23] 1 QSviii.1 and 5–6.

[24] 4QMMTii.88–89

[25] See vaiourly in Chapter 4-7 above and Ps. *Hom.* 7.8, Koran 2.173, 5.3, 6.146, 16.115, etc.

[26] This counter indication is expressed in the Gospels in several ways: since 'Jesus' is the Temple, the various scenes of 'Jesus' keeping table-fellowship with and approving of various classes of persons, such as *prostitutes,* *tax-collectors,* *Sinners,* *gluttons* (i.e., in Gospel 'code': persons not keeping Mosaic dietary regulations), and the like in Matthew 9:10, 11:19, 21:31 and *pars.* and miraculously curing *the deaf,* *the dumb,* and *the blind* in Matthew 9:32, 10:51, 11:5, 12:22, 15:30 and *pars.,* provide vivid examples of this sort of reversal.

[27] 4QMMTii.68–70.

[28] 1QMi.2–3.

[29] Cf. CDvii.13–21 with 1QMi.2–3. and 4QMMTii.68–70 above and see Chapter 14 below.

[30] We have discussed the situation in Northern Syria variously, including Chapers 3 above and will do in 28, but see our map in the back.

[31] See n. 25 above, but for our original discussion of *strangled things* in James' rulings as *carrion,* see *James,* pp. 294–6. For this ban on *carrion* as applicable specifically to *Priests* or *Sons of Zadok* in the Temple, see Ezekiel 44:31.

[32] See, for instance, the bans on such persons in *the Camps of Holiness* in 1QMvii.3–7 and in the Temple in 11QTxvi–xvii and cf. n. 20 above; for *touching,* see Matthew 8:2 (a leper)-15, 9:20–34 (a woman with a flow of blood, a blind person, and a dumb one), 14:36, Mark 3:10, 5:25–34, 7:32–35 (a deaf and dumb man and including *spitting on his tongue*!), 8:22–25 (again a blind person), 10:13 (*little children*, which even *the Disciples* get angry about), Luke 7:14–16 (the bier of the dead, accompanied by the cry *God has visited His People*—thus!—and cf. CDiv.7–8 above about *God visiting them* and *causing a Root of Planting to grow*), 7:37–40 (*a woman in the city...a Sinner*), 8:43–47, 22:51 (here 'Jesus' heals the High Priest's servant's ear!); but *par contra,* see John 20:17 forbidding Mary Magdalene to *touch* him in his post-Resurrection state for he had *not yet risen* (sic!), implying that *touching* in this way (in the Jewish manner, this would particularly apply to women) was somehow *polluting.*

[33] See above n. 18 and variously; *War* 2.408–20.

[34] See 11QTxlvi.10 and the general allusions, in the same context, to *skins sacrificed to idols* in xlvii.13ff. (a variation of James', *MMT's,* and Hippolytus' *Essenes'* *things sacrificed to idols*) and my full Appendix on this subject in *JJHP,* pp. 87–94 above.

[35] Cf. 4QMMTii.66–70 above.

[36] The point is that *the Temple* is directly mentioned in 4QMMTii.67, which then leads into ii.68–70 about *Jerusalem being the Holy Camp* and *the foremost of the Camps of Israel* (this being clearly not a 'Samaritan' document but very obviously a nationalist 'Judean' one!). But see, too, the ban relative to *Priests* in the Temple in Ezekiel 44:31's *Zadokite Statement* above.

[37] The first such allusion would appear to be Irenaeus in *Ad. Haer.* 1.23.2. But also see Justin Martyr, *First Apology* 1.26, Hippolytus 6.15, Eusebius, *E.H.* 2.13.4, Epiphanius, *Haeres.* 21.2.1–3.6, and Ps. *Rec.* 2.8–12, where she is called *Luna;* and see Chapter 8 above.

[38] See specifically Josephus, *War* 2.409–10.

[39] See, in particular, Ezekiel 44:6–13 disqualifying *the Levites* in favor of *the Sons of Zadok* on this

basis and note that, when the Habakkuk *Pesher* describes '*the Wicked Priest*' as '*not circumcising the foreskin of his heart*' in xi.13, it is disqualifying him from Temple Service on this basis as well.

[40] See Hippolytus 9.21 above.

[41] *War* 2.152–53.

[42] See *E.H.* 3.33.1–4, which recapitulates the substance of Pliny's Letter 96 and Trajan's reply no. 97. For Simeon's purported death, by crucifixion, which also seems to have occurred during the Reign of Trajan, see *E.H.* 3.32.3–7; for the examination of Judas' two sons, which seems to have occurred under Domitian (d. 96 CE), see 3.20.1–10.

[43] See my remarks on this subject in Chapters 1, 4, and 8 above and *James*, pp. 808–50.

[44] See Chapter 10 and n. 57 above.

[45] Of course, '*Meroe*' could not be mistaken for '*Ethiopia*' even in Roman times, but '*Ethiopia*' as a pejorative for someone 'dark' is something else. See the reference to the last-documented '*Candakes*' in Strabo's *Geography* 17.1.54 and Pliny's *H.N.* 6.35. But this '*Candakes*,' who was killed in approximately 22 BC, certainly was not '*Rich*' enough to send any '*Treasury Agents*' up to Jerusalem at this time as Queen Helen had done. Nor is there any evidence that '*Christianity*' as such had yet penetrated either into Egypt or further South into Nubia or Ethiopia—while the opposite is true of Northern Syria/Iraq!

[46] These '*Arizei-Go'im*' are obviously pro-Revolutionary foreign fighters, either '*Herodians*'—like '*Niger of Perea*' and his '*Idumaeans*'—or descendants and servitors of Queen Helen and her two sons, Izates and Monobazus; but for 1QpHabii.1–10, where they are simply called '*Arizim*,' they participate in the scriptural exegesis sessions of the Righteous Teacher—'*the Priest in whose heart God put (the discernment) to interpret all the words of His Servants the Prophets (through whom) God foretold all that was going to happen to His People.*' 4QpPs 37ii.19–21 and iv.8–12 go further. There, using the language of 1QpHabxii.2–3 and Isaiah 3:10 of '*paying him his reward*,' they are the ones who are specifically specifically denoted as '*taking vengeance upon*' the Wicked Priest, for what he seems to have done to the Righteous Teacher and '*the Congregation*'/'*Assembly*'/or '*Church of the Poor*'; see *James*, pp. 179–84 and below, Chapters 23 and 25.

[47] *War* 2.520.

[48] See, for instance, our nn. 125 and 70 in Chapters 6 and 9 above, Dio Cassius 68.3–4, and Origen's comment in *Contra Celsus* 2.13 that the judges even in his time were particularly zealous in applying this law and few escaped death who had run afoul of it.

[49] Dio Cassius 68.3–4.

[50] See *Git.* 44a, 55b, 58a, and *B.B.* 47b, etc.

[51] For this '*remembering before God*' language, one should see Ps. *Rec.* 1.70 about how, after the riot led by '*the Enemy*' on the Temple Mount in which James broke either one or both his legs, the Community fled to Jericho but escaped the '*Enemy*'s pursuit because they went outside the city to visit the tombs of two of the brothers which, because they '*were remembered before God*,'

'miraculously whitened of themselves every year'; and the crucial Column xx.18–20 of Manuscript B of the Damascus Document, referring to *'the God-Fearers'* and/or *'those who feared God,'* for whom *'a Book of Remembrance would be written out before Him'* because *'they reckoned His Name'* (the *'reckoning'* vocabulary again), and for whom *'God would reveal Salvation (Yesha^c) and Justification.'*

52 *Contra Celsus* 2.13 and see Jerome, Letter 84 to Pammachius and Oceanus..

53 For fornication, marriage, monogamy, divorce, and adultery, see CDiv.17–v.11, vii.1–3, viii.3–15, 11QTlvi.11–lvii.19, lxvi.12–17, etc. But one should also note 1QpHabxii.4—*'the Simple Ones of Judah'* and 4QpNahii.9 and iii.5–6—*'the Simple Ones of Ephraim'* basically paralleling in signification these expressions in the Gospels such as *'these Little Ones'* or *'the Little Children.'*

54 In Hippolytus' testimony in 9.21 above, it is because these *'Sicarii'* or *'Zealot Essenes,'* when meeting such an uncircumcised person discussing the Laws of God, *'threaten to slay such a person if he refuses to undergo the ritual of circumcision'* that they are called by these names—in other words, this is the reason for these appellations. For Josephus' derivation, in which he only emphasizes the *'Terrorist'* aspect of the appellation, see *War* 2.254–7 and *Ant.* 20.186–7.

55 CDi.14–8 and cf. viii.12–xx.16.

56 See *Ant.* 20.38–48 which tells the whole story, including the controversy between Helen's teachers *'Ananias'* and his unnamed companion (Paul?) and the countermanding of their position by one *'Eleazar of Galilee,'* who sees *'circumcision'* as the *sine qua non* for conversion. One should also compare this picture with Gen R. 46.10, we have already pointed out above and elsewhere, which actually knows the passage Izates and his brother Monobazus were reading when they understood *'Eleazar'* had the correct approach—Genesis 17:11–27, on Abraham circumcising his whole household and all those traveling with him. It has correctly been pointed out by scholars that this argument very much resembles the one between R. Yohanan's two students on the same subject in j. *Kid.* 3:14—R. Joshua and R. Eliezer b. Hyrcanus, who typically holds the more severe position (just as *'Eleazar of Galilee'* here—is there some mix-up?); while R. Joshua (like *'Jesus'*), the more lenient or accommodating.

57 CDxvi.4–7. The passage in question actually refers to *'the Angel Mastemah'*/*'Satan'* and the oath that had been taken *'to circumcise,'* the *'keeping'* of which turned aside the pursuit by this *'Angel.'* CDxii.11 also alludes inadvertently and in passing to such entry into *'the Covenant of Abraham.'*

58 For this *'Land'* and its association with *'Abraham'*—to say nothing of *'Noah'* and *'Ad and Thamud'*—see Koran 11.25–49, 26.105–49, 29.14–35, etc.

59 The *'going'* or *'leading astray'* vocabulary is so widespread in the Scrolls that it is difficult to list all the occurrences of it. But some important ones come in CDi.13–6 above in the description of *'the waters of Lying which the Man of Scoffing pours over Israel,'* ii.13–7 in the primordial history of Israel, vii.22 on *'betraying and turning aside from the Fountain of Living Waters,'* and xx.10–12 on *'turning aside'* from *'the House of the Torah'* and *'rejecting the New Covenant in the Land of Damascus'*—but also in 1QSiii.21–22 on how *'the Sons of Righteousness (sic) are led astray'* by

'the Angel of Darkness' ('Mastemah' again?), 1QpHabx.9–10 about 'the Spouter of Lying who leads Many astray to build a Worthless City upon Blood and erect an Assembly ('Church'?) upon Lying,' etc.

[60] See the Preamble of the Gospel of Thomas and *E.H.* 1.13.10 and the account Eusebius translates from the Syriac about *'Judas Thomas'* sending *'Thaddaeus'* to Agbarus/Abgarus in Northern Syria. Also see the *The Acts of Thomas* and the Syriac *Doctrine of the Apostles.*

[61] See Chapter 4 above and *James*, pp. 844–70.

[62] Cf. Matthew 26:6–13/Mark 14:3–9, having all the elements of John 12, including the *'precious alabaster flask/jar of pure spikenard oil'* and 'Jesus'' self-centered utterance *'the Poor you have with you always, but you don't always have me'*—which is used to introduce the betrayal by *'Judas Iscariot'*—and Luke 7:39–50, including more *'anointing'* of his *'feet'*, and more Dionysus-like rebukes. We have already expressed the opinion that cognomens like *'the leper'* or *'the Pharisee'* are more of the kind of *'Code'* we have been following in this book—the former, in some warped manner, perhaps standing for *'the Iscariot'/'Sicarios'* and for that matter the partisans of James.

[62(2)] The Adiabene family are proverbial for their *'wealth'* and largesse in Josephus and Talmudic tradition. See, for instance, the palace that Helen and her sons built in Jerusalem in *War* 5.252 and 6.355. their tomb, 5.55, 5.119, 5.147, and *Ant.* 20.94–5, the Golden Candelabra depicted on the Arch of Titus which was ultimately taken to Rome and probably melted down to help pay for the Colosseum (see Plates 85–8), and the golden handles for vessels used in Temple services on *Yom Kippur*—*Yoma* 3:10 (37a)—and her famine relief in *B.B.* 11a, *j. Pe'ah* 1:1, 15b/*Tos. Pe'ah* 4:18, and *Ant.* 20.49–51, in which Josephus actually remarks the *'great amounts of money (Izates) sent to the Leaders in Jerusalem'* (*B.B.* 11a even records how his brother Monobazus—the members of whose family are even described in *Men.* 32b as being so *'Pious'* that they carried *mezuzoth* with them when they traveled and set them up in inns where they stayed, even though temporary dwellings of this nature did not require them—and just about beggared the Kingdom with so much charity); so if she was a supporter of the kind of *'Nazirite Judaism'* exemplified at Qumran, there is no reason to suppose that she or her sons could not have supported that installation as well.

[63] This is the implication of *'the suspected adulteress'* plaque containing the passage from Numbers 5:12–31 she had erected on the wall of the Temple and the three successive, seven-year Nazirite oath penances she observed according to Rabbinic tradition in *Naz.* 3:10 (19b–20a) above and *Git.*60a.

[64] *Ibid.*

[65] We have already compared Helen to Simon *Magus'* consort of the same name (see, for instance, *Ps. Hom.* 2.23–4). It is curious that the inscription found in *'The Tomb of the Kings,'* mentioned above, bears the formulaic *'Malchat-Zedan'* ('The Queen of Zedan'), repeated twice both in Hebrew and Palmyrene Syriac, which can imply *'Sidon'* in Phoenician *'Tyre'*—this being the very place Simon was legended to have picked his consort/mistress out of a brothel there (early Church hyperbole aside), to say nothing of 'Jesus'' various excursions and the women he meets

there we have covered sufficiently above. But equally curious, is another obscure passage in *Ket.* 7a about a decision R. Yohanan was supposed to have given *'at Zedan'* relative to Queen Helen—the why and wherefore is unclear—but recalling the imposition by the Rabbis of *Beit-Hillel* on her of an *'additional seven-year'* Nazirite-oath Penance Period as illustrative of or a precedent for forbidding the performance of *'the first intercourse on the Sabbath.'* This certainly is a peculiar notice and more lurks beneath its surface than is immediately apparent, but it does go a certain way perhaps towards helping elucidate these strange *'Zedan'* evocations.

[66] See *Ant.* 20.51–53 and, for instance, *E.H.* 2.12.1–3 above (*n.b.*, that Eusebius directly follows this up in *E.H.* 2.13:1–7 with the notice about Simon *Magus'* consort *'Helena, who had formerly been a prostitute in Tyre of Phoenicia,'* saying more about her than the *'Helen'* who preceded her, which—all things being equal—is certainly very peculiar placement indeed. The author has no explanation for it other than to remark it). That the New Testament is not totally unaware of this *'Queen,'* as I have already argued in connecting her with *'the Ethiopian Queen'* who sent her *'Treasury Agent'* (and a *'eunuch'*) up to Jerusalem in Acts 8:27–39; but her plight is also to be found reflected in the story in Luke 7:11–17 of *'the Widow of Nain'* (an otherwise unidentifiable Palestinian locale—as we have suggested, *'Adiabene'*?), who has lost her *'only-begotten son'*—a title, as we have seen, Josephus applies to Helen's son *'Izates'* and which, of course, the Synoptics apply to *'Jesus'*!—and Jesus raises him, at which point all the People there cry out, *'A Great Prophet has appeared among us* (*'the True Prophet'* ideology) *and God has visited His People'* (cf. the like-minded usages, we have already pointed out, in the Damascus Document and will point out further below).

[67] Though the *'King,'* her husband (whom some sources also call her *'brother'*) had children by numerous wives, Izates and Monobazus stand out as favorites; and it was Monobazus who stood in for his brother in difficult times and had the Pyramid monuments known significantly as *'The Tomb of the Kings,'* built for both Helen and Izates in Jerusalem—see Josephus, *Ant.* 20.92–6 above. One should note that Josephus promised at the end of this passage to *'narrate'* the rest of *'the acts of King Monobazus during his lifetime later,'* though for some reason he never performed on this promise (possibly because he made it in *The Antiquities,* after which publication in 93 CE he himself soon disappeared from the scene. That this Tomb was also connected in Jewish tradition with what was known as *'the Cave of Kalba Savuᶜa'* (i.e., *'Ben Kalba Sabuᶜa'* above, whose daughter, Rachel, seems to have married the famous Rabbi Akiba, also known for his Revolutionary and Messianic sentiments) should not be underestimated— see the article *'Izates'* in *The Encyclopaedia Judaica,* vol. 9, p. 1158. We have already commented upon Monobazus' extreme *'Piety'* in *Men.* 32b and *B.B.* 11a in n. 62 above. *'Monobazus'* seems to have been the Persian designation for principal members of this family and it is possible to point to at least four by that name in the small amount of information we have: Helen's husband *'Bazeus'* (clearly a corruption of *'Monobazus'*), *'Monobazus'* himself, the Monobazus who gave his life at the Pass at Beit Horon at the start of the 66 CE Uprising, and in the final generation of this family, as we shall argue below, R. Akiba's important associate by this name, *'Monobaz.'* It is interesting that, according to Tacitus, *Annal.* 15.1 and 15.4, the Herodian *'Tigranes'* was

ravaging his Kingdom from neighboring Armenia in 62 CE and, in any event, under Trajan (98–116) the area was conquered and absorbed into the Roman Province of Assyria, but the date of Monobazus' passing remains a mystery. Was it one of his sons or of Izates that was the 'Monobazus' who martyred himself at the beginning of the War against Rome or could it have been 'Monobazus' himself?

68 See *Naz.* 3:10 (19b–20a) and *Git.* 60a above. See too Josephus in *Ant.* 20.95, who comments as well on her great sorrow. which seems to have been a contributing factor to her death almost directly thereafter—'She died of a 'broken heart.' But also see the story of 'the Widow of Nain,' we have called attention to in Luke 7:11–7 and how 'Jesus' as a favor to this grieving 'Widow' resurrects her son (*thus*)!

69 The relation between all these 'Abgarus'es and 'Monobazus'es, as far as I am aware, has never been completely investigated but we first called attention to the matter in *James*, pp. 887–92 , 906–14, and variously.

70 Josephus, *loc. cit.* above, but also see Pausanius, *In Arcadicis* 8.16.5 and Eusebius *E.H.* 2.12.3. Moses of Chorene, *History of Armenia* 2.35 in the Sixth Century comments on her 'remarkable' tomb 'before the gates of Jerusalem' and he is sure she is 'the principal of Abgar's wives' (*thus!*).

71 We have covered this 'Primal Adam' ideology in *James*, pp. 423–34 and 585–8 and in Chapter 7 above and variously.

72 See the allusions to James 'being a Nazirite from his mother's womb' in *E.H.* 2.23.4 and Epiphanius, *Haeres.* 78.7.7; but also see n. 74 below. It should be appreciated that, relative to John 3:10–3's contention that 'the Son of Man' knew 'Heavenly things'; in 1QpHabii.8–10 and vii.4–10, not unsimilar things are said about 'the Priest'/'Teacher of Righteousness, to whom God made known all the Mysteries of His Servants the Prophets' and 'in whose heat God put the Knowledge to interpret all the words of His Servants the Prophets and through whom God foretold all that was going to happen to His People.'

73 For this expression 'only-begotten' as applied to Helen's favorite son Izates, see *Ant.* 20.20 where Josephus, though seemingly designating Izates as younger than Monobazus, was nevertheless willing to support him. For 'the Subbaᶜ of the Marshes,' see Chapter 3 above and *James*, pp. 324–32 and 836–9.

74 The point that we have emphasized is the 'fourteen years' in both Paul's references to going up to see James in Galatians 2:1 and here in 2 Corinthians 12:1–5. It is hard to imagine that Paul had anyone else in mind than James. This would be particularly true if James were 'the Righteous Teacher' from Qumran in view of documents there like 'Songs of the Sabbath Sacrifice' describing just such Heavenly Wisdom, not to mention the lost work Epiphanius and others describe, known as *The Anabathmoi Jacobou* ('The Ascents of James'), which by its very nature—aside from discussing James' discourses on the Temple steps as reflected in Book One of the Pseudoclementine *Recognitions*—would seem to be implying something of what Jewish Mysticism (*Kabbalah*) would refer to as 'the Literature of Heavenly Ascents,' i.e., 'Hechalot Mysticism.'

⁷⁵ For these accounts, see *Ket.* 62a–63b, where R. Akiba is called '*Ben Kalba Sabuᶜa's shepherd*' and *Ned.* 50a, both of which tell the story of R. Akiba's two 12-year periods of study and his 24,000 '*Disciples*' (i.e., an army!) and include an allusion to a vow and its annulment (this time *Ben Kalba Sabuᶜa's* vow to disinherit his daughter—*thus!*). For the matter of grain storage, one should see *Git.* 56a which mentions the four '*Councilors of Great Wealth*,' all of whom '*could keep the city in provisions for twenty-one years*'; for Lam R. 1.5.31, this is reduced to '*ten years*.' For *ARN* 6.3 (21a), as we have seen, this is '*twenty-two years*' (and what '*Kalba Sabuᶜa*' does alone, but which '*the Zealots*' wish to burn—see *War* 5.24–6 and Tacitus, *Hist.* 5.12 above). However, he objects (*n.b.*, *Ben Kalba Sabuᶜa*—unlike the other Councilors—is both endlessly generous and a patriot!) and rather has baked into '*loaves of bread*'—'Jesus'' miracle of the loaves again? They rather '*bricked into the walls and had them plastered over with clay*' (an alternate translation is: '*cut with saws and soiled with mud*').

⁷⁶ Ps. *Rec.* 1.72, 2.7–8, and Ps. *Hom.* 2.22–4 and above Chapters 1, 3, 4, etc.

⁷⁷ See *Ket.* 62a–63b, *Ned.* 50, and *ARN* 6.1 (20a) above. For *Kethuboth*, Rachel's father kisses R. Akiba's feet (thus!) and gives him all his wealth when he hears he is '*a great man*'; for *Nedarim*, which contains the '*straw*' episode, Ben *Kalba Sabuᶜa* comes before R. Akiba and asks him to remit his vow—presumably because he is so great.

⁷⁸ *Shab.* 68b. In our view, this notice clinches the relationship of R. Akiba to the family of the Royal House of Adiabene and its constant sponsorship of Revolutionary Action against both Herodians and Romans. If one takes the death of the first Monobazus at around 68 CE and the second at about the same time, then this third '*Monobazus*' can either be the son or grandson of the first or the son of the second, or he may have been a descendant of Izates. In any event, in our view, this would make him either Rachel's brother or close cousin. It is interesting that the context of the discussion recorded here is that of '*a child taken captive among the Gentiles*' or '*a convert among the Gentiles*,' including reference to both the consumption of '*blood*' and '*idolatry*' (the '*food sacrificed to idols*' of James' ruling and as Hippolytus' '*Sicarii Essenes*' above?) with '*Monobaz*' adopting the more lenient position regarding the necessity of one '*sin offering for breaking the Sabbath*' only and R. Akiba ultimately deferring to him.

⁷⁹ See *ARN* 6.3 (21a) and *Taᶜan* 19b–20a.

⁸⁰ See Chapters 1, 4, and variously and Ps. *Rec.* 1.72, 2.7–8, Ps. *Hom.* 2.22–4, and Epiphanius, *Haeres.* 21.2.3–5.1 above.

⁸¹⁽⁸²⁾ In Psalm 69:9, of course, it is only '*zeal for Your House consumes me*' not as John 2:16 applies it: '*You have made My Father's House a house of commerce*.' We have already commented upon this previously but elsewhere in this Psalm in 2:8 we have the theme of '*being a stranger to my brothers and an alien to my mother's other sons*.' In 69:15, there is the language of '*the Pit*' and in 69:21, '*being given vinegar to drink*.' Then, of course, there is: '*Let their encampment be desolate and let none dwell in their tents*' (69:26, preceded by allusion in 69:25 to God's vengeance and the '*fierceness of His Anger*'—hardly very 'Christian' sentiments), quoted so tendentiously in Acts 1:20's discussion of the election to succeed Judas *Iscariot* and '*occupy his Office*' (*Episkopon*). Of course the Psalm ends in 69:36–7 with the statement that '*God will save Zion and rebuild the*

cities of Judah. The Seed of His Servants shall inherit it and they that love His Name shall dwell therein'—the very language, as we have been pointing out, of CDxx.19–20 regarding *'the Book of Remembrance that would be written out for those fearing God'* and *'God-Fearers'* above. It is hard to imagine anything more *'Zionist'* than this. Such are the pitfalls of taking scriptural passages out of context.

[82] M. Ta'an 3:8, Ta'an 23a/j. Ta'an 66b, and *Ber* 19a.

[83] For *'Honi,'* who is called—prefiguring James—*'Onias the Righteous'* in Josephus (missing from the account in the *War*), see *Ant.* 14.22–8; for the account of how Aristobulus—whose part *'Honi'* appears to have taken with his rain-making before he was stoned—refused to humble himself before Pompey (which differs from the account in the *Antiquities*), see *War* 2.128–141.

[84] See *Ant.* 2.24–8 above in the aftermath of Honi's (*'Onias the Righteous'*) stoning and cf. 1 Kings 17:1 and 19:9–14 where Elijah, as we have seen, as the prototypical *'Zealot'* is *'filled with a burning zeal for the Lord'* and note too in 1 Kings 21:19, following the murder of Naboth of Jezreel, how Elijah prophesies to Ahab that *'the dogs will lick your blood too'* (thus!)—meaning, that all male members and descendants of his family will *'be swept away.'*

[85] *Ta'an.* 20a. That the *Talmud* knows five *'Disciples'* of *'Jesus the Nazorean',* known as *'Matthai, Nakai, Nezer, Boni, and Thodah,'* all of whom were supposedly put to death for various bizarre reasons, is to be found in *San.* 43a. It is clear, as we shall discuss, that these names are euphemisms, but the passage itself, which has been questioned—except for the names—would appear to be mostly dimly-remembered obscure nonsense.

[86] See M. Ta'an 3:8–9, Ta'an 19a, 23a–b, and j. Ta'an 66b. In this story, as told in a kind of *'Rip Van Winkle'* manner in the Babylonian *Talmud*, Honi the Circle-Drawer goes into a mountain cave and sleeps for seventy years. When he awakes and asks for his son, he is told about his grandson, either another such Honi the Circle-Drawer, whom we identify with *'Hanan the Hidden'* or *'John,'* or *'Abba Hilkiah'* who like his grandfather also made rain (see *James*, pp. 366–85, 419, 474–5 and 820 and above Chapters 6 and 8). For the Jerusalem *Talmud*, this all occurred *'near the time of destroying the Temple,'* its *'destruction,'* and *'its being rebuilt a second time after seventy years,'* though what this might mean is impossible to say. Of course, the *'Seventy Years of Wrath'* are important chronological pegs for Jeremiah 25:11 and 29:10, Daniel 9:2–27, and the War Scroll from Qumran. In these passages in the two *Talmuds*, the *'seventy years'* of Honi's *'sleep'* are equated in the former with the time between the planting and germination of *'the carob tree';* in the latter, with a *'world changed utterly',* where *'vineyards produce olive orchards'* and *'olive fields produce grain'* (thus)!

[87] *'The Branch'* / *'Netzer'* is important vocabulary in the Scrolls. It is to be found in 4Q285 as *'the Branch of David'* and identified with *'the Nasi ha-'Edah'* and in 4QpIs^a on Isaiah 11:1–4, where it is again identified, as we have seen, with *'the Branch of David'.* This is also the case for 4QpGenv.5 on Genesis 49:10, which introduces a new identity, *'the Messiah of Righteousness',* and 4QFlori.11–2 which we shall analyse further below. Of course, the terminology is based on Jeremiah 23:5 and 33:15 as well as Zechariah 3:8 and 6:12. Still, at Qumran and in early Christianity, one cannot ignore the *'Nazirite'* component to the vocabulary, even though it is

based on a slightly different root.

[88] *San.* 43a. The choice of scriptural passages given here as reasons for the death of these five would seem to be totally tendentious. Still the reversals involved are quite typical.

[89] See Psalm 10:9, 12, 17, etc.

[90] *War* 2.451 and 628 and *Vita* 197ff., 290, 316, and 322. It would be interesting to know just who this 'Ananias' was. At this point in the narrative, he is certainly part of 'the Peace Party' and allied with the High Priest responsible for James' death, Ananus ben Ananus. On the attribution of the tomb, otherwise known as 'The Tomb of the Kings'—and now known to be dedicated to Queen Helen of Adiabene and her sons—to 'Ben Kalba Sabuʿa,' see n. 67 above and the article on 'Izates' in *The Encyclopaedia Judaica*, vol. 9, p. 1158. As already remarked, that this tomb is known significantly to Jewish tradition as 'the Cave of Kalba Savuʿa'—i.e., the individual whose daughter Rachel married the famous 'Zealot' Rabbi we have been describing above and supporter of the Bar Kochba Revolt for which he seems to have been executed in the most excruciating manner conceivable—cannot be be underestimated.

[91] See Koran 7.59–79, 9.70, 11.25–68, 14.9, 22.42, 26.106–59, 27.20–53, 29.14–40, 51.41–6, 69.5–8, etc. For our discussion of these matters, see Chapter 3 above and Chapter 28 below.

[92] The comparison to Abraham's 'Salvationary' state in Genesis 15:6 and the references to it in such contexts as Paul's Letters to the Romans, Galatians, and James is crucial We have covered the importance of Northern Syria and Edessa ('Antioch-by-Callirhoe') in Chapters 3-4 above

[93(94)] *War* 2.451–56. Here Mitelius saves himself by agreeing to convert and be circumcised (i.e., forcibly—our 'Zealot'/'Sicarii Essenes' practices again). Here, too, Josephus shows his obsequiousness by stating that, not only was 'the City polluted by such a stain of guilt,' it would not be able to avoid 'some Visitation from Heaven (the 'Visitation' language again, which we shall discuss further below) *if not the Vengeance of Rome*'; but he even adds to this the fact of the massacre of the garrison having occurred on the Sabbath, '*a day on which Jews with religious scruples* (meaning 'caring about Mosaic Law'—paralleling Paul's 'weak conscience' language in 1 Corinthians 8:10–12) *abstain even from the most innocent acts*'!

[94] *War* 2.451–56. This would appear to be the same 'Eleazar son of the High Priest Ananias'—'the Captain of the Temple'—who argued for 'the stopping of gifts or sacrifices on behalf of foreigners' in *War* 2.409 and the 'Party' of whom in 2.440–44 was responsible for the death of 'Menachem'— the descendant of 'Judas the Galilean' and the Head of 'the Sicarii Party' at Masada—whom he blamed for the death of his father and who had just put on the Royal Purple in the Temple! It certainly was not 'Eleazar ben Jair', who in *War* 2.447 is described as fleeing back to Masada, leaving his kinsman 'Menachem' to be 'tortured with all sorts of torments and slain.' Nor does it seem to be the 'Eleazar' of Galilee, who taught the necessity of circumcision to Helen's two sons some two decades before.

[95] *War* 2.418, 556–58, and *Ant.* 20.214, where the two are called 'brother's. These people are clearly—like Paul—of the Generation of Agrippa I. We give their probable genealogy in the Chart at the end of this book. Costobarus along with Saulos is probably a descendant through

Herod's sister Salome of her Idumaean husband by that name—also seemingly executed by Herod in a fit of jealousy—*Ant.* 15.252–66. We treat '*Saulos*' relation to '*Paul*' and the whole '*Costobarus*' line in Chapter 17 below.

[96] *War* 2.556–58. Afterwards the two, along with 'Philip the son of Jacimus' ('*Philip the father of four virgin daughters who were prophetesses*' in Acts 21:6–9?), seem to have gone to Corinth to report to Nero who was then building the Corinth Canal (a favorite venue, as we can see from Paul's Letters, of Paul's activities).

[97] *War* 2.557 and 4.140–46. It is at the point of executing this man '*of Royal lineage and most powerful in the whole City*' in prison by cutting his throat (here he mentions one '*John the son of Dorcas*' as instigating the deed; cf. Acts 9:36) and abrogating the previous High Priest Lines (*War* 4.147–48) by '*electing by lot*' an ignoble and unknown commoner named '*Phannius*' (i.e., '*Phineas*'—4.155–56, also known as '*the Stone-Cutter*') that those Josephus has, up to now, been calling '*Lestai*'/'*Brigands*' (the Gospels'' '*Thieves*') start to be called '*Zealots*' (4.160–365). It is here that Josephus, not only introduces his friend '*Jesus ben Gamala*' as—along with '*Ananus ben Ananus*'—an '*anti-Zealot*'; but, like Paul in Galatians 4:17–8—who calls his '*Zealot*' opponents '*zealous to exclude*' and not '*zealous in the right way*'— challenges such person as not '*zealous in the cause of virtue*' but rather '*in the cause of Evil works in their lowest and basest sense*' (sic)!

[98] *War* 2.254–7 but in *Ant.* 20.162–68 he only uses the term '*Brigands*' again and blames Felix for '*bribing*' them to accomplish this assassination. In *War* 4.400–409, he starts to describe the *Sicarii* and how they took over Masada and overran the surrounding countryside.

[99] *Loc. cit.* and see 1QpHabviii.12–4 and xii.8, where it is used—harking back to the '*pollution of the Temple*'/'*breaking the Covenant*' parameters—to disqualify '*the Wicked Priest*' from service in the Temple for things like his violent tax-collecting and '*robbing the Poor*.' Also see 11QTxlviii.6, lxvi.11ff., lx.17ff., and lxii.16, where it is related to forbidden foods and '*things sacrificed to idols*,' niece marriage and relations with Gentiles generally.

[100] See n. 93 above and *War* 2.451–56.

[101] See CDi.7, vii.9, xix.6, etc. and above, Chapters 1, 7, 10-12 and below, 21-24.

[102] See n. 99 above and 1QpHabxii.8 and 11QTXLviii.6.

[103] See n. 96 above and, in particular *War* 2.558, *Ant.* 17.30–31, and *Vita* 46–61, 177–84, and 407–409. For Josephus' references to Philip's '*daughters*'—relating to '*Philip the father of four virgin daughters who were prophetesses*' with whom Paul stayed in Acts 21:9–9—who escaped from the Roman massacre at Gamala (see Plates 102-103) by hiding in a ditch, see *War* 4.80–83.

[104] See n. 95 above and *War* 2.418. For his further activities as a Leader of a gang of thugs and final going over to Roman Forces, whose agent he seems to have been all along, see *War* 2.556–8 and *Ant.* 20.214.

[105] See *War* 2.556–58 above. For Vespasian's dispatch from Britain to Judea by Nero in Corinth, see *War* 3.1–8.

[106] See *War* 2.648–53, 4.162–238, and 4.314–18 where he praises him in the most extravagant

terms and declares his murder by 'Zealots' and 'Idumaeans' was 'the beginning of the destruction of the City' and 'the ruin of her affairs' (meaning Jerusalem)—a speech which seems rather to embody much phraseology applied in early Church Literature to James, whose death he engineered. But also see *Vita* 193–216 and 309, where his attitude towards Ananus with whom he seems to have been closely involved is almost exactly the reverse.

107 See n. 90 and *War* 626–31 and *Vita* 197ff., 290, 316, and 322 above—the last illustrating Josephus' leniency towards this man. For his involvement with 'Gurion the son of Nicodemus' (i.e., 'Nakdimon') and their mutual attempt to have the Roman Garrison of Jerusalem released, see *War* 2.451 above too.

108 See *Ant.* 18.1–25 and note that in this description of the so-called 'Fourth Philosophy'—which we prefer to call 'the Messianic Movement'—he admits that 'our young men were zealous for it' and seemingly, borrowing a piece from his description of 'the Essenes' in the *War*, 'they did not hesitate to die a death of any kind, nor the deaths of their relations and friends. Nor could any such fear induce them to call any man Lord.' This is the 'Movement' which he ascribes to 'Judas the Galilean and Sadduk' and later, from the 50's to the mass suicide at Masada, he starts rather to designate 'Sicarii.'

109 See *ARN* 4.5 (20a), *Git.* 56a, and *Lam R.* 1.5.31 above.

110 Cf. *Ps. Rec.* 1.65–68 (who is described as 'secretly our brother') and 1.71 with Acts 5.34–40, which includes the anachronism about 'Theudas' and 'Judas the Galilean' and where Gamaliel is pictured as persuading the Sanhedrin to be lenient with 'Peter and the Apostles' (James missing). Also see Acts 22:3 for Paul's alleged claim to have 'been brought up at the feet of Gamaliel'— whatever this might have meant—in the same breath as 'being zealous for God, even as all of you today' (sic)!

112 See Josephus *Vita* 1–8, where he identifies both his father and his brother as named 'Matthias' and claims to be a direct descendant of the first Maccabean High Priest Jonathan (obviously the brother of Judas Maccabee and Simon).

113 *Ps. Rec.* 1.72, 2.7–8, and *Ps. Hom.* 2.22–4 and cf. nn. 71 and 76 above.

114 It should be appreciated that everywhere the term 'Righteous Teacher' is mentioned at Qumran in the Pesharim, the underlying Biblical text—as we have noted—subjected to exegesis is a 'Zaddik' one. See, for example, 4QpHabi.10–11, v.8–12, vii.17–viii.3 (on Habakkuk 2:4), 4QpPs 37ii.22 and iii.9–16, etc.

115 See *Ant.* 20.20 and cf. John 1:14, 3:15, 3:19 (the last two lecturing 'Nicodemus'), etc.

Chapter 14

1 See above Chapters 8, 10, 13, etc.

2 See 1QMxi.13–xii.18 and xix.1–5 and cf. Eusebius, *E. H.* 2.23.13–14, Epiphanius *Haeres.* 78.14, etc.

3 This episode, as we have seen, is mentioned in *Ant.* 20.97–99 and occurs right after the long description of Queen Helen's conversion and her family—most notably that of her and her son Izates' 'famine-relief' activities—but curiously it is missing from the narrative of *The Jewish War*,

written a decade or two earlier, though Josephus obviously knows quite a few details about it. Josephus repeatedly condemns such *'impostors and deceivers, leading the People out into the desert'* in 20.168–72 and *War* 2.259–64 (this exactly after he introduces the new group of agitators he calls the *'Sicarii'* and, of course, all of the so-called *'lestai'/'brigands'* Felix crucified).

[4] See Chapters 4-8 above. In particular, what he wishes to do is a reverse Joshua Exodus, to lead the people once more out into the wilderness—there, no doubt, to show them *'the signs of their impending freedom.'*

[5] One should note that this description of *'Theudas'* activities occurs in *Ant.* 20.97–99, just following the long description of Helen and her sons and just before the one continuing that to 'the *Famine*' and the crucifixion (on the order of Tiberius Alexander, Philo's nephew) of the two sons of Judas the Galilean, *'James and Simon.'* Of course the anachronism in Acts 5:36 regarding *'Theudas'* is easily explained on this basis because, in describing these crucifixions, Josephus explains how Judas the Galilean *'aroused the People to revolt against the Romans when Quirinius was taking the Census in Judea.'* Acts' author was just reading—and in the process, *compressing*—his Josephus a little too rapidly. For the reference in Eusebius, see *E.H.* 2.11.1–3, who does get his sequence for the most part correct, i.e., Philo's Mission to Gaius, Pilate's suicide (*sic*—he doesn't either acknowledge or consider Judas *Iscariot*'s suicide worthy of note), 'the Famine', the beheading of *'James the brother of John'* (*sic*), Agrippa I's death, Theudas' beheading, Helen's famine-relief activities, Simon *Magus*, the preaching of Peter in Rome—obviously based on the Pseudoclementines—etc., etc.

[6] Cf. *Ant.* 20.97 with Acts 5:36.

[7] *Ant.* 18.20. The same number is given by Philo in *Quod Omnis Probus Liber Sit* 7.5.

[8] *Ibid.*, 8.13–14.

[9] *War* 1.95.

[10] See Ps. *Rec.* 1.71. In 1.72, continuing the parallel, Simon *Magus* is introduced and described as *'the Standing One'* (*'that is, the Christ and the Great Power of the High God which is Superior to the Creator of the World'*), as are his *'performance ('Christ'-like) of many miracles.'* The reference to *'Simon a Magician'* as being responsible for the riot in which James was injured and thrown down the Temple steps in 1.70 is probably an interpolation on the order of the deletion of this whole first part from the account from the *Homilies*—and probably as a result of the same embarrassment—since it is clear from the continuing description and from a marginal note on one of the manuscripts that this individual is Paul.

[11] 1QSix.11. N.b., his *'coming'* here is grouped together with that of *'the Messiah of Aaron and Israel'* (here, as already explained, we take the *'yod'* in the word *'Messiah'* as an idiosyncratic singular usage as elsewhere in the Scrolls). For the actual appearance of this *'True Prophet'* proof-text of Deuteronomy 18:18–19 in the Scrolls, see 4QTesti.5–8. For *'works of God'* in the Damascus Document, see CDi.1–2, i.9, vi.8, etc. One should note that in the War Scroll, these *'works'* are not the miracles, raisings, curings, etc., as here in the Gospels and in the Pseudoclementines descriptive of Simon *Magus'* Messianic claims (i.e., *'works of magic'*); but rather God's *'mighty*

works and wonders' are the battles God wins on behalf of His People (cf. 1QMxi.5–xii.17—in exposition of *'the Star Prophecy'*— and 1QMxvii.7–xix.14).

[12] Here, the only difference is that this is not at the *'Last Supper'* as later in Matthew 26:26ff. and *pars.* in the Synoptics.

[13] For *'the Last Times'/'Last Day'/'Day of Judgement'* at Qumran, see 1QpHabvii.7, ix.6, xii.14–xiii.4, etc.

[14] This *'eating and drinking'* the flesh and blood of the living and dying god is the very essence of Greek *'Mystery'* Religion; for *'the Mysteries of God'* here at Qumran, see 1QpHabvii.12–15 above in exposition of Habakkuk 2:3 leading into the pivotal Habakkuk 2:4: *'the Righteous shall live by his Faith'.*

[15] See above *Ant.* 20.168–72 and *War* 2.259–64. This, of course, is not the entirety of such references. Moreover, it is very interesting and certainly not incurious that most of these episodes occur on Passover—the National Liberation Festival of the Jews. For Paul on *'Freedom'* and his sophistical Philo-like, yet almost always pointedly (as in the Gospels generally) antagonistic-to-the-Jews, allegorical method, see Galatians 4:21–5:1—where he even admits he is using an *'allegorical methodology'.*

[16] *Vita* 10 and *War* 2.119–161. The points of contact in these two well-known descriptions are *Banus'* repeated cold-water baths (*War* 2.129) and the description of *Banus'* clothing as *'growing on trees,'* i.e., vegetable matter or *'linen'* (again see *War* 2.129, but also the descriptions of James in Early Church Literature as wearing only *'linen'*); but perhaps, even more germane, the Essenes generally as *'not anointing themselves with oil'* (cf. *War* 2.123 with Eusebius, *E.H.* 2.23.5–6 and *pars.*).

[17] *E.H.* 2.23.8 and *pars.* In this passage, Eusebius makes it clear that this is a direct quote from Hegesippus' account (c. 165 CE) and the lost Five Books of his *Memoirs.*

[18] 1QMxi.11. This is an incredibly important reference, as we shall see as we proceed further below, because it is delivered, not only in the context of the exegesis of *'the Star Prophecy'* from Numbers 24:17–19, but also amid reference to how *'the Enemies of all the Lands will be delivered into the hand of the Poor'* and how *'those bent in the dust (i.e., 'the Meek') would pay the Reward on Evil Ones* (a term used in both the Community Rule and Habakkuk *Pesher*—further solidifying the common vocabulary and, therefore, the contemporaneity of all these texts) *on the Mighty Ones of the Peoples and justify* (God's) *True Judgement on all Mankind'!*

[19] See 1QMxi.11.1–14 and *pars.* above.

[20] Numbers 24:17–19. As already noted above, one should also connect with this the citation from Isaiah 10:33–4 about *'Lebanon falling by a Mighty One'* (itself followed up by the *'Shoot from the Stem of Jesse and a Branch growing out of his Roots'* material from Isaiah 11:1–5), itself subjected to exegesis in 4QpIs[a] as well as in Rabbinic literature, where it is definitively connected to the fall of the Temple in 70 CE. Not only is this *'Star'* ideology to be found in the Damascus Document, but it is also at the basis of the *'Star'*-over-Bethlehem material found in Matthew 2:2–10's account of the birth of Jesus. Also see the two pictures in *JBJ* of the wall paintings in

the Catacombs of Rome of Balaam pointing at *'the Star'*, Plates XX and XXIX.

[21] See Chapters 21, 22, 28, and vairously below.

[22] 1QMxi.7 (the usage here is again idiomatic as we saw—but probably singular), xii.9–10, and xix.2.

[23] *Haeres.* 78.7.7 and 14.1–3.

[24] *E.H.* 2.1.2. *N.b.,* this 'crown' imagery too in 1QSiv.7. Eusebius makes this statement in the course of presenting the two 'James'es—one 'the Lord's brother' 'James the Just,' the first 'Bishop of Jerusalem,' and the other 'James' (whom he hardly describes at all and clearly views as secondary) —and 'Thomas' (in our view, 'Judas Thomas', who is hardly differentiable from 'Judas of James' in Apostle lists and who is himself indistinguishable from 'Thaddaeus surnamed Lebbaeus' in these same lists)—having sent 'Thaddaeus,' 'under a Divine impulse,' to 'the Land of the Edessenes' in Northern Syria and 'the King of the Osrhoeans' there, i.e. 'the Assyrians,' and also, no doubt, the area known as 'Adiabene'.

[25] *War* 6.312–15.

[26] It should be appreciated that the reference to 'the ships of the Kittim' in Daniel 11:30 is very definitely a reference to the Romans in the Eastern Mediterranean. Where the War Scroll reflecting Roman military behaviour is concerned, one should have reference to the works of Roth and Driver—also to some extent reflected in those of Yadin—and, once more, we should emphasize that regardless of the 'results' of palaeography and other similarly imprecise forms of measurement, on the basis of internal parameters alone and the use of common vocabulary and replicating *dramatis personae,* all Documents of this kind—generally referred to as 'sectarian' or 'extra-biblical' documents—should be seen as more or less coming from the same place and being written at similarly contemporary times.

[27(26)] As we just saw above, this allusion found in 1QMxi.13–4 is also more or less replicated (in the context of like-minded references to 'the Poor'/'the Ebionim') in 1QpHabxii.2–3, 1QSii.6– 7, and 4QpPs 37iv.12. It should be appreciated, too, that it also comprises some of the imagery attached to the Isaiah 3:10–11 passage, applied to James' death in early Church Literature.

[28] 1QMxi.6–14 above. Of course, the imagery of 'Justification' is important, as is that of allusion to 'the Meek' and 'the Poor'; but so too is that to 'Enemy'/'Enemies,' well known to the Ps. *Rec.* 1.71, the Letter of James 4:4, *the Parable of the Tares* (Matthew 13:25) and, of course, Paul in Galatians 4:16 and 1 Thessalonians 2:15.

[29] 1QpHabxii.2–4 above. Here, the allusions to 'Judging him to destruction' and '*lechelot'/'destroy'* very definitely refer to the kind of Apocalyptic Scene of '*the Last Judgement'* depicted in 1QpHabvii.10–viii.3 (in interpretation of Habakkuk 2:3–4), x.3–5, and x.13–15 and alluded to in xii.14–xiii.4.

[30] *Ibid.*

[31] Cf. 4QpPs 37 ii.10, ii.19, iii.1–2, iii.10–11, iii.16, iv.9–11 (here, too, the same *'paying him his reward'* in the sense of 'Divine Vengeance'), and iv.19–20.

[32] 1QMi.3.

33 1QMi.2. '*Ethnon*' should always be read as the Greek parallel to the Hebrew '*Amim*.'

34 Cf. CDiv.2–3 and vi.4–5. For Theudas' reverse exodus, see *Ant.* 20.97 above and for 'Jesus"—where he too '*leads*' or '*feeds*' some 4–5000 people—cf. Matthew 10:1, 14.13–21 and 15.29–39, and *pars.* above.

35 Acts 9:1–25, Galatians 1:17, and *Ps. Rec.* 1.71.

36 See *Haeres.* 19.1.2–10 and 29.7.7.

37 *Ibid.*, 20.3.2–3, 30.1.7, 53.1.1, etc.

38 1QMi.1–2, ii.10–4, etc. There can be little doubt that what we are speaking about here is the Desert between Transjordan and Iraq and all the 'Arab' Nations bordering thereon—i.e., '*the Fertile Crescent.*'

39 1QMi.6–7. *N.b.*, that in the line preceding this (i.5), one actually baldly states that 'this is the time of "*Jesus for the People of God*'"—i.e., '*Yeshuᶜa le-ᶜAm-El.*'

40 We describe the reason for this below, but the point is that the multiple descriptions of '*the Kittim*' in 1QpHabii.12–iv.14 and v.16–vi.11—most notably, '*trampling the Earth with their horses and pack animals and coming from far off, from the islands of the Sea*' (hardly the Seleucids in Syria), '*collecting booty like the fish of the sea,*' '*sacrificing to their standards and worshipping their weapons of war*' (the key allusion as most thinking scholars have recognized and the military practice of Imperial Rome, the Emperor's bust at this time being on their standards and adored after every victory), '*portioning out their yoke and their taxes* (i.e., '*tax-farming*', another definitive allusion), *consuming* (literally '*eating*') *all the Peoples*' (in the East, '*the Peoples,*' as we have seen, were called '*Ethnoi*' and their Rulers, '*Kings of the Peoples*'), '*and having no pity, even on the fruit of the womb*' (n.b., Josephus' description of the butchery carried out by the Romans around the Sea of Galilee where he uses almost the precise language. Again, hardly the Seleucids). But what is definitive here as well is the passage in 4QpNahii.3, which makes it clear that '*the Kittim*' come after '*the Greeks*', i.e., '*God did not permit the City* (meaning Jerusalem) *to fall into the hands of the Greeks—from the time of Antiochus to the* (time of the) *coming of the Kittim,*' that is, the coming of Pompey and the Romans and, after that, the final conquest and destruction by Vespasian and Titus.

41 1QMi.1. Vermes gives '*Satan*' here, as he does most frequently in his translations; but the usage here is '*Belial*'—'*the Devil*' or '*Diabolos*'—not '*Satan.*' '*Satan* is a different word. This may confuse the unsuspecting reader.

42 1QMi.3, 8–9, 14–6, vii.1–7, xii.8–9, etc.

43 1QMi.5 above.

44 1QMi.2.

45 Both '*Belial*' and '*the Sons of Belial,*' of course, are widespread usages throughout the Qumran corpus. For its part '*Balaam*' is one of '*the Enemies of God*' along with Doᶜeg, Cain, Korah, and Gehazi delineated in b. *San.* 105a–109b. Where these '*Sons of Belial*' are concerned, in the Bible some of the most vivid usages are to be found in Judges 19:22–20:13. It should be appreciated that in these passages from Judges, '*the Sons of Belial*' being talked about are for the most part

'Benjaminites'. For reference to '*Belial*' (corrupted, as we have seen, into '*Beliar*') and '*Balaam*' in the New Testament, one should see 2 Corinthians 6:15, 2 Peter 2:15 and Revelation 2:14. For 'Balaam' in the Old Testament, see Numbers 22:5 and Deuteronomy 23:4. But perhaps the best discussion of any of these things is to be found in my Appendix to *JJHP*, pp. 87–94: '*The "Three Nets of Belial" in the Zadokite Document and "Balla*ᶜ*"/"Bela*ᶜ*" in the Temple Scroll*. This has been further developed in my article: '*The Final Proof that James and the Righteous Teacher are the Same*' in *DSSFC*, pp. 332–51 (first presented to the Society of Biblical Literature in 1994).

[46] For a Genealogical Chart of the '*Herodians*,' see the back of the book and *Ant.* 18.136–7, where Josephus makes it clear that it is this 'Salome' who is married to 'Philip' and not her mother 'Herodias' as in New Testament reformulation. Also that she then later marries the son of Herod of Chalcis, Aristobulus—more marriage with nieces and close family cousins so abhorred at Qumran!

[47] Since these salutations at the end of Romans do refer to '*the Littlest Herod*'—hardly a common name at this juncture of Roman History—it is our view that this individual is the son of said 'Salome' and 'Aristobulus', making it ever more likely that the reference to '*the household of Aristobulus*' in 16:10, followed by that to '*Herodion*' in 16:11, is none other than the one of these two, '*Aristobulus and Salome*' now living in Rome. This makes it even more likely that 'Paul' or 'Saul' is actually the descendant of Herod's sister (the first '*Salome*'), a first cousin of both Agrippa I and Herod of Chalcis, and, therefore, the individual who was brought up with '*Herod the Tetrarch*' as per Acts 13:1. One should also note that the reference to his '*kinsman Junius*' in Romans 16:7 is, in the author's view, none other than the son of '*Saulos*' sister '*Cypros*' by Helcias/Alexas, the Temple Treasurer, and therefore probably Paul's nephew in Acts 23:16, who has access to and warns the Centurions in the Fortress of Antonia of plots against his uncle. In this passage, it should be appreciated that Paul's 'sister' is specifically listed as residing in Jerusalem. We know, too, that this 'Julius' was an avid reader of Josephus' works in Rome and therefore specifically retired in Rome (the destination of Paul's letter) because Josephus proudly tells us so in his *Vita*.

[49] For '*Bela*ᶜ' as a descendant of '*Benjamin*', see Genesis 46:21 and 1 Chronicles 7:6. This makes the curious reference to barring one '*Bela*ᶜ' from the Temple in 11QTxlvi.10–11 all the more riveting.

[50] See Koran 2.130–40, 3.65–67, 4.125, etc. and Paul in Romans 4:1–20, 9.8–9, Galatians 3:6–18, 4:22–28, etc.

[51] See, for instance, CDxx.17–20 and my article in *DSSFC*, "'*Joining*'/'*Joiners*,' '*Arizei-Go'im*,' and '*the Simple of Ephraim*' Relating to a Cadre of Gentile '*God-Fearers*' at Qumran' (first presented to the Society of Biblical Literature in 1991), pp. 313–31; and Acts 9:31, 10:2, 13:16, Romans 3:18, 2 Corinthians 7:1, etc.

[52] CDiv.2–10 and vi.3–11.

[53] 4QpNahiii.3–8 and iv.3–7 (in the second instance, anyhow, clearly tied to an allusion to '*joining*,

'i.e., 'ger-nilveh'). It should be appreciated that 'Ephraim' became 'Samaria' when the capital was moved from Shechem to Samaria somewhere in the middle of the Israelite History in 1 Kings 16:24–32 during the Reign of Ahab and Jezebel.

54 The usage 'ger-nilvim' is actually used in 4QpNahiii.9 introducing these passages in iv.3–7 above, but one can also see the outlines of it in the exegesis in CDiv.2–3 above as well. It is not incurious that the further exegesis concerning 'going out from the Land of Judah to dwell in the Land of Damascus' in CDvi.3–10 also relates to 'the Penitents of Israel' ('Priests' in the exegesis of CDiv) and 'the Nobles of the People' or 'Peoples'—the 'Ethne' of Paul's 'Mission to the Gentiles.' But see too, my 'Joining/Joiners…' article in DSSFC above.

55 For Monobazus and Kenedaeus, see War 2.520; for 'the Idumaeans,' War 4.228–358; for 'the Peoples' and/or 'the Violent Ones'/'Violent Ones of the Gentiles' at Qumran, see 1QpHabii.6, iii.5, iii.11, iv.14, v.3–4, vi.7, viii.9–ix.7, and 4QpPs 37ii.20 and iv.10.

56 For Niger, see War 2.520, 566, and 3.11–28. For his death, so reminiscent of that of Jesus, see 4.359–63.

57 4QpPs 37ii.20 and iv.10 above.

58 1QpHabii.6 above.

59 See Acts 13:21, Romans 11:1, Philippians 3:5, and 1QMi.2 above.

60 See E. H. 1.12.4–13.20 and ANCL: Appendix to Hippolytus and Codex Baroccian 206.

61 Cf. 1QMxviii.8 with 4Q252–54v.3

62 1QMxi.4–11 and xix.3–4.

63 1QpHabvi.6–11 and xi.7–xii.6.

64 1QMxix.11.

65 1QSv.2 and 9 above.

66 1QMxviii.7. As we have seen, the term 'Yeshuᶜa' in Hebrew actually does mean 'Salvation'; cf. the very last line of the substantive portion of the Damascus Document—CDxx.34 above.

67 E.H. 2.23.13 above.

68 Aside from the references to the 'delivering up' of 'Jesus' in Matthew 18:34, 27:2, 27:26, etc. and pars., see CDi.17 (meaning, 'delivered up to the Avenging Sword of the Covenant'), iii.10–1 (likewise), viii.1, etc.

69 War 2.599, 3.450–531, and Vita 66–67, 134–36, 271–301.

70 War 3.448, 3.463, and Vita 65–67 and 134. The word 'Innovation,' as Josephus uses it throughout these descriptions of troublemakers, agitators, and malcontents, is very interesting and can mean 'those desirous for Religious Innovation' or, quite simply, 'Revolutionaries.' The two are not always distinguishable.

71 Vita 65–67.

72 Vita 66, 134–36, 143.302–311, etc.

73 War 3.450. This last ('Lestai'), of course, is exactly the vocabulary used in Matthew 27:38 and pars. to describe 'the two thieves' (sic), between whom 'Jesus' is crucified. It would, moreover,

be more accurate to translate this term as '*Bandits*', as it usually is in Josephus, as these were certainly not two '*pickpockets*' or such like.

74 *War* 3.499–502 (here Josephus, in describing the massacring that went on in Tarichaeae, specifically comments on Titus' '*valor*' and several times mentions Trajan's father '*Trajan*' in a not unsimilar light) and 3.522–30; cf. Matthew 4:18–22, 8:23–24, 14:13–34, Mark 3:9, 4:36–5:2, 5:18–21, 6:32–54, 8:10–14, Luke 5:1–7, 8:23–25, John 6:1, 6:17–23, 21:1–8, and *pars*.

75 I have treated this subject extensively in '*The Final Proof that James and the Righteous Teacher are the Same*' in *DSSFC*, pp. 332–51 and the Appendix to *JJHP*, pp. 87–94: '*The "Three Nets of Belial" in the Zadokite Document and "Balla^c^"/"Bela^c^" in the Temple Scroll*', already mentioned above; but for several interesting examples of this '*casting nets*' or, for instance, even themselves '*into the sea*,' see Matthew 4:6 (this, '*Jesus*' himself), 4:18, 7:22–10:34 ('*casting out devils*' and '*spirits*'), 13:42–50 ('*cast into a furnace of fire*'), 15:17–30 ('*cast down the toilet bowl*'), 17:19–23, John 21:6–8 (here Peter, however absurdly, puts on his clothes '*for he was naked*'—this probably based on some very good Etruscan or Roman wall paintings—in order '*to cast himself into the sea*' with his '*net full of fishes*'—thus!), and *pars*.

76 *War* 3.459–85

77(76a) *Ibid.*, 3.522–542

78 *Ibid.*, 3.532–8. Of course, Josephus is completely either enamored of or obsequious to both Agrippas, not only in his narration of the Tiberias Palace episode, but also in *Vita* 364–7 where he admits that Agrippa II supplied him with sixty-two letters testifying to the truth of his narrative!

79 *War* 2.181–83 and *Ant.* 18.240–55. Though, in the *War*, Josephus calls the place of his exile '*Spain*'; in the *Antiquities*, he corrects this to '*Lyons, a city in Gaul*' (perhaps he benefited here from Agrippa II's 62 letters!).

80 *Epistle of Peter to James* 4.1–2.

81 1QSix.17–8.

82 *War* 3.522–9. Here, of course, there is *real* '*blood*' being '*poured out.*'

83 *War* 4.478.

84 See Matthew 14:24–35 and *pars.* above.

85 *The Qumran Chronicle* in December, 1992 (vol. 2, no.1), '*The 1990 Survey of Qumran Caves*,' p 49. Also see my '*The 1988–92 California State University Dead Sea Walking Survey and Radar Groundscan of the Qumran Cliffs*'; Michael Baigent's and my '*A Ground-Penetrating Radar Survey Testing the Claim for Earthquake Damage of the Second Temple Ruins at Khirbet Qumran*'; and Dennis Walker's '*Notes on Qumran Archaeology: The Geographical Context of the Caves and Tracks*' in *The Qumran Chronicle*, December, 2000 (vol. 9, no.2), pp. 123–30, pp. 131–37, and December, 1993 (vol. 3, no. 1), pp. 93–100.

86 See 4QMMTii.66–67 above.

87 1QMi.1–3 above.

[88] 1QMvii.5.

[89] See *MZCQ*, pp. 12–16 and 19–27 and *DSSU*, pp. 32–43 and 49–80.

[90] Cf. my discussion of this in *DSSU*, pp. 273–80.

[91] 4Q448. The scholars who originally found this were A. Yardeni, E. Eshel, and H. Eshel. See their article 'A Qumran Composition Containing Part of Psalm 154 and a Prayer for the Welfare of King Jonathan and his Kingdom,' *Tarbiz* (60), 1991, pp. 297–300 and in *Israel Exploration Journal* (42), 1992, pp. 199–229 and the version of this Document, Michael Wise and I published in *DSSU*, pp. 280–1.

[92] 4Q448ii.6–8 (now called by some 'Apocryphal Psalm and Prayer'—we called it 'Paean for King Jonathan').

[93] Cf., for example, 1 Maccabees 2:26–7 and 54–8 and 2 Maccabees 4:2 with 1QSii.15, iv.4–18, ix.12, 1QHi.6–7, ii.31, ix.5, x.15, xii.14, xvii.3, xx.14, etc.

[94] *War* 2.152–53, but also see 'John the Essene'—*War* 2.567 and 3.11–9—who participated along with one 'Silas' and a 'Niger' in the early battles of the War and died along with the former at Ashkelon.

[95] See, for instance, J. T. Milik, *Ten Years of Discovery in the Wilderness of Judaea*, London, 1959 whose attitude in pp. 44–98, 142–43, etc. is fairly typical of this way of looking at the Documents, that is, dismiss anything that doesn't easily fit into one's preconceptions. Don't worry about what the documents themselves say! These can always be explained away as, for instance, with the Copper Scroll—to paraphrase—'it was dropped by a passer-by' or 'it represented a child's exercise tablet'!

[96] Aside from the War Scroll, there is the Community Rule itself in which we have already encountered the expression 'the Day of Vengeance', which in the Qumran Hymns (vii.20) is called 'the Day of Massacre.' But there is also the finale of the Habakkuk *Pesher*, xii.12–xiii.4, which twice refers in the manner of Muhammad in the Koran to 'the Day of Judgement' and ends with the pious hope that 'on the Day of Judgement, God will destroy all the Servants of Idols and Evil Ones off the Earth.' This is to say nothing of the 'Paean to King Jonathan' just elucidated above.

[97] 1QSix.20–4 above.

[98] See our comments, Chapter Two above.

[99] Cf. 1QSviii.12–16 and ix.20 with Matthew 3:1–3/Mark 1:2–4/Luke 3:4–11.

[100] Cf. CDiv.6–9, vi.17–vii.5, etc.; but opposed to this—in addition to Paul's endless remonstrances that 'for me, there are no forbidden things'—see Acts 10:14–16, 10:28, and 11:2–10 where, as we have seen, Peter learns from a 'Bat-Kol' not to 'make distinctions between clean and unclean, Holy or profane.'

[101] (100a) 1QSviii.1–16.

[102] 1QSviii.10–15.

[103] Cf. CDiv.8, xx.2, xx.21, 1QSi.2, i.7, i.16–17, v.20 (repeated in viii.15 in exposition of Isaiah 40:3 as we just saw), ix.20, 1QpHabvii.11 and viii.1 (in exposition of the all-important Habakkuk

2:4), xii.4–5, etc.

[104] One can see the '*Piety*' part of this dichotomy in CDxx.21 just cited above. But it permeates the whole Qumran corpus as it does the Letter of James—cf. James 2:4 on how '*God chose the Poor... as Heirs to the Kingdom Promised to those who Love Him*'. In this regard, see CDvii.6 of Ms. A, repeated with the term '*love*' added in xx.21 of Ms. B (just cited above), and cf. 1QHviii.21. For my comments about the '*Righteousness*'/'*Piety*' dichotomy generally see *JBJ*, pp. 62, 109, 235–7, 261–4, 333, and 365 and Chapters 4 , 9-10, and variously above.

[105] *Epistle of Peter to James* 3:1 and 4:4.

[106] 1QSix.13–24.

[107] For our comments on '*internal data*' as opposed to '*external data*', see Chapter 2 and variously above.

[108] In these Documents there are numerous such references. But in the Habakkuk *Pesher*, for instance, there are the descriptions of '*the Kittim*' as '*sacrificing to their standards and worshipping their weapons of war*,' '*tax-farming*,' '*having no mercy even on the fruit of the womb*,' the exegesis of Habakkuk 2:4: '*the Righteous shall live by his Faith*' in terms of '*the Delay of the Parousia*' and '*the Last Judgement*' and circumscribed to '*the Doers of the Torah in the House of Judah*'. In the Isaiah *Pesher* there is, of course, the exegesis of '*the Messianic Prophecy*' of Isaiah 10:33–11:5; in Nahum, there is the note about '*the Kittim coming after the Greeks*'; in the *Florilegium*, there are the Messianic promises to David and '*his seed*' including Amos 9:11 (evoked in Acts 15:16 in James' speech at the so-called '*Jerusalem Conference*' and quoted in conjunction with '*the Star Prophecy*' in the all-important Column vii of CD); and in The Testimonia, there are '*the True Prophet*' Prophecy of Deuteronomy 18:18–9, so dear to '*Ebionites*' according to the Pseudoclementines and, of course following this, the full citation of '*the Star Prophecy*' itself.

[109] 1QHvii.20 and cf., for instance, 1QMi.10 and vii.5.

[110] 1QMvii.6.

[111] Cf. 1QSviii.16–25, ix.19, CDxv.17, 4Q266, 4Q270, etc.

[112] CDvi.19–vii.6. N.b., the allusion to '*all those rejecting (the Commandments of God) being paid the reward on Evil Ones when God visits the Earth*' in CDvii.9 directly following these '*Promises*'.

113 For these categories of '*unclean*' persons at Qumran see, for instance 1QMvii.3–7 and 11QTxlv.5–xlvii.18. Many of these are precisely the kind of persons that '*Jesus*' in the Gospels is presented as either '*curing*' or '*keeping table fellowship with*'. The same is true for what '*Peter*' learns in Acts 10–11 and how, in particular, in 11:2–3, '*those of the Circumcision (i.e., James' Party in Galatians 2:12) opposed him, complaining that* '*you went in to uncircumcised men and ate with them*.'

[114] 1QMvii.6–7—cf., for instance, Mark 7:20's version of 'Jesus'' analogy of the '*toilet bowl*' situation.

[115 (114a)] 11QTxlvi.13–16. Recently there has been quite a bit of discussion about these latrines at Qumran and some have even claimed to have found them by following these parameters.

[116] *War* 2.147–9. Josephus even mentions—obviously for the benefit of his non-Jewish readers— that, even though such easement is natural, yet is it a rule among them to wash their hands

thereafter, as if it were a defilement to them.' No doubt Mark 7:1–23/Matthew 15:1–20's 'Jesus' would consider this 'a Tradition of the Elders', required only by 'the Pharisees coming down from Jerusalem' (cf. Acts 15:1–4 on the commencement of 'the Jerusalem Council'), i.e., only 'a Tradition of Men', and binding only in so far as not opposed by one 'given by God'—such as that 'to honor one's father and mother'!

[117] B. Ta‘an 23b.

[118] A.Z. 16b–17a, Eccles. R. 1.8.3, and *Tos. Hul.* 2:24 and see above Chapter Six.

Chapter 15

[1] 1QHxi.22–23. For 'the soul of the Righteous One' and 'of the Poor One' (nephesh-Ebion), see the attack on 'the Righteous One and all the Walkers in Perfection' in CDi.20 and 1QHix.9–10, x.32–34 (nephesh-Ebion and 'nephesh-‘Ani'), xi.25, xiii.6, xiii.13, etc. below.

[2] 1QHxi.22–23 and cf. xvii.25–36, xix.24–27, xxvi.7–12, etc. One should also note in passing passages like xi.35–36 about 'the Foundations of the World staggering and swaying' picturing a kind of 'Last Judgement' and paralleling imagery so characteristic of the early *Surahs* of the Koran. Moreover, it is not surprising that the same kind of imagery is to be found in the Pauline corpus as well.

[3] For 'the Standing One,' see *JBJ*, pp. 705–90 and above Chapters 4-6 and 8-9, etc. For 'standing' at Qumran, see CDiv.4, xii.23, xiv.19, 1QHxv.31, xxi.13–14, xxiii.9–10, etc.

[4] For Synoptic parallels to this 'shoe latchet' allusion, see Mark 1:7 and Luke 3:16. At Qumran this 'Shiloh' Prophecy (Genesis 49:10) is actually to be found in the so called Genesis *Pesher* (4Q252–54 above), v. 1–7, which actually mentions 'the Messiah's 'feet' and probably explains all these 'feet' references we have been variously following above.

[5] See 1QHxii.22–25, xx.13–17, and xxi(top).13–15. It would be well for the reader to trace both this 'Power' and 'Light' language throughout the Scrolls.

[6] See 1QHxii.18–22 and 30–33. Also note 1QH.xv.31–32 and, whereas before we had 'the Scoffers of Lying' preceding these passages. here there is a reference to 'the Man of Emptiness' (cf. James 2:20 and 1QpHabx.12 on 'the Emptiness' of the Lying Spouter's 'works') that follows this.

[7] We have covered this 'swallowing' language at Qumran in many works—particularly 1QpHabv.8–9 (Habakkuk 1:13), xi.5, and xi.15—but see *JJHP*, pp. 62–64, 87–90, and 96 and *DSSFC*, pp. 182–4, 208–17, 339–51, 425, and 428.

[8] 1QpHabxi.2–15 above.

[9] 1QSviii.3–11.

[10] 1QSviii.6–7, but note too 1QMvi.6, xi.13 and 4QpPs 37iv.9—further solidifying the homogeneity of all these documents.

[11] CDi.7.

[12] For Paul's 'building' language (to say nothing of 'planting' and 'plantation' imagery), see 1 Corinthians 3:6–14, 2 Corinthians 5:1, and Ephesians 2:19–20 (if authentic).

¹³ For 'Precious Cornerstone' language as applied to 'Jesus,' see Matthew 21:42 and *pars*. But also see Acts 4:11, Ephesians 2:20, and 1 Peter 1:20 and 2:6–7.

¹⁴ Cf. Ephesians 5:2, 1 Peter 2:5, Hebrews 9:26, 10:5–11:4, 13:15–16, etc.

¹⁵ 1QSviii.3–4 above.

¹⁶ 1QSviii.10.

¹⁷ Of course, this links up with '*the Son of Man came eating and drinking*' theme in Matthew 11:18–19 and pars. (*n.b.*, here it is specifically remarked that John '*did not come eating and drinking*'!) and is the very opposite of those in Acts 23:12–21 who took an oath (obviously a '*Nazirite*' one) '*not to eat or drink until (they) had killed Paul*.' In the end, the whole issue revolves around the '*pure foods*' debate we have signalled in our discussion of the '*Toilet Bowl*' Parable above. For Qumran, of course, '*Judgement*' is a very serious matter and we have also been following it closely in passages (some of which also mention '*Vengeance*') like 1QpHabviii.1–2, x.3, xii.14–xiii.3, CDvii.16–25, 1QSviii.3–9, viii.24, ix.7, and 1QMiv.6, vii.5, xi.14, xii.10, xv.2–17 (here and in vii.5, '*the Day of Vengeance*, as in 1QSix).

¹⁸ Cf. 1QMi.2–5, xv.14–17, xviii.1–3, etc.

¹⁹ 1QHxix.10–14.

²⁰ 1QMxii.9. For '*Jinn*' in the Koran, see 6.101–30, 18.51 (together with '*Iblis*'/'*Belial*'), 34.41, 72.1ff. etc.

²¹ 1QSii.23–25.

²² Cf. Matthew 22:37–39 and *pars*., James 1:12–2:8, Justin Martyr in *Dial*. 23, 47, and 93, etc.

²³ Cf. 1QSii.24–25, viii.2, CDvi.17–vii.2, xx.18–21, etc.

^{24.} *War* 2.128, 2.139, *Ant*. 15.375–79, and 18.117. Josephus also applies these two categories to his description of the first '*Zaddik*,' '*Simeon the Righteous*,' in *Ant*. 12.43.

²⁵ *Epistle of Peter to James* 4:5.

²⁶ The interpolation, of course, which was first recognized by A. von Harnack in the Nineteenth Century, is the first line '*Cephas and the Twelve*' (in the Gospel view, there were only '*Eleven*' at the time and who '*Cephas*' was is a matter of debate—possibly the '*Cleopas*' mentioned in Luke 24:18—the first post-resurrection appearance according to that Gospel—or, if one prefers '*Simeon bar Cleophas*,' the second Successor to James in the History of '*the Jerusalem Church*'). Of course, this depends on whether one acknowledges the '*suicide*' of '*Judas Iscariot*.' On the other hand, the reference to '*James, then all the Apostles, and last of all to me*' in 1 Corinthians 15;7 is far less precise and far more sensible.

²⁷ Cf. CDi.4, i.16, iii.10, iv.6–8, vii.2, viii.16–17, etc.

²⁸ For Qumran, '*the First*' are quite literally the '*First*,' the first of whom in CDiii.3–10 is Abraham himself in his role as '*Friend of God*.'

²⁹ For '*Last*'/'*Last Times*,' see CDi.11–12, iv.4, xx.8–9, 1QSi.1, iv.16–17, 1QpHabii.7, ii.5–6, vii.2–12, ix.4–6, etc.

³⁰ CDvii.14–23.

³¹ Cf. Matthew 17:1–8 and *pars*. with Galatians 2:5–9.

[32] 1QSviii.1–7.

[33] Of course, *'Perfection'* and *'Perfection of the Way'* are basic Qumran doctrines; cf. 1QSi.8, ii.2, iii.9, v.24, vii.22–5, viii.6–9, viii.20, ix.19, xi.2, xi.10–11, CDi.20–21, ii.15–16, vii.4–5, viii.24–30, etc.

[34] Cf. 1QpHabx.5–13 and below Chapter 27.

[35] 1QSviii.8, 1QHxiv.24-27, xv.8–9, etc.

[36] Cf. Chapter 10 above and CDi.6–11.

[37] Cf. Matthew 22:37–9 and n. 22 above.

[38] Cf. 1 Corinthians 8:1 with 1QpHabvii.14–6.

[39] Cf. 1QpHabx.5–13 above.

[40] *War* 2.128–48 (*n.b.*, the use of *'casting out'* and *'separation'* language in 2.143 to describe the treatment meted out to backsliders, the allusion to *'not spitting in the midst of'* the Assembly in 2.147—paralleling allusions linking the Community Rule to the Damascus Document, and 2.148 on their *'toilet'* habits and latrine situation certainly increases these parallels to Qumran Documents).

[41] *Ibid.*

[42] *Ant.* 18.117—*'Righteousness,'* of course being the basic doctrine at Qumran, which is why I have *inter alia* continually capitalized it in my work to show its importance.

[43] Cf. *War* 2.123, 129, and 161, *Vita* 11–12, and pp. 4, 22, 34–36, 71–82, 93, 100, 114–15, 124–25, 210, 259, 264, 392, etc. above.

[44] 1QSiv.6–8, but see also 1QSiii.14–19 and ix.17–22 where *'Visitation'* and *'concealing the Truth of the Marvelous Mysteries'* are concerned.

[45] Cf. Chapter 14 above, Acts 6:5ff., *JBJ*, pp. 223, 240–47, 304, and 344, and Eusebius in *E.H.* 2.1.2.

[46] See *War* 2.155, Hippolytus 9.21, Eusebius, *E.H.* 3.32.6, and Epiphanius, *Haeres.* 78.14.5–6

[47] Cf. *Haeres.* 19.4.1, 30.3.1–6, 30.17.5, and *Abstract* 30.2.

[48] 1QSiv.19–21.

[49] 1QSiv.21–23

[50] See CDiii.18–20 (in a passage referring to *'building a House of Faith,' 'standing,' 'His marvelous Mysteries,'* and *'forgiving sin'*) and 1QMiii.20 and xi.11.

[51] 1QSii.23–iii.4.

[52] For a selection of references to *'the Man of Lying'*/*'Spouter of Lying,'* see CDi.14–15, iv.19–20, xx.15, 1QpHabv.11, x.9–13, etc.—more testimony to the homogeneity and contemporaneity of the Documents at Qumran.

[53] Aside from all the other parallels, it is Paul, as we shall see, who constantly refers to the fact that he *'does not lie'*—cf. Galatians 1:20 (in the context of averring to having met James), 2 Corinthians 11:30 (in the context of escaping from Damascus *'in a basket'* and *'knowing a man in Christ, who was caught up into the Third Heaven'*—sic!), Romans 3:7 and 9:1, 1 Timothy 2:7, etc.

[54] 1QSiii.9–12. Note he is *'the pleasing atonement'* and it is he who *'will be washed by purifying waters and sanctified by cleansing waters.'* Also see 1QSi.15 and iii.10 and cf. 4Q266, Lines 17–18 on expelling a person who *'departs from the right or the left of the Torah.'*

[55] 1QSiii.7–9.

[56] *Ant.* 18.117 above.

[57] For *'Sons of Zedek,'* see 1QSiii.20 and 22; for *'Sons of the Zaddik,'* see ix.14. For *'the Sons of Zadok'* as *'the Elect'* or *'Chosen'* (*'of Israel called by Name, who will stand up in the Last Days'*), see CDiv.3–4 and cf. 1QSv.2–10 above.

[58] 1QSxi.5–9

[59] Cf. 1 Corinthians 12:14–27 and Ephesians 2:19–22.

[60] *Haeres.* 30.15.3 and 21.1 and *Hom.* 10.1, 11.1, 11.26–30, 12.6, 13.4–5 (just like *'Essenes,'* calling these things *'Piety towards God'*), etc.

[61] 1QSii.15, iv.7, viii.10–16, and ix.19–23.

[62] 1QMx.4–5 and cf. vii.5–6.

[63] Cf. 1QSi.19–26, x.18, 1QMi.5, iv.13, xi.11–2, xiv.4–5, xviii.7, CDxx.19–34, etc.

[64] See Acts 9:31 (this describing all the Churches in Judea), 10:5 (describing *'Cornelius, a Roman Centurion!'*), 13:16 (here Paul really uses the term to describe *'Gentiles associated with the Synagogue'* he is addressing in Antioch at Pisidia); but also Paul's own use of the formulation—sometimes even sarcastically—in Romans 3:18, 8:15, 13:7, 2 Corinthians 7:1 (perhaps the most *'Perfect'* formulation of the usage), Ephesians 5:21, etc.

[65] Cf. Acts 2:21, 3:6, 4:7–17, 5:28, etc. with CDiv.3–4 (the definition of *'the Sons of Zadok'* at Qumran).

[66] Cf. CDvi.15, vii.1, and viii.8.

[67] Cf. 1QSvi.12–20, CDix.18–22, xiii.5–16, xiv.8–12, xv.7–14, 4Q266.16, etc.

[68] CDxx.34, basically the last line of the revised historical exhortation in the Damascus Document.

[69] Cf. 1QMxi.5–xii.14 and xvii.7–xix.13.

[70] Cf. 1QSi.8, ii.2, iii.9, v.24, viii.9, ix.19, x.22, xi.10–11, CDi.20–21, ii.15–16, xx.2–8, etc.

[71] See Hippolytus 9.21, *JBJ*, pp. 309, 709, 764, 898, and above, Chapters 3, 5, and 12.

[72] Cf. Jeremiah 35:10–7.

[73] For Paul's contempt for *'the Torah as given by the hand of Moses,'* see in particular Galatians 2:16–21, 3:17–4:11, 4:24–4:30, and 2 Corinthians 3:1–18.

[74] Of course, for *'the Way'* at Qumran, see 1QSi.28, iv.22, viii.19–21, ix.5–8, xi.10–11, CDi.9–11, ii.6, iii.10–11, etc.

[75] The *'Separation'* ideal is, of course, the key—see Jeremiah 35:6–18 and Chapter 15 above.

[76] 1QSviii.13–18.

[77] Cf. 1QMvii.5 and 4Q448ii.7.

[78] See, for instance, Acts 9:18–41, but in particular Paul's greetings in Philippians 4:21–22 to *'the*

Saints in Caesar's household'—clearly meaning, '*Nero Caesar*'! Such conceptions are obviously a complete turnaround. There are many more such allusions.

[79] See 1QMxi.6–xii.10 above.

[80] Cf. Matthew 24:30 and 26:64 and *pars,*

[81] 1QMxi.10–15.

[82] See A. N. Sherwin-White, *The Roman Citizenship*, Oxford, 1939, pp. 270–75, the Romans being '*the Lord of the Peoples*' ('*Princeps Gentium*')—in Greek '*Ethnon*'—Paul, not only being '*the Apostles to the Peoples*' (as Muhammad is), but the Arab King Abgar/Agbar (we have been following throughout this work) being '*the Great King of the Peoples beyond the Euphrates.*' Also see 1QpHabvi.7, viii.5–x.7, CDvii.9–11, *JBJ*, pp. 190, 429, 636, etc. and Chapters 1-3 above.

[83] John 14:22. For '*delivered up,*' see Matthew 10:4, 26:14–6 and *pars*. and cf. John 6:71, 12:4, and 13:3.

[84] 1QMxi.13–15.

[85] Cf. CDxx.27–34 with 1QpHabii.1–10 and v.9–12.

[86] Note that, as Eusebius sees it in *E.H.* 2.23.7, one of James' cognomens (besides '*the Zaddik*'/'*the Just*') is '*Oblias*'—as some would have it, '*Ophel-ᶜAm*'/'*Fortress*' or '*Bulwark of the People*'; as others would have it, '*ᶜOz-le-ᶜAm*'/'*Strength of the People,*' a phrase well known in the Psalms. Elsewhere in *E.H.* 3.7.9 Eusebius, seemingly quoting Hegesippus, alludes to how James' dwelling in Jerusalem provided the City while he was still alive '*the Surest Bulwark.*' Cf. phrases in 1QHxi.37, xiv.25–27 and xv.8–9 like '*a Strong Wall,*' '*a Fortified City,*' '*a High Wall,*' '*a Foundation on Rock,*' '*a Tried Cornerstone,*' '*a Bulwark that will not shake,*' etc. and my discussions in *JBJ*, pp. 353–67 and Chapters 1, 3, and 5-6 above.

[87] Cf. n. 65 above and *JBJ*, pp. 226, 270–71, 386, 434, 461–62, 564–76, 728, 741, and 824–25.

[88] *Vir. ill. 2*

[89] See *Zohar* on '*Balak and Balaam*', 193a–97a.

[90] 1QpHabviii.2–3.

[91] Cf. CDxx.19–34 above.

[92] Cf. 1QpHabviii.2–3 with x.3–5 and xii.14–xiii.4.

[93] 1QpHabxii.14 and xiii.2–3 above.

[94] Cf. Matthew 10:15, 11:22–24, 12:20 and 36. etc. (*n.b.*, this language is mostly unique to Matthew), 2 Peter 2:9 and 3:7, Jude 1:6 and 15.

[95] For the widespread allusions to '*the Day of Judgement*'/'*the Last Day*' in the Koran, see 78.17–18, 81.1–14, 82.12–19, 83.11, 85.2, etc.; for the categories of persons known as '*idolaters*' and '*hypocrites,*' see 2.8–20, 105, 113–14, 135, 3.167, 4.48–89, 4.136–43, 5.60, 5.82, 8.49, 9.1–64, etc.

[96] 1QpHabv.3–5.

[97] Cf. CDi.19 with iv.7.

[98] Cf. 1QpHabv.3–5 above.

⁹⁹ Jude 1:14–15.

¹⁰⁰ Cf. *DSSU*, pp. 17–23 and 4Q521ii.5 ('*the Lord will visit His Pious Ones*') and variously.

¹⁰¹ 1QMxii.8; cf. CDi.7 and variously throughout that Document and elsewhere.

¹⁰² 1QMxi.16–xii.10; for '*the Army of the Ginn*' elsewhere in this Document, see xix.1.

¹⁰³ Cf. 4Q521ii.5 above.

¹⁰⁴ 1QMxii.5–9. This allusion occurs in 1QMxii.7.

¹⁰⁵ See 1QMxii.9–10 and xix.2–3 above.

¹⁰⁶ Hebrews 1:13 (followed in 1:14 by allusion to '*ministering spirits*' and '*Heirs of Salvation*') and 10:12–13 (followed in 10:14 by the '*Perfection*' ideology and '*being made Holy*' and allusion to '*the Holy Spirit*') and cf. Matthew 5:35 and 22:44 and *pars.* and Acts 2:35 and 7:49.

¹⁰⁷ See, for instance, Psalm 110:2–3: '*The Lord will send the Rod of Your Strength out of Zion to rule in the midst of Your Enemies…on the Day of Your Warfare*' or 110:5–6: '*The Lord at Your Right Hand dost crush King in the Day of His Wrath. He will judge among the Nations*' —'*the Last Judgement*' again!

¹⁰⁸ Cf. 1QpHabv.16–vi.7 above.

¹⁰⁹ 1QMxix.3–8, the allusion to '*eating*' occurring in xix.4.

¹¹⁰ See, for instance, Koran 73.12, 82.15, 92.14, 111.3 or 96.1–5 on '*The Night of Power*.'

¹¹¹ Cf. 1QMxii.10 and xix.2 above.

¹¹² 1QMxii.10–16 and xix.2–8.

¹¹³ See James 4:4–8 and Chapters 5-6 above.

Chapter 16

¹ *Haeres.* 30.16.1.

² See *DSSU*, pp. 145–56 and 4QMessianic Apocalypseii.12 and cf. 4Q179 (note here, another allusion to God's '*Visitation*') and 501 (paralleling 4QTestament of Kahat/542 below). Also see, Robert Eisenman in *BAR* (vol. 17 no.6), Nov/Dec, 1991, '*Long-Secreted Plates from the Unpublished Corpus*.'

³ 4QTestament of Kahati.4–7.

⁴ 4QApocryphal Psalm and Prayerii.7.

⁵ Cf. *Vir. ill.* 2 under his discussion of James.

⁶ *Haeres.* 30.16.4.6.

^{7(6a)} See *DSSU*, pp. 17–22 and my first publication of this document in *BAR* (v. 17, no. 6), Nov/Dec, 1991, '*Long-Secreted Plates from the Unpublished Corpus*.' Also see the two articles on this document by J. Tabor and M. Wise in *BAR* (18.6), Nov/Dec, 1992, '*The Messiah at Qumran*' and '*The Messiah Text: 4Q521*.'

⁸ Koran 2.30–37. This picture of '*Adam*' is, of course, so unique that it can only owe a debt to the previous Centuries' thinking about '*the Primal Adam*' in Judeo-Christian tradition. For

more on *'Adam'* and *'Iblis'*, see 7.11–18, 17.61–70, and 20.115–24 but, in particular, see 3.59 which actually expresses the total *'Essene'/'Ebionite'* concept of *'Adam'*: *'Lo, the likeness of Jesus with Allah is the likeness of Adam. He created him from the dust.'* For Paul on the same subject, see 1 Corinthians 15:22 and 45–9 which actually includes the phrase *'made from the dust'* three times!

9 Of course, *'Belial'* is a widespread usage in the Scrolls (though some, as we have seen, like Vermes were originally translating the term *'Satan'*. He has corrected this under criticism to *'Belial'* or *'the Devil.'* *'Satan'* in the somewhat clumsy Hebrew usage of the Scrolls being *'the Angel of Mastemah'* which includes something of the *'fallen Angel'* ideology). The most important of which are to be found in CDiv.15–vi2: *'the Three Nets of Belial'* and its exposition—including reference to how *'Belial in his guilefulness raised up Jannes and his brother.'* For the corruption, *'Beliar'* in see Paul in 2 Corinthians 6:15 above; for other references to *'Iblis'* in the Koran, see 7:11–18, 15:29–37, 17:61–70, 38:72–86, etc.

10 See 4QFlori.10–14 and below Chapters 21-23 and 4QpGenv.1–8 and my discussion in *DSSU*, pp. 75–86.

11 4Q521ii.6 and 12 (here *'cAnavim,'* which as used at Qumran is a synonym for *'Ebionim'* or, for that matter, *'Dallim.'* In our translations we have always used the English *'Meek'* for the first; *'the Poor'* for the second; and *'the Downtrodden'* for the third while others, not realizing how important these terms really are, have not been as scrupulous or consistent). For the most famous usage of *'the Meek'* in the New Testament, see Matthew's *'Sermon on the Mount'* 5:5, but also Matthew 11:29 and 21:5 and *pars.*

12 4Q521ii.5 and 12. The parallel with the definition of *'the Sons of Zadok'* in CDii.12 and iv.3–4 makes it very clear that *'the Sons of Zadok'* and *'the Righteous Ones'/'Zaddikim'* are synonyms. In New Testament usage—particularly in Acts—the variation often becomes *'called by this Name'* or *'called by his Name.'*

13 4Q521ii.1. For the *'Heaven and Earth'* theme in the Gospel of Thomas, see *Logion* 12; in the New Testament, see Matthew 3:18 and *'the Little Apocalypse'* in 24:35 and *pars.*, and above, Chapters 5, 9, and 10.

14 The first person, who suggested this at the very time the Damascus Document was first discovered and printed, was R. H. Charles. He saw the single nature of the roots, ajectivals, and verbs associated with the this usage and realized that what we were, in fact, dealing with here was an idiomatic usage which actually implied a singular person, such as the Davidic and Aaronite roots ascribed to a character like 'Jesus' in the Gospels; see *DSSFC*, pp. xix and 14 and R. H. Charles *APOT*, pp. 9, 32, 61, 309, 418, etc. Unfortunately since that time, scholars following the work of F. M. Cross, J. T. Milik, R. de Vaux, G. Vermes, and others—as we have emphasized—have all assumed that what we were dealing with here was *'two Messiahs'* (always, of course, a possibility). But more recent texts, such as the Genesis *Pesher* above, our Messiah of Heaven and Earth, the *Florilegium*, and all texts incorporating *'the Star Prophecy'* distinctly show that the concept of a singular (even *'Davidic'*) Messiah was alive and well at Qumran.

15 1QMxvii.6–9

[16] These kinds of phrases, such as '*Sons of His Truth*', '*Sons of His Covenant*', and even '*Sons of Righteousness*', are found generously sprinkled throughout the Literature of Qumran; see, in particular, 1QHvi.29, vii.29, ix.35, 1QMxvii.8, 1QSiii.20–25, ix.14, etc.

[17] 1QMxvii.6.

[18] See Hebrews 5:6–7:21 and cf. 11QMelchizedekii.5–8 and J. T. Milik, '*Milki-sedeq et Milki-resa[c] dans les ecrits juifs et chretiens*', *JJS*, 23, 1972, pp. 95–144, M. de Jonge and A. S. van der Woude, '11 QMelchizedek and the New Testament', *NTS*, xii, pp. 301–26, J. A. Fitzmyer, '*Further Light on Melchizedek from Qumran Cave 11*', *JBL*, 86, pp. 25–41, and my discussion in *MZCQ*, p.44.

[19] E. Hennecke, *New Testament Apocrypha*, Philadelphia, 1963, i, p.163.

[20] See, for instance, Hippolytus 5.2 and 10.5 and cf. 1 Apoc. Jas. 40.25 and 2 Apoc. Jas. 44.15.

[21] *Haeres.* 30.16.2–4. Also cf. John 3:36.

[22] 1QSviii.3–10. In these columns, it is the '*separation*' ideology—'*separation from the Men of Unholiness*' or '*the Men of the Pit*'—which is pivotal.

[23] 1QSviii.3–4.

[24] Matthew 16:21, 17:12, and *pars.*, Acts 17:2–3, 29:23, 1 Corinthians 5:7, 12:26, Hebrews 9:26, 11:25, etc.

[25] 1QSviii.6–7, 10 and ix.5. This is the same '*Elect of Israel who will stand in the Last Days*' in CDiv.3–4 above—more contemporaneous imagery.

[26] 1QpHabx.3.

[27] 1QSviii.1.

[28] 1QSviii.9.

[29] 2 Corinthians 2:16–17.

[30] 1QpHabix.5 and cf. CDvii.7.

[31] Cf. Ps. *Hom.* 11.35 (Peter preaching at Tripoli) and Epistle of Clement to James 20.

[32] There can be no doubt what Paul is implying here in his two-fold attack both on the Tablets of the Law of Moses and the Certification Letters required by James''*Jerusalem Church*'. For more such attacks by Paul on the Law as bringing '*death*', see Romans 5:10–21, 6:13–23 (using the language of '*Righteousness*' and '*Unrighteousness*' of 1QSviii–ix), 7:5–8:14 (using the language of '*Heirs*', '*adoptionist sonship*', and '*Sons of God*'), etc.

[33] 1QSix.2.

[34] 1QSix.3–6.

[35] For some of the first examples of this sort of ideology in Judaism, see Tobit 1:7–8, 4:7–12, 12:8–10, etc.

[36] Cf. 1QSviii.4–11 and ix.6 above. Of course, we have already seen that Paul uses the very same '*offering up a pleasing fragrance*' language in 2 Corinthians 2:14–5 to describe what his newly-minted followers of '*Jesus*' are to offer up.

[37] 1QHxiv.25–7 and xv.8–9.

[38] Cf. Matthew 21:42 and *pars.*, Acts 4:11, Ephesians 2:20, and 1 Peter 2:7.

39 Cf. Eusebius, *E.H.* 2.23.7, 3.7.9, etc. above.

40 *Ant.* 19.332–34.

41 See above, pp. 29 and 343–44 and *JBJ*, pp. 502–636, *MZCQ*, pp. 42, 46–48, 61, 78, etc..

42 Cf. Luke 6:15 and Acts 1:13 with Matthew 10:4 and Mark 3:18.

43 Eusebius, *E.H.* 2.23.17.

44 The point here is that this '*Peter*' begins very much to resemble '*Simeon bar Cleophas*,' the Second Successor to James in the Leadership of '*the Jerusalem Church*' and purportedly his '*cousin*'— but, in all probability, most likely his second brother '*Simon the Zealot*' just mentioned (along with '*Judas the brother of James*') above—see *JBJ*, pp. 817–50.

45 See, for instance, the crucial attack on '*the Righteous One and all the Walkers in Perfection*' in CDi.20 and such '*soul*' language, not only in Isaiah 53:11—its probable origin—but also in 1QHix.9–10, x.32–34 (*nephesh-Ebion* and '*nephesh-ᶜAni*'), xi.25, xiii.6, xiii.13, etc.

46 See Revelation 2:28, 8:10–11, 9:1 (along with the language of '*the Fountain of Living Waters*' and '*the Pit*' of the Damascus Document), and 22:6 (defined as '*the Root and Offspring of David*'). Of course, the '*Star*' imagery is that of Numbers 24:17 and various Qumran Documents such as the War Scroll, the Damascus Document, Testimonia, etc.

47 4QpIsaᵃiii.11–24, interpreted in terms of '*the Branch of David*'—a term. as we shall see, found throughout the important Documents at Qumran. Also see the newly-published fragment 4Q437 where the term '*sharp arrow*' is used.

48 For more on the whole complex of these '*nets*,' see my Appendix to *JJHP*: '*The Three Nets of Belial in the Zadokite Document...*, etc.,' pp. 87–94.

49 CDiv.16–19.

50 See *MZCQ*, pp. 19–31 and 35–38 and *JJHP*, pp. 1–20 and the Appendix in pp. 87–94 above and variously.

51 See the Herodian Family Genealogy at the end of this volume. That marrying nieces and close family cousins was the family dynastic policy of the Herodians and *not the Maccabeans* should be obvious.

52 One should note the easy-going relationship between Felix and Drusilla (whom Acts 24:24 dissimulatingly calls '*a Jewess*,' though it knows very well she is an '*Herodian Princess*' and that even Josephus remarks in *Ant.* 20.141–4 how *she left the Jewish Religion*). Nor is this to say anything about the one ultimately between Titus and Bernice—her sister—none of whom were likely to have observed Jewish scrupulousness about '*not sleeping with women during their periods*.' This is the key allusion since, whatever the Maccabeans were—as Jews and certainly claiming '*High Priestly descent*'—they most certainly did.

53 CDv.14–15. This significantly follows the material banning on the basis of legal analogy with Leviticus 18:13, marriage with close family cousins (unknown to Jewish Law previously) and the John the Baptist-like imprecations (in Josephus, also based on objections to '*Herodian*' marital practices) about '*kindlers of Fire*' and '*their offspring being those of vipers*' in v.7–14.

54 For these traditions about Jacob of Kfar Sechania, see Chapter 6 above and b. *A.Z.* 27b, *Tos.*

Hul. 2:22–23, and j. *Shab.* 14:4 and *A.Z.* 2:2, 4QD as well as *JBJ*, pp. 217–29. One should note that during her purported 21 years of 3 successive seven-year Nazirite-oath periods, Helen, for some reason (unexplained), was considered too impure to be involved in the Temple. As we have seen, Christian tradition also places its '*Helen*'—Simon *Magus*' consort—in the brothels of Tyre!

55 See *JJHP*, pp. 62–74 and my article on this subject in *DSSFC*, pp. 332–51: '*The Final Proof that James and the Righteous Teacher are the Same*'—first given to the Society of Biblical Literature in 1994.

56 *vacat.*

57(58) *War* 2.143 (*ekballousai*).

58(61) Cf. 11QT xlvii.8–18—this too is pretty specific about '*defiling the Temple*'—and *MMT* ii.3–9.

59 Cf. Hippolytus 9.21 and n. 55 above.

60 4QTesti.1–13.

61 Ps. *Rec.* 1:39. One should note that the Pseudoclementine *Recognitions* explores this theme of '*the True Prophet*', *inter alia*, from 1.37–41 (this last even incorporating imagery clearly picked up and employed by Muhammad in the Koran) and actually evokes the destruction of the coming War and exile.

62 Cf. CDiii.21–iv.10 and v.7–17, etc. with Hebrews 4:14–16 and 7:26–8:2.

63 See how Peter, John, and the other Apostles seem to go to the Temple every day in Acts 3:1–4:3, 5:12–16, 5:19–25, etc. This picture is, of course, paralleled in the Pseudoclementines and in Epiphanius' quotes from the *Anabathmoi*.

64 Cf. Eusebius, *E.H.* 2.23.6–17 and *pars.*

65 Cf. Acts 23:12–13 with the '*plotting*' language, mentioned above in 1QpHabix.5 and CDvii.7 (in both instances, describing the sins of the Establishment and, in particular, those of '*the Wicked Priest*'/'*High Priests*').

66 Cf. Paul in 1 Corinthians 8:1–9:1, 10:14–32, and 11:26–30.

67 See *War* 2.405–429.

68 This language of '*separation*' is all important; see CDv.6–8 and 1QSviii.12–5 in exposition of Isaiah 40:3 and note Paul in 2 Corinthians 6:17–7:1. Note, too, that it is possible to view Qumran as a Community of life-long '*Nazirites*' (i.e., '*those who have separated themselves*') or '*Rechabites*.'

69 See *War* 2.7/*Ant.* 17.207.

70 See 1QSviii.7–8 above.

71 See, for instance, in the War Scroll, Columns xii.12–3 and xix.3–4 and cf. nn. 105–9 of Chapter 15 above.

72 See Koran, *Surah* 97.

73 See Eusebius, *E.I.* 2.23.5 and pars. and Luke 1:15.

[74] See *War* 2.117–8 (introducing his diversion to talk about the '*Three Jewish Philosophies*') and *Ant.* 18.1–10 (introducing '*the Sicarii Movement*' of Judas the Galilean and Sadduk and only after this the '*Three Jewish Philosophies*'—the shift is significant).

[75] Ben Sira 44:1. The Hebrew version of this Document, found at the end of the Nineteenth Ccentury along with the Damascus Document at the Cairo *Genizah*, and now at Qumran and Masada, confirms this reading, '*Anshei-Hesed*.' One should note the importance of this individual in the train of transmitters in the Rabbinic Document known as '*the Pirke Abbot*' and in our '*Abbot de R. Nathan*' above—as well as in *Ant.* 12.43, where his cognomen is explained in terms of the '*Piety*'/'*Righteousness*' Dichotomy.

[76] 2 Peter 2:6 in the context of allusions to '*the Morning Star*,' '*Balaam the son of Bosor*' (*sic*), and '*the dumb beast*.' See n. 45 above and the crucial attack on '*the Righteous One*' in CDi.20 and in 1QHix.9–10, x.32–4, xi.25, xiii.6, xiii.13, etc.

[77] *Vita* 11–12. It is interesting that three aspects of '*Banus*" behaviour that Josephus lists are '*daily baths in cold water*' (he says to quell sexual desire—but there may have been other reasons for such an '*Essene*'/'*Ebionite*'-like practice), consuming '*food growing only of itself* (i.e., like Judas Maccabee's behaviour here and more or less the behaviour signalled. in '*Rechabite*' tradition), and finally wearing only clothing that '*grew on trees*,' i.e., only vegetable-matter clothing or '*linen*,' the clothing of '*the Essenes*' and also that of James '*Jerusalem Church*' followers.

[78] For '*the Rechabites*,' see Jeremiah 35:1–19, which we claim would have been part of the missing Introduction of James in the New Testament according to Palestinian tradition (in this context, note the mistaken attribution of the Scriptural passage about the '*thirty pieces of silver*' and '*the Temple*,' used to characterize '*Judas Iscariot*' in Matthew 27:3–10, as being from '*Jeremiah the Prophet*' when it is in fact, as we have seen, a loose paraphrase of '*Zechariah*') and our discussion of said '*Rechabites*' and other such related matters in Chapter 12 above and *JBJ*, pp. 229–47, 456–69, and 728–72.

[79] Ben Sira 48:1–3. See the parallel to this kind of language in Mattathias' final speech to his sons in 1 Maccabees 2:58–59 and in CDv.13–16: '*they are all kindlers of Fire and lighters of Firebrands* (cf. Isaiah 50:11).

[80] See *Vita* 11 above.

[81] This allusion is to be found in the missing material from Ben Sira, Chapters 50–51, signalled by the Hebrew versions of this document found at the *Geniza* and, after that, Masada and Qumran, which applies both '*the Covenant of Phineas*' and '*the 'Sons of Zadok*' terminology to Simeon's heirs, thereby linking both the '*Zaddikite*' and '*Zadokite Covenant*'s.

[82] Cf. 1QSiii.20–5 and ix.14 and n. 16 above.

[83] See my general discussion of this inability to relate to literary metaphor and word play in *MZCQ*, pp. 3–16, 19–27, and 41–46.

[84] The reason for this difference is that the Catholic Recension, which is based on both the *Septuagint* and Jerome's *Vulgate* while the Rabbinic, which seems to have been collected after the 66–73 CE Revolt around 100 CE and therefore incorporated a certain hostility to books

that may have inspired this Uprising, contains 1 and 2 Maccabees while the Masoretic does not. This is manifestly very peculiar since Jews, in theory (and more and more in latterly following the birth of the State of Israel and their attempts to provide an alternative for their assimilated children to Christmas' powerful hold), celebrate *Hanukkah*—the reason for which is explained in these books and in Josephus, but not in the *Talmud* which is for the most part hostile to the Maccabees; while Catholics have never been known to celebrate it at all.

[85] Cf. 1 Maccabees 4:36–61, 2 Maccabees 1:1–2:24, and 10:1–8, *Ant.* 12.323–26, and my discussion of these matters in *MZCQ*, pp. 12–16.

[86] See *Ant.* 12.414 and 419–34. Josephus refers three times here to the *'High Priesthood'* of Judas and makes it clear that he was *'elected by the People'* in the *'Zealot'* manner!

[87] See John 2:13–22 and the Synoptic parallels (though without the cry of *'zeal'* from the totally *'Zionist'* Psalm—rifled by Gospel artificers—69:9) in Matthew 21:12–17 and *pars.*

[88] See *Surah* 2.43. There is little doubt that the usage *'zakat'* here, which is usually translated in terms of *'paying the poor-due'*, is to be understood (as Muhammad makes clear in subsequent admonitions) as *'charity'* and is based on the Hebrew root—here condensed—*'zedakah.'*

[89] The term *'Zedakah'*—the closest meaning for which, based on a 4th form causative root, is *'Justification'*—occurs throughout the Qumran corpus. In CDi.18–21 and iv.3–9, the verb upon which it is based, *'lehazdik,'* occurs in two separate instances—each, as I have several times remarked, with mutually-reversed emphases—i.e., *'they ('the Seekers after Smooth Things'* and *'the Man of Lying') justified the Wicked and condemned the Righteous One,' 'pursuing the Walkers in Perfection with the sword'* and *'the Sons of Zadok are the Elect of Israel, called by Name, who will stand up in the Last Days'* and *'justify the Righteous and condemn the Wicked.'* Another pregnant use of this term *'Zedakah,'* that we have been calling attention to, occurs in CDxx.19–20: *'and a Book of Remembrance would be written out before Him for God-Fearers and for those considering His Name until God would reveal Salvation (Yesha[c]) and 'Justification' (Zedakah) to those fearing his Name'*—in my view, including Gentile *'God-Fearers'* just mentioned above and several times previously.

[90] See n. 35 above and Tobit 1:7–8, 4:7–12, 12:8–10, etc. It is interesting that Eusebius, too, places this *'Tobit'* or *'Tobias the son of Tobias'* (his descendant?) in far-off Edessa—or, as the case may be, Adiabene—when he describes in *E.I.* 1.13.10 how, after 'Jesus'' death, *'Thomas sent Thaddaeus'* to see the Great King Agbar/Abgar there. For my understanding of these events, see *JBJ*, pp. 853–82 and Chapter 28 below.

[91] Also see Paul in Acts 26:5, complimented to some extent by Galatians 1:14.

[92] Note how Paul puts this in Philippians 4:15–9 in the very terms of the *'odour of a sweet small, an acceptable sacrifice, well-pleasing to God,'* when referring to the contributions Epaphroditus is bringing from them—exactly the terms of Tobit and, for that matter, those at Qumran and in the Koran, we have been discussing—but there can be no doubt he is speaking in terms of monetary contributions, charity or otherwise. He also makes this very clear in Romans 15:25–32 and in 1 Corinthians 16:1–9; and Acts, too, makes it very clear that he does not wish to go

up to Jerusalem without the contributions he has raised—further delineating what he meant in Galatians 2:10 by describing James as admonishing him *'not to forget to remember the Poor.'*

93 This idea of Jewish *'backsliders'* is made very clear in at the end of the Habakkuk *Pesher,* when it speaks in xiii.2–4 of *'the Day of Judgement,'* at which time *'God would destroy all servants of idols and Evil Ones off the Earth.'* The *'Evil Ones'* recapitulates the usage *'Wicked Priest'* and previous references to *'the Evil Ones of His own People'* in categorizing this genre of wrong-doers. The Damascus Document, too throughout, refers to such *'backsliding'* among *'His own People'*—but one that particularly stands out occurs in CDvii.21–24/xix.33–xx.1 when, in referring to *'all the men who entered the New Covenant in the Land of Damascus,'* it particularly cites those who *'turned back and betrayed and turned aside from the Fountain of Living Waters.'* This is to say nothing of the repeated allusions to *'the Seekers after Smooth things'* in this Document and elsewhere in the corpus.

Chapter 17

1 *Haeres.* 30.16.7–8

2 These debates on the Temple steps are variously pictured in Acts 3:1–4:3 (unlike in the Pseudoclementines only *'Peter and John'*—James for some reason clearly missing. The reason is not hard to contemplate) and 5:20–33 (including abundant *'standing'* imagery), in the Pseudoclementine *Recognitions* 1.55–71 in exquisite detail (not only do we have here the material concerning the *'Pharisee Gamaliel',* paralleled in Acts, but also the number of those listening to Peter—put in Acts 4:4 as *'some five thousand'*—the exact number the *Recognitions* says flee with James' battered body down to Jericho to escape the *'Enemy'* Paul), and clearly here in Epiphanius' *Anabathmoi* (he also mentions *'The Travels of Peter'*), *Haeres.* 30.15.1–34.6.

3 See Hennecke, *New Testament Apocrypha,* ii, pp. 88–111 and also Epiphanius' *Haeres.* 30.15.1, just mentioned above.

4 Here the powerful outside forces, I refer to, are clearly Roman and Herodian, not Maccabean. But, of course, the *leit-motifs* are there—in this case, *'the Teacher of Righteousness,' 'the Spouter of Lying,' 'the Wicked Priest,'* and what is perhaps the most revealing, *'the Kings of the Peoples'* in CDvii.10, in this instance identified as *'the viper'.* This is the very allusion we have heard attached to John and clearly identifiable with *'the Herodians'* since, as I have made clear elsewhere, *'Kings of the Peoples'* is a definitive Roman juridical term bearing with it the meaning of *'the Kings in the Eastern Part of the Empire'* where *'the Peoples'* were considered to be located and full Roman Citizenship had not yet been applied to them. The *'Herodians'* are clear exemplars of this.

5 See *The Nag Hammadi Library in English,* ed. by J. M. Robinson, Harper and Row, 1977, pp. 242–55. In *'The Second'* anyhow, v. 4, 61.20–25, James is pictured in some manner in the Temple. But in both, he is the recipient of a kind of mystic *'Kiss'* of Knowledge (something like the beloved Disciple in the Gospel of John). In the First, v.3, 35.5–10 and 36.5–10, *'the immortal Sophia' / 'Wisdom'* is specifically invoked.

6 Cf. 1QpHabvii.17–viii.3 with James 2:8–11) and Romans 13:7–8 (here using it to defend

Roman taxation in Palestine—as I have already pointed out, could anything be more cynical? But where Paul is concerned, anything goes!) and Galatians 3:5–29 (using this passage as a long polemic to attack *the Law*—the very opposite, it would appear, of how it is used in the Letter of James).

7 This is not completely accurate. The *'Kiss'* in both Apocalypses is from *'Jesus'* (1 Ap Jas. 31.5 and 32.5–10 and 2 Ap Jas. 57.14–20); but only in the Second does it appear to be the mystic *'Kiss'* of Knowledge. In 1 Ap. Jas. 40.25–30, this appears simply to be one or the other *'Mary's* in the Gospels, though here she is called *'Mariam.'* It is in the Second Apocalypse that *'Mareim'* is mentioned as *'one of the Priests'* and the narrator who gave the account to *'Theuda the brother of the Just One'* (*'Thaddaeus'/'Addai'/'Judas Thomas'/'Judas of James'*?). It is in Hippolytus 5.2 above that the group he calls the *'Naassenes'* receive their knowledge from the numerous discourses which *'James the brother of the Lord handed down to Mariamme'* or *'Mareim.'*

8 This is a subject that has been argued over very extensively in Dead Sea Scrolls Studies and the consensus concerning it is clear. See my comments concerning *'the Wicked Priest'* in *MZCQ* and *JJHP.*

9 1QpHabii.7–10 and cf. vii.4–8.

10 Here the verb *'hodiᶜa'/'to make known'* (based on the usage *'yodeᶜa'/'to know'* carries with it the same root a *'Daᶜat'*—in Hebrew *'Knowledge'*; in Greek, *'Gnosis'*) is pivotal and should be catalogued throughout the Qumran corpus. It is particularly strong, *inter alia* not surprisingly, in the Damascus Document where it occurs almost from the very first line addressed to *'all Knowers of Righteousness'/'Yodᶜei-Zedek'* (CDi.1) and, of course, in line ii.3, which intones: *'God loves Daᶜat, Hochma, and Bina'* and, for which, *'Habad'* is the reverse acronym.

11 1QpHabvii.7–8—in other words, He informed him about *'the Delay of the Parousia.'*

12 In Judaism of the mystic orientation, this is the companion Literature to that of *'the Chariot'* or, what is referred to as, *'Merkabah Mysticism.'* The idea of *'Heavenly Ascents'* is a strong motif, not only in the Koran, but also in Islamic Literature and Tradition. For Paul, the man he knows in 2 Corinthians 12:2–4 below *'ascended'* or *'was caught away—whether in body or out of body, I know not—to the Third Heaven.'* He then adds that he know such a man *'was caught away into Paradise* (and in Kabbalistic Hebrew too, *'Pardes'*), *where he heard unutterable words which it is not permitted a man to speak'* (*sic*)! He then goes on to allude in 12:7 to *'the magnificence of* (his own) *Heavenly Visions'* (Apocalypseon). It should be appreciated, too, that this is one of the sections in his corpus in which he makes in 11:31 his defence against *'not lying.'*

13 Here too, he makes another defence against *'Lying,'* asserting in 1:20: *'Now the things I write to you, behold, I do not lie.'*

14 For the exposition of *'reading and running'* in Habakkuk 2:2, see 1QpHabvii.3–16 above. Paul also uses this expression *'running'* in a crucial passage in 1 Corinthians 9:24, following his attack on *'those who are so weak'* in 8:7–13 as to be unwilling to eat *'things sacrificed to idols'* and where he outlines his own *modus operandi* (such as it is) —using the imagery of Greco-Roman *'Stadium'* athletics!

15 This word *'Apocalypsin'/'Apocalypseon'* is crucial in Paul and he uses it at key moments in his

corpus, as for instance in Galatians 1:2 in connection with the words *'running'* and *'ran'* and also in connection with the number *'fourteen years'* again, where he uses it to insist that he was not summoned up to Jerusalem *'by those reckoned as important'* (i.e., James and the others of the so-called *'Jerusalem Church', 'whose importance—as far as he was concerned—nothing conferred'*), but rather as a result of a private *'revelation'* or *'vision'* (apocalypsin) and because of accusations *'of the false brothers who stole in by stealth to spy on the freedom which we enjoy in Christ Jesus* (i.e., *'the Circumcision Party'* or *'the Circumcisers'*), so that they might enslave us.'

[16] Eusebius, *E.I.* 2.23.12–3.

[17] In *Surah* 70, we again have reference to *'the Angels and the Spirit'* who ascend with him (4), *'the Day of Judgement'* (26), and *'the Garden of Delight'* (38). The reason we say this is probably James is the peculiar coincidence of the two allusions to *'fourteen years'* concerning Paul's references to the *'Heavenly Voyager'* in 1 Corinthians and his two visits to Jerusalem, both of which times he saw James.

[18] Cf. 4Q*ShirShabb* (400–7) and 11Q17 and C. Newsom, *Songs of the Sabbath Sacrifice: A Critical Edition*, Atlanta, 1985. It is not insignificant that fragments of this work were also found at Masada (see Y. Yadin and C. Newsom, *'The Masada Fragment of the Qumran Songs of the Sabbath Sacrifice,' IEJ* 34, 1984, pp. 77–88).

[19] Koran 22.23. For more on these *'Gardens,'* see *Surahs* 19, 37, 38, 43, 55, 56, 76, etc.

[20] For additional material on the Mysticism of the Throne in the Koran, see *Surahs* 7.45 and 85.15, and 53.5 on *'being taught by One Mighty in Powers.'*

[21] See 1 Apoc. Jas. 31.5 and 32.5–10 and 2 Apoc. Jas. 57.14–20 above.

[22] Cf. for *'the Sons of Zadok'* as *'Keepers,'* see 1QSv.2 and 9 above. This directly follows an allusion to *'the Service of Righteousness'* in 1QSiv.9. For more of this kind of the language of *'Servant'* in 1QS, see i.13 referring to *'the Prophets,'* ix.22 below, and xi.15–6 encased in the language of *'Righteous works'* and following allusion to *'joining the Community to the Sons of Heaven'* as *'a Foundation of a Building of Holiness to be an Eternal Plantation'* in xi.8–10; in CD, see xx.20.

[23] Cf. 1QpHabii.8–9 and vii.4–14 and for *'the Mebakker's mastery of all the secrets of Men and all their respective Tongues'* in the Damascus Document, see xiv.8–9.

[24] For the Habakkuk *Pesher*, see vii.5, 8, and 14; for the Community Rule, xi.19 and, *inter alia*, the Document, I entitled, *'The Children of Salvation (Yesha^c) and the Mystery of Existence'* (4Q413–24), *DSSU*, pp. 241–54 (entitled by some *'A Sapiential Work'*—whatever is meant by this); also, for instance, the mystical 4Q286–7 (*Berachot*), *DSSU*, pp. 222–30 and 1QSix.18 and the *'Servant'* language that follows. In addition, the Qumran Hymns are steeped in this sort of language.

[25] Koran 2.4, 27.66, 32.7, 49.19, etc. The Arabic here is *'gheib'*—*'absent'/'hidden'/'unseen'*—but it is the equivalent to what would otherwise be called *'Mystery.'*

[26] See in the *Homilies*, Epistle of Peter to James 4.1–5.1 and 1QSix.16–21—not only including reference to the *'Love'* Commandment, but also the second citation of *'the Way in the wilderness.'*

[27] See S. G. F. Brandon in *Jesus and the Zealots*, New York, 1967, pp. 114–141.

[28] Acts 21:24 and cf. 1QSi.8–9 and 15–16 and now the Last Column of the Damascus Document 4Q266.17–18.

[29] *'Asia'* is, of course, Paul's main center of activities and his alleged place of origin. If anyone knew what Paul was doing and saying or preaching in these areas, such Jews would. This is what begins to lend this picture credibility.

[30] It is interesting that in the events leading up to this, in addition to picking up the voice of *'the We Narrative'* on 20:6, Acts 20:2–16 specifically mentions another *'plot being made against him (Paul) by the Jews'* (sic!) and that his intention was *'to sail to Syria'* (i.e., Palestine and the Lebanon/Phoenician Coast—20:3), *'Trophimus'* for the first time in 20:3, his stopping at *'Miletus'* to deliver a kind of farewell sermon (20:15–21:1—*'so that I may finish my course with joy and the Ministry I received from the Lord Jesus'*—he does not say exactly how, but he is using the *'running'* vocabulary again), and finally his decision *'to sail past Ephesus so as not to lose time in Asia,'* for *'he was hurrying so as to be in Jerusalem on the Day of Pentecost'*—the time of the Annual Reunion of *'all the Sons of Levi and all those dwelling in the camps'* under the Leadership of either *'The (High) Priest Commanding the Many'* or *'the Mebakker'* or *'Bishop'* to *'curse those departing from the right or the left of the Torah'* according to 4Q266.17–8 above. What could be more explicit or more relevant to these scenes in Acts than this?

[31] For more on this, see the teacher Josephus calls *'Simon,'* who could *'get together an Assembly'* (*Ecclesian*—in other words, he was the Head of *'a Church'*) of his own in Jerusalem in *Ant.* 19, 332–34, who wanted to bar Agrippa I (c. 44 CE) from the Temple, *'which belonged only to native-born Jews,'* *'as a foreigner'* or, as some would have it, *'ritually unclean.'* Not only does this relate to the demand made by the Lower Priesthood and *'the Innovators'/'Revolutionaries'* in the run-up to the War against Rome in 66 CE not to accept gifts from or on behalf of Romans and other foreigners in the Temple, which we have covered above and which Josephus rails against as *'an innovation which our Ancestors were before unacquainted with,'* but I have made much of this episode as the *'real Historical Peter'* and the reason for his arrest, c. 44 CE in Acts 12:3–21—see above Chapters 1, 12, and 16 and *JBJ*, pp. 105–9, 282–9, 534–8, etc. and *MZCQ*, pp. 42–8.

[32] See *War* 2.402–408.

[33] See CDvi.3–21, including reference to *'separating between polluted and pure and distinguishing between Holy and profane'* and *'each man loving his brother as himself.'*

[34] See above, *Haeres.* 30.16.1–8.

[35] We have discussed the issue of Qumran chronology, in Chapter 2 above and throughout my work, but it is quite clear that both the group Epiphanius dubs as followers of James (called *'Ebionites'*—the terminology is extant at Qumran, as we have seen, and widespread there) have an ambivalent attitude towards sacrifice and the Temple—depending on the *'purity'* of those both offering it and the situation surrounding the process—and both are, *inter alia*, clearly *'Daily-Bathing'* groups.

[36] CDvi.14–6 above.

[37] Of course, the *'N-Z-R'* root is found throughout the Damascus Document. It is even found in

missing passages leading up to Column i in the new Cave 4 materials in 4Q266–67—the first line of the first fragment. Also see, vii.1 and viii.8. The way we see this is, not only does this usage link up with the expression in Greek *'keep away from'* of James instructions to Overseas Communities in Acts; but the fact that it is based on an *'N-Z-R'* root in Hebrew testifies to the life-long *'Nazirite'* aspect of the Community represented by these Documents—not only in terms of its *'Holiness'*, but also its command to *'separate from all pollution.'* In our view, too, this is something of the confusion that has permeated Greek and other translations, ending up in the phraseology *'Nazrene'/'Nazoraean'/*and ever *'Nazareth.'*

[38] See *Ant.* 20.181 and 206.

[39] See 1QpHabxii.2–10 (*'the Poor'* or *'Ebionim'* mentioned three times, though the terminology does not appear in the underlying Habakkuk until 3:14 and here it is only *'Ani'/'the Meek'*— the associated verb being *'to eat'/'consume'/*or *'destroy'*). In the *Pesher*, the underlying sense is: *'He (the Wicked Priest) would be paid the reward with which he rewarded the Poor,' 'because he conspired to destroy the Poor,'* and *'stole the sustenance* (literally *'Riches'*) *of the Poor'*—in Josephus, this is exactly what Ananus, James' destroyer, is described as doing.

[40] Cf. CDvi.15 above.

[41] CDvii.1.

[42] Cf. CDviii.5–12. For evocation of the second *'Love'* Commandment, see CDvi.20–21 above, but also see xx.17–18, followed by the first *'Love'* Commandment in xx.21.

[43] CDviii.6 and cf. v.5–11 and vii.1, where the point in both cases is *'approaching near kin for fornication.'* We have discussed Herodian marital practices above, but see Josephus, *Ant.* 18.130–42 and 19.354–5 and our Herodian Genealogical Chart below and.

[44] 1QSvi.1, 7–25, vii.3–25, etc.

[45] This usage *'People'/'Peoples'* is an important one at Qumran and should be catalogued, as we have insisted. Perhaps the most important incidence of it is in the Habakkuk *Pesher* ix.4–7: *'Amim'* and *'Yeter ha-'Amim'/'the Peoples'* and *'the Additional ones of the Peoples,'* where the second clearly implies the Army of the Romans—who *'in the Last Days'* clearly do take over *'the Riches'* of the Temple. But as in CDvii.10, *'the Kings of the Peoples'*—the *'Amim'* here, in our view, manifestly representing *'Herodians.'* See *JJHP*, pp. 76–93 and its Glossary, p.94. The parallel in Pauline parlance is *'Ethnon'* or *'Gentium'* and, of course, the term *'Apostle to the Gentiles.'* In Rabbinic literature, there is the term *'Am ha-Aretz'* which has a slightly different, if parallel, connotation.

[46] CDvii.7–8 introducing the material about *'Kings of the Peoples.'*

[47] See A. N. Sherwin-White, *The Roman Citizenship*, Oxford, 1939, pp. 270–5, the Romans being *'the Lord of the Peoples'* (*'Princeps Gentium'*). But also see how Eusebius uses the term in *E.H.* 1.13.2 when he speaks of Abgarus, *'the King of the Peoples beyond the Euphrates.'*

[48] CDvii.10–2. This exegesis will play, as we shall see below, on two parallels or homonyms in Hebrew *'yayin'* meaning *'wine'* in Hebrew and *'Yavan'/'Greece'* and *'Rosh'* meaning *'Head'* in Hebrew (as *'Head of the Greek-speaking of the Peoples,'* i.e., the Roman Emperor) and *'rosh'*

meaning *'poison.'* This double entendre cuts two ways—not only *'wine'* (a word which might have originally come from Greece) and *'venom,'* but also *'yayin'* and *'Yavan,'* their ways being *'Hellenized'* or *'Greek.'*

49 This is the famous *'Generation of Vipers'* in Matthew 3:7, 12:34, and 23:33 and pars., sometimes attributed to John the Baptist and sometimes attributed to Jesus, the vituperation of which is clear—but see the additional parallel in v.13–15, the sense of which directed against the ruling Establishment in Jerusalem is also clear. There is almost no way one can harmonize these things with Maccabean times except for a superficial reading of the term *'Grecian Kings,'* which is as I have just shown, is a play on words and how these *'Kings of the Peoples'* (all of whom would have been *'Greek-speaking'*) would have appeared to Palestinian eyes from 333 BC onwards.

50 I use this term in the way Acts 6:1, 9:29, and 11:20 uses the term *'Hellenists.'* As I have already argued in Chapters 1, 9 13, etc. above, these don't all represent *'Hellenists,'* but often actually a *'code'* that can even transform an underlying meaning of *'Zealotry.'*

51 CDvii.12–13. The point here is that someone preaching a doctrine such as *'baptism by the Holy Spirit'* or who himself claims to be in touch with *'the Spirit,'* might just as easily be parodied by his ideological opponents in terms of the Hebrew double entendre *'wind'* or *'windiness'*—or in modern terminology *'a (big) Windbag.'*

52 See Chapter 2 above.

53 For my critique of carbon dating, see again Chapter 2 above; for palaeography, see *MZCQ*, pp. 28–31 and 78–91; for archaeology, *MZCQ*, pp. 32–4 and 91–4—reproduced in *DSSU*, pp. 80–104.

54 I cannot emphasize this too strongly and, though I have reiterated it several times in this book, these points about *'the Kings of the Peoples,' 'the wine of their ways,' 'walking in the spirit,'* and *'the Lying Spouter'* just add definitively to the weight of the *'internal evidence'* arguing for a Firt Century CE date generally for Documents of this kind using common vocabulary and allusions across the board.

55 Cf. James 2:8–10 with CDvi.20–1 above and note, as we have already done that, whereas the former is preceded by the *'Piety'* Commandment of *'loving God'* in 2:5 (itself connected to *'the Poor'*), the latter is followed by it in CDxx.21–22

56 CDvi.19–20.

57 For the *'Priesthood,'* see Exodus 22:31, 28:2–31:10, 39:1–41, Numbers 16:3, etc.; for the *'Nazirite,'* see Numbers 6:1–21.

58 See notes 23, 28, and 30, 4Q266.17–8, and CDxiv.8–9 above. It should be appreciated that F. M. Cross in *The Ancient Library of Qumran*, pp. 232–3, was probably one of the first persons to understand this equivalence.

59 CDvii.18–9 and xx.8–12 (here in conjunction with *'the Scoffer,'* which shows the expression is used to characterize his activities as it does *'the Liar'*—and this definitively—who in 1QpHabv.11–2 *'rejected the Torah in the midst of the whole Congregation'* or *'Church'*). But also see the more general 1QpHabi.10, 1QSiii.5f., CDvii.9, and *JJHP*, pp. 23–32 and 91.

60 CDvii.21–22.

[61] Cf. Plates 6 and 54 both fragments of 4Q266. On the second, the empty space of the right-hand Column is clearly visible.

[62] See *DSSU*. pp. 212–19 and Plates nos. 19–20.

[63] See 1QSi.15 above.

[64] See n. 51 and CDvii.12–13. above.

[65] See n. 58 and CDxiv.8–9 above. What is generally not appreciated by the public at large when presented with these translations is that the expression *'languages'* in Hebrew is *'tongues'* and, therefore, to *'master all secrets of men and the tongues in their enumeration'* as *'the Mebakker'* is defined as being able to do is, in effect, *'speaking in tongues.'*

[66] Hippolytus 9.21.

[67] 1QSix.23 and 4QpNahi.3–11 (another *'Lebanon'* text, this one being completely anti-*'Kittim'* or anti-Roman,' *the Kittim'* clearly being the ones who are going to be destroyed via *'the whirlwind'* of God's Fury. This also, no doubt, relates to the stormy *'whirlwind'* of Ezekiel 13:12–4 which God will unleash against *'the Plasterers on the Wall,'* another notation alluded to in the Damascus Document.

[68] Cf. *DSSU*, pp. 180–200 and i.2–24, including in particular the allusion to *'things sacrificed to idols'* in 8–9 and the rejection of *'the skins of unclean animals'* in the Temple (i.e., *'skins sacrificed to an idol'*) in 18–24.

[69] See Ps. *Rec.* 1.36–37 above.

[70] Eusebius, for instance, in *E.I. 1.7.11–3* is well aware of Herod's non-Jewish origins which, therefore, included the rest of his family as well and see the incident, noted above, where *'Simon'* the *'Head of an Assembly'* of his own in Jerusalem wants to bar even the most observant of the Herodians, Agrippa I, from the Temple as a foreigner; *Ant. 19.332–4.*

[71] *M. Sota* 8.12; cf. *M. Bik.* 3.4. This is a mirror reversal of the portrayal of *'Peter'* denying the Messiah three times on his death night in the Synoptics or the Heavenly Voice crying out to him in Acts three times on the rooftop in Jaffa *'not to make distinctions between men'* in the Literature so familiar to and beloved by us.

[72] To think of any of the troops of the *'Caesarean Regiment'* (which Josephus describes as the most violent in Palestine and after the War, Titus had banished from the country for such unrestrained violence and obvious disapprobation by the People; *Ant.* 19.366—one should also note that before the War, these same troops seem to have been responsible for the manhandling and rape of the young Herodian Princesses Mariamme, Drusilla, and possible even Bernice—later Titus' mistress; *Ant.* 19.355–5) being described in this way is beyond the pale and calls the whole account into question. We have already seen the importance of the terms *'God-Fearer'* and *'fearing God'* at the end of CDxx.19–20 and cf. Paul in Romans 3:18, 8:15, 2 Corinthians 7:1, Ephesians 5:21, etc. In fact, the description here seems more like what one would wish to say of James.

[73] *Ant.* 19.332–48. Agrippa dismisses him with a gift as if he is some nobody and so easily

bought off, but this 'Simon' really would have been arrested in the manner so disingenuously portrayed of 'Simon Peter' in Acts 12:3–19 (in the midst of its first real introduction of 'James' and the beheading of a 'brother of' someone preceding it in 12:1–2) by the next 'Herodian', his brother 'Herod of Chalcis' after Agrippa I's death under mysterious circumstances; cf. *Ant.* 19.343–20.16 and *War* 2.218–22. This 'Herod' had even married Agrippa I's daughter—the notorious Bernice above (another case of 'niece marriage'—the preferred 'Herodian' family marital policy)—and most certainly did not have the lightness of touch of this first Agrippa. Note, for instance, how one 'Silas', Agrippa I's Commander of the Guard and friend, had been imprisoned by Agrippa owing to some personal dispute but whom he had declined to have executed' but who was then slain in *Ant.* 19.353 immediately upon this 'Herod''s assumption of power and by his express command.

[74] See Dio Cassius 68.14.5–33.3 and 67.14.1–18.2. Trajan, of course, whose father had participated under Vespasian in the campaigning in Palestine, had virtually decimated the Jewish population of Egypt in the wake of seeming 'Messianic' disturbances there around the period 105–115 CE and Hadrian, of course, had done the same in Palestine during the Bar Kochba Revolt from 132–36 CE.

[75] See our discussion of this episode above and in *JBJ*, pp. 286–9, 534–7, 623–42, etc.

[76] See 11QTlvi.10–15.

[77] 11QTlvii.15–17.

[78] See CDiv.17–v.15 and viii.5–8 and 4QMMTii.3–57. But also see 11QTxlvi.6–12 and xlvii.8–18 above.

[79] See *War* 2.409–426 above.

[80] See *Ant.* 20.189–196. The fact that this episode is, for all intents and purposes, missing from the *War* is of the utmost importance. Moreover, it precedes the notes about the death of James and the High Priest plundering the 'Poorer' Priests tithes by means of Herodian 'bully-boys' like 'Saul' from Ant. 20.197–214—also missing from the *War*. These omissions from the *War* are quite astonishing and can only be explained by the fact of their importance and that Josephus was unwilling at that point to either communicate them or make such things clear. I have treated this 'Affair' and the sequentiality relating to it in some detail in *JBJ*, pp. 487–521 and 778–98.

[81] The first person to propose this position was S. G. F. Brandon in his two books, *Jesus and the Zealots*, New York, 1967, pp. 115–25 and 158–89 and *The Fall of Jerusalem and the Christian Church*, London, 1951. But he was basing himself for the most part on Robert Eisler, *The Messiah Jesus and John the Baptist*, New York, 1931, pp. 141–52, 221–80, 449–53, 518–27, 540–61, and 593–4, whom he mentions throughout and who really was the first to critically recognize the important of James in this regard and his role as an 'Opposition High Priest'—a position which I too have adopted.

[82] In Eusebius, *E.I.* 2.23.18–21, 'immediately Vespasian besieged them' (i.e., Jerusalem). Moreover,

he follows this up with the notice that Josephus testified that *'the siege of Jerusalem'* occurred because of *'his martyrdom'*—of course, totally contradicting Christian theology as we know it and, in particular, the portrait of the Gospels. This position is also supported by and possibly even based on Origen, *Contra Celsum* 1.47, from where Eusebius and Jerome, *Vir. ill. 2*, might have taken it—if not directly from the copy of Josephus they themselves may have seen in the library at Caesarea. For similar accounts, see Clement, *Hypotyposes* 6.13 and Epiphanius, *Haeres*. 66.20.1 and 78.14. The problem is the whole sequentiality of these matters and the *'fall'* James takes—which seems to relate to the attack on him, described in the Pseudoclementine *Recognitions* and paralleling that on the character called *'Stephen'* in Acts around 44 CE (which actually seems to be based on that on another *'Stephen'* in Josephus, but I have covered these matters in detail in *JBJ* above).

83(82a) See *War* 2.409–426 above.

84 See 1QpHabxi.12–13.

85 This is particularly obvious in CDiii.23–iv.9 where Ezekiel 44:15 is quoted and elaborated upon, but also CDvii.12–4, where Ezekiel 13:10 about *'the builders'* and *'the Daubers on the Wall with Plaster'* is quoted and related to *'the Spouter of Lying'* or *'Windbag'* above. Also see CDxix.9–13, where Ezekiel 9:4 about *'putting a mark on the foreheads of those who weep and cry'* is quoted and related to the *'coming of the Messiah of Aaron and Israel'* (singular) nd the *'escape (of 'those who hold fast to the Torah') in the Era of the Visitation.'*

86 See 4QMMTii.3–9 above.

87 For these *'complaints,'* see Epiphanius, *Haeres*. 30.16.5–7.

88 Cf. *Ant*. 20.216 with Eusebius' testimony regarding James in *E.I.* 2.23.6 and *pars*. above.

89 Cf. n. 82 above and *E.I.* 2.23.18–21, Origen, *Contra Celsum* 1.47, and Jerome, *Vir. ill. 2* above.

90 See 1QpHabxi.4–xii.10 and 4QpPs 37ii.18–20 and iv.8–10.

91 *Haeres*. 30.16.6–9.

92 See, for instance, *E.I.* 3.27.1–6 on *'the Heresy of the Ebionites.'*

93 Cf. 1QMxi.10–15 in exposition of the Numbers 24:17–19's *'Star Prophecy'* and ending in the *'humbling of the Enemies of all the Lands...and the Powerful Ones of the Nations by the hand of the Poor (Ebionim)'* and *'the hand of those bent in the dust.'*

94 Cf. 1QpHabxi.11–12 above about *'not circumcising the foreskin of his heart'* and 4QpPs 37ii.18–19—this about *'the Righteous Teacher'* in his role as *'Opposition High Priest.'* One can see the same ideology at work in 1QpHabii.7–10 above.

95 See Jerome, *Preface to Book I of Ezekiel*, but also see Letter 84 to Pammachius and Oceanus.

96 *Haeres*. 30.16.8–9 above.

97 See the Genealogy at the end of the book. These two were both called *'Tigranes'* and, as Josephus traces their genealogy, they are descendants of that *'Mariamme,'* the last true Maccabean Princess via her older son by and in due course executed by Herod, Alexander, and Glaphyra, the daughter of the King of Cappadocia—see Josephus, *Ant*. 18.139–40 and *War* 1.552 and

2.221–22.

98 See, for instance, the third descendant of this Alexander, who was also called '*Alexander*' and was married to Jotape, the daughter of Antiochus, the King of Commagene. Alexander's own wife, as we just saw, was the daughter of the King of Cappadocia. But then there was also Herod, Agrippa I's brother, just mentioned above, who was King of Chalcis in Lebanese or Coele Syria, and Drusilla who was originally married to Azizus, King of Emesa (modernday '*Homs*' in Syria), before she ran off with the Roman Governor Felix and left the Jewish Faith altogether; see Josephus, *Ant.* 19.276, l9.355, 20.139–41, *War* 2.18–22, 7.221–41, etc.

99 See note 98 above and how, in *Ant.* 18.139, Agrippa I required Azizus, King of Emesa, to circumcise himself before he would give his daughter Drusilla to him to marry (the same '*Drusilla*', Acts 24:24 calls '*a Jewess*', as we have seen, but whom at the same time neglects to mention that she was an '*Herodian*'!); but also see *Ant.* 19.355, on '*Antiochus, the son of the King of Commagene*', who would not!

100 See our Genealogy at the end and Josephus, *Ant.* 20.140 and 147. Like his father before him, he was 'the Temple Treasurer' for awhile and originally married to Agrippa I's third daughter, '*Mariamme*', before she divorced him in order to marry someone even '*Richer*' than—Philo's nephew, '*Demetrius, the Alabarch of Alexandria*'—the Richest man in Alexandria. He like Josephus later enjoyed comfortable retirement in Rome and in *Apion* 1.51, Josephus cites him (as he did Agrippa II, Vespasian, and Titus) as willing to vouch for the veracity of his writing. If he was Paul's '*nephew*', then this would make that '*aunt*', referred to in Acts 23:16, Paul's sister '*Cypros*'—a daughter of the Idumaean line of the Herodian Genealogy and the wife of the Temple Treasurer Helcias—all descendants of Herod's sister Salome.

101 For the two '*Helcias*'es, see our Herodian Genealogy and Josephus, *War* 1.566–666 and *Ant.* 17.9–10, 17.175–94, 18.138, 18.273, 19.353–55, 20.140, and 20.194–95. Actually there is some confusion in these genealogies and, after Salome died, the first Helcias seems to have married someone else. So it looks as if there were three '*Helcias*'es, though it may be that this was just the first '*Cypros*'—the mother of the second Costobarus, Saulos, and the second '*Cypros*' (the person we identify as Paul's '*aunt*' and married to the second—or third—'Helcias'), Nonetheless, all were Temple Treasurers (because they were close colleagues of the original Herod and intimately trusted by him) and all descendants of the third husband of Herod's sister Salome after both the first, '*Joseph*', and the second, *Costobarus*'—the original '*Idumaean*' in these genealogies—fell afoul of Herod in some way.

102 The point here is that Paul also mentions '*the household of Aristobulus*' in Romans 16:10 preceding this, who would seem to be no other than the son of Agrippa I's brother Herod of Chalcis and the ultimate husband of that 'Salome' supposedly involved in some way in the death of John the Baptist, whom Josephus says was originally married to the notorious '*Philip the Tetrarch*' and not Herodias her mother as per Synoptic retelling (see *Ant.* 18.136–7 above and note that she, too, then was named after Herod's sister, the first 'Salome' in these genealogies). But also see *Apion* 1.51 above on this '*Julius*' being—like Josephus himself—in Rome and note that, if our genealogies are correct, this '*Julius*' ('*Junius*'?) really was '*a kinsman*' of Paul. Furthermore, if

the relationships are as set forth, this would make 'Julius Archelaus' Saulos' or Paul's 'nephew' and 'the Littlest Herod' or 'Herodion' of Romans 16:11, the son of said Aristobulus and Salome (John's alleged murderess)—all by this time living in Rome.

103 See *War* 1.566, 660–6 and *Ant.* 17.9–10, 17.175–94, and 18.138 above.

104 For the whole story of this affair, see *War* 1.441–3, *Ant.* 15.65–87, and variously.

105 See n. 100 above and *Ant.* 20.147; for Tiberius Alexander, his presumable uncle or brother, see *War* 2.220–3 and *Ant.* 20.100–3; as later Governor of Alexandria and Titus' military Commander of the Siege of Jerusalem, see *War* 2.492–7, 4.616–18, 5.45, 205, and 510, and 6.237–42.

106 See *Ant.* 20.102–3 above. Interestingly, Josephus mentions this in the same breath as he does Queen Helen's *'famine relief'* activity (20.100) and the *'the Census taken by Quirinius'*—the source of the anachronism concerning these same in Acts.

107 See *War* 4.616–18, 5.45, 5.205, 5.510, and 6.237–42 above.

108 See *War* 2.418, 2.556–59, 4.140–46, and *Ant.* 20.214.

109 For Niger of Perea, see Chapter 23 below and *JBJ*, pp. 537–49 and 885–92; for his execution, see *War* 4.359–63.

110 This refrain was clearly started by Paul in 1 Thessalonians 2:15 and picked up by Muhammad, though he is hardly a *'Paulinist'* except in mehodology, in the Koran (e. g., 2.61, 2.91, etc.). In both cases, it would be interesting to name anyone besides 'Honi' (who was stoned during civil strife) and Zechariah (the reason behind whose death—if in fact he was killed and this is not just the *'Zechariah the son of Bariscaeus'* we are discussing here—remains murky) before the usual condemnations—almost all of which tendentious—one hears so much about in the First Century CE.

111 *Ant.* 20.214, but also see their later exploits in *War* 2.418 and 556–9.

112 Seen my nn. 100–101 above and the Herodian Genealogy.

113 For the original 'Costobarus,' clearly an 'Idumaean,' see Josephus, *War* 1.486 and *Ant.* 15.252–66, 16.227, and 18.133. The line descending from Costobarus was definitely 'Idumaean.'

114 Cf. *Ant.* 20.214 with Acts 8:1–3. The overlap between the stoning of James and the stoning of Stephen was first suggested by H. J. Schoeps in *Theologie und Geschichte des Judenchristentums*, Tubingen, 1949, pp. 408–45. We have discussed it quite extensively in *MZCQ*, pp. 38, 76, *JJHP*, pp. 4, 22, 39, and *JBJ*, pp. xxxii, 166–87, 444–53, 599–612, 834–6, etc.

115 Cf. *Ps. Rec.* 1.70–71. Here, the use of the word 'headlong' is the same word used to describe the fate of Judas *Iscariot* and the 'fall' he supposedly took into 'the Field of Blood'/'the Akeldama' in Acts 1:18–19 contradicting the account in Matthew 27:3 that 'he hung himself' (*thus*)!

116 Cf. *Ant.* 20.214 with 1QpHabix.3–7 and xii.2–10 and CDvii.5–12.

117 Cf. 1QpHabix.5 with CDvii.7 above. It is here, too, that the 'Belial'/'Bela'/'Balaam' complex of language becomes of interest. We have already seen how the confusions over 'Bela' being listed in the Hebrew genealogies as both the first King of the Edomites and also as a 'Benjaminite' and the whole parallel represented by 'Balaam' both in Rabbinic and Christian

literatures contributed to this. But at the same time, that said, 'Idumaeans' were virtually indistinguishable from those that were being called 'Arabs' in those days (as they are today), both deeply imbedded in the 'Herodian' genealogies, as we have been showing, which added to the problem—see my Appendix on 'The Three Nets of Belial and Balla^c/Bela^c', etc. in *JJHP*, pp. 87–94. Both Muhammad and Paul, before and with them, no doubt appreciated and exploited these issues, wisely claiming their mutual descent from Abraham, though not necessary via Jacob or Israel—in Muhammad's case, via Ishmael, though 'Herodians' would probably have been quite satisfied with Isaac as well.

118 See 1QpHabix.2–12 (the last part of the exposition being missing, but it is based on Habakkuk 2:8–9's *'profiteer's profiting'*). It should be appreciated that throughout this exposition, we are using the expression *'Peoples'*/*'^{c}Amim*,' in particular, *'the Additional Ones of the Peoples,'* which in this context we claim specifically applies to *'Herodians.'*

119 For *'^{c}Arizei-Go'im,'* see 4QpPs 37ii.20 and iv.10. In our view, these specifically correspond to those in the final phase of the Revolt Josephus is calling *'Idumaeans'*—who cooperate with those, he has begun calling *'Zealots',* to take Vengeance for the death of James. For *'the 'Violent Ones'* in 'the Assembly' of 'the Priest'/'Righteous Teacher'* who are privy to his scriptural exegesis sessions, see 1QpHabii.6–11.

120 For this kind of 'persecution,' see Acts 9:4–5, 22:4–8, 26:11, and Galatians 4:29. 1 Thessalonians 2:15, as we have seen, even turns the whole sense around and transforms it into the Jews 'persecuting' a whole host of persons historically—including Paul. For *'the Assembly'*/ *'Congregation of His Elect'* see, for instance, in 4QpPs 37ii.5, iii.5, and iii.16; *'the Assembly'* or *'Congregation of the Poor'* in ii.10 and iii.8; *'the Assembly of the Men of Perfect Holiness'* in CDxx.2, *'the Disciples of God'* in xx.4, or *'the House of the Torah'* in xx.10 and 13; or *'the House of God'* in 1QSii.23 or *'the Community of His Truth'* in ii.24 or *'a Holy Community'* in ix.2, etc.

121 See Matthew 10:33, 24:9, 27:2, etc., and *pars.* and note that the Dead Sea Scrolls are replete with the use of this verb *'delivered up'*—particularly in the Damascus Document (which we shall cover below), but there it is usually God *'delivering them up to the sword'*!

122 See, for instance, *JJHP*, pp. 4 and 22 and Josephus, *Ant.* 1.5–9, *Vita* 423–30, and *Apion*, 47–52. As we have been implying above, there are many important characters and episodes for one reason or another left out of the War, including Honi, John the Baptist, Theudas, James, and many others. The why of this is impossible to determine except that Josephus may have felt more comfortable in the 90's than he did in the 70's (this, perhaps falsely so). Still, the *'Stephen'* in Josephus is only beaten underneath the walls of Jerusalem and *not stoned* (as he is clearly *not Jewish* but rather 'the Emperor's Servant' from Corinth). Clearly, too, the *'stoning of Stephen'* is taken from the Literature surrounding the *'stoning of James.'* In turn, it replaces the attack on James by *'the Enemy'* (probably Paul—this manifestly intended to be *a mortal attack*). All the rest of the mistakes in sequencing, both in Acts or in Josephus, stem from these original fundamental errors.

123 See Eusebius in *E.I.* 2.25.5 and 3.1.2, claiming to rely on an earlier tradition from Origen's

Commentary on Genesis (but similar testimony also appears in Clement, *Ad. Cor.* 5 and Tertullian, *Praescrpt. Haer.* 36), claiming he was beheaded. Jerome, *Vir. ill.* 5 gives the date of 'the Fourteenth Year of Nero' or 67–68 CE. What is most strange, however and as I have remarked elsewhere, is that Acts—which surely knows all these things—chooses to end its account in 62 CE with Paul under light house arrest in Rome while the same year in Jerusalem witnessed the stoning of James, perhaps the most significant fact in the life of the Early Church. Acts ignores this event—why? The answer should be obvious to all but the most close-minded reader. That someone, Paul or even his alter-ego in Josephus 'Saulos', might ultimately have been beheaded in the political turmoil of this time—either before or in the aftermath of Nero's assassination in 68 CE—would not be at all surprising, particularly if they were Roman citizens, though what the reason for such a beheading might have been is debatable and must remain an open question. Nor is there any reason to suppose that after Paul's initial quasi-house arrest in Rome in 62 CE, he might not have gone back to Palestine. In fact, given the nature of his contacts in Palestine—in both Jerusalem and Caesarea even according to Act's narrative—he may very well have. Acts' reticence on these matters and the manner of his death is unsatisfactory and leads one to suspect he did. Luke, the reputed author of Acts, certainly must have known more. In any event, as we are seeing, the narrative in Acts is incomplete, leaving both James' and Peter's deaths in limbo as well and just trailing off. Again one must ask, why?

[124] See the important apocryphal '*Correspondence between Seneca and Paul*,' alluded to in Jerome, *Vir. Ill.* 12, Hennecke, ii, pp. 133–41 and M. R. James, *The Apocryphal New Testament*, Oxford, 1924, pp. 480–84. It is also referred to by Augustine, *City of God* 6.11, and his *Epistle* 153.14. Also see Tertullian *De Anima* 20 and 42, who considers Seneca to have been '*on our side*.' For his part, Gallio may himself have been executed with another brother Mela and his son Lucan, in the aftermath of the Piso Conspiracy in 65 CE; cf. Tacitus, *Annals* 15.65–16.17.

[125] Paul, as we have seen, already knew persons '*in the household of Caesar*' (cf. Philippians 4:22), as did his '*fellow soldier and worker Epaphroditus*' (Philippians 2:25), whom he was actually sending to Rome and to whom, in our view, Josephus was dedicating his *Antiquities* (cf. *Ant.* 1.5–9 above). In any event, if Paul was an '*Herodian*,' this was most certainly the case.

[126] See *War* 2.411–22. As Josephus puts it, this message delivered by '*Saulos, Antipas* ('the Temple Treasurer'), *and Costobarus, all of the King's kindred*,' made a very deep impression on Florus, the Roman Governor; though he claims Agrippa II tried to calm the situation. But however, these things may be, it is clear that this is the Alliance that invites the Romans into the City.

[127] For this '*Mission*,' see *War* 2.556–58.

[128] See *Ant.* 18.130–42 and 20.138–39, but also see Josephus' story of the conversion of Queen Helen and her sons, which we have often spoken of above—*Ant.* 20.38–48. If we take the unnamed companion of the merchant Ananias in this story, who did not insist on 'circumcision' as a sine qua non for conversation, as Saulos or Paul—then we have an almost perfect convergence of materials. For Paul's attitude towards 'circumcision,' one should have regard for almost the whole Letter to the Galatians— but particularly his remarks in 2:8–12 about '*those of the circumcision*' and 5:12 about '*wishing they would themselves cut off*.' But also see Romans

2:25–4:12, 1 Corinthians 7:19, and Philippians 3:2 warning against *'the Concision.'*

[129] Josephus himself remarks that Agrippa I seemed to have had ambitions of founding an Empire of some kind with other petty Kings in the East and Saulos' conduct seems to have fallen under a cloud of some kind, which is why he was urged by Agrippa II to report to Nero in Corinth (the last one hears of him), especially with the butchering of the Roman garrison in Jerusalem and the circumcision of its Commander. For Paul's attitude towards such a polity of *'Jews and Greeks,'* which his religious efforts seemed aimed at establishing, see Romans 1:16, 2:9–10, 10:12, 1 Corinthians 1:24, Galatians 3:28, and Colossians 3:11.

[130] The whole tragic story of this Antiochus, who had been loyal to Rome and whose son had fought in the War as Head of *'the Macedonian Legion,'* is told by Josephus in *War* 7.219–43. At one time he had been friendly with Agrippa I; cf. *Ant.* 18.140, 19.338 and 355, and 20.136.

[131] Cf. *Ant.* 20.139–43 above.

[132] See *Ant.* 20.139–40.

[133] For Paul's *'cozy'* relations with Felix, Claudius' freedman, who even Acts opines *'knew a lot about the Way,'* and his (Paul's) appeal to Caesar, see Acts 23:24–24:27 (this is in *'the We Document'* and includes Drusilla) and 25:10–27:1 (this includes Festus, Agrippa II, and Bernice—pictured as his consort—and Agrippa II making the final decision concerning Paul's *'Appeal to Caesar',* just as he seems to have done with *'Saulos'* later). Moreover, it should be appreciated that this is the longest continuous narrative episode in the New Testament (almost five chapters!).

[134] See *Ant.* 20.142 and cf. *'Peter'*'s confrontations with *'Simon Magus'* in Acts 8:18–25 for largely unfathomable reasons. The reasons for the confrontations in the Peudoclementines are not very much better. But the real reasons have to be seen as those being alluded to here in Josephus, *'Cyprus'* as we have suggested elsewhere being a stand-in for *'Samaria,'* the connecting pieces being *'Simon'*'s place of origin *'Gitta'* (or *'Kitta,'* i.e. *'Crete'*) and the denotation of *'Samaritans'* in classical Hebrew as *'Cuthaeans.'* The overlap or confusion in the various manuscripts of Josephus between *'Atomus'* and *'Simon,'* of course, reflects nothing more than this *'Simon'*'s basic doctrine, *'the Primal Adam.'*

[135] See *Ant.* 15.105, 17.11–80 and 324–38 on a false *'Alexander'*), and 18.139–40 and *War* 1.552–56. That this is the preferred line, because of the actuality of its Maccabean blood, is proved by the pre-eminence of both Agrippa I, Agrippa II, and of course all their sisters—and made clear by all those who want to become a part of it, as for instance both husbands of Herodias, to say nothing of Salome's.

[136] *Ant.* 18.140.

[137] See the section of my Chapter *'Jesus' Brothers as Apostles'* in *JBJ*: *'Epaphroditus and his Intellectual Circle,'* pp. 793–801. This section might just as well be called, *'Who Wrote the Gospels,'* and it identifies the outlook of the original traditions behind these Documents as stemming from persons such as Epaphroditus, Paul, Josephus, Agrippa II, and a number of other *'Herodians'* in the circle surrounding Tiberius Alexander and not a few anti-Semitic Greek Alexandrians in the Hellenizing and *'Allegorical'* Philonic tradition.

[138] *Ant.* 18.141.

[139] See 1QpHabxii.2–10.

[140] The portrait in Matthew 14:1–12 and *pars*. (but see also Mark 12:19–27, a nonsense episode parodying *'the Seven Brothers'* in the Maccabee Books, on the level of Gospel understanding, of the issue of *'raising up seed' unto one's brother*) is certainly archaizing, as its Greco-Roman authors knew very little about the true kind of objections that were being raised against the 'Herodians'—such as niece marriage, divorce, polygamy, marriage with close family cousins, and the like, as outlined in such Qumran documents as CD, *MMT*, the Temple Scroll, etc. and were forced (in this case erroneously) to consult their ancient Hebrew texts to come up with some rationale for John's objections to Herodian marital activities. But, in this case, *'Philip'* as Josephus tells us (*Ant*. 18.136–7), did *'die childless,'* so Herod Antipas could have been *'raising up children'* unto his half-brother—but he did not since this *'Philip'* was not married to Herodias. Rather he was married to her daughter *'Salome'* as we have seen—another case of 'niece marriage.' Herodias' first husband was actually called *'Herod'* and he was the son of Herod's second wife who was also called *'Mariamme'*—the daughter of the High Priest Boethus he had imported from Egypt in place of the Maccabeans (again see our *Genealogy* below). Now the issue of their marital state is unclear but, in any event, the issues here are *'divorce'* and 'marriage with nieces.' These are clearly what John was objecting to. Plus, the fact that Antipas divorced his *'Arab'* wife in order to marry Herodias, causing a mini-war with her father Aretas, which Josephus actually remarks. And what was the moving force behind all these machinations? Herodias' 'Maccabean' blood—to say nothing of her great *'wealth.'*

[141] See *Ant*. 18.137 above and 20.13 and 104. It is interesting that these two were ultimately given the Kingdom of Lesser Armenia by Nero *Ant*. 20.158), another example of *'Herodian'* penetration into these areas of Asia Minor.

[142] See Suetonius 6.49.3–4 and 8.14.4 and Dio Cassius 63.28.1–2 and 67.15.1. We have already identified these two in *JBJ*, pp. 791–7 and variously. As we can see here, the *'Epaphroditus'* under Nero, to whom Josephus dedicates all his works—later blamed by Domitian, whether justly or unjustly and even though he had also been his Secretary, as Nero's assassin—was executed along with Flavius Clemens, Domitian's own cousin (Clement?) in 96 CE. Later another Epaphroditus, perhaps his son or a relative, appears as Trajan's secretary.

[143] See, for instance, how Tacitus in *Histories* 5.13 expresses this—an almost perfect copy of Josephus' similar statement at the end of the War and an almost precise statement of *'the World Ruler Prophecy.'* Suetonius—among other prodigies—expresses the same thought in 8.5.6 under *'Vespasian'* even mentioning Josephus, so the Romans were obviously very much taken by this *'Prophecy.'* Yet in 7.9.2 under *'Galba'* (who became Emperor for awhile in 68 CE, following Nero's assassination), Suetonius alludes to a similar ideology, but rather adds (in line with the 'Spanish' origins of many of these claimants, successful or otherwise—Galba, for instance, had been a Governor there for a long time) *'would one day arise in Spain'* (*thus!*). Later Emperors like Trajan (98–117) and Hadrian (117–138) also came from Spain. Trajan's father—also Trajan—was, as we have seen, one of Vespasian's bravest Legion Commanders in Palestine and mentioned several times in Josephus.

[144] For this crackdown, in particular in regard to Flavius Clemens, Flavia Domitilla, his wife or

niece, and others, in regard to which Epaphroditus and Josephus were, in the author's view, undoubtedly swept up; see Suetonius 8.15.1, 8.17.1–2, Dio Cassius 67.14, and *E.I.* 3.18.3–5.

[145] This report to Nero is covered in *War* 2.556–8 above. If that *'Saulos,'* Agrippa's *'kinsman'* already alluded to above, did somehow run afoul of Nero's unpredictable and volatile temperament, it would not have been surprising. Being sent to Nero, as we have seen also in Corinth, Greece where Nero was supervising the digging of the Canal, to report to him on the turmoil in Palestine, was the last trace of him in Josephus' work after being the intermediary between *'the Peace Party'* in Jerusalem—the Pharisees, principal Sadducees, and Herodians—and the Roman Army outside it. This was right before Vespasian's appointment as Commander in Palestine. It is also around the time most people think Paul was beheaded in Rome in 66 CE or thereabouts—if he was beheaded.

[146] See *Ant.* 19.299–325 (here is another character missing in the *War*).

[147] See *Vita* 407–409—this in addition to the material in *War* 2.556–58 above. It is clear that Philip goes to Nero on the advice of both Vespasian and Agrippa II. One can make more or less the same conclusion about *'Saulos'*—a *'kinsman'* of Agrippa—though he is not mentioned in the *Vita*.

[148] Cf. *War* 2.556–58 and n. 123 above.

[149] See *War* 2.214–22 and *Ant.* 19.353, 20.13–16, 104, and 158.

[150] *Ant.* 20.143–44.

[151] For our tracing of the identities of these two individuals (Julius Archelaus and his mother, Saulos' sister *'Cypros'*—the wife of the second Temple Treasurer named *'Helcias'*), see nn. 100–1 and 145 above and the Herodian Genealogy below. For Antipater's relations with the Romans and the bestowal upon him and his progeny after him of Roman citizenship in perpetuity, see *War* 1.187–203 and *Ant.* 16.52–54 (also cf. 14.127–49, which gives the whole Senatorial Decree, and 14.491 on the *'meanness'* of Herod's birth when compared to his own ancestors— the Maccabeans!). This would, therefore have encompassed the whole *'Herodian'* family after him and, in particular, if *'Saulos'* = *'Paul'* and Paul was an *'Herodian,'* Paul himself.

[152] See how Aretas, the *'Arab'* King of Petra, took control of Coele Syria and Damascus in the early First Century BC in *Ant.* 13.392 and 14.34, 40, and 74. After that, it seemed to have a variety of Roman Governors—but in the mini-war between Herod the Tetrarch and Aretas, his descendant, after the execution of John the Baptist; the *'Arab'* King Aretas seems to have retaken control of it for awhile if Acts 9:22–5 is at all credible. See *Ant.* 18.109–25.

[153] Cf. Acts 9:1–2 with the far more detailed account in Ps. *Rec.* 1.70–71

[154] See, for instance, *War* 1.401–28, 7.172–77, *Ant.* 15.267–364, 16.136–59, and variously. He even named cities after Julius Caesar, Augustus, Tiberius, Temple Guard Towers after Anthony (how symbolic) and his own brother funded Olympic-style games at home and abroad, etc.

[155] *War* 1.437 and *Ant.* 15.25–64 and 20.247–48.

[156] See his description in *Haeres.* 30.16.8–9 of how Paul was a convert who came up to Jerusalem because *'he wanted to marry the High Priest's daughter'* (which I take to be a reflection of Herod and what he/Herod actually did. He married two of them!) and cf. his description of Herod's

origins in 20.1.1–6, which shows he has really read his Josephus very carefully too.

[157] See Josephus' description of how Agrippa I treated the 'Simon' the Head of an Assembly (*Ecclesia*) of his own in Jerusalem, who wanted to have him barred him from the Temple as a foreigner, in *Ant.* 19.332–34 above. Also see *M. Sot.* 7:8 where Agrippa weeps when it comes to reading the Deuteronomic King Law in the Temple and the assembled Rabbis cry out, '*You are one of us, you are one of us, you are one of us*' three times on *Succot*, mentioned above and cf. *M. Bik.* 3:4, *M. Kel.* 1:8, b. *Pes* 107b, *Keth* 17a, Leviticus *R.* 3.5, *Ant.* 19.328–34, etc.

[158] See Eusebius, *E.I.* 1.7.11 and 14.

[159] *Ibid.,* 1.7.13. Eusebius claims to be taking this information from Julius Africanus (170–245 CE) but one need not go here to discover Herod's base origins. One has only to read Josephus comments, noted in n. 150 above—but, particularly, in *Ant.* 14.491 where uncharacteristically (because he is comparing him with his own ancestors, the Maccabees), he shows his utter contempt for Herod's '*base*' origins.

[160] Cf. *War* 2.422–8. But also see 4.411–22—the principal issue here, of course, being '*sacrificing on behalf of foreigners*' or '*accepting their gifts in the Temple*' and the various opposing interpretations of '*pollution of the Temple*' as we have outlined them above.

[161] See *War* 2.520.

[162] See *War* 4.491–93, Suetonius 6.49.3–4, 8.14.4, and Dio Cassius 63.28.2 and 67.15.1.

[163] See n. 143 above and Suetonius on '*Galba,*' 7.8.1–9.2.

[164] See Dio Cassius 68.14.4.

[165] Cf. CDxx.19–20 above.

[166] See n. 124 and Tacitus, *Annals* 15.65–16.17 above.

[167] Cf. Acts 9:22–25. The key passage for solving this riddle, as we have elsewhere demonstrated, is the note in Acts 9:23 about how Paul was escaping '*the Jews who plotted to kill him*.' This is the usual tendentious dislocation one encounters in this genre of secondary narrative. More likely is Paul's own firsthand testimony in 2 Corinthians 11:32–3 that he was escaping '*the Ethnarch of Aretas the King*' who '*was desirous of arresting*' him. No wonder those wishing to take these testimonies seriously want to postulate 'two' escapes down the walls of Damascus '*in a basket*.' The alternative is too unpleasant to contemplate—but it will not fly!

[168] Cf. Acts 23:35, 24:23, and 28:30–31 and see *E.I.* 2.22.2–8, immediately introducing the Chapter on the martyrdom of James. Also see Romans 15:24–28 where Paul expresses his intention to visit Spain.

Chapter 18

[1] For Eusebius, see *E.I.* 3.5.3; for Epiphanius, see *Haeres.* 29.7.7, 30.2.7, and *De pond. et mens.* 15; for 1 Apoc. Jas., see 5.25.15 and 5.35.15–20,

[2] *E.I.* 3.5.3–4

[3] CDiv.2–3 and vi.4–5.

4 1QpHabxii.5.

5 The Hebrew word here is *'Ebionim'* even though the underlying Hebrew, usage, *'Ani'*/*'the Meek,'* doesn't occur until Habakkuk 3:4. Here we are only at Habakkuk 2:17. This is repeated in 1QpHabxii.10 and xii.15 and in 4QpPs 37ii.10 and iii.8, as we have seen, where it is tied to the expression *'the Church'* or *'Congregation'* as well, i.e., *'the Church of the Poor'.*

6 1QpHabxii.13 and 1QpHabxiii.2. This is paralleled in Paul's mocking characterization of the *'Hebrew'* *'Super Apostles'* in 2 Corinthians 11:15, who go around presenting themselves as *'Servants of Righteousness,'* but who actually are *'Pseudo-Apostles'* and *'Servants of Satan.'* Paul is nothing if always blunt and full of malevolence. For *'the Assembly'*/*'Congregation of His Elect'* see, for instance, in 4QpPs 37ii.5, iii.5, and iii.16—*'the Assembly'* or *'Congregation of the Poor'* in ii.10 and iii.8;

7 Cf. *'the Assembly of the Men of Perfect Holiness'* in CDxx.2–7, *'a Holy Community'* in 1QSix.2, *'the House of God'* and *'the Community of His Truth'* in 1QSii.23–24, *'the Disciples of God'* in CDxx.4. For John as consecrated *'from his mother's womb,'* see Luke 1:15. We know this was how James was described in all Early Church texts. Also see various references to *'Tamimei-Derech'*/*'Perfect of the Way'* and *'Tamim-Kodesh'*/*'Perfect Holiness'* in 1QSi.8, ii.3, iii.9, viii.8–21, and ix.5–19

8 See *Git* 56a, 1.15, and *ARN* 6(20b–21a). For R. Akiba, see also *Ket* 62b–63a.

9 See *E.I.* 3.5.1–6.32.

10 See *War* 6.312–5.

11 *War* 6.288–300.

12 See the end of this Chapter below and *War* 6.301–9.

13 Of course all this comes from *'the Star Prophecy'* of Numbers 24:17, since it is clear from numerous sources and now authentic actual letters that Bar Kochba's original name was *'Bar Kosiba'.*

14 *Haeres.* 29.7.7.

15 See *The Haran Gawaita and the Baptism of Hibil-Ziwa,* tr. E. S. Drower, Biblioteca Apostolica Vaticano, Citta del Vaticano, 1953, pp. viii–xi and 2–17 above.

16 *E.I.* 1.7.14 and cf. Epiphanius in *Haeres.* 29.7.7 above, who both knows that *'Cocaba'* is based on *'Star'* and places it *'in Bashan'* (see the general map at the end ot this book), which is on the way to *'Damascus'* or *'the Land of Damascus'* not far from *'the region of Pella'* and *'the Decapolis'*—a little further South. There is a discrepancy here.

17 *E.I.* 1.7.14.

18 See our maps at the end of this book. It should be appreciated that *'Chozeba'* is where the presentday *'Wadi Kelt'* or *'Monastery of St. George'* really is. The presence of *'Kaukaba'* in Southern Lebanon is an extremely interesting anomaly, as it is in the middle of what one would term the Shi'ite Area of the Country where most to the ongoing fighting between Hezballah and Israelis takes place.

19 *E.I.* 4.6.4.

20 For Paul's use of the term *'Apocalypseos,'* see Galatians 2:2 where he claims he was not summoned up to Jerusalem to give an account of *'the Gospel which (he preaches) among the Gentiles'*; but

rather, on the contrary, he came as a result of *'a private Revelation'*—but he would claim this, wouldn't he?

21 1 Apoc. Jas. 5.25.10–20.

22 Cf. Paul in 1 Corinthians 11:25–9 on his presentation of *'Communion with the body and blood of Christ,'* where he suddenly becomes quite aggressive speaking in 11:27 about *'drinking the Cup of the Lord in an unworthy way'* (whatever he might mean by this) and, thus, *'being guilty of the body and blood of the Lord.'* But, of course too, once one dispenses with the dissimulation of *'the two sons of Zebedee,'* there is little doubt that what one is really referring to—and this in all sources—is the martyrdom of the two brothers *'James and Simon',* whether one is talking about *'the two sons of Judas the Galilean'* by those names or *'Simon the Zealot'* or, for that matter his double *'Simeon bar Cleophas'* or *'James'* himself/*'James the son of Alphaeus'* (i.e., *'Cleophas'*).

23 Luke 24:13–35. That this is parallel to Jerome's Gospel of the Hebrews, where the *'Cup'* is now given to Jesus' brother James, should be obvious. So now basically we have two family members, one *'Cleopas'* (allegedly Jesus' *'uncle'*) and the unknown other—obviously James.

24 John 21:2. *'Nathanael of Cana of Galilee'* we have already identified as a parallel in John to James. But here we also have *'the sons of Zebedee'* again (unnamed) *'and two other of his Disciples'* again also unnamed, but there is no doubt who they are supposed to be—the same *'two'* that Jesus appeared to 'on the Emmaus Road' in Luke. One should also note the *'standing'* imagery (i.e., *'the Standing One'* of the Pseudoclementines) that permeates this episode in John. Moreover, we know from Josephus what really happened in those days by *'the Sea of of Tiberius'*—utter mayhem, devastation, and massacre. This at least is correctly recounted in the Dead Sea Scrolls.

25 Jerome, *Vir. ill.* 2. As this appears in *'The Gospel of the Hebrews,'* according to the report of Jerome, it reads in full: *'He took the bread, blessed it, broke it, and gave it to James the Just* (there no longer being any doubt as to which individual is missing in Luke's *'Emmaus Road'* account) *and said to him, "My brother, eat your bread, for the Son of Man is risen from amongst those that sleep."'*

26 Ps. Rec. 1.71.

27 *Vir. ill.* 2 above.

28 Cf. 1QpHabxi.9–15.

29 1QpHabxii.15.

30 1QpHabxi.13–4. This has been misinterpreted by almost all commentators, since it has nothing to do with *'the Wicked Priest'*'s alleged *'drunkenness'* but rather his *'drinking his fill'* or *'drinking to satiety of the Cup of the Wrath of God,'* just as here in Revelation. Inability to relate to literary metaphor has always been a weak point of the *'run-of the-mill'* of Qumran commentators. For *'Cup,' 'drunkenness,'* and *'wine'* imagery for Divine Vengeance, see Jeremiah 13:13, 25:28, 48:26, 49:12, 51:7, Ezekiel 23:32–34, Zechariah 12:2, and Lamentations 4:21.—but, in particular, Psalm 75:8, which seems to be the basis of the imagery here in Revelation. Nor is this to say anything of Habakkuk 2:15–16, the subject of this exegesis. *'Poured out,'* of course, is also always important imagery, not only in the various renditions of *'Last Supper'* pronouncements

but, in particular, in Isaiah 51:17 on *'the Cup of the Wrath of God being drunk to the dregs'* as here in the Habakkuk *Pesher* it is actually set forth.

[31] See 1QpHabx.2–5 introducing all this.

[32] See Chapter 28 below.

[33] See my article: *'An Esoteric Relation between Qumran's "New Covenant in the Land of Damascus" and the New Testament's "Cup of the New Covenant in (his) Blood"?', Revue de Qumran*, v. 21, n. 83, 2004, pp. 439–56.

[34] *Ps. Rec.* 1.71.

[35] This is already implied earlier by the saying, ascribed allegedly to 'Jesus' on his leaving the Temple in Matthew 24:1–2/Mark 13:1–2/Luke 21:5–6 that *'There shall not be left here one stone upon another that shall not be thrown down.'* Here the *'balla'* language is abjured because it has just been used in the previous material (in Mark and Luke) about the widow *'casting her two mites'* into the Temple Treasury!

[36] See 1QpHabxii.14–xiii.3

[37] CDi.14–6. This individual, quite literally, is *'the Pourer out of Lying.'*

[38] Cf. CDvii.13, xix.12–13, and 1QSii.5–7.

[39] See 1QpHabxi.4–xii.10 and 4QpPs 37 ii.18–20 and iv.8–10 above.

[40] In flurry of scholarly activity in the 50's and 60's, the authenticity of *'the Pella Flight'* Tradition was being questioned, particularly by S. G. F. Brandon in *Jesus and the Zealots*, New York, 1967, pp. 208–18 and in his earlier *Fall of Jerusalem*, pp. 168–73 and 263–4, but also by W. Farmer, *Maccabees, Zealots and Josephus*, New York, 1957, p. 125 and G. Strecker, *Das Judenchistentum in den Pseudoklemintinen*, Berlin, 1959, pp. 229–31; and cf. *MZCQ*, pp. 80–81 and 89–91. The main point they were arguing was that conditions on the other side of the Jordan in this Revolt Period were too unsettled to allow such a flight to *'Pella'* and that the *'Tradition'* was taken over by a later more Paulinized Community in Pella—which may or may not have been true. But this did not rule out other kinds of *'flight'*s, as I am arguing here, either to Qumran, Masada, or even further afield to Northern Syria.

[41] Cf. Acts 5:36 and 1 Apoc. Jas. 5.25.15–29—the reference to *'giving the Cup of Bitterness to the Sons of Light.'*

[42] *Ant.* 20.97–98.

[43] Cf. Acts 9:1–3 with Ps. Rec 1.70–71 above.

[44] We say *'grandson,'* because *'son'* would perhaps be a little precarious given the chronology involved. But Josephus does mention the preventive crucifixion of his *'two sons, James and Simon'* in *Ant.* 20.102, which we have mentioned above and which gave rise to the anachronism in Acts 5:36–7 as we have previously explained (the point was that, in mentioning these *'two sons'*, Josephus did mention *'the Judas'* who *'had roused the people to revolt against the Romans when Cyrenius was taking the Census in Judea.'*

[45] *War* 2.433–49 and *Vita* 21.

[46] See *War* 7.252–406.

[47] See *War* 2.405–456 above and *Ant.* 20.160–78.

[48] See 4Q266 (The Last Column of the Damascus Document) and my discussion in *DSSU*, pp. 212–9.

[49] CDxiv.8–9.

[50] CDvii.12–3 and xix.24–6. Here, we have more intertextuality, once again, implying a contemporaneous date with other documents mentioning this 'Lying Spouter.' That this is the same 'Spouter of Lying' one encounters in the Habakkuk *Pesher* and in the First Column of CD is hardly to be doubted

[51] CDvii.7–12/xix.20–25.

[52] Cf. CDvii.11–12 and 18–19/xix.23–4 and 31–32.

[53] *Ant.* 20.22–23 and 34–48. Izates meets the 'Ananias', Josephus calls 'a merchant', in the town of Charax Spasini at the Head of the Persian Gulf—the city we now call 'Basrah' and a hotbed of Shi'ism. Then it was a hotbed of the 'Mandaean Elchasaites' or those Muhammad calls 'Sabaeans'—after their 'bathing' habits, not their supposed place of origin in Southern Arabia (this is a simple confusion of consonants).

[54] See E. S. Drower, *The Haran Gawaita and the Baptism of Hibil-Ziwa*, pp. viii–xi and 2–17 above.

[55] See our pictures in Plates 53–4. Plate 54 depicts a volcanic hot river that flows past Machaeros and into the Dead Sea more or less opposite the mouth of the Wadi Kedron, depicted in Plates 1–15, and Qumran.

[56] *War* 2.93–5 and *Ant.* 17.188 and 318–20. This is why the picture in Luke 23:7–15, on the one hand, is a little worrisome (unless 'Herod''s opinion is being sought concerning 'Galilee' matters; while, on the other, it is fairly accurate in that Antipas is not pictured as having any Authority in Jerusalem.

[57] See n. 40 above and *War* 2.457–68.

[58] *Ibid.* and *Vita* 341–42 and 410. This is what makes the picture of 'Jesus' in the Gospels visiting and seeming to make headway in 'the Decapolis' and 'beyond Jordan' in Mark 3:8, 5:20, 7:31, 10:1, Matthew 4:15, John 10:40 and *pars.* so compelling; because these areas were definitely the scene of much civil strife during the Uprising.

[59] This tradition probably began with the work of Aristo of Pella, magnifying the importance of his place of origin, after Hadrian had forbidden Jews 'from ever going up to the country around Jerusalem' or 'even seeing from a distance the Land of their Fathers'—Eusebius, *E.I.* 3.6.4 above. It is probably in this Period, too, that the Movement, we have stressed, known as 'the Mourners for Zion,' which not only gave birth to Karaite Judaism, but several returns to the Land of Zion or Jerusalem at the time of the first discovery of the Dead Sea Scrolls in the 8th–9th centuries CE, developed. For 'the See of St. James,' see *E.I.* 7.19. For my view of Santiago de Compostella, see *JBJ*, pp. 621–22 and 861–62; for the 'Myth of 'Santiago de Compostella,' see James Bentley, *The Way of St. James*, London, 1992, pp. 7–15 and J. Marshall-Cornwall, 'The Myth of Santiago' in *History Today*, March, 1981, pp. 46f. This 'Myth' is certainly very curious and turns on the

story that *'James the Brother of John'* both had time to accomplish considerable *'evangelization'* in Spain and yet return to Palestine to be beheaded (thus!). The meaning of the term *'Compostella'* is debated, some considering it related to *'Tomb'*; others to *'Field of Stars.'* The latter rests on a story that a hermit shepherd named Pelayo, *'guided by a star'* around 810 CE found the corpse of *'St. James'* buried in a *'field'* in Northern Spain which became *'Compostella'*—hence *'Santiago de Compostella.'* Everyone knows this mushroomed into a major Christian Pilgrimage site, dedicated to *'the Order of St. James'* and the famous *'Way of St. James.'* Thus far the *'myth,'* but what does seem authentic is that there is a *'Star'* and *'a Field'* (*'the Akeldama'* of the Judas Iscariot *'bloody fall'*?—a story I have already shown related to the picture of James' fall and death in most Early Church sources and the Pseudoclementines) once more associated with the happenings. Moreover, if one views the gold-plated Ossuary, which sits underneath the altar of the Cathedral at Santiago; one cannot escape the feeling that the *'rosettes'* on it give the impression of something very *'Palestinian'* from the Firsst Century. My conclusion: Spanish Pilgrims did probably bring an ossuary back to Northern Spain (one notes there is often a *'boat'* theme associated with these legends) sometime after the Muslim conquest of the area in the Seventh Century when such ossuaries would have been easily acquired (as they are today). Since it is questionable if there ever was a *'James the brother of John'* and not simply a *'James the brother of Jesus'* (as I have argued, calling the former an *'overwrite'* of the latter throughout *JBJ;* cf. pp. xviii, xxviii, 51, 95–119, 190–2, and variously)—moreover, the recent controversies over the so-called *'James Ossuary'* has focused attention on such ossuaries and since the site of James' burial was known even in Eusebius and Jerome's time in the 4th and 5th Centuries, but lost thereafter—I would conclude that, if the bones in the Ossuary underneath the altar of the Cathedral of Santiago are authentic and belong to any James, they would belong to *'James the brother of Jesus'* (not *'James the brother of John'*—a product of theological transformation), brought to Spain by pious pilgrims sometime after the Muslim conquest of Jerusalem. If this is true, how ironic and yet how fitting.

[60] See above Chapter 5 and *Zohar* 59b on Noah, quoting Proverbs 10:25.

[61] See Eusebius, *E.I.* 2.23.18–21, Clement in *E.I.* 2.5.3, Origen, *Contra Celsum* 1.47, Jerome, *Vir. ill.* 2, Epiphanius, *Haeres.* 78.14, etc.

[62] Eusebius, *E.I.* 2.23.20–1, Origen, *Contra Celsum* 1.47, and Jerome, *Vir. ill.* 2 above.

[63] *Ant.* 20.200–202. I have theorized elsewhere that, since these authors state they saw this testimony in the War, the place it occurred was probably in Book Four on the death of James' nemesis, the High Priest Ananias, or Book Seven on *'the Signs and portents'* for the fall of Jerusalem.

[64] See *War* 7.300–309.

[65] In Daniel, the seven and a half-year chronology appears in 7:25 and 8:12–14. The first speaks of *'three and a half years'* (*'a time two times and a half'*), which could certainly have been taken (even if mistakenly) by the Revolutionaries as signifying the time between James' stoning (*Succot*, 62 CE) and signal for the beginning of the War against Rome. This is to say nothing about the denouement four years later (*'two thousand three hundred evenings and mornings all told'*). Here

is the *'seven and a half years'*, but I prefers not to comment about this as certainly those following such chronologies would not have known the the War was going to end at its start.

[66] Cf. *War* 7.300–308 with *Ant.* 20.200–202 above.

[67] 1QpHabvi.12–vii.8 and CDiv.11–12.

[68] See *Ant.* 20.17. That this King also had a large harem—the custom in *'the Land of the Edessenes'* and beyond in *'Adiabene'*—is testified to in Ant. 20.20.

[69] See Moses of Chorene, *History or Armenia* 2.25. In Roman and Latin sources, this King is often called *'Acbarus'* and he is referred to as *'King of the Arabs'*—see, for instance, Tacitus, *Annals* 12.12 (but also see 6.44 calling these people *'Arabs'*). This is what makes Acts 8:25's allusion to *'the Ethiopian Queen'* all the more untenable. In any event, the name of a *'prophet called Agabus'* is clearly a nonsense designation

[70] There are so many references to the quintessential *'coming down to Antioch'* that it would be difficult to catalogue them all, but we have already explained why this *'Antioch'* is not the one *'on the Orontes'* in Syria, as it is normally taken to be; but rather *'Edessan Antioch'* on a tributary of the Euphrates in Northern Syria above in Chapter 1. Strabo, in Books 5–7 of his *Geography*, identifies five different *'Antioch's* in the Seleucid Empire at this time—the reason being, as we have pointed out previously, that he honored his father so exceedingly (in 16.1.28 he considers, like Tacitus above, almost all Mesopotamians *'Arabs'*—as did the Romans after him—and the inhabitants of Edessa, *'Osrhoeans'* or *'Assyrians'*). It is left to Pliny, *H.N.* 5.21 to make the final identification of *'Antioch-by-Callirhoe'* with *'Edessa.'* For additional comments on this situation see J. B. Segal, *Edessa: The Blessed City*, Oxford, 1970, pp. 6 and 46. Even in the story Eusebius recounts about the conversion of *'King Abgar'* or *'Agbar'*, echoed thereafter too in Syriac and Armenian sources (see *The Teaching of Addai the Apostle* and *Moses of Chorene* 2.33–6), *'Ananias'* plays the key role in the proceedings, as he does in Paul's alleged conversion *'on a Street called the Straight'* in Acts 9:10–7 and Josephus' parallel story of the conversion of Izates (one of these *'Agbarus'es'* putative sons).

[71] On *'Land of Judah,'* see CDvi.5 and the parallel archaism *'House of Judah'* in iv.11 above. For this last, also see 1QpHabviii.1, limiting the efficacy of Habakkuk 2:4.

[72] Both are *'beheaded'* contemporaneously in the mid-40's CE and, in our analysis, both are *'brother's* of someone. In the latter case, we identify him with *'Judas the brother of James'* and his various look-alikes; cf. *JBJ*, pp. 866–958.

[73] The key here is Peter's arrest and subsequent escape from prison; cf. Josephus, *Ant.* 19.277–20.15 and *War* 2.178–2.223

[74] Cf. CDxii.22–xiii.1, xiv.19, xx.1, and 4QFlori.11–4. This is also the case in CDii.12–3, the second part of which translators like G. Vermes of Oxford inexplicably omit. See also 1QMxi.11–2 on *'the sword of No Mere Man'* in exegesis of Numbers 24:16–7.

[75] For this kind of *'laying on of hands,'* see Plate no.36 in *JBJ*. Also see the Frontispiece in E. S. Drower, *The Mandaeans of Iraq and Iran*, Leiden, 1962.

[76] Cf. *Ant.* 20.201–203.

[77] Cf. 1QpHabix.1–11, x.1–5, xi.10–xiii.4 and 4QpPs 37ii.18–19 and iv.6–11.

78 *Ant.* 20.197–203 above. It is really curious how many things, Josephus packs into this last Book Twenty of the *Antiquities*, including Theudas, James, the whole story of Queen Helen of Adiabene and her sons, ending with the rioting led by Costobarus and Saulos before the enumeration of all the High Priest up to the fall of the Temple, almost all of which missing from the *War*. We say, '*perhaps unwisely so*,' because Josephus seems to have disappeared from sight not long after the publication of these works, along with many other putative '*Christians*' in Domitian's Court such as Epaphroditus and that '*Clement*' (probably '*Flavius Clemens*') —the presumable hero of the Pseudoclementines.

79 Cf. *War* 4.314–25 and Josephus' own comments in *Vita* 193–96 (where he rather calls '*Ananus the High Priest*,' '*corrupted by bribes*') and 202–204, where Josephus is saved by '*Jesus*" warning.

80 For '*Banus*,' see *Vita* 10–12; for my presentation of '*Banus*' as a '*Rechabite*,' see *JBJ*, pp. 319–54.

81 We have touched on the sequentiality of this Book above n. 78. We shall touch on it further below when discussing the importance of '*the Temple Wall*' Affair.

82 Cf. *Ant.* 206–58 and his comments about the help Agrippa II and others in Rome provided him in the intervening years in *Vita* 359–67 and *Apion* 1.51. Where '*goading*' goes, one should note that perhaps Josephus' last comment about Albinus in *Ant.* 20.215 is that '*he took money*' from many prisoners (those he had not already put to death) and '*by this means, the prisons were consequently emptied and the countryside filled with Robbers*' (often the designation for '*Revolutionaries*' as we have seen).

83 *War* 2.254–60. It is with this assassination that Josephus actually first describes exactly who these '*extreme Zealots*' (or '*Essenes*', as Hippolytus might prefer to term them) he is calling '*Sicarii*' are—nor is this definition either comprehensive or adequate. There had to be more than this— for instance, why the Masada suicide?

84 *Ant.* 20.168 and 188 and cf. *War* 2.258–59 above, descriptions chronologically preceding that of the death of James. One should note that the word for '*Deliverance*'/'*er*' in Greek is '*Soter*' and should appreciate that there are many references to such '*signs and wonders*' both at Qumran and in the Gospels—though, as we have pointed out, at Qumran '*the signs and wonders*' are the mighty battles God has won for His People; whereas in the Gospels, in typically Hellenizing style, these same '*signs and wonders*' are the raisings, curings, healings, exorcisms, loaf multiplications, wine transubstantiations, and the like that '*Jesus*' and his '*Apostles*' do for the people. It is almost as if we have Asclepius vs. Yahweh.

85 *Ant.* 20.206–7 and 2.213–14, the second being the riotous plundering led by Saulos and his bully boys, with which the historical part of the *Antiquities* effectively comes to an end.

86 For Belaᶜ as both the first Edomite King and one of the principal sons of Benjamin, see Genesis 14:2–8, 36:32–33, 46:21, Numbers 26:38–40, 1 Chronicles 1:43–44 and 7:6–8:3.

87 See 11QTxlvi.9–12 and my Appendix on same in *JJHP*, pp. 87–94.

88 For '*the Temple Wall Affair*,' see *Ant.* 20.189–96, which just precedes his account of the death of James and probably explains why Josephus himself—like '*Ishmael the High Priest*' and '*Helcias the Temple Treasurer*' who were taken into the actual household of Poppea (before she was kicked to death by Nero) — went on an Embassy to Nero and, in particular, went to see this

same Poppea (see *Vita* 13–6—he calls the vegetarianism, those on whose behalf he had gone to Rome '*to secure deliverance for*', displayed by '*eating nothing but dates and nuts*' an example of their '*Piety towards God*') and, moreover, why he was not in Jerusalem at the time of the death of James.

89 '*Blasphemy*,' for instance would have included '*pronouncing the forbidden Name of God*,' which James would have done had he gone into the Inner Sanctum of the Temple, as all Early Church sources insist he did (cf. *E.I.* 2.23.11–8 and *pars.* above), '*pleading on his knees until they became tough as camel's hide*' (what vivid similes), '*to ask forgiveness on behalf of the People*.' That he and his followers '*transgressed the Law*' and were, therefore, '*delivered up to be stoned*' in *Ant.* 20.200–201, can imply no other charge than '*blasphemy*.' For 'Jesus''*'blasphemy*,' see Matthew 26:65 and *pars.* For *Talmud Sanhedrin*, it should be clear that the punishment for either insurrection or sedition was quite different, including a variety of things like '*beheading*' but not '*crucifixion*' which, as the world by now has perhaps come to appreciate (even if movie-makers like Mel Gibson have not), was a Roman exemplary punishment imposed on subject '*Peoples*,' not Citizens, and absolutely forbidden in all Jewish Legal Contexts.

90 *War* 4.288–322 but cf. *Vita* 193–204 above where he calls him '*corrupted by bribes*.'

91 *Ant.* 20.200, also reproduced in Eusebius, *E.I.* 2.23.23–5. It is doubtful that the term '*the Christ*' (which is really first encountered in the Letters of Paul) had gained prominence in Palestine or even, perhaps, the Josephus' circle. It is impossible to separate out interpolations of this kind from authentic testimony, so the reader will have to judge passages like this for him or herself. Still, I am not among those who doubt the general authenticity of the timing embodied here, as it certainly makes much too much sense to doubt the reliability of the whole passage.

92 See 1QpHabxi.10–xii.6.

93 Cf. *Ant.* 20.201 with Matthew 26:25, 27:1–10, and *pars.*

94 Cf. the use of the term '*breaking*' or '*Breakers*' in CDi.20 (*par contra* ii.18–iii.2), 1QpHabii.6, 1QSi.24, etc.

95 1QpHabxi.14–xii.10 above.

96 Cf. for instance, the classic Romans 13:1–15:13.

97 For the illegality of passing the death sentence when the Sanhedrin was '*exiled*' from the Stone Chamber on the Temple Mount to another place of sitting, which it seems to have been for much of the Period from 30–70 CE, see *inter alia* Talmudic Tractates *R.H.* 31a–b, *San.* 41a, 88b, *A.Z* 8b, and *j. San.* i.1. Also see my article on '*Interpreting "Abeit-Galuto" in the Habakkuk Pesher*' in *DSSFC*, pp. 247–71. This paper was first presented to '*The Groningen Conference*' in Holland in 1989, where the promise was that all papers given there would be published in the *Revue de Qumran*. It was not, breaking the assurances given at that time. This was not the fault of Florentino Garcia-Martinez, who fought hard to have it included, but of others. Afterwards, it was published by Zdzislaw Kapera as an Addendum to the *Proceedings* of his Conferences in Poland, Mogilany 1989, vol. ii., Crakow, 1991, pp. 177–95.

98 *Ant.* 20.201–203.

99 It should be appreciated that it is here in *Ant.* 20.215 that Albinus is portrayed as taking '*bribes*'

and *'clearing the prisons, so that the Country was completely overrun by Brigands (Lestai as in the Gospels)'.*

[100] *Ant.* 20.160–81, for which even Josephus provides his *mea culpa* in *Ant.* 20.166: *'This is the reason why, in my opinion, even God Himself out of hatred of their Impiety, rejected our City; and, as for the Temple, he no longer considered it a pure enough place for His dwelling and brought the Romans upon us, purified our City by fire, and brought Slavery upon ourselves, our wives, and our children, for He wished to chasten us by our calamities.'* How obsequious!

[101] Cf. 1QpHabii.5–10 and my comments about this in *JJHP*, pp. 17–26, 44–48, and 93–97, etc. These episodes are also reprised in the Talmud in *Pes* 57a and *Tos. Men.* xiii.21: *'The Zealot Woes'.* It is here, too, that the Habakkuk *Pesher* and the Damascus Document actually use the same verb, *'steal'/'gazal,'* to describe the activities of the High Priests vis-à-vis *'the Poor'*; cf. 1QpHabviii.11, xii.10, and CDvi.16.

[102] See *Ant.* 20.204–15 above.

[103] Cf. 1QpHabxii.2–10 above.

[104] Ananus crystallized his relationship with Agrippa II in Rome in the Early Fifties when Ananus and others had been sent to Rome in bonds and Agrippa intervened on his behalf both with Agrippina and Claudius; cf. *War* 2.241–46 and *Ant.* 20.125–34. This was in the wake of the Samaritan—Jewish disturbances when Quadratus *'crucified'* (at Lydda, as Pontius Pilate had done before him) and *'beheaded'* a good many individuals whom Cumanus (the previous Governor 48–52 CE) had imprisoned. Furthermore, on Agrippa's recommendation, Claudius banished Cumanus and sent the Tribune Celer—who had been involved in many of these bloody outrages—back to Jerusalem and *'delivered him over to the Jews'* to be tortured, paraded around the City, and finally beheaded (sound familiar?). We know the date for this must have been 52 CE, the date of Cumanus' removal and ten years before James' death. This was the date too for the beginning of Felix's Governorship.

[105] See *Ant.* 19.332–34 above.

[106] See *Ant.* 19.328–31

[107] See *War* 2.214–23 and *Ant.* 19.343–53.

[108] See *War* 2.426.

[109] 1QpHabix.5.

[110] (114) See *War* 2.409–413 above. It is here that Josephus starts talking about the charge preoccupying the Dead Sea Scrolls. *'pollution of the Temple.'*

[111] For the best treatment of the Slavonic Josephus, see Robert Eisler, *The Messiah Jesus and John the Baptist*, New York, 1931, pp. 113–82.

[112] *War* 7.312–15. There is very little that could be more self-serving or cynical than Josephus' interpretation of this *'Prophecy'* (except perhaps R. Yohanan's interpretation of it in Rabbinic literature—which is largely parallel).

[113] (118) *War* 7.288–300, displaying both the same cynicism but also the most humorous credulity.

[114] (118a) *War* 7.300–301.

[115] Matthew 9:15, 25:1–12, John 3:29–30, and *pars*. Also see Jeremiah 7:34 on '*bridegrooms*' and '*brides*,' etc.

[116] *War* 7.302–305.

[117] See Eisler, *The Messiah Jesus and John the Baptist*, pp. 113–82 above and the Penguin, *Jewish War*, 1959 Edition, tr. by G. A. Williamson, *Appendix on the Slavonic Josephus*, pp. 402–405.

[118] *War* 7.316. *N. b.*, how he follows this up with the descriptions of the spoils the Roman soldiers took from the Temple and how Titus put '*the Priests*' to death who, even though amid the carnage had surrendered, explaining that: '*as the time of pardon had passed*,' it was only fitting that '*Priests should perish with the House, to which they belonged.*' Little doubt about who destroyed the Temple here. For '*Yeter ha-ᶜAmim*,' see 1QpHabix.4–7, which describes this '*taking of spoils*' or '*plundering*,' refers to '*the Last Priest of Jerusalem*,' and identifies this term with '*the Army of the Kittim*' or '*Romans*'—it can be no other. For '*sacrificing to their standards and worshipping their weapons of war*,' see 1QpHabv.12–vi.11. There can be no other possible interpretation here too. Josephus also tells the story of a boy who tricked the Romans into giving him some water and then fled. These passages from Josephus (*War* 7.317–22) are among the most vivid and tragic of any period of History writing.

[119] For the Roman *Lex Cornelia de Sicarius et Veneficis*, which outlawed such procedures or practices, see *JBJ*, pp. 183–4, 814–6, and 922 and Chapter 28 below; also cf. Josephus, *Ant.* 20.34–48, on how Izates and his brother Monobazus were convinced to adopt the practice regardless of the teachings of Ananias and his companion (Paul?) and their mother's misgivings. This controversy, as we have seen, is also reported in Gen. R. 46.10. along with the very passage on which it was based and which Izates and his brother seem to have been reading, Genesis 17:11.

[120] See *Ant.* 20.17–20, 51–53, and 101–102.

[121] For the Syriac tradition on '*Judas the Zealot*' who parallels '*Judas of James*' and, therefore, '*Thaddaeus*'/'*Lebbaeus surnamed Thaddaeus*' in Synoptic Apostle Lists, see the two variant notices in *Apost. Const.* 8.25, which read: '*Thaddaeus, also called Lebbaeus, who was surnamed Judas the Zealot, preached the Truth to the Edessenes and the People of Mesopotamia when Abgarus ruled over Edessa and was buried at Berytus.*' It is also clear that this character parallels the character Josephus is calling '*Theudas*'—in the Second Apocalypse of James, '*Theuda the brother of the Just One.*' In the fragment that is attributed to '*Hippolytus on the Twelve Apostles*,' this is reproduced as '*Judas who is also called Lebbaeus preached the Truth to the People of Edessa* (*Aidesinous*, i.e., something to do with '*Addai*'/'ᵗ*Ad*'/or '*Adi*' as '*Adiabene*' probably does), etc., etc., and in the Latin document known as the *Epistula Apostolorum 2*, '*Judas Zelotes*' is also listed as one of the Eleven Apostles. Some have considered this a mistake for '*Simon Zelotes*,' but since neither '*Judas of James*' or '*Thaddaeus*'/'*Lebbaeus*' is anywhere mentioned, while '*Peter*' and '*Cephas*' are listed separately (i.e., the second probably meant to be '*Simeon bar Cleophas*' *cum* '*Simon the Zealot*'), this is probably not a mistake. Still, taken as a whole, the variant manuscripts of the Syriac *Apostolic Constitutions*, backed up to some extent by the above fragment attributed to Hippolytus, probably come closer to the truth of the situation than anything else. See my

discussion of the whole range of these kinds of complexities in *JBJ*, pp. 807–16, 853–82, and 930–8.

122 *War* 2.520.

123 Cf. Gen R. 46.10 and variously above and my full discussion of these kinds of correspondences in *JBJ*, pp. 883–922.

124 Cf. Strabo, *Geography* 17.1.54 with Pliny, *H.N.* 6.35. The latter—along with an assortment of other prejudices and burlesques—was probably Acts' source. It was very convenient to confuse *'the Queen of Sheba'* and *'Ethiopia'* with *'the Sabaean* Queen' or *'the Queen of Adiabene.'* She was only an *'Arab'* in any case. Plus her sons had—in a manner of speaking—*'castrated themselves'* anyhow and *they had fought against Rome!* No matter that they were martyrs! Josephus did tell us in *Ant.* 20.96 that he was going to tell us more about these things *'later'*; but he never did.

125 *Ant.* 18.118–19.

126 See *War* 2.418–19, 556–57, and *Ant.* 20.214.

127 Otherwise known as *'Philip the son of Jacimus.'* See *War* 2.421, 556, *Ant.* 17.30–31, and *Vita* 46. With *'Saulos and Costobarus,'* he is the intermediary between *'the Peace Party'* in Jerusalem and Cestius' Army outside it. He helps convince the Romans to come into the City and crush the Rebellion. In *Vita* 46–61, Josephus goes into great detail about this *'Philip'* (probably on the basis of information supplied to him by Agrippa II—whose friend he was). It turns out he also acted as a *'messenger'* or *'apostle'* of sorts (in Line 52, Josephus actually calls him an *'Apostle'*). As this is expressed by Josephus, he was one of *'the Twelve'* who was sent to their Jewish compatriots in Ecbatana (referred to by the adjective *'Babylonian,'* i.e., Babylon and Persia—Philip's family having originated there) to dissuade them from revolting against Rome. It even turns out *'Seventy'* others were required to go with them who are even called by Josephus *'the Seventy'*—i.e., *'the Seventy'* and *'the Twelve Apostles,'* *'Philip'* is always being confused with in Early Church texts—but these *'had no intention of seeking Innovations'* (thus)! Also see *Vita* 177–84 for more of Philip's story, which very much preoccupies Josephus, probably to exonerate him of certain charges of treason. It also even turns out, as we shall see below, that Philip has *'two daughters'* (cf. Acts 21:8–9's *'Philip the Evangelist who'* had *'four virgin daughters who were prophetesses'*—sic)! These are mentioned as having miraculously escaped Gamala when it was overrun, by hiding in a ravine when *'no other children were spared'* (thus!)—*War* 4.81–82.

128 Acts 20:15–17. It is here the narrator of the *'We Document'* explains that Paul *'was hurrying, so as to be in Jerusalem in time for Pentecost,'* which we now know from 4Q266 above was the time of the Reunion of *'all those in the Desert Camps'* under the Command of both *'the (High) Priest Commanding the Many'* or *'the Camps'* and/or *'the Mebakker'*—*'the Bishop.'*

129 Of course, as we have seen, the usage and allusion to *'Lying'* fairly permeates Qumran Literature—the most important of which being: CDi.14–15 about how *'the Man of Jesting poured out the waters of Lying over Israel'* and viii.13 about how *'the Windbag'* or *'Spouter of Lying spouted to them'*; 1QSiii.18–iv.11 on *'the Two Spirits'*—the second being *'of Wickedness and Lying,...Deceitfulness and duplicitousness'*; and finally in 1QpHabv.11–12 on *'the Man of Lying*

who rejected the Law in the midst of their whole Assembly' or 'Church' and x.9–11 on 'the Spouter of Lying who led Many astray,' 'tired out Many with a worthless Service,' and 'erected an Assembly' or 'Church upon Lying for the sake of his Glory'; etc.

130 *E.I.* 3.32.5–8. This testimony, which is attributed to Hegesippus, comes on the heels of the account of the crucifixion of Simeon bar Cleophas *'at the age of one hundred and twenty'*— seemingly during the Reign of Trajan during the disturbances in Egypt but more probably earlier during the persecutions under Domitian already delineated above.

131 Acts 6:5. Another name parallel is *'the Gate of Nicanor'* in the Temple, named after the gift by an important Rich overseas donor—cf. the various references to it in the *Talmud* (to say nothing of one of the enemy generals in the Maccabee Books, whose head was hung from the Citadel in 2 Macc 15:35–36 and who even had a Festival named for him, *'Nicanor's Day'*—the day apparently before *Purim*).

132 Cf. *War* 1.574–638, 2.14–92, *Ant.* 1.94 and 108, and variously.

133 See n. 127 above and *War* 2.421, 556, 4.81–82, *Ant.* 17.30–31, and *Vita* 46–61, 177–84, and 407–409. It is interesting that in these last notices, Philip is evidently under a cloud of some kind and Agrippa II with Vespasian's counsel is most anxious to have him go to Rome to give an account of what he had done to Nero. After this, like Saulos before him, he is heard of no more although, in his case, Josephus does mention that he returned to the King, having been unable to see Nero whose troubles were already well underway. The issue seems to have related to his improper surrender of Agrippa II's Palace in Jerusalem or, at least, his escape from there, along with Saulos and Costobarus, while Antipas was left behind; but the amount of time Josephus spends on Philip, evidently at Agrippa II's prompting and the ostentatious mention of Vespasian's intercession on his part, does betoke some concern relating to Philip's ultimate fate. It is interesting too that, as we saw above, Philip seems to have gone directly from Gamala after his escape from there to Ecbatana in Babylonian Persia for his *'Apostolic'* Mission to the Jews of the East—along with *'the Twelve'* and *'the Seventy'* above—to persuade them not to revolt against Rome and not to join their confederates in Galilee and Judea. At the same time, he seems to have left his *'daughters'* in Gamala (see our Plates nos. 102–3 below) to fend for themselves—or did he?

134 We have covered this in n. 127 above, but see *War* 4.54–82 where Josephus recounts some nine thousand perished, four thousand of whom slain outright by the Romans who *'did not even spare the children, many of whom were flung down by them from the citadel'*; cf. 1QpHab vi.10–1 on *'sacrificing to their standards and worshipping their weapons of war'* and *'the Kittim,'* who *'have no pity even on the fruit of the womb'*!

135 *Loc. cit.* As already noted, they seem to have been the only ones to have escaped. Curious. No wonder, Acts refers to their alter egos as *'prophetesses.'*

136 Cf. Galatians 2:10 with Romans 15:25–32 , 1 Corinthians 16:1–18, and 2 Corinthians 9:2–13, etc.

137 Cf. 4Q266.17–18 and *DSSU*, pp. 212–19 above.

138 *Ibid.*

139 CDvi.12–13 and 19–21.

140 Cf. CDvii.14–16 and viii.5–12 above with *Ant.* 20.206–207 and variously.

141 *Ant.* 20.206–14.

142 See, for instance, CDi.4, i.17, vii.13, and 1QMxi.13 above (in interpretation of *'the Star Prophecy'*) and variously.

143 Cf. 1QpHabviii.9–13 and ix.4–12 (including an allusion to *'delivered into the hand of'*) with *Ant.* 20.214.

144 1QpHabviii.11–13.

145 Cf. Ps. *Rec.* 7.9–10 and *Hom.* 12.8–17 and 14.6

146 See Eusebius, *E.I.* 3.39.9–10.

147 See *A.Z.* 27b–28a and Eccl. *R* 1.8.3–4 where Jacob comes to cure an individual known as *'Ben Dama'* (an obvious *nom-a-clef* for one or another worrisome individual of some kind; cf. *Ber* 56b) of snakebite. Also see *A.Z.* 16b for the main Jacob of Kfar Sechania story.

148 1QMxi.13 above.

Chapter 19

1 CDi.19.

2 All such *'casting down'* allusions should be compared with CDiv.15–7 on *'Belial casting down nets to deceive Israel'* and the corresponding material in Revelation 2:14 about *'Balaam teaching Balak (two 'B-L's here) to cast a net before the Sons of Israel to eat things sacrificed to idols* (the terms of James' Directives to Overseas Communities in Acts) *and commit fornication'* (also a part of these *Directives* and banned at Qumran, specifically here in the Damascus Document); and see my article in *DSSFC*: *'The final Proof that James and the Righteous Teacher are the Same'*, pp. 332–51.

3 Ps. *Rec.* 1.49–52.

4 *Ant.* 20.142.

5 *Ant.* 20.139–41 and cf. M. *Sot.* 6:8, where the actual passage being discussed is that found in the Temple Scroll, Deuteronomy 17:15: *'Thou shall not put a foreigner over you.'* As we have already seen, Agrippa I is so *'Pious'* that those assembled on the Temple Mount cry out; *'You are our brother, you are our brother, you are our brother'* three times.

6 See our Herodian Genealogy below. There, it should be appreciated, Agrippa I (Drusilla's father) is descended on his mother's side from the *'Costobarus'/'Salome'* (Herod's sister) or *'Idumaean'* side of the relationships (drawing us ever closer to *'Saulos,'* the *'Helcias'es/'*Temple Treasurer's, and *'Julius Archelaus.'* Of course, on his father's side, he is descended from the last Maccabean Princess (Herod's wife by coercion) Mariamme. It is here that the Rabbinic stricture that you are *'Jewish'* if your mother was *'Jewish'* probably developed; but it is doubtful if the *'purists'* at Qumran would have accepted such a tenuous connection. Even the Rabbinic groups would

have had to have been given pause by Agrippa I's mother—to say nothing of both Drusilla's mother and grandmother. In any event, as Josephus attests, once her father was dead, '*Judaism*', as it were, seems to have hung very lightly on her shoulders.

7 11QIvii.15–9. This continues from the quotation of the Deuteronomic King Law (17:15) in 11QIvi.13–5. The first to have really called attention to the importance of this notation to Second Temple history was Robert Eisler. If he could have seen the Temple Scroll, he would have been very excited. Of course, one should also note 11QIxvi.8–17, where the Scroll breaks off.

8 See *Ant.* 18.253–6, 20.145–6, and *Vita* 119. Note that Bernice's first marriage in *Ant.* 19.276–77 was to Marcus, the son of Alexander the Alabarch of Alexandria (and probably Philo's nephew), the Richest man in Alexandria. Note, too, that in *War* 2.183, Josephus tells us Herodias and Herod the Tetrarch were banished to Spain—whereas in *Ant.* 18.252, he says that they were banished to Lyons in Gaul.

9 See *Ant.* 19.363–65, 20.173–84, and cf. *War* 2.457–93. Also note how in *Ant.* 19.355–59, the inhabitants of this city even go so far as to rape Agrippa I's still virginal daughters, when they were only girls, after his death.

10 *Ant.* 20.197–215. The sequentiality here is of the utmost importance and even parallels that in Acts 20 years earlier of Stephen to Saulos. Here in the *Antiquities* it goes James to the riots and finally to the enumeration of the last Priest of Jerusalem. This—including the ending here in the *Antiquities*—is all very curious.

11 *Vita* 13–6. Note Josephus begins this excursus on his trip to Rome on behalf of some priests who were sent there by Felix and who would '*eat nothing but dates and nuts*' by saying he '*had completed his twenty-sixth year*'—meaning it was approximately 61–63 CE, just around the time of James' stoning. It would be also be well to add that this was also approximately the time Paul made his first plea to go to Rome—also just following the end of Felix's Governorship. These link-ups are curious indeed.

12 *Vita* 16. It was not long after this that Nero kicked his wife to death when she was pregnant, whether in Dio Cassius' words in 62.28.1, '*by accident or design*.' One always harbours the niggling suspicion that this child might have been Josephus,' since he describes how well-received he was by Poppea and it is not clear when he finally left Rome. Only that he was back to Jerusalem in time to witness the events culminating in the Revolt against Rome.

13(12a) *Vita* 13. As usual, these are 'certain Priests.' In addition the '*Piety of their practices*' is noted and, it should not be forgotten that under the Essene '*Piety to God*,' i.e., the First '*Love*' Commandment, just such practices are noted. It should be noted that many individuals were sent to Rome at this time to plead their cause before Caesar, including the High Priests Ananus and Ishmael ben Phiabi and the Temple Treasurer Helcias—the last two of whom Josephus actually notes in *Ant.* 20.189–96 stayed with Poppea in her own house. Our warrant is to try to figure out what the disturbance was that was causing all this disruptions and '*the Temple Wall Affair*' seems to fit all the parameters.

[14] *Vita* 13.

[15] As we saw, in *Vita* 364–67, Agrippa II is described by Josephus as writing some sixty-two letters attesting to his veracity and adding to his information in between the writing of the two works, several passages from which Josephus actually quotes.

16 We note in Acts 25:9–26:32, Paul's appeal to Caesar occurs in the presence of Festus around 61 CE and in the company of Agrippa II and Bernice—both of whom are present. In *Ant.* 20.214, the riot led by '*Saulos and Costobarus*' some 3–4 years later at the end of Albinus' Governorship when Gessius Florus was on the way to succeed him.

[17] Cf John 12:10–11 with the more extensive '*plotting*' preceding it in John 11:45–54, the duplication of which shows how tendentious these accounts generally are.

[18] See, for instance, the allusion to '*joining*'/'*Joiners*' (in Esther, as we have seen, an expression for '*Gentile Converts*') in CDiv.3—in esoteric exposition of '*Levi'im*'/'*Levites*' in Ezekiel 44:15—and 4QpNahiii.8 and iv.5, with generally the same meaning of '*convert*' or, in the case of '*Ephraim*' perhaps, those backsliders who have since come back to Judaism. One should also note '*the Joiners in the War of* ' of the last decipherable line of *The Paean for King Jonathan* (4Q448) in *DSSU*, pp. 273–81 and '*joining*' Christ's body in 1 Corinthians 6:16–17 banning '*fornication*.'

[19] Cf. Acts 6:11 with *E.I.* 2.23.16–25 and *pars*. The unexplained '*stoning*' (the penalty for '*blasphemy*') is the same in both cases, but the '*why*' is not clear. Moreover, in '*Stephen*''s case—despite the somewhat '*fuzzy*' picture of him in Acts—'*Stephen*' can hardly be reckoned a '*Jew*,' so why the stoning? One should also note the '*blasphemy*' charge depicted against '*Jesus*' in John 10:31–39, introducing the two passages about '*the Jews plotting*' against both '*Jesus*' and '*Lazarus*' in Chapter 11, just noted above. Here the writer obviously understands more about the '*blasphemy*' charge and thinks it has to do with '*claiming to be the Christ*' or '*Son of God*' (very Pauline), though '*Jesus*' corrects them with the claim—as at Qumran and elsewhere—of multiple sons.

[20] Here it is the Jews who are '*blaspheming*' while Paul and the Gentile Christians, he represents, are presumably doing just the opposite. One should also note the repetitive picture in Acts 13:45–50, 14:19, 17:4 (including the word '*joined*' again), 17:10–13, etc.

[21] See *War* 3.536–41 and cf. Suetonius 6.19 on '*Nero*.'

[22(25)] *Ant.* 1.8–9. Despite much scholarly controversy over this, Epaphroditus was executed in approximately 95–96 CE (see Suetonius 8.14.4 on '*Domitian*' and cf. 6.49.4 on '*Nero*') in the same upheavals which seem to have taken the life of Flavius Clemens ('*Clement*') and probably Josephus himself—this, despite the fact, that some think Josephus (and therefore a second '*Epaphroditus*') lived into the Second Century and Trajan's time—an unlikely proposition. It is for this reason, it is possible to conclude that Paul's '*Epaphroditus*,' who has entrance into Nero's Household, and Josephus' '*Epaphroditus*' are identical.

[23] Despite the seemingly mutually-exclusive references to '*Timothy*' and '*Titus*' in 2 Timothy 1:2 and 4:10, it is difficult to escape the impression that both are the same person. *N.b.*, also, the reference to '*Epaphras*' in Philemon 1:23.

24 Cf. *War* 2.227 with *Ant.* 20.112. The former gives the figure of either *'ten'* or *'thirty thousand'* depending on the redaction; the latter, *'twenty thousand.'*

25 *War* 2.223–24/*Ant.* 20.108. Interestingly, the latter actually calls this *'a blasphemy against God.'*

26 It should be appreciated that the *Homilies*, which came down through the Greek, begins with the Letters from Peter and Clement to James—the latter in Chapter 20—explaining that all that follows are the reports of Clement to James. The whole of Book One of the *Recognitions*, which came down through the Latin and the Syriac and contains the meeting with James and the attack on him by Paul, is missing from the *Homilies*; while the Peter and Clement Letters are missing from the *Recognitions*.

27 *War* 2.228–31 and *Ant.* 20.113.

28 See *E. H.* 2.1.1–2 and 23.5 and *pars.* .

29 See Ps. Rec. 1.72–3, where James sends out Peter from somewhere outside of Jericho on his first 'Missionary' journey to stay at the house of one Zacchaeus and confront Simon Magus in Caesarea (note that in Luke 19:2–8, Zacchaeus is *'a little man,' 'a tax-collector,'* who shimmies up a Sycamore Tree as 'Jesus' is passing through Jericho and invites him to stay at his house— a very curious parallel). In Josephus (*Ant.* 20.142), the *'Cypriot magician'*, he calls *'Simon'* or *'Atomus'*, is presumably also in Caesarea where he persuades Drusilla to divorce her previous husband Azizus—who had specifically circumcised himself to marry her in deference to her father Agrippa I's wishes—and marry Felix.

30 For this squabbling between Greeks and Jews, see notes 9 and 10 above (*Ant.* 19.357–65, 20.173–84, and cf. *War* 2.457–93). For Samaritans and Jews, see *Ant.* 20.118–36.

31 *Ant.* 20.124 and cf. *War* 2.238.

32 *Ant.* 20.127 and cf. *War* 2.232–46.

33 For Petronius (later the author of the *Satyricon*), see *War* 2.185–203 and *Ant.* 18.209–61; for Cestius, see *War* 1.20–21 and 2.280–364 and cf. Quadratus—the base of whose Governorship was Antioch in Syria—here in *War* 2.238–46 and *Ant.* 20.125–36.

34 Cf. *War* 2.239–44 with *Ant.* 20.130–31. For Tacitus' comment, see *Annals* 12.54.

35. See n. 25 in Chapter Seven above and *San.* 32a. For how the sages led by R. Akiba brought R. Eliezer's body back to Lydda, see ARN 25.3 (27a); also see Lam R. 1.5.31 on R. Eliezer and R. Judah going back into Jerusalem to take R. Zadok out via the Gate to Lydda at Vespasian's bidding (*sic!*) and *Suk.* 2b–3a/*Tos. Suk.* 1:1 on the construction of Queen Helen's giant *Sukkah* there.

36 See *Ant.* 20.130 above and *War* 2.241. Also, for the various crucifixions at Lydda in Talmudic tradition, see *JBJ*, pp. 494–97 and 1018 and *Suk.* 52a–52b, which considers that *'the Messiah ben Joseph'*—probably the Samaritan Messiah—who was supposed to precede *'the Messiah ben Judah'* (the Judean one) was crucified there. Also, another curious *nom-a-clef* (probably for 'Jesus' or 'Simon Magus'), *'Ben Stada,'* is mentioned in *San.* 67a—cf. *San.* 43a and *Shab.* 104b, which says he brought *'magic from Egypt'*—as having been crucified there. For more on *'the martyrs at Lydda,'* see *B.B.* 10b and *Pes.* 50a.

[37] See Chapter 4 above on the Samaritan *'Messiah'* or *'Taheb'* and Acts 9:32–43 on how Peter meets all *'the Saints that lived at Lydda'*, just prior to his *'tablecloth vision'*, in 10:1–32, among whom are *'Dorcas'* a.k.a. *'Tabitha'*—a woman whom, quite naturally, he raises from the dead! In any event, *'Ben Stada'* is probably another corruption of *'the Standing One'* and one should note that for the Pseudoclementines (*Rec.* 2.7–12 and *Hom.* 2.17–32), *'Dositheus'* (i.e., *'Doetus'*) is a Samaritan Disciple with Simon Magus of John the Baptist. For Josephus, though the *'Doetus'* who is executed here at Lydda by Quadratus is a Samaritan, he is *'a Leader of the Jews'* (thus!). Curiously enough, in *War* 4.145–46, Josephus identifies another individual, *'John the son of Dorcas'* (i.e., *'Doetus'*) as the *'Zealot'* assassin who creeps into the Temple prison and assassinates Saulos' and Costobarus' kinsman, Antipas, the Temple Treasurer who is awaiting trial as a *'Traitor'* preceding the murders of James' executioner Ananus ben Ananus and Josephus colleague Jesus ben Gamala that follow. For Justin Martyr, a Samaritan himself, in the early Second Century, *'the Sotadists'* are definitely related in 2 Apology 14–15 in some way to the Samaritan Simon *Magus*. Further, one cannot go but, as we have noted, *'Tabitha'* is definitely a variation on *'Tirathaba'*, the location of the activities and Pontius Pilate's subsequent crucifixion of the Samaritan *'Taheb'*, as described by Josephus *Ant.* 18.87–89. Nor, can there be any doubt, that *'Dositheus'* is in some manner a Samaritan.

[38] See *War* 2.225–49 and *Ant.* 20.115–38 above. The point is that in *Ant.* 20.142–43 *'Simon'* or *'Atomus'* (i.e., *'the Primal Adam'*) is a *'magician'*, who convinces Drusilla to marry Felix, while at the same time one can hypothesize that he was the *'Samaritan who informed'* Quadratus in Lydda that the instigators of the Jewish mob against the Romans there were *'Doetus together with four other Religious Innovators'* or *'Revolutionaries.'*

[39] See Chapters 1 and 9 above.

[40] Cf. Acts 11:19–26 with Ps. *Rec.* 1.70–71.

[41] See *Ant.* 20.51 and 101, which make it clear that Helen spent large sums of money to send her treasury agents to Egypt and Cyprus to purchase grain and dried figs to relieve the Famine in Jerusalem. It is Helen who comes up to Jerusalem, not necessarily Paul—but Paul may have accompanied her as the merchant Ananias, who got in among her husband's harem to convert her, might have done.

[42] Cf. 1QSviii.20–25.

[43] Since he is speaking mainly about *'circumcision'* in many of these passages, it can be assumed this is what he means. But cf. 1QpHabxi.2–15, where the subject is Habakkuk 2:15 *'spying on their Festivals'* but which in the received Habakkuk is *'spying on their privy parts'* (*me*^{c}*oreihem'* vs. *'me*^{c}*odeihem'*—very similar spellings in Hebrew) and ends up with the assertion that *'the Wicked Priest did not circumcise the foreskin of his heart'* and that in the end he would drink from *'the Cup of the Right Hand of the Lord.'* One should also note that in 1QpHabxi.8–9, quoting Habakkuk 2:16, the words: *'Drink also and stagger'*, are substituted for the received version, *'Let your foreskin be uncovered'*—which, however, as we just saw, is picked up in the exegesis in 1QpHabxi.13. These substitutions and transformations are too insistent to be accidental; see my article *'Interpreting Abeit-Galuto in the Habakkuk Pesher: Playing on and Transmuting*

Terms,' DSSFC, pp. 247–71.

[44] See, for instance Galatians 4:11–5:12 where he is making just these sorts of complaints and ends up with an expletive about *'circumcision.'*

[45] Jerome, *Vir. ill.* 2.

[46] 1QpHabxi.8–15.

[47] Ps. *Hom.* 11.15.

[48] 1QpHabxi.13 above.

[49] See CDiii.5–12 (giving the eschatological picture of the History of Israel) and 1QSi.2, ii.13–18, iv.9–14, etc.

[50] For this kind of *'building'* imagery and *'puffed up'* language in the Habakkuk *Pesher*, see x.9–12 on *'the Worthless City,'* the Spouter of Lying *'builds upon blood'* and *'the Church,'* he *'erects upon Lying'*; and vii.14–viii.15 on Habakkuk 2:4, introducing the all-important *'the Righteous shall live by his Faith,' 'Behold his soul is puffed up and not Upright within him'* which ends with how the Wicked Priest's *'heart became puffed up and he deserted God and betrayed the Laws for the sake of Riches'* and how *'the sins'* of persons like him (presumably meant to include *'the Spouter of Lying'/'Liar'*) *'would be doubled upon them and they would not be pleased with their Judgement.'*

Chapter 20

[1] Cf. *inter alia*, 1QMxi.7–14, in interpretation of *'the Star Prophecy'* of Numbers 24:17–19, referring to God's *'hands'* (plural), *'the hands of the Messiahs'* (interpreted in terms of *'the Seers of Your/God's Testimonies*—presumably *'the Prophets'*), *'the hand of the Poor One'* (Ebion—singular), *'Yours (God's) hand'* (singular), and *'the hands of the Poor'* (Ebionim—plural), in the context of the language very much resembling that of John the Baptist in Matthew of *'setting a flame like a torch of fire in the straw until all Evil is devoured'*; and *'the Visitation for their Punishments'* and *'Reward'* by *'His (God's) hand'* and *'the hand of the Prince of Lights...and that of the Angel of Darkness'* in 1QSiii.14–21.

[2] 1QpHabx.9–12 above.

[3] Cf. 1QpHabxi.12–xii.12.

[4] See 1QpHabviii.9–x.5 and xi.12–xii.12 above, CDiii.21–iv.7, v. 7–15, vi.11, viii.4–19, etc.

[5] Cf. 1 Corinthians 12:20 and 2 Corinthians 5:1.

[6] Of course, the same language permeates the Dead Sea Scrolls; cf., in particular, 1QpHabviii.9–x.5 and xi.12–xii.12 and CDiii.21–iv.7, v.6–15, vi.11–vii.4, and viii.3–12, etc. above. Also cf. 1 Corinthians 4:18, 6:11, 8:7, 10:7–9, 12:28, etc.

[7] Cf. Acts 21:28, 1 Corinthians 3:9–17, and 2 Corinthians 7:1 (including the language of *'Perfecting Holiness in the fear of God'* also found in the Damascus Document) with 4QMMTii.2–23.

[8] 1QpHabx.9–13.

[9] For others like J. Murphy-O'Connor in *The New Jerome Biblical Commentary*, 1990, pp. 826–27, these are the so-called *'Judaizers'* (*sic*—a derogatory euphemism if there ever was one); for

The New English Bible of Oxford University, they are *'the Jewish Christians'*—a more neutral euphemism—whatever this might mean.

[10] That James required *'written authorizations'* or *'credentials,'* much like modern Rabbinical *'smichut,'* is made quite clear in Ps. *Hom.* 11.35, echoed in Ps. *Rec.* 4.35. But also see *The Epistle of Clement to James* 20 and variously—in particular, Paul own view of *'written credentials'* in 2 Corinthians 3:1–11, comparing them to the two Tablets on Sinai, which he characterizes as *'the Ministry of Condemnation'* as opposed to his own *'Ministry of the Spirit in Glory.'* Cf., too, 2 Corinthians 5:11–12 and 10:8–18 above, where he begins his *'boasting'* and condemns those *'who recommend themselves'* or *'write their own letters of recommendation.'* Note here, too, the *'works'/'labor'* dichotomy, also extent at Qumran in 1QpHabx.9–13 above—*'labor'* for *'the Liar'* and *'works'* for *'the Righteous Teacher.'*

[11] Cf., where all these *'coming down's* to Antioch in Acts are concerned, n.b., Acts 11:27–8 where it is *'prophets'* who are *'coming down from Jerusalem to Antioch.'* In Acts 13:1 *'there were in the Assembly which was in Antioch certain prophets and teachers.'* Regardless of whom such *'prophets and teachers'* could have been thought of as being, there is no doubt that the *'some'* or *'certain ones'* who are *'coming down from Judea'* in 15:1 (should one read here rather *'from James'?*) and *'teaching the brothers'* are the representatives of the author of precisely these kinds of *'letters of authorization'* or *'recommendations'* as we have been explaining.

[12] 1QpHabviii.1–3 in interpretation of the all-important Habakkuk 2:4. That it is eschatological is made clear from all that precedes it in 1QpHabvii.2–16, where the whole subject is *'the Last Generation,' 'the End,' 'the Last Age,' 'the Time of the End,'* and the *'Judgement.'* For more on *'the Day of Judgement'* and *'the Last Days,'* see ix.6, xii.14–xiii.4, CDiv.4.4, etc.

[13] See Josephus' description in *War* 2.143–44. Here the word Josephus uses, as we have seen, is *'ekballonsi.'*

[14] For *'the Enemy'* in the Pseudoclementines, see Ps. *Rec.* 1.71 and *The Epistle of Peter to James* 2; in Matthew, see the anti-Pauline *'Parable of the Tears'* (13:25–39) and, in the Letter of James, see 4:4. For the *'Zealots for the Law'* as the followers of James *par excellence,* see Acts 21:20.

[15] CDiii.6–7 and 9–11. Also see xix.25–26.

[16] It will be recalled that for *'Jesus'* in the Gospels, this is expressed in terms of the famous *'not one jot or tittle shall disappear from the Law until all these things are accomplished'*—whatever might be meant by *'being accomplished'*—see Matthew 5:18/Luke 16:17. In the Habakkuk *Pesher,* this *'stumbling'* idea is reflected in xi.6–8.

[17] *Ant.* 20.38–46 and Gen. *R.* 46.10 on Genesis 17:11.

[18] 1QpHabvii.11 (on Habakkuk 2:3–2:4), viii.1, and xii.4–5. For the same idea in CD (*'doing according to the precise letter of the Torah'*), see iv.8. For being a *'Doer'* in James, see 1:22–26 and 2:13.

[19] Cf. 1QpHabx.9–12 above.

[20] The point here is that Paul seems consciously to avoid the term *'Jew'* or *'Jewish'* where it relates to himself. He does speak in Galatians 1:13–14 of *'being advanced in the practice of Judaism'*—a

new term, which he seems to have been one of the first, if not the first, to coin and where he does actually use the term *'race'*/*'genous'* again, but again not *'Judah'* or *'Jew'*—rather unspecified.

21 See *JBJ*, pp. 502–15 and 653–56 and see Chapters 14-15 above.

22 Cf. CDiv.11 and 1QpHabviii.1

23 Genesis 36:32–33 and 46:21; cf. Numbers 26:38–40 and 1 Chronicles 1:43–44, 7:6–7, and 8:1–3.

24 The point is that *'being of the Tribe of Benjamin'* is an Israelite notation while *'being an Edomite'* or *'Idumaean'* is an *'Hebraic'* one—so Paul ingeniously makes use of both—but the unique Biblical commonality might have been what made it all possible. While the spelling in Genesis 46:21 is slightly different than in 36:32, still that in 1 Chronicles 7:6 and 8:1 is the same. Interestingly enough, there is even another *'Bela^c'* listed as a descendant of Reuben in 1 Chronicles 5:8.

25 If one wanted to be cruel or deprecating here, one could substitute the euphemism *'Judaizers'*, as some above prefer to do, or even the more neutral *'Jewish Christians'*; but those in Jerusalem at this time—the *'some from James'* of Galatians 2:12 below—certainly had no knowledge as yet that they were to be called *'Christians'* and all of this language reflects the new attitude of the Pauline *'Gentile Mission'* or, of what we we would now call, *'Pauline Christianity'*, and is retrospective. *'The Jerusalem Assembly'* is more appropriate or 4QpPs 37's *'the Assembly of the Poor'.*

26 There is no comparable work found at Qumran, unless it be the Temple Scroll or even *MMT* which are compendiums of re-arranged Old Testament passages on various subjects, as Qumran is firmly against *'Traditions'*—clearly, against even *'Traditions of the Fathers'*—as the parody in CDi.18 and variously of *'Seekers after Halakot'* or *'Smooth Things'* for *'Halachot'* makes plain.

27 We have already discussed the *'Enemy'* terminology of Ps. Rec. 1.71, *The Epistle of Peter to James* 3, Matthew 13:25–39, and James 4:4 above. For the *'Zealots for the Law'* as the followers of James *par excellence*, see Acts 21:20.

28(29) CDxx.17. There is certainly a disconnect here.

29 For verification of this, see Romans 4:1–16, 9:7, Galatians 3:6–29, 4:28, and 2 Corinthians 11:22, as well as Paul's purported speech in Antioch of Pisidia in Acts 13:26 which uses both the *'Genous'* and the *'fearing God'* terminologies—to say nothing of the *'Salvation'* one.

30 CDi.14–16.

31 *War* 2.143–44 and see my reference to Josephus' use of the same term, *'ekballonsi,'* n. 13 above. We have covered the use of this *'casting out'* language in all of my work over the last fifteen years but, particularly, in *'The final Proof that James and the Righteous Teacher are the Same,'* DSSFC, pp. 332–51 (first given to the Society of Biblical Literature in Chicago in 1994) and *JBJ*, pp. 219–25, 505–509, and 710–59

32 This *'slavery'* and *'attachment to the flesh'* imagery of Paul is a favorite one—see, for instance, Romans 1:3, 7:1–9:8, 11:14, 13:1–15, 1 Corinthians 10:18, 2 Corinthians 11:18–24, Galatians 1:16 (definitely pointing to *'the First'* or *'Super Apostles'*), 6:8–13 (he writes it *'in large letters'*

worthy of Goebbels), Philippians 3:2(*'look out for dogs'*)–6, etc.

33 Note 1QpHabvi.7 and see, for instance, 2 Corinthians 11:20 above. For the *'Belial'*/*'Bela^c'*/ *'Balaam'* allusions, see CDiv.14–17, 1QHiv.10, and variously at Qumran, Revelations 2:14, 2 Peter 2:15, and Jude 1:11, and 11QTxlvi.10 above.

34 See 1QpHabv.12–vi.11 above.

35 1QpHabxi.15–xii.10.

36 See in general, *San.* 105a–106b.

37 Cf. CDiv.18–20, viii.13, 1QpHabx.9–15, 1QSiv.9–11, etc.

38 Cf., for instance 1QSix.22–25 and 1QpHabx.9–12.

39 See, for instance, how *'the Jews'* seem to persecute *'Jesus'* as if he were not Jewish in John 1:19, 5:16–18, 6:52–7:11, 8:48–57, and variously. The same for *'Stephen'* in Acts 6:1–7:60 or, for that matter, Paul in Acts 9:22–23.

40 See, for instance, *The Epistle of Peter to James* at the beginning of the *Homilies* 2–5.

41 1QSii.22–5.

42 See below at the end of this Chapter and 11QTlxiv.9–11.

43 The actual word Deuteronomy 21:23 uses is *'tetamme'*/*'to be polluted,'* an expression so widespread at Qumran it would be hard to catalogue all its occurrences/derivatives.

44 4QpNahii.7–8.

45 See John Allegro in *DJDv—Qumran Cave IV—4Q158–4Q186*, Oxford, 1958, whose reconstruction it originally was, and F. G. Martinez in *The Dead Sea Scrolls Study Edition*, Leiden, 1997, i, p. 337. But see Vermes in *The Complete Dead Sea Scrolls in English* (revised edition), New York, 2004, p. 505, who (always temporizing) leaves out the reconstructed phrase *'a thing not done'*—though in previous editions he had included it.

46 See *War* 1.97–98 and *Ant.* 13.380–81.

47 See Vita 420–21, War 2.308, 5.449–51, 7.17, and Appian, *Civil Wars* 1.116–20, Plutarch, *The Fall of the Roman Republic*, 8.1–2 on Pompey referring to this Crassus, and Seneca in *The Dialog to Marcia on Consolation* 6.20.3. Actually the events during the Spartacus Uprising appear to have been even closer to those during Alexander Jannaeus' reign—c. 71 BC; and the individual involved in its brutality, the Roman plutocrat Crassus, later followed this up in Judea—succeeding Pompey's lieutenant Gabinius there—where he proceeded to do what even Pompey had not done, *'taking away all the rest of the gold belonging to the Temple* (Josephus reckons this as *'two thousand talents which Pompey had not touched'*—sic!) *in order to outfit his Persian Expedition'* where, in fact, he was killed—see *War* 1.179.

48 See, for instance, how John 19:31–33 understands this. Josephus, too, explains this as a kind of Jewish *'scrupulousness in the matter of the burial of the dead'* to emphasize in his description of the brutalities inflicted upon the corpses of the High Priest Ananus ben Ananus and his friend Jesus ben Gamala by *'the Zealots and Idumaeans'* in *War* 4.314–52 (specifically 4.317) and even uses the Temple Scroll's language of *'pollution'* in describing in 4.323 how, because of these things, *'God had condemned (Jerusalem) to destruction as a polluted City and resolved to*

purge His Temple by fire'—chilling words anticipating and justifying Titus' final actions against the City two years later!

[49] 11QTlxiv.7.

[50] There is no way to avoid this conclusion as this is certainly not the point of Deuteronomy 21:22–23, which only speaks generally about '*a man who commits a sin worthy of death*' and, here too, the point is specifically made that he is '*put to death*' first and only afterwards his body is to be '*hung upon a tree*,' clearly in some exemplary manner, to display to others the heinousness of his crime. Again, the point is specifically made that the '*pollution*' has to do with '*his body remaining all night upon the tree*', not the act of '*hanging*' itself, which is recommended as long—it seems—as the body is already dead. Once again, the Gospels seem to have this wrong—as the portrayal there, in the words of John 19:31 and *pars.*, has to do with how for '*the Jews, because it was the Eve of the Preparation, the bodies should not remain on the cross upon the Sabbath for the day of the Sabbath is a Holy Day.*' Again, this was not the point of '*the breaking of the legs*' for the vast majority of the Jews—though perhaps it was for the Romans. Who knows? Moreover, this point seems to have '*bled into*' the portrayal of (or *vice versa*) both the attack on James by Paul in Ps. *Rec.* 1.71–72 and his stoning according to the account by Jerome in *Vir. ill.* 2, in which he '*had broken*' either one or both '*his legs*'! That in the Temple Scroll, the charges are made more specific than in any other context—namely spying on or betraying your People to foreign power and, what is even more interesting, committing a capital offence and escaping to a foreign country and thereafter cursing your People or the Children of Israel—bespeaks a very different political situation, one mainly having to do with Dominion or impending Dominion by foreign powers.

[51] See Y. Yadin, who originally published it, in *The Temple Scroll*, Oxford, 1983, p. 362, F. Garcia Martinez in *Near Eastern Archaeology*, 2000 on the Temple Scroll, p. 172, and B. Z. Wacholder, *The Dawn of Qumran: The Sectarian Torah and the Teacher of Righteousness*, Cincinnati, 1983, pp. 1–9.

[52] Both of these situations, as described—however tendentiously—in Acts, certainly involve either fleeing abroad to escape charges of some kind—the first perhaps even causing someone's death and the second appealing to foreign power to save oneself from charges involving either sacrilege, betraying others to death, slandering one's own People, and even perhaps idolatry or blasphemy.

[53] See n. 43 above and John 19:31–33 and *pars.* and *War* 4.317, all of which (as we have seen) focus, however tendentiously, on the issue of not leaving '*the body on the tree overnight.*' But what is riveting here is that the Temple Scroll, lxiv.7–9, is actually different from Deuteronomy 21:22–23 and lists crimes for which it is appropriate to '*hang (a man) alive upon a tree until he dies*' (here again the caveat is that '*the corpse shall not spend the night upon the tree*')—namely, '*fleeing to the Gentiles*' to escape an appropriate death sentence, '*cursing*' one's own People and '*the Children of Israel*' (with some justice, one could in fact describe both Paul and Josephus in this manner), and treacherous activities like '*slander*' and '*betrayal*'—all particularly appropriate to Judea in the mid-First Century (more internal dating parameters).

⁵⁴ 11QTlxiv.7–13.

⁵⁵ See the antagonism to backsliders, turncoats, traitors, and the like in 1 Macc 1:12–16, 1:36–38, 1:44–56, 3:5–7, etc. and 2 Macc 4:33–35, 5:15–16, 6:1–9, 14:3–14, etc.

⁵⁶ Josephus' self-justifications in the *Vita* are numerous—see, in particular, *Vita* 62–79, 82–113, 336–367, 414–30, etc.

⁵⁷ See *War* 4.335–43 above. It is hard to think that the author of Luke has not mixed up these two characters with such similar sounding names, nor that the precision involved in making such an assertion existed concerning the Prophet Zechariah.

⁵⁸ We have already discussed Saulos, Costobarus, and Antipas above but Antipas, in particular, was executed by this combination of the Zealots and the Idumaeans just as Ananus, Jesus ben Gamala, and Zechariah ben Barachias were (and, even seemingly, later *'Niger of Perea,'* though it is not at all clear that he was considered Jewish and not simply Idumaean). Cf. *War* 2.418, 556–57, 4.140–46, 314–18, 359–63, and *Ant.* 20.214.

⁵⁹ 11QTlxiv.12. Though the expression *'he that is hanged is the accursed of God'* is found in the Septuagint and most Biblical redaction, the general thrust has to do with the act of *'putting him to death'* which precedes the exemplary exhibition of *'hanging him upon a tree'* and in most Biblical redaction the phraseology *'upon a tree'* is missing at this point in relation to *'the accursed of God.'* The emphasis, therefore, is appreciatively different. In the Temple Scroll, Paul, and, by implication, the Gospel of John however the emphasis shifts to the pivotal *'hanging alive upon a tree'* (seemingly in accord with the tenor of the times)—a phraseology just not found as such in received Biblical writ except here, as just noted, in the Temple Scroll. It is clearly this, therefore, that Paul is playing off as his *'Christ Jesus'* is certainly for him someone *'hung live upon a tree.'* On the other handonce again, for John and, by implication, the other Gospels, their author or authors show their total ignorance of the real parameters of existence in Palestine and demonstrate that they are working off sources—largely second or even third-hand—since they misunderstand that the hurry to get the *'crucified ones'* down *'from the tree'* has nothing *per se* whatever to do with the coming *'Sabbath'* or *'Feast Day'*—whether Passover or some other— but rather the general Commandment, reiterated in all sources, that the body whether dead at the time of the exemplary *'hanging'* or *'hung up alive,'* according to later Roman practice, could not remain *'upon the tree overnight'*—as it was this that was the affront to the God of Israel and *'polluted the Land',* weekday or Festival Day.

⁶⁰ See *Septuagint* Deuteronomy 21:22. For Paul, this reads approximately: *'Cursed (is) everyone hung upon a tree'* while here in the Septuagint it reads: *'for everyone that is hung upon a tree is the cursed of God'* or *'Cursed is everyone that is hung upon a tree by God'*—not a precise fit. Moreover, it follows the caveat that the malefactor has already *'been put to death'* and must, therefore be taken down before sunset so as not to *'pollute the land.'*

⁶¹ These words are to be found in Galatians 3:10 and precede the quotation of Habakkuk 2:4: *'the Righteous shall live by Faith'* (not *'his Faith'*) in Galatians 3:11—the difference having to do with *'epikatapatos'* as opposed to *'kekatepamenos.'* The Septuagint reads, *'Cursed is every man*

that continues not in all the words of this law to do them' and does not contain the word *'Biblio'* or 'Book' which, interestingly enough, Paul uses. For the way the Temple Scroll renders this, see lxiv.12 above. Interestingly enough, in addition to Deuteronomy's *'of God'* above, it adds as well *'and of men'* (plural).

[62] See, for instance, the kind of phraseology he sets forth in 2 Corinthians 6:14–7:2. Not only does he know the *'Light'* vs. *'Darkness'* imagery, so much in evidence at Qumran; but also that of *'the Perfection of Holiness'* of the Damascus Document—to say nothing of *'so come out from among them and be separate'* of the Community Rule and *'touch nothing that is unclean'* and *'and I will be a Father to you and you will be sons and daughters to Me'* of Hymns. There is much more, including *'the Servants of Righteousness'* of 11:15.

[63] See, for instance, his comments in *War Preface* 1.11–12 and *Against Apion* 38–46, 82–124, and 271–96.

[64] See, for instance, 1QSi.15–18 and note how the *'cursing'* begins in ii.4–9 and 11–18 and continues. *N.b.,* the same expression, *'not deviating to either the right or the left'* from *'the Covenant of our Ancestors'* or *'the Law and its observances'* occurs in 1 Macc 2:21–22 above.

[65] This was the whole reason of our request to John Strugnell in 1989 to see the unpublished fragments of the Dead Sea Scrolls—in particular, those of the Damascus Document—to compare them with the extant work in the Cairo Genizah. Thereafter Michael Wise and myself published this all-important fragment—which was clearly the Final Column of the Damascus Document—in DSSU, pp. 218–19. My commentary on it—which includes many of the points being made here—is to be found on pp. 212–18 of that volume and the particular passage being referred to here is what is now referred to as 4QD266, Lines 13–18. One should also compare this to the picture in Acts 20:16ff. of Paul hurrying to get to Jerusalem with his contributions in time for *'Pentecost,'* i.e., the time of the Reunion of the *'Inhabitants of the Desert Camps.'* One should note that the allusion here to *'breaking the boundary markers'* recalls and recapitulates the First Column of CD which also refers to both *'removing the boundary markers'*—which seems to have been the hallmark of *'the Lying Spouter'*—and *'delivering them up to the Avenging Sword of Vengeance of the Covenant'* and *'calling down on them the curses of His Covenant'* (CDi.16–18)

[66] 4QD266, Lines 4–5—possibly a loose quotation of Joel 2:12. Since the whole passage ends up in a kind of *'Penance Prayer,'* as does CDxx.28–32 from the Cairo Genizah, it is possible to look upon the individuals practicing these things as a species of *'Mourners for Zion.'* Before this, too, in Lines 3–4 is an extremely-doctored quotation from Leviticus 26:31—*'Highest Heaven'* being very revealingly substituted for 'ruined cities' (one doubts if there ever was a concept such as *'Highest Heaven'* in the days when Leviticus was written) —*'I shall ascend to the Highest Heaven and there not smell the fragrance of their offerings.'*

[67] For the use of this language of *'rejecting'* / *'rejection'* at Qumran—particularly in relation to *'the Lying Spouter'* and those of his persuasion (who *'rejected the Torah in the midst of their whole Assembly'* or 'Church')—see 1QpHabv.11–12. For more general usage, but in the same tenor, see 1QpHabi.10, CDvii.9, 18–19, xx.8–9, 1QSiii.5–6, etc.

[68] I have discussed this idea of a *'penance'* or *'repentance'* in n. 66 above, but the use of this word *'reckoned'* is all-important. It is the basis of the pivotal proof text for Early Christianity from Genesis 15:6, found in Galatians 3:6 and elsewhere: *'And Abraham's Faith was reckoned to him as Righteousness'* (or, in other language, *'justifying him'*); but it also forms the backbone of the more recently come-to-light—as result of our agitation—Document known as *'MMT'*; cf. 4QMMTii.1–2 and the concluding sentence of the Second Letter or Third Column, Lines 32–4: *'Thus, it will be reckoned to you as Righteousness, your having done what is Upright and Good before Him, for your own Good and for that of Israel.'*

[69] The first to have made this suggestion about James about being *'the Opposition High Priest'* and the Head of *'the Opposition Alliance'* was Robert Eisler and he did this on the basis of Early Church Testimonies, but without the Dead Sea Scrolls which had not yet come into full prominence; see his *Messiah Jesus and John the Baptist*, pp. 518–26, 540–6, etc. We have carried through these arguments in almost all our work, particularly *MZCQ* in 1983 (pp. 35–43), *JJHP* in 1986 (pp. 3–22), *JBJ*, 1997, pp. 353–408 and variously; but note, in particular, the reference to *'the Righteous Teacher'* as *'the Priest'* in 1QpHabii.6–9 and, of course, the references we have just highlighted at the end of 4QD266—the previously-unpublished Last Column of the Damascus Document. Moreover, as a concomitant of this, just noted as well, *'the Priest'* in whatever context in this Period—Rabbinic, sectarian, or even *'Christian'*—always means *'the High Priest,'* further solidifying this identity of *'the Righteous Teacher'* with *'the Opposition High Priest'*/*'Zaddik'*/*'Righteous One'* James.

[70] These are the same *'Boundary Markers'* of CDi.16–18, we noted in n. 65 above—the *'breaking'* or *'removal'* of which seems to have been the hallmark of *'the Lying Spouter'*'s activities. This, in turn, just like the inverted and reversed activity of the hypothetical *'Judas Iscariot'* according to Gospel presentation, *'delivers them (not him) up to the avenging sword of Vengeance of the Covenant'* and *'calls down upon them (again, not him) the curses of His Covenant.'*

[71] Cf. *War* 2.138–44. The materials outlined here make identification with the aggressive *'Final War'* mentality at Qumran almost a certainty.

[72] 4QD266, Lines15–6.

[73] Cf. 1QSi.8–12 and iii.17–iv.26 and note the description of *'Two Ways'* in the *Didache* 1–6. In the latter, one actual has in the First Section, the presentation of the two *'Love'* Commandments, directly paralleled in 1QSii.24–5; but also note how the description of *'the Way of Death'* in Part 4 directly parallels that of *'the Spirit of Unrighteousness'* in 1QSiii.9–14.

[74] Cf. Romans 8:1–27, 2 Corinthians 3:3–18, Galatians 4:29–5:28, etc.

[75] 1QSii.5–9

[76] Cf. 4Q286–87 in *DSSU*, pp. 222–29 and note Ms. A, Fragment 1, Line 1. In normative vocabulary, this reference occurs in 4QBer²ii.1.

[77] See 4Q287, Fragment 3, Column 2 on pp. 227–30 or 4QBer², Fragment 7, Column 2.

[78] CDi.4–5, iii.10–11, vii.13, viii.1, and xix.6–16 and cf. 4QpPs 37ii.21.

[79] Cf. Chapter 9 above and Matthew 24:9, 26:15, 26:24, 27:3, and *pars*.

[80] 1QSii.5–7 and cf. CDvii.9, 1QpHabxii.2–3, and 4QpPs 37iv.9–10.

[81] Cf. James 3:4–8.

[82] James 3:8–10. For this kind of imagery at Qumran, see CDvii.13 and the whole imagery of *'spouting'* and *'the Lying Spouter'* there. For specific *'Tongue'* imagery, aside from the *'speaking in Tongues'* of CDxiv.10 already alluded to above, see 4QBeat525iv.21–28 (*'guard against the stumbling block of the tongue'*)—a text we have called (after an allusion in Column v.5), *'The Demons of Death'* (4Q525—*DSSU*, pp. 168–73); but which scholars—as we have seen—call *'Beatitudes'*.

Chapter 21

[1] 1QpHabv.8–12. One should note that this is a *'swallowing'* passage about *'the Wicked swallowing one more Righteous than he,'* but here the exposition is not about *'the Wicked Priest'*—which is usual in *'Wickedness'* vs. *'Righteousness'* prophetical passages such as this. This time, the *Pesher* has to do with *'the Man of Lying'* and, in fact, the exposition continues later into the *Pesher* when it comes to describing his doctrines and the *'ᵗAmal'* of *'the Spouter of Lying.'* One should be very clear that the Hebrew word *'ᵗEdah'* in use here actually means *'Assembly'* or what in Greek or English goes under the title of *'Church'*—and this is not *'Yahad'* at Qumran, which many take it to be and which actually means *'Community'*. Moreover, it has strong parallels elsewhere in the literature at Qumran—particularly in the Psalm 37 *Pesher*, where the usage *'Assembly of the Poor'*/*'the Church of the Poor'* actually occurs several times as we have seen, *'The Liar rejected the Torah in the midst of their whole Assembly.'* So this must be seen as something like what goes in the Literature as *'the Jerusalem Council'* or *'the Jerusalem Conference'*—where Paul must have been perceived by at least *'some'* as having done likewise.

[2] Though the explanation in 20:16 had to do with being *'anxious to avoid spending time in Asia—though he was already in Samos and Miletus—in order to get to Jerusalem, if possible, in time for the Day of Pentecost.'* Since this is in what we call *'the We Document',* the narrative is more straightforward, logical, and believable and 20:6 had already even referred to *'leaving Philippi by ship after the Days of the Unleavened Bread'*—n.b., the reference again to *'a plot being made against him by the Jews'* (sic!) in 20:3 *'after staying in Greece for three months'* and *'being on the verge of setting sail for Syria,'* i.e., *'Lebanon'* and *'Phoenicia.'* But where was this *'plot'*? Certainly not in *'Greece'* or *'Macedonia,'* to where Paul then returned instead of then *'setting sail for Syria.'* The *'plot'* had to be in *'Syria'* or *'Jerusalem'*—most likely the latter (we take this material more seriously because, as we just said, it is in *'the We Document'* and much more prosaic and straightforward, lacking either exaggeration or supernatural phenomena)—but the explanation for his rushing past Ephesus also had to have something to do with *'the Silversmiths' Riot'* at *'the Temple of the Great Goddess Diana'* and its aftermath, already just described—tendentiously or otherwise—in Acts 19:23–20:2.

[3] *DSSU*, pp. 24–29, 68–71, and 83–89 and note that this term *'House of Judah'* is particularly important as an archaism in 1QpHabviii.1–2's exposition of Habakkuk 2:4: *'the Righteous shall live by his Faith'* and CDiv.10–11 on *'with the Completion of the Era of the number of these years,*

there being no more joining' to 'the House of Judah' per se.

[4] See *JBJ*, pp. 468–9, 778–83, and 951–5 and Chapters 1 and 16 above.

[5] See, for instance CDi.11, ii.11, vii.16, vii.19, xx.12, etc., and 4QFlori.10–13, citing 2 Samuel 7:2–4, and Amos 9:11; and 4QTesti.5 and 12, citing Deuteronomy 18:18–9 ('the True Prophet' Prophecy) and Numbers 24:15–17 ('the Star Prophecy').

[6] See CDi.10–11, 14–21, viii.7–8, xx.9, xx.33, etc.

[7] CDi.10–11 above.

[8] CDvii.7–8 above. This imagery of 'nazru'/'lehinnazer' (vi.15) is fundamental to the ethos of the Damascus Document—and, therefore, Qumran. As a result, it defines them as a 'Nazirite Community' of 'Perfect Holiness' in the Wilderness—what 'Christianity' was trying to express by its somewhat puzzling usage 'Nazarene' and its variations.

[9] 1QSiii.18–iv.26.

[10] Note that this term is actually used, as we have seen in 1QpHabx.8–12, to describe the 'building', 'works', 'Service', and 'Assembly' of 'the Spouter of Lying who leads Many astray'.

[11] See CDi.11–ii.1 and cf. 1QpHabii.1–10.

[12] Cf. CDiv.3–9.

[13] Cf. James 2:14–26 with Kor 3.113–14 on some very congenial 'People of the Book', who 'recite the Revelations all the night season' and are 'of the Righteous'. See also Kor 2.25, 2.62 (evoking 'Sabaeans'), 2.82, 2.277, 4.125 (with Abraham as 'Friend'), 84.25, 103.3, etc. Of course, 'doing' is a usage we have met throughout the Dead Sea Scrolls—to say nothing of the Letter of James. Also see Ps. *Rec.* 1.69.

[14] CDxx.9–10.

[15] See CDi.12–16 above.

[16] CDxx.10–13 and cf. n. 1 above.

[17] Cf. CDvii.16–17 and 4QFlori.11–13, specifically interpreted—as we have seen and will see in more detail below—in terms of the Davidic Messiah.

[18] This usage is perhaps definitive of the relationship to points being made in Acts to the Literature at Qumran. One can find it throughout the Qumran corpus, but especially in CDi.7–8, v.15–16, vii.9, viii.2–3 (here, one should appreciate that the word 'Command' is the same as 'Visit'), xiii.23–24, 1QMxii.4, xiii.10, etc.

[19] Here the 'Visitation' implies a kind of positive process—i.e., the 'Gentiles' of 'the Gentile Mission' are turning to God—a blessing. Wereas in CDv.15–16, vii.9, viii.2–3 xiii.23–24 above, it is for 'Judgement' or 'Destruction'—that is, it is for 'Payback'.

[20] See the Document, we entitled, 'the Messianic Leader' (4Q285), now considered part of the War Scroll and called 4QSM—but one also encounters this 'Zemach' or 'Branch of David' language in 4QFlori.11 and the Genesis *Pesher* (4Q252 or 4QCommGenB)v. 3–4 above.

[21] See, for instance, how a translator like G. Vermes of Oxford translates CDii.12–13 which refers to 'making known to them His Holy Spirit' by 'the hand of His Messiah'. While the usage is certainly idiomatique, Vermes and others translate this—in the writer's view, tendentiously—as 'His

anointed ones', even though the usages surrounding it are—like CDi.7–8 preceding it—all singular. The same holds true for CDv.21–vi.1 and occurs in 1QMxi.7 directly following the citation of '*the Star Prophecy*' from Numbers 24:17–19 where, knowing this directly involves what we would call '*the Messiah*,' he deliberately translates this as '*by the hand of Thine anointed*'— again indirectly implying plural usage (others like Garcia Martinez go further and translate it '*Your anointed ones*'—though here too it is again completely clear the adjectival and verbal usages surrounding it are singular). This is typical of attempts, subconsciously or otherwise, by a plethora of scholars to divert the public's attention away from the clear '*Messianic*' character of these texts. But in Vermes' case, what is more disturbing—as I have already pointed out in *DSSFC*, pp. 357–69—the next sentence, despite its admitted arcaneness (CDii.13: '*and he*' or '*it is Truth and, in the explanation of His Name, their names*' presumably '*are to be found*'), is completely left out or bowdlerized into '*and He proclaimed the Truth (to them)*' —without any indication of missing text or lacuna! The reason for this is quite clear. The missing sentence shows completely singular usage—as opposed to the plural this translator and others have given '*His anointed ones*.' The present writer does not pretend to understand the meaning of the passage such translators so tendentiously omit—but one thing is certain, all the surrounding usages are singular and the intent of the writer here has to be seen as singular. The same can be said for the War Scroll's exposition of '*the Star Prophecy*.' This kind of agenda-driven translation (even going so far as to omit whole lines of difficult text without even giving an indication of it) is shameful and misleads the public.

22 CDii.11–13 and cf. CDxii.23–xiii.10–14 and xiv.18–19 about the '*arising of the Messiah of Aaron and Israel*' is, once again, itself utterly singular as are all usages surrounding it, e.g., the reference to '*the coming of the Messiah of Aaron and Israel*' in xix.10–11 (preceding another telltale reference—this time to '*the First Visitation*'—with the express meaning of '*Destruction*') and '*the standing up of the Messiah from Aaron and from Israel*' in xx.1. The same is true of the reference in CDv.21–vi.1 to '*speaking rebellion against the Commandments of God (as given) by the hand of Moses and also against His Holy Messiah*' (singular) and that to '*the coming of the Prophet (i.e., 'the True Prophet' of 'Ebionite' usage) and the Messiah of Aaron and Israel*' in 1QSix.11. Once again, the usage in such places is clearly idiomatique and singular.

23 Not only does Galatians 2:11–15 make it clear that '*Cephas*'/'*Peter*' is absolutely subject to James' rulings, though Paul in his dialectical polemicizing thinks he is not; the episode in Acts 15:5–23—the so-called '*Jerusalem Council*', which ends with James ('*the Bishop of Bishops*' or '*Archbishop*' as per the Pseudoclementines and other Early Church Testimony) making his '*rulings*' (Acts 15:19) and everyone, including Paul, is required to obey them.

24 Cf. 1QpHabii.8–10 and vii.4–5.

25 Cf. CDxx.17: '*the Penitents from sin in Jacob*.'

26 Cf. Matthew 3:8–12 and *pars*.

27 CDii.2–7.

28 CDii.8–10.

29 CDiv.3–4. The point is that, as I have explained elsewhere and will do so further below, *the Nilvim*—which means *'Joiners'*—is another word in the Hebrew of Isaiah and Esther for Gentiles *'joining'* themselves to the Jewish Community. This is something of the meaning of *'the Residue of Men seeking out the Lord and all the Peoples upon whom My Name has been called'* above.

30 See my explanations in n. 21 above.

31 CDii.11–13.

32 Cf. nn. 21–22 above.

33 We have already several times commented upon the *'works'* language at Qumran. But for *'works of God'*, see CDi.1–2—the very first line of the *Genizah* copy of the Damascus Document, addressed to *'all those who know Righteousness and understand the works of God.'* The circularity and consistency here is impressive.

34 CDii.14–15.

35 CDii.16–iii.12.

36 CDiii.12–13.

37 For this *'Heirs'* language, see Romans 4:13–4 and Galatians 3:29–4:7; for the *'Rechabite,'* see Jeremiah 35:2–19 and cf. 1QSv.2, v.9, and CDiii.21.

38 CDiii.18–20.

39 See the *'building'* imagery used above to attack *'the Lying Spouter'* in 1QpHabix.9–10 above. But also see CDiii.19–20 on the *'building of a House of Faith in Israel'* and the later material about the *'House of the Torah'* in xx.10–13—as well as that on the *'Fortress of Strength'* and *'the Foundation,' 'Walls,'* and *'Rock'* that will not *'sway or shake'* in 1QHvi.24–26 and vii.7–10.

40 CDiii.19–iv.4. This is not the only place where such imagery is used—also see 1QSiv.23, CDv.4–5, vi.10–11, viii.20–24, xii.23–xiii.1, xiv.18, etc.

41 The point here is that the whole of Column One of the Damascus Document from the reference to God *'visited them'* in i.7 ends up in i.8–9 with the allusion to: *'and they understood their Guiltiness and knew that they were Sinners'*—which, of course, is nothing other than *'seeking remission of their Sins'* as put here in Luke 1:78. Further to these usages, see CDiii.18 and also note xx.20 and 34 on *'Salvation.'*

42 Cf. CDvi.3–11 and viii.21–22, directly followed in xx.1 by another allusion to *'the Standing up'* or *'arising of the Messiah from Aaron and from Israel'* (again the verbal usages are singular).

43 CDiv.4–8.

44 What we would call *'the Last Judgement'* is definitely being evoked, as we shall see, in 1QpHabvii.16–viii.3 (on Habakkuk 2:3–4), x.3–5, and xii.12–xiii.4.

45 CDi.19–22

46 CDiv.7–10.

47 See CDiv.10–12 and note how this archaism for *'Jews'* reappears, as we have already pointed up, in 1QpHabviii.1 above.

[48] For Paul, exclusive allegiance to *'the House of Judah'* is a downright negative and he is looking forward to a Community where Greeks and Jews can live harmoniously as *'equal citizens'*—cf. Romans 1:14–16, 2:9–3:1, and 10:12, 1 Corinthians 1:22–24, Galatians 3:28, and Ephesians 2:19–21 (using again, of course, the Qumran *'building'* and *'Cornerstone'* imagery). `

[49] See Solomon Schechter, *Fragments of a Zadokite Work*, Cambridge, 1910, whose publication it originally was and our Plates nn. 55 and 71. 71 is Column i of Ms. A and 55 is Column xx of Ms. B—which, to some extent, *'overlaps'* Columns vii-viii of Ms. A. It should be clear that the Document in Plate 71 is in typical Babylonian Block Script (which, of course, makes it late); but actually that in Plate 55 is in a somewhat older Hebrew hand—perhaps even an original, though this is sheer hypothesis.

[50] Cf. xix.33–35 with viii.21 which breaks off tantalizingly with the words *'the New Covenant in the Land of Damascus.'*

[51] CDvi.19–vii.9.

[52] CDi.7–ii.10, iii.7–12, and vii.9–viii.19.

[53] Cf. *E.I.* 2.23.15 and *pars.*, probably based on Hegesippus' now-lost Second Century CE testimony. But note how in the Hebrew rendition of this Isaiah 3:10 passage (not the Septuagint one, which is being reproduced in Greek texts such as Eusebius' here), the reference in Isaiah 3:9 and 3:11 is to *'gamul,'* i.e., *'reward,'* which is omitted in most Greek-language based presentations—that is, *'the reward on Evil'* or *'of their hands would be paid'* of *'done to them.'* This is the exact sense of the culminating passages of the Habakkuk *Pesher* given below—to say nothing of the Psalm 37 *Pesher*—on the fate of *'the Wicked Priest'* because of what he had *'paid'* the Righteous Teacher and those of his followers among *'the Poor.'* I have also covered this in my revised version of *JJHP* in *DSSU*, pp. 84–8.

[54] Cf. 1QpHabxii.2–6, 4QpPs 37iv.9, and 1QSii.6–7—but also see, CDvii.9. The commonality here (and by implication the contemporaneity) could not be more pronounced.

[55] 1QpHabxii.2–6, 4QpPs 37ii.19–20, and 4QpPs 37iv.9

[56] Cf. CDxx.19 with 1 Corinthians 11:25 and Luke 22:19 (*n.b.*, this phraseology, reflecting Paul in 1 Corinthians, only occurs in Luke).

[57] CDxx.34. Significantly, this is the last line of the Last Column of Ms. B.

[58] CDv.15–16.

[59] CDvii.21–viii.3/xix.13–16 and cf. *Surahs* like Kor 74.16–48, 78.17–40, 81.1–14, 82.1–19 (the purest expression of it), etc.

[60] Cf. CDxix.6–15—again beginning with the word *'gamul.'*

[61] CDxix.16 (at this point, both mss., which have now linked up again, actually allude to *'the Way of Traitors'*/*'Bogdim'*).

[62] CDxix.6–13.

[63] CDvi.3–11 and cf. CDiii.16 (in Ms. A) and xix.34–35 (in Ms. B).

[64] CDvi.17–vii.9.

[65] CDvii.2–8.

[66] CDvii.16 and 18–19/xix.13–14, 29, 32, and xx.1. As for ᶜ*Am*'/ᶜ*Amim*', though here the usage is singular, the usage ᶜ*Amim*' and '*Yeter ha* ᶜ*Amim*' in 1QpHabix.4–7 would clearly appear to relate to groups like '*the Herodians*' and '*Romans*' and the context here in the Damascus Document would seem to dictate a similar conclusion. There can be little doubt it relates to the Establishment and we discuss allusions such as these '*Kings of the Peoples*' and '*the Princes of Judah*' in these same Columns of the Damascus Document in Chapters 24 and 28 below—to say nothing of in '*Interpreting Some Esotericisms: "The Kings of the Peoples", "the Princes of Judah", and "Gehazi" in the Damascus Document*,' *DSSU*, pp. 313–31.

[67] CDvii.21–22/xix.33–34.

[68] A synonym for '*the Righteous*'—CDxx.1–3—cf. 1QSviii.13–18 on Isaiah 40:3.

[69] CDxx.3–7. Note that this same expression '*Midrash ha-Torah*' also occurs in the Qumran interpretation of '*the Way in the Wilderness*' passage of Isaiah 40:3 in 1QSviii.13–18 above and, by way of summing up the whole, in the very Last Column of the Damascus Document—now found in 4QD266, Line 19—and also the very last words of the whole Document!

[70] CDi.14–ii.1, viii.13/xix.25–26, xx.15, and, of course, 1QpHabii.1–2, v. 11, and x.9 and 1QHii.31 and iv.9–10.

[71] CDxx.2–12.

[72] Cf. CDvii.4–5 with 1QSi.13, iv.20, viii.1, viii.21, viii.25, ix.6–8, ix.19, etc.

[73] CDvi.19–vii.5. As we have repeatedly shown, Paul is not too interested in either of these '*Covenants*'— though he does repeat something of the same words in his version in 1 Corinthians 15:3 of how the post-Resurrection appearance Traditions (regardless of the interpolations involved) were communicated to him—but not in his rendition of '*the New Covenant*' tradition in 11:24–5 (his version of '*the Last Supper*') which, in 11:23 as we have seen, he says he '*received directly from the Lord*' (*thus*—though, of course, he never explains how this transpired)!

[74] CDxx.12–13 and 21–22.

[75] CDvii.5–6/xix.1–2.

[76] Cf. CDxii.23–xiii.1, xiv.18, and xx.1.

[77] Cf. CDxix.10 with xix.13.

[78] CDvii.13–4. This is then followed by the quote from Amos 5:26–7 in vii.14–15 about '*exiling the Tabernacle of your King*' and '*My Tent in Damascus*,' which is not paralleled in Ms. B and does not read anything like the received version of this passage in Amos.

[79] Cf. CDxix.9 with viii.13–14.

[80] CDvii.10–11 and xii.23–xiii.1, xiv.18, and xx.1.3–14 above.

[81] We have discussed the problem with this above in nn. 21–22 above.

[82] Cf. the verbal noun '*coming*' in '*the coming of the Messiah of Aaron and Israel*' in CDvii.11 or, for that matter, the '*rising*'/'*arising of Zadok*' in v. 5 or '*the Standing up* (singular) of *the Messiah from Aaron and from Israel*' in xx.1 above, *et. al.*

[83] This is particularly true in a Document like 4Q*Flor*i.11, which we shall consider in detail in the next chapter (Chapter 22) below and which in exegesis of 2 Samuel 7:12–14: '*I will raise up*

your seed after you and establish the Throne of his Kingdom forever. I will be a Father to him and he will be a son to Me'—singular—refers to *'the Branch of David who will stand up'* or *'arise with the Doresh ha-Torah, who will (also) rise in Zion* (here a different verb—*'yakim'*—which does not mean *'stand up')* at *(end…) time.*

84 Cf. *DSSU,* pp. 19–23 and 4Q521 ii.1–3, the references throughout are singular.

85 See *DSSU,* pp. 76–88 and 4Q252v.3–4 expounding *'the Shiloh Prophecy'* of Genesis 49:11 and the reference there to *'the coming (again singular) of the Messiah of Righteousness, the Branch of David, because to him and his seed was given the Covenant of his Kingdom forever* (also elaborating on 2 Samuel 7:12–4 in the Messianic *Florilegium* about the promises *'to the seed of David'* above—again, all singular usages). For those who think there is no Davidic *'Messiah'* at Qumran, it is hard to get more specific than this and the allusion to *'the Messiah of Righteousness'* is particularly significant.

86 See, for instance, CDi.11, vi.4–11, vii.18–19, xiii.5–13, xiv.12, xx.14, 4QD266, Lines 1, 8, and 16, 1QSiii.13, vi.12–20, ix.12–21, etc.

87 Cf. CDi.7, vii.19–20, 4Q285v.4–6 and vii.3–4, 4QFlori.11, and 4Q246i.9–ii.1.

88 Cf. CDxix.12–3. For *'the Mourners for Zion,'* see *JBJ,* pp. 709, 764, 868 and Chapters 3, 4, 7, 9, 12, 15, and 19 above.

89 Cf. CDxix.10–13 with vii.21–viii.1. The reason why in Ms. B this is clearly the time of the fall of the First Temple is that these passages from Ezekiel—which can only refer to the First Temple—are specifically applied to it. The passages from Isaiah and Amos—and, for that matter, Numbers—in Ms. A are less specific and, time-wise, more general.

90 CDiv.17–vi.2.

91 Cf. CDvii.12–13/xix.24–26.

92 Matthew 3:4 and Mark 1:6. It is missing as well from Luke, though perhaps the *'camel'* part of it comes once again from Early Church Testimony about the skin on James' *'knees becoming hard as a camel's nobules.'* Cf. too Josephus, *Ant.* 18.116–19—a testimony likewise which is missing from the *War.*

93 That is, the *'called by Name'* in CDii.11–12 and iv.3–4. The former—*'He raised up to Himself men, called by Name, so a Remnant might remain in the Land and fill the face of the Earth with their seed'*—perfectly anticipate these lines, put into James' mouth at the so-called 'Jerusalem Council' by Acts 15:16–17, as they even include references to both *'Remnant'* and *'men'* (of course, this passage, too, is followed in the very next line by *'He made known to them His Holy Spirit by the hand of His Messiah'*). CDiv.3–4 is the exposition of Ezekiel 44:15, we should be by now so familiar with, defining *'the Sons of Zadok'* as *'the Elect of Israel, called by Name, who would Stand Up in the Last Days'* and *'Justify the Righteous and Condemn the Wicked.'* One should also note that, not only is *'the Remnant'* language used here and throughout the Damascus Document (especially in Columns vii–viii and xix), but so too is the *'seeking'* language, which first appears in these lines from CDi.9–11. These enunciate, it will be recalled, how *'God considered their works, because they sought Him with a whole heart* (here the precise *'seeking out the Lord'* of

Acts 15:17 above), *and raised up for them a Teacher of Righteousness to guide them* ('*the Guide*' language of Matthew's '*Blind Guides*') in *the Way of His heart*. Nor is this to say anything about the whole issue of '*the Doresh ha-Torah*' in CDvi.7–vii20 and 4QFlori.11–13 above which also relates to Amos 9:11's '*fallen Tent of David*,' the presumable subject of James' words here in Acts 15:16–17 as well. With this in mind, there can be little doubt of the intertextuality of all these documents.

[94] Cf. CDxix.1–2 and xx.17.

[95] CDiv.1–4.

[96] CDvi.16 and 21 and cf. CDxix.8–10.

[97] CDxx.14–15. In this connection, '*the Man of Lying*' is once more mentioned, but the timeframe is clearly after the fall of the Temple in 70 CE since the fact of there being '*no Prince, no King, no Judge, none to Judge with Righteousness*' of Hosea 1:4 is distinctly evoked.

[98] Cf. CDvii.14–18.

[99] See Chapter 2 above and the parts of the actual text of provided by Michael Baigent and Richard Leigh in *The Dead Sea Scrolls Deception*, London, 1991, pp. 77–83—as well as my article in *Midstream*, December, 1991, pp. 13–17 at the same time.

[100] This is a very important proposition and relates to what I was noting above about the handwriting on Ms. B, which seems obviously much older than that of Ms. A., identifying the latter certainly as a recension. Both of these two important Columns vii of Ms. A and xix-xx of Ms. B are now extant in 4QD267, paralleling CDv–viii about '*digging the well*' and '*Jannes and his brother*' (though the order reverses that of Ms. A) and '*Ephraim separating from Judah*' from CDvii.12–13 (again out of order) and '*God visiting the Earth*' from viii.2–3. The fact that the text was not finalized at the time of the deposit in the caves means of course that CD is not the Early Second Century BC Document, those dominating Scrolls Studies uniformly take it to be; but rather one relatively late in the life of the Community and one still in flux at the time of its seeming destruction or initial composition.

[101] Aside from meaning that the text of CD was not finalized by the time of the deposit of the Scrolls, it may mean that the text we have of Ms. B—as already suggested—is a very old one indeed and may represent a further development of the ideas, as they were being expressed at the time of the abandonment of the installation at Qumran.

[102] That the Scrolls are '*Ebionite*'—though perhaps a variety of '*Ebionitism*' unknown to our sources (except perhaps the kind of notices about '*Sicarii Essenes*' preserved in Hippolytus)—is made clear by the frequent allusion to '*the Poor*' throughout the corpus, most notably, in CDvi.21, xiv.13, 1QHii.32, iii.25, v.15–18 (*nephesh-Ebion*), v.23 (*Ebionei-Hesed*—'*the Poor Ones of Piety*'), 1QMxi.13 (in interpretation of '*the Star Prophecy*'), 1QpHabxii.3–10 (used three times in as many lines for the rank and file of the Community), 4QpPs 37ii.10 and iii.10 ('*the Assembly*' or '*Church of the Poor*'), and now finally '*The Hymns of the Poor*' (4Q434 and 436—*DSSU*, pp. 233–40).

[103] CDvii.13–15.

[104] Acts 7:42.

105 CDvii.17, called *'the bases of the statues,'* and 1QpHabii.9 and vii.5: *'the words of His Servants the Prophets.'*

106 See 4QD266iii.18–22.

107 CDvii.16–18.

108 See, for instance, the Bar Kochba coin depicted on Plate 51 above.

109 Cf. *War* 2.520 and note 6.354–57, where Josephus describes the surrender of *'the sons and brothers of King Izates'* amid the burning of their palace, whom—though supposedly angry at their disloyalty—Titus refrained from executing but rather *'put in chains and brought to Rome as hostages for the allegiance of their Country'*—interesting!

110 Cf. CDxx.18 and 4QFlori.3.

111 CDxx.34.

Chapter 22

1 Cf. *4QFlori.10–13*, in exposition of 2 Samuel 7:12–4 about the promises to *'the Seed'* of David and see John Allegro in *DJD V: Qumran Cave iv: 4Q158–4Q186*, Oxford, 1958 above. This should certainly disabuse anyone who is suffering under the misapprehension that a Messianic *'Son of David'* is not in evidence at Qumran.

2 *4QFlori.11–13*

3 See AP article by Lee Siegel, *'Messiah-like Leader Mentioned in the Scrolls,'* 11/8/91; John Noble Wilford writing in *The New York Times*, 11/8/91, *'Messianic Link to Christianity Is Found in Scrolls'*; and *DSSU*, 4Q285, pp. 24–29—in particular, Fragment 7, Lines 2–4, in exposition of Isaiah 10:34: *'Lebanon shall fall by a Mighty One'* (extant as well elsewhere at Qumran in a *Pesher*—*'*The Isaiah *Pesher'*), the signification of which in Rabbinic Literature we have also discussed above. Also see Richard N. Ostling the next year writing in *Time Magazine*, 9/21/92, *'Is Jesus in the Dead Sea Scrolls?'*

4 Cf. *4QFlori.10–13* with CDvii.16–21—more of the homogeneity which implies contemporaneousness at Qumran. This would then extend to its Paulinized bowdlerization in James' speech in Acts 15:16–17.

5 *4QFlori.11–13*. We have discussed the significance of this verb *'standing up'* above. There would appear to be three *'arise's* in these two lines (depending on the reconstruction) and, if one adds, Line 10, three *'yakim's* or *'establish's*/*'raise up's*.

6 Cf. 1QpHabviii.1–3 in exposition of Habakkuk 2:4. This is a very important use of the verb *'to save'*/*'lehoshi*ᶜ*a'*. For another, its verbal noun (*'Yeshu*ᶜ*ah'*), see the last line of the Damascus Document—CDxx.34 above.

7 CDxix.10–11. The only difference, of course, is that here in Ms. B the verb is *'coming'*; while in *4QFlori.10–11* *'the Branch of David'* is to *'arise'* or *'stand up.'* One should note again that in Ms. A of CDvii.20—in line with its quotation of Numbers 24:17—*'the Sceptre'* is described as *'standing up'* again.

8 Cf. CDi.7–8 with Amos 9:12 and this bowdlerization in Acts 15:17. Obviously with the new

'*Pauline Gentile Mission*,' there is no need to emphasize the '*inheritance of the Land*' anymore!

9 The '*Zionist*' aspects, of course reappear 2 Samuel 7:11–16, not only in the promise of the '*Establishment of the Throne of His Kingdom forever*,' but in the instruction to '*build a House in (God's) Name*.' Nor is this latter lost on the *Flori*.11–12 which, combining this with Amos 9:11 ('the Fallen Tent ot David' in CDvii), now has both '*the Branch*' and '*the Doresh ha-Torah*' of CDvi.6–9 '*rise up in Zion in the Last Days*.'

10 Cf. CDxx.10 (which in xx.1 preceding this, as we have seen, also speaks of the '*Standing up of the Messiah from Aaron and from Israel*'—the only difference being that here it is '*from Aaron and from Israel*' and not '*of Aaron and of Israel*;' but the surrounding usages, once again, are all singular).

11 Cf. 1QSviii.5 and ix.6 and note the whole exegesis of Psalm 89:23 and Exodus 15:17–18 in 4QFlori.1–7, which is about '*establishing the Temple for him (David) in the Last Days*,' in which '*the Lord shall reign forever and ever*' and in which '*no foreigners*' or the like (including '*Ammonites*' and '*Moabites*' which would seem to imply—in the code of the time—'Herodians') '*shall ever enter*' or '*lay it waste*'—which would seemingly mean here, too, that the Temple has already been destroyed, i.e., after 70 CE.

12 4QFlori.3–5.

13 4QFlori.3–4 and cf. 11QTxlv.7–xlvi.12 and 4QMMTii.3–9—also see Chapter 2 above.

14 We have already covered all these things in n. 4, Chaper 2 as just noted above, and variously. Since all these Documents use more or less the same internal parameters and the same *dramatis personae*, they have to have been written—as remarked ad nauseum—at more or less the same time and it is a matter for the 'internal evidence' to indicate precisely when, not 'the external' (such as the latter may be).

15 4QFlori.4 and cf. 1QMvii.6–7 and CDxv.17.

16 4QMMTii.68–70.

17 Cf. 4QpNahiii.9 and iv.5, which uses the expression '*nilvu*'—the same root as '*Nilvim*'/'*Joiners*' in iii.9 and CDiv.3 above— addressed to '*the Simple of Ephraim*' (in our view, a euphemism for groups like Pauline '*Gentile Christians*' paralleling '*the Simple of Judah doing Torah*' in the Habakkuk *Pesher*), expressing the hope that '*they would abandon those who mislead them and join...Israel*,' which is certainly more accommodating than this regarding the '*ger-Nilveh*'/ '*Resident Alien*.' Also see the key interpretation regarding '*the Nilvim*,' just signaled, in CDiv.2–4, based on Isaiah 56:3–6 (and Esther 9::27), my further analysis below and my article, '*Joining/ Joiners, ᶜArizei-Go'im, and the Simple of Ephraim* Relating to a Cadre of Gentile God-Fearers at Qumran,' *DSSFC*, pp. 313–31.

18 Cf. 4QFlori.5–6. This would also seem to be the implication of the new inscription (called '*A Dead Sea Scroll in Stone*' and attributed, not unlike the Koran, to the Angel '*Gabriel*')—if it is authentic—and cf. 4QFlor i.10–17 and A. Yardeni, '*A New Dead Sea Scroll in Stone*,' *BAR*, January/February, 2008.

19 4QFlori.6–8. Note here that the '*lehachshil*' usage found in 4QFlori.7–8—'*He will comfort*

them from all the Sons of Belial who cause them to stumble' or *'cast them down on account of their sins'*—also forms a key aspect of the passage in the Habakkuk *Pesher* describing what the Wicked Priest did to the Righteous Teacher and those of his persuasion on *Yom Kippur*—*'cast them down'* (xi.7–8). A parallel allusion to *'destroy them'* also appears in the follow-up passage in 1QpHabxii.5–6 about what the Wicked Priest did to *'the Poor'* (*Ebionim*) —denoting the followers of the Righteous Teacher—i.e., *'plotted to destroy them.'* It should not be necessary to add that this *'causing to stumble'* or *'casting down'* in Greek forms the central thrust of descriptions of the death of James—the followers of whom were also known as *'the Poor'* as we have seen—in all Early Church accounts, as it does the attack by *'the Enemy'* (Paul) on James in the Pseudoclementine *Recognitions*.

20 4Q*Flor*i.9; for *'Sons of Belial'* elsewhere at Qumran, see 1QHiv.10, but also see *'Anshei-Gorel Belial'* in 1QSii.4–5 and *'Gedudei-Belial'* in 1QMxi.8.

21 See my Appendix to *JJHP*, pp. 87–94, 'The "Three Nets of Belial" in the Zadokite Document and "Balla^c"/"Bela^c" in the Temple Scroll' and San. 105a–106b on *'Balaam'* as *'the Swallower of the People.'*

22 4Q*Flor*i.12–13.

23 1QHix.35.

23a Cf. 4Q*Flor*i.10–11.

24 Also cf. Matthew 19:21 and note the *'Perfection'* doctrine throughout the Documents at Qumran—as, for instance, 1QSi.8, ii.2, viii.9–21, ix.6–22 (*'Perfection of the Way'* combining the *'Perfection'* doctrine with the Isaiah 40:3 *'Way'* doctrine), CDi.20–21 (*'the Walkers in Perfection'*), ii.15–16 (*'the Church of the Men of the Perfection of Holiness'*), xx.5–7, etc. Also note James 1:4–25 and 2:22 to the same effect.

25 Cf. CDiv.2–4 with 4Q*Flor*i.11–17 and ii.3–4.

26 For this kind of shift, see how in the Gospels (Matthew 3:17 and *pars.*), Hebrews 1:5, 5:5, Jerome's Gospel of the Hebrews, and Psalm 2:7's *'You are My son; at this moment I have begotten you,'* is changed into *'This is My beloved son; in him I am well pleased.'*

27 Cf. Ps. *Rec.* 1.71 and the *'strengthening'* imagery of CDxx.18 and 33 above; but also see the *'whitening'* imagery (together with the *'strengthening'*), based on Daniel 11:32 and 12:10, at the end of 4Q*Flor*ii.3–4 above too.

28 Cf. 4Q246ii.1–9, obviously based on Daniel 2:46, where there is no mention of either *'David'* or *'his seed'* as there is in 4Q*Flor*i.10–13.

29 The first to suggest such an interpretation was D. Flusser in his *'The Hubris of the Antichrist in a Fragment from Qumran,'* Immanuel 10 (1980), pp. 31–37; but it was also hinted at by J. T. Milik when he first revealed the text in a Harvard Lecture in 1972. Also see F. García Martínez's *'The Eschatological Figure of 4Q246'* in his *Qumran and Apocalyptic*, Leiden, 1992, pp. 162–79, J. A. Fitzmyer in *'The Contribution of Qumran Aramaic to the Study of the New Testament,'* NTS 20 (1972–4), pp. 382–407, and E. Puech, *'Fragment d'une apocalypse en araméen (4Q246) et le Royaume de Dieu,'* Revue Biblique 99 (1992), pp. 116–7.

[30] Cf. 4Q246ii.5-6 and 9.

[31] See Daniel 2:40 on the *'Kingdom of Iron,'* normally thought to represent the Macedonian one, 7:7 on *'the fourth beast'* with *'iron teeth'* and *'ten horns,'* and 8:5–8 on the *'goat with one majestic horn between its eyes'*—Alexander, which is even interpreted as such by *'Gabriel'* in 8:21–2—*'Yavan'* of course being the Hebrew word for *'Greece.'*

[32] 4Q*Flori*.16–7 which even refers to the same passage from Ezekiel (44:7–15) which is referred to in CDiv.2–4 above in defining *'the Sons of Zadok'*—more intertextuality, implying a more or less contemporaneous date—and seems to refer to *'pursuing Righteousness'* or *'Justification'* (this is a reconstruction).

[33] 1QHxvii.29–30 (old numeration, ix.29–30).

[34] 1QHxvii.34–35/ix.34–35; for *'Ebionei-Hesed,'* see 1QHviii.23.

[35] 4Q*Flori*.14.

[36] Cf. CDvii.9 for *'the Way of Evil Ones,'* but viii.16 for *'the Penitents of Israel* (another important phraseology) *who turned aside from the Way of the People'*—in our view, *'Herodians'* and those whom they have infected, i.e., the whole Jewish Establishment from BC 50 to CE 50. This word *'People,'* of course, now follows the interpretation of Isaiah 8:11 in 4Q*Flori*.15–16—again, more proof that both Documents are operating on exactly the same wave-length.

[37] 4Q*Flori*.15. It is after this and an unreadable portion of the text that the word *'the People'* starts the Line at *Flori*.16.

[38] That is, the *'strength'* imagery in James' cognomen, *'Oblias'*—though never actually decoded, thought to imply the phraseology from Psalms *ᶜOz-le-ᶜAm'*/*'Strength of the People'*—and the description of him in Early Church literature as providing a *'strong Bulwark'*; cf. E.I. 2.23.7 and 3.7.9 and Psalms 39:11, 68:35, and 77:14; but also see Psalms 37:39, Isaiah 25:4 (*'Strength to the Poor'*), and Habakkuk 3:19.

[39] Note the several allusions to *'by'* or *'into the hand of'* in the crucial section of 1QMxi.7–14 in exegesis of Numbers 24:17–19 (*'the Star Prophecy'*) and Isaiah 31:8, which must now be looked upon as part of these *'Messianic'* Prophecies: *'Ashur will fall by the sword of no mere man'*—exegeses applying to *'the hand of Your Messiah(s),'* *'Your hand,'* and being *'delivered into the hand of the Poor' (Ebionim).'*

[40] CDvii.8–10/xix.20–21.

[41] CDvii.4–5/xix.17 and xix.35.

[42] CDvii.21/CDxix.32–xx.7 and cf. *War* 2.143.

[43] Cf. CDi.3, i.17, vii.13, xix.10, etc.

[44] Isaiah 8:23–9:1.

[45] Cf., for instance, the passages in CDiii.21–iv.4, CDvii.12–13, CDxix.11–13, and 4Q*Flori*.15 (here the references to *'the Book of Ezekiel,'* to say nothing of *'the Book of Isaiah'* which precedes it and *'the Book of Daniel'* that follows it—just as we would refer to them—shows this Document to be a fairly late one in terms of chronology).

[46] See Daniel 11:25, 12:2 below, and 12:10–13.

47 Cf. CDiv.3–7 above and note this *standing up in the Last Days* of iv.4 which is, in our view, an allusion to *the Last Judgement*. Also note what follows this in iv.8 about *doing the precise letter of the Torah* which also parallels, now, what follows in 1QFlorii.2–3 below about *doing the Torah of Moses.*

48 Cf. 1QSVi.1–21, vii.1–25, and viii.18–ix.2, CDxiii.7–8 and xiv.5–11, and see its reversal in 1QpHabx.11 and 4QpNahii.8 above.

49 4QFlorii.3–4 and see the reference to *whitening* in Ps. *Rec.* 1.71 below.

50 Cf. CDiv.4 and its reversal in i.19–21, 1QpHabi.10–11, v.4–12, vii.17 (in interpretation of Habakkuk 2:4), xii.10, 4QpPs 37ii.12–23, iv.5–22, etc. In fact, as we have already suggested, this seems to have been one of the ways in which many of these Documents were chosen for exposition.

51 4QFlorii.2.

52 Cf CDxx.18 and 33 and Ps. *Rec.* 1.71.

53 See n. 38 above and Psalms 39:11, 68:35, and 77:14.

54 See *E.I.* 2.23.7 and 3.7.9 above.

55 See Ps. *Rec.* 1.71.

56 See nn. 36 and 41 above and CDvii.4–5, viii.9, viii.16, xix.17, and xix.35

57 Not only compare this with the description of James' followers in Acts 21:21, but also see the use of this term in 1QSii.15, iv.4, ix.23, 1QHii.15, etc.

58 Cf. CDiv.4 and 1QpHabv.4–5,

59 1QpHabix.9–12.

60 Hippolytus 9.21.

61 *War* 2.205–10.

62 CDvi.10–11, viii.17–18, xii.23–xiii.1, xiv.19, xx.1, etc.

63 4QFlori.7–8.

64 1QpHabxi.8–ix.5.

65 *'The Moreh'* and *'the Yoreh'* are often interchangeable—since they are based on the same root in Hebrew—cf., for instance, in CDxix.34–xx.1 and xx.13–4, as well as vi.10–1 above.

66 CDvii.20–21.

67 See 4Q246 ii.5–6.

68 4QFlori.10.

69 Acts 15:22. Note that the previous *'Barsabas'* we met in Act was in 1:23, where he was the defeated candidate called *'Joseph surnamed Barsabas and known as Justus'* (was this the way members of *'the Messianic family'* were referred to? Is this the same person as *'Judas Barsabas'* or just another name for James—see JBJ, pp. 853–63) for the supposed *'election'* to succeed the *'Judas Iscariot*,' who had just *'fallen headlong'* (like James in the Pseudoclementines when he was attacked by the *'Enemy'* Paul) and *'his guts burst open'*—James' head being crushed in Early Church accounts of his death? Also note that *the We Document* intrudes in 16:10 right

after the break between Barnabas and John Mark and Paul and Acts' introduction of *'a certain Disciple named Timothy, the son of a mother who was a believing Jewess* (who was this?), *but whose father was a Greek'*!

70 CDvi.3–4. In the original Numbers 21:18 the words *'be-mish*ᶜ*anotam'*/*'their staves'* also appear in vi.9, however this is changed into *'bemehokkekot'* for obvious exegetical reasons—we shall analyse below.

71 CDvi.9—literally *'be-mehokkekot asher hakkak ha-Mehokkek.'*

72 CDiv.2 and vi.4–5. That this is obviously esoteric is borne out by the use of the same term later in the Document in different formulations; see my *'Joining/Joiners,* ᶜ*Arizei-Go'im, and the Simple of Ephraim Relating to a Cadre of Gentile God-Fearers at Qumran,' DSSFC*, pp. 313–31. That it is basically another form of what we would be referring to as *'repentance from Sin'* is made clear in CDii.5, 1QSx.21, 1QHii.8–9, vi.6, and xiv.21–22.

73 CDxx.17 and cf. the *'breaking'* allusion in James 2:8–11.

74 CDvii.16/xix.29, which make is more clear than anything else, that these *'Shavim'* are repenting from sin, as in the Gospel portrayal of the followers of John the Baptist, and, that there were people who could *'turn aside from'* this *'Way'* among them, means this is not a normative definition of *'Priests.'*

75 Cf. CDiv.20–v.2 and see 11QTLvii.17–19.

76 CDv.11–16 and cf. how Paul uses this *'Deliverer out of Zion'* in Romans 11:26 where he identifies *'the Israelites'* or *'the Jews'* as *'the Enemies'*—another one of his now farcical polemical reversals!

77 I have discussed these *'Kings of the Peoples'* as a Roman juridical term for the petty *'Kings'* in the Eastern part of the Empire, among whom *'the Herodians'* were especially prominent, in Chapters 3, 15, and 17, etc. above and throughout *JBJ*. But see also A. N. Sherwin-White, *The Roman Citizenship*, Oxford, 1939, pp. 270–5—the Romans being *'the Princeps Gentium'*/*'the Lord of the Peoples'*—and see Eusebius' description of the Arab King Abgar as *'the Great King of the Peoples beyond the Euphrates.'* Nor is this to mention, as we have seen, how Paul terms himself in Romans 11:1–13 as *'Ethnon Apostolos'*/*'the Apostle to the Gentiles'*—a variation of which Muhammad also employs. Of course the whole Chapter 11 of Romans, where Paul explains how he is *'of the seed of Abraham of the Tribe of Benjamin'*, is pregnant with Qumranisms—including (this same) *'seed,' 'Salvation,' 'snare,' 'net'* and *'stumbling block,' 'Riches,' 'zeal'* and *'zealotry,' 'Branches,' 'Root'* (and now *'Grafts'*), *'cut off,' 'stand,'* and, to be sure, *'the Deliverer.'*

78 CDvii.9–12.

79 CDvii.8–9 and note that this *'venom of vipers'* is employed in regard to *'walking in the Way of the Evil Ones'* in viii.9 above. Also see my translation of documents such as CD, 1QS, and 1QpHab, which could prove particularly useful to the reader, in *DSSFC*, pp. 355–431.

80 Cf. n. 77 above and A. N. Sherwin-White, *The Roman Citizenship*, Oxford, 1939, pp. 270–5

81 CDvii.10–11/xix.23–24. This imagery is so clever and yet so little understood in Qumran Studies where the greatest flaw, as I have explained, is the inability to relate to literary metaphor. It plays, as we saw earlier, on the relationship of *'yayin'* (*wine*) in Hebrew to *'Yavon'* in Hebrew

(*Greece*) and the homonyms in Hebrew '*Rosh*'/'*Head*' to '*rosh*'/'*poison*'/'*venom*'. It is interesting to remark, too, how much the consumption of strong drink plays in the unruly and untimely death of Alexander the Great.

82 Cf. CDvii.12–13 with CDxix.24–26. Once again, there are the homonyms here denoting '*wind*' and '*Spirit*' and one should see the differences in the two texts where the description of '*the Mattif*' is concerned, which shows the Damascus Document was still in a state of flux when these two documents were penned—that is, it is a comparatively late document. The text we provide here in this particular description is from Ms. A. Also see the previous description in CDiv.19–22 above, which has to do with '*fornication*' and '*polygamy*', a clear attack on the Herodians and not the Maccabeans, since it was Herod who was this polygamist—and this with a vengeance!

83 Cf. CDi.7–8 with CDvii.18–19.

84 CDvii.14–18/CDxix.17–21. The reason I call this the Palestinian form of '*Grace*' is that over and over again in CD and other documents at Qumran, the concept is repeated that it is not for one's '*own sake*' or what one has personally done or not done, but because of '*the Fathers*', that is, it is not a '*free gift*' as Paul puts it, where '*Gentiles*' are concerned, but a consequence of promises God made to '*the Fathers*'!

85 1QSviii.13–14—'*they shall separate from the midst of the habitation of the Men of Unrighteousness*'.

86 This '*only-begotten*' usage, as we have seen, is very interesting—the more so since Josephus uses it to describe the nature of Helen of Adiabene's love for her favorite son, Izates, who circumcised himself in order to convert to Judaism contrary to the teaching of one '*Ananias*' and another (Paul?) and for whom the Burial Monuments known as '*the Tomb of the Kings*' in Jerusalem was built; see *Ant.* 20.20 and 95.

87 1QpHabv.11–12.

88 Cf. 1QpHabx.9–13 with CDiii.5–12, in which are outlined those '*who deserted the Covenant*' and '*did not hold fast to the Commandments of God*'.

89 CDvii.18–21/xix.32–33 (missing the '*Elisha*'/'*Gehazi*' allusion).

90 These '*Enemies*' are the ones listed in *San.* 90a and 105a–107b above.

91 This is certainly true of the supposed allusions to '*Jesus*' as '*ben Panthera*', the son of a Roman Legionnaire named '*Panther*'; but the best place to look for these Talmudic esotericisms and the like is in R. Eisler, *The Messiah Jesus and John the Baptist*, pp. 80–112 and 405–11. References such as this occur in *Yeb.* 49a and are combined in uncensored versions of *San.* 67a, which combines this with another Talmudic euphemism for Jesus, '*Ben Stada*'. Also see *Tos. Hul.* 2.22–24 and note that Morton Smith in *Jesus the Magician*, 1973, pp. 47 and 61, speaks about a tombstone found in Binkerbruck, Germany in the name of one '*Tiberius Julius Abdes Panthera, an archer from native of Sidon, Phoenicia who was transferred for service in the Rhineland in 9 CE*'—a statement which is backed up to some extent in Origen's *Contra Celsus* 1.28 and Epiphanius' *Haeres.* 77.7.

[92] Cf. *San.* 107a above and the emphasis on his leprosy which was the seeming result of his selling his master's teaching. For Paul's sensitivity to the latter accusation, see 1 Corinthians 9:5–18, following his mention of *'Cephas and the brothers of the Lord'*; for the former, also see 2 Corinthians 10:10 and 2 Kings 5:27.

[93] CDvi.2–11.

[94] CDvii.21/CDxix.34–xx.1.

[95] CDxx.1, paralleled in xii.22–xiii.1 and xiv.19 above, but also 4QD266, Frag. 10, i.12. This should be clear from the verbal noun associated in all instances with the phraseology.

[96] CDvi.3–9, literally *'be-mehokkekot asher hakkak ha-Mehokkek*, and see nn. 70–71 above.

[97] CDv.16–19. This is clear from the whole ambiance—particularly the references to *'Moses and his brother'* and their opposition in the wilderness to *'Jannes and his brother.'* Note too the parallelism here.

[98] See, for instance, the work known as *The Acts of Pilate* 5.1 and, not surprisingly, 2 Timothy 3:8.

[99] Cf., for instance, CDi.1, i.8–9, CDi.11–14, ii.4–5, ii.6, iv.3–5, iv.9–10, iv.15–16, viii.16–22, xx.17–25, 1QpHabvii.14–6, and x.12 above, etc.

[100] See *San.* 90a and 105a–107b above.

[101] CDi.14–16; for *'the Lying Spouter,'* see 1QpHabx.9–13—but also CDiv.19–20 and viii.13.

[102] CDv.20–vi.1 and viii.3–4.

[103] Cf. CDi.13–ii.1, ii.16–17, iii.5–12, iii.16–8, iv.19–21, v. 20–vi.2, vi.5–21, viii.18–21/xix.32–4, xx.8–13, etc.

[104] Cf. CDv.20–vi.1—but also see ii.12 and xx.1. Those who would translate this otherwise should be clear.

[105] CDvi.2–5 and cf. CDi.4–6, ii.2–21, and Matthew 11:15 and 13:9–43 and *pars.*

[106] Cf. CDvi.6–7 with 4QD266.19; but also see CDi.10, the *'seeking Him with a whole heart',* which precedes God *'raising up for them a Teacher of Righteousness'* in i.11, xx.6, and my *DSSU*, pp. 212–19.

[107] CDvi.4–5.

[108] 4QpNahiii.5.

[109] *'The Simple of Ephraim'* as a parallel to *'the Simple of Judah doing Torah'* in the Habakkuk *Pesher* is particularly suggestive in this regard—*'Ephraim'* being *'Samaria'.* See Chapters 4, 12, and 14, etc. above and my article *'Joining/Joiners, ᶜArizei-Go'im, and the Simple of Ephraim* Relating to a Cadre of Gentile *God-Fearers* at Qumran,' in *DSSFC*, pp. 313–31.

[110] See *'Joining/Joiners, ᶜArizei-Go'im, and the Simple of Ephraim* Relating to a Cadre of Gentile *God-Fearers* at Qumran,' in *DSSFC*, pp. 313–31 above and note, this was first given in 1991 to the Society of Biblical Literature. Also see *JJHP*, pp. 7, 17, 55, 68–9, and the Glossary on p. 99/*DSSFC*, p. 429.

[111] See Josephus' *War* 1.6, which is addressed to just such persons further East—but also his

description of the conversions of Queen Helen and her family in *Ant.* 20.17–96 and *E.I.* 1.13.1–20's parallel picture of the Conversion of King Agbarus in Northern Syria and its parallels in Syriac literature.

[112] Isaiah 56:3. In fact, the whole Chapter 56 of Isaiah is about the subjects being addressed here in CDvi—namely '*Keeping Judgement and doing Righteousness*' and '*holding fast by keeping the Sabbath and not profaning it and holding his hand back from any Evil doing*', the '*foreigner who joins himself to the Lord*' (3), and again '*holding fast to My Covenant*' and not '*being cut off*'. The parallels of these to these passages in the Damascus Document should be obvious.

[113] CDiii.12–13, iii.20, vi.21, vii.13–14, xiv.14, viii.2, xix.14, xx.18, xx.27, and xx.33.

[114] Cf. CDi.11, vi.11–12 (here '*Yoreh ha-Zedek*'), xx.1 (here '*Teacher of the Community*'/'*Moreh ha-Yahad*'), xx.14 ('*Yoreh ha-Yahad*'), xx.32, 1QpHabi.11, v.10, xi.5, etc.

[115] Cf. Eusebius—relying on Hegesippus—in his *E.I.* 2.23.7.

[116] CDxx.33–34. In xx.19–20, '*those fearing God*' and '*fearing his Name*' are actually mentioned in the context of '*reckoning His Name and revealing Salvation*' (*Yesha*ᶜ), as we saw.

[117] Cf. CDvi.10–11 with 4QFlori.11–13. Once again, this kind of intertextuality, like that above we have been illustrating, demonstrates these documents to all have been written at approximately the same time and actually very late in the life of the Community. Again, this is the kind of '*internal data*' we have been talking about, regardless of the more tenuous '*results*' of palaeography and A.M.S. C-14 dating. Moreover, since these documents all consistently use the same allusions and the same turns-of-phrase, embodying the same '*zealous*' and aggressive attitude, they are the documents of '*a Movement*'. But, even more to the point, as parallels to Columns xix-xx of the Cairo Damascus Document do not yet seem to have been found among the extant finds from Cave 4, though the parallel Columns viii–viii to some extent have; it is perhaps a reasonable conclusion that the Damascus Document itself had not yet achieved a fixed final form and the materials that somehow made their way down to Egypt, to be found in our time in the Cairo *Genizah*, may not even have been written yet in their present form—but only after the abandonment of the settlement at Qumran.

[118] Cf. CDvii.1 with CDxix.10–11. In vii.19–20, as we shall see below, this is '*the Sceptre that shall arise*' from '*the Star Prophecy*' of Numbers 24:17; but though the usage in xix.10 is actually '*coming*' and not the usual '*standing up*' or '*arising*; there is no doubt that again the usage is singular and this is reinforced by the verbs in both cases, i.e., '*the Sceptre*', as we shall see as well below, is '*the Messiah of Aaron and Israel*.' The version in xix.8–13 is simpler and only refers to '*the Little Ones*' or '*the Meek of the Flock*' of Zechariah 13:7 (followed as we saw by Ezekiel 9:4) escaping while, '*with the coming of the Messiah of Aaron and Israel*' (the '*Sceptre*')—very definitely singular here and very definitely '*coming*' and, moreover, a vengeful war-like Messiah as in the War Scroll—'*the rest will be given over to the Avenging Sword of the Covenant*.'

[119] CDvi.5–6.

[120] CDvi.9.

[121] Cf. CDxx.11 and xx.30–33.

122 CDvii21/xix.34–35.

123 Cf. 1QpHabxii.14 and CDxx.34 above.

124 Cf. CDxx.2 and xx.5 and note CDvi.3–11, CDvii.16–21, and 4QFlori.12–13.

125 CDvi.14–15.

126 CDvi.17–18.

127 For 'the Mebakker' at Qumran, see CDxix.17–18, xiii.5–16, xiv.10–12, xv.7–14, 4QD266.16, 1QSvii.12–20, etc.

128 CDvii.8–9/xix.20–25.

129 Cf. CDvii.1 and note CDv.7–8.

130 See CDiv.19–21 and viii.12–13/xix.24–26.

131 CDv.6 and cf. vi.17–18.

132 CDv.7–8

133 CDv.11–15.

134 For MMT, see 4QMMTii.3–33, 47–60, and 83–89.

135 CDvi.18–19 and Cf. 1QpHabxi.8, which uses the same expression, calling it 'the Sabbath of their Rest.'

136 CDvi.19–20 and Cf. 4QMMTii.3–33 above.

137 CDvi.19–21.

138 Cf. War 2.139 and Ant. 18.117.

139 CDvi.20–vii.1.

140 CDvii.1–4 and cf. iv.15–18.

141 CDvii.4–5; for 'Rechabites,' see above, Chapters 6 and 16 and JBJ, pp. 229–42, 302–308, 467–69, etc.

142 Cf. CDvii.13–4 with xix.4–7 and, of course, vi.21, xx.18, 27, and 33 above.

143 Cf. CDxix.12–3 of Ms. B with vii.21–viii.1 of Ms. A.

144 CDvii.19–21.

145 (148)Cf. 4QFlori.12–13 with 1QMxi.6–15.

146 1QMxi.12. This same 'eating' verb is used in 1QpHab vi.7–8 to describe what 'the Kittim' (in our view, the Romans) do to 'all the Peoples year by year' —and here, too, our 'Peoples' expression once again.

147 CDvii.14 and 21–viii.1. Note in viii.2 the use of the same 'holding fast' expression again (also in xix.14).

148 See the coin on Plate no. 51: 'Shim'on Nasi-Israel.' As we just saw, this 'Nasi' is mentioned in CDvii.20 in exposition of 'the Star Prophecy' of Numbers 24:17 in CD vii.17–21. It is also quoted verbatim at this point in 1QMxi.5–7 and the exegesis is set forth, as we also saw, in terms of the 'no mere Man' citation from Isaiah 31:8 above.

149 CDvii.1–2 and CDxix.13–16 above.

[150] See an allusion of this kind in CDvii.16/xix.28–xx.16, which reiterates both this *'Judgement'* and this *'Visitation for Destruction'* over and over again.

[151] CDvii.2–3/xix.15. It is important to catalogue these *'Command'* / *'visitation'* usages—as we have been trying to do.

[152] See DSSU, pp. 24–29 and, in particular, 4Q285, Frag. 7, Lines 1–5. When we released this text at the height of the Scrolls controversy, we were roundly criticized for not appreciating whether it was *'the Nasi ha-ᶜEdah' / 'the Branch of David'* who was doing the *'executing'* or *'being executed'*; but the original find and its translation was the work of Prof. Wise and his University of Chicago Team, not mine, though at the time I did not quibble with it because I did not consider this to be what was most important about the text. It was the height of the struggle to free the Scrolls in 1991 and those in *'the Consensus'* and *'Official Team'*, who controlled the Scrolls at the time, were saying there was little or nothing of importance in the unpublished materials. I disagreed and, in order to gainsay this, I released this text so full of Messianic usages like *'the Branch of David,' 'the Root of Jesse,' 'the Nasi ha-ᶜEdah*, and, in particular, *'woundings,'* and almost no one has stopped talking about it ever since, including those in *'the Official Team'*, but also others. As I have been emphasizing, our purpose in releasing it was to show that there were important materials in the unpublished corpus that the Public had a right to see—not that we thought we had arrived at a definitive translation. On the contrary, the Scholarly Community has since worked this out to its satisfaction and that was the point of the whole exercise to begin with.

[153] Cf. 4Q285, Fragment 7, Line 5 and 4Q252 (The Genesis *Pesher*, DSSU, pp. 77–89)v.1–4.

[154] 4Q285, Fragment 7, Lines 2–4.

[155] Cf. CDvii.18–20 and 4QFlori.10–13 with 4Q252v.2–5, which also speaks of *'the Mehokkek'*—in this context, *'the Staff*—and a new, but absolutely beautiful, expression, *'the Messiah of Righteousness'*!

[156] See the coin on Plate no. 51: *'Shimᶜon Nasi-Israel'* and above, n. 148.

[157] (160) Cf. CDvii.20 above and compare this with 4Q285, Fragment 7, Lines 3–4 and 4Q252v. 2–4.

[158] The verb in Amos 9:12 is *'yarshu' / 'possessing,'* which only differs by a single consonant from and is homophonic with *'darshu' / 'seeking'* as we have it in James' speech and here in the Dead Sea Scrolls.

[159] CDvii.13–18. Everything is transformed here. First of all, this is not looked upon as an *'Exile'* but rather an *'escape.'* In addition, the *'beyond Damascus'* of Amos 5:27 (from which the document gets its name) now becomes *'My tents of Damascus'*—an expression to be used exegetically in both these passages in CD and in Acts. Finally, *'the Star of your God'* of Amos 5:26 is missing altogether, but reappears and is exploited in the exegesis that follows to pave the way for the citation of *'the Star Prophecy'*—incredibly fecund exegesis as we have and shall see.

[160] Cf. CDvii.18–21 with vii.14–15.

[161] Once again, we have a homophonic transformation from *'me-hal'ah'* to *'me-ohali'*—cf. Amos 5:28 with CDvii.14–15. This is incredibly creative and tendentious Biblical exposition—as

Nietzsche might put it, *'philosophizing with a hammer.'*

162 Cf. CDvii.15–16 with CDiii.19 and 4Q252 v.2–4.

163 Cf. CDvii.16–7 with 4Q252v.3. There is some dispute here about whether this should read *'the thousands of Israel'* or *'the Leaders of Israel'*—as in both cases the first word is a reconstruction. Probably *'thousands'* is more to the point in the context of what follows concerning *'the Kingdom of His People'* in v.4. In any event, in all cases the exposition is esoteric as can be seen.

164 CDvii.15–18. What is impressive here is that a basically idolatrous allusion is esoterically transformed into a negative allusion to Israel's religion—once again, *'exposition with a hammer'*!

165 Cf. Acts 15:14–15 with CDvii.17 and 4QMMTiii.15–16.

166 1QpHabii.9 and vii.5. The correspondence is almost exact.

167 Cf. CDi.7 and CDv.16, clearly using the same language as John the Baptist is pictured as using in the Synoptics.

168 Cf. CDvii.2 and 18–19 with Koran, *Surah* 82:12–19: *'on that Day ('the Day of Judgement'), the Command is Allah's.'*

169 Cf. Acts 15:17–19 (just before the first expression of James' directives to these *'Gentiles'* or *'Overseas Communities'*) with 4QMMTiii.33 (the last line).

170 See *War* 1.6 and n. 116 above.

171 See nn. 77, 80, and variously above

172 Cf. 4Q285, Fragment 7, Line 4 and 4Q252v.4 and note this incredibly original new phraseology *'the Messiah of Righteousness'*—as just indicated, definitively singular! Also see n. 153 above.

173 CDxix.6–16—by extrapolation with all these other characterizations, again, clearly a singular.

174 CDvii.9–12/xix.20–24.

175 Cf. CDvii.9 with 1QpHabxi.5–6. The allusion to such *'hemah'/'anger'*, human or divine. also appears in Ezekiel 13:13 which depicts a *'storm'* or *'torrential rain'*—not unlike, in our view, that which is portrayed in the previously-missing First Column of the Nahum *Pesher* in n. 177 below. One should also note here the *'rodef'* or *'pursuit'* ideology, well-known to Rabbinic Literature and even to the Modern Period where, recently, it was applied by the assassin of Prime Minister Itzhak Rabin as the reason for his act. Interestingly, too, recently high-placed Rabbis have used this ideology to forbid the surrender of any land to idolators; see *Ha-Aretz*, 6/30/04: *'Top Rabbi: Din Rodef on Anyone Ceding Land.'* Be this as it may, the ideology is to be found in *San.* 73a–74a (see also Laban's *'pursuit'* of Jacob in Genesis 31:23). However, what is most interesting from our point-of view and what might surprise the reader the most, *'the Rodef'* or *'Pursuer'* is not the one *'pursuing after'* someone to kill him or her (or the like— the Law also applies, for instance, to the rapist), but rather the bystander or third party who is obliged to warn or stop *'the Pursuer'*! It is at this point, too, that the individual doing the *'pursuing'* is to be judged guilty of death. In other words, here in the Habakkuk *Pesher*, it is *'the Wicked Priest'* by *'the Law of the Rodef'* who is guilty when the situation is framed in this manner and upon whom, the death sentence is to be pronounced. This is exactly the case here,

whether with knowledge of the Mishnaic position on this matter or coincidentally. The writer, obviously, considers the allusion to be framed in this manner purposefully. This is reinforced by exactly the same kind of linguistic presentation in CDi.19–21 where those who '*transgressed the Covenant and broke the Law banded together against the soul of the Just One* (James?) *and against all the Walkers in Perfection*' and '*pursued them with the sword*'—more intertextuality demonstrating the contemporaneity of all these kinds of Documents regardless of either '*the results*' of palaeography or AMS C-14 dating, (such as these may be).

176 CDvii.1–13/xix.25–26. The point here is that '*the Spouter*' is the one who '*spouted*' to '*the Daubers*'/'*Plasterers on*' or '*Builders of the Wall*' and '*kindled God's Wrath against his entire Congregation*' or '*Church.*' In the first, he is '*one of confused spirit*' or '*windiness*'; in the second, '*he walked in windiness*' or '*the Spirit and poured out confusion*'—very vivid! In both cases, he is called '*the Spouter of Lies.*'

177 Cf. *Ant.* 14.22 and 28 with 4QpNahi.2–11.

178 CDi.14–18.

179 Cf. CDi.20–1 with CDvii.13/xix.25–26. This very well could be '*the Lying Spouter's Congregation*' or '*Church.*' Once again, it is the internal sense which must decide the meaning.

180 Cf. CDvii.18–21/xix.30–33 with *San.* 90a and 105a–107b and see nn. 21 and 89–90 above.

181 (180)CDxix.33–35.

182 CDxx.2–4.

183 Cf. CDxix.34–35. The same expression is used in CDxx.19–20 concerning '*those reckoning His (God's) Name*' and/or '*God-Fearers*' as we have seen. But also see 4QMMTiii.33: '*reckoned to you as Righteousness*' above—i.e., in Paul's languageof '*justifying you.*'

184 CDxx.6–7. Also see ii.15–16, vii.4–7, 1QSi.15, viii.2, 18, ix.6–19, etc. and cf. especially James' instructions to Paul in Acts 21:24 that '*you show you yourself still walk regularly keeping the Law.*'

185 Literally, '*House of the Torah.*' Cf. CDxx.10 as expressed previously in CDxx.6.

186 1QSii.15–18; also see iv.9–14.

187 Cf. CDxx.8–10 with Acts 15:19–29 and 4QMMTii.8–9 and iii.6–7 and 23–24.

188 CDxx.10–13.

189 CDxx.17–20.

190 CDxx.25–26.

191 CDxiii.6–8.

192 CDxiii.9 and xiv.14–15.

193 CDxv.8–17.

194 1QMvii.4–5.

195 CDxiv.17–19. It is hard to imagine anything that could be more '*Messianic*' than this—nor that anyone could imagine this '*Messiah*' in this context to be plural. *Pace* research in the first days of Qumran Studies—much of which now appears as tendentious (just as those who disagree

with my approach would consider mine to be!).

[196] 1QpHabviii.2

[197] Cf. '*the Priest Commanding the Many*' described in CDxiv.6–7 and the new fragment in 4QD266, Fragment 11, Line 8 (see Plate 54 and also 4QD267, Fragment 9, Lines 10–1, which parallels CDxiv.6–7). It is not clear if this is or can be the same person as '*the Mebakker*' or '*Bishop*' or not.

[198] CDxii.19–23 and xiii.21–22.

[199] Cf. 1 Corinthians 5:9–11 (contradicting the picture of '*Jesus*' eating with '*harlots*' in the Gospels) and 6:9–7:2 (including both the '*idolatry*' language and, following in 7:35, that of the '*snare*') with CDiv.14–18 and v. 7–11.

[200] Cf. CDxx.3 and 1QSviii.17–23.

[201] CDix.1–7.

[202] Cf. Eusebius, *E.I.* 3.7.9 and *pars.* and our discussion of this point in Chaper 3 above, *JBJ*, pp. 353–64, and *JJHP*, pp. 10–12.

[203] For '*the Many*' (probably based on the language of Isaiah 53:11f.), see '*the (High) Priest Commanding the Many*' above in CDxiv.6–7, 4QD267, Fragment 9, Lines 10–11, and 4QD266, Fragment 11, Line 8, CDxiiii.7–xiv.6, 1QSvi.1–vii.27, viii.18–ix.2, 1QpHabx.11, 4QpNah. ii.8, etc.

[204] 1QpHabx.9–12.

[205] CDv.17–19.

[206] See *Ps. Jonathan* on Numbers 22:22 and R. Pattai, *A Book of Jewish Legends: Gates to the City*, 1981, pp. 312 and 788. Also see the *Encyclopedia Biblica* entry on '*Jannes and Jambres*,' *Apocryphon of Jannes and Jambres the Magicians*, Leiden, 1994, Logion 34, and *San.* 105a–106b and *Men.* 35a above.

[207] See CDv.7–11 above and note how this is preceded by the charge of '*every man of them sleep with women during their periods*'—a charge obviously directed against Herodians and the curious basis of the '*not separating clean from unclean in*' and, therefore, the '*polluting the Temple*' charge; but also followed in v.12–19 by the John the Baptist-like '*offspring of Vipers*' characterizations we have already discussed above.

[208] CDv.14–15—the addition of '*unless he was forced*' in Line 15 obviously also being significant.

[209] CDv.13–14 and cf. Matthew 3:7, 12:34, 23:33, and *pars.* and n. 207 above.

[210] Cf. CDvi.7–10 above and 1QSix.23.

[211] CDv.11–12.

[212] CDv.12–16 and nn. 207 and 209 above.

[213] See n. 184 above and CDii.15–6, vii.4–7, xx.6–7, 1QSi.15, viii.2, 18, ix.6–19, etc.

[214] CDvi.11–vii.5 and note vi.15 and vii.1, as well as viii.9/xix.20 on the same subject ending again with '*the venom of vipers.*' For the Wicked Priest '*robbing the Riches of the Poor*,' see 1QpHabxii.10 and cf. as well viii.11–12 where '*he stole from*' and '*profiteered from the spoils of the Peoples*' (in our

view, as repeatedly observe, 'Herodians'—also called here 'the Men of Violence').

215 CDv.15 and n. 208 above. This is an important exception and generally completely unappreciated because of poor translations—Hebrew to English.

Chapter 23

[1] See my Introduction to *DSSU*, pp. 2–16.

[2] See, for instance, 4Q521 ('*The Messiah of Heaven and Earth*'), Frag. 1, Col. ii.12, 4Q434 and 436 ('*The Hymns of the Poor*'), Frag. 2, Col. i.1–3, etc. in *DSSU*, pp. 19–23 and 232–41.

[3] See, in particular, nn. 85 of Chapter 21 and 118 of Chapter 22 above; but also see nn. 21–22, 42, and 82 of 21 and 3, 10, 39, 172, and 195 of 22 as well.

[4] See 4Q*MMT*ii.1–3 and iii.29–34.

[5] Cf. 1QSviii.12–23 and ix.16–24; for '*the stumbling block of the Tongue*,' see 4Q525(*Beatitudes*)ii.1.

[6] For '*puffed up*' in the Habakkuk *Pesher*, see vii.14–16 which introduces the all-important exposition of Habakkuk 2:4: '*the Righteous shall live by his Faith*.'

[7] Cf. CDiii.6 and v.7.

[8] See Romans 14:1–4 and cf. 1QHix.29–35 and Jerome's '*Gospel of the Hebrews*.'

[9] See CDiii.19–iv.12 and 1QSix.22–25.

[10] See Plate 54 (4QD266), but also the last fragment of 4QD270—both of which contain this empty space at the bottom as well as on the left.

[11] Cf. CDi.10–16.

[12] Cf. 4QD266.5–7 with CDi.15–16, but also see CDvii.18–19 on '*the Judgement upon all those who reject the Commandments of God and forsake them*'—in particular '*the Builders of the Wall*' (probably '*the Pharisees*'), mentioned earlier as '*following the Spouter of Lying*' in iv.19–20 and note xx.3–15 which also continues on to mention both '*the Men of Scoffing*' and '*the Liar*.'

[13] Cf. 4QD266.7–8 with xx.3–11, but also see 1QSviii.20–24.

[14] See Chapter 21 and n. 118 of Chapter 22 above.

[15] Cf. 1QSii.4–19, words more or less repeated in 4Q286–87 ('*The Chariots of Glory*'—DSSU, pp 222–30): '*The Community Council Curses Belial*' (now known as '*Blessings*'—4QBer), Frag 3, Col ii.1–12.

[16] See Chapter 20 and, in particular, nn. 50, 53, and 59–60 above.

[17] Cf. CDix.1.

[18] 4QpNahii.7–8.

[19] See CDxiv.9 on the '*Mebakker*' and cf. 4QD266.10.

[20] For a discussion of the relationship of '*the Mourners for Zion*' with the birth and development of the Karaite Movement, see A. Paul, *Ecrits de Qumran et Sectes Juives aux Premiers Siecles de L'Islam: Recherches sur l'origine du Qaraisme*, Paris, 1969 and Chapers 3, 4, 7, 15, and 21 above.

21 4QD266.18 and see, for instance, G. Vermes, *The Complete Dead Sea Scrolls in English (Revised Edition)*, 2004, p.154, *et. al.*

22 4QD266.18–9 (see *DSSU*, pp. 212–9).

23 See Numbers 6:1–21 and *JBJ*, pp. 222–63 and 939–52.

24 This notice in Acts 18:18–22 would appear to be defective, as it speaks of Paul *'sailing away to Syria,' 'shaving his head,' 'coming to Ephesus,' 'sailing from Ephesus,'* and finally *'landing at Caesarea (and) going up and greeting the Church before going down to Antioch'* —when the *'shaving his head'* probably should have come in connection with activities *'up'* in Jerusalem, as it does in Acts 21, and not at Cenchrea (the Aegean-side seaport of Corinth) unless, even here, he was involved in a *'temporary Nazirite oath'* procedure of some kind.

25 Cf. Acts 21:22–23 and for more on the requirements of *'cutting off one's hair,'* see *M. Naz.* 3:4–6 (which even includes reference to Queen Helen's Seven-year Nazirite oath), 6:1–10, and 7:1–9:2 and commentaries. One point of relevance to Paul in 18:18 would be *M. Naz.* 1:6 which seems to put a minimum of *'thirty days'* on a traveler's *'Nazirite oath'* before shaving his head and *M. Naz.* 3:1–3 which pursues this point further.

26 Cf. 1QSii.2, viii.21–25, ix.6, CDxx.2–5, xx.7, etc.

27 1QSi.16–18.

28 1QSiii.9–11.

29 Cf. Matthew 5:18/Luke 16:17.

30 1QSii.24, ii.26, v.10, etc.

31 Cf. 1QpHabv.11–12 with CDi.15–16.

32 In particular, the kind of texts we are talking about are 4QFlor, 4QTest, 4QTanh, and 4Q252–253 (otherwise known as 4QCommGen).

33 The extant Documents of this latter kind are materials like Ben Sira, Jubilees, Wisdom, Enoch, The Testament of Levi, and the like—most from a previous Period and not specifically *'new'* as such. But even many of these display the characteristics of this *'Opposition'* or *'Sectarian'* Movement.

34 These usages occur in CDvi.2, vi.7, vi.11, xii.20–21, xiii.2, xx.14, etc.; whereas the actual allusion to *'the Teacher of Righteousness'* occurs in i.11 as we have seen.

35 Cf. 1QSvi.12, vi.19–20, CDix.17–19, ix.22, xiii.5–7, xiii.13–16 (these last three references include allusion to being *'over all the camps,'* just as references to *'the High Priest Commanding the Many'* do), xiv.8–12, xv.7–8, xv.11, xv.14, etc. —that to *'the Cohen,'* xiv.6–7 and 4QD266.8–9.

36 Cf. CDxiii.6.

37 CDxiv.8–10.

38 CDiv.19–21 and viii.13/CDxix.31–32 and cf. CDi.14–15, xx.10–11, 1QpHabv.11, x.9–12, etc.

39 Cf. CDvi.10–11 above.

40 CDxx.10–12.

41 CDxx.14–15.

[42] Ibid. Note that this is followed in CDxx.15–17 with the quotation from Hosea 1:4 that *'there is no King, no Prince, no Judge, and none to judge with Righteousness.'* If we were to associate this with *'Christian'* tradition, this would approximately agree with the period between the death of the Gospel *'Jesus'* and that of Paul (if we could precisify it)—approximately 40 years later.

[43] See 1QHii.31 and iv.9–10 and cf. CDxx.10–11 above.

[44] The material about *'the Dajjal'* in Islamic tradition is generally to be found in the *Hadith* literature but it is a deep-seated belief among Sunnis.

[45] We shall cover this *'remembrance'* notation further below but, not only is it found in Gospel renditions of *'the Last Supper,'* a variation of it occurs in CDxx.19 in *'the Book of Remembrance that would be written out for God-Fearers.'* Another variation of it also occurs in the Pseudoclementine *Recognitions'* scene of the miraculous *'whitening'* of the tomb of the two brothers, who were *'remembered before God.'*

[46] This is true of passages from CDvii–viii, which can be found in 4QD266, Frag 3, Col. iii; but unfortunately, few if any parallels have yet been found to CDxix/xx (i.e., Ms. B) as far as they are not paralleled by vii–viii. This means, of course, that the Damascus Document was probably still in a state of flux or developing at the time of the deposit or abandonment of the Scrolls in the caves, as I have already alluded to above.

[47] Cf. 4QD270, Frag. 2, Col. ii.13–14 and cf. 4QD266, Frag. 8, Col. ii.

[48] Cf. *The Complete Dead Sea Scrolls in English* (Revised Edition), p.130 and my *DSSU*, pp. 361. I have contended that this usage *'Mashichehu'/'His Messiah(s)'* in Hebrew is idiomatic. For me, this is proven by the singular adjective *'ha-Kodesh'/'Holy'* attached to it. If understood as a plural, normally the adjective should be plural as well—but in all cases, as already explained, there are exceptions.

[49] CDv.21–vi.2.

[50] Cf. CDi.14–16 with 4QD266, Frag. 11, Lines 10–14

[51] CDi.20–21; cf. Vermes in *The Complete Dead Sea Scrolls in English*, p. 130 above.

[52] Cf. CDi.21 with Galatians 5:16, Romans 8:1–8:4, etc.

[53] See 1QpHabii.1–10.

[54] Cf. *MZCQ*, pp. xv, 35, 41–43, etc, and *JJHP*, pp. vii–viii, 22–41, 52–64, etc.

[55] He started this kind of derogation in his 1995 edition (*The Fourth Edition*) of *The Dead Sea Scrolls in English*, pp. xxx–xxxi above (even though, as he himself admits on p. xxi, he benefited mightily from the publication of almost all the previously unpublished plates by Prof. James Robinson and myself in 1991) and continued this on through all subsequent editions up to *The Complete Dead Sea Scrolls in English* (Revised Edition), pp. 21 and 65, grouping me with Barbara Thiering and remarking *'Only the sensation-seeking media have been taken in by their theories (sic!)'*—this from the brave and insightful Oxford don! But look at his insightful conclusion in this section on p. 25: *'Essenism is dead... and though the Teacher of Righteousness clearly sensed the deeper obligations implicit in the Mosaic Law, he was without the genius of Jesus the Jew (thus!—his own designation), who succeeded in uncovering the essence of religion as an existential relationship*

between man and man and man and God'—my, my, such profound detachment and insight. This is scholarship? He acts like he were really there. Two hundred years of research into *'the Historical Jesus'* have just completely passed him by!

[56] *'The straw man,'* I am speaking about I described in nn. 64–6 of Chapter 2 above, confusing me with the theories of J. Teicher of Cambridge University in his own *Journal of Jewish Studies* in 1951 and 1955, who in the early days of Qumran research considered Jesus *'the Righteous Teacher'* and Paul *'the Wicked Priest.'* While I am flattered to be grouped in such illustrious company, obviously if Paul is the Establishment Wicked Priest, he can laugh as much as he wants; but he hasn't a clue, as I have explained above as well, that in my theories I have always distinguished between *'the Wicked Priest'* and *'the Liar'/'Spouter of Lying'*—which he, manifestly lacking in historical perspicuity and text critical acumen, does not—identifying *'the Wicked Priest'* as Ananus ben Ananus responsible for the death of James, and the internal adversary, known as *'the Liar'/'Windbag'/'Spouter of Lying'/'Comedian',* as Paul. In so doing, as I have explained in detail above, he demonstrates with certitude and conclusively that he has not read my articles or books to any extent before criticizing them and, moreover, hasn't a clue what they are about. Nevertheless, this doesn't prevent him from criticizing my works by meticulously pinpointing them in footnotes in his own, so the reader will not be unaware of all the times he has done so and even giving a reference to the *DSSU*, 1992 as a source—page number (as I have noted previously) missing—not surprisingly, since the point he is alluding to is not there! Was he relying on a student or hearsay for this citation or did he make this amazing discovery about my position himself? This is what is meant by *'setting up a straw man'* and then proceeding to demolish him.

[57] Cf. the first paper I gave to the Society of Biblical Literature in 1976: *'James the Just as Righteous Teacher'* and my upgrading this and other papers in the two books *MZCQ*, Leiden, 1983 and *JJHP*, Leiden, 1986 and the references in n. 54 above. I continue this below in Chapter 26: *'He rejected the Law in the Midst of their Whole Assembly'.* That means I have been talking about this for thirty years. I hope that will be sufficient for Prof. Vermes (and others like him) to understand!

[58] 1QpHabi.11, viii.8 and 16, etc. and 4QpPs 37iv.8–10.

[59] 1QpHabviii.16–17 and xi.12–14.

[60] See *The Messiah Jesus and John the Baptist*, New York, 1931, pp. 540–46.

[61] See Romans 2:25–3:1, 3:30, 4:9–12, 8:1–9:8, 15:8, Galatians 5:2–6:5, etc.

[62] *War* 2.8/*Ant.* 17.207

[63] See also Hebrews 1:17, 4:14, 9:9–10, 10:21–2, etc.

[64] See, for instance, how *'the Sons of Zadok'* are described in CDiv.2–4 or *'the Priesthood after the Order of Melchizedek'* in Hebrews 5:4–11 and 7:5–28. The point is that both these designations are parallel and playing off the usage *'Z-D-K'* or *'Righteousness'* in Hebrew.

[65] 1QpHabviii.13 and xii.8

[66] Cf. *War* 2.409–16 with 1QpHabii.3–6.

[67] 1QpHabii.1–6, but also see CDxx.14–15.

⁶⁸ Cf. James 1:22–27, 2:9–12, 4:11, and 4:17 and the *'doing,' 'keeping,'* and *'breaking'* usages in CDi.20, ii.18–iii.3, iii.12, iv.1, vi.14, xx.2, xx.17, xx.21–22 and 1QpHabii.6, vii.11, viii.1, etc.

⁶⁹ Cf. 1QpHabxii.4–5 with 3–5 and 4QpNahiv.5–7 with 4QpPs 37ii.9–10, iii.10, 1QSvi.20, vii.10–25, viii.19, etc.

⁷⁰ 4QpNahiv.4–8.

⁷¹ That the Northern Kingdom was referred to throughout the Prophets as *'Ephraim'* (Joseph's more powerful son according to the blessings of Jacob), one has only to consult Isaiah 7:2–17, 11:13, Jeremiah 31:6–20, Ezekiel 37:16–19, Hosea 4:17–18, etc.

⁷² Cf. CDxx.19–20 with 1 Corinthians 11:24–25 and Luke 22:19.

⁷³ Ps. *Rec.* 1.70–71.

⁷⁴ This is to be found in 1QpHabvii.5–14 and clearly involves *'the Last Era,' 'the Final Times,'* and *'the End'* and just as clearly states the proposition that these *'shall be prolonged'* and *'exceed anything the Prophets have foretold.'* Moreover the passage under exposition is Habakkuk 2:3, preceding Habakkuk 2:4: *'The Righteous shall live by his Faith',* and the exegesis is attributed to *'the Righteous Teacher,'* and the application (just as the exposition of Habakkuk 2:4 following it) only to *'the Doers of Torah'*—i.e., by implication, it did no apply to *'non-Doers'* either within or without *'the House of Judah.'* Nothing could be closer to *'the Delay of the Parousia'* in Christian theology to follow except it has, once more, been *'Paulinized,'* i.e., extended, reversed, and applied now to *'non-Torah-doing Pauline Gentile Christians.'*

⁷⁵ See S. Goranson, *'Essenes: Etymology from ᶜAsah,' Revue de Qumran,* XV, 1984, pp. 483–98.

⁷⁶ See Epiphanius, *Haeres.* 29.1.3–4, 4.9, and 5.1–7.1.

⁷⁷ Cf. 4QpNahiii.1–10 and 1QpHabx.5–13.

⁷⁸ 4QpNahiii.1–2.

⁷⁹ See, for instance, M. Allegro and A. A. Anderson, *DJDV:1* (4Q158–4Q186), Oxford, 1968 and J. Strugnell, *'Notes en marge du volume V des DJD,' Revue de Qumran,* VII, 1976, pp. 163–276.

⁸⁰ Cf. CDxix.10–11, but also see iii.19, iv.4, vi.10–11, vi.21, xx.5, xx.18, xx.33–34, etc. and cf. *E.I.* 2.23.33 and *pars.*

⁸¹ See 4QSD265, Frags. 1–2 and cf. 1QSvii.13–17, CDxiv.22, and 4QD270, Frag. 7. I had already called attention to this overlap without recourse to the new manuscripts, observing that CD and 1QS were therefore virtually parts of the same ongoing document, in *MZCQ* in 1983.

⁸² Psalm 37:17–9 and cf. 4QpPs 37.iii.1 which overlaps CDiv.2–3, vi.4–5, and viii.16, to say nothing of xx.17.

⁸³ Cf. 4QpPs 37.iii.1–2, which also mentions *'the inheritance of Adam'* and *'Salvation'* in the same breath, with CDvii.5–6 and xx.21–22.

⁸⁴ CDvi.5 and viii.16,

⁸⁵ CDiv.2–3 and Chapter 22 above.

⁸⁶ CDvi.14–vii.5.

⁸⁷ See my comments in Chapter 2 above—in particular nn. 57 and 62—and in J. Atwill and S.

Braunheim (with charts and with my participation), 'Redating the Radiocarbon Dating of the Dead Sea Scrolls' in DSD (11/2), Leiden, 2004, pp. 144–57.

88 Cf. Chapter 2 above and Chapters 24-25 and 28 below.

89 1QpHabvi.3–8.

90 See *War* 6.316.

91 See *JJHP*, pp. 27–28 and *War* 3.132–34, 141–339, 409–54, 4.11–83, etc.

92 See *Ant.* 18.65–84 (an episode, of course, missing from the *War*) and cf. 18.56–9/*War* 2.171–74.

93 *Ant.* 18.288–309/*War* 2.190–205.

94 1QpHabviii.11–13 and ix.4–7.

95 Cf. *Ant.* 20.181 and 206–7.

96 See *War* 2.409–416 above.

97 Cf. 1QpHabvii.8–viii.3.

98 1QpHabvii.4–5.

99 1QpHabii.1–10. This, of course, is the same *'believing'* we encounter in the Pauline Corpus and would be all the more meaningful if we should find a play in it on just this sort of thing.

100 1QpHabii.6–10.

101 The description of these *'Kittim'*—their ferocity, ruthlessness, and unstoppability—dominate Columns 1QpHabii.10–iv.14 and v.13–vi.11.

102 1QpHabii.10–iii.11.

103 The description of these *'Fortresses'* as being *'of the Peoples,'* once more reinforces our understanding of this term as descriptive of *'Herodians'*—cf. *War* 1.364, 1.402–21, 2.484, *Ant.* 16.143, etc.

104 1QpHabvi.11. This is certainly borne out by what Josephus describes happened around the Sea of Galilee in 67 CE—particularly Tarichaeae; *War* 3.532–42 (n.b., it is here that Josephus observes that Vespasian's advisers insisted that, where *Jews* were concerned, *'no offence could be considered an Impiety'*—thus!).

105 Cf. 1QpHabix.3–10 in Chapters 3 and 18 above and *JJHP*, pp. 44–8 and 100. This formula is so simple that it is hard to envision any other explanation.

106 See 1QpHabviii.10–ix.12 and cf. 4QpPs 37ii.18–20 and iv.9–10.

107 1QpHabxii.2–6.

108 See Chapter 2 above, particularly n. 57, and in J. Atwill and S. Braunheim (with charts and with my participation as just noted above), *'Redating the Radiocarbon Dating of the Dead Sea Scrolls'* in DSD (11/2), Leiden, 2004, pp. 144–57.

109 Cf. 4QpPs 37.ii.18–20 and iv.9–10 above.

110 Note the *'Judgements upon Evil'* performed upon the *'corpse'* of the Wicked Priest in 1QpHabix.1–2 and *'the Judgement'* (here literally, *'the House of Judgement'* and probably *'the Last Judgement',* as I have explained in detail elsewhere and will further below) described in such

detail in ix.9–x.5.

111 1QpHabxii.2–6 and *E. H.* 2.23.15. Note that, whereas Eusebius quoting Hegesippus only gives Isaiah 3:10: *'they shall eat the fruit of their doing',* Isaiah 3:11 follows this up with: as for 'the Wicked' (in Qumran exposition usually the catch phrase for 'the Wicked Priest'), *'the reward of his hands will be done to him'*—just as here in Habakkuk *Pesher.* Nor can such an exposition be considered accidental. Note, *inter alia,* also 4QpPs 37iv.9–10 and CDvii.9–10/xix.5–6.

112 Cf. CDxix.8–9.

113 4QpPs 37ii.4, iii.12, and iv.18 and cf. CDiii.7, xx.27, etc. above and Paul in Galatians 5:12.

114 1QpHabxii.3–9 and *E.I.* 3.27.1–6 on the followers of James as 'the Ebionites.'

115 See Jerome, *Vir. ill.* 2.

116 Cf. 1QpHabxii.10–xiii.4 with 4QpPs 37iii.12.

117 Cf. 1QpHabxii.9–10 with *Ant.* 20.181 and 206–7—and cf., too, *Pes.* 57a.

118 1QpHabxi.4–9 and Chapters 24-25 below.

119 *Ant.* 20.105–132 and 194–97 and cf. *War* 2.228–46.

120 1QpHabviii.8–9.

121 1QpHabviii.12.

122 Cf. *E.I.* 1.9.2–3 and 11.9. It is these 'Acts' that cause him to give the interpolated material from Josephus about 'Jesus' and also even the counter indicative material about John the Baptist in order to contradict these.

123 4QpPs 37ii.18–20.

124 4QpPs 37iv.8–10.

125 1QpHabix.1–2.

126 4QpPs 37iii.1.

127 Cf. 4QpPs 37ii.19–20 and iv.9–12 with CDi.7–9.

128 4QpPs 37ii.6–11.

129 4QpPs 37ii.11–13.

130 4QpPs 37i.26–27 and cf. 1QpHabx.9–12.

131 Cf. CDxx.13–15 with 4QpPs 37ii.7–10.

132 4QpPs 37ii.7 with CDvii.4–5 and cf. too i.12–3.

133 4QpPs 37ii.12–3 and cf. 1QpHabvii.10–viii.3.

134 4QpPs 37ii.9–10 and 18–20.

135 For 'Salvation,' see 4QpPs 37iii.19 and iv.19–20 and cf. ii.7–8 and 19–20.

136 Cf. 4QpPs 37ii.19 with *Ant.* 20.200–201 and also see 1QpHabxii.3–10.

137 This is what Eusebius is railing about in *E.I.* 1.9.2–1.11.9, where he himself actually quotes the two passages from Josephus about Jesus and John the Baptist from *Ant.* 18.63–64 and 18.116–19.

138 1QpHabii.1–10.

139 1QpHabii.6–8.

140 See 1QpHabviii.9–13 above.

141 1QpHabix.4–7.

142 *Ant.* 20.214.

143 *War* 1.486–87 and *Ant.* 15.253–66 and note the individuals called '*the sons of Baba*' here (some consider this to be '*sons of Saba*'), who are described as popular with the citizens of Jerusalem and who are protected by Costobarus (triggering his execution, because they wanted to resist the Roman take-over). Who are they? Why do we hear so little about them?

144 *War* 1.486–87 and *Ant.* 15.252–59.

145 Cf. *Ant.* 15.259–62 with 20.139–47. It is here he also describes the marriage of Mariamme to Demetrius the Alabarch of Alexandria after divorcing Polemo. The latter had expressly circumcised himself at the request of her father, Agrippa I, to marry her. In doing so, he also describes how Drusilla married Felix under similar circumstances and the death of their son in the eruption of Vesuvius in 79 CE. Moreover, here too, he mentions the role of the infamous '*Simon Magus*'/'*Atomus*' in this divorce!

146 *Ant.* 15.164–267.

147 *Ant.* 15.365–69 with 18.116–19.

148 4QMMTii.3–9.

149 Cf. CDi.20–21 and 1QHi.9–10, ii.32–4, iii.25 (all '*nephesh-Ebion*'—'*the soul of the Poor One*'), and v.14 (this is '*nephesh-ᶜAni*'—'*the soul of the Meek One*').

150 *War* 4.228–353 and 566–72 and cf. *Ant.* 20.200 on the death of James.

151 See *War* 2.566, 3.11, 20–28 (here Niger is called '*the Pereaite*' and emerges from the ground after being thought dead for three days!).

152 *War* 2.520.

153 Cf. *War* 2.520, 2.567, and 3.11.

154 *War* 4.359–63. As we have been suggesting, much in Niger's life and death recalls the picture of '*Jesus*' life and death in the Gospels.

155 *War* 4.335–43.

156 See 2 Chronicles 24:20–22, where the individual killed in this manner is called '*Zechariah son of Yehoiada the High Priest*,' not '*Zechariah son of Iddo*' as described in Zechariah 1:1–2. Moreover, this is sometime in the 700's before the Assyrian conquest. Of course, Ezra 5:1 and 6:14 have the chronology right and, naturally, there is nothing in these about the death of one '*Zacharias son of Barachias whom you slew between the Temple and the altar*.' The only such individual that even remotely resembles this description is the traitorous collaborator described in *War* 4.335–43.

157 These are the names ascribed to these tombs by tradition though, recently, there has been a plaque discovered attached to one of the neighboring tombs known as '*the Tomb of Absalom*' which ascribes it to that '*Zachariah*' considered to be the father of John the Baptist (see n. 130 in Chapter 2 above and the article by J. Zias and E. Puech referred to there). For pictures of

these tombs, see Plates 83, 86, and 90 and, for their relationship to *the Pinnacle of the Temple* and these tombs, see Plate 81.

[158] See *War* 2.18–20 above.

[159] See *War* 4.81–82.

[160] *War* 4.140–46.

[161] 4QpPs 37iii.7–8.

[162] CDvii.6–8/xix.18–20.

[163] 4QpPs 37iii.11–12.

[164] 1QpHabix.9–12.

[165] 1QpHabv.3–5.

[166] For this *'Day of Judgement'* and these same *'Evil Ones,'* see 1QpHabxii.12–xiii.4 above. For *'the hand of the Messiah,'* *'the hand of the Poor'*, and *'the sword of no mere Man,'* see 1QMxi.7–13.

[167] 4QpPs 37iii.5–7.

[168] 4QpPs 37iii.1–8.

[169] See *Vita* 193–204 and cf. *War* 4.160, 238–83, and 316–25.

[170] *War* 4.238–42 (Jesus speaking) and 4.326–33 (Josephus' own words).

[171] *War* 4.314–25.

[172] 1QpHabviii.11–13 and ix.4–7. The allusion to *'collecting taxes'* or *'tax-farming'* literally occurs in vi.1–7.

[173] Cf. *War* 1.152–53/*Ant.* 14.72 for Pompey; *War* 1.354–57/*Ant.* 14.481–86 for Herod.

[174] See 1QpHabix.4–5 above.

[175] Cf. 1QpHabix.5 with CDix.7.

[176] Cf. Vermes, *op. cit.*, p. 514, etc.

[177] 1QpHabviii.13.

[178] 1QpHabix.6–7 above.

[179] Cf. *Ant.* 20.139–47 above.

Chapter 24

[1] *War* 2.197 and 409–16 and cf. *Apion* 2.77.

[2] CDv.8–11 and viii.6–7 above and see our Table of Herodian Genealogies and note the number of niece marriage and marriage with close family cousins.

[3] See *Vita* 2–5.

[4] Again, see our Table of Herodian Genealogies.

[5] For a description of this situation, see *War* 2.407–32 and for Josephus' command and activities in Galilee, see *War* 2.568–76. This use of the term *'Innovators'* and *'Innovations'* is widespread in Josephus and relates very closely to a combination of Religious *'Innovation'* with Revolutionary activity.

[6] *Ant.* 19.328–31.

[7] *Ant.* 19.332–34.

[8] Cf. 1QMxii.1–12., CDiv, 3, xx.10, xx.13, 1QSviii.9, ix.6, etc.,

[9] Cf. *JBJ*, pp. 532–9, 600–4, 640–4, etc., *Ant.* 332–4 above, and Ps. *Rec.* 1.171.

[10] *M. Sota* 7:8 and cf. *M. Bik.* 3–4.

[11] 11QTlvi.12–9 and lvii.15–20.

[12] 11QTxlvi.9–12, xlvii.5–18, and lxvi.13–6

[13] Cf. 11QTxlvi.9–12 above and my Appendix in *JJHP*, pp. 86–94.

[14] See F. M. Cross, *The Ancient Library at Qumran*, pp. 135 and 140 (and, in general, pp. 127–60), who set the tone for this whole approach. But also see G. Vermes in his first *Dead Sea Scrolls in English*, London, 1962, pp. 62ff., J. T. Milik, *Ten Years of Discovery in the Wilderness of Judea*, London, 1959, pp. 44–98, and F. F. Bruce, *Second Thoughts on the Dead Sea Scrolls*, Exeter, 1956, p. 100, who sums up their general position quite succinctly; and cf. *Ant.* 12.414, 419, and 434.

[15] Cf. 1QMi.4–ii.13, CDi.5–12, xx.13–17, Matthew 3:7, 18:22, 24:15 and *pars.*, Revelation 6:17, 14:10ff., etc.

[16] *War* 2.7.

[17] *War* 2.406–502, 6.236–43, *Vita* 340–67, 402–10, *Apion* 1.51, etc. and see, *JBJ*, pp. 67–69 citing Tacitus, *Annal.* 2.85 and 15.44 and Sulpicius Severus, *Historia Sacra* 2.30–31.

[18] *War* 2.427.

[19] Note the peculiar usage '*be-ᶜorot*' in 11QTXLvii.4–18 (following allusion to '*ballaᶜ*' and protecting the purity of the Temple) and 4QMMTii.18–24 (following allusion to beginning '*things sacrificed to idols*' as representative of all '*Gentile*' offerings in the Temple) and cf. *San.* 105a–106b.

[20] See 2 Samuel 16:7, 20:1, and 2 Chronicles 13:7. In 1 Kings 21:13, for instance, two '*sons of Belial*' are directly involved at the instigation of Jezebel in the stoning of Naboth for blasphemy and for opposing the King.

[21] See *San.* 105a above and my Appendix on '*Ballaᶜ/Belaᶜ in the Temple Scroll*' in *JJHP*, pp. 87–94, which also includes a discussion of Job 20:15 and is replete with Qumranisms such as '*stealing from the Poor*,' '*the Tongue*,' '*the poison of asps*,' etc. and contains the original of the passage found in the Temple Scroll, Column xlvi, alluding to '*Ballaᶜ/Belaᶜ*' and playing on '*swallowing*.'

[22] See *War* 3.445–502.

[23] Cf. 1QpHabvi.1–11 above and note that this has been interpreted as '*the Year of the Three Emperors*' (68 CE) and how these changes in the Senate Chamber were perceived abroad.

[24] See, for instance, Josephus' description of Pontius Pilate's attempt to introduce the military standards which carried '*the busts of the Emperor*' on them into the City of Jerusalem in *Ant.* 18.55–59 and *War* 2.169–74 and cf. A. D. Nock, '*The Roman Army and the Roman Religious Year*,' *HTR*, XLIV, 1952, p.239, Tacitus, *Hist.* 4.62 and *Annals* 1.39.7 and 2.17.2, Tertullian,

Apology 16.8, and Pliny, *N. H.* 13.3.23. Also note, Suetonius on Vespasian 6.2 and Titus 4.1 on the number of busts and statues of the latter there actually were among his former legionnaires.

[25] 4QpNahii.2–4 and note how, in the rest of this *Pesher*, usages like overseas 'Apostles,' a '*Lying Tongue*,' '*walking in Lying*' 'deceitful lips,' 'the Last Days,' 'the Simple of Ephraim,' 'joining,' etc., are pervasive.

[26] This accusation is very strong in Christian theology as it develops and Josephus himself even several times uses it—starting with his Introduction to the Jewish *War* 1.10.

[27] Such a reference may be found in that to '*Mezad-Hassidim*'/'the Fortress of the Hassidim' in the parallel documents from the Wadi Murabba'at (*Mur.* 45.6) which may, in fact, actually refer to Masada—if not to the actual structures at Qumran.

[28] For a general description see *Ber.* 47b. But for the widest employment of this description in the *Mishnah*, see *M. Dem.* 1:1–2:3. *M. Sh.* 3:3–4:6, *Hag.* 2.7, *Git.* 5.9, etc.

[29] CDvii.5–10 and cf. v.13–14.

[30] CDvii.6.

[31] CDv.11–12

[32] CDvii.3/xix.16

[33] CDvii.12–3/xix.24–6. There are two versions here: the first (Ms. A) literally mentions '*the Spouter of Lying*.' The second (Ms. B) actually speaks of '*the Spouter of Adam for Lying*,' which is obviously corrupt but still trying to say something. Nevertheless, it contains the material about '*walking in the Spirit*' from Micah 2:11, upon which the whole passage is based.

[34] CDvii.13/xix.21.

[35] 4Q434–37 and cf. *DSSU*, pp. 233–41.

[36(16)] 4Q434ii.5–6 and ii.8–9/4Q437ii.8–10 amid reference 'vipers,' 'cursing' and a general picture of Hell and cf. the parallels in 4Q525(*Beatitudes*)v.1–8.

[36] See A. N. Sherwyn-White, *The Roman Citizenship*, Oxford, 1939, pp. 270–5 and Chapter 23, n. 77 above—the Romans being 'the Princeps Gentium'/'the Lord of the Peoples.'

[37] 1QpHabviii.11 and 16 and cf. CDi.3 and 20 and viii.3/xix.15–16.

[38] 1QpHabix.1–2 and cf. Vermes, *op. cit.*, p.514 and *pars.* and note my full discussion of this passage and this word in *JJHP*, pp. 49–51 and 97.

[39] See Vermes above, Cross, pp. 142–60, Milik, pp. 59–70, etc. and note the word '*woundings*'/ '*mahalalot*' with the feminine plural in the Document, Prof. Wise and myself discovered (4Q285: '*The Messianic Leader*'—since considered part of the War Scroll) and the verb based on the same root in 11QTxlvi.11—clearly meaning, not '*to cause disease*', but to '*defile it*,' i.e., '*the Temple*.'

[40] *Ibid.* and cf. 4QpPs 37iv.8–11 with 1QpHabix.1–2 and 9–12 above.

[41] *War* 2.647–51 is his first use of it and it is not insignificant that it occurs in conjunction with the mention of Ananus and what he calls the 'misinterpretation' of certain '*omens*' (among which

he most certainly includes his later mention of 'the Messianic Prophecy'). His second is in *War* 4.160–61 where he discusses the opposition of '*the Zealots*' to Ananus (whom at one point he even opposed himself), as usual turning the usage around, saying it did not mean '*zealous in the cause of virtue, as they claimed, but rather for vice in its most disgusting and unbridled form*.' Cf. the way Paul makes the same reversal in describing his more '*zealous*' opponents in Galatians 4:16–8, who are obviously calling him '*the Enemy*' and/or '*the Liar*' and whom he feels '*are not zealous in the right way*'!

42 *War* 4.314–15. One should note that in 4.316, in describing the desecration of the bodies of these High Priests, he actually uses the word '*corpse*' just as the Habakkuk *Pesher* does here in relation to '*the Wicked Priest*.'

43 *Vita* 193–216 and 309. In these passages, Josephus, contrary to here in the *War*, shows real animus towards Ananus. This is very odd—something peculiar has transpired between 75 and 96 CE.

44 *War* 4.318–23

45 Here, one should note 1QpHabxi.4–11 which, in discussing the '*pursuit*' and obviously death or destruction of '*the Righteous Teacher*,' alludes to '*the completion of the Fast Day, the Sabbath of their rest*.'

46 4.318.

47 The use of this word '*Arab*' for Greco-Roman historians was, as we have seen, a very general one that certainly encompassed areas such as Northern Syria; cf. *JBJ*, pp. 886–90 and Strabo, *Geography* 16.1.28, Tacitus, *Annals* 6.44 and 12.12 (who calls King Agbar, '*Acbar King of the Arabs*'), etc.

48 See *War* 1.6 and cf. Origen, *Contra Celsus* 1.47, 2.13, and Comm. in Matt. 10:17 and Eusebius, *E.I.* 2.23.20–21.

49 Cf. *War* 4.317 with 4.316 above.

50 *War* 4.319–20.

51 Cf. Eusebius, *E.I.* 2.6.1–8, 2.23.20–22, 3.6.32, 3.7.8–9, etc. and *pars.*

52 4QpPs 37ii.19–20 and iv.8–11 and cf. 1QpHabix.1–2, ix.9–x.5, and xi.12–xii.3.

53 1QpHabxii.6–10.

54 1QpHabix.4–7.

55 Cf. 1QpHabviii.2–3 (in interpretation of Habakkuk 2:4) and xii.14–xiii.4 with x.3–5.

56 Eusebius, *E.I.* 2.23.15–16 and *pars.*

57 Cf. CDi.18–21.

58 1QpHabviii.2–3, CDv.4–5, etc.

59 Eusebius, *E.I.* 2.23.12.

60 1QpHabx.3–4 and x.9–12.

61 Cf. *E.I.* 2.1.4, 2.23.3, and 2.23.16–18 and *pars.* with Ps. *Rec.* 1.70.

62 See *War* 4.335–43 and cf. n. 157 in Chapter 23 above about the Tombs of Zechariah and

the neighboring one on the other side of the one attributed to James—the so-called *'Tomb of Absalom'*—Plates 83, 86, and 90.

[63(62)]In Apocryphal Literature, as for instance in *'the Gospel of the Hebrews'* reported by Jerome in Vir. ill. 2, James will also drink *'the Cup of the Lord'*, but this will be an entirely different kind of *'Cup'* or so it might seem. Here in 1QpHabxi.2–11, the *'Cup'* which the Wicked Priest will have to drink for what he did to the Righteous Teacher will be *'the Cup of the Right Hand of God'*, which will more or less parallel what it is here in the Gospels and what it will be in Revelation.

[64]I coined this term to make things comprehensible to journalists and in television appearances and described this *'Consensus'* and its erroneous outlooks and preconceptions in the Introduction to *MZCQ* (Brill, 1983, pp. xi–xvii and 1–3), but Baigent and Leigh in *Dead Sea Scrolls Deception*, Jonathan Cape, 1991 (under my tutelege), popularized it.

[65] See n. 39 above.

[66] Cf. 1QpHabxi.5–6 with viii.2 and x.3–5 above.

[67] *Loc. cit.*

[68] *Loc. cit.*

[69] Matthew 24:30, 26:64, Mark 13:26, 14:62, Luke 22:69, Acts 2:33, 7:55–56, Romans 8:34, etc.

[70] *Loc. cit.*

[71] Cf. *'the ʿArizei-Goʾim'*/*'the Violent Ones of the Gentiles'* in 4QpPs 37ii.20 and iv.10 above.

[72] 1QpHabv.6–8.

[73] We have already seen how this theme of *'the Day of Judgement'*/*'the Last Judgement'*—all synonyms—is repeated in the last two summing-up columns—the conclusion: 1QpHabxii.14 and 1QpHabxiii.2–3.

[74] 4QpPs 37iv.9–10. The word here, which is reconstructed, may either be *'Vengeance'* or *'Judgement.'* It is *'Judgement'* in ii.20.

[75] *'Blasphemy'* is defined, as we have seen, in *M. San.* 7:5–6 and it does not include the expression of sentiments of this kind. It only relates to *'pronouncing the (Forbidden) Name'* of God. In any event, the punishement for such an infraction is *'stoning'* and not *'hanging'* or, in this instance, supposedly being handed over to the Gentiles for crucifixion.

[76] CDi.19–21 and see n. 175 in Chapter 22 above. One should note that, in the original expression of this in Deuteronomy 19:6, even the term *'lehamem'*/*'heated'* or *'to become hot'* is employed to characterize how *'the avenger'* or *'the pursuer of blood'*/*'the goʿel'*'s *'heart'* may have become *'overheated'*. But this is exactly, as we shall see below, how 1QpHabxi.5–6 will express this in describing the *'anger'* or *'fury'*/*'hemah'* of the Wicked Priest in his *'pursuit'* or *'pursuing after'* the Righteous Teacher *'to cast him down'* or *'destroy him.'*

[77] *Ibid.*

[78] Cf. *War* 2.254–56. In *Ant.* 20.162–66, this account is contradicted somewhat by having the Roman Governor Felix complicit in this murder. This makes the whole approach of Josephus at

this point somewhat suspicious. What is going on here? Does he mean that James was complicit in this murder as a putative inspirer of *'the Sicarii'*? If Felix is involved in this murder, it makes no sense to then go on to assert that it was because of these *'Impieties'* that God withdrew his support from the City and brought the Romans in to set *'fire'* to it and the Temple and reduce *'our wives and out children to Slavery'* as he does in 20.166.

[79] *Euthyphro* 2a–3b.

[80] See *R.H.* 31a. and cf. *A.Z.* 8b and *San.* 41a—this last having both *'ha-bayit'* and *'galtah'* in direct conjunction.

[81] *A.Z.* 8b and *San.* 41a and see my article in *DSSFC*, pp. 247–71: *'Interpreting Abeit-Galuto in the Habakkuk Pesher: Playing on and Transmuting Terms'*—in particular, pp. 268–69.

[82] This is made particularly clear in *ARN* 4 which actually refers to Isaiah 10:34 and Zechariah 11:2 and likewise even asserts that *'Lebanon'*/*'the Strong Forest that is going to fall refers to the Temple'*. Moreover, it does so in the course of a conversation R. Yohanan is having with Vespasian (of course, an anachronism, but no matter—Josephus is probably the original anyhow), in which he applies to him the *'Lebanon being felled by a Mighty One'*, as Josephus had doubtlessly done before him and as we have it in 4QpIs³iii.7–11 (directly followed by *'a Shoot will spring from the Root of Jesse and a Branch from its roots'*). A stronger First Century dating confirmation could not be found. However, one can find it as well in *Git.* 56a, also referring to Isaiah 10:33–34 and *Yoma* 39b referring to Zechariah 11:1 as here in *ARN*. Actually 4QpIs^c, in fact, combines Isaiah 30 with Zechariah 11.

[83] Cf. *R.H.* 31a–b above. For this issue of *'swallowing'*, see my *'The Historical Provenance of the "Three Nets of Belial" Allusion in the Zadokite Document and Balla^c/Bela^c in the Temple Scroll'*, *Folia Orientalia*: U. of Cracow/Mogilany, xxv, 1988, pp. 31–66 and *'The Final Proof that James and the Righteous Teacher are the Same'*, *DSSFC*, pp. 332–51 and Chapter 25 below.

[84] See *M. San.* 6:3–4, *San.* 45a–b, which is directly followed by all the discussions about *'being hung upon a tree'*, and 2 Apoc. Jas. 62.1–14; for *'the Enemies'*, see 105a–107a and Chapter 23 above.

[85] See, in particular, *A.Z.* 8b above, which actually sets forth this proposition. The same by implication in *San.* 41a although with less specificity. Both are concerned with the fall of the Temple in 70 CE.

[86] Cf. 1QpHabix.1–x.5, xi.12–5, and xii.2–10 above.

[87] 1QpHabxi. In received Habakkuk, this is significantly different: *'looked upon their privy parts'* which, of course, would have the most profound meaning for what Paul is so concerned about in Galatians 2:3–5—with particular emphasis on what turns out to be *'circumcision'* or the lack thereof (a reference to which will now directly follow in Line 13 of the *Pesher*). Also see my translation of this line and my comments in *DSSFC*, pp. 412–14. It is impossible to say which is correct.

[88] 1QpHabxi.13 and see n. 87 above.

[89] 1QpHabxi.6–9 and see my article in *DSSFC*, pp. 247–71: *'Interpreting Abeit-Galuto in the*

Habakkuk Pesher: Playing on and Transmuting Terms' in n. 81 above. Also see n. 45 above. This article was first given at the Groningen Conference in 1989, but the promise to publish all papers at this Conference in the *Revue de Qumran* was broken by the Editors of the Journal at the time (including E. Puech of the *Ecole Biblique*) and that is the reason it was finally published by Z. Kapera—to his credit—in Cracow in 1991 as part of his Second Volume of '*Mogilany 1989: Papers on the Dead Sea Scrolls,*' pp. 177–96 and, after which, then reprinted in *DSSFC* in 1996.

[90] 1QpHabxi.6–8.

[91] Cf. 1QpHabxi.14–5 with 1QpHabxii.2–6.

[92] 1QpHabxiii.1–4. It should be noted that these *'Evil Ones of His (Own) People, who kept His Commandments only when convenient',* have already been referred to in 1QpHabv.4–7 in its description of how *'by the hand of the Elect* (i.e., *'the Sons of Zadok'* in CDiv.2–4 above) *God would execute Judgement on all the Nations'*—and not the other way round as people like Josephus, Paul, the authors of the Gospels, and theologians like Eusebius seem to think in the light of their observation of history and, in the course of this, their reversal of this proposition!

[93] See, for instance Kor 2.39, 126, 174–5 (including the palpably 'Jamesian' dietary regulations), 3.185, 73.12, 74.26 (including use of *'the Day of Judgement'* in 46, as we have seen), 82.15 (again, alluding to *'the Day of Judgement'*), 84,12, 92.14, etc.

[94] See, for instance, J. T. Milik, *op. cit.*, p. 67f., F. M. Cross, *op. cit*, p. 153, S. Talmon, *'The Calendar Reckoning of the Sect from the Judaean Desert'* in *Aspects of the Dead Sea Scrolls*, Jerusalem, 1958, pp. 162–99, A. Jaubert, *'Le calendrier des Jubiles et de la secte de Qumran: Ses origines bibliques,'* *V.T.*3, 1955, pp. 250–64, etc.

[95] This is the position of G. Vermes, *op. cit.*, p. 515 and, in fact, in all his previous published translations starting in 1962. For my complete translation of the Habakkuk *Pesher* (which I hope to be a little more accurate) with Hebrew transcription, so the reader may judge for him or herself; see *DSSFC*, pp. 403–21.

[96] See the *'Translator's Foreword,'* Line 28, which explains that *'It was in the 38th Year of the Late King Euergetes'* (probably Ptolemy VII and, therefore, around 132 BC) upon his arrival in Egypt that the translator—who identifies himself in Ben Sira 50:27–9 as *'Jesus ben Sira Eleazar of Jerusalem'*—found the work. One should also note the additions in Hebrew *Ben Sira* from 50:4–51:55, which have now been found at both Masada and in the materials in the Cairo *Genizah*. These, not only speak of *'the Pious Ones,'* but also attribute to this Simeon the Righteous at the point of this Yom Kippur Atonement in the Holy of Holies in the Temple, the Zealot *'Covenant of Phineas'*—identifying it to some degree with that of *'the Sons of Zadok'*; see too *MZCQ*, pp. 6–15.

[97] Cf. Eusebius, *E.I.* 2.23.2–1, quoting Hegesippus and Clement, Jerome, *Vir. ill.* 2, Epiphanius, *Haeres.* 29.4.1–4, 78.7.7–9, and *pars.*

[98] *War* 2.7 / *Ant.* 17.207 in the aftermath of the disturbances in 4 BC at Herod's death and leading up to the imposition of direct Roman Rule and the Census of Cyrenius in 6–7 CE. It is interesting

that these are the two times associated in the Gospels of Matthew and Luke respectively with the birth of 'Jesus'—the first, '*Seventy Years*' before the outbreak of the final War against Rome in 66 CE. But, what is equally if not even more interesting, it is precisely at this moment that Josephus takes time out to describe the sects among the Jews as he knows them—in the first, in particular, 'the Essenes', whom he dotes over in loving detail as if they were first established at this time (for the Pseudoclementines, they were); in the second, the '*Movement*' initiated by '*Judas the Galilean*' we now all know of as '*the Zealots*' or '*Sicarii*.' Why?

[99] For the issues behind this event, see Josephus, *Ant.* 20.197–207; for this matter of '*blasphemy*' and unlawfully pronouncing the Divine Name God, see *M. San.* 7:6 and n. 75 above.

[100] Cf. 1QpHabv.3–5, viii.2–3, ix.1–2, ix.8–12, xi.7–15, xii.10, 4QpPs 37ii.14–20, iii.12, iv.8–11, 4QpIsᵃiii.1–10, 4QpIsᶜ, Frags. 8–10 and 21–3, etc. and see how many parallels there are to this kind of language. One should also note all references to '*yeshaᶜ*'/'*salvation*' and the like there are in this Chapter 3 of Isaiah. In fact, this is the way—as I have tried to point out—Biblical passages were probably chosen for exposition at Qumran, i.e., in order to bring this sort of exegesis out of the text.

[101] Cf. Eusebius, *E.I.* 2.23.15 and <u>pars</u>. and see my JBJ, pp. 466–88. etc. One should also note that similar versions of this passage—with slight linguistic variations—are to be found in the Greek in Justin Martyr, *Dial.* 133 and Tertullian, *Adv. Marc.* 3.22.

[102] Cf. 1QpHabix.1 and xii.2–3 and 4QpPs 37iv.9–11 above and see my revised discussion of the parallel of this passage from Isaiah 3:20—with its insertion into Column xii of the Habakkuk Pesher—in JJHP in DSSFC, pp. 184–95.

[103] For '*the Poor*', as the followers of the Righteous Teacher in the Habakkuk *Pesher*, see this description in xii.2–10. But see also the introduction of this term in crucial contexts at Qumran, such as in 1QMxi.9ff., xiii.13f., and 1QHii.32ff., iii.25, v.18, and v.23 (in conjunction with '*Hesed*,' i.e., '*the Ebionei-Hesed*'/'*the Poor Ones of Piety*').

[104] Cf. 4QpPs 37ii.9 (here '*Anayyim*'/'*the Meek*'—plural), ii.10, ii.15 and ii.23 ('*Doers of the Torah*' as in 1QpHab), ii.16 ('*Ani*' and '*Ebion*'), and iv.11 with 1QpHabvii.10–11, viii.1–23, and xii.4–5.

Chapter 25

[1] *War* 1.32.

[2] 1QMxii.10/xix.2.

[3] See *ARN* 4.4, 19b–20a and cf. Epiphanius, *Haeres.* 30.16.4–6.

[4] *Taᶜan.* 5b and also see 6a–6b, evoking Isaiah 45:8: '*the day on which rain falls is as great as the day Heaven and Earth were created*' (note the allusion '*Heaven and Earth*' again, so often associated with James' name in the sources), and my article '*Eschatological "Rain" Imagery in the War Scroll and the Letter of James*,' *Journal of Near Eastern Studies* 49(2), U. of Chicago, reprinted in DSSFC, pp. 272–87.

[5] Cf. CDvi.10–11 and xx.13–14.

[6] See n. 173 in Chapter 23 above and cf. for Pompey, *War* 1.152–53/*Ant.* 14.72 and for Herod,

War 1.354–57/*Ant.* 14.481–86.

[7] See above, Chapters 19 and 23 and cf. Matthew 26:59–65 and *pars.*

[8] See nn. 75 and 84 in Chapter 24 above and cf. *San.* 45a–b and *M. San.* 6:3–4 and 7:5–6.

[9] See Matthew 26:57–66/Mark 14:53–64, and by implication Luke 22:66–71 and the curious discussion in John 10:22–38, which tries to explain the whole issue in terms of claiming to be *'the Son of God'*. However, these are all framed in terms of later 'Christian' theology and claiming to be *'the Christ, the Son of God'*, as Matthew/Mark/and Luke would put it in their own various ways, but this is not a blasphemous offence according to *M. Sanhedrin* above. From the material we have already seen, too, about the death penalty being withdrawn from the Sanhedrin in the forty years before the fall of the Temple when the Sanhedrin was transferred from *'the Chamber of Hewn Stone'* to a *'House'* called *'Beit-Hanut'* outside the City (not very different from the note about *'the House of the High Priest'* here in the Gospel of Luke). In any event, Pilate had the power to impose the death sentence for sedition by crucifixion, which was never in the lexicon of Jewish capital punishments, as we have seen.

[10] Cf. 11QTxlvi.9–12 above.

[11] *Ant.* 20.214–16.

[12] See, for instance, references such as those concerning the Final Apocalyptic War against Evil in 1QMii.9–14, etc. and chronology relating to *'the Righteous Teacher'* and *'the Community'* in CDi.5–10 and xx.14–15.

[13] 1QpHabix.9–11.

[14] See, for instance, F. M. Cross who, as in most things concerning the Scrolls, sets the tone for the debate, *The Ancient Library of Qumran*, 1958, pp. 149–52 and like Vermes in 1962 and thereafter, even includes the translation *'drunkenness'* in his rendering of this passage (1QpHabxi.12–14). So sure is he of his translation that he even comments—somewhat casually by way of humor—*'Simon* (his candidate for *'the Wicked Priest'*) *consumed one cup too many'.* This is typical—cf. Milik, *op. cit.*, pp. 68–72, Vermes, in his earliest work in 1953, pp. 99–100, *et. al.*

[15] Cf. Vermes in his Third Edition of *The Dead Sea Scrolls in English*, 1988, p. 33.

[16] This is the reference incorporating the all-important citation from Isaiah 3:10-11—applied in Early Church Literature to the death of James, I referred to above—1QpHabxii.2–3.

[17] Cf. 1QpHabxi.14–15 with 1QpHabxi.4–7.

[18] *Loc. cit.*

[19] Cf. how D. H. Lawrence puts this in his fulsome attack on the language of *The Apocalypse* in his autobiographical treatise by that name and see Revelation 2:9, 6:10, 11:18, 13:1–36, 14:7, 14:10, 15:4, 16:1–17, 16:21, 17:1–3, 18:10, 18:8, 19:2, 20:4, 20:12–13, etc.

[20] *Loc. cit.*

[21] Cf. CDvii.21 (which breaks off here) and xix.33–xx.13 and note the parallels in language found throughout the Pseudoclementines and even a work like Ibn Gabirol's *Fons Vitae*.

[22] Cf. Paul in 1 Thessalonians 2:15, Matthew 5:12, 23:30–37, and *pars.*, Acts 3:25 and 7:52, and Koran 1.61, 1.87, 4.157, *et. al.*

[23] In Revelation, see all the references to *'blood'*—but, in particular, 1:5, 5:9, 7:4, 12:11, 16:6, 17:6, 19:2, etc. Of course, for a *'Christian'* man, Eusebius' ire and call for Vengeance against *'the Jews,'* is *'blood-curdling'*; cf. 1.1, 2.5, 2.6, 2.26, 3.5, but particularly 3.6 where he rises to a fever pitch of *'blood'* lust, and then, of course, 3.7, etc.

[24] *Loc. cit.* and cf. CDi.21–ii.1, iv.14–16, v.16, viii.13, etc.

[25] See *DSSU*, pp. 222–30, 4Q286 (now called 4Q*Berachot*/Blessings^a), Fragment 1, Column ii.4–6—including allusion, not only to *'the Fountain,'* but also, *'the Fountain of Understanding'* and *'the Fountain of Discovery.'* Where the titles of such manuscripts were concerned and their section headings, we chose such names to capitalize on the vividness of some of the allusions in them.

[26] Cf. 1QpHabix.12–15 and 1QpHabx.3–5. Again, this *'cutting off'* will be an expression found throughout the Damascus Document, especially in Columns i–iii.

[27] CDvii.12–13/xix.25–6. One should note that it is here that most translations prefer to use the English language in translating *'spouting'*—but it should be appreciated this verb is based on the underlying real Hebrew usage implying *'pouring.'*

[28] We have explained this whole issue of *'the Pierced Messiah'* as opposed to *'the Messianic Leader'* language above. Primarily, the former was popularized by Hershel Shanks in his *Biblical Archaeological Review.* For our presentation of these things, see *DSSU*, pp. 24–29. The passages we are talking about are 4QpIs^aiii.11–22 (this really is *'the Messianic Prophecy'* of Isaiah 10:34: *'Lebanon with its grandeur shall fall'* or *'Lebanon shall fall by a Mighty One',* obsequiously applied by Josephus and R. Yohanan b. Zacchai to Vespasian); cf. 4Q285, Fragment 7, Lines 1–6. The expression *'woundings'* appears, as we have seen, in Line 5.

[29] *Ibid.*—especially Lines 17–22 above.

[30] Cf. 4QpIs^aiii.11 with 4QpIs^aiii.20, speaking of *'the Throne of Glory'* and *'the Crown of His Holiness',* and cf. 4Q285, Fragment 7, Line 4. But also see 4Q252 (The Genesis *Pesher*)iv.2–5, which also makes reference to *'the Staff'* of CDvi–vii and, in no uncertain terms, identifies *'the Branch of David'* with *'the Messiah of Righteousness.'* As we have already noted, one can't get much more singular and specific than this! But also see 4QFlorii.13, which speaks of *'raising up the Branch of David* (here now designated as *'the Zemach David') along with the Doresh ha-Torah'* who would themselves *'raise up the fallen Tent of David'* of Amos 9:11 *'in the Last Days'*—and all of this supposedly Second Century BC and *two-Messiah* ideology? Hardly.

[31] Ibid., 4QpIs^aiii.11 and 4QpIs^aiii.20. On this *'Netzer'/'Nazir'/'Nazirite'* confusion, see Chapter 13 above and *JBJ*, pp. 222–47.

[32] 4QpNahi.1–11.

[33] See 1QpHabviii.13 and cf. 1QpHabxii.1–9. It is interesting that *'the dumb beasts'* are identified with *'the Simple of Judah doing Torah'*—themselves apparently the same as the followers of *'the Righteous Teacher',* designated as *'the Poor'* or *'Ebionim.'*

[34] Cf. 1QpHabxi.10–11 with 1QpHabxi.12–15.

[35] CDvii.13/xix.25–26 and cf. n. 27 above. Also see my article *'Playing on and Transmuting Words—Interpreting Abeit-Galuto in the Habakkuk Pesher'* in *Folio Orientalia: Mogilany, 1989*

and in *DSSFC*, pp. 247–71 above as well.

36 Cf. CDiii.20–iv.12. These allusions to *'circumcision'* have to be seen as relating to some degree to *'the Party of the Circumcision'* associated with James in Jerusalem in Paul's Galatians 2:12–13 above.

37 Cf. *E.I.* 2.1.4–5, 2.23.4 and 18, Epiphanius, *Haeres.* 78.14.5–6, etc. and also see *San.* 45a–b and *M. San.* 6:3–4 and 7:5–6, mentioned above as well.

38 Cf. CDix.17–20—but see too xii.21–23, xiii.7–13, and xv.10–14.

39 Cf. CDvi.17–vii.5. This is in the context of *'separating between polluted and pure,' 'Holy from profane,' 'setting up the Holy Things according to their precise specifications,' 'loving each man his brother as himself* (James 2:8's *'Royal Law according to the Scripture'*)*,' 'keeping away from fornication'* (*lehazzir*—using the *'Nazirite'* language of James' directives to overseas Communities in Acts 15 and 21), *'separating from all pollutions according to their Statute,'* and *'walking in these things in Perfect Holiness'* (cf. Paul in 2 Corinthians 7:1).

40 1QpHabxiii.1–4. Here we have the same allusion to *'Evil Ones'* as we have in 1QpHabv.4–6 above (i.e., the *'Evil Ones of His own People'*).

41 Cf. *War* 4.146–61 with Matthew 12:5–6 and *pars.* and Acts 24:6–25:8.

42 1QpHabviii.13 and xii.8–10.

43 Cf. 4Q286 (*'The Chariots of Glory'*—4Q*Ber*ᵃ), Fragment 1, ii.9–12.

44 1QpHabxii.5–10 and cf. the same usage in 1QHiv.7–10, surrounded by allusions to *'the Sons of Belial'* and their *'nets',* not to mention, *'the Scoffers of Lying'* who lead the People astray *'with Smooth Things,' 'give vinegar to drink,'* and whose *'works are of boasting.'*

45 1QpHabxii.7–10.

46 Cf. 4Q*MMT*ii.2 and iii.29–32 (*DSSU*, pp. 180–200)—itself based on Genesis 15:6 and Psalm 106:31.

47 *Loc. cit.* and cf. with CDvi.15–vii.3 and viii.4–8/xix.15–20.

48 Cf. Ps. *Rec.* 1.71 with Matthew 17:2, 28:3, Mark 9:3, Luke 9:29 and *pars.* and see *JBJ*, pp. 680–7 and 753–56.

49 1QSviii.4–10.

50 Cf. 1QSviii.1 with Matthew 17:1–8 and *pars.* and Galatians 2:9.

51 Cf. Galatians 2:9 with Matthew 17:1–8 and *pars.* above and Galatians 1:19 and 1 Corinthians 15:7 in *E.I.* 1.9–12, ass well as in my section on *'The Brothers of Jesus as Apostles'* in *JBJ*, pp. 644–850.

52 For *'Balaam'* as *'Swallower of the People,'* see *San.* 106a and cf. my Appendix on *'The Three Nets of Belial'* in *JJHP*, pp. 87–94. For Herod as the first *'Innovator'* in the Religion of the Jews, see *Ant.* 15.365–69.

53 Cf. 1QSv. 2 and v. 9 above.

54 *E.I.* 2.23.2–7 and *pars.* Cf. Ezekiel 44:15–31, Numbers 6:1–27 (following up *'the Suspected Adulteress'* passage, so dear to the thoughts of Helen of Adiabene, in Chapter 5), Jeremiah

35:2–19. and see *JBJ*, pp. 229–47, etc.

[55] 1QpHabv.13–vi.11.

[56] This '*balla^c*'/'*ballo*' language has many parodies and parallels among Josephus' '*Essenes*' (*War* 2.143) and at Qumran (1QSviii.22) and cf. my article in DSSFC, pp. 332–51: '*The Final Proof that James and the Righteous Teacher are the Same.*'

[57] Cf. Ananus in *War* 4.317; Zachariah, *War* 4.344.

[58] Cf. 4QpIs^aii.9–11 and iii.15–17 with Revelation 1:7, 14:8–20, 16:17–21, 18:2 19:21 and Hebrews 1:13 and 10:13.

[59] Cf. 4QpIs^aii.9–11, iii.15–17, 1QMxi.9–xii.11, xix.4–14, CDvii.20–21, and 1QHvii.2 with Matthew 22:44 and *pars.*, Acts 2:35, Hebrews 1:13 and 10:13, James 2:3, etc.—all based on Psalms 110:1, a psalm which itself speaks of the cognomen applied to James, '*the ^cOz-le-^cAm*' and '*the Day of His Wrath.*'

[60] This ideology of the '*only begotten*', as we have seen, is an important one and we find it primarily applied in Josephus by Helen to her favorite son—her '*only-begotten*' son Izates—*Ant.* 20.18.

[61] *Haeres.* 30.13.7–8. The Qumran position on this is best seen in 1QHvii.25–27 and ix.29–33.

[62] Cf. See Jerome, *Vir. ill.* 2 and cf. Ps. *Rec.* 1.71, where James was '*still limping*' from his broken leg when he sent Peter out on his first Missionary Journey from outside Jericho.

[63] Cf. *E.I.* 2.1.4, 2.23.3, and 2.23.18 and *pars.*

[64] Cf. *JBJ*, pp. 444–54 and note how the words and vision attributed to Stephen—about '*crying out*' (repeated three times), the mob being '*cut to their hearts*,' and '*the Heavens opening and the Son of Man standing on the right hand of God*' in Acts 7:55–60—more or less duplicate the account of the stoning of James here in these Early Church Sources. Only the date, as we have seen, has been inverted—the early 40's taking the place of the early 60's.

[65] See *War* 1.566 and 1.666 for the '*Helcias*' in Herod's time, who was married to his sister '*Salome*.' However in *Ant.* 18.273 and 20.140, as we have seen, we have a second '*Helcias*'—also a '*Temple Treasurer*'—who was married to another woman in the Herodian family and evidently the aunt of that '*Saulos*' under consideration. As above, see our Herodian Genealogical Table.

[66] See *War* 2.556–58.

[67] *War* 2.418 and see my article '*Paul as Herodian*' in *The Journal of Higher Criticism*, iii, Spring, 1996, pp. 110–22—reprinted in *DSSFC*, pp. 226–45.,

[68] Cf. CDi.19–21 with QpHabi.6–8,

[69] Cf. 1QpHabi.10 and note that this word '*Crown*', not only incorporates the usage of '*the Netzer*' worn by the High Priest, but is also the basis of a Greek name like '*Stephen*' who is said in *E.I.* 2.1.2 to have earned the '*First Crown of the Martyrs*' (thus!).

[70] 1QpHabi.11, which goes on in ii.2–10 to describe the Scriptural Exegesis sessions of the '*Righteous Teacher*' and his identification with '*the Priest*'/'*High Priest*.'

[71] 1QpHabxii.11–xiii.1.

[72] CDi.19.

 THE NEW TESTAMENT CODE COMPANION

73 *E.I.* 2.23.7 and 15.

74 1QpHabv.11–12.

75 This is the preoccupying background concern of the *Pesher*, starting with the reference to '*God raising up the Chaldeans, a cruel and aggressive nation,*' in Habakkuk 1:6—distinctly interpreted in terms of '*the Kittim in who are swift and strong in way, causing Many to perish by the sword and all the world to fall under (their) Dominion*' in 1QpHabii.10–4. Nor could this hardly be any other group after Alexander except the Romans. *Certainly not the Seleucids,* even taking into account possible hyperbole! This continues throughout in iii.1–iv.13 and the reference to '*their Guilty Council House*' and '*their Leaders coming one after another to despoil the Earth*'—again hardly descriptive of any People other than the Romans except in the tendentious eyes of those with an agenda. This has generally been interpreted to mean '*the Year of the Four Emperors*'—68–69 CE.

76 This is certainly true if one interprets '*Babylon*' in passages like Revelation 14:8, 16:19, 15:5, and 18:2–21 as Rome, as we have here, i.e., '*Chaldeans*'/'*Kittim*'='*Babylon*'/'*Rome,*' another strong piece of internal verification and correspondence. Here the passage is 1QpHabv.6–8. Not only is it preceded by condemnation of '*the Evil Ones of His People who kept His Commandments only when convenient*' (we know who these are), but it is—so typically—followed by like-minded and fulsome condemnation of '*Traitors*' and the passages in vi.3–11 about '*their eating being plenteous*' and '*sacrificing to their standards and worshipping their weapons of war*'—as if we don't know who these were.

77 Cf. 1QpHabv.6–8 with 1QpHabxi.4–15 and see my whole discussion of this in '*The Final Proof that James and the Righteous Teacher are the Same,*' DSSFC, pp. 332–54, first given to the Society of Biblical Literature in Chicago in 1994.

78 Cf. 1QpHabv.12–14. This of course has everything to do with the picture of '*Jesus*'' '*Galilean*' Disciples on the Sea of Galilee '*casting out their nets*' and that of '*Jesus*'' own action in Matthew 17:27 of sending Peter '*to the Sea to cast down a hook*' (this directly following the Paulinizing statement: '*Truly the Sons are free*'). And what comes up, why '*a Stater*' (even this in perfect Romanized language)—the coin to pay the Roman taxes, of course—referred to here in 1QpHabvi.5–7 concerning '*parceling out their yoke and their taxes, consuming all Peoples year by year*'—and moreover, the perfect statement of '*Christian*' tax-paying policy. See also above, Chapters 2, 11, 23, etc.

79 *Loc. cit.* and see as well, 1QpHabvi.6–11, ending with the blood-curdling '*the Kittim who destroy Many by the sword, young men, grown-ups, and old people, women and children, and have no pity even on the fruit of the womb*'—which is exactly what Josephus describes as happening following the brutal Roman decimation of the towns along the Sea of Galilee in 67-68 CE!

80 *Loc. cit.* But see, in particular, 1QpHabvii.4–5.

81 1QpHabii.6–10.

82 CDxx.14–15. This expression is quite literally '*Men of War*'/'*Milchamah*' and certainly recalls the kind of companions in '*the Herodian family*', with whom the '*Saulos*' in Josephus is pictured

as keeping company, in *War* 2.556–8 and *Ant.* 20.214 (directly following the death of James), themselves so roundly condemned in the so-called *'Zealot Woes'* in the *Talmud*.

Chapter 26

[1] 1QpHabv.8–12.

[2] *Ibid.*

[3] Cf. *Ant.* 18:8–10 and note that his description of their 'Philosophy' from 18.23–26, not only disagrees with *War* 2.117–18 about who the actual founder of this particular *'school'* or *'sect'* was, but actually basically substitutes for the much longer description of the *'Essenes'* in the *War* which follows in both.

[4] Matthew 17:27—here 'Jesus' doesn't wish to *'offend,' 'scandalize,'* or *'cause to stumble'* those charged with *'collecting the tax'*; but see Paul in 1 Corinthians 8:13 about *'food causing the (weak) brother to stumble'* and therefore (like James) proclaiming his intent *'not to eat flesh again forever'*—a vow he promptly gainsays in 10:25 (also amid the language of *'conscience'* and *'stumbling'*). But also see 1 Corinthians 1:23, 8:9, and 1QpHabxi.8.

[5] Matthew 17:26—the same *'Freedom,'* of course Paul is referring to in Galatians 3:28, 4:26–31, Romans 5:15–18, 6:18–22, 1 Corinthians 7:21–22, 9:19, 12:12, etc.

[6] Cf. 1QSvii.13 (*'the Way in the Wilderness'* exposition in the Community Rule) and CDvi.14–15, xiii.14–15, and xv.7.

[7] Epistle of Peter to James 4.1–2 and see the reference to *'the Pit of Destruction'* in 3.1.

[8] Cf. the introductory salutations to both *The Epistle of Peter to James* and *Clement to James*, prefacing the *Homilies*.

[9] See *Epistle of Peter to James* 3.1 above and cf. passages among the Qumran documents like CDvi.14–15, xiii.14–15, and xv.7 above and 1QSix.16, ix.20–21, etc.

[10] Cf. Epiphanius, *Haeres.* 30.21.1 and cf. Ps. *Hom.* 8.2, 9.23, 10.1, 11.26–31, etc.

[11] Ps. *Hom.* 11.35.

[12] *Epistle of Peter to James* 2.1.

[13] Cf. 1QpHabv.11–12 above.

[14] Cf. *War* 2.130 with 1QSvi.20–21.

[15] CDxiv.6–10.

[16] CDxii.1–5.

[17] Cf. *Epistle of Peter to James* 4.2 and 5.1 with 1QSi.24–ii.18.

[18] CDxv.2–3, an injunction which relates to that of *'profanation of the Name'* of Leviticus 19:12.

[19] *Epistle of Peter to James* 4.4 and cf. CDi.14–15, vii.13, 1QpHabii.1–2, v.11, x.9, etc. and Romans 1:25, 9:1, 2 Corinthians 11:31, Galatians 1:20, etc.

[20] *Epistle of Peter to James* 4.4.

[21] 1QSii.5–17. The translation of some of these lines in Vermes is questionable.

[22] Cf. *War* 2.141–42—which is also the opposite of Paul—to passages like 1 Corinthians 2:7–16

and 4:5.

23 Cf. *Epistle of Peter to James* 5 with Josephus in *War* 2.139–40 on the 'Essenes' and *Ant.* 18.117–18 on John.

24 *Epistle of Peter to James* 4–5.

25 *Epistle of Peter to James* 5:1.

26 1QSiii.3–5.

27 1QSv.11–14

28 1QSv.12–13 and cf. CDiii.14.

29 1QSv.18–23.

30 Cf. *Epistle of Peter to James* 4.4 with 1QSv.2–9.

31 *Ibid.*

32 Cf. 1QMvii.5–7, xii.7–10, and CDxv.15-17.

33 See Romans 13.1–3 and cf. Josephus in *War* 2.140–41.

34 Cf. 1QSiv.10–11 and CDv.11–13. Also see 1QSx.23 and 1QHvii.11–12.

35 CDv.11–vi.2.

36 1QSiii.18–iv.15.

37 Cf. *DSSU*, p. 170 and 4Q525 (*Beatitudes—The Demons of Death*) iv.24–26 (repeated three times in three lines).

38 Cf. Galatians 1:10–12.

39 1QSviii.20–24.

40 Cf. CDxx.7–10 and 4QD266, Fragment 11, Lines 14–6.

41 Cf. Koran 2.124–39, 3.65, 4.125, etc.

42 Koran 37.102–16 which, though note naming Ishmael per se, is generally interpreted by commentators in this manner and is probably the only possible interpretation of the phraseology of the passage.

43 See above, Chapters 3-4, 13, and 16, etc. and *JBJ*, pp. 886–95, 907–24, and 939–46.

44 *Ant.* 20.20 above and cf. John 1:14–18 and 3:16–18.

45 Again see our Herodian Genealogy and Josephus on Agrippa I's two daughters, Bernice and Mariamme—*Ant.* 19.276–7 and 20.147

46 See *Naz.* 19a–19b and n. 14 of Chapter 8 above.

47 See CDiii.4–12.

48 CDiii.6–7 above.

49 See Jubilees 19:9; cf. 17:18, 19:30 and especially 30:19–22 on how Levi ('*zealous in the exercise of Righteousness*'—in the passage about '*living for a thousand generations*,' also quoted twice in the extant Damascus Document) and others '*not transgressing the Ordinances or breaking the Covenant*' would be '*recorded on the Heavenly Tablets as a Friend (of God) and a Zaddik*' (R. H. Charles translation).

[50] See James 2:21–23 and CDiii.2–4.

[51] See above, Chapters 4, 9-10, 15, etc. and cf. CDvi.20–1, vii.5–6/xix.18–20, xx.17–18, xx.21, etc.

[52] CDvii.1 and cf. vii.3.

[53] *Loc. cit.* Of course, for Paul's attitude towards the consumption of '*blood*,' see 1 Corinthians 10:14–11:29 and his innovative new ideas on '*Communion with the blood of Christ.*' One should also note that in Jubilees, there is an especially strong antagonism to the consumption of '*blood*' as, for instance in 21:6–7, 21:18–19, etc. and, to be sure—where Paul is concerned—in some redactions '*Beliar*' is used in 15:33.

[54] Cf. Koran 2.111–146.

[55] Cf. 1 Corinthians 1:3: '*If anyone loves God, he is known by him*' (whatever this is supposed to mean— more rhetorical obfuscation) and see James 2:5 on '*the Kingdom promised to those who love Him*' and Josephus' '*Essenes*' in *War* 2.139 and their '*Piety towards God.*'

[56(35)] Cf. 1QSii.10–18 and 4Q286 (*Ber*ᵃ—*The Chariots of Glory*), Fragment, ii.1–11: '*The Community Council Curses Belial*' in *DSSU*, pp. 229–30.

[57] Cf. 1QpHabx.5–10 above.

[58] Cf. 4QD266, Fragment 11, Lines 5–18 with 1QpHabv.11–12.

[59] 4QD266, Fragment 11, Lines 6–7.

[60] Cf. CDvii.4/xix.17, viii.19–22/xix.32–35, xx.8–10, xx.23, xx.29–31, etc.

[61] Cf. CDxiv.8–10 and 4QD266, Fragment 11, Lines 9–10 above.

[62] 1QSv.10–18.

[63] Cf. 4QD266, Fragment 11, Line 19, with 1QSviii.15.

[64] 1QSviii.15–16.

[65] Cf. 4QD266, Fragment 11, Lines 10–12.

[66] Cf. n. 49 above and Jubilees 30:19–22 on how Levi ('*zealous in the exercise of Righteousness*'—in the passage about '*living for a thousand generations*'—also quoted twice in the extant Damascus Document) and others, '*not transgressing the Ordinances or breaking the Covenant*', would be '*recorded on the Heavenly Tablets as a Friend (of God) and a Zaddik.*' This could not be a more telling expression of '*the Zealot Covenant*' adhering to '*the Sons of Levi*' and their heirs. It also parallels, almost precisely, the material in CDiii.2–4—or, to mention additional parallels, in *Surah* 2 of the Koran about who the first '*Muslims*' were.

[67] 4QD266, Fragment 11, Lines 12–13.

[68] This of course runs in the face of Paul's contention in Galatians 3:6–26, which also speaks of the '*promises to Abraham and his seed*' in general exposition of Genesis 15:6 how '*Abraham believed God and it was reckoned to him as righteousness*' or '*Justification.*' As against this, see CDxvi.2–7 above.

[69] See 4QpNahii.5–8 and Chapter 20 above

[70] See nn. 21 and 56 and cf. 4Q286 (*Ber*ᵃ—*The Chariots of Glory*), Fragment, ii.1–11 in *DSSU*,

pp. 229–30 above

71 1QpHabx.12–13.

72 Cf. Wisdom 2:16.

73 CDi.1.

74 For Paul's references to 'Lying,' see n. 19 above and Galatians 1:20 (regarding his 'seeing no other Apostles' except 'Peter' and 'James the brother of the Lord'), 4:16 (on the opposite: 'Have I your Enemy become by telling Truth to you?'—sic!), 2 Corinthians 12:31 (preceding his attestation to 'being lowered through a window down the walls of Damascus in a basket'), Romans 1:25 and 9:1, etc.

75 Similar sayings are to be found in Romans 1:14 and Acts 14:1, 18:4, 19:10 and 17, 20:21, etc.

76 Cf. CDvi.17–20, ending with James' 'Royal Law according to the Scripture' and leading into the ban on 'fornication' in vii.1–2, and cf. 4Q486 ('The Chariots of Glory' in the Section we entitled: 'The Splendor of the Spirits'), Ms. B, Fragment 1, Lines 6–8 in DSSU, pp. 222–30 above.

77 4QMMTii.56–66 in the section following illegal 'mingling' (including marrying 'Ammonites,' 'Moabites,' and presumably non-Jewish foreigners generally) and followed by the ban on 'bringing dogs into the Holy Camp,' that is, James' ban on 'carrion,' i.e., 'because Jerusalem is the Holy Camp' and 'the Chief of the Camps of Israel' and they 'might bring some of the bones into the Temple while the flesh is still on them.'

78 1QSiii.18–iv.26 and cf. Didache 1.1.

79 4QNahiii.5–8 and cf. 4QNahiv.4–8 and the definition of these same 'Nilvim' in CDiv.2–4, Esther 9:27, Isaiah 56:3–6 (in the context of 'the Song of the Well'—above Chapter 22 and below Chapter 28), and my article '"Joining"/"Joiner," "ʿArizei-Go'im, " and "the Simple of Ephraim, "Relating to a Cadre of Gentile "God-Fearers" at Qumran,' first given at a National Meeting of the Society of Biblical Literature in 1991 as we have seen and, thereafter, reprinted in DSSFC, pp. 313–31 above.

80 Cf. 4QNahiii.8–9 with CDiv.2–4 above and Romans 2:13, 3:20–28, 4:2–5:9, Galatians 2:16–17, 3:11, 3:24, 5:4, etc,

81 Cf. CDvii.12–13/xix.25–26.

82 Loc cit. Actually, as we have already seen, Ms. A is different from Ms. B though both are based in this case on the same Biblical passages. In Ms. A we have 'one of confused Spirit' ('Ruah'—'wind' and 'Spirit' being the same word or homonyms in Hebrew) 'spouted to them'—so one could possibly read here 'Windbag' as we saw. Ms. B has 'and spilled windiness' or 'storms' and, instead of Ms. A's 'the Spouter of Lying spouted to them,' 'the Spouter of Man for Lying spouted to them'—'Man' being quite mysterious here. In this instance, Ms. A is possibly superior, but both are saying approximately the same thing. Still, as a by-product of this, one can see—as we have been suggesting—that the Damascus Document was still in a process of development when the copies found in the Cairo Genizah were produced.

83 This seems to be true throughout the Qumran corpus. These infuriating circumlocutions were certainly developed for reasons of self-preservation. Of course, members of the Community

would know whom they referred to but they provided plausible deniability. They also seem to prove that these things occurred during the Herodian or Roman Periods when powerful outside forces were certainly the over-riding concern. These people *used their power for Riches and profiteering* and *wallowed in the ways of fornication and Evil Riches,* *each man approaching the flesh of his flesh for fornication* (certainly an allusion to *Herodians*!). For these *Visitation* and *Wrath being poured* usages, cf. CDi.3, i.17, ii.6–8, v.15–16, viii.2–3/xix.13–15, viii.5–7/xix.17–20, xx.15–16, etc.

[84] CDvii.9–23/xix.23–35.

[85] CDxx.2–4.

[86] CDxx.6–7. It is interesting that this word *ʿavodah* in the sense of *work* as *labor,* *mission,* or *service* is different in Hebrew from *works*/*maʿasim,* based on the Hebrew root *to do,* *doing,* or *Doers* (*ʿOseh*/*ʿOsei* usually *of the Torah*). Cf. the way *the Spouter of Lying* is described in 1QpHabx.11 and see, as well, 1QSiv.9–10, v.14, or CDxx.7. On the other hand, I have been particularly insistent on consistently translating *maʿasim* as *works*—a subtlety many of my colleagues in the field seem to feel unobliged to recognize. Cf., for instance, 1QSi.5, i.19, iii.14, iv.3–4, iv.15–16, viii.18, ix.23, CDi.1–2, i.10, ii.1, ii.7–8, ii.14–15, iv.5–6, v.5, v. 16, xiii.11, xx.3–6, 1QpHabx.12 and xii.8. etc.

Chapter 27

[1] CDi.21–ii.1.

[2] CDi.4–5. The chronology here has confused many—Paul helps explain it in Galatians 3:17, where he is speaking *of the Covenant confirmed in advance by God to Christ.* It would appear that things were thought of in periods of either 490 or 430 years. For him, it is the *430 years—* spoken of in Exodus 12:40—from Abraham to Moses,* which he considers somehow to be related to the issue of the Period from *God to Christ.* The *390 years,* referred to in CDi.5–6 as relating to *the Era of Wrath,* obviously has something to do with Daniel 9:24's *seventy weeks of years*—itself harking back, to some extent, to Jeremiah 29:10's *70 years* (also mentioned by Daniel 9:2–3 and relating to the time of the *Captivity* in Babylon)—cannot be taken literally and should not be. It either relates to one of these two chronological schemes, or a third—the *390 days* of Ezekiel 4:5. This is the amount of time that Ezekiel's tongue stuck to the roof of his mouth after he heard about the destruction of the Temple, but which is also interpreted in 4:9 as the number of years *the House of Israel will sin*—*one day equaling one year.* If one takes this together with Paul's version of the Exodus reckoning, then one could imagine we are *40 years* before the destruction of the Second Temple in 70 CE, i.e., 30 CE. If one, rather, goes with the *490* of Daniel's *seventy weeks of years,* then it is *one hundred* years. In any event, I would imagine that the *390* here absolutely relates to the Period of Israel's *sinning,* as in Ezekiel. As to total chronological reckoning, not even Josephus—to say nothing of the *Talmud,* has a firm hand on this. Therefore, one cannot just reckon *390 years* from the time of the destruction of the First Temple by Nebuchadnezzar.

[3] CDi.10–11.

[4] CDi.10 and cf. Acts 9:2, 16:17, 18:25–26, 19:9, 22:4, 24:14, 24:22, etc.

[5] CDi.11–12.

[6] *Loc. cit.* As we shall see below, there are also in the Qumran corpus two additional *Peshers* on Hosea and Micah—the former alluding to the typical things such as *'leading Israel astray,' 'rejecting the Law,'* or *'following the festivals of the Peoples'* (4QpHos[a–b]/4Q166–67); the latter, *'the Righteous Teacher who expounded the Law correctly'* and those who *'joined'* him *'who would be saved on the Day of Judgements'* (this is an idiomatique plural here)—to say nothing of *'the Spouter of Lying'* who, as in the Nahum *Pesher,* *'leads the Simple astray'* (cf. 4QpMic/4Q168 i.5–10).

[6a] 4QD266, Fragment 11, Lines 11–13. Also see 1QpHabvii.17–viii.3 above.

[7] 1QpHabvi.6–8.

[8] See the points I first made in my conclusion to *MZCQ* in 1983, pp. 35–38.

[9] 4QpNahiii.2–3 and 8

[10] I have explained the importance of this term *'ger-nilveh'* and/or *'Nilvim'* in n. 79 of Chapter 26 above, but cf. 4QNahiii.5–8, 4QNahiv.4–8, and see the definition of these same *'Nilvim'* in CDiv.2–4, Esther 9:27, Isaiah 56:3–6 (in the context of *'the Song of the Well'* in Chapter 22 above and Chapter 28 below), and my article *'"Joining"/"Joiner","Arizei-Go'im," and "the Simple of Ephraim", Relating to a Cadre of Gentile "God-Fearers" at Qumran,'* 1991 in *DSSFC,* pp. 313–31 above.

[11] 4QpIs[c] Frag. 23, ii.10–14.

[12] 4QpMic(4Q168)i.5–10.

[13] 4QpMic(4Q168)i.10.

[14] Cf. CDi.19–20 above.

[15(33)] 1QpHabvi.12–13 and note that the word for *'my Fortress'* here (*'Metzuri'*) is very likely what originally appeared in CDiv.12 (*'metzudo'*), i.e., a *'dalet'* for a *'resh'*—virtually indistinguishable anyhow—where the Cairo *Genizah* transcription reads: *'each man standing upon his own net'*—but which, more than likely, originally echoed the phraseology here in Habakkuk 2:1, *'taking one's stand upon one's Fortress'.* However, since the passage has not turned up so far among the extant Cave 4 fragments, it is impossible to say.

[16] Cf. 1QpHabv.8–9 with 1QpHabxi.5–15.

[17] Cf. 1QpHabvii.7–14 with CDiv.3–10.

[18] See n. 15 above on 1QpHabvi.12–13 and its possible relevance to CDiv.12 (*'metzudo'*) being discussed here.

[19] 1QpHabvii.4–5.

[20] Cf. 1QpHabvii.12–13 with Matthew 5:16–8 and 24:34 and *pars.*

[21] 1QpHabvii.7–8.

[22] 1QpHabvii.10–12.

[23] See n. 86 of Chapter 26 above and, for instance, CDxx.6–7, 1QpHabx.11, 1QSiv.9–10, v.14, etc. vs. 1QSi.5, i.19, iii.14, iv.3–4, iv.15–6, viii.18, ix.23, CDi.1–2, i.10, ii.1, ii.7–8, ii.14–15, iv.5–6, v. 5, v.16, xiii.11, xx.3–6, 1QpHabx.12 and xii.8. *et. al.* Where Paul is concerned, see Romans 12:7, 13:4, 15:8, 15:27, Galatians 2:17, 1 Corinthians 3:5, 16:15, 2 Corinthians 3:3–9, 4:1, 5:18, 6:3–4, 9:11–13, 11:15–23, all relating to *'diakonen'*/*'Service'*/*'Servant'*—the root of the *'Stephen'*/*'Deacon'* appointment episode in Acts 6:1–7. For *'works,'* see the famous Romans 3:27, 4:2–6, 9:32 (usually associated with *'the Law'*), 13:3, 13:12, Galatians 2:16, 3:2–10, 5:19, 2 Corinthians 11:13, etc.

[24] 1QpHabvii.14–16.

[25] 1QpHabviii.1–3.

[26] Cf. Vermes, *op. cit*, p.239, etc.; but they miss the eschatological nature of what proceeds this in 1QpHabvii.1–12 in interpretation of Habakkuk 2:2–2:3 (including *'the Delay of the Parousia'*) and, of course, the use of the key phrase *'House of Judgement'* in viii.2, which repeats in x.3 and which is defined in x.4 as *'the Judgement God will give in the midst of Many Peoples'* which, in turn, can be nothing other than what is generally called in contemporary parlance, *'the Last Judgement.'*

[27] Cf. Vermes above, p. 241, where in 1QpHabx.3, he changes this phrase from *'House of Judgement'* here in viii.2 to *'Condemned House'*—thus obscuring the relationship of the two, to say nothing of word translation consistency and generally reducing the whole to incomprehensibility. He repeats this in *The Complete Dead Sea Scrolls in English* (the publication of which, to some extent, he owes to our efforts in opening the previously-unpublished materials to the Scholarly Community as a whole), Penguin, 1997, p. 514. Yet so pervasive is the influence of his translations and so rarely do commentators actually go to the Hebrew of the texts themselves to check their translations, that it is picked up in almost all contemporary discussions of the matter as both reliable and normative. For a proper translation of both passages, see my *DSSFC*, pp. 410–11.

[28] 1QpHabxii.2–4 and note, as we have done earlier, that the allusion to these *'Evil Ones'*/*'Risha^cim'* recapitulates the earlier one in 1QpHabv.5 to *'the Evil Ones of His own People, who kept the Commandments only when convenient'* and makes it fairly clear that this ultimate allusion at the time of *'the Day of Judgement'* has to do, not only with *'idolators'* as in the Koran, but *'Backsliders among His own People'*—something like ones finds in the Koran, too, concerning those designated there as *'Hypocrites'*/*'Munafiqun.'*

[29] Cf. 1QpHabxii.14 with 1QpHabviii.2 and—among numerous examples in Paul—see Romans 5:9, 11:14, 1 Corinthians 9:22, 15:2, etc. One particularly impressive occurremce of this language comes in Revelation 21:24, which describes *'the Holy Jerusalem coming down out of Heaven from God'* and actually speaking of the *'Ethne'* or *'Peoples'* who would be *'saved'* in terms of *'walking in its Light.'* One should note that the other kind of *'Salvation'* in Hebrew, *'lehoshi^ca',* is to be found in passages like CDxx.20 (*Yesha^c*) and xx.34 (*Yeshu^cato: 'They would see His Salvation because they took refuge in His Holy Name'*—the last line of the Cairo *Genizah* version of the Damascus Document as we have seen).

[30] 1QSviii.2–10.

[31] 1QpHabvii.14–15.

[32] Cf. 1QpHabxi.14–15 above.

[33] 1QpHabx.10–15. We already saw this '*filling*' in 1QpHabxi.14 above.

[34] Cf. 4QpPs 37iv.11–12 (also see ii.4–5 and iii.3–5), CDiv.3–4, and 4QpMic(4Q168) i.10 above.

[35] 4QpPs 37 ii.4–5 and cf. iii.3–5 above.

[36] See *DSSU*, pp. 241–55, 4Q416 and 418 (now called 4QInstruction[a–f]) and, in particular, Fragment 9, Column I: '*The Salvation (Yesha[c]) of His Works*' and Fragment 8: '*The Mystery of Existence*,' from which I derived its name.

[37] 4Q416 and 418: *The Children of Salvation and the Mystery of Existence*, Fragment 9, Column i.8–12; cf., too, the evocation of this '*amal*' (i.e., '*suffering works*' or '*travail*') in 4QInstruction[a] (4Q416), Frag 2, i.5 and 4QInstruction[c] (4Q417), Frag. 1, Col. i.10. Note, too, that in one of the more recently-published fragments 4QInstruction[d] (4Q418), Fragment 81, Line 12, one even has the phraseology '*called by His Name*,' as opposed to '*called by Name*' in the Damascus Document (CDii.11 and iv.4), which has its well-known parallels in Acts 2:21, 3:16 ('*made strong in this Name*'), 4:7, 8:12, 9:21 ('*called by this Name*'), 15:17 ('*all the Gentiles upon whom My Name has been called*'), etc.

[38] 1QSviii.3–4.

[39] 1QpHabxi.15–xii.3.

[40] 1QSviii.4–5.

[41] 1QpHabx.11–12 above.

[42] *Loc. cit.*

[43] 1QpHabx.13.

[44] 1QpHabx.9–10.

[45] Cf. CDvii.15–16, playing off Amos 5:26–27 and 9:11 and 4QFlori.10–13 playing off Samuel 7:12–14 and Amos 9:11 again too. Such circularity should never be overlooked.

[46] 1QpHabx.12–13, i.e., '*They would be brought to the same Judgements of Fire, by which they insulted and vilified the Elect of God*.' What could be both more vivid and illustrative than this?

[47] Cf. 4QpNahiii.9 (*ger-nilvim*) and iv.5 (*nilvu*) with CDiv.2–3 ('*the Nilvim*,' playing off the term '*Levites*' being expounded from Ezekiel 44:15 and attached to '*the Priests*,' identified there with '*the Penitents of Israel who went out from the Land of Judah*'—a fundamental designation); and see nn. 10 above and 79 in Chapter 26, preceding it. Also note the kind of definitions in Esther 9:27 and Isaiah 56:3–6 (in the context of the material about '*singing out to the Well*') and my article '"*Joining*"/"*Joiner*", "*Arizei-Go'im*", and "*the Simple of Ephraim*" Relating to a Cadre of Gentile "*God-Fearers*" at Qumran,' first delivered to the Society of Biblical Literature at the height of the controversy over the freeing of the Scrolls in 1991 and later collected—as we gave severak times remarked—in *DSSFC*, 1992, pp. 313–31.

48 4QpNahiii.1–2, here identified with *the City of Ephraim* (another circumlocution, which we have already seen parodied in other expositions as ᶜ*Amraphel*), but which, with reference to the double references to *the Seekers after Smooth Things* (*Halakot*) in iv.5–8, can easily be seen to be *an Assembly* or *Congregation* of some kind which most scholars identify—because of the play on *Halachot*/*Legal Traditions*, i.e., *seeking Legal Traditions*—with *the Pharisees*.

49 4QpNahii.2–4. Note here how Demetrius, though a Seleucid, is considered to be a *Grecian King* and see Josephus, *War* 1.92–99 and *Ant.* 13.370–79.

50 4QpNahii.2–iii.8, a terrifying indictment, which seems to know very well about the coming of the Romans and the endless piles of wounded and corpses and the way that whole cities and families will perish *because of their guilty counsel*. It is a terrible picture and a terrifying indictment, as just stated.

51 1QpHabx.9–10

52 4QpNahii.1, literally referring to *Apostles to the Gentiles*—here *Goʻim*.

53 4QpNahiii.2–4. For the relationship to the indictment of *the Spouter of Lying*—also based on an allusion to *City of Blood* and who has so many characteristics, in my view, in common with *the Historical Paul*—see 1QpHabx.9–16. For the relationship to the issue of ᶜ*Amraphel* in the Psalm 37 *Pesher* and Rabbinic Literature generally, see above Chapters 12 and 14.

54 4QpNahiii.8–9.

55 4QpNahiii.2–4

56 CDxx.19–20 and note there too how *God will reveal Salvation* (*Yesha*ᶜ) *and Justification* (*Zedakah*) *to those fearing His Name*. One can now see there are many parallels in the new Document, which we called *The Children of Salvation and the Mystery of Existence*. See, in particular, 4QInstructionᶜ (4Q417), Fragment 2, Column i.15–16 (*a Book of Remembrance for those who keep His word*—repeated twice), 4QInstructionᵈ (4Q418), Fragment 55, Line 11, etc.

57 CDiii.8.

58 Cf. Matthew 26:27–9 and *pars.* and note how this is directly followed in both Matthew and Luke with vow-like assertion that he *would drink no more of the fruit of the vine* (like James) *until that day when* he *should drink it with you in the Kingdom* or, as Luke 22:30 puts it, *so that you may eat and drink at my table in my Kingdom*; and see my articles, already mentioned several times above: *Qumran's "New Covenant in the Land of Damascus" and the New Testament's "Cup of the New Covenant in (his) Blood,"* in *The Journal of Higher Criticism*, Spring, 2003 (10/1), pp. 121–36 and *An Esoteric Relation between Qumran's "New Covenant in the Land of Damascus" and the New Testament's "Cup of the New Covenant in (his) Blood"*, *Revue de Qumran*, March, 2004 (83/21/3), pp. 439–56.

59 Cf. CDi.16, iii.10, iv.6–10, vi.2, viii.15–18, xx.8–9, and xx.30–32.

60 *Cf. CDiv.8-10 above—that 'Covenant' which is explained in terms of having 'to do according to the precise letter of the Torah.'*

61 Cf. CDvi.2, CDiii.10, and iv.9 above.

62 1QpHabii.2–10.

63(62)1QpHabii.1–8 and cf. Paul in 2 Corinthians 3:2–6.

64 See my conclusions in *'Qumran's "New Covenant in the Land of Damascus" and the New Testament's "Cup of the New Covenant in (his) Blood,"'* in *The Journal of Higher Criticism*, Spring, 2003 (10/1), pp. 121–36 and *'An Esoteric Relation between Qumran's "New Covenant in the Land of Damascus" and the New Testament's "Cup of the New Covenant in (his) Blood,"'* *Revue de Qumran*, March, 2004 (83/21/3), pp. 439–56 above and my detailed discussion of the palaeography of the Damascus Document and other crucial Documents at Qumran in *MZCQ*, pp. 28–31 and 78–91.

65 See 1QpHabx.5–12 and cf., as well, 1QpHabxii.1–10.

66 1QpHabx.9–12 and cf. James 2:20 on the parallel picture of its opponent whom it calls *'the Man of Emptiness.'*

67 1QSviii.1–10.

68 Cf. CDi.3, i.17, ii.5–11, iii.8–9, v.16–21 (including the language of 'works'), viii.1–5/xix.13–17, viii.16–22/xix.28–34, and xx.15–16 and 25–26.

69 See, for instance, 1QSii.26–iii.1, iii.25, v.5, vi.26, vii.17, viii.7–10, ix.3–4, CDii.7–8, iv.21, x.6, 1QpHabv.1, 1QHix.12, xii.7–8, etc.

70 Cf. 4QpNahiii.9 and iv.5 above.

71 1QSviii.6–9.

72 See also the whole ethos in 1 Peter 2:5 (it, too, strongly replete with Qumran language usage and imagery), 2 Corinthians 5:1, Galatians 2:18, Colossians 2:7, and Hebrews 3:3–4—another telling passage, this time referring to *'Moses' House'* as we have generally implied here in the Damascus Document (cf. *'the House of the Torah'* in Column xx.10 and xx.13) but, for Paul of course, *'the House built by God'* (*'the House'* he is *'building'*—to be sure) is superior.

73 Cf. 1QHvii.7–10, preceded by references to both *'Belial'* and *'swallowing'* (vii.3–5—based on the same root in Hebrew) and followed by the familiar ones to *'Yeshaᶜ,' 'Netzer,' 'the Sons of Piety'/'Hesed,'* and *'Faithfulness'* (vii.19–21).

74 Cf. 1QHvii.8–12 (including what can only be called a plethora of *'Lying,' 'Tongue,'* and *'lips'* imagery) with 1QHv.35–38 and vi.25–28—passages themselves preceded in v.13–4 with allusion to *'saving the soul of the Meek One'* and, then, *'curing the soul of the Meek'* (*ᶜAni*); in v.19, *'the soul of the Poor One'* (*Ebion*); and in v.23–24, allusions to *'all the Poor Ones of Piety'* (*'Ebionei-Hesed'*, combining both *'Ebionite'* and *'Hassidaean'* imagery) and *'zeal.'*

75 *Ibid.* but, in particular, 1QHvii.12 above.

76 1QHviii.30–37 ending with another allusion to *'Homat-ᶜOz'*—*'Wall of Strength'* (*'ᶜOz-le-ᶜAm'* or *'Oblias'?*). Of course this is the imagery of *'the Last Judgement'*—cf. Isaiah 24:19–20, Joel 2:10–11, 2 Peter 3:5–13, and Koran 70.8–10 (again on *'the Day of Judgement'*), 78.17–20, 81.1–7 (*'the Day of Decision'*—the best expression of this imagery), 82.1–5, etc.

77 For allusions to this kind in the Scrolls, see CDiii.19 (*'holding fast to the House of Faith'*), viii.13–14/xix.27 (*'holding fast'* or *'steadfast'*), xx.18 (*'strengthening'*), xx.27 (*'holding fast'*), xx.33 (*'their hearts will be strengthened'*), 1QSiv.5, viii.7–7 (*'a Tested Rampart, a Precious Cornerstone, the*

Foundations of which will not shake or sway in their place'), and 1QHiii.35–36, vi.25–29, vii.7–10, ix.28, etc. above.

78 Cf. 1QpHabvi.16–vii.6.

79 Cf. 1QpHabx.11–12 above.

80 *'The Dajjal'* is a kind of *'Lying'* eschatological figure who makes war both on *'the Christ'* and/or *'the Mahdi'*—depending on which tradition one is following. He is recognized in both *Sunni* and *Shiʿa* Islam even though he is not mentioned in the Koran at all. Rather, he is to be found in some extremely detailed *Hadith*. For Sunnism, see al-Buhari, *al-Sahih* 3.106, 4.55–54, 4.574, 9.453, Muslim, *al-Sahih* 1.296, 4.1224, 7.3197, 40.692–93, 40.7015, 40.7023, 40.7034 (identifying him with the *'70, 000 Jews of Isfahan'* who marched on Jerusalem—probably reflecting the very real Jewish *'Messianic'* Revolts there of individuals like David Alroy, anticipating *'the Mourners for Zion Movement,'* I have covered elsewhere—to say nothing of both *Karaism* and *Shiʿism* itself), 46.7028, 50.6979, and Abu Daʿud, *al-Sunan* 35.4230–32, 37.4281–82, 37.4283, 37.4292, 37.4306, 37.4311, 40.4738, etc. For 12–*Imam Shiʿism*, he is defeated at the end of time by the returning Twelfth, *'The Hidden Imam', al-Mahdi*; while in Sunnism, he appears to be defeated either by the Prophet himself or Jesus Christ! But all forms of Islam recognize him in their eschatology as a kind of *'Antichrist.'* In fact, in most Islamic eschatology, *'the Dajjal'* and *'Christ'*, who also returns, are at war when ultimately *'the Mahdi'* then also returns and, either separate from or together with *'Christ'*, defeats *'the Dajjal.'* In the Damascus Document as well as in Hymns at Qumran, *'the Liar'* is also referred to as *'the Scoffer'* or *'Ish ha-Lazon'*—*'who poured over Israel the waters of Lying'*—which I interpret, not simply as *'The Scoffer,'* but actually *'The Joker'* or *'Comedian'*—*'Comedian'*, in the sense that his ideas are so ridiculous, they are not to be taken seriously; cf. CDi.14 and xx.34 (here *'the Men of Scoffing'*) and also see 1QHii.31 (ii.14: *'the Scoffers of Error'*) and iv.9–10 for parallel materials about *'the Scoffers of Lying'* (plural).

81 1QpHabx.12.

82 1QpHabx.11–13 above.

83 Cf. CDvii.9 and xiii.24 among numerous other allusions to such *'Visitations.'*

84 Cf. 1QpHabviii.8–ix.12.

85 1QpHabvi.9–11. We have already discussed just this kind of violence demonstrated by Vespasian, Titus, and their troops around the Sea of Galilee—particularly Tarichaeae; cf. *War* 2.573–641, 3.445–532, and Chapters 14 and 24 above.

86 4QpNahiii.4–69 and cf. *War* 5.3–25, 5.252–308, and variously. Note in 5.290 the *'Jewish prisoner, whom Titus had crucified before the wall, in the hope that the spectacle might lead the rest to surrender in dismay'*—a possible model, in my view, for the Gospel crucifixion of *'Jesus.'* Note, too, how this is followed by the equally unsettling death of *'John'*, who seems to have been *'the brother'* of a *'James'*, and that of both Leaders of the Idumaeans. It is difficult to know what all this portends.

87 See 1QpHabv.5–6 above and cf. *Ant.* 20.100–103, but also see *War* 2.220–23; for his role as Governor of Egypt, see *War* 2.309; as Commander after Vespasian departed for Rome and,

along with Titus at crucial points in the siege of Jerusalem, *War* 4.616–18 and 6.237–43.

[88] 1QpHabxii.10–14.

[89] For some examples of Muhammad's use of these terms or concepts in the Koran, see 2.8–20, 88–91, 96–98, 105–108, 135, 142; 3.94–95, 167; 4.48–52, 76, 88, 116–19, 132, 142; 5.60, 82; 6.138, 8.49, 9.1–36, 64–66, 113, etc. —they are, indeed, widespread. Cf. 1QpHabv.5–6, 1QpHabxiii.3–4, and CDi.2–3, 16–17, ii.5–9, iii.10–12, v.11–17, viii.1–2/xix.13–14, viii.21–22/xix.34–35, xx.1–5, 8–17, 22–27, and 32-33.

[90] 1QpHabxiii.1–4.

Chapter 28

[1] See *The Holy Quran: Arabic Text with English Translation and Short Commentary*, Midrat Mirza Tahir Ahmad, Islam International Publications Ltd., 1994, nn. 995–09 on 7:66–85; but also see the comments in all commentaries below on 11.61–66, 26.124–60, 41.13–18, 46.22–26, 51.41–45, 69.4–6, etc.

[2] See *The Holy Quran: Text, Translation, and Commentary* by A. Yusuf Ali, Beirut, 1968, p. 360.

[3] See *The Holy Quran: Arabic Text with English Translation and Short Commentary* by Midrat Mirza Tahir Ahmad above, n. 998, p. 341 on 7.74.

[4] See, for instance, *The Holy Quran*, IFTA, Medina and cf. *Surah* 46.21, n. 4798, p. 1551, *Surah* 77.11, n. 5866, p. 1872, and *Surah* 4.150–60, n. 580, pp. 227–29 and those on 23.45–54, nn. 909–910, pp. 883–84 in Yusuf Ali's *The Holy Quran* above.

[5] See my article 'Who were the Koranic Prophets ʿAd, Thamud, Hud, and Salih?', *Journal of Higher Criticism*, vol. xi/n. 2, 2005, pp. 96–107—originally given to the American Academy of Religion, San Francisco, 1992 as ʿAd, Thamud, Hud, and Salih as Reflecting Edessene/Northern Syrian Conversion Stories about Thomas, Addai/Thaddaeus, Yehudah (Judas Thomas/Judas the Zealot/Judas Barsabas), and James' — and A. Yusuf Ali, *The Holy Quran*, n. 1048, p. 362 on *Surah* 7.79 above.

[6] See *JBJ*, pp. 191–93 and 883–88 and Moses of Chorene 2.30–35 who calls her 'the first of Agbar's wives,' to whom—not insignificantly—he gave the town of Haran!

[7] This comes through both 'Mandaean' ('the Subbaʿ of the Marshes') emigration accounts and lists of 'Jewish *Heresies*' such as those in Eusebius and Epiphanius—e. g., 'the Masbuthaeans' in *E.I.* 4.22.5; in *Apost. Const.* 6.6, 'the Basmuthaeans', an evident verbal reversal; and *Haraes.*19.2.10, 20.3.2–4, 30.3.2, etc., 'the Sampsaeans,' another evident corruption but obviously part and parcel of 'the Elchasaites' who are, in effect, what Muslims are calling 'the Subbaʿ' or 'Sabaeans' (for Hippolytus, 'the Sobiai') — cf. the *Haran Gawaita* and Chapter 4 and variously above.

[8] See, for instance, *Annals* 6.44 and 12.12 but also Strabo, *Geography* 16.1.28. For Juvenal, for instance, *Satire* 1.33, the Jewish 'Alabarch's of Alexandria are, rather, 'Arabarch's—thus!

[9] Cf. Chapter 3 above and Moses of Chorene, *History of Armenia* 2.26, who notes—as we saw earlier—the kind of difficulty Westerners had pronouncing Semitic Languages.

[10] See *Annals* 12.12 above.

[11] See *E.I.* 1.13.6, Moses of Chorene, *History of Armenia* 2.30–5, J. B. Segal, *Edessa 'The Blessed City,'* pp. 62–82 above, and the Syriac *Doctrine of Addai* which, not surprisingly, has strong links to the Document known obviously as *The Acts of Thaddaeus.* In Syriac, *'Uchama'* or *'Ukkama',* means *'the Black.'* There are many explanations for this name but the best perhaps, as we have been alluding to, is the way Acts parodies it in its episode regarding *'the Ethiopian Queen's eunuch.'*

[12] Also cf. Josephus' *Ant.* 1.220.

[13] Cf. *Ant.* 20.38–45.

[14] See *JBJ*, pp. 882 and 890 and *Ant.* 20.25. But also see *Ant.* 1.90–95, which mentions the Third Century Armenian historian, *'Berosus the Chaldaean',* who calls the Mountain—that of *'the Cordyaeans',* i.e., *'the Kurds'*—and Hippolytus 9.8 and 10:26. For Adiabene, see Chapters 8, 13, 14, and variously above.

[15] See Benjamin of Tudela, *Travels: Years 1163–1165.*

[16] See, for instance, the Babylonian *Targum* on Jeremiah 51:27 and Ezekiel 27:23, Gen R. 37.1–4 on the location of Adiabene and Corduene, *Yeb.* 16b on the legitimacy of converts from there (also echoed in the Jerusalem *Talmud* in a tradition ascribed to R. Nahman b. Jacob), *Kid.* 72a, j. *Meg.* i.71b, and *Yalqut* Daniel 1064. But also see *Wikipedia* article on 'Corduene' (i.e., 'Kurdistan, the linguistic equivalent to *'Adiabene',* and the sources cited there—in particular, J. Neusner *'The Jews in Pagan Armenia', JAOS,* 1964, p. 233) and *Ant.* 1.90–5 and 20.25 above.

[17] See Kor 7.59–67, 9.70, 11.25–69, 14.9, 22.42, 26.106–59, 29.14–38, etc. above. These are all passages where *'Noah'/'the Land of Noah'* are mentioned in the same breath as ʿAd', 'Thamud', 'Salih', and 'Hud'.

[18] For references such as this about *'minim',* see *Ber.* 9a, *San.* 37b–39b, j. *San.* 105b, *Hul.* 13a-b, *Tos. Hul.* 2.24—but, in particular, for the *'Birkat ha-Minim'* (*'Cursing of Minim'*—which includes 'the *Saddukim'*), *Ber.* 28b–29a, *Shab.* 116a and *Tos. Shab.* 13.5; for *'the Saddukim'* per se, see also *Ber.* 7a, 10a, 56b, 58a, *San.* 38b, 90b, 106a, *Git.* 45b, 57a, *Ket.* 112a, *Shab* 14b, 88a, *A.Z.* 40b, *Ned.* 49b, *Suk* 48b, *Hul.* 87a, *Yeb.* 63b, etc., and *Eccles. R.* 1.8.

[19] *Haraes.* 19.2.10, 20.3.2–4, 30.3.2, and 53.1.1–2.2 (which identifies them as *'the Elchasaites'*—an obvious equivalence).

[20] See Benjamin of Tudela, *Travels: Years 1163–1165* above.

[21] See Muhammad ibn al-Nadim, *Kitab al-Fihrist* 9.1.

[21a] 4QTesti.5–8.

[22] 1QSix.11—the allusion is to *'the Prophet and the Messiah of Aaron and Israel.'*

[23] See, for instance, Koran 2.82, 2.277, 3.114 (on a 'James'-like Community Muhammad both recognizes and is familiar with), 84.25, etc.

[24] Cf. Koran 2.173, 5.3, 6.146, 16.115, etc.

[25(26)] The point was, as we have already explained previously, that *'strangled things'* was probably a way of rendering into Greek a rather technical Hebreo-Arabic usage like *'carrion'*—particularly as it had something to do with carnivorous animals preying on more *'cud-chewing'* ones usually via choking the windpipe. Cf. Ps. *Hom.* 7.3–4, 7.8, and 8.19 above, all of which make it very clear we are talking about '*carrion*' and even describe it.

26 See n. 11 above and J. B. Segal, *Edessa 'The Blessed City,'* pp. 62–82. Note, as well, the Greek *Acts of Thaddaeus* and the Syriac *The Doctrine of Addai.*

27 Moses of Chorene 2.26–29 above.

28 Cf. Koran 9.70 and its reference to the '*disasters which came upon them,'* 29.38, 41.15–19 ('*loosening upon them a raging wind in Evil Days*'), 41.41–45, 54.18–21, and 59.4–7; and see also 14.9, 22.40–42, 46.21, and 26.123–50,

29 Cf. the Syriac *Doctrine of Addai.*

30 This matter has been widely discussed, but perhaps the best-known book detailing these origins and, in effect, starting the whole series of subsequent investigations, was Ian Wilson's *The Turin Shroud: The Burial Cloth of Jesus Christ?*, London, 1979.

31 See Gospel of Thomas 1.1.

32 Cf. *The Acts of Thomas* 1.1, *The Doctrine of Addai, The Acts of Thaddaeus, The Teaching of the Apostles,* etc.

33 Though Eusebius himself only calls '*Thomas,'* '*Thomas,'* in *E.I.* 1.13.4; in the actual correspondence, he includes, there the sentence reads '*Judas, who was also called Thomas, sent to him Thaddaeus, an Apostle—one of the 70*' (1.12.10). Not only is the confusion between '*Apostle*' and '*Disciple*' manifest here, but '*Thomas*' is actually called by his real name '*Judas Thomas*'—probably also '*Jesus*" brother. One should note that in the Syriac version of this, in *The Teaching of the Apostles* above, the reading is '*Thomas, the Apostle, sent Judas—who is also called Thaddaeus—one of the Seventy, etc., etc.,'* and here the larger problem is clarified even more. Both of these individuals are called '*Judas*' and, in fact, the best ungarbled reading should probably read '*James sent Judas, his brother, etc., etc.'*—the only one which makes any sense after one removes all the layers of disinformation or poorly-digested facts.

34 Cf. *Apost. Const.* 8.25. A note identifies a variant manuscript as reading: '*Thaddaeus, also called Lebbaeus and who was surnamed Judas the Zealot, preached the Truth to the Edessenes and the People of Mesopotamia, when Abgarus ruled over Edessa, and was buried in Berytus of Phoenicia.'* In Matthew 27:56 and Mark 15:40, this '*Mary*' is seemingly called '*the mother of James and Joses*' or of '*James the Less (thus!), Joses, and Salome'.* However, all is fairly definitively clarified in a Fragment X of Papias stating: '*Mary the wife of Cleophas or Alphaeus was the mother of James the Bishop and Apostle and of Simon and Thaddaeus, and of one Joseph*' (need I say more?). See also my *JBJ,* Chapter 26: '*Judas Thomas and Theuda the Brother of the Just One,'* pp. 923–63.

35 *E.I.* 2.23.7.

36 Cf. n. 34 above and *E.I.* 1.12.1–4, which gives way to the '*Agbarus*' story in 1.13. But also see Papias, Fragment X, who expresses himself totally confused about all these matters, falling on the horns of the dilemma as it were of how '*Mary the wife of Cleophas*' could be the sister of her own sister '*Mary*'!

37 See '*Addai*' in 1 Apoc. Jas. v.3:35.15 and cf. '*Theuda the brother*' or '*father of the Just One, since he*

was a relative of his' (*sic*!) in 1 *Apoc. Jas.* v.4, 44:15–20

[38] Cf. Eusebius in *E.I.* 1.13.1–20 with *The Doctrine of Addai*, Moses of Chorene, 2.32–33, *The Acts of Thaddaeus*, *The Teaching of the Apostles*, etc.

[39] The Prophet 'Ad' or 'Adi'—obviously connected to 'Addai,' 'Edessa,' and 'Adiabene'—has always been represented in this Region (and is even today), though the origins of this connection are clouded in obscurity. This is also true for the 'Yazidis' in the same Region, themselves following their saintly progenitor the Sufi 'Shaykh 'Adi'—and as are his origins!

[40] *E.I.* 2.1.2–5 and cf. my discussion of the substitution in Acts of *'the election to replace Judas Iscariot'* for this *'election'* above in Chapters 4 and 6 above and *JBJ*, pp. 166–209.

[41] Cf. 4QMMTiii.24–33 and see my discussion in *DSSU*, pp. 180–88 and above Chapter 19 and in *JBJ*, pp. 900–902 and 949–59. Also see my *'A Response to Schiffman on MMT'* in *The Qumran Chronicle*, 1990/91, Cracow, pp. 95–104. The point is that he Letter is addressed to a *'King and His People'*, whom it wishes to compare or who wishes to compare himself to David. Since there was no 'King' in Jerusalem at this time, we are almost in all likelihood speaking about a foreign convert who knows little about Judaism. Certainly no *'Herodian'*, including Agrippa I, would either require or wish such tuition. In fact (as I argue in *'MMT as a Jamesian Letter to the Great King of the Peoples or Izates,'* *Journal of Higher Criticism*, Spring, 2005, pp. 55–68—a paper I first gave at a National Session of the Society of Biblical Literature in 1991), it is a *'letter to the Great King of the Peoples beyond the Euphrates'*!

[42] Cf. CDvii.14–21 on *'re-erecting the fallen Tent of David'* and xvi.4–9 on *'taking upon oneself the Covenant'* and Abraham *'circumcising all the members of his household'* in Genesis 17:10-14.

[43] Cf. Moses of Chorene 2.35, who specifically asserts this. But also see Josephus' note in *Ant.* 20.17–22 on Helen's husband, though going under the Persian title 'Bazeus' or 'Monobazus,' being—as in the Biblical story of Abraham and Sarah—her brother.

[44] Cf. *Ant.* 20.34–48 with Gen. R. 46.10, But also see *E.I.* 1.13.6–8 and Acts 9:12–7.

[45] See Josephus, *War* 4.567 concerning the palaces of *'a kinsman of King Izas of Adiabene'* in Jerusalem, War 5.147 where he seems to think Helen is *'the daughter of King Izas,'* and J. B. Segal, *Edessa the Blessed City*, pp. 12 and 67-71 above.

[46] Note how in *Surahs* 7.65–72, 9.7, 14.9, 11.50–60, 22.42, 25.37–40, 26.123–40, etc., these *'warnings'* and imprecations always follow the story of 'Noah' and 'the Flood'. In fact, 11.52 actually alludes to rain-making as part of the 'Hud'/'Ad' tradition—the same for 25.40. See, too, the comments of A. Yusuf Ali, *The Holy Quran*, Beirut, pp. 358–60 and 527–30. In n. 1040 on 7.65, he actually refers to this *'three year* period of drought' and in n. 1546 on 11.52, he makes much of this drought and its end being in some way associated with 'Hud and 'Ad'. One might wish to associate the *'three years'* with James 5:17–18 and its *'efficacious prayer of the Righteous One'* and actual allusion to Elijah and his paradigmatic *'three year'*-plus bout of rain-cessation and rain-making in 1 Kings 17:1–18:46, already signaled earlier.

[47] Cf. how in 6:9, Noah is described as *'Just and Righteous in his generation'* and how the whole episode of *'the Flood'* is preceded by the allusion 'the Sons of God' having intercourse with *'the daughters of men'* in 6:1–4. Nor is this to say anything about CDii.16–iii.1's actual reference to

'fornication' in its paradigmatic retelling of this occurrence. In the Koran, cf. 7.80 11.45–49, 26, 83, 27.53, etc., where both are mentioned in one way or another.

48 Cf. these kinds of allusions in Kor 11.61, 26.42, 46.21, etc.

49 See his note at the beginning of the *War* 1.4–6 that, in the context of the death of Nero and the subsequent disorder, he felt it prudent to accurately inform *'those of our People beyond the Euphrates with the Adiabeni'* (and here is the precise language of the Syriac tradition of *'the Letter to the Great King of the Peoples beyond the Euphrates'*—to say nothing of the specific allusion to *'those in Adiabene'*) *'concerning how the War began, the miseries it brought, and in what manner it ended.'*

50 Cf. Hippolytus 9.21 with *War* 2.150 and *Ant.* 18.11–25. In the latter, he speaks of *'Four Philosophies'*, seemingly evaluating them all equally on this basis. But in *War* 2.119, he rather speaks of one *'Jewish Philosophy'* with *'three forms'*—specifically calling the Movement founded by 'the *Sophist* Judas' in the previous line (2.118), *'an heresios'* or *'heresy'/*'sect.' It is in 2.150 that he speaks of *'the four grades'* of 'Essenes', which mainly appear to break down according to descending order of *'Holiness'* or *'Purity,'* but his application of the term 'Sophist' here to 'Judas the Galilean' is especially interesting.

51 Hippolytus 9.22.

52 Hippolytus 9.23 and cf. this with War 2.160–61, both of which then seem to go on to talk of *'the Pharisees'.* Nor is it completely clear how these *'Pharisees'* would differ from this last *'order'* or *'grade'* of so-called *'Essenes.'*

53 Cf. Hippolytus 9.21 above.

54 This issue was particularly strong in the early days of Qumran research, I having particularly focused upon it in MZCQ, pp. 17–34, 55–59, and 66–78—but also see Cecil Roth, *The Dead Sea Scrolls: A New Historical Approach*, Oxford, 1959 and G. R. Driver, *The Hebrew Scrolls*, Oxford, 1959 and *The Judaean Scrolls*, Oxford, 1965 who—being Oxford colleagues—worked together and who, like myself, on p. 394 of the last-named work, stated that *'internal evidence afforded by a document must take precedence over external evidence.'* But *par contra*, note F. M. Cross' severe criticism of both and others (in fact, anyone who stood in his way) in *The Ancient Library of Qumran*, New York, 1958, pp. 73–77—criticism which was followed up by his many colleagues: Milik, de Vaux, Strugnell, Tov, *et. al.*, sweeping over all subsequent work and which, as it were, *'won the field'* and still reigns supreme even today. But which was not really either subtle, succinct, or historically-incisive enough to have done so.

55 Cf. Hippolytus 9.21 with Matthew 17:24–27 (which contains the typical Paulism: *'but truly the Sons are free'*; cf. 1 Corinthians 6:12, 9:18–19, 10:24–29, Galatians 2:4, 4:31, etc.) and *pars.* The point here is that the Gospel 'Jesus' is quite willing to pay the *'two drachma'* tax and recommend to others to do so as well, but he does not carry coinage on his own person and seems unwilling to touch it either—rather recommending to 'Peter', as we saw, to fish up a fish with a *'stater'* in its mouth. The knowledge of foreign coinage here is also quite impressive— again adding to the impression of non-Palestinian authorship. The same for the famous issue

of the *'tribute money'* in Matthew 22:15–22 and *pars.*, ending up in the *'render unto Caesar and God what is God's'* admonition and directed against tell-tale *'Pharisees'* and *'hypocrites'* again. He does not touch this or handle this either but merely looks upon it.

[56] The implied picture here of itinerant *'preachers,'* *'messengers,'* or *'disease-carriers,'* as the case may be, is very much in keeping with that of 4QpNahiii.1, we have highlighted above, to say nothing of Paul in Acts 16:20–21, 17:6–7 and 24:5 (pictured as another of these *'pests'* or *'disease-carriers,'* *'turning the world upside down'* and *'stirring up trouble among the Jews around the World'*—*'a Ringleader of the Nazarene Sect'*—thus!), reflected too in the letter of caution Claudius sends to the Jews of Alexandria— obviously around 50 CE—cautioning them against the carriers of just such an *'infection'* and conserved in H. Idris Bell, *Jews and Christians in Egypt*, London, 1934, pp. 25–28.

[57] I have traced this development in all my previous work. Note how Josephus first introduces *'the Sicarii'* around 55 CE in *War* 2.254–57 and *Ant.* 20.186–204. However, he doesn't actually really start using the term *'Zealot'* until much later—in the latter stages of the War in 69 or even 70 CE (though, earlier he did apply the term, *'zealous for the Law'*, to the Revolutionaries in the Temple in *War* 1.655 around the time of Herod's last illness just before his death in 4 BC), Moreover, at this point, he does so in the context of allusion to individuals like *'Simeon the son of Gamaliel,'* Josephus' friend *'Jesus ben Gamala,'* and James' murderer *'Ananus ben Ananus,'* who incited the crowd against them as *'disease-carriers and infectors of their Freedom'* and *'Temple polluters'* (*War* 4.158–62—note the ideological reversal again here and furthermore that they are using the exact language Paul is using in Galatians 4:17–18 above of *'not being zealous of good works'*—for him, *'in the right way*—but rather *'zealous in the pursuit of Evil'* or, again, as he puts it, *'to exclude'.* Par contra, relative to their charge of *'polluting the Temple,'* see the opposite one of *'polluting the Temple of God'* leveled against *'the Wicked Priest'*—Ananus ben Ananus?—in 1QpHabxii.8–9). For his part, Josephus applies the term *'Zealot'* to one particular group only—the one led by *'Eleazar ben Simon'* actually in and occupying the Temple (*War* 5.3–28). Nor does he do so until after the Vengeance they and their confreres take on the above individuals seemingly, as we saw, for the death of James (*War* 4.302–10), already delineated above.

[58(52)] Hippolytus 9.22 above.

[58(49)] See nn. 54 and 57 above and C. Roth, *The Dead Sea Scrolls: A New Historical Approach*, Oxford, 1959, G. R. Driver, *The Hebrew Scrolls*, Oxford, 1959 and *The Judaean Scrolls*, Oxford, 1965, and my *MZCQ*, pp. 17–34, 55–59, and 66–78, as well as F. M. Cross, *The Ancient Library of Qumran*, New York, 1958, pp. 73–77.

[59] See, in particular, the actual use of this term in 1QSii.15 (*'zeal for His/God's Ordinances'*), iv.4 (*'zeal for the Ordinances of Righteousness'*), and ix.23 (*'being like a man zealous for the Law'*) and their opposite in iv.10 (*'the Way of Darkness of the Evil soul'* and *'zeal for lustfulness'*), iv.17–8 (*'zeal for division'*), x.19–20 (*'not zealous in a spirit of Evil'*), etc. But also see these aggressive attitudes surrounding these *'Last Days,'* *'the Torah of Moses,'* *'zeal against Backsliders and Traitors to the New Covenant'* in CDi.17–ii.1, ii.5–8, ii.15–iii.12, iii.20, iv.4–7, v.12–16, v.21, vi.10–

vii.9, vii.14–viii.10/xix.9–21, viii.14–21/xix.24–34, xx.6–13, xx.22–34, 1QpHabii.1–6, v.3–12, vii.2–14, viii.1–3, ix.4–8, x.3–5, xi.15, xii.10–xiii.4, etc.

60 See, for instance, Eusebius' version of these names and my comments in n. 53 of Chapter 8 above and in *JBJ*, pp. 866–82. For '*Augurus*,' see *ANCL*: *Codex Baroccian* 206 (and compare the spelling here with Dio Cassius 68:18–21). For '*Acbarus*' and '*Albarus*' also see Tacitus 6.44 and 8.12, Strabo, *Geography* 16.1.28, and various Latin versions of some of the Documents mentioned above and in the *ANCL Fragments*. In my view, this error was already occurring in Acts transference of '*Agbarus*' to the patently nonsensenical name '*Agabus*.'

61 Note in a variant mss. in *ANCL*: *Apost. Const.* 8.25, and above, nn. 5 and 24. One should compare this to another work, attributed to Hippolytus in *ANCL's Appendix on Hippolytus*: *Hippolytus on the Twelve Apostles*, '*Judas, also called Lebbaeus, preached to the people of Edessa and to all Mesopotamia and fell asleep at Berytus and was buried there*' and cf. too *Epist. Apost.* 12 and *JBJ* above, pp. 807–16, 860–64, and 930–38.

62 See Josephus, *War* 7.253–444, particularly 7.410–19 and 437–44.

63 *Ibid.*, 7.437, 439, 444 and *Vita* 424 and his narrative about Jonathan of Cyrene, who accused him of sending both weapons and money to support the Uprising there; but who—on Josephus' very testimony that he was '*a Liar*'—was put to death by Vespasian.

64 *Ad. Haer.* 1.31.1

65 Cf. Gospel of Judas 45 with CDvii.19–21, 1QMxi.6–7, and 4QTesti.9–10.

66 Cf. Galatians 2:3–4, 2:7–9, 2:12, 5:6–7 but most of all 5:12, where he makes, as we have frequently remarked, a ribald joke about it—all the time using the language of both '*the Essenes*' and the Qumran sectaries about '*cutting off*'—for them, meaning '*to excommunicate*'; but for him, a double entendre playing off their '*zealousness to exclude*' (cf. Galatians 4:17 above).

67 Cf. Hippolytus 9.21 with *War* 2.152. Note the difference here. One has the '*Jamesian*' and Koranic refusal—and this on pain of death—'*to eat things sacrificed to idols*'; the other, merely the more general refusal '*to eat forbidden foods.*' Which is more precise or more accurate? The reader must judge for his or her self, but for the writer it is obvious.

68 Cf. Hippolytus 9.21 with *Ant.* 18.23 and *War* 2.118, both of which emphasis the refusal '*to call any man Lord*'—including the Roman Emperor. No wonder there was so much trouble.

69 One can see this by comparing *War* 2.151–53 with *Ant.* 18.23–24. For this, Hippolytus' version is perhaps better—combining the two into '*Zealot*' or '*Sicarii Essenes.*'

70 *War* 4.310–25 above (of course, who exactly these '*Idumaeans*' were, whom Josephus conveniently links with '*the Zealots*' in the execution of these bloody deeds, is a subject which needs explanation).

71 Cf. *War* 4.241–43, 352–58, etc. By this time, he seems to be including descriptions of this kind to please persons like Agrippa II but, by then, his own animus following the brutal dispatch of his friend Jesus ben Gamala, mentioned above, was perhaps motivation enough.

72 For these kind of allusions to '*the First*' or '*the Forefathers*' or '*the Ancestors*—usually associated with '*the Brit*' or '*the Covenant of the Forefathers*'—see CDi.4, iii.10, iv.6–9, vi.2, viii.16–17 (a Qumran form of Pauline '*Grace*,' as we have explained), xx.8–9—this actually contrasting '*the*

First' with '*the Last*' as in the Gospels (Matthew 20:16 and *pars.*) but, of course, to opposite ideological effect—and xx.31. In another Document, see also 1QSix.10—but this framed rather in terms of '*the Ordinances of the First*.' This expression, of course, should be linked up with '*the Last Times*'/'*the Last Days*,' i.e., in the view of the Sectarians—that time presently transpiring.

73 Hippolytus 9.21.

74 *Ibid.* and cf. Peter in Acts 10:28, somewhat tendentiously speaking to those of the household of the '*God-fearing*' Centurion ('*well-spoken of by the whole of the Jewish People*'—sic!) Cornelius: '*You know it is not Lawful for a Jewish man to go with or come near one of another race*' and a similar notice in Josephus' description of '*the Essenes*' about '*being touched by an inferior member*' in *War* 2.151.

75 *War* 7.253–406.

76 Cf. n. 74 above and *War* 2.151.

77 In these episodes, of course, something miraculous is usually achieved; cf. Matthew 9:20–29 and 14:35–36 and *pars.* concerning '*touching the hem of his garment*' (echoing, to some extent, what Jerome in *Vir. ill.* 2 and *Commentary on Galatians* 1:19 tells us about James in the tradition he recounts that, '*so Holy was he that the People sought to touch the hem of James' garments as he walked by*'), 8:3–15, 14:36, 17:17, 20:34, etc. and *pars.*

78 Hippolytus 9.21.

79 Cf. Hippolytus 9.21 with *War* 2.151–53 with *Ant.* 18.23–24.

80 Cf. *War* 2.151–53 and also note the extremely important early Leader of the Uprising, '*John the Essene*'—*War* 2.567 and 3.11–19, which ends with the picture of his death at Ashkelon. He is involved in this engagement with two companions with the curious names of '*Niger*' and '*Silas the Babylonian*'—names also familiar in Early Christian History. Odd.

81 *War* 2.152.

82 Hippolytus 9.21 above.

83 Cf. 4QMMTii.2–22 and 11QTxlvii.13–17 and see my Appendix on '*Balla^c^/Bela^c^ in the Temple Scroll*' in *JJHP*, pp. 87–94. Also note the whole section on '*pollution of the Temple*' in 4QMMTii.2–24 and 11QTxlv.7–lv. 8, ending with the imprecation '*not to eat the blood, but pour it out on the ground*' (*thus!*) and then leading into, significantly, the exposition of '*Nazirite*' oaths.

84 CDiv.15–18 and v.6–8, but see our note above about Josephus in *War* 4.157–61 and 241–43, putting this charge both in the mouths of the son of Paul's alleged teacher '*Simeon ben Gamaliel*,' '*Jesus ben Gamala*,' and '*Ananus ben Ananus*' attacking '*the Zealots*', and Paul himself in 1 Corinthians 3:16–17 and 8:2–10:21, against '*those claiming to have Knowledge*' and/or the Leadership of '*the Jerusalem Church*'. Also see how Paul reflects this in 2 Corinthians 6:16–7:3, including the defective allusion to '*Beliar*,' we have seen, as does Josephus himself in *War* 2.423.

85 Cf. *War* 2.254–57, 425, and *Ant.* 20.186.

[86] Cf. *War* 2.409–16.

[87] *War* 2.259, 274, 407, etc. and cf. *Ant.* 18.10 on the effects of the beginning of 'the Movement' led by 'Judas and Sadduk.'

[88] See my comments on the 'Lex Cornelia de Sicarius et Veneficis' in *JBJ*, pp. 183–84, 996, and 1005–1006 and in Chapters 1, 6, 9, and 11 above and in 'Sicarii Essenes, "Those of the Circumcision," and Qumran,' *Journal of Higher Criticism*, vol. 12, Spring, 2001 and in *Revue de Qumran* 70, 2008, pp. 247–60; and cf. Origen in *Contra Celsus* 2.13, defining 'Sicarii' as those attempting to forcibly circumcise others—just the sort of behavior, ascribed to Hippolytus' 'Sicarii'/'Zealot Essenes' in 9.22 above and Josephus in War 2.450–55 after the fall of the Citadel at the beginning of the Uprising and the punishment meted out to the Roman Commander Metilius there who had surrendered (thanks to the intermediation of 'Gurion son of Nicomedes' and 'Ananias son of Zadok,' an individual involved with the High Priest Ananus ben Ananus in undermining Josephus' Command in Galilee according to *Vita*, pp. 197–203)—and Dio Cassius 68.3–4 on how this set of Roman legal traditions (ascribed to Publius Cornelius Scipio—therefore its appellation) came into effect in Nerva's time but gained particular force in Hadrian's.

[89] 2.13 above.

[90] This is made clear in Jerome's Letter 84 to Pammachius and Oceanus.

[91] *Ibid.*

[92] See nn. 54 and 57 above and Paul in Galatians 4:17–18, but also see his typical practice of reversal in 1 Corinthians 14:12, 2 Corinthians 7:11 and 9:2, Galatians 1:14, and Philippians 3:6.

[93] Cf. Dio Cassius 68.3–4 above.

[94] See the article in The Encyclopaedia Judaica, 'Sicaricon,' and note that Origen, as we saw, actually calls the person who forcibly circumcises either himself or others, a 'Sicarion'—a displacement of only one letter in both the Hebrew and the Greek—and, of course, the sobriquet 'Iscariot.' For this matter of 'the Sicaricon,' imposed after Hadrian's suppression of the Bar Kochba Revolt and, most probably (if Dio Cassius' note about Nerva is correct), after the First Jewish Revolt too and widely reported in the *Talmud*—a document beginning to be formed in these times (not to mention those following)—which related in Palestine to the confiscation of 'Enemy Property' or, in fact, the property of those who had participated in some manner in the Uprising or given support to those who had, a typical practice of Roman Occupation; cf. *Git.* 55b, *B.B.* 47b, etc. But why such a confiscation should have been called 'Sicaricon,' both in Latin/Greek and in Hebrew, surely relates to it having been imposed upon those participating in these Uprisings and, by extension, circumcision both of themselves and others!

[95] *Ibid.*

[96] CDxvi.4–6 above.

[97] For this position, see CDvii.4–9 on Deuteronomy 9:7—repeated in xx.12 and 21–23.

[98] CDxvi.8–9.

[99] See nn. 68 and 79 above and cf. Hippolytus 9.21 with *War* 2.152–53 and *Ant.* 18.23–24.

[100] *Loc. cit.*

[101] For other usages of this term which we have also listed earlier, see 1QSiii.23: '*His Mastemah*,' 1QMxiii.4 and possibly 11, 4Q390(PsMoses), Frag. 1, Line 11: '*Angels of Mastemoth*,' 4QPsEzek, Frags. 4–6, Col. 2, Line 13: '*Angels of Mastemoth*' again, 4QBer^a(286–87), Frag. 3, Col. 2, Line 2 (here meaning something like '*Satanic*'), 4QBeat, Frag. 4, Col. 5, Line 4: '*Mastemah*,' etc.

[102] CDxvi.4–6 above.

[103] Cf. *Ant.* 20 and *Gen. R.* 46.10, but on the conversion of Helen in general, also see *A.Z.* 19b.

[104] See 1QSiii.23 and cf. CDxvi.5.

[105] CDix.1.

[106] Cf. 4Q*MMT*ii.2–24 with *War* 2.409–16.

[107] 4Q*MMT*ii.8–9.

[108] See nn. 63 and 75 above and cf. *War* 7.253–454—particularly 7.410–36.

[109] See *War* 437–54 and *Vita* 424 above and the Revolution led by Jonathan of Cyrene there, unrest which obviously continued beyond its suppression. See, for instance, Dio Cassius 68.31–32 and 69.12–14, Sallust, *Histories* 2.40–42, Eusebius, *E.I.* 4.21–24, etc.

[110] Matthew 6:44, 15:38, 16:9–10 and pars. above; also cf. John 6:10 and Acts 4:4. For 'the wilderness,' of course, one should see, as well, CDiv.2–3 and vi.5 about 'the Penitents going out from the Land of Judah to dwell in the Land of Damascus,' 1QMi.2–3 about '*the Sons of Levi, Judah, and Benjamin*—'*the Golat of the Desert*' and/or '*the Sons of Light*' who '*would return from the Desert of the Peoples to camp in the Desert of Jerusalem*,' and 1QSviii.13–14 and ix.19–20 about '*going out into the wilderness to prepare* (John the Baptist-like) *the Way of the Lord*' (this is also the implication of '*the Penitents*' in CDiv.2-3).

[111] Cf. n. 109 above and *War* 7.437–54 and *Vita* 424.

[112] For examples of this, see CDiii.1, iii.6–9 (one could even call this an historical sermon on '*abstention from blood*,' '*Friendship to God*,' '*cutting off*,' and '*delivering up those who desert the Covenant of God*'), and xx.25–26—but also cf. 1QSii.16, 1QHiv.26–27, etc.

[113] Cf. CDiv.3, vi.8–9 ('*the Nobles of the People*' equivalent in this exegesis to '*the Nilvim*' in CDiv.3), CDx.2, xx.19–20, 1QpNahiii.7–9 and iv.5, 4Q448('*The Paean to King Jonathan*')ii.7; and cf. Acts 9:31 on the multiplication of the Churches in Judea, Galilee, and Samaria (but also 2:43 on the '*fear*' engendered by '*the descent of the Holy Spirit*'), 10:2 and 10:35, designating (somewhat laughably) the Roman Centurion '*Cornelius*' of the '*Italica Regiment in Caesarea*,' '*God-Fearing*' (*sic*!); and Paul, too, in Acts 13:16, 13:36, and 16:38, Romans 3:18, 8:14–15 (talking about becoming '*Sons of God by adoption*,' but not through '*bondage*' and '*fear*' and echoing the '*slave woman*' parody of Galatians 4), 11:20 (followed by several significant allusions to '*cutting off*'), 13:7, 2 Corinthians 7:1 (the most perfect statement of the concept using, of course, the vocabulary of Qumran), Ephesians 5:21, etc.

[114] We have discussed '*Iblis*' above, but see Kor 2.34, 7.11 15.30–32, 17.61, 18.51, 20.116, 26.95, 38.75–76, etc.

[115] Cf. Paul in 1 Corinthians 11:25 (of course, this is '*the Covenant of consuming blood*'—the total opposite of at Qumran and James' Directives to Overseas Communities and, one might add,

Islam) and 2 Corinthians 3:6 with Jeremiah 31:31–32, Ezekiel 11:20, 18:21, 36:27, etc.

[116] Among such allusions in this speech, one might count 26:6: *'the promises made to the Fathers by God'* (cf. CDvii.15, incorporating this same idea of *'Grace'*), 26:16: *'Stand up'* (usage, as we have been showing, found throughout the Qumran corpus), 24:18: *'turning from Darkness to Light'* (again imagery so familiar at Qumran that it is hardly worth enumerating), 24:20: *'preaching first to those in Damascus'* (cf. CDvii.18–19: *'the Star who came to Damascus'*) and then *'to all the Region of Judea'* (cf. CDiv.3 and vi.5: *'the Land of Judah'* above), and *'the Peoples'* (*'Amim'* at Qumran, as we have been alluding to throughout), *'turning to God, doing works worthy of Repentance'* (here the Qumran language of *'doing'* and *'works'* together; cf. CDi.8–10, not to mention the tell-tale language of *'Penitents'* in CDiv.2-3 above, vi.5—here *'the Diggers'*, viii.16, and, most particularly, at the end in xx.17 where they are called *'the Penitents from Sin in Jacob'*), etc.

[117] Cf. n. 113 and, for example, in CDxx.19–20 and variously above.

[118] CDxx.21–34

[119] Cf. 4QD266, Frag. 1, Line 1–Frag. 2, Line 6 (Plate 6) and 4QD268, Frag. 1, Lines 1–8 (Plate 74).

[120] CDvi.17–19.

[121] See *JBJ*, pp. 353–64 and *E.I.* 2.23.7.

[122] See n. 37 in Chapter 27 above. For *'called by Name'* at Qumran, see the passage, oft-quoted, in CDiv.2–4 above; but also CDii.11, 1QpHabviii.9 (*'called by the Name of Truth'*), and 4QInstruction[d] (4Q418), Fragment 81, Line 12: (*'called by His Name'*)—in Acts, see 2:21, 3:16 (*'made strong in this Name'*), 4:7, 8:12, 9:21 (*'called by this Name'*), and finally 15:17 (*'all the Gentiles upon whom My Name has been called'*)—all cited above.

[123] Cf. CDvii.13–14, vii.21–viii.3, xix.13–14 and, perhaps most importantly, xx.27–34. But also see notices like 1QMi.6–7, etc. For *'seeking,'* see *inter alia* the all-important CDi.10 above (*'seeking Him with a whole heart'*) and *'the Seeker of the Torah'* in CDvi.7 and vii.8–9—not to mention 4QFlori.11 that parallels it.

[124] Cf. Paul in Galatians 5:2–3: (*'If you are circumcised, Christ will not profit you'*—a true statement of his *'Christ'* idea); but see 5:6: *'For in Christ Jesus, neither circumcision nor uncircumcision is worth anything, but rather Faith working with love'*—always an attractive ideology, of course, but clearly missing the *'Jamesian'* ideology of *'works,'* i.e., *'Faith working with works'*; and finally (following his ribald slur on *'circumcision'* in 5:12 and using the *'cutting off'* language: *'I even would that those who are confusing you would themselves cut off*—sic!), Galatians 6:12–15: *'As many desire to make a show in the flesh, these force you to be circumcised, only so that they may not be persecuted for the cross of Christ* (repeating and clarifying to some degree a similar odd accusation in 1 Corinthians 11:27, following upon his delineation of *'Communion with the body and blood of Christ'*)...*They desire you to be circumcised so they might boast in your flesh'* (again sic!). Also see 1 Corinthians 7:19: *'Circumcision is nothing and not being circumcised is nothing, but keeping God's Commandments is everything'* (here he does use the word *'keeping,'* but does he really mean *'the Commandments of God'* or something more like Romans 13:1–2: *'Everyone must*

submit to the governing Authorities—there is no Authority but by the act of God'?) and Romans 2:25–29 (very diffuse and somewhat dissembling). *Par contra*, see Romans 3:1: *'What profit circumcision?'* as in Galatians 6:15 and finally Romans 4:9–12, echoing 1 Corinthians 7:19 and Galatians 5:6 above and which can be considered his general conclusion: *'not in circumcision, but in uncircumcision.'*

[125] See n. 115 above and Jeremiah 31:31–34 and Ezekiel 11:19–20 and 36:26.

[126] For some parallel usages here, see CDi.8–9 above: *'And they understood their sinfulness and knew they were Sinners, etc., etc.'* and xx.17: *'But the Penitents from Sin in Jacob kept the Covenant of God'* (here the *'keeping'* language again, but from a Qumran point-of-view).

[127] For particularly important instances of this *'camp'/'camps'* usage, see 4QMMTii.66–70: *'One is not to bring dogs into the Holy Camp because they may eat some of the bones in the Temple with the flesh still on them. Because Jerusalem is the Holy Camp, the Place that He chose from all the Tribes of Israel. Thus Jerusalem is the foremost of the Camps of Israel.'* One should also have regard for 4QD266, Fragment 11 (as we have seen above, the last Column of the Damascus Document—Plate 54), Lines 17–9, CDvi.8–9, vii.6, x.23–xi.1, xii.22–23, xiii.4–7, 12–20, xx.26 (perhaps, most importantly), 1QMiii.4–5, 13, iv.9, vii.1–7. x.1, xv.2, xviii.4, etc. Also cf. Chapter 14 above.

[128] Cf. CDiv.11 with 1QpHabvi.12 and see the way these usages are compared in *DSSFC*, pp. 359 and 409.

[129] See my Appendix on *'The Three Nets of Belial in the Damascus Document and Balla^c/Bela^c in the Temple Scroll'* in *JJHP*—in particular, pp. 88–93 explaining *'Balaam'* as *'Swallower of the People'* and *'Be^{c}or'* as *'be^{c}ir'/'animal'* in *San.* 105a. Cf. too Chapters 14 and 23-25 above, *JBJ*, pp. 505–12, 637–38, and 706–13, and note the mix-ups in the Biblical genealogies where *'Bela^c'* is the name of the first Edomite King (Genesis 14:2–18, 36:31–33, and 1 Chronicles 1:43–44). In Genesis 46:21, Numbers 26:38, and 1 Chronicles 7–8, he is also the firstborn son of Benjamin which sets up interesting resonances, as we have been pointing out, with Paul's claim to be *'of the Tribe of Benjamin'* and his possible *'Herodian'* origins. For Judges 19:20, *'the Sons of Belial'* are also *'Benjaminites'*, the inhabitants of Saul's Gibeah and their reprehensible sexual acts put them in particular ill-repute and make their name a byword for demonic characterization; cf. 2 Samuel 16:76, 20:1, and 2 Chronicles 13:7 where the usage is often applied to *'Benjaminites'* in close association with *'Saul'* who, moreover, oppose the Davidic King line. Likewise, in 1 Kings 21:13, two *'Sons of Belial'* are directly involved at the instigation of *'Jezebel'* (another name with interesting *'Bela^c'*-like connections) in the stoning of Naboth for *'blasphemy'* and *'opposing the King'*. Finally, in these genealogies, *'Bela^c'*s father is *'Be^{c}or'*—just as *'Balaam'*s is in the genealogies relating to him (cf. Numbers 22:5–24:15, 31:8, Deuteronomy 23:4, Joshuah 13:22, 24:9, etc.—a point also noted in the pregnant allusions in 2 Peter 2:15 which bring us full circle regarding all these *'Bela^c'/'Be^{c}or'/* and *'Balaam'* interplays and allusions while tying up these relationships to both *'Benjaminites'* and *'Herodians'* who were obviously exploiting these genealogical lacunae, weaknesses, and/or interplays to make a variety of Hebrew or Israelitish (if not *'Judaistic'*) claims for themselves.

ABBREVIATIONS

Acts Th.: Acts of Thomas

Ad Cor.: Clement of Alexandria, Letter to the Corinthians

Ad Haer.: Irenaeus, *Against Heresies*

Ad Rom.: Ignatius, Letter to the Romans

ADAJ: *Annual of the Department of Antiquities, Jordan*

Adv. Hel.: Jerome, *Against Helvidius*

Adv. Marcion: Tertullian, *Against Marcion*

ANCL: *Anti-Nicene Christian Library* (1867–71 Edition)

Ant.: Josephus, *The Antiquities of the Jews*

Apion: Josephus, *Against Apion (Contra Apion)*

1 Apoc Jas.: First Apocalypse of James

2 Apoc Jas.: Second Apocalypse of James

Apoc. Pet.: Apocalypse of Peter

Apost. Const.: Apostolic Constitutions

APOT: *Apocrypha and Pseudepigrapha of the Old Testament* (ed. R. H. Charles)

ARN: *Abbot de Rabbi Nathan*

As. Moses: Assumption of Moses

b.A.Z.: Babylonian *Talmud,*Tractate cAvodah Zarah

b. B.B.: Babylonian *Talmud*, Tractate *Baba Bathra*

b. Ber: Babylonian *Talmud*, Tractate *Berachot*

b. Bik: Babylonian *Talmud*, Tractate *Bikkurim*

b. Git: Babylonian *Talmud*, Tractate *Gittin*

b. Hul: Babylonian *Talmud*, Tractate *Hullin*

b. Kid: Babylonian *Talmud*, Tractate *Kiddushim*

b. Ket: Babylonian *Talmud*, Tractate *Kethuboth*

b. Ned: Babylonian *Talmud*, Tractate *Nedarim*

b. Pes: Babylonian *Talmud*, Tractate *Pesahim*

b. R.H.: Babylonian *Talmud*, Tractate *Rosh Ha-Shanah*

b. Shab.: Babylonian *Talmud*, Tractate *Shabbath*

b. Sot: Babylonian *Talmud*, Tractate *Sotah*

b. Suk: Babylonian *Talmud*, Tractate *Sukkah*

b.Taᶜan: Babylonian *Talmud*, Tractate *Taᶜanith*

b. San.: Babylonian *Talmud*, Tractate *Sanhedrin*

b.Yeb: Babylonian *Talmud*, Tractate *Yebamoth*

b.Yom: Babylonian *Talmud*, Tractate *Yoma*

BAR: *Biblical Archaeology Review*

Baroccian.: *Codice Barocciano*

BASOR: *Bulletin of the American Scholls of Oriental Research*

CD: Cairo Damascus Document (Ms. A and Ms. B)

Comm. on Gal.: Jerome, *Commentary on Galatians*

Comm. on John: Origen, *Commentary of John*

Comm. on Matt.: Origen, *Commentary on Matthew de Carne* Tertullian, *On the Body of Christ*

de Mens. et Pond.: Epiphanius, *De Mensuris et Ponderibus*

de Monog.: Tertullian, *On Monogamy*

de Verig. vel.: Tertullian, *On the Veiling of Virgins*

Dial.: Justin Martyr, *Dialogue with Trypho*

Deut. *R.*: Deuteronomy *Rabbah*

DSD: *Dead Sea Discoveries*

DSSNT: *The Dead Sea Scrolls: A New Translation* (ed. M. Wise, M. Abegg, & E. Cook)

DSSFC: *The Dead Sea Scrolls and the First Christians* (R. Eisenman)

DSSU: *The Dead Sea Scrolls Uncovered* (ed. R. Eisenman and M. Wise)

Eccles.: R. Ecclesiastes *Rabbah*

EH: Eusebius, *Ecclesiastical History*

Enarr. in Ps. 34:3: Augustine, *Discourses on the Psalms*

Eph.: Ignatius, Letter to the Ephesians

Epist. Apost.: Epistle of the Apostles

Epist. B.: Epistle of Barnabas

FEDSS: *A Facsimile Edition of the Dead Sea Scrolls* (ed. R. Eisenman and J. Robinson)

Gen. *R.*: Genesis *Rabbah*

Gos Th.: The Gospel of Thomas

Haeres.: Epiphanius, *Against Heresies* (*Panarion* in Latin)

H.N.: Pliny, *Natural History*

Haer.: Tertullian, *Against Heretics*

Hennecke: *The New Testament Apocrypha* (ed. E. Hennecke and W. Schneemelcher)

Hippolytus: Hippolytus, *Refutation of all Heresies*

Hom. in Luc.: Origen, *Homilies on Luke*

HUCA: *Hebrew Union College Annual*

JJHP: *James the Just in the Habakkuk Pesher* (R. Eisenman)

IEJ: *Israel Exploration Journal*

j.Taʿan: Jerusalem *Talmud*, Tractate *Taʿanith* Lam R. Lamentations *Rabbah*

M. San.: *Mishnah Sanhedrin*

Mur.: Wadi Murraba'at, Cave 1

MZCQ: Maccabees, Zadokite,Christians and Qumran (R. Eisenman)

Opus imperf.: Augustine, *Opus Imperfectum contra Secundum C. Iul Juliani pars.* parallels

Protevang.: Protevangelium of James

Ps *Hom.*: Pseudoclementine *Homilies*

Ps Philo: Pseudo Philo

Ps *Rec.*: Pseuclementine *Recognitions*

Quod Omnis: Philo, *On the Contemplative Life*

4QD: The Qumran Damascus Document (Cave 4)

4Q*Ber*: The Qumran Blessings (The Chariots of Glory)

4Q*Flor*: The Qumran *Florilegium* (on Promises to David's 'Seed')

1QH: The Qumran Hymns

1QM: The Qumran War Scroll

4Q*MMT*: The Qumran Letter(s) on Works Righteousness

4QpGen: The Qumran Genesis *Pesher* (Genesis *Florilegium*)

1QpHab: The Qumran Habakkuk *Pesher*

4QpIs: The Qumran Isaiah *Pesher*

4QpNah: The Qumran Nahum *Pesher*

4QpPs 37: The Qumran Psalm 37 *Pesher*

1QS: The Qumran Community Rule

11QT: The Qumran Temple Scroll

4QTest:The Qumran Testimonia

Song of Songs *R.*: Song of Songs *Rabbah*

Suet.: Seutonius, *The Twelve Caesars*

Tos. Kellim: Tosefta Kellim

Trall.: Ignatius, *Letter to the Trallians*

Vir. ill.: Jerome, *Lives of Illustrious Men*

Vita: Josephus, *Autobiography of Flavius Josephus*

War: The Jewish War

Appendices

Chronological Charts

Genealogies

Maps

and

Photographs

CHRONOLOGICAL CHART

MACCABEAN PRIEST KINGS

Mattathias, 167–166 BCE
Judas Maccabee, 166–160
Jonathan, 160–142
Simon, 142–134
John Hyrcanus, 134–104
Alexander Jannaeus, 103–76
Salome Alexandra, 76–67
Aristobulus II, 67–63
Hyrcanus II, 76–67 and 63–40
Antigonus, 40–37

HERODIAN KINGS, ETHNARCHS, OR TETRARCHS

Herod, Roman–supported King, 37–4 BCE
Archelaus, Ethnarch of Judea, 4 BCE–7 CE
Herod Antipas, Tetrarch of Galilee & Perea, 4 BCE–39 CE
Philip, Tetrarch of Trachonitis, 4 BCE–34 CE
Agrippa I, Tetrarch and King, 37–44
Herod of Chalcis, 44–49
Agrippa II, 49–93

ROMAN EMPERORS FROM 60 BC TO 138 CE

Caesar, 60–44 BCE
Mark Anthony and Octavius, 43–31 BCE
Octavius (Augustus), 27 BCE–14 CE
Tiberius, 14–37
Caligula, 37–41
Claudius, 41–54
Nero, 54–68
Galba, 68–69

Otho, 69
Vitellius, 69
Vespasian, 69–79
Titus, 79–81
Domitian, 81–96
Nerva, 96–98
Trajan, 98–117
Hadrian, 117–138

EARLY CHURCH AND OTHER SOURCES

Philo of Alexandria, c. 30 BCE –45 CE
Clement of Rome, c. 30–97 CE
Josephus, 37–96
Ignatius, c. 50–115
Papias, c. 60–135
Pliny, 61–113
Polycarp, 69–156
Justin Martyr, c. 100–165
Hegesippus, c. 90–180
Tatian, c. 115–185
Lucian of Samosata, c. 125–180
Irenaeus, c. 130–200

Clement of Alexandria, c. 150–215
Tertullian, c. 160–221
Hippolytus, c. 160–235
Julius Africanus, c. 170—245
Origen, c. 185–254
Eusebius of Caesarea, c. 260–340
Epiphanius, 367–404
Jerome, 348–420
Rufinus of Aquileia, c. 350–410
Augustine, 354–430
St Cyril of Jerusalem, 375–444

The Maccabeans

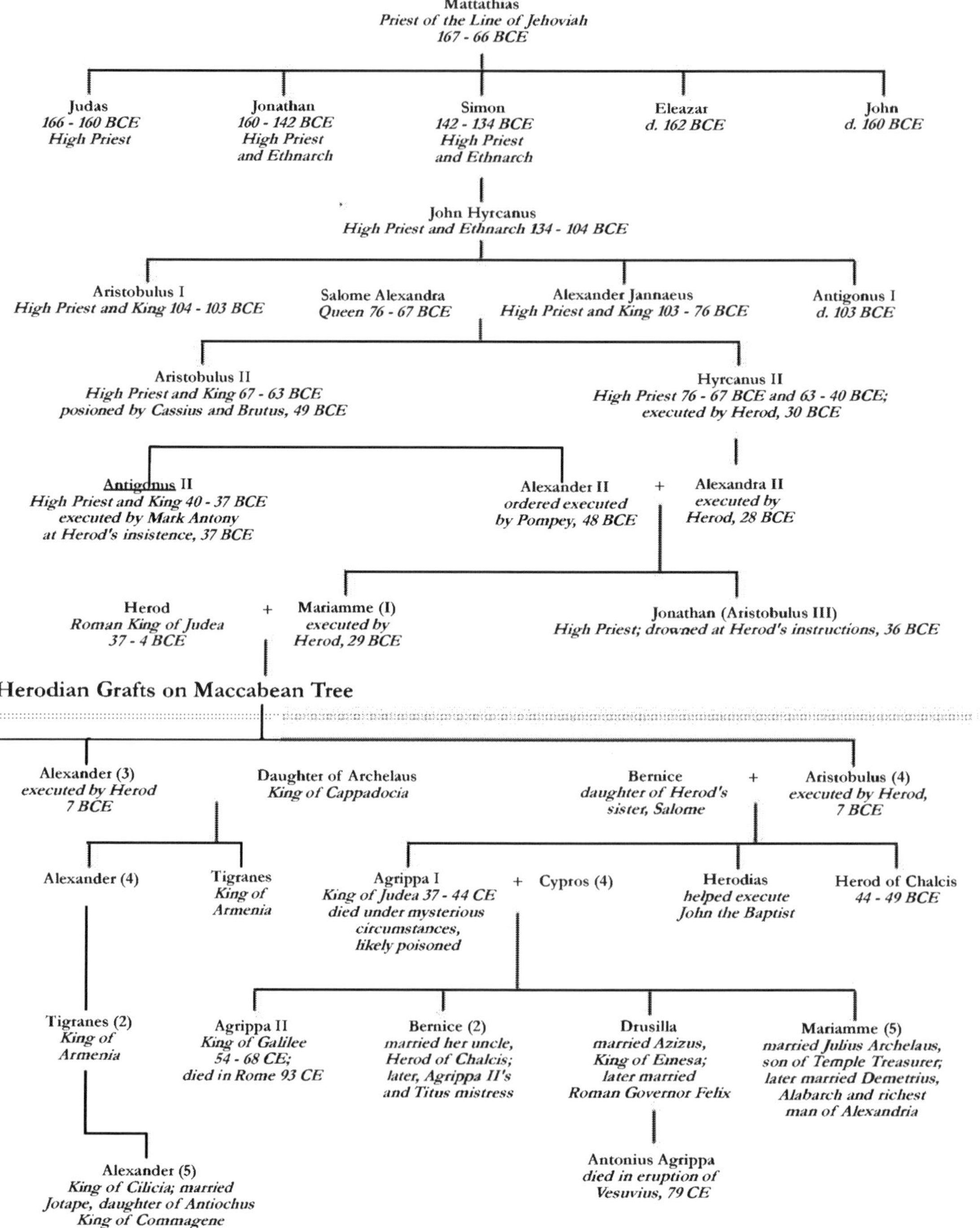

The Herodians

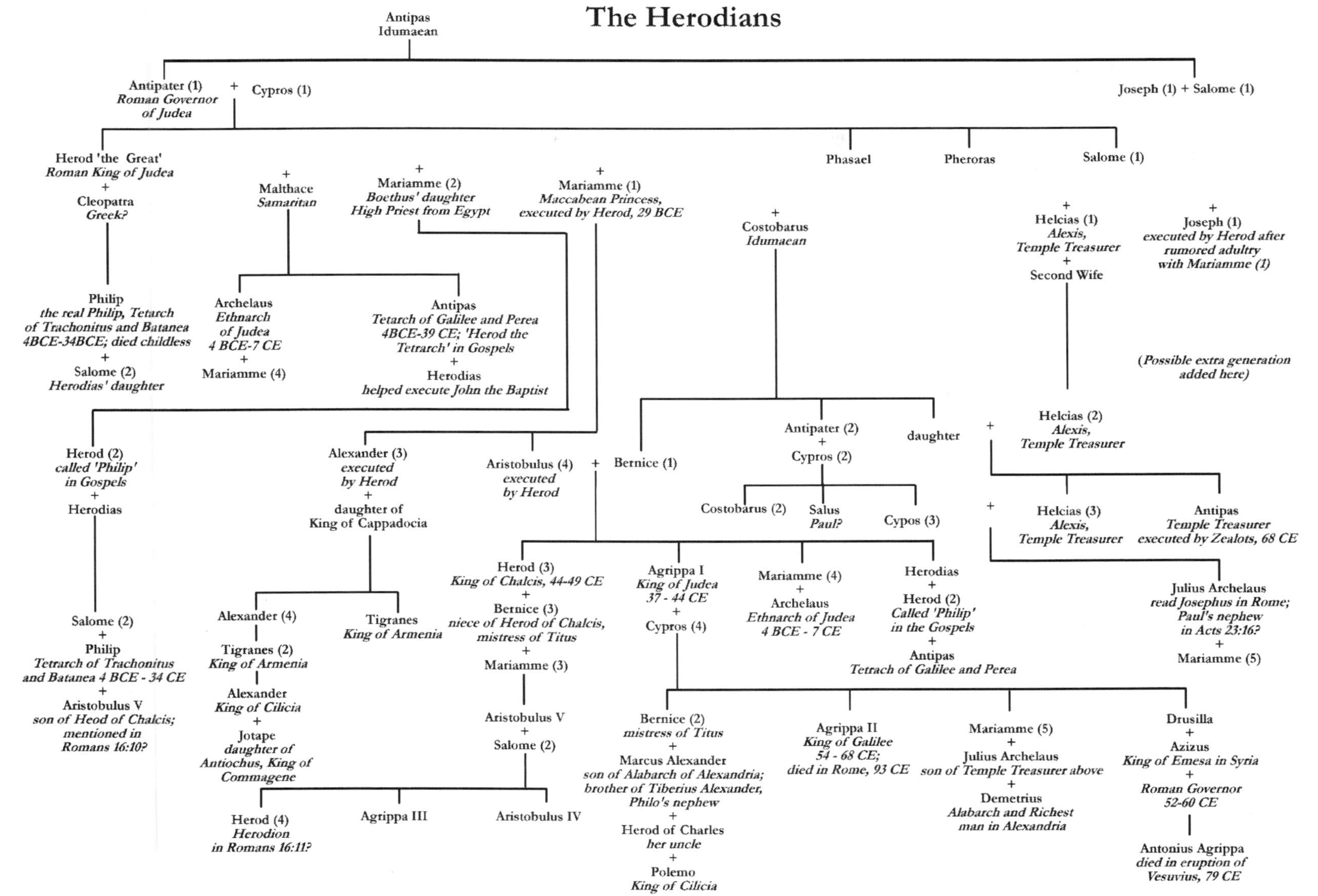

UPPER ARMENIA
MT ARARAT (Modern location)
LOWER ARMENIA
MT ARARAT (Classical location)
LAND OF THE EDESSENES
PARTHIA
PERSIA
Ecbatana
BITHYNIA
GALATIA
THESSALONICA
MACEDONIA
Philippi
GREECE
PHRYGIA
CAPPADOCIA
Samosata
Nisibis
Arbela
Edessa(Antiochia)
Haran(Carrhae)
ADIABENE
COMMAGENE
Hierapolis
Tigris
Antioch of Pisidia
CILICIA
Iconium
Lystra
Tarsus
Aegean
Sea
Euphrates
BABYLONIA
Ephesus
ASIA
Antioch
Beroea (Aleppo)
Seleucia
Athens
Miletus
Orontes
Palmyra
Babylon
Corinth
Cenchrea
ACHAIA
Sparta
Rhodes
CYPRUS
Tripolis
COELE SYRIA
ARABIA
Charax Spasini
(Antiochia or Basra)
Crete
Sidon
Damascus
Tyre
Jordan
Mediterranean Sea
Caesarea
Jerusalem
Ashkelon
Qumran
Gaza
IDUMAEA
Petra
Alexandria
Heliopolis
CYRENE
Memphis
EGYPT
Oxythynchus
N
500 miles

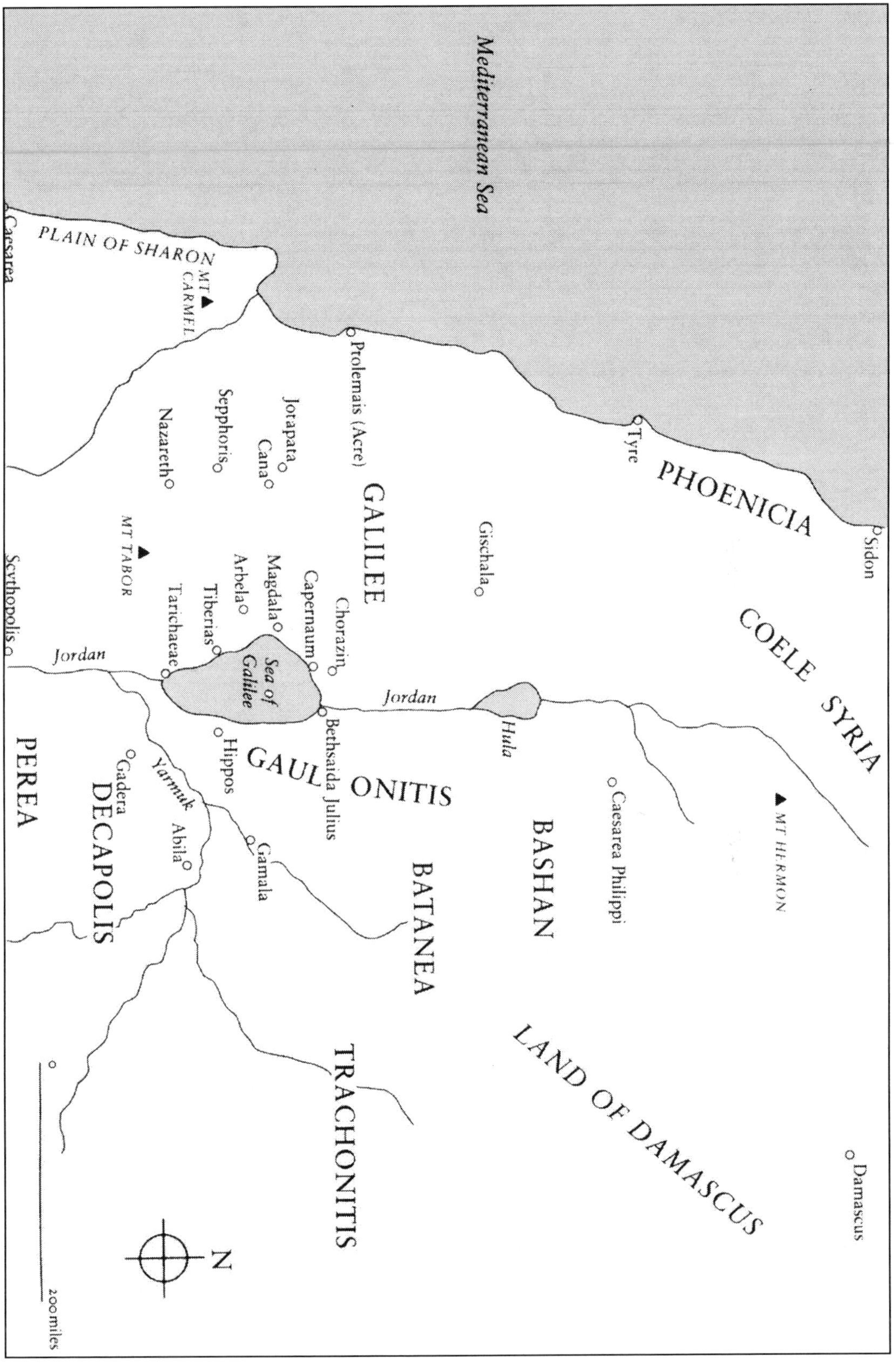

Mediterranean Sea

PLAIN OF SHARON

Caesarea

MT CARMEL

Ptolemais (Acre)

Sepphoris

Jotapata

Cana

Nazareth

GALILEE

Gischala

Tyre

PHOENICIA

Sidon

MT TABOR

Magdala

Arbela

Chorazin

Capernaum

Tiberias

Taricheae

Scythopolis

Jordan

Sea of Galilee

Bethsaida Julius

Jordan

Hula

COELE SYRIA

GAULONITIS

Hippos

PEREA

Gadera

DECAPOLIS

Yarmuk

Abila

Gamala

BATANEA

BASHAN

Caesarea Philippi

MT HERMON

TRACHONITIS

LAND OF DAMASCUS

Damascus

N

200 miles

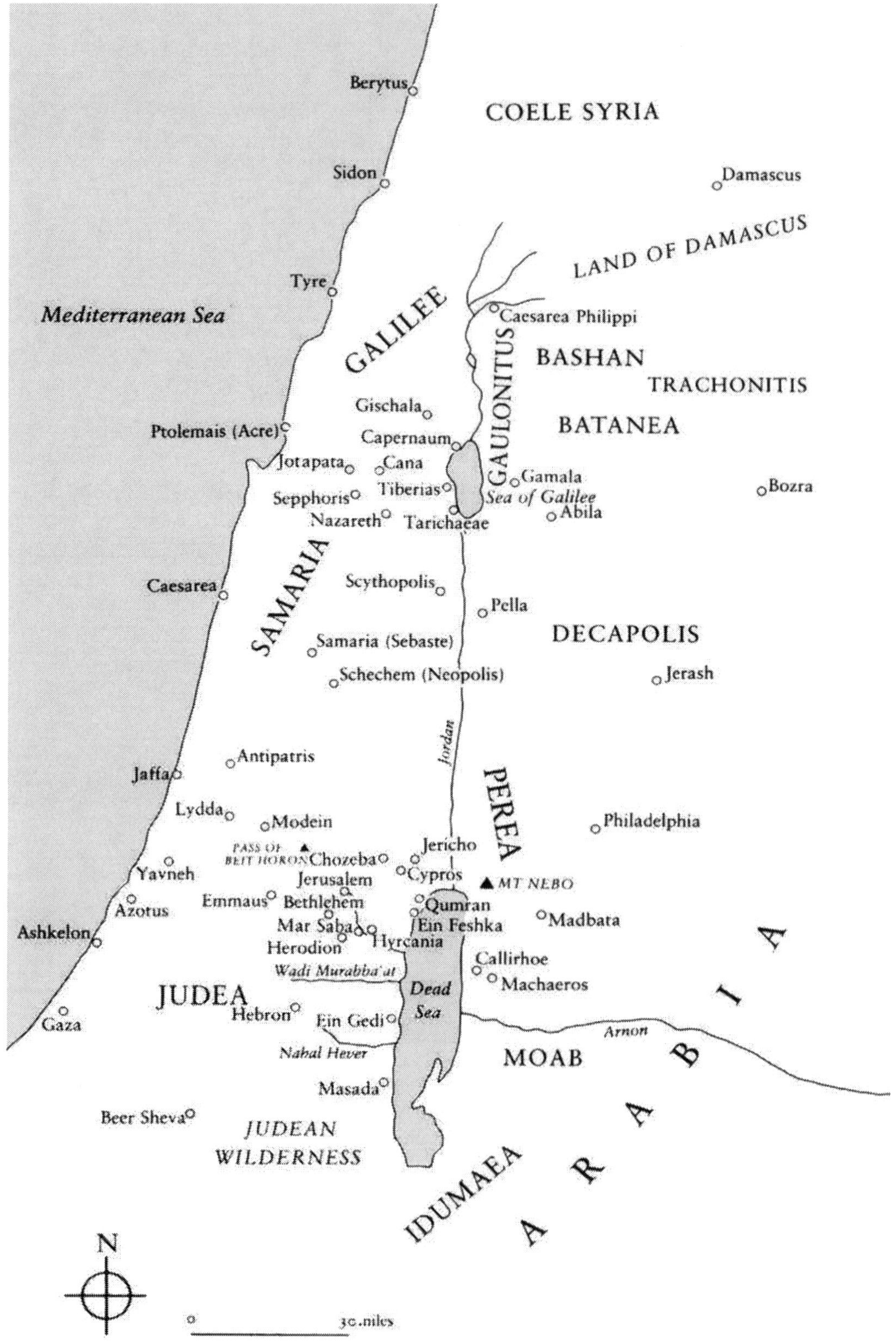

Berytus
COELE SYRIA
Sidon
Damascus
LAND OF DAMASCUS
Tyre
Mediterranean Sea
GALILEE
Caesarea Philippi
GAULONITUS
BASHAN
TRACHONITIS
BATANEA
Gischala
Capernaum
Ptolemais (Acre)
Jotapata
Cana
Gamala
Bozra
Sepphoris
Tiberias
Sea of Galilee
Nazareth
Tarichaeae
Abila
Caesarea
SAMARIA
Scythopolis
Pella
DECAPOLIS
Samaria (Sebaste)
Schechem (Neopolis)
Jerash
Jordan
Antipatris
PEREA
Jaffa
Lydda
Modein
Philadelphia
PASS OF
BEIT HORON
Chozeba
Jericho
Yavneh
Jerusalem
Cypros
MT NEBO
Azotus
Emmaus
Bethlehem
Qumran
Madbata
Ashkelon
Mar Saba
Ein Feshka
Herodion
Hyrcania
Wadi Murabba'at
Callirhoe
Machaeros
JUDEA
Hebron
Ein Gedi
Dead
Sea
Arnon
A R A B I A
Gaza
Nahal Hever
MOAB
Masada
Beer Sheva
JUDEAN
WILDERNESS
IDUMAEA
A R A B
N
30 miles

1. Left: View of the Qumran marl, mainly consisting of Cave 4 but also 5–6, with the settlement across the wadi and Dead Sea in the background.

2. Right: The Mausoleum or Burial Monument at the Head of the Qumran Cemetery (discovered by two CSULB students) with the Dead Sea in the background.

3. Left: Another view of the Mausoleum, discovered by two CSULB students, containing the so-called 'Burial Monument of the Righteous Teacher' and dominating the graveyard.

4. Above: Graves in front of the Mausoleum showing the north/south orientation of 'Essene'/'Sabaean' bathing groups.
5. Below: Another view of the north/south orientation of the some nine hundred graves in the main cemetery.

6. Right: The excavated Mausoleum showing its splendid location over-looking the Dead Sea and the east/west orientation of its burials.

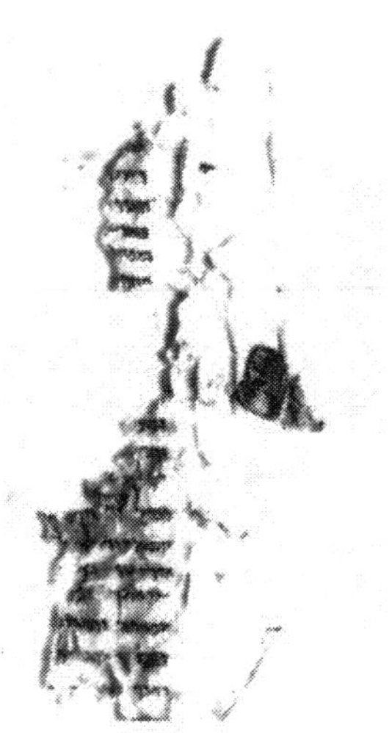

7. Right The fragment from 4QD266 preceding Column I of the Cairo Damascus Document mentioning 'the Sons of Light keeping away from' (linzor/ Naziritism).

8. Right Above: Column III of the Psalm 37 Pesher mentioning both 'the Penitents of the Wilderness' and 'the Assembly' or 'Church of the Poor' (Ebionim). (The Huntington Library courtesy of Bill Moffett)

7. Above: The excavated Mausoleum showing its splendid location over-looking the Dead Sea and the east/west orientation of its burials.

9. Left: A view of the excavated grave, in which one adult male buried in an east/west orientation facing Jerusalem and two secondary females burials were found so far.

10. Right: The lookout overlooking the Kedron's effluence to the Dead Sea, discovered by the author's son Hanan Eisenman by following the Second Temple Period pottery-trail leading to it. (CSULB Judean Desert Explorations)

11. Below left: Another view of the lookout around which rare coins from Year 4 of the Revolt against Rome were found.

12. Above right: The impressive doorway of the structure connected to the lookout.

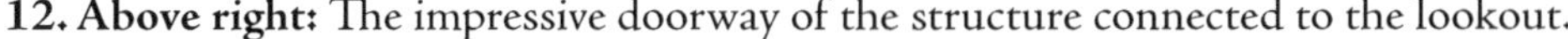

13. Below: Columns vii–viii of the Habakkuk Pesher containing 'the Delay of the Parousia' and the anti-Pauline exposition of Habakkuk 2:4: 'The Righteous shall by his Faith.'

14. Below: The terrace of the lookout, showing its strategic location over-looking both the mouth of the Kedron and the wharf.

15. Below: The wharf at Khirbat Mazin at the effluence of the Wadi Kedron on the Dead Sea.

16. Right: Columns viiiix of
the Community Rule, twice
quoting Isaiah 40:3's 'Preparing
a Way in the Wilderness' and
referring to 'zeal for the Day of
Vengeance.'

17. Left: Cave 4 overlooking
the Wadi, from which the lion's
share of the Qumran manuscripts
came.

18 .Right: Periodic water
pouring down into the Wadi
Qumran from the Bethlehem
Plain, the storage of which made
habitation at Qumran possible.

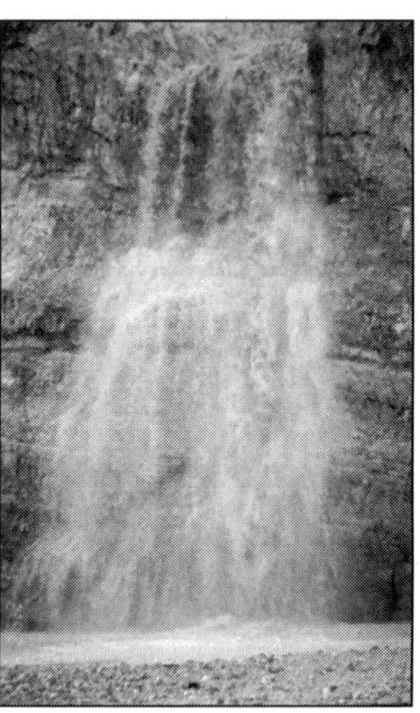

19. Left: Columns i-ii of the Community Rule, like 4QD266, 'cursing' all those departing from
the right or left of the Torah.

20. Above: The author standing in the mouth of Cave 4 during the 1991-2 CSULB radar ground scan.

21. Above Left: The artificially hollowed-out water channel at the top of the Wadi Qumran, the *raison d'etre* of the Community.

22. Above right: The also artificially hollowed-out interior of Cave 4 where most of the manuscripts appear to have been stored.

23. Above: Cave I where the first and most complete manuscripts were found in 1947 in neat storage jars.

24. Below Left: Cave 11, the last manuscript-bearing cave found in the mid-fifties, from which the Temple Scroll apparently came.

25. Bottom Left: A piece of the *Pesher* on Isaiah 10:33-11:5, containing the Messianic Prophecy on *'Lebanon being felled by a Mighty One'* and *'the Branch'* from *'the Root of Jesse.'* (The Huntington Library)

26. Bottom Right: Column II of the Nahum *Pesher* describing how *'the Kittim'* came after the Greeks and in which, contrary to Paul, crucifixion or *'hanging a man alive upon a tree'* is condemned. (The Huntington Library courtesy of Bill Moffett)

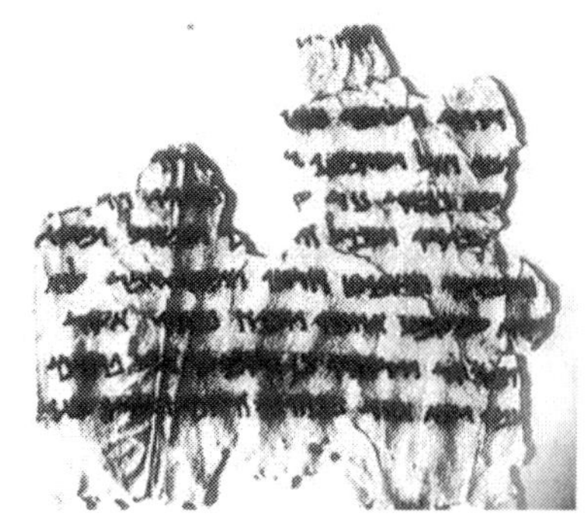

27. Right: The first radar ground scan of the Qumran cliffs, carried out by the author together with the CSULB Team in the winter of 1991–2.

28. Below: The first ground scan of the ruins on Qumran plateau in which it became clear that no real earthquake damage had occurred to the installations at Qumran.

29. Below right: Members of the CSULB Team and author's son ground scanning inside Cave 4.

30. Left: The CSULB Survey of 1990–2 charting caves from Qumran in the North to Ein Gedi in the South.

31. Below: Member of the CSULB Survey Team inspecting lintel doorway of a cave 20 kilometers south of Qumran.

32. Below: The 1990 Walking Survey visiting the ruins of the Judean Desert Fortress of Hyrcania (also Khirbat Mird) not far from Mar Saba where Herod kept all his treasure.

33. Right: The Herodian three-tier step Palace at the northern end of Masada, the Dead Sea in the distance at dusk.

 THE NEW TESTAMENT CODE COMPANION

34. Left: A view from Masada of the Roman siege camp, the Dead Sea in the distance.

35. Below: The ramp the Romans built using Jewish prisoners as slave-labor to finally take Masada in 73 CE, but not before all its inhabitants committed suicide.

36. Left: The storage bins at Masada, the contents of which were not burned when the inhabitants committed mass suicide, to show they 'chose death over slavery' not hunger.

37. Below Left: The entrance to the large water cistern that made life tenable at Masada.

38. Below Right: The text mentioning 'the Son of God' from Cave 4.

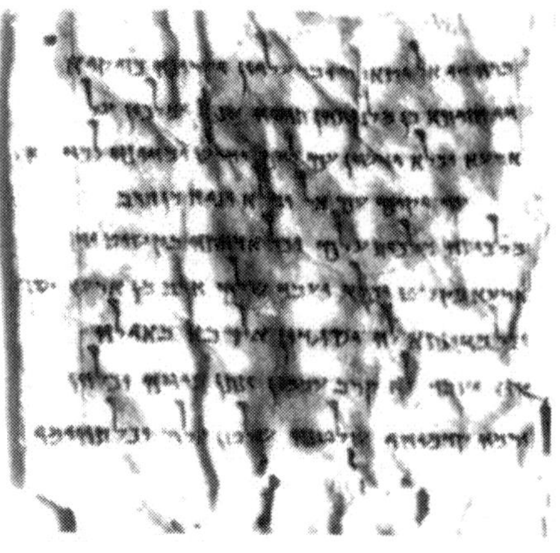

39. Above: The pilings of the Roman-style hot steam bath at Masada.

40. Right: One of the frescoed murals and pillars in the three-tier luxurious palace built by Herod on Masada.

41. Below Left: Herod's Palace at Herodion, the Fortress dedicated to his name and in which he is reputed to be buried—author sitting in the distance.

42. Right Below: 4Q285 identifying 'the Root of Jesse' from Isaiah 11:1–5 with 'the Branch of David' and, in turn, 'the Nasi of the Assembly' ('the Nasi Israel' found on Bar Kochba coins).

43. Below Left: Herod's winter Palace in Jericho where he had Jonathan, the last Maccabean High Priest, drowned when he came of age.

44. Below Right: The Greek Orthodox Monastery in Wadi Kelt, also possibly the site of Kochabe, from where Bar Kochba might have come.

45. Below Left: The mouth of the Wadi Murabbacat south of Qumran on the Dead Sea leading up to the Bar Kochba Caves further inland.

46. Below Right: Further along the Wadi Murabbacat in the Judean Desert leading inland to the Bar Kochba Cave.

47. Below: The Cave further into the Wadi Murabbacat where letters actually signed by Bar Kochba and his lieutenants were found.

48. Below: The walls of the Judean Desert Monastery of Mar Saba (note its name), one of the oldest—the Wadi Kedron flowing down to the Dead Sea from Jerusalem in the background.

49. Right: The Qumran proof-text called 'The Testimonia,' including 'The True Prophet' of Deuteronomy 18:18–9, 'the Star Prophecy' (from which 'Bar Kochba' took his name), and the anti-Herodian Joshua 6:26.

50. Below: The Qumran Florilegium, containing the promises to 'David's seed' and referring to 'the fallen Tabernacle of David,' 'the Scepter to save Israel,' and 'the Branch.'

51. Left: Palm tree coin from Bar Kochba mentioning 'Shimcon' (Nasi Israel) on the obverse and 'the Freedom of Jerusalem' on the reverse.

52. Right: The Herodian Fortress of Machaeros where John the Baptist was executed in Perea across the Dead Sea from the Wadi Kedron, the wharf, and Qumran.

53. Left: Hot volcanic river flowing down on the East side of the Dead Sea beneath Machaeros where Herod probably bathed during his final fatal illness.

54. Below left: The Last Column of the Damascus Document from 4QD266, mentioning a reunion of the Desert 'Camps' every year at Pentecost 'to curse' (as in 1QS but unlike in Paul) 'those who depart to the right or left of Torah.'

55. Below: Column xx of Ms. B of CD, which actually refers to 'the Standing up of the Messiah of Aaron and Israel,' 'seeing Yeshuca' ('Jesus' or 'Salvation'), and 'a Book of Remembrance for God-Fearers.'

THE NEW TESTAMENT CODE COMPANION

56. Below Left: Augustus under whom Judea was pacified and given over to the Herodians as tax-farmers and the first Imperial deifications occurred.

57. Below Right: Presumed bust of the Jewish historian Josephus.

58. Above: A coin issued by Nero in honor of Poppea, whom he kicked to death in 65 CE and who was visited by Josephus not long before.

59. Left: Columns ix–x of the Habakkuk Pesher mentioning 'the Riches of the Last Priests of Jerusalem" given over to the Army of the Kittim' and 'the Worthless City' the Liar 'built upon Blood.'

60. Left: The entrance to Petra, Herod's mother's place-of-origin and the capital of the 'Arab' King Aretas, her possible kinsman (and also, therefore, the possible 'kinsman' of Paul).

61. Below: Column XVI of 4QD271 describing how Abraham was threatened by 'the Angel Mastemah' ('Satan') for not circumcising all members of his household, whereupon he promptly did so.

62. Two below: The amphitheater at Hellenistic Petra, a city Paul may have visited when he speaks in Galatians 1:17 of 'going into Arabia.'

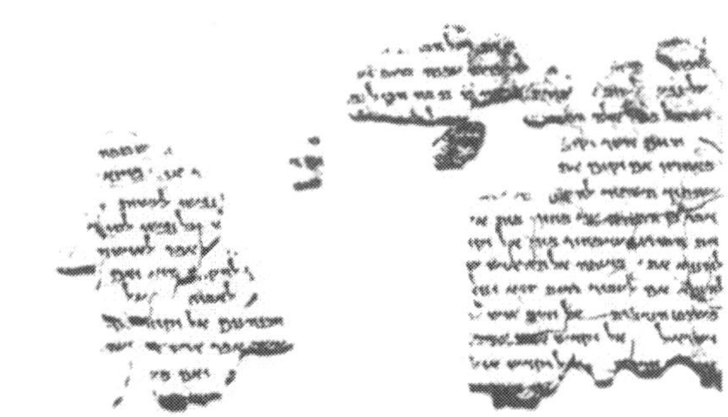

　THE NEW TESTAMENT CODE COMPANION

64 Right: The ruins of Palmyra, a key city on the trade route going North to Syria, Adiabene, and beyond.

65 Below: The Cave 4 parallel to CDVI where the all-important 'going out to dwell in the Land of Damascus,' 'digging of the Well,' and 'the New Covenant' to be erected there are mentioned.

66 Below right: The ruins of Hellenistic Jerash, like Pella, another city of 'the Decapolis' but further inland.

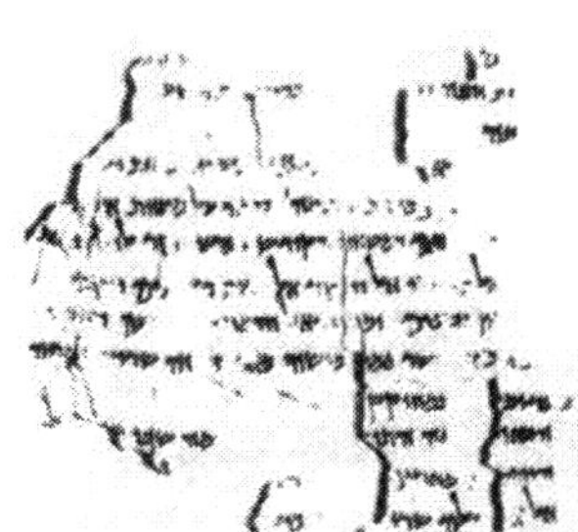

67. Left: A scene from old Damascus, down the walls of which Paul allegedly escaped 'in a basket' from the 'Arab' King Aretas and the venue of many important allusions at Qumran.

68. Below: The City of Edessa ('Antioch Orrhoe') with the Pool of Abraham and the Plain of Haran—Abraham's childhood home—in the background.

69. Below Left: The end of the Second Part ('the Second Letter') of MMT speaking of 'the works of the Torah which would be reckoned for your Good' as per Abraham in Genesis 15:6, James, and Paul.

70. Below Right: The MMT passage banning 'things sacrificed to idols' so important to James' directives to overseas communities and 'Sicarii Essene' martyrdom/resistance practices.

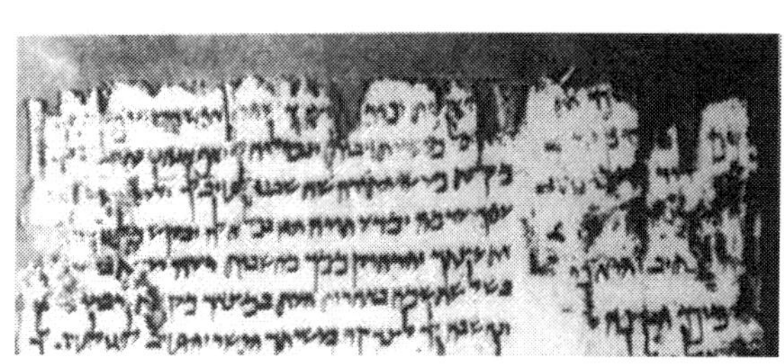

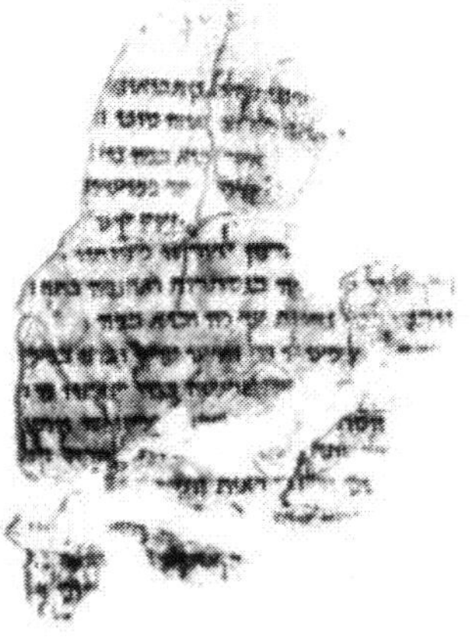

73. Above Left: The First Column of CD mentioning 'the Root of Planting,' 'the Teacher of Righteousness,' and 'the Pourer out'/'Spouter of Lying.'

74. Above Right: 4Q268, paralleling the First Column of the Cairo Genizah version, showing the link with earlier material instructing 'the Sons of Light to keep away from the Paths'/'the Ways (of pollution).'

75. Below Left: A Hellenistic sculpture found around Italica in Spain, the birthplace of Trajan (98–117 CE) and Hadrian (117–138 CE).

76. Below Right: Bust of Hadrian who suppressed the Bar Kochba Revolt and rebuilt Jerusalem under his own name as 'Aelia Capitolina.'

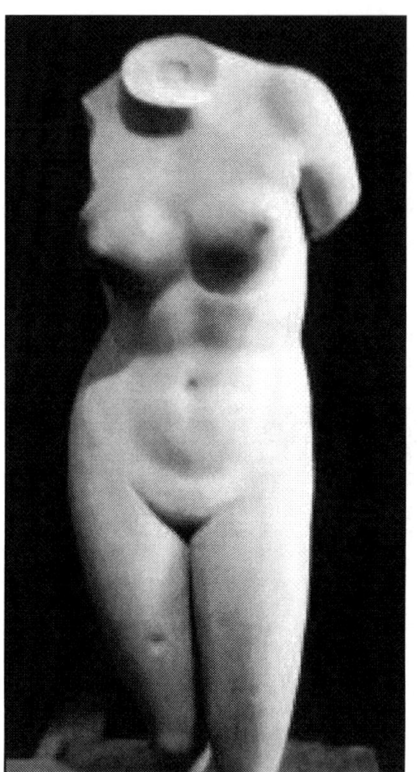

77. Above: Amphitheater at Italica, birthplace of Trajan and Hadrian and perhaps home of 'the Regiment' mentioned in Acts 10:2.

78. Below: Sumptuous reconstructed floor mosaic found in ruins in the area of Italica.

79. Left: Silver Sestertias with portrait of Trajan, under whom Egyptian Jewish Community was wiped out in disturbances around the years 105–115 CE.

80. Right: Silver dinar with portrait bust of Hadrian.

81. Left: The Pinnacle of the Temple with the Kedron Valley tombs—in particular, the Monument of Absalom just visible below.

82. Right: Rock-cut 'Tomb of Zadok' in the Kedron Valley below the Pinnacle of the Temple next to James'—a hiding place mentioned in the Copper Scroll.

83. Below: The Tomb attributed by pilgrims to James, but an inscription identified it as that of the 'Bnei-Hezir' Priest Clan ('the Boethusians') and probably at the root of the burial legends about Jesus.

84. Below: Burial chambers inside 'the Tomb of St. James.'

85. Below Center: The excavated entry to the family Tomb of Queen Helen of Adiabene built for her and her son Izates by her second son Monobazus.

    THE NEW TESTAMENT CODE COMPANION

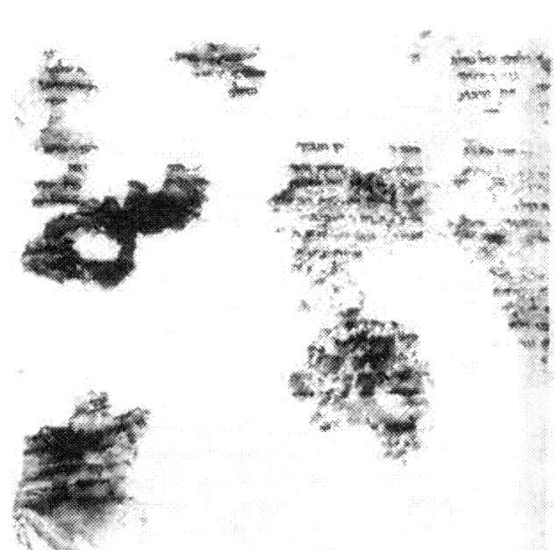

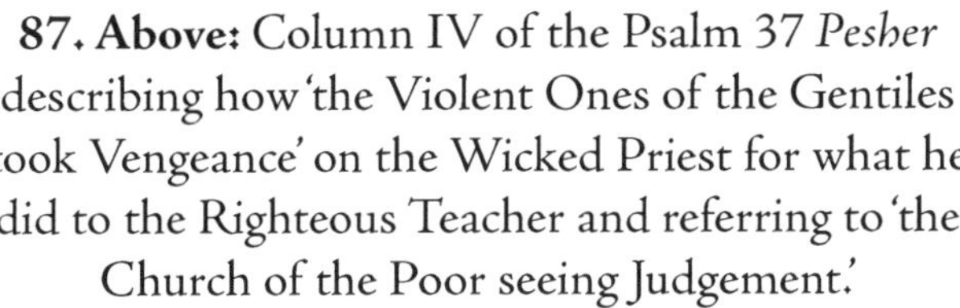

87. **Above:** Column IV of the Psalm 37 *Pesher*
describing how 'the Violent Ones of the Gentiles
took Vengeance' on the Wicked Priest for what he
did to the Righteous Teacher and referring to 'the
Church of the Poor seeing Judgement.'

88. **Right:** Burial niche inside the Family Tomb of
Queen Helen of Adiabene.

89. **Above:** Ruins surrounding the steps of the Temple in Jerusalem with the Pinnacle and
Mount of Olives Cemetery in the background.

90. Right: Tomb directly alongside James,' attributed to Zechariah the Prophet, but the designation probably has more to do with 'Zachariah ben Bariscaeus,' the 'Rich' collaborator 'cast down' by Revolutionaries from the Temple wall into the Kedron Valley below.

91. Above: The Temple steps upon which James lectured the People when he was supposedly 'cast down' by 'the Enemy' Paul.

92. Below Left: The Third Column of the Nahum Pesher referring to 'messengers'/'Apostles' to 'the Gentiles' and 'deceiving' converts with 'a Lying Tongue.'

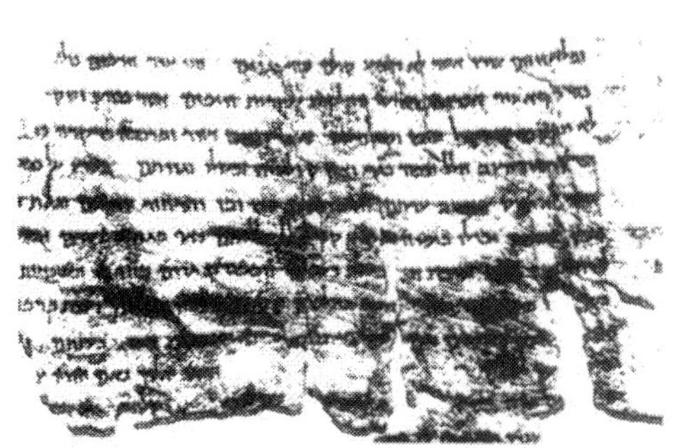

93. Right: 'The Golden Gate,' towards which the Romans made their final adoration of their standards after storming and burning the Temple in 70 CE.

94. Right: What is left of 'Herod's Palace' in Jerusalem where Saulos and his Herodian colleagues took refuge at the beginning of the Uprising.

95. Below: Greek/Hebrew warning block in the Temple forbidding non-Jews to enter its sacred precincts on pain of death.

96 Right: Fragment from the Genesis Pesher (49:14) identifying 'the Scepter' as 'the Messiah of Righteousness' (singular) and 'the Branch of David.'

97 Below: 4QBerachot/'The Chariots of Glory' 'cursing' Belial as 'the Angel of the Pit.'

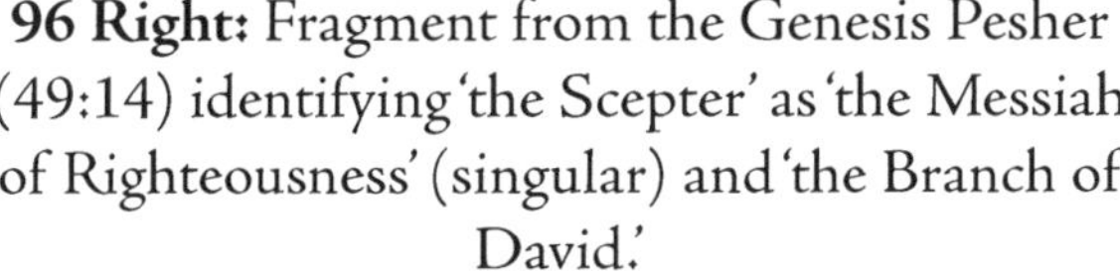

98 Left: The ruins of strategic Emmaus where Jesus appeared to 'Cleopas' and Jewish defenders were sealed in their caves and starved to death by the Romans.

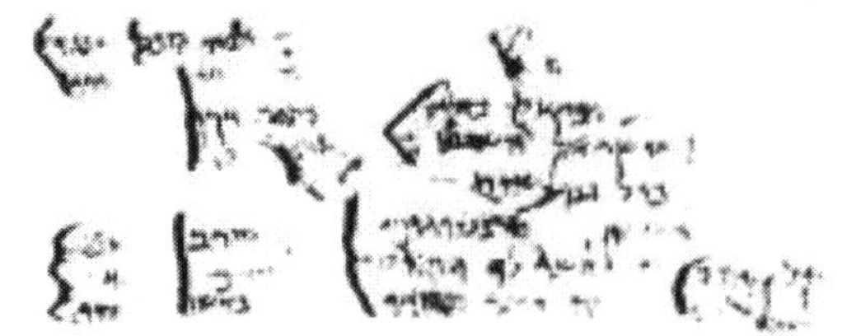

99. Right: A passage verifying the presence of CDvii at Qumran evoking 'the Star who came to Damascus,' 'the Doresh,' 'the Scepter,' 'the Nasi,' and 'destruction by the hand of Belial.'

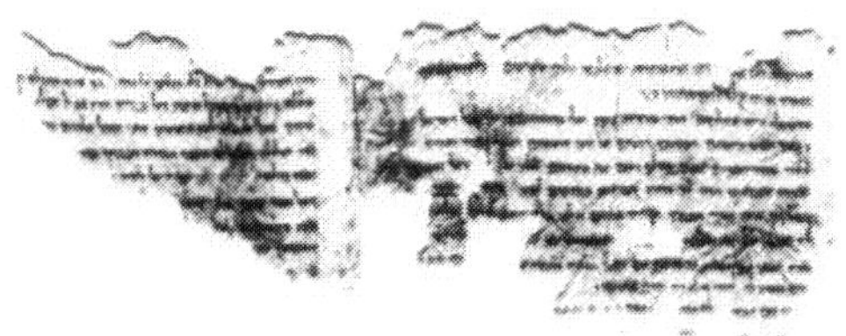

100. Left: Columns iv–v of the Nahum *Pesher* referring to 'the Nilvim' rejoining 'the Glory of Judah,' 'the Cup,' 'perishing by the sword,' and 'going into captivity'

101. Below: The ruins of the seaport at Caesarea, where Paul visited 'Philip' and was incarcerated for two years by Felix in the Palace of Agrippa II, his putative 'kinsman.'

102 Right: The Synagogue at Gamala just above the Sea of Galilee in the Gaulon, the birthplace of 'Judas the Galilean' (the progenitor of 'the Zealot Movement').

103. Right: The two 'Camel'-like humps from which Gamala received its name and from which the first Jewish mass suicide occurred in 67 CE as the Romans made their bloody way down from Galilee.

104. Above: Ruins near Mt. Gerizim in Samaria where the Samaritan Redeemer figure, 'The Taheb,' crucified by Pontius Pilate, performed his 'Signs.'

105. Above: The Western or 'Wailing Wall,' the only part of Temple left standing after its destruction in 70 CE.

106. Above: Columns xi–xii of the Habakkuk Pesher referring to how the Wicked Priest both 'swallowed' the Righteous Teacher and 'destroyed the Poor' and how 'the Cup of the Right Hand of the Lord' would then 'come around' and 'swallow him.'

107. Right: The last Column XIII of the Habakkuk *Pesher* evoking 'the Day of Judgement' on 'Idolaters' and 'Evil Ones' and announcing that 'God is in His Holy Temple, let all the world be still.'

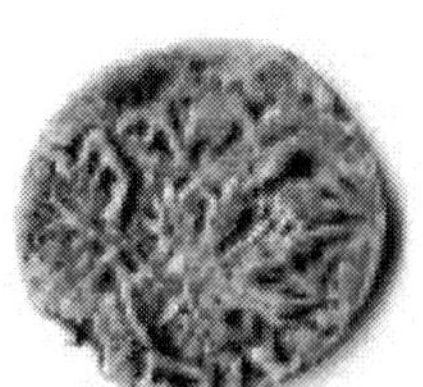

108. Left: 'Year 2' coin of the Uprising depicting a ceremonial amphora on the obverse and a grape leaf with the logo 'the Freedom of Zion' on the reverse.

 THE NEW TESTAMENT CODE COMPANION

109. Above: The Colosseum, built by Vespasian from the proceeds of the Temple Treasure and the numerous slaves he took, the survivors among whom (martyrs all) probably died in it.

110. Below Left: The underground walkways of the Priests in the Jerusalem Temple which survived its destruction by Vespasian, Titus, Titus' mistress Bernice, and Philo's nephew Tiberius Alexander.

111. Below Right: The Arch of Titus, celebrating his victory over the Jews, still standing in the Roman Forum today—his father Vespasian's Colosseum visible just behind it.

112. Above: Vespasian's 'Judea Capta' coin, displaying his image on its obverse and the Roman dominion over a weeping Judean woman on its reverse—the palm tree signifying the Jewish State.

113. Above Left: The image on the Arch of Titus showing his great Triumph, the Jewish captives carrying their sacred objects, particularly the seven-branched, gold candelabra given by Queen Helen to the Temple—presumably melted down to help to pay for the Colosseum.

114. Above Right: Jewish Revolutionary coin from the rare Year 4 depicting the real 'Cup of the Lord' ('the Cup' of Divine Vengeance?) and bearing the logo 'the Redemption of Zion.'

Robert Eisenman is the author of *James the Brother of Jesus: The Key to Unlocking the Secrets of Early Christianity and the Dead Sea Scrolls* (1998), *The Dead Sea Scrolls and the First Christians* (1996), *Islamic Law in Palestine and Israel: A History of the Survival of Tanzimat and Shari'ah* (1978), and co-editor of *The Facsimile Edition of the Dead Sea Scrolls* (1989), *The Dead Sea Scrolls Uncovered* (1992), and *James the Brother of Jesus and the Dead Sea Scrolls Volumes I and II* (2012).

Author standing in Cave 4 mouth on first CSULB Radar Groundscan of Qumran marls, cliffs, and environs in 1989–90.

Robert is an Emeritus Professor of Middle East Religions and Archaeology and the former Director of the Institute for the Study of Judeo-Christian Origins at California State University Long Beach and Visiting Senior Member of Linacre College, Oxford. He holds a B.A. from Cornell University in Philosophy and Engineering Physics (1958), an M.A. from New York University in Near Eastern Studies (1966), and a Ph.D from Columbia University in Middle East Languages and Cultures and Islamic Law (1971). He was a Senior Fellow at the Oxford Centre for Postgraduate Hebrew Studies and an American Endowment for the Humanities Fellow-in-Residence at the Albright Institute of Archaeological Research in Jerusalem, where the Dead Sea Scrolls were first examined.

In 1991–2, he was the Consultant to the Huntington Library in San Marino, California on its decision to open its archives and allow free access for all scholars to the previously unpublished Scrolls. In 2002, he was the first to publicly announce that the so-called 'James Ossuary', which so suddenly and 'miraculously' appeared, was fraudulent; and he did this on the very same day it was made public on the basis of the actual inscription itself and what it said without any 'scientific' or 'pseudo-scientific' aids.

     THE NEW TESTAMENT CODE COMPANION